HOW INTERPRETATION MAKES INTERNATIONAL LAW

How Interpretation Makes International Law

On Semantic Change and Normative Twists

INGO VENZKE

OXFORD
UNIVERSITY PRESS

OXFORD
UNIVERSITY PRESS

Great Clarendon Street, Oxford, OX2 6DP,
United Kingdom

Oxford University Press is a department of the University of Oxford.
It furthers the University's objective of excellence in research, scholarship,
and education by publishing worldwide. Oxford is a registered trade mark of
Oxford University Press in the UK and in certain other countries

First Edition published in 2012
First published in paperback 2014

Published in the United States of America by Oxford University Press
198 Madison Avenue, New York, NY 10016, United States of America

British Library Cataloguing in Publication Data
Data available

Library of Congress Cataloging in Publication Data
Data available

ISBN 978–0–19–871297–8

Meinen Eltern Jürgen und Elisabeth Venzke

Kein Imperativ ohne Imperator.
Hans Kelsen, *Allgemeine Theorie der Normen* (1979), 23.

Preface to the Paperback Edition

Main Threads

The present book has spelled out with theoretical and practical nuances a rather basic idea: interpretation makes international law. Interpretations shift meanings and provide new reference points for legal discourse. My argument has thus relocated international legal normativity in large parts from recognized sources of law to the interpretative practice. Other work before mine has certainly seen how law springs from communicative practices. But I have argued that it has over-emphasized either the interpreting actor who creatively uses the law in political struggles, on the one hand, or the structural conditions that permeate and constrain the international legal discourse, on the other. Drawing on theories of language, general sociology and more specific international relations scholarship, I have developed a theoretical perspective on the *practice* of interpretation. It purports to transcend divides in an attempt to understand interpretation as both creative and constrained. My argument has not stopped there.

It did not only proceed to *show* how interpretation makes international law in two concrete legal fields—refugee law and trade law—but also offered a new concept to guide understanding and, ultimately, to focus normative inquiry. The book introduces the concept of *semantic authority* in an attempt to capture actors' capacity of finding acceptance for their claims about international law. An inquiry of—bluntly—where international law comes from, the argument goes, needs to redirect attention from the recognized sources of the law to the actors who enjoy semantic authority. I have placed the authority of international institutions, both bureaucracies (the UNHCR in refugee law) and judicial bodies (adjudicators in the GATT/WTO context) in the spot light. The choice of these examples responds to the increased weight of international institutions in international legal discourse. It further prompts specific normative challenges.

The law cannot be tied down at any moment of formal (quasi-)legislation, in terms of legal sources or otherwise. It develops dynamically in the interplay between different actors who all pull and tug on what the law 'really' says. If all that is so, the received narrative of legitimacy, which connects so closely to the consent of sovereign states, surely suffers. It has always been challenged from a variety of angles, to be sure. My argument critiques its semantics and opens up towards the practice of interpretation as a main locus of lawmaking. I confront the normative challenges and first zoom in on the rhetoric of justice, which imbues parts of the interpretative discourse. To think of justice as a basis for normative assessments of how interpretation makes international law is, however, plainly inconclusive—it leads into an open end, if not a dead end. Further steps in this part on the *normative twists* of creative interpretations include a critique of the theory of communicative action and the logic of arguing. It is here, too, that I connect to doctrinal debates of soft-law and subsequent practice in treaty interpretation.

Approaches in the line of global administrative law or research centred on the exercise of international public authority, I argue, are well suited to meet the normative challenges of international institutions' semantic authority. State sovereignty, in any event, can no longer function as an exclusive building block for legitimate order. It evaporates between levels of governance. The semantic authority of actors in international legal discourse ultimately needs to be justified and negotiated in a normative pluriverse.

The above presented the book's main threads at a fast pace. Behind it are three closely intertwined ambitions. First and foremost, there was a critical ambition in the classic sense of working against the alienation of power. I have criticized received narratives of the making and the legitimacy of international law so as to expose eclipsed sites of power. For that purpose I have offered an alternative theoretical perspective that comes with, second, conceptual development. The notion of semantic authority aims at redirecting attention and purports to focus normative inquiry. Third, I have tried to contribute to outright normative questions about the legitimacy of international lawmaking and here, too, aimed at critique and conceptual development by highlighting the drawbacks of justice rhetoric, the shortcomings of doctrinal arguments, and, finally, the promise of justifying semantic authority in a normative pluriverse where state sovereignty evaporates.

For everyone in the process of writing a first book, I should hasten to add that this neat summary of main threads and ambitions by no means implements a programme that was clear from the start. What I had in mind those seven years ago, roughly, was to beef up Jürgen Habermas and his theory of communicative action to knock down Martti Koskenniemi's indeterminacy thesis. It did not work. But the fight was immensely productive for me and out of it came the present book. It shows some traces of that early setup but ultimately does something rather different. I even started my doctoral studies with a quite clear research proposal (something still rather unusual in Germany). That was not without use, but the result, I am sure, is much better (I leave it to your imagination and judgment as to how bad the proposal must have been). I grew more certain of what I was doing only late in the process, and in some ways only after I had dropped the pen, not the least through the eyes of others.

I am truly grateful for the opportunities to discuss the present book. I have certainly learned more about it and more about what is left to do.[1] A number of

[1] André Nollkaemper and Jean d'Aspremont organized and opened a book launch with the support of OUP in the Hague where Christina Hoss and Fausto Pocar acted as discussants. Ulf Linderfalk and Gregor Noll offered an opportunity for discussing the book during a Pufendorf Reserch Seminar in Lund, Mikael Rask Madsen arranged a luncheon at iCourts in Copenhagen, Christina Binder and August Reinisch organized an exchange in Vienna, Maria Gavouneli and Ilias Plakokefalos in Athens, Tanja Aalberts set up a workshop at the VU University in Amsterdam and Iris van Domselar gave the book a thorough reading for a faculty seminar at my academic home, the University of Amsterdam. I am indebted to all of them for their very kind efforts.

reviews and review essays further spurred my thinking.[2] In the following, I first wish to concentrate on debates surrounding the central concept of semantic authority, and then on ways that lie ahead. In that outlook beyond the confines of the present book, I will connect to thinking about the language of international law, subsequent practice in treaty interpretation, and on legal scholarship between political philosophy and sociology.

Semantic Authority

The book offers the concept of semantic authority in an attempt to redirect and refocus inquiries on where international law comes from. It understands semantic authority as an actors' capacity to influence and shape meanings as well as to establish its interpretations as authoritative reference points in legal discourse (p. 63). It is notably a capacity that is not necessarily justified, nor does it necessarily justify action that is based on it. Moreover, semantic authority is communicative in nature. It unfolds its force and works as a constraint in the dynamic practice of interpretation. Especially in the short period since the book's publication the concept of authority has received increased attention in a variety of conferences and publications. As a melting point and meeting point of different disciplines, it is an inevitably slippery. A brief follow-up on how I understand authority in this context first of all connects to these ongoing debates and, second, allows me to rearticulate the book's disciplinary place. It opens up to both sociology and political philosophy. But it can make its specific contributions to those flanks as well as to the discipline of international law only by not becoming either.

Semantic authority, understood as an actors' capacity to influence legal discourse by shifting meanings and establishing new reference points, provides a focus. It draws attention to specific actors and away from the recognized sources of international law. I have expanded elsewhere on the dynamic and communicative construction of such authority.[3] It goes beyond both delegation and persuasion. It may certainly connect to moments of express delegation. Interpreters frequently do precisely that in order to try and find recognition for their claims. As Pierre Bourdieu put it:

> The rational (or rationalizing) formalism of rationalist law...participates in the symbolic effectiveness of law at its most rational. The ritual that is designed to intensify the authority

[2] At this time, I am aware of the following reviews: Jan Klabbers in (2013) 24 *European Journal of International Law* 718–22; Ralph Christensen in (2013) 68 *JuristenZeitung* 994–5; Irina Buga in (2013) *British Yearbook of International Law*; Gelijn Molier in (2013) 60 *Netherlands International Law Review* 503–7; and the following review essays: Maria Panezi, 'Of Tortoises and Hares: Exploring the Roles of International Administrations and Tribunals in the Development of International Law' (2013) 4 *Transnational Legal Theory* 283–300; Chris Thomale, 'Sprache und Recht [Language and Law]' (2013) 99 *Archives for Philosophy of Law and Social Philosophy* 420–32.

[3] 'Between Power and Persuasion: On International Institutions' Authority in Making Law' (2013) 4 *Transnational Legal Theory* 351–70. The contribution is part of a special issue on 'Authority Beyond the State', just one instance of the increased emphasis placed on that concept.

of the act of interpretation...only adds to the collective work of sublimation designed to attest that the decision expresses not the will or the world-view of the judge but the will of the law or the legislature.[4]

References to moments of express delegation (to the mandate bestowing interpretative authority, to the law that is being applied and, possibly, to the procedures that placed the interpreter into his or her position) thus serve to intensify authority. But such delegation only provides the starting point of authority because in its dynamic practice it then builds up distance and autonomy. Hannah Arendt recalls in this vein, that *auctoritas* derives from *augere* (to augment). It has its roots in the past, she argues, and builds on earlier foundations.[5] This is a very apt formulation for the exercise of authority through interpretation. References to foundations —'the will of the law or the legislature'—intensify the authority of the interpreter. The effect is twofold. This dynamic places moments of delegation into the centre. Crucially, it also explains how authority grows out of those moments and possibly overshadows what once might have been (with all idealistic and romantic excess) the will of sovereign states in international law.

At the same time, authority cannot solely lean on the persuasiveness of what it suggests or demands. As many voices agree, it implies a minimal degree of content-independence. Actors enjoy semantic authority solely if they have the capacity of finding recognition for interpretative claims also in the absence of agreement in substance. Foreshadowing the book's demonstration of how interpretation makes international law in the context of trade law, the WTO Appellate Body, for example, enjoys semantic authority because interpreters can practically not escape from referring to its earlier decisions even if they disagree. Disagreeing, in any event, is usually a much less promising strategy than giving a specific spin to what was said.

The present book develops a theoretical perspective of communicative lawmaking that is attuned to these discursive practices and that lead towards the concept of semantic authority. It does not explore in detail the sociological forces that underpin the authority of some actors rather than others. It offers some suggestions in that regard and hopes to feed into further studies of those questions by mostly staying attuned to the argumentative dynamics of international law. For any sociological inquiry into what sustains an actor's semantic authority, in any event, the internal logic of the legal discourse needs to be taken seriously.[6]

This consideration also accounts for my general caveat that explaining why international law changes one way or another through interpretative practice does not form part of the book's agenda (p. 14). I do explicitly hark back to that initial note when I turn to the normative implications of lawmaking through

[4] Pierre Bourdieu, 'The Force of Law: Toward a Sociology of the Juridical Field' (1987) 28 *Hastings Law Journal* 814–53, 828.

[5] Hannah Arendt, 'What is Authority?' in *Between Past and Future* (Penguin 2006) 91, 121.

[6] Pierre Bourdieu and Loïc Wacquant, *An Invitation to Reflexive Sociology* (Chicago: University of Chicago Press 1992) 9 (arguing—here against materialism—that any science of society 'must recognize that the consciousness and interpretations of agents are an essential component of the full reality of the social world').

interpretation and to the inconclusive role that justice rhetoric plays in that regard (p. 199). Maria Panezi suggests in her review essay that the caveat might have been all too cautious.[7] I agree with her that an account of legal change almost inevitably creeps into any account of the operation of law. As she puts it, '[i]t may in fact be difficult, if not impossible, to form a theoretical account that separates the process from the jurisgenerative reasons behind it.'[8] When I turn to the normative implications of interpretation, the problems of grand narratives (of progress and scepticism, their tendency towards reification and kitsch) at first support a continued separation of the process from the reasons. A unified account needs to come with a more elaborate social theory. In the book's last passages I offer pointers in that regard. The account of international law as a product of actors' semantic struggles needs to be combined with an argument on whose and which interpretations find recognition in legal discourse. Here and elsewhere lay further paths yet to be explored.

Ways ahead

Much remains to be done. My hope is that it can be done more productively on the basis of the present book.[9] Among the ways that lay ahead, I wish to briefly focus on two. They branch out according to the main disciplinary outlooks of international relations and international law proper. With regard to the first, uneasy and problematic understandings of international law continue to plague quite large parts of most social scientific research. Problematic features include ideas about almost self-applying norms in compliance literature, reductionist understandings of international law as a mere side product of power play as well as constructivist accounts that do open up to dynamic approaches to norms that count, but then seem to turn pale in light of the apparent complexities of the law (see p. 34). This is not the place to rehearse and to try and advance debates in the discipline of international relations. Nor is it my main concern. But an emphasis on the practice of interpretation may, yet again, heed the thought that the logics of the legal system, to which the present book stays attuned (p. 42), matter also in the so-called 'external' or second-order descriptions of the law. The book's theoretical perspective on the practice of interpretation thus aspires to speak to ongoing debates about inter-disciplinarity, including the anxieties it stirs. It offers an account of interpretation that does not aim at directly instructing interpreters (though it wishes to inform practice about itself and to thus influence indirectly).[10] All the same it does not break with the demands of legal practice and takes into account the power of the 'outward show' of legal argument (p. 46). As such, it might well be taken further in research of a more social scientific bent and hopes to be instructive in that regard.

7 Panezi, 'Tortoises and Hares', 289. 8 Ibid.

9 See Christensen's review (note 2) for further suggestions in that regard.

10 See Klabbers (note 2).

A second way ahead could focus on questions that lie more squarely within the core business of international law scholarship.[11] Dissonances between the view that legal doctrine holds of the operation of the law and more distanced descriptions will differ even if the latter needs to include the former to some extent. Strong dissonances, however, invite further reflection about the development of legal doctrine. It might thus be asked whether the international legal theory of sources should change in light of lawmaking by way of interpretation. More specifically, for example, should a judgment by an international court with semantic authority count as a source of law?[12] That might at one point become a fair question. At the moment I do not see that it would be very productive. Questions about what is legally relevant should not be tied up all too closely with the sources of law or even the concept of law. The concept of authority provides a better focal point of inquiry and charts a different path ahead.[13] What is more, I do not see any normative foundation strong enough to carry arguments as to how sources doctrine should be reconstructed (see pp. 245–428, 264–5).

Smaller and more promising steps would pertain to the doctrine of interpretation and how it may accommodate complementary and competing claims to authority in a normative pluriverse. The project of the International Law Commission on treaties over time, which turned into the topic of 'subsequent agreements and subsequent practice in relation to the interpretation of treaties', offers one avenue. But it resolutely stays within the universe of state sovereignty (see pp. 238–40).[14] Another avenue zooms in on specific institutions and would continue to see how the shape and form of their interpretations can adapt to complementary or competing authorities. Armin von Bogdandy and I have taken this strand further with regard to many international courts and how they should go about the business of interpretation.[15] There we suggest further strides. The development of legal doctrine needs many more.[16] It inevitably develops at glacial speed. But it does so continuously in light of a lasting phenomenon: the shift of (lawmaking) authority beyond the state and towards international institutions with semantic authority.

[11] See also Thomale (note 2), 'Sprache und Rechte', 431, who offers a complementary agenda on what might further be done in that regard on the basis of the present book.

[12] Such is the question, for instance, by Molier (note 2).

[13] In that vein, too, Matthias Goldmann, 'We Need to Cut Off the Head of the King: Past, Present, and Future Approaches to International Soft Law' (2012) 25 *Leiden Journal of International Law* 335–68.

[14] Now taken further in International Law Commission, Report on the work of its sixty-fifth session(6 May to 7 June and 8 July to 9 August 2013), A/68/10, chapter 4.

[15] Armin von Bogdandy and Ingo Venzke, *In Whose Name? A Public Law Theory of International Adjudication* (Oxford: Oxford University Press 2014), chapter 4c.

[16] Buga (note 2), too, points in that direction.

Acknowledgements

The path leading to this book has taken numerous turns and I am profoundly indebted to many people for their input along the way. This work is the product of my doctoral studies at the Max Planck Institute in Heidelberg, conducted under the supervision of Armin von Bogdandy. I am grateful for his generous support and subtle guidance. I have learned an immense amount through his insightful comments and our vivid discussions over the years. Among the colleagues and guests at the Institute, I wish to thank Sergio Dellavalle and Alec Walen who both kept me from falling into too obvious philosophical traps. Jochen von Bernstorff, Isabel Feichtner, and Matthias Goldmann critiqued my work and shaped my arguments through many debates. I am also obliged to the input of Jelena von Achenbach, Jürgen Bast, Miriam Clados, Marie von Engelhardt, Jürgen Friedrich, Felix Hanschmann, Marc Jacob, András Jakab, Thomas Kleinlein, Matthias Kottmann, Niels Petersen, Julia Sattelberger, Stephan Schill, and Maja Smrkolj. The Institute's administrative and library staff offered superb assistance.

This book leans on developments in linguistic theory and gained key inspirations from stimulating exchanges in the Heidelberg-Mannheim juristic-linguistic discussion group. Special thanks are due to Ralph Christensen, Ekkehard Felder, Friedrich Müller, Marcus Müller, and Rainer Wimmer.

Beyond the homestead of the Heidelberg Institute, I am grateful for the opportunities I gained as a Visiting Scholar at the Cegla Center at Tel Aviv University where I again benefited from rich discourses. Eyal Benvenisti, Assaf Likhovski, Ziv Bohrer, Shai Dothan, Aya Shalom, and others made my stay truly enriching. As did Orna Ben-Naftali.

With Georg Nolte's support I was able to participate in the International Law Commission's yearly seminar and debate on the topic of 'treaties over time'. I appreciate his candid criticism and our discussions of this book's argument in Geneva and Berlin.

I embarked on new projects as a Hauser Research Scholar at New York University, but the present work ripened all the same. I am thankful for the sponsorship and input of Robert Howse and Richard Stewart. Joseph Weiler engaged with my work, invited me to conduct a workshop on its basis, and thus offered a wonderfully vigorous and very enriching experience. I am also indebted to friends and colleagues at NYU, specifically to Mattias Kumm, Federico Mucciarelli, Maxi Scherer, Fuad Zarbiyev, and Josephine van Zeben.

I defended my doctoral thesis at the University of Frankfurt and thank Michael Bothe for a swift and reflective second opinion. In the aftermath, Sabino Cassese read the manuscript and offered valuable feedback, as did Horatia Muir Watt. I would also like to thank anonymous reviewers and appreciate OUP's professional editorial work.

At my current (academic) home at the University of Amsterdam new discourses opened up and inspired the final touches to the manuscript. Many thanks to Jean d'Aspremont, Maarten den Heijer, Hege Elisabeth Kjos, Joana Mendes, Anne van Mulligen, André Nollkaemper, Tim Staal, and Marjoleine Zieck for their careful reading and feedback.

I would also like to thank my friends who have supported me despite the fact that this book sometimes took priority over my time with them. Among them, Kate Emery deserves special mention. Seline Trevisanut's limitless and continuing support lifted my spirit and smoothed my writing. Finally, without my parents' wholehearted backing over the years I could not have come close to writing this book—I therefore dedicate it to them.

Amsterdam, April 2012

Contents

Table of Cases xvii
List of Abbreviations xxiii

I. In the Beginning was the Deed 1
Problématique 2
Agenda 10
Programme 14

II. The Practice of Interpretation: A Theoretical Perspective 16
A. Lawmaking in communicative practice 18
1. On the sources of international law 19
2. Sovereignty, sources, and semantic change 27
3. From sources to communicative practice 29
B. Semantic struggles in the practice of legal interpretation 37
1. Practice between agency and structure 38
2. On the form and substance of legal interpretation 46
3. Power and authority in semantic struggles 57
C. Actors in the practice of interpretation 64
1. Private norm entrepreneurs 65
2. The disaggregated state 67
3. International institutions: Bureaucracies and judicial bodies 69

III. UNHCR and the Making of Refugee Law 72
A. International bureaucracies as actors in legal discourse 76
1. Delegation from principals to agents 77
2. The authority of international bureaucracies 82
B. The expansion of UNHCR's Statute 87
1. Expectations and concerns 90
2. International protection and humble beginnings 95
3. Material assistance, good offices, and displaced persons 98
4. Humanitarian aid and voluntary repatriation 104
C. UNHCR and the meaning of the Convention 109
1. UNHCR's role in developing the Convention 110
2. Semantic change at work: Shifting elements in the meaning of 'refugee' 122
D. Conclusions: Change and contexts 130

IV. Adjudication in the GATT/WTO: Making General Exceptions in Trade Law 135
A. International adjudicators as actors in legal discourse 139
1. Historiography: Longing for international adjudication 140
2. Judicial decisions and precedents 144
3. The GATT/WTO context 147
B. Article XX in the era of the GATT 150
1. General exceptions: A general prologue 150
2. The creation of a high threshold 157
3. A territorial limitation? 163
C. Article XX in the era of the WTO 167
1. Institutional changes and the working of precedents 167
2. A new beginning with the Appellate Body 172
3. Proportionality, interpretation, and legitimacy 180
D. Conclusions: Adjudication, precedents, and legitimacy 190

V. Creative Interpretations: Normative Twists 196
A. The bittersweet taste of justice in legal discourse 198
1. Narratives of progress and advents of justice 200
2. Scepticism and realism 207
3. The practice of interpretation and communicative action 214
B. The centrality of law: Dissonances and developments in legal doctrine 223
1. The appeal and futility of soft law 225
2. Intertemporal law and subsequent practice: shortening the leash? 230
3. Global administrative law and international public authority 240
C. Evasive foundations: Semantic authority in a normative pluriverse 245
1. Principles of democracy and ultimate authority 248
2. Architectural renovation and institutional design 252
3. Attitudes and interpretation at critical junctures 256

VI. Epilogue: In the End there is Eternity 262

Bibliography 266
Index 313

Table of Cases

EUROPEAN COURT OF JUSTICE (COURT OF JUSTICE OF THE EUROPEAN UNION)

Amministrazione delle Finanze dello Stato v Simmenthal SpA (Case 106/77), [1978] ECR 629 . . . . 260 n291
CIMADE and GISTI v Ministry of the Interior (Case C-179/11) 121 n257
Costa v ENEL (Case 6/64), [1964] ECR 585 . . . . 260 n291
Debus (Cases C-13/91 and C-113/91), [1992] ECR I-3617 . . . . 182 n231
Federal Republic of Germany v Y (Case C-71/ 11) 121 n257
Federal Republic of Germany v Z (Case C-99/11) 121 n257
Foto-Frost v Hauptzollamt Lübeck-Ost (Case 314/85), [1987] ECR 4199 . . . . 260 n291
Internationale Handelsgeselleschaft mbH v Einfuhr-und Vorratsstelle für Getreide und Futtermittel (Case 11/70), [1970] ECR 1125 . . . . 260 n291
Kadi v Commission (Case T-85/09), Judgment of 30 September 2010 . . . . 260 n297
Kadi & Al Barakaat v Council & Commission (Cases C-402 P and 415/05 P), [2008] ECR I 6351 260
Sandoz (Case 174/82), [1983] ECR 2445 . . . . 182 n231

EUROPEAN COURT OF HUMAN RIGHTS

Bayatyan v Armenia, Judgment of 27 October 2009 . . . . 39 n116
Emonet and others v Switzerland, Judgment of 13 December 2007 . . . . 39 n116
Gillow v The United Kingdom, Judgment of 24 November 1986 . . . . 183 n232
Johnston and others v Ireland, Judgment of 18 December 1986 . . . . 39 n116
M.S.S. v Belgium and Greece, Judgment of the Grand Chamber of 21 January 2011 . . . . . 121 n255
Scoppola v Italy (No. 2), Judgment of the Grand Chamber of 17 September 2009 . . . . 39 n116

GENERAL AGREEMENT ON TARIFF AND TRADE

GATT Panel Report, *Canada—Measures Affecting Exports of Unprocessed Herring and Salmon*, L/6268, adopted 22 March 1988, BISD 35S/98 158–9
GATT Panel Report, *Thailand—Restrictions on Importation of and Internal Taxes on Cigarettes*, DS10/R, adopted 7 November 1990, BISD 37S/200 162
GATT Panel Report, *United States—Measures Affecting Alcoholic and Malt Beverages*, DS23/R, adopted 19 June 1992, BISD 39S/206 . . . . 153 n90
GATT Panel Report, *United States—Prohibition of Imports of Tuna and Tuna Products from Canada*, L/5198, adopted 22 February 1982, BISD 29S/91 . . . . 157–8, 165, 166
GATT Panel Report, *United States—Section 337 of the Tariff Act of 1930*, L/6439, adopted 7 November 1989, BISD 36S/345 . . . . 161, 174 n191
GATT Panel Report, *United States—Taxes on Petroleum and Certain Imported Substances*, L/6175, adopted 17 June 1987, BISD 34S/136 . . . . 137, 153 n90
GATT Panel Report, *Uruguayan Recourse to Article XXIII*, L/1923, adopted 16 November 1962, BISD 11S/95 137
GATT Panel Report, *United States—Restrictions on Imports of Tuna*, DS29/R, 16 June 1994, unadopted 154, 163–4, 166–7, 174 n194

INTERNATIONAL CENTER FOR THE SETTLEMENT OF INVESTMENT DISPUTES

Saipem S.p.A. v The People's Republic of Bangladesh, ICSID Case No ARB/05/7, Award, 30 June 2009 . . . . . 139 n18

INTERNATIONAL COURT OF JUSTICE

Aegean Sea Continental Shelf (Greece v Turkey), Judgment of 19 December 1978, ICJ Reports 3. . . . . 39 n117, 179, 232
Application of the International Convention on the Elimination of All Forms of Racial Discrimination (Georgia v Russian Federation), Preliminary Objections, Judgment of 1 April 2011, Dissenting Opinion of Judge Cançado Trinidade. 201 n16
Armed Activities on the Territory of the Congo (New Application: 2002), Jurisdiction of the Court and Admissibility of the Application, Judgment of 3 February 2006, ICJ Reports 1. 203
Case Concerning Kasikili/Sedudu Island (Botswana v Namibia), Judgment of 13 December 1999, ICJ Reports 1045. . . . . 236 n182
Case Concerning the Dispute Regarding Navigational and Related Rights (Costa Rica v Nicaragua), Judgment of 13 July 2009. . . . . 39 n117, 232–4
Certain Expenses of the United Nations (Article 17, paragraph 2, of the Charter), Advisory Opinion of 20 July 1962, ICJ Reports 151 . . . . . 236 n182
Competence of the General Assembly for the Admission of a State to the United Nations, Advisory Opinion of 3 March 1950, ICJ Reports 4 . . . . . 50, 52
Corfu Channel Case (United Kingdom of Great Britain and Northern Ireland v Albania), Judgment of 9 April 1949, ICJ Reports 4. . . . . 25 n40, 174 n191, 203
Gabíkovo-Nagymaros Project (Hungary v Slovakia), Judgment of 25 September 1997, ICJ Reports 7. . . . . 183 n235, 231 n164
Fisheries Jurisdiction (Great Britain and Northern Ireland v Iceland), Judgment of 25 July 1974, ICJ Reports 3 145
Legal Consequences for States of the Continuing Presence of South Africa in Namibia (South West Africa) notwithstanding Security Council Resolution 276 (1970), Advisory Opinion of 21 June 1971, ICJ Reports 16 . . . . . 73, 179, 236 n182
Legality of the Threat or Use of Nuclear Weapons, Advisory Opinion of 8 July 1996, ICJ Reports 226. . . . . 73, 183 n234, 238
Military and Paramilitary Activities in and Against Nicaragua (Nicaragua v United States of America), Judgment of 27 June 1986, ICJ Reports 14 . . . . . 25 n40, 183 n234
South West Africa (Ethiopia v South Africa; Liberia v South Africa), Judgment of 18 July 1966, ICJ Reports 6 25
Territorial Dispute Case (Libyan Arab Jamahiriya v Chad), Judgment of 3 February 1994, ICJ Reports 6. . . . . 174 n192

INTERNATIONAL CRIMINAL TRIBUNALS

Prosecutor v Akayesu, Case No ICTR-96-4-T, 2 September 1998. . . . . 127 n290
Prosecutor v Jelisic, Case No IT-95-10-A, 5 July 2001. . . . . 127 n290
Prosecutor v Jelisić, Case No IT-95-10-T, 14 December 1999 . . . . . 238 n194
Prosecutor v Krstic, Case No IT-98-33-T, 2 August 2001 . . . . . 127 n290

PERMANENT COURT OF ARBITRATION

Arbitration Regarding the Iron Rhine ('Ijzeren Rijn') Railway (Belgium v The Netherlands), Award of 24 May 2005 . . . . . 231 n163
Island of Palmas Case (Netherlands v United States of America), Award of 4 April 1928 . . . . . 230 n159

PERMANENT COURT OF INTERNATIONAL JUSTICE

Case of Readaptation of the Mavrommatis Jerusalem Concessions, Jurisdiction, Judgment of 10 October 1927, PCIJ Series A, No 11 147
The Case of the S.S. Lotus (France v Turkey), Judgment of 7 July 1927, PCIJ Series A, No 10 21–22

WORLD TRADE ORGANIZATION

Appellate Body Report, *Brazil—Measures Affecting Imports of Retreaded Tyres*, WT/DS332/AB/R, 3 December 2007 187
Appellate Body Report, *Canada—Measures Affecting the Export of Civilian Aircraft (Article 21.5)*, WT/DS70/AB/R, 21 July 2000 178
Appellate Body Report, *Chile—Price Band System and Safeguard Measures Relating to Certain Agricultural Products*, WT/DS207/AB/R, 23 September 2002 . . . . . 235 n182
Appellate Body Report, *China—Measures Affecting Trading Rights and Distribution Services for Certain Publications and Audiovisual Entertainment Products*, WT/DS363/AB/R, 21 December 2009 . . . . . 8, 39 n117, 179, 233 n170
Appellate Body Report, *European Communities—Customs Classification of Frozen Boneless Chicken Cuts*, WT/DS286/AB/R, 12 September 2005 . . . . . 234, 235 n182
Appellate Body Report, *European Communities—Measures Affecting Asbestos and Products Containing Asbestos*, WT/DS135/AB/R, 12 March 2001 . . . . . 153 n89, 154, 178, 186, 193
Appellate Body Report, *European Communities—Measures Affecting the Importation of Certain Poultry Products*, WT/DS69/AB/R, 13 July 1998 179
Appellate Body Report, *Japan—Measures Affecting the Importation of Apples*, WT/DS245/AB/R, 16 November 2003 . . . . . 187 n257
Appellate Body Report, *Japan—Taxes on Alcoholic Beverages*, WT/DS8, 10 & 11/AB/R, 4 October 1996 . . . . . 154, 155, 156 n103, 170, 192 n274, 193 n277, 235 n182
Appellate Body Report, *Korea—Measures Affecting Imports of Fresh, Chilled and Frozen Beef*, WT/DS161 & 169/AB/R, 11 December 2000 . . . . . 184–6, 187, 191 n271
Appellate Body Report, *United States—Anti-Dumping Measures on Certain Hot-Rolled Steel Products from Japan*, WT/DS184/AB/R, 24 July 2001 . . . . . 171 n180, 172 n182
Appellate Body Report, *United States—Continued Existence and Application of Zeroing Methodology*, WT/DS344/AB/R, 4 February 2009 . . . . . 8 n29, 172 n182, 192 n275, 256 n273
Appellate Body Report, *United States—Definitive Safeguard Measures on Imports of Circular Welded Carbon Quality Line Pipe from Korea*, WT/DS202/AB/R, 15 February 2002 . . . . . 184 n239
Appellate Body Report, *United States—Final Anti-Dumping Measures on Stainless Steel from Mexico*, WT/DS344/AB/R, 30 April 2008 . . . . . 8 n29, 171, 172
Appellate Body Report, *United States—Import Prohibition of Certain Shrimp and Shrimp Products*, WT/DS58/AB/R, 12 October 1998 . . . . . 39 n117, 50, 176–7, 178, 179, 180–1, 182 n227, 193

Appellate Body Report, *United States—Measures Affecting the Cross-Border Supply of Gambling and Betting Services*, WT/DS285/AB/R, 7 April 2005 . . . . 187, 235 n182
Appellate Body Report, *United States—Measures Affecting the Production and Sale of Clove Cigarettes*, WT/DS406/AB/R, 4 April 2012 . . . . 187 n252
Appellate Body Report, *United States—Measures Relating to Shrimp from Thailand*, WT/DS343/AB/R, 16 July 2008 . . . . 172 n182
Appellate Body Report, *United States—Standards for Reformulated and Conventional Gasoline*, WT/DS2/AB/R, 29 April 1996 . . . . 173–4, 175 n193, 180–1, 182 n227
Appellate Body Report, *United States—Sunset Reviews of Anti-Dumping Measures on Oil Country Tubular Goods from Argentina*, WT/DS268/AB/R, 17 December 2004 172
Appellate Body Report, *United States—Transitional Safeguard Measure on Combed Cotton Yarn from Pakistan*, WT/DS192/AB/R, 8 October 2001 183
Panel Report, *Canada—Continued Suspension of Obligations in the EC—Hormones Dispute*, WT/DS321/R, 31 March 2008 . . . . 256 n273
Panel Report, *Canada—Measures Relating to Exports of Wheat and Treatment of Imported Grain*, WT/DS276/R, 30 August 2004 . . . . .190 n269
Panel Report, *European Communities and its Member States—Tariff Treatment of Certain Information Technology Products*, WT/DS375, 376 & 377/R, 16 August 2010 . . . . 179 n218, 233 n170
Panel Report, *Mexico—Taxes on Soft Drinks*, WT/DS308/R, 7 October 2005 . . . . 155 n102
Panel Report, *Japan—Taxes on Alcoholic Beverages*, WT/DS8, 10 & 11/R, 11 July 1996 . . . . 170 n176, 238
Panel Report, *Korea—Measures Affecting Imports of Fresh, Chilled and Frozen Beef*, WT/DS161 & 169/R, 31 July 2000 . . . . 185 n248
Panel Report, *United States—Import Prohibition of Certain Shrimp and Shrimp Products*, WB/DS58/R, 15 May 1998 175–6
Panel Report, *United States—Standards for Reformulated and Conventional Gasoline*, WT/DS2/R, 29 January 1996 . . . . 160, 173, 174 n191

NATIONAL COURTS

Australia

Minister for Immigration and Multicultural and Indigenous Affairs v QAAH of 2004, High Court of Australia, 15 November 2006, [2006] HCA 53 118–9

Canada

Canada (Attorney General) v Ward, Supreme Court of Canada, 30 June 1993, [1993] 2 SCR 689 129

Germany

Görgülü, Constitutional Court, 111 BVerfG 307, 14 October 2004 258
Lissabon, Constitutional Court, 123 BVerfGE 267, 30 June 2009 .259, 260
Maastricht, Constitutional Court, 89 BVerfGE 155, 12 October 1993 . . . . 260 n292
Rundberg et al. v Bundesrepublik Deutschland, Federal Administrative Court, 1C 118.62, 1 June 1965 125
Solange I, Constitutional Court, 37 BVerfGE 271, 29 May 1974 . . . . 259 n290
Solange II, Constitutional Court, 73 BVerfGE 339, 22 October 1986 . . . . 259 n290
Wencker, Constitutional Court, 19 BVerfG 342, 15 December 1965 . . . . 182 n228
Zweckentfremdung von Wohnraum, Constitutional Court, 38 BVerfG 348, 4 February 1975 . . . . 182 n228

New Zealand

Re S.A., Refugee Appeal No 1/92, New Zealand, Refugee Status Appeals Authority, 30 April 1992 118

United Kingdom

AE and FE v Secretary of State for the Home Department, Court of Appeal (England and Wales), 16 July 2003, [2003] EWCA Civ 1032. 286
Islam v Secretary of State for the Home Department; R v Immigration Appeal Tribunal and Another, ex parte Shah, House of Lords, 25 March 1999, [1999] UKHL 20. 128
R v Secretary of State for the Home Department, ex parte Adan and Aitseguer, 19 December 2000, [2001] 2 AC 477 118
R v Uxbridge Magistrates' Court and Another, ex parte Adimi, English High Court (Divisional Court), 29 July 1999, [1999] Imm AR 560, [1999] 4 All ER 520 117
Secretary of State for the Home Department v Fornah, House of Lords, 18 October 2006, [2006] UKHL 46. . . . . . 118, 130
Secretary of State for the Home Department v Khalif Mohamed Abdi, Court of Appeal (England and Wales), 20 April 1994, [1994] Imm AR 402. 117
Sepet and Bulbul v Secretary of State for the Home Department, House of Lords, 20 March 2003, [2003] UKHL 15 118
T v Secretary of State for the Home Department, House of Lords, 22 May 1996, [1996] 2 All ER 865. 118

United States

Immigration and Naturalization Service v Cardoza-Fonseca, US Supreme Court, 480 US 421, 107 S Ct 1207, 9 March 1987. 118
Immigration and Naturalization Service v Juan Anibal Aguirre-Aguirre, US Supreme Court, 526 US 415, 119 S Ct 1439, 3 May 1999 . . . . . . 118 n239
Murray v The Schooner Charming Betsy, (1804) 6 US (2 Cranch) 64 260

List of Abbreviations

AB	Appellate Body
ACHPR	African Charter on Human and Peoples' Rights
ACHR	American Convention on Human Rights
ADA	Anti-Dumping Agreement
ArabCHR	Arab Convention on Human Rights
CAT	Convention against Torture and Other Cruel, Inhuman or Degrading Treatment or Punishment
Cf.	Confer
CIL	Customary International Law
DSB	Dispute Settlement Body
DSU	Dispute Settlement Understanding
ECHR	European Convention on Human Rights
ECJ	European Court of Justice
ECOSOC	Economic and Social Council
ECtHR	European Court of Human Rights
EJIL	European Journal of International Law
EU	European Union
ExCom	Executive Committee of the High Commissioner's Programme
FAO	Food and Agricultural Organization
GA	General Assembly
GATT	General Agreement on Tariffs and Trade
IACtHR	Inter-American Court of Human Rights
IASC	Inter-Agency Standing Committee
IBDR	International Bank for Reconstruction and Development
ICC	International Criminal Court
ICCPR	International Covenant on Civil and Political Rights
ICESCR	International Covenant on Economic Social and Cultural Rights
ICJ	International Court of Justice
ICRC	International Committee of the Red Cross
ICSID	International Centre for Settlement of Investment Disputes
ICTR	International Criminal Tribunal for Rwanda
ICTY	International Criminal Tribunal for the Former Yugoslavia
IDP	Internally Displaced Person
ILC	International Law Commission
IMO	International Maritime Organization
IO	International Organization
IRO	International Refugee Organization

ITLOS	International Tribunal of the Law of the Sea
Mn	Margin number
MPEPIL	Max Planck Encyclopedia of Public International Law
OCHA	Office for the Coordination of Humanitarian Affairs
PCIJ	Permanent Court of International Justice
PPM	Production and Process Method
RSD	Refugee Status Determination
SC	Security Council
TEC	Treaty of the European Community
TEU	Treaty on European Union
TFEU	Treaty on the Functioning of the European Union
UDHR	Universal Declaration of Human Rights
UNC	United Nations Charter
UNCLOS	United Nations Convention on the Law of the Sea
UNDRO	Office of the United Nations Disaster Relief Coordinator
UNHCR	Office of the United Nations High Commissioner for Refugees
UNREF	United Nations Refugee Fund
UNRRA	United Nations Relief and Rehabilitation Administration
VCLT	Vienna Convention on the Law of Treaties
WCO	World Customs Organization
WHO	World Health Organization
WTO	World Trade Organization

I

In the Beginning was the Deed

Texts cannot talk—they are talked about. They passively submit to the need for interpretation and gain meaning in their use. Also legal texts are not immediately palpable but only come to life in acts of interpretation. Meaning is a product of practice and every effort of trying to fix it outside fluctuating practice is evasive. Ludwig Wittgenstein pinned down the problem when he wrote that 'any interpretation... hangs in the air along with what it interprets, and cannot give it any support'.[1] In the last days of his life, Wittgenstein closely identified with Goethe's tragic figure *Faust* who was troubled by the insecurity of knowledge to such an extent that he sold his soul to the devil if only the devil could bring him satisfaction.

For Wittgenstein this must have been bitterly ironic because in his opinion *Faust* had already found the answer to his sorrows. In one of *Faust's* early quarrels with the futility of his studies, he opens the Bible in search of comfort and seeks to console himself by translating the holy original into his beloved German mother tongue. He starts with the first sentence of the Gospel according to John. The moment he sets out to write 'In the beginning was the word!' he hesitates and cries out in despair that he could not possibly value the *word* to such an extent. He tries to write *sense* instead of *word* but remains unconvinced. He then ponders the thought of writing *force*, which again fails to satisfy him. At last he sees the solution and writes 'in the beginning was the *deed*!'[2] Wittgenstein was so impressed with this scene and its ultimate conclusion that he confessed it could well serve as the motto for the whole of his later philosophy.[3] In the notes *On Certainty*, published only posthumously, Wittgenstein summed up his insights: 'You must look at the practice of language, then you will see it.'[4]

For the language of international law this means not to look at the sources of the law but at its practice in search of what the law is. The common narrative of international lawmaking tells quite to the contrary, however, that international legal norms are based on the consent of those subject to them—in international law it has for long been rather clear that those subjects of the legal order are unitary states. Even if individuals, international organizations, and maybe even multinational corporations have by now become bearers of rights and obligations, the

[1] L Wittgenstein, *Philosophical Investigations* (Oxford: Blackwell 1958), para 198.

[2] German: 'Auf einmal seh' ich Rat/Und schreibe getrost: Im Anfang war die *Tat*!'

[3] R Monk, *Ludwig Wittgenstein. The Duty of Genius* (London: Vintage 1991), 306 and 578–9; S Krämer, *Sprache, Sprechakt, Kommunikation* (Frankfurt am Main: Suhrkamp 2001), 113.

[4] L Wittgenstein, *On Certainty* (Oxford: Blackwell 1969), para 501.

doctrine of sources reserves the making of law for states alone. There is some flux and some sound controversy in this regard. But with a bit of distance, this bedrock belief still seems to stand rather firm. Legal norms are understood as expressions of state consent or, with slightly more archaic overtones, of state will. The doctrine of sources in international law is part of a normative construction that gives effect to the idea that legal normativity—a sense of obligation to follow a legal rule—is rooted in prior consent to be bound by that rule. This holds true above all for treaty law. International norms whose validity rests on custom merit distinct treatment and for now recede into the background. Treaty texts are supposed to carry the consent to be bound into legal practice. But how exactly are they supposed to do so? This was a hotly disputed issue at the time of the drafting of the Vienna Convention on the Law of Treaties (VCLT) which remains tremendously intriguing.

Problématique

When the International Law Commission (ILC) completed its first reading of the draft articles on the law of treaties in 1964, its chairman Roberto Ago recalled that 'the reason why the United Nations had entrusted it with the codification of international law, and in particular the law of treaties, was that the main objective was certainty of the law; and certainty of the law of treaties depended mainly on certainty of the rules of interpretation'.[5] How would this certainty be achieved? Running through the answers that were voiced in this context, it is quite fitting to loosely follow the steps that Goethe's miserable *Faust* took in search for the beginning of things.

The first step, it may be recalled, was the *word*. According to the final outcome of the deliberations on the VCLT, also any interpreter should first look at a treaty's wording. Article 31 VCLT crowns the ordinary meaning of a treaty as the starting point of interpretation. This is to a large extent the legacy of Sir Humphrey Waldock, the last Special Rapporteur in the ILC on the issue, who maintained that the text of a treaty 'must be presumed to be the authentic expression of the intentions of the parties'.[6] Abundant voices from scholarship and legal practice chime in and uphold this view.[7] But what should be done if the meaning of the text is contested, as is frequently the case? The wording itself immediately seems unsuited to give away the answer. Each actor who disagrees with the other coats the legal text with a specific meaning and takes the law to be on its side. Words provide the battleground for semantic struggles but not the answers for their resolution. Disputing parties use the same words with different meanings.[8]

[5] ILC, Yearbook, vol I, (1964), 23, para 34.

[6] ILC, Yearbook, *Third Report on the Law of Treaties*, vol II, (1964), 5, 56.

[7] See below Chapter II, section B.2(b).

[8] See below Chapter II, section B.2(c)(on the notion of semantic struggles).

In response, the task of interpretation could be to carve out the real meaning of the text—its true *sense*. After all, Art. 31 demands that the ordinary meaning should be given to the terms of a treaty 'in their context and in the light of its object and purpose'. Words do not stand alone but come with company. Not the word itself but its sense in the totality of what surrounds the words, their *con*text, would then provide certainty about a treaty's meaning (a standard position in classical hermeneutics). A dispute between competing claims about 'ordinary meaning' should be settled in such a holistic view of the words in their context. To cut a long story short, there is considerable purchase in this proposition, but it ultimately cannot help to see but many other words which again need interpretation.[9]

Not only *Faust* dismissed this approach but also some protagonists in the ILC strongly suggested that it is finally futile. In turn, they rather preferred to look to the *force* that makes the treaty—the will behind the text. Myres McDougal was of the opinion that the rule of treaty interpretation regrettably falls for the outdated thought that there could be such a thing as an 'ordinary meaning' of words. Also Hersch Lauterpacht vehemently argued that looking at the text without determining the will of the parties would be as bad as engaging in a kind of *Begriffsjurisprudenz* of the worst kind.[10] He continued to argue that something so mysterious as an ordinary meaning, even if placed in its context, should at best create a refutable presumption; it should most certainly not be decisive. He averred that importance should rather be attached to the *travaux préparatoires* as 'a fundamental, if not the most important, element in the matter of treaty interpretation'.[11] Lauterpacht also firmly rejected the idea that treaties should have a life independent from the preceding negotiations. To isolate the text from the intentions of its drafters, he argued, is simply not permitted.[12] The text means what its drafters wanted it to mean.

There are a number of quite evident problems with reaching through the text towards the force behind it. On the fragile assumption that the drafting process was neatly documented and readily available, even in 'good faith' it is frequently impossible to find a uniform intention on the part of the drafters.[13] Anything

[9] I still say that it has fundamental purchase because it credits the idea that all meaning is relational.

[10] H Lauterpacht, 'De L'Interprétation des Traités: Rapport' (1950-II) 43 *Annuaire de l'Institut de Droit International* 366–460, 397. The term 'Begriffsjurisprudenz' may be translated as 'conceptual jurisprudence'. It commonly denotes a kind of legal scholarship that embraces conceptual investigation far removed from practice as the true modus of its discipline. The label is mockingly pejorative and attaches first of all to the work of the nineteenth century jurist Georg Friedrich Puchta. See R v Jhering, *Scherz und Ernst in der Jurisprudenz* (Leipzig: Breitkopf und Härtel 1884); F S Cohen, 'Transcendental Nonsense and the Functional Approach' (1935) 35 *Columbia Law Review* 809–49.

[11] Lauterpacht, 'De l'Interprétation des Traités', 397 ('un élement fondamental, peut-être le plus important, en matière d'interprétation des traités').

[12] Ibid., at 389. Also see the classic critique of McDougal's policy-oriented jurisprudence, G Fitzmaurice, 'Vae Victis or Woe to the Negotiator! Your Treaty or our "Interpretation" of it?' (1971) 65 *American Journal of International Law* 358–73. Cf. J Klabbers, 'International Legal Histories: The declining importance of *travaux préparatoires* in treaty interpretation?' (2003) 50 *Netherlands International Law Review* 267–88, 277.

[13] P Allott, 'The Concept of International Law' (1999) 10 *European Journal of International Law* 31–50, 43 (drastically suggesting that '[a] treaty is a disagreement reduced to writing').

that might be found in the negotiating records would also be expressed in the form of texts that again need to be interpreted. Resorting to the force behind the treaty, with all the methodological challenges this would involve, might also render the law rather outdated.

Finally, as a matter of fact and in spite of the fierce critique of McDougal, Lauterpacht, and others, the rules of interpretation refer to the *travaux préparatoires* only as a last resort after all other means of interpretation have failed. As Rudolf Bernhardt then already remarked at the time: 'If the *text* of a treaty is recognized as the object of interpretation [*Auslegung*], then nothing stands in the way of assuming that the text can experience a change of meaning in the course of its development even without any tacit modification of the treaty.'[14] Also Jan Klabbers observed more recently that

> [t]he meaning of a treaty is not carved in stone at the moment of its conclusion: instead, debates continue, albeit no longer on what words to use in the treaty, but on how to give meaning to the words that are used. Whoever controls this process controls the meaning of the treaty, and therewith controls whether or not the obligations resting upon him are bearable or onerous, and controls whether the acts of States are faithful implementations of a text, or amount to breaches of that same text.[15]

After the wording itself, its true sense, and the will of parties have failed as fixed points for determining a treaty's meaning, the only available alternative is the *deed*.[16] The meaning of norms is the product of legal practice. Practice itself has to bear the burden of completing the lawmaking process in concrete instances by interpreting the relevant texts. A norm's meaning does not lie hidden in or behind the norm text itself but is a product of interpretation. The practice of interpretation then also accounts for the semantic change and legal developments. Interpretations may further provide new reference points for legal discourse and they structure the space for legal argument. The practice of interpretation shifts and generates legal normativity. If nothing else, this position fundamentally challenges the common narrative according to which international law owes its existence and normativity to the consent of its subjects. Both the idea of semantic change by way

[14] R Bernhardt, *Die Auslegung völkerrechtlicher Verträge. Insbesondere in der neueren Rechtsprechung internationaler Gerichte* (Heidelberg: Heymann 1963), 132 ('Wird der *Vertragstext* als Gegenstand der Auslegung anerkannt, so steht nichts der Annahme entgegen, daß der Text im Laufe der Entwicklung auch ohne stillschweigende Vertragsänderung einen Bedeutungswandel erfahren kann').

[15] J Klabbers, 'On Rationalism in Politics: Interpretation of Treaties and the World Trade Organization' (2005) 74 *Nordic Journal of International Law* 405–28, 406–7. Cf. W Karl, *Vertrag und spätere Praxis im Völkerrecht. Zum Einfluß der Praxis auf Inhalt und Bestand völkerrechtlicher Verträge* (Berlin: Springer 1983), 1 ('Der förmliche Abschluß ist ein wichtiger Augenblick in der Entstehung eines völkerrechtlichen Vertrages, doch ist er nicht eigentlich ein "Abschluß". Kaum ins rechtliche Leben getreten und wirksam, ist der Vertrag auch schon Kräften ausgesetzt, die auf seinen Inhalt und Bestand einwirken.'); G Scelle, *Théorie juridique de la révision des traités* (Paris: Recueil Sirey 1936), 11 (stating that 'l'application elle-même des traités n'est... qu'une révision continue').

[16] Roughly, writing *sense*, *force*, or *deed* would correspond to three main semantic theories: *formal semantics*, *intentionalism*, and *pragmatism*. For a concise overview of these semantic theories see J Habermas, Zur Kritik der Bedeutungstheorie, in: *Nachmetaphysisches Denken: Philosophische Aufsätze* (Frankfurt am Main: Suhrkamp 1988), 105–35.

of interpretation as well as the notion of legal normativity merit an introductory word of explanation.

On a preliminary note, it may be useful to stress in these beginnings of the book that placing meaning within practice does not mean that anything goes, nor does it take away from the standing of words or from any appreciation of legal text. Exposing the productivity of legal practice and shifts in meaning by way of interpretation does not involve a statement about the degree of freedom and constraint in interpretation other than the uncontroversial proposition that it is not *determined* by way of deduction from the text. Interpretations have to live up to the standards of legal argument and need to find acceptance within a relevant community in order to succeed. They are embedded in societal practice and past uses of the law. The text is the first and foremost authoritative reference point in legal argument. The plain proposition is that norm texts do not come with a fixed meaning that lies behind the level of expression, ready to be uncovered by the interpreter.[17] Legal interpretations contribute to creating what they find.

I take legal normativity to refer to a sense of legal obligation that is located at the junctures between validity and effectiveness, between the sphere that speaks on what *should* be a norm and the sphere that speaks on what *is* a norm. It is neither one nor the other but a mixture of the two. What it means that a rule is *normative* is rather basic and may well be explained by looking at how it relates to its application. This relationship between a rule and its application may simply be *descriptive*. Such is the case for the rule of gravity for instance. If the world does not correspond to the rule, the rule needs to be modified. The relationship may also be *normative*. If the world does not correspond to the rule, the rule and the expectations to which it gives rise persist.[18] This is not the case for the rule of gravity but it is a characteristic trait of legal rules. Law is normative in this sense and different legal theories share the view that one of law's principal functions lies with stabilizing normative expectations.[19] To further clarify the point with the words of Hans Kelsen: 'it is one thing to say that *A* is legally obligated to turn over 1,000 talers to *B*, and quite another to say that there is a certain chance that *A* will in fact turn over 1,000 talers to *B*.'[20] This might seem to border on simplicity but on further thought it is rather

[17] S Fish, *Doing What Comes Naturally. Change, Rhetoric, and the Practice of Theory in Literature and Legal Studies* (Durham: Duke University Press 1989), 141–2 ('what would be in dispute would be the interpretative "angle" from which the text was to be seen, and in being seen, made.').

[18] In the theory of language this distinction is developed further under the heading of 'direction of fit', see in detail J R Searle, A Taxonomy of Illocutionary Acts, in: *Expression and Meaning: Studies in the Theory of Speech Acts* (Cambridge: Cambridge University Press 1979), 1–19, with reference to G E M Anscombe, *Intention* (Oxford: Blackwell 1963), 56. Cf. S A Kripke, *Wittgenstein on Rules and Private Language* (Harvard University Press 1982), 37; J Liptow, *Regel und Interpretation. Eine Untersuchung zur sozialen Struktur sprachlicher Praxis* (Weilerswist: Velbrück 2004), 89–90. In systems theory this distinction is taken up in the juxtaposition between *cognitive* and *normative* expectations and the (un)willingness to learn from the disappointment of expectations, N Luhmann, *Rechtssoziologie* (Wiesbaden: Verlag für Sozialwissenschaften 2008 [1972]), 42.

[19] J Habermas, *Between Facts and Norms* (Cambridge, MA: MIT Press 1998), 427; N Luhmann, *Das Recht der Gesellschaft* (Frankfurt am Main: Suhrkamp 1993), 151.

[20] H Kelsen, *Introduction to the Problems of Legal Theory* (Oxford: Clarendon Press 1992), 33; cf. S L Paulson, Introduction, in: S L Paulson and B Litschewski Paulson (eds), *Normativity and Norms.*

significant and not without difficulty. Kelsen recognized that normativity could only prosper in a context in which rules are to a certain degree generally effective. 'A legal order is regarded as valid,' he wrote, 'if its norms are by and large effective (that is, actually applied and obeyed).'[21] At the same time, it matters why *A* turns over the money to *B*; that is, the reasons *A* has for doing so (rather than the explanation that an outsider may give for *A*'s action). Normativity refers to a sense of obligation. In other words, it is the force that makes a rule binding. Like any force, it can come in different degrees.

In the orthodox positivist picture of international lawmaking, a norm is considered binding because those subject to that norm have themselves created it in accordance with certain recognized procedures (commonly known as *sources*). The norm rests on their consent. Yet, the law's reach towards consent is severed when it comes to a provision's meaning. Semantic content is negotiated in the legal practice of interpretation. This is significant. Part of legal normativity is thus removed from formal pedigree and placed into the practice of interpretation itself. The practice of applying the law makes law. It sets free normative force.

This partial relocation of legal normativity from sources to practice will require further explanation. For now it should suffice to introduce in a few more words the thought that transformations of legal normativity in the practice of interpretation challenge the common narrative on the legitimacy of international law that clings to state consent. Tensions will become yet more conspicuous if one considers the increasing authority of international institutions in legal practice and their ways of contributing to the making of international law by way of interpretation.[22]

The theoretically backed analytical move away from exploring legal texts in search of their true meanings towards an understanding of *practice* as the fundamental *locus* for the generation of meaning and normativity first of all shifts emphasis and attention. When law is a product of interpretative practice, crucial questions would be who the actors are and how they argue.

Before sketching this book's agenda, it merits emphasis that the development of legal norms and semantic change through practice is a pervasive phenomenon in any legal order.[23] Manley O. Hudson speaks for many when he writes that

Critical Perspectives on Kelsenian Themes (Oxford: Oxford University Press 1998), xxiii–liii, xxxiii–xxxiv.

[21] H Kelsen, *Pure Theory of Law* (Berkeley: UC Berkeley Press 1967), 212. Kelsen employs the concept of 'validity' in an equivocal fashion and tends to use it synonymously with 'bindingness', see H Kelsen, *General Theory of Law and State* (Cambridge, MA: Harvard University Press 1945), 30 ('To say that a norm is valid is to say that . . . it has "binding force" for those whose behaviour it regulates'). Cf. E Bulygin, Das Problem der Geltung bei Kelsen, in: S L Paulson and M Stolleis (eds), *Hans Kelsen: Staatsrechtslehrer und Rechtstheoretiker des 20. Jahrhunderts* (Tübingen: Mohr Siebeck 2005), 80–95. For critiques of the sociological foundations of validity and its challenge to a *pure* theory of law, see J Raz, Kelsen's Theory of the Basic Norm, in: *The Authority of Law* (Oxford: Oxford University Press 2009), 122–45; H L A Hart, 'Kelsen Visited' (1962) 10 *UCLA Law Review* 709–28.

[22] See J E Alvarez, *International Organizations as Law-Makers* (Oxford: Oxford University Press 2005), especially at 601–8.

[23] Analogies in municipal legal orders relate to constitutional change that unfolds without any amendment; for the German context see A Voßkuhle, 'Gibt es und wozu nutzt eine Lehre vom Verfassungswandel?' (2004) 43 *Der Staat* 450–9; B-O Bryde, *Verfassungsentwicklung. Stabilität und*

[n]o system of law can depend solely on legislation for its development; however; the day-to-day application of the law must supply one of the elements of growth, and it is in this way that courts make their contribution.[24]

For a number of reasons, however, this phenomenon is of amplified importance and gives rise to particular concerns when it comes to the international legal order. First of all, the grand picture of the development of international law of the last couple of decades by and large shows large changes that stand in contrast to little legislative activity; that is acts passing through the channels of the sources of law. When compared to domestic contexts, it is then above all noteworthy that there is no functionally equivalent legislator on the international level that could either claim a central role in developing the law, or that could react to changes in the law that have come about in the practice of interpretation.[25] In domestic contexts, when norms change through interpretative practice in ways to which the legislature objects, there are political avenues to redirect legal argument by enacting new norm texts. The international legal order, to the contrary, is little politicized in this sense. Thresholds for treaty amendments frequently erect practically insurmountable obstacles. Changes in the meaning of norms typically also work to the advantage of at least one of the parties to a treaty who can then obstruct any amendment in reaction to shifts in meaning, especially where unanimity is required to change the treaty text. In short, there is an asymmetry between the 'powers of government'. While law-applying institutions have moved ahead, legislative mechanisms lag behind.[26]

The development of international norms in the practice of interpretation deserves special attention because of an increased authority of international institutions and their growing impact in the practice of interpretation in international law. International bureaucracies as well as international courts have built up considerable interpretative authority. They are weighty actors in disputes about meaning and their legally relevant communications represent reference points in later legal discourse. At times, they understand the development of international law by way of interpretation as their main target of action. Their authority largely exceeds the control of their creators. The price states would have to pay if they attempted to formally draw back from their influence, if possible at all, may be exceedingly high

Dynamik im Verfassungsrecht der Bundesrepublik Deutschland (Baden-Baden: Nomos 1982). Also see Hans Vorländer, Der Interpret als Souverän. Die Macht des Bundesverfassungsgerichts beruht auf einem Vertrauensvorschuss, der anderen Institutionen fehlt, in *Frankfurter Allgemeine Zeitung*, 17 April 2001, p 14.

[24] M O Hudson, *Progress in International Organization* (Littleton: Rothman 1981 [1932]), 80. Also see, more recently, R Howse, 'Moving the WTO Forward—One Case at a Time' (2009) 42 *Cornell International Law Journal* 223–31, 231 (noting that 'any legal system, if it is going to be effective, has to be able to evolve incrementally through practice').

[25] M Koskenniemi, 'International Legislation Today: Limits and Possibilities' (2005) 23 *Wisconsin International Law Journal* 61–92 (stating that many actors actually see avenues for increased legislation as a potential threat to the dynamism that does prevail in different regimes).

[26] A v Bogdandy and I Venzke, 'In Whose Name? An Investigation of International Courts' Public Authority and its Democratic Justification' (2012) 23 *European Journal of International Law* 7–41, 19–21.

and it usually involves reputational costs that do matter. The authority of international institutions in the practice of interpretation thus constitutes the principal focus of this book.

The work of the UNHCR serves as a first prime example. The UNHCR has thrown its authority into changing international refugee law by way of interpretation when it became evident that neither new treaty law nor amendments to the 1951 Geneva Convention relating to the Status of Refugees were forthcoming in order to adapt the legal frame to changing needs and circumstances.[27] The context of the WTO, the book's second main case in point, is just as replete with examples of how adjudicators developed the law in areas where the political-legislative process could not come to an agreement or where it even was in direct opposition to such developments.[28] In the saga about zeroing—a specific way of calculating anti-dumping duties—it was clear that member states had not agreed to prohibit the zeroing method (they had even made their disagreement explicit in the anti-dumping agreement). The Appellate Body still found, repeatedly reversing panel reports on this issue, that zeroing was not allowed.[29] It is also intriguing that in the recent *China—Publications and Audiovisual Products* dispute China appealed against the Panel's finding that the scope of its commitments could expand simply by semantic shifts.[30] To no avail: the Appellate Body resolutely maintained that it 'consider[s] the terms used in China's GATS Schedule . . . to be sufficiently generic that what they apply to may change over time'.[31]

Legal development and change by way of interpretation thus seems to sap the flow of legitimation that springs from the consent of the unitary and sovereign states, or, by extension, from the consent of democratically governed citizens. International lawmaking by way of international interpretative practice runs counter to the idea of legitimation in international law, which is nested in the narrative that no subject can be bound without its consent and that consent is expressed in the formal acts of lawmaking.

At the same time, it is frequently a blunt necessity and desirable fact that also international law develops in its practice, *especially*, where there is no functional legislator that can do the job. To be clear, legal development and semantic change in the practice of interpretation is certainly not of necessity a bad thing, not even under democratic premises. In view of changing circumstances it may be in the will of the legal subjects that the law develops in this way. From the perspective of comparative institutionalism, it may also be that independent agents like bureaucracies and courts might be the better lawmakers when compared to political bodies

[27] See below Chapter III.

[28] See below Chapter IV.

[29] Appellate Body Report, *United States—Final Anti-Dumping Measures on Stainless Steel from Mexico*, WT/DS344/AB/R, 30 April 2008; Appellate Body Report, *United States—Continued Existence and Application of Zeroing Methodology*, WT/DS344/AB/R, 4 February 2009.

[30] Appellate Body Report, *China—Measures Affecting Trading Rights and Distribution Services for Certain Publications and Audiovisual Entertainment Products*, WT/DS363/AB/R, 21 December 2009, para 47.

[31] Ibid., at para 396.

of state representatives. That requires further study. The challenge persists either way for the positivist idea of legitimation in international law to offer a convincing account of how these developments relate to the consent of those governed. The phenomenon of lawmaking by way of interpretation—specifically under the impact of international institutions—draws attention to the need for updated accounts of international lawmaking as well as revised narratives of legitimacy (and it reveals the paucity and poverty thereof). Seeing the phenomenon more clearly may also be expected to have repercussions in the development of legal doctrine, in sketches of institutional design, and in thinking about law in the international order more generally.[32]

Apart from problems connected to the asymmetry of powers, it may further be expected that power relations have a rather immediate bearing in the amorphous international legal discourse that shapes the law. In contrast, formalized settings of treaty making have the potential of levelling the playing field to some extent.[33] What is more, formalized legislative processes in international law tend to portray features that increase the chances and the significance of legal change once the norm text is out there. For example, the principle of unanimity in political-legislative lawmaking leads to norm texts that are often particularly vague. It also remains very much context specific and subject to further research, whether global or sectoral publics may perform a critical role, contribute to discursivity, and feed into political processes in a way similar to domestic publics. The relative paucity of judicial proceedings and little overarching doctrine with relatively stable concepts further render international law more vulnerable to projections of power. Conversely, fragmented regimes that portray a greater normative density and more stability might at the same time stabilize power projections by fortifying the preferences of a particular part of society—valuing trade over labour protection or investment protection over environmental concerns, for instance.[34] Not least, actors' normative convictions, policy preferences, and cognitive frames tend to be more diverse on the global level. With regard to certain issue areas, actors might just live in different worlds and be subject to different socialization processes that bear on their interpretations. When compared to the domestic level, this suggests that the societal basis that can possibly sustain legal developments by way of interpretation is more fragile.

Having listed what I take to be the reasons that make international lawmaking through the interpretative practice of international institutions in principle problematic and interesting, I should clarify at the beginning that I do not consider it to

[32] The Project of 'Treaties over Time' at the International Law Commission may be read as a response to this challenge, ILC, Report of the 60th Session 2008, (A/63/10), 365–89 ('Annex A'). See below Chapter V, section B.2.

[33] When comparing institutional settings, independent international courts may however level playing fields to a yet greater extent—more empirical research is needed to provide a more solid foundation for normative assessment. See E Benvenisti and G W Downs, 'Prospects for the Increased Independence of International Tribunals' (2011) 12 *German Law Journal* 1057–82.

[34] Jürgen Bast, 'Das Demokratiedefizit fragmentierter Internationalisierung', in: Hauke Brunkhorst (ed), *Demokratie in der Weltgesellschaft* (2009), 177–85.

be a solution to tie all international action closely to the influence of individual states. Such is the thrust of accounts looking at all international authority that is not responsive to the input of democratic states as wholly undemocratic and categorically illegitimate. They miss the mark simply because international action is also a mechanism for overcoming the democratic deficit that results from the projection of one state's power onto the people of another domestic polity.[35] The solution does not usually lie in dismantling international authority but in accommodating spheres of authority in the interplay between different levels of governance and in strengthening its democratic justification from the vantage point of cosmopolitanism.[36]

Agenda

The sources of international law are chronically myopic with regard to changes in the law by way of semantic shifts and what concerns any normative force other than that enjoy their blessing. This blind spot shall be this book's focus. The book looks at the jurisgenerative processes of legal interpretation and thereby provides a complementary account of where international law comes from. It then places emphasis on features of practice, its actors and their reasoning.

Many actors have traditionally remained hidden behind the overarching shadow of unitary states. But they actually have an increasing influence on the making of international law in communicative practices. Apart from state representatives, the scope of actors in international legal discourse includes domestic and international courts, international organizations, legal scholars as well as non-governmental organizations. Over the past decades, the international legal order has come to be especially marked by the growing impact of international institutions that partake in processes of global governance. The analysis of concrete examples of how the practice of interpretation develops international norms will therefore concentrate on international bureaucracies and international judicial institutions as actors.

The outward show of legal reasoning presents itself as an activity of finding the law that is already out there. There is then no creative part to interpretation—no agency, no politics, and no problem (except for the methodological squabble of how best to interpret). The theoretical move of locating law in the performative act of interpretation turns this view of legal reasoning on its head. Apart from a shift towards interpreters that this swing in perspective entails, actors' reasoning comes to be of primary interest. If the meaning of norms is a product of interpretative practice, the projections of power within, via, and by the interpretative discourse are of evident importance. From such a point of view, it appears that '[p]ersuasive discourse, or argumentation, has been a key technique in the development of

[35] Of course there are different conceptions of democracy at play, A v Bogdandy, 'Globalization and Europe: How to Square Democracy, Globalization, and International Law' (2004) 15 *European Journal of International Law* 885–906.

[36] See below Chapter V, section C.

international law'.[37] The power of rhetoric steps to the fore. One of the first items of this contribution's agenda then is to develop an understanding of interpretation in law as an exercise of power. Or put better, as an exercise of authority. Interpreters strive to find recognition for claims about (il)legality; thereby they seek to bend law's distribution of payoffs to their advantage and struggle to tap law's symbolic power.[38]

Apart from the exercise of authority, looking at semantic struggles in international law highlights the structures that bear on an interpretation's chances for success. Such chances depend on the legal material. But they also depend on the sociological structures of the society in which the interpretations take place. Disputes about meaning and their outcomes are reflective of the more general distributions of power within a society, of preferences embedded in prevalent belief systems, and of cognitive frames.[39] This is the power of the international law discourse that is not in the hands of any individual actor. In keeping with linguistic concepts, society's structures could be termed its grammar. Grammar, Wittgenstein says, 'lets us do some things with language and not others; it fixes the degree of freedom'. And further: 'Grammar is a mirror of reality.'[40]

The items on the agenda have so far aimed at analysis and understanding. This is true to Wittgenstein's insightful yet overdrawn contention that all explanation should be set aside for the benefit of description.[41] But description also paves the way for entertaining normative twists. First of all, and this is probably one of the safer suggestions, elucidating legal practice may bring to light potentials for improvement: a better grasp on practice for the sake of a better practice, or so goes the recurrent Aristotelian theme.[42] For example, Bhupinder Chimni insightfully analysed struggles about what it means that refugees may only be 'voluntarily' repatriated. He suggests that legal interpretation in this case should not be understood as an exercise that attempts to find out what 'voluntary' really means. Quite to the contrary, 'any attempt to solve the problem of terminology without paying

37 L V Prott, 'Argumentation in International Law' (1991) *Argumentation* 299–310, 299.

38 P Bourdieu, 'The Force of Law: Toward a Sociology of the Juridical Field' (1987) 38 *Hastings Law Journal* 814–53, 838 ('Law is the quintessential form of the symbolic power of naming that creates the things named ... It confers upon the reality which arises from its classificatory operations the maximum permanence.').

39 M Foucault, *Discipline and Punishment* (London: Tavistock 1977), 27. It is helpful to keep in mind the distinct concepts of discourse that are floating around. For an overview see R Keller, A Hirseland, W Schneider, and W Viehöver, Zur Aktualität sozialwissenschaftlicher Diskursanalyse—Eine Einführung, in: R Keller, A Hirseland, W Schneider, and W Viehöver (eds), *Handbuch Sozialwissenschaftliche Diskursanalyse*, vol 1 (Wiesbaden: Verlag für Sozialwissenschaften 2006), 7–30.

40 Quoted in Monk, *Ludwig Wittgenstein*, 291. Cf. M Koskenniemi, *From Apology to Utopia. The Structure of International Legal Argument* (Cambridge: Cambridge University Press 2005), 568 (speaking of grammar in a very similar vein).

41 Wittgenstein, *Philosophical Investigations*, para 107.

42 O Höffe, Einführung in Aristoteles' *Politik*, in: O Höffe (ed), *Aristoteles. Politik* (Berlin: Akademie Verlag 2001), 5–19. Exercises in what has been termed 'reflexive sociology' have made it their principal goal to improve the understanding of practice in order to widen the basis for action and critique, P Bourdieu and L J D Wacquant, *An Invitation to Reflexive Sociology* (Chicago: University of Chicago Press 1992).

attention to the social forces and practices which give meaning to the concerned words is to partake in a relatively futile, if not deliberately misleading, exercise.'[43]

Showing legal change in the practice of interpretation may serve to provide a better understanding of the transformation of international society and—philosophically pompous—its promise. The vast variety of approaches to international law, the views on its relation to morality, its sources of legitimacy, and the reasons that can be offered for why actors should accept its constraints, appear to emanate from deep-seated disagreements. Such disagreements concern the degree to which the international legal order does in fact reflect aspirations of all those affected by it (virtually everyone), the extent to which it does already work towards justice, and the promise that international law can actually sustain. In other words, under the surface of distinct theoretical approaches in international law linger diverging judgements of the status quo of the current international legal order, of its history, its achievements, and its future.[44] There is probably no better basis for judgement than historical analysis.

There are still more immediate normative dimensions to the present endeavour of showing how the practice of interpretation develops international norms. To the extent that meaning moves from the text into practice, so does normativity. In classical positivism, a norm *is* and *should be* because actors who are authorized to make new law have done so according to the rules they are required to follow. In international law this process is roughly sketched by the sources listed in Art. 38 ICJ Statute, complemented by jurisprudence and more specific rules on treaty making. When the norm (together with the meaning with which it has travelled through the process of formal norm production) is then applied to the concrete case, everything has gone well. However, if applying a norm depends on establishing a certain reading of the norm (it always requires a certain reading before it can be applied) and if meaning is the product of practice, then legal normativity also depends on that practice.[45] The practice of interpretation brings a norm into operation and at the same time it will have to bear part of the burden of providing an account for why a norm should be. To illustrate the point: if there is dispute over provision *X*, a judicial decision that simply states that *X* means *Y* and not *Z* without giving any reasons cannot explain why that should be.[46] In sum, legal normativity not only depends on formal pedigree but also on the practice of interpretation (leaving aside

[43] B S Chimni, 'The Meaning of Words and the Role of UNHCR in Voluntary Repatriation' (1993) 5 *International Journal of Refugee Law* 442–60, 443.

[44] J v Bernstorff and I Venzke, Ethos, Ethics and Morality in International Relations, in: R Wolfrum (ed), *MPEPIL* (Oxford: Oxford Universtiy Press 2011), Mn 29.

[45] See U Fastenrath, 'Relative Normativity in International Law' (1993) 4 *European Journal of International Law* 305–40, 316 ('By virtue of linguistic openness, legal positivism even in its purest form is never immune to such changes in meaning and to the consequent informal development of law.').

[46] The renowned English judge of the eighteenth century, Lord Mansfield, once told a newly appointed colonial governor: 'consider what you think justice requires and decide accordingly. But never give your reasons; for your judgement will probably be right, but your reasons will certainly be wrong.' This runs counter to any idea of how the conditions for just decisions may be advanced. Taken from A Sen, *The Idea of Justice* (Cambridge, MA: Harvard University Press 2009), 4–5.

a whole host of further fundamental critiques of legal positivism that cannot be entertained here).[47]

Three implications follow. One is the task of improving the institutional conditions under which legal developments by way of interpretation take place. At present, the institutional design is still shaped by repercussions of thinking in terms of formal sources in international law and by the already waning thought that only states make international law. The impact of international bureaucracies and international judicial institutions in the development of international law is largely neglected. Improvements could for example be rather pointed responses geared towards building or developing specific fora in which actors can participate in the practice of interpretation. Those affected by a norm should be able to challenge its use, to demand and give reasons for how a norm is used. The task would be to construct spaces of reasons in which actors can contest interpretations, refute arguments, and introduce their own views.[48] This is for now only a broad and vague suggestion and there is no guarantee that it would lead to better outcomes, but it might open up possibilities and increase probabilities.

A second implication is that power comes with responsibility. Interpretation is not just the recognition of a norm's meaning, nor is it determined by omnipresent and all pervasive structures. It is an act that in most practical circumstances involves a considerable degree of freedom and amounts to an exercise of authority.

The question persists how this authority can be justified. Drawing specific attention to the actions of international institutions in the practice of interpretation and understanding interpretations as acts of authority finally points to the relationship between levels of governance. While the orthodox narrative on the legitimacy of international law only recognized the state or, in a more modern and individualist reading, the sum of state citizens as legitimating subjects, the way in which international institutions develop international norms carries the law away from this legitimatory foundation. But this foundation itself has crumbled. International actors can draw on broader constituencies as sources of their authority—a potential that they have to set free in their interpretative practice and in negotiation with other actors in a normative pluriverse.

[47] R Christensen and H Kudlich, *Theorie richterlichen Begründens* (Berlin: Duncker und Humblot 2001), 171–8; F Müller, *Strukturierende Rechtslehre*, vol 1 (Berlin: Duncker und Humblot 1994), 167. In a very similar vein, A Somek, Ermächtigung und Verpflichtung: Ein Versuch über Normativität bei Hans Kelsen, in: S L Paulson and M Stolleis (eds), *Hans Kelsen: Staatsrechtslehrer und Rechtstheoretiker des 20. Jahrhunderts* (Tübingen: Mohr Siebeck 2005), 58–79, 67. Also Jürgen Habermas' legal theory presents itself as an attempt to account for sources of legitimation in the application of the law, J Habermas, *Faktizität und Geltung* (Frankfurt am Main: Suhrkamp 1992), 238–91.

[48] I borrow the expression 'space[s] of reasons' from R Brandom, *Making it Explicit: Reasoning, Representing, and Discursive Commitment* (Cambridge, MA: Harvard University Press 1998), 4–5 and 275. Brandom follows a programme that is specifically tailored to the needs and interests of theoretical philosophy. For a more detailed discussion see below Chapter II, section B.2(c). For a similar point in the more practical realm of political philosophy see R Forst, *Das Recht auf Rechtfertigung. Elemente einer konstruktivistischen Theorie der Gerechtigkeit* (Frankfurt am Main: Suhrkamp 2007), 356; P Pettit, *A Theory of Freedom. From the Psychology to the Politics of Agency* (Cambridge: Polity 2001), 164–74.

I wish to close the agenda by pointing out two limitations. First, the question *why* norms change does not form a focus of the book. An *explanation* of semantic change would run the risk of projecting an outside perspective onto semantic change in law—be it the benevolent force of justice, the rationality of economics, the working of power balances, or changes in a general notion of culture. Such explanations are likely to be oblivious to the intrinsic logic of legal practice as well as to the myriad factors that would not fit the particular explanatory rationality. Sure enough, without any focus everything would be blurred and nothing could be seen. It seems to be the burden of grand theory to provide explanations that threaten to be totalizing.[49] This is not my battleground. Histories of interpretation in international law shall not be told as parts of a grand scheme. The task is to understand and show *how* the practice of interpretation makes international law.[50]

Second, in comparison to treaty law, customary international law is considered much more dynamic and also, in part precisely because of its dynamics, much more prone to reflect projections of power.[51] It is also in the field of customary international law where the thought has found currency that interpretations contribute to creating what they find.[52] Customary international law could foreshadow a theoretical perspective that seeks to draw attention to jurisgenerative legal practice. But the differences between the two sources—the argumentative patterns, and the expectations with regard to what interpretation is about—are so significant that the change of norms in customary international law requires distinct discussions that will not form part of the present agenda.

Programme

The book approaches the question of how the practice of interpretation makes international law in three big strides. The first stride recalls the common narrative

[49] Cf. Fish, *Doing What Comes Naturally*, 153 ('It would seem that if change can be understood at all, it is only in the context of a historical reconstruction of its empirical conditions and not in the context of any (impossible) general account').

[50] D Busse and W Teubert, Ist Diskurs ein sprachwissenschaftliches Objekt? Zur Methodenfrage der historischen Semantik, in: D Busse, F Hermanns, and W Teubert (eds), *Begriffsgeschichte und Diskursgeschichte* (Opladen: Westdeutscher Verlag 1994), 10–28, 18–19.

[51] O Schachter, New Custom: Power, Opinio Juris and Contrary Practice, in: J Makarczyk (ed), *Theory of International Law at the Threshold of the 21st Century. Essays in Honour of Krzysztof Skubiszewski* (The Hague: Kluwer Law International 1996), 531–40; M Byers, 'Custom, Power, and the Power of Rules: Customary International Law from an Interdisciplinary Perspective' (1995) 17 *Michigan Journal of International Law* 109–80, 115 (noting that '[t]he customary process gives weight to power because, rather than involving quasi-contractual agreements, it concerns patterns of legally relevant behavior which, if not effectively opposed, may develop into legal rules.'). Others might however be disappointed with the glacial pace by which customary law changes, see B Simma and P Alston, 'The Sources of Human Rights Law: Custom, Jus Cogens, and General Principles' (1988) 12 *Australian Yearbook of International Law* 82–108, 90.

[52] M Mendelson, 'The Formation of Customary International Law' (1998) 272 *Recueil des Cours* 155–410, 174–5, and 196 (noting that because of the performative side to interpretations in customary international law it is of utmost importance to focus on *who* says what the law *is*).

of legitimacy in international law which is reflected in its doctrine. The principal aim of this part then is to set the scene by introducing a theoretical perspective on the practice of interpretation for better understanding and analysis. It critiques past approaches to lawmaking in communicative practices, tackles the question of how interpretation can be both creative as well as constrained, and introduces the space of interpretation as a site for the exercise of power and authority. Shifting attention from sources to the legal discourse, it argues that what matters in the practice of legal interpretation is an actor's semantic authority (Chapter II). The theoretical perspective paves the way for analysing two concrete cases of international lawmaking through the interpretative practice of international institutions in the second stride. Emphasis falls on the influence of an international bureaucracy, the UNHCR, in the making of refugee law (Chapter III) and of an international judicial institution, the GATT/WTO adjudicating bodies, in developing the general exceptions in trade law (Chapter IV). In view of these concrete cases, the third big stride then turns to the normative implications of lawmaking by way of interpretation under the spell of international institutions' semantic authority (Chapter V). It discusses the bittersweet taste of justice in legal discourse, pays close regard to the legitimatory potential of processes of arguing, and ultimately (re-)connects to developments in international legal doctrine to test them against public international law's task of contributing to the justification of authority. The book closes on suggestions for architectural innovation and with the proposition that interpreters need to be guided by a sense for respective spheres of authority and by the possibilities for democratic governance in the postnational constellation (Chapter VI).

II

The Practice of Interpretation: A Theoretical Perspective

Sources doctrine and rules of interpretation attempt to tie international law to the consent of unitary states. As part of a classical liberal framework, they promise to ensure that no legal subject—be it the individual in the domestic context or the state on the international level—is bound by legal obligations against its will. Such a promise is certainly hard to maintain in any legal order and classical liberal propositions run into a variety of theoretical and practical problems. The focus on how the practice of interpretation contributes to the making of international law only points towards one particular problem that thinking of lawmaking in terms of sources encounters: it cannot see how norms develop in the practice of legal interpretation. The following theoretical perspective sets out to elucidate interpretation as a practice that takes part in lawmaking—as a practice that gives meaning to norms and that generates legal normativity.

This theoretical outlook significantly redirects the view on lawmaking and legal practice in two principal ways. First, orthodox sources doctrine justifies a narrow focus on a small scope of actors in lawmaking. Article 38 ICJ Statute and Arts 6–17 VCLT support the view that states are the only subjects that create international law. Article 9 VCLT illustratively provides that '[t]he adoption of the text of a treaty takes place by the consent of all the States participating in its drawing up'. For some time, such a view has come under increasing stress. For now I do not wish to tackle questions of sources doctrine head on. I do not explore whether other actors in international law can create new norm texts that form the basis of legal rights and obligations—something which can hardly be doubted for certain international or supranational organizations, among others. I leave this aside and rather explore the thought that even if the text of a norm was tied to the signature of state representatives participating in its drawing up, its interpretation is not in their hands alone. International and domestic courts, international institutions, non-governmental organizations as well as legal scholars raise interpretative claims about what the law says and contribute to its development. What is more, to the extent that these actors enjoy a certain authority among the participants in legal discourse, their legally relevant communications might in effect gain a normative force similar to that of traditional sources. This is especially the case where the social practices of the legal system vest them with an institutional authority, which in turn sustains the attitude that their interpretations are determinative of what the law is. Legal practice in the context of the WTO demonstrates for example very well how actors cannot escape the normative force of judicial precedents. There is both a force as a matter of fact as well as an attitude that interpretations should relate to precedents. The scope of actors in lawmaking that need to be considered is thus considerably wider than those that enjoy the blessing of sources doctrine.

With actors comes agency and with agency comes power. A second aspect that looks crucially different from the present theoretical perspective when compared with most other accounts is the act of interpretation. Assumptions embedded in judicial methods strongly suggest that the nature of interpretation is about finding the meaning of a norm text. It is about finding what parties to a treaty had intended the text to mean or what the (international) community requires the law to be—its true *sense*, or the *force* behind it. The outward show of legal argument unequivocally supports the thought that the law is already there, contained and conserved in the norm text. This chapter develops a perspective on the practice of legal interpretation that turns this understanding on its head and sees that interpretations take part in the creation of what they purport to find. From this vantage point, the reasoning interpreters employ in seeking acceptance for their claims is of critical importance. Actors' motives in legal interpretation are manifold and hard to discern. The rules of interpretation provide the form in which actors have to pursue their aims. Following Hersch Lauterpacht they are 'not the determining cause of judicial decisions, but the form in which the judge cloaks a result arrived at by other means'.[1] It may be worth clarifying, however, that looking at the law-creative side of interpretations does not categorically rule out that finding the right legal answer may well be an interpreter's motive. The arguments work on different levels of analysis.

In spite of the fact that international lawmaking by way of interpretation is of amplified importance in international law it has received only scant attention. A compelling legal ethos has largely overshadowed the phenomenon of change through interpretation. Actors trying to win any legal dispute need to base their arguments 'on the law as it is', everything else would defeat their claims from the outset. Stanley Fish wrote pertinently that 'every point of the legal enterprise requires that its practitioners see continuity where others, with less of a stake in the enterprise, might feel free to see change'.[2] Most actors and observers have remained faithful to the enterprise. Thus changes in the law that are carried by communicative practices have been observed from more distanced outside perspectives. From such standpoints, however, observers of the legal enterprise have either neglected the intrinsic logic of legal interpretation or they have tried to stay attuned to the logic of the legal system but have done so with the consequence of losing an adequate grasp on interpreters as actors.

[1] H Lauterpacht, 'Restrictive Interpretation and the Principle of Effectiveness in the Interpretation of Treaties' (1949) 26 *British Yearbook of International Law* 48–85, 53.

[2] S Fish, *Doing What Comes Naturally. Change, Rhetoric, and the Practice of Theory in Literature and Legal Studies* (Durham: Duke University Press 1989), 157.

This chapter first traces the conception of lawmaking in terms of sources in international law to its origins in the projection of domestic contractual theories onto the international level. This original form of classical liberalism in international law and its corollary of orthodox legal positivism were crucial for shaping international law as it continues to present itself. The chapter then focuses on one persistent challenge relating to the implicit assumption that the law can in fact be found at its positive source and argues that the moment the law is spelled out in black letters, it needs to be interpreted and gains meaning in its use. With semantic change the law notably moves away from its legitimatory foundation. In order to understand the production of law by way of interpretation, a number of theoretical approaches to lawmaking have thus shifted their focus from sources to communicative practices of interpretation (A.).

The chapter's second step turns from the background of sources to interpretation and argues that past approaches to communicative lawmaking lack a refined concept of practice that mediates between opposing poles of theoretical approaches. With such a concept at hand, it discusses freedom and constraint in the form and substance of legal interpretation and introduces a dynamic understanding of interpretation that takes into account past and future practices. It develops the argument that interpreters negotiate the content of legal commitments in struggles over what the law means. A clearer view of such semantic struggles opens up possibilities for exploring the exercise of power and authority in legal interpretation (B.). In a last step, this chapter briefly presents the main actors in the practice of interpretation (C.).

A. Lawmaking in communicative practice

The quest for understanding how legal practice develops international norms and contributes to lawmaking might first translate into questions about the sources of law. At law's origin, it might be suggested, there must remain hidden the key for understanding its change. Unfortunately, the exploratory journey in search of sources is fraught with obstacles. It is taken in by the metaphorical insinuation that legal norms spring from dark and hidden places into daylight. This is of course a presumption that overshadows incremental lawmaking in processes of interpretation where actors make claims about what the law really says. Legal doctrine has been caught in this image.[3] It has been held prisoner in the confines set by the metaphor, systematically pointing to a narrow segment of reality while blinding out the rest.[4]

[3] L Wittgenstein, *Philosophical Investigations* (Oxford: Blackwell 1958), para 115 ('A *picture* held us captive. And we could not get outside it, for it lay in our language and language seemed to repeat it to us inexorably.').

[4] See A v Bogdandy, *Gubernative Rechtsetzung* (Tübingen: Mohr Siebeck 2000), 156. On metaphor and perception see P Sarasin, Diskurstheorie und Geschichtswissenschaft, in: R Keller, A Hirseland, W Schneider, and W Viehöver (eds), *Handbuch Sozialwissenschaftliche Diskursanalyse*, vol 1 (Wiesbaden: Verlag für Sozialwissenschaften 2006), 55–83, 68–9; M Reiner and E Camp, Metaphor, in:

By and large, first conceptions of international lawmaking that employ ideas about sources can be traced to the predominance of a positivist understanding of international law that posits state consent as the exclusive basis for legal validity. This way of thinking mirrors the projection of domestic contractual theories onto the international plane: the state in its international relations is set equal to the individual in its domestic order. Neither can be bound without consent—explicit or hypothetical (1.).

Taking a brief step back to the foundational times of the French Revolution helps to clarify the normative import of positive sources doctrine. At the same time, it points to one of the key challenges for the normative framework of which sources form part: changes in the law through semantic developments. French revolutionary thinkers tried to design a language that would carry their ideas into the future. But they immediately saw that the power of words that they tried to use could just as well be turned against them. They realized that the meaning of words would be subject to change and thus argued that meaning should be tied back to the legitimating subject, the people. They saw clearly that words are powerful, that their content shifts in semantic struggles, and that this has strong normative implications (2.).

Also an analysis of international lawmaking should thus shift from sources to communicative practice. One of the most powerful attacks on sources doctrine, of which Kant struck the first blow, has been launched precisely on its semantics. The concept of source builds on the presumption that legislation can be distinguished from norm-application in terms of lawmaking: once it is set in place, the rest is about applying it. However, the categorical distinction between acts of setting it in place expressed in doctrines of sources or in terms of legislation, on the one hand, and acts of applying the law as a matter of finding the law that is already out there, on the other, is untenable. A number of approaches to where law comes from have accordingly focused on legal communications rather than sources. But they are either centred on the actor while almost oblivious to the particular workings of legal interpretation (its structures), or they attempt to stay attuned to the intrinsic logic of legal interpretations with the downside of unduly abstracting from actual communicative practices and its actors (3.).

1. On the sources of international law

Thinking of international lawmaking in terms of sources gained currency in the heyday of classic liberalism in international law when domestic contractual theories were applied by analogy on the international level. The development of such a conception of the international legal order and the emergence of sovereign and equal states as constituent subjects of international law has gone hand in hand with processes of secularization and decentralization; roughly, from a centralized hierarchical system with the pope or the emperor at its top towards a decentralized flat

E Lepore and B C Smith (eds), *The Oxford Handbook of Philosophy of Language* (Oxford: Oxford University Press 2006), 845–63.

order of territorial states.[5] The fundamental individual rights carved out in the French Revolution were cast onto states in their international affairs.[6] This is evident, for instance, in Immanuel Kant's projection of Hobbesian contractual theory onto the international level in his *Metaphysik* (1797)[7] as well as in the classic liberal conception of international law that Jeremy Bentham developed a year later in his influential *Principles of International Law* (1798).[8] Also the famous first article of the 1933 Montevideo Convention on the Rights and Duties of States defines '[t]he state as a *person* of international law'.[9] The international legal order has undergone significant transformations ever since. Yet, the conception of state sovereignty as a foundational corner stone and as an element in the legitimation of international law remains omnipresent in scholarly and practical discourses.[10] The concept also pervades accounts that, in view of mass atrocities committed by sovereign states, rather wish to relax its importance.[11] International law, the argument goes, is based on state consent.[12]

The rise of state sovereignty has been part of a decidedly normative construction of the international legal order. It is part of a classical liberal justification of why autonomous subjects of law should accept to be bound by legal obligations; namely, because they have agreed to be bound. Sure enough, facts never fully

[5] J Goebel, *The Equality of States: A Study in the History of Law* (New York: Columbia University Press 1925), 34; A Carty, *The Decay of International Law?* (Manchester: Manchester University Press 1986), 87; G Simpson, 'Imagined Consent: Democratic Liberalism in International Legal Theory' (1994) 15 *Australian Yearbook of International Law* 103–28; S Kadelbach, 'Wandel und Kontinuitäten des Völkerrechts und seiner Theorie' (1997) *Archiv für Rechts- und Sozialphilosophie*, Beiheft 71, 178–93, 181–3; G Simpson, *Great Powers and Outlaw States* (Cambridge: Cambridge University Press 2004), 30–56.

[6] The *Déclaration du droit des gens* (1795), for example, treats states and peoples like individuals—the people has many of the relevant attributes of individuals and forms part of the human family. See W G Grewe, *The Epochs of International Law* (Berlin: de Gruyter 2000), 415.

[7] I Kant, *Die Metaphysik der Sitten* (Frankfurt am Main: Surhkamp 1977 [1797]), 466–7, § 53.

[8] J Bentham, *Principles of International Law*, vol 2 (Edinburgh: William Tait 1843 [1798]).

[9] Convention on the Rights and Duties of States ('Montevideo Convention'), 26 December 1933, 165 LNTS 19, (italics added).

[10] A v Bogdandy and S Dellavalle, Ad hostes docere—Zu den Ursprüngen und zur Präsenz partikularistisch-holistischen Denkens, in: A Fischer-Lescano, H-P Gasser, T Marauhn, and N Ronzitti (eds), *Frieden in Freiheit. Festschrift Bothe* (Baden-Baden: Nomos 2008), 847–63; J L Cohen, 'Whose Sovereignty? Empire Versus International Law' (2004) 18 *Ethics & International Affairs* 1–24; David Kennedy, 'International Law and the Nineteenth Century: History of an Illusion' (1996) 65 *Nordic Journal of International Law* 385, at 403; B Kingsbury, 'Sovereignty and Inequality' (1998) 9 *European Journal of International Law* 599–625. See, however, to the contrary S Oeter, Souveränität—ein überholtes Konzept?, in: H-J Cremer, T Griegerich, D Richter, and A Zimmermann (eds), *Tradition und Weltoffenheit des Rechts. Festschrift für Helmut Steinberger* (Berlin: Springer 2002), 259–90 (arguing that the concept of sovereignty has lost its place in accounts of legitimacy).

[11] See, e.g., A Peters, 'Humanity as the A and Ω of Sovereignty' (2009) 20 *European Journal of International Law* 513–44.

[12] Arguments about sources were used before this move to voluntarism, but only in this context did they become key. For an overview of earlier conceptions of sources in the works of Hugo Grotius, Emmerich de Vattel, and Georg Friedrich de Martens, see J d'Aspremont, *Formalism and the Sources of International Law: A Theory of the Ascertainment of Legal Rules* (Oxford: Oxford University Press 2011), 63–6. Cf. R Collins, 'Constitutionalism as Liberal-Judicial Consciousness: Echoes from International Law's Past' (2009) 22 *Leiden Journal of International Law* 251–87.

lived up to the construction of state sovereignty as the highest and unlimited authority.[13] This did not, however, shake the concept of sovereign consent as the building block of the international legal order. The moment international law was based on the consent of the sovereign, legal theory and doctrine had to approach the question of how that law could be binding on those same sovereigns.[14] The projection of liberal contractual theories onto the international arena met with critiques, which mirrored controversies in the theory of the state: Was the sovereign state the source of all law? How then could that law bind that same sovereign? Or was some law prior and beyond the sovereigns' reach? What then was the basis of such law? These questions marked legal scholarship throughout the emergence of an international legal order built on state consent in the nineteenth century and have continued to divide international lawyers ever since. Their answers let international law appear in different lights. At the time of the positive explication of the sources of international law, however, approaches that rejected any authority apart from the consent of the sovereign state were in their prime with little opposition.[15] The classical positivist understanding of international law found its famous epitomizing expression in the PCIJ's *Lotus* case:

[13] H Kelsen, *Das Problem der Souveränität und die Theorie des Völkerrechts* (Tübingen: Mohr 1920), 5–8; D Croxton, 'The Peace of Westphalia of 1648 and the Origins of Sovereignty' (1999) 21 *International History Review* 569–91, 571; C Destol, 'Mythologies de l'international' (2006) *Politique Étrangère* 1075–83. Karl Marx prominently argued that sovereigns have always been subject to the economic conditions of their time and could never impose their laws on those economic relations, see H Boldt, Staat und Souveränität IX–X, in: O Brunner, W Conze, and R Koselleck (eds), *Geschichtliche Grundbegriffe*, vol VI (Stuttgart: Klett-Cotta 1990), 129–54, 149. Further see H J Laski, *The Foundations of Sovereignty* (New York: Harcourt, Brace and Company 1921) (suggesting in the vein of Marx that the concept of sovereignty lacks explanatory force in the real world); L Duguit, *Le droit social, le droit individuel et la transformation de l'État* (Paris: Alcan 1922), 1–2 (noting that '[l]a croyance à l'éxistence d'une puissance souveraine étatique ne correspond à rien de réel, qu'elle est en train de disparaître').

[14] Martti Koskenniemi juxtaposes a 'pure fact approach' with a 'legal approach' to sovereignty in this regard. The former includes protagonists in the tradition of Thomas Hobbes, reaches all the way to Carl Schmitt, and maintains that it is implausible to think of the sovereign at the same time as the source of all law and as legally bound by that same law. The social fact of sovereignty comes prior to its legal frame. The latter approach stands in the tradition of Jean Bodin, reaches all the way to Hans Kelsen, and maintains that sovereignty is a legal concept that is not premised on factually highest authority. M Koskenniemi, *From Apology to Utopia. The Structure of International Legal Argument* (Cambridge: Cambridge University Press 2005), 228–33. Also see M Hardt and A Negri, *Empire* (Cambridge, MA: Harvard University Press 2002) (distinguishing normative from descriptive uses of sovereignty).

[15] Georg Jellinek concurred with Hegel that once there is no higher authority reigning above the sovereign state there could be no international law that does not find its origin in their will, G Jellinek, *Die rechtliche Natur der Staatenverträge. Ein Beitrag zur juristischen Construction des Völkerrechts* (Wien: Hoelder 1880), 2, with reference to G W F Hegel, *Grundlinien der Philosophie des Rechts* (Frankfurt: Suhrkamp 1986 [1821]), §333. Jellinek responded to the question of how international law could constrain the state with an answer that turned on sociology. A community of states and the interconnection between their interests made international cooperation a purpose of the state and a basis for constraints in its contractual freedom. This was a very influential argument even if it was fraught with problems. Also Heinrich Triepel took up the challenge and remained faithful to positivist premises, see H Triepel, *Völkerrecht und Landesrecht* (Leipzig: Hirschfeldt 1899). Cf. H Lauterpacht, *Private Law Sources and Analogies of International Law* (Hambden, CT: Archon Books 1970 [1927]), 41–50; M Koskenniemi, *The Gentle Civilizer of Nations* (Cambridge: Cambridge University Press 2001), 179–206; J v Bernstorff, *Der Glaube an das universale Recht* (Baden-Baden: Nomos 2001), 22–33.

International law governs relations between independent States. The rules of law binding upon States therefore emanate from their own free will... Restrictions upon the independence of States cannot therefore be presumed.[16]

The need for a sophisticated positive doctrine of sources increased while natural law thinking receded into the background.[17] Now that international law came to be premised on the consent of sovereign states, the contours of any doctrine of sources could have been expected to be clear-cut. Yet, scholarly work on the matter has oftentimes groaningly lamented continuous confusions and shortcomings.[18] H L A Hart still observed prominently in 1961 that 'international law not only lacks the secondary rules of change and adjudication which provide for legislature and courts, but also a unifying rule of recognition specifying "sources" of law and providing general criteria for the identification of rules'.[19] And also such an ardent international lawyer as Robert Jennings found that international law is weakest when it comes to its procedures for changing the law and to lawmaking generally.[20]

In spite of much dissatisfaction with Art. 38 ICJ Statute and its reading as a statement on the sources of international law, it has in fact come to frame disputes about what amounts to a source and what does not.[21] It is still the widely accepted reference point in legal practice—even if this understanding might have begun to unravel in light of global governance phenomena.[22] Art. 38 is a product of work undertaken by legal scholars at the Advisory Committee of Jurists established by the Council of the League of Nations. It already formed part of the Statute of the PCIJ and with minor modifications and without much controversy it then also entered

[16] *The Case of the S.S. Lotus (France v Turkey)*, Judgment of 7 July 1927, PCIJ 1927, Series A, No 10, p 18.

[17] P Guggenheim, 'Contribution à l'histoire des sources du droit des gens' (1958) 94 *Recueil des Cours* 5–82, 20–35; R Ago, 'Positive Law and International Law' (1957) 51 *American Journal of International Law* 691–753.

[18] G J H v Hoof, *Rethinking the Sources of International Law* (Deventer: Kluwer 1983), 13–16 (referencing many instances of disillusionment); R Higgins, *Problems & Process* (Oxford: Oxford University Press 1994), 17; d'Aspremont, *Formalism and the Sources*, 73–4 (observing persistent reluctance of international legal scholars, by and large, to think hard about sources doctrine).

[19] H L A Hart, *The Concept of Law* (Oxford: Oxford University Press 1997 [1961]), 214.

[20] R Y Jennings, 'What is International Law and How do we Tell it when we See it?' (1981) 37 *Schweizerisches Jahrbuch für Internationales Recht* 59–88, 87–8. Also see Higgins, *Problems & Process*, 17 (noting that 'we have become so preoccupied with jurisprudential debate about the sources of international law that we have, I think, lost sight of the fact that it is an admission of an uncertainty at the heart of the international legal system.').

[21] See G Abi-Saab, Les sources du droit international: Essai de déconstruction, in: M Rama-Montaldo (ed), *El derecho internacional en un mundo en transformación. Liber amicorum en homenaje al Profesor Eduardo Jiménez de Aréchaga*, vol 1 (Montevideo: Fundación de Cultura Universitaria 1994), 29–49, 36; H W A Thirlway, *International Customary Law and Codification* (Leiden: Sijthoff 1972) (concluding on the basis of a nuanced analysis rather categorically that ultimately international law is what the ICJ finds it to be).

[22] Hart, *Concept of Law*, 100–10 (arguing that there is no better test than such practice for finding the rules that decide on the sources of law). The concept of 'soft law' is but one piece of evidence suggesting that the understanding might unravel. See in further detail below Chapter V, section B.

the ICJ Statute.[23] Once Art. 38 was spelled out in black letters, it exerted a guiding influence on legal practice.[24] Its well-known first paragraph reads:

The Court, whose function is to decide in accordance with international law such disputes as are submitted to it, shall apply:

a. international conventions, whether general or particular, establishing rules expressly recognized by the contesting states;
b. international custom, as evidence of a general practice accepted as law;
c. the general principles of law recognized by civilized nations;
d. subject to the provisions of Article 59, judicial decisions and the teachings of the most highly qualified publicists of the various nations, as subsidiary means for the determination of rules of law.

The remainder of this section briefly illustrates how each particular source pretends to be a manifestation of state consent.[25] This is most straightforward with regard to treaty law coming closest to what can plausibly be called a wilful act of legislation.[26] Article 2(1)(a) VCLT defines a treaty as 'an international agreement concluded between States in written form and governed by international law, whether embodied in a single instrument or in two or more related instruments and whatever its particular designation'. The consensual element of the particular state is further strengthened in the ratification process and in the conditions for the treaty's validity.[27] There are many odd cases and especially in some treaties that create an international organization there are noteworthy tendencies to curtail the consent requirement in amendment procedures.[28] Yet, the understanding of a treaty as agreement between states premised on their individual consent remains the yardstick against which 'anomalies' are judged.

The source of international custom gives rise to more protracted difficulties.[29] The trite commonplace is that customary international law (CIL) consists of state

[23] A Pellet, Article 38, in: A Zimmermann, C Tomuschat, and K Oellers-Frahm (eds), *Statute of the International Court of Justice: A Commentary* (Oxford: Oxford University Press 2006), 677–792, Mns 17–48.

[24] M Sørensen, *Les sources du droit international* (Copenhague: Munksgaard 1946), 40; T Skouteris, The Force of a Doctrine: Art. 38 of the PCIJ Statute and the Sources of International Law, in: F Johns, R Joyce, and S Pahuja (eds), *Events: The Force of International Law* (Abingdon: Routledge 2011), 69–80.

[25] M Bos, 'Recognized Manifestations of International Law—A New Theory of Sources' (1977) 19 *German Yearbook of International Law* 9–76; M Bos, *A Methodology of International Law* (Amsterdam: North-Holland 1984); v Hoof, *Rethinking the Sources*, 76–82.

[26] K Oellers-Frahm, The Evolving Role of Treaties in International Law in: R Miller and R Bratspies (eds), *Progress in International Law* (Leiden: Nijhoff 2008), 173–95, 176–9; A Aust, *Modern Treaty Law and Practice* (Cambridge: Cambridge University Press 2007), 16–32 and 94–121.

[27] Arts 9–18 VCLT.

[28] J Klabbers, *The Concept of Treaty in International Law* (The Hague: Kluwer 1996), 15–36; R Wolfrum and V Röben (eds), *Developments of International Law in Treaty Making* (Berlin: Springer 2005); M A Fitzmaurice, 'Modifications to the Principle of Consent in Relation to Certain Treaty Obligations' (1997) 2 *Austrian Review of International and European Law* 275–317.

[29] Difficulties start with the odd definition in Art. 38(1)(b) that has stirred surprise about how customary international law could ever be created, or changed, if the practice that *creates* it needs to be thought of as a practice that *follows* that same law. One of the most pointed critiques is set out by J L Kunz, 'The Nature of Customary International Law' (1953) 47 *American Journal of International*

practice and *opinio juris*.[30] Some have conceived customary law in close analogy with treaty law as a form of tacit agreement,[31] but such an understanding is now certainly quaint and well out of touch with the reality of the formation of CIL.[32] The prevalent understanding of CIL still holds that state practice and *opinio juris* are decisive precisely because they are manifestations of state consent.[33] This is also evident in the notion of the persistent objector—if a state persistently objects to being bound by an emerging rule of CIL that state may not be considered bound by that rule.[34] However, it is with regard to CIL that sources doctrine has started to accept a more lenient standard of proof for state consent to the extent that it embraces an outright deductive technique in legal reasoning.[35] Bruno Simma and Philip Alston have suggested that neglect for the element of practice distorts the understanding of CIL to such an extent that the source of general principles might be a better alternative for anchoring claims about what international law is.[36]

A look at general principles as sources of law is most dizzying.[37] Some sobering focus might be gained by emphasizing that what is at issue are general principles as a source of international law in the sense of Art. 38(1)(c) ICJ Statute. Many agree

Law 662–9, 667. Also see M Byers, 'Custom, Power, and the Power of Rules: Customary International Law from an Interdisciplinary Perspective' (1995) 17 *Michigan Journal of International Law* 109–80, 129–46.

[30] P Guggenheim, Les Deux Eléments de la Coutume en Droit International, in: C Roussel (ed), *La Technique et les Principes du Droit Public—Etudes en l'Honneur de Georges Scelle*, 1950), 275–84; P Haggenmacher, 'La doctrine des deux élements du droit coutumier dans la pactique de la Cour internationale' (1986) 90 *Revue Générale de Droit International Public* 5 (Paris: LGDJ); M Akehurst, 'Custom as a Source of International Law' (1976) 47 *British Yearbook of International Law* 1–53, 35. From the body of case-law, see in particular *North Sea Continental Shelf (Federal Republic of Germany v Denmark; Federal Republic of Germany v The Netherlands)*, Judgment of 20 February 1969, ICJ Reports 3, 44.

[31] D Anzilotti, *Corso di diritto internazionale* (Roma: Athenaeum 1923), 66 and 72. Also Triepel, faithful to his will theory of international law, conceived custom in this fashion, Triepel, *Völkerrecht und Landesrecht*, 95.

[32] M Mendelson, 'The Formation of Customary International Law' (1998) 272 *Recueil des Cours* 155–410, 264. Also consider that new states are usually not granted the option to object to already existing custom, see v Hoof, *Rethinking the Sources*, 77–8.

[33] Pellet, Article 38, 677–792, Mn 207–29; L Boisson de Chazournes, Qu'est-ce que la pratique en droit international?, in: Société française de droit international (ed), *La pratique et le droit international* (Paris: Pedone 2004), 13–47; v Hoof, *Rethinking the Sources*, 76–81.

[34] T L Stein, 'The Approach of the Different Drummer: The Principle of the Persistent Objector in International Law' (1985) 26 *Harvard International Law Journal* 467–82; R Müllerson, 'On the Nature and Scope of Customary International Law' (1997) 2 *Austrian Review of International and European Law* 341–60, 349–51.

[35] See A Roberts, 'Traditional and Modern Approaches to Customary International Law ' (2001) 95 *American Journal of International Law* 757–91.

[36] B Simma and P Alston, 'The Sources of Human Rights Law: Custom, Jus Cogens, and General Principles' (1988) 12 *Australian Yearbook of International Law* 82–108.

[37] For an attempt at clarity see M Koskenniemi, 'General Principles: Reflexions on Constructivist Thinking in International Law' (1985) 18 *Oikeustiede-Jurisprudentia* 120–63, 125 (noting that '[r]eference to principles seem to come from such differing views that even the possibility of general understanding seems excluded.').

that the article refers to general principles recognized in municipal legal systems that are transposable into international law.[38] Yet, general principles remain also closely intertwined with notions such as equity that are usually not themselves sources of law but guiding yardsticks for interpretation or a rescue kit if gaps in the law need to be fixed.[39] Case-law has been most scarce and ambiguous in its use of Art. 38(1)(c). Where the ICJ did use the expression 'general principles' it was precisely not in a way that relates to municipal legal systems. It rather spoke with a natural law overtone of 'general and well-recognized principles [such as] elementary considerations of humanity'.[40] These are curious statements whose reception has been most welcome or repellent depending on the overall view the onlooker usually casts on international law. On another occasion the ICJ clarified its decidedly legalistic ethos:

> It is a court of law, and can take account of moral principles only in so far as these are given a sufficient expression in legal form. Law exists, it is said, to serve a social need; but precisely for that reason it can do so only through and within the limits of its own discipline. Otherwise, it is not a legal service that would be rendered. Humanitarian considerations may constitute the inspirational basis for rules of law... Such considerations do not, however, in themselves amount to rules of law.[41]

Some have suggested that general principles can also emanate from the context of international relations directly and need not necessarily be derived from municipal legal systems. They see such a construction of general principles as a deliberate and preferable alternative to exceedingly deductive approaches to CIL.[42] Advocates of the idea that the international order itself can also generate general principles as a source of law tend to note a certain proximity to remnants of a natural law tradition and, by way of distinction, emphasize that general principles in their use of the term 'essentially depend on an established consent'.[43] Thus, also in such an extended approach to Art. 38(1)(c) the normative basis of state consent remains

[38] Pellet, Article 38, 677–792, Mns 250–64.

[39] U Fastenrath, *Lücken im Völkerrecht* (Berlin: Duncker und Humblot 1991), 127–34; M Akehurst, 'Equity and General Principles of Law' (1976) 25 *International and Comparative Law Quarterly* 801–25.

[40] *Corfu Channel Case (United Kingdom of Great Britain and Northern Ireland v Albania)*, Judgment of 9 April 1949, ICJ Reports 4, 22. Cf. *Military and Paramilitary Activities in and Against Nicaragua (Nicaragua v United States of America)*, Judgment of 27 June 1986, ICJ Reports 14, 113–14 (speaking of 'fundamental principles of humanitarian law').

[41] *South West Africa (Ethiopia v South Africa; Liberia v South Africa)*, Judgment of 18 July 1966, ICJ Reports 6, para 49.

[42] Simma and Alston, 'Sources of Human Rights Law' 82–108; S Kadelbach and T Kleinlein, 'International Law—a Constitution for Mankind? An Attempt at a Re-appraisal with an Analysis of Constitutional Principles' (2007) 50 *German Yearbook of International Law* 303–48, 338–42; N Petersen, 'Customary Law without Custom? Rules, principles, and the role of state practice in international norm creation' (2008) 23 *American University International Law Review* 275–310.

[43] S Kadelbach and T Kleinlein, 'International Law—a Constitution for Mankind? An Attempt at a Re-appraisal with an Analysis of Constitutional Principles' (2007) 50 *German Yearbook of International Law* 340.

unchallenged and surprisingly solid. Retaining the ultimate authority over what counts as law, legal practice has not, at least not yet, given central significance to a more detached and dynamic use of general principles. As a source of law they have in any event remained slumbering most of the time. This is without prejudice to other kinds of 'principles' that construct the law from particular vantage points and influence interpretation.[44] They bear on the meaning and work on the level of interpretation but are not themselves recognized as a source of international law.

Article 38(1)(d) ICJ Statute speaks of 'judicial decisions and the teachings of the most highly qualified publicists' as 'subsidiary means for the determination of rules of law' and thus gives them a standing similar to factors influencing the meaning of a legal norm. They are not themselves considered sources but means for identifying legal norms.[45] No court statute and no judgment holds otherwise. Moreover, parties to a regime providing for third party adjudication as well as members who have accepted a court's jurisdiction frequently seek to contain the effect of judicial decisions. Article 59 ICJ Statute stipulates for example that the 'decision of the Court has no binding force except between the parties and in respect of that particular case'.[46] Most telling and intriguing is certainly Art. 3(2) Dispute Settlement Understanding (DSU) providing that the recommendations and rulings of the WTO Dispute Settlement Body (DSB) 'cannot add to or diminish the rights and obligations provided in the covered agreements'. This provision makes little sense in orthodox doctrine and reflects the apprehension that reality frequently does not live up to its categorical order of things.[47]

Just as there are problems with linking recognized primary sources of international law—treaty, custom, and general principles—back to the will of unitary states, there are problems with thinking of judicial decisions as subsidiary means of interpretation for identifying legal norms. With only a bit of distance to the legal enterprise it may frequently be observed that they do take part in lawmaking.[48] By authoritatively stating what the law is, they partake in its creation. Chapter IV below examines in closer detail how judicial practice has created the general exceptions of Art. XX GATT. The treaty source of the law in this example has practically remained the same since it was spelled out in 1947 while changes in its

[44] A v Bogdandy, 'General Principles of International Public Authority: Sketching a Research Field' (2008) 11 *German Law Journal* 1909–38; cf. V-Đ Degan, *Sources of International Law* (The Hague: Nijhoff 1997), 1 (speaking of principles as factors influencing the development of law).

[45] Pellet, Article 38, 677–792, Mns 298–300 (noting that 'the intention behind the final wording of this provision was that jurisprudence and doctrine were supposed to elucidate what the rules to be applied by the Court were, not to create them.').

[46] Cf. R Bernhardt, Article 59, in: A Zimmermann, C Tomuschat, and K Oellers-Frahm (eds), *The Statute of the International Court of Justice: A commentary* (Oxford: Oxford University Press 2006), 1231–51, 1233 (noting that this provision 'was primarily intended to underline the opinion that the Court should not be considered a lawmaking or law-creating institution.'). Also see A E Boyle and C M Chinkin, *The Making of International Law* (Oxford: Oxford University Press 2007), 266–9.

[47] See below Chapter IV, section A.3.

[48] See Armin von Bogdandy and Ingo Venzke (eds), 'Beyond Dispute: International Judicial Institutions as Lawmakers' Special Issue (2011) 12 *German Law Journal* 979–1370.

meaning—developments of what the law is—have been carried by interpretative practice. Adjudicators have structured the space of legal discourse with their precedents as new reference points that no interpreter can escape.

Other legal phenomena like certain unilateral acts of states, binding as well as non-binding resolutions, and other acts of international organizations are only rarely discussed in terms of sources of law; they find no mention in Art. 38.[49] A plethora of concepts and approaches have been offered to handle such phenomena. In some ways, the debate surrounding their categorization within sources doctrine resembles the treatment of judicial decisions. Their impact on the law can hardly be denied and some authors have therefore suggested that they be characterized as indirect or auxiliary sources of law.[50] Another approach might be to characterize them as 'soft law', with unsure purchase.[51] As a matter of fact, acts of international organizations bring sources doctrine under such stress that it might be better to untie questions of legal validity to some extent from primary sources and to discuss them with reference to categories of legal instruments instead.[52] All this is indicative of profound problems of sources doctrine—if not in principle, then at least what concerns Art. 38 as a statement on the sources of international law. Documents issued by UNHCR such as its Handbook or Guidance Notes do not, on the face of it, fall under the heading of any specific source of law and still they contribute to the making of refugee law—the focus of Chapter III below.

2. Sovereignty, sources, and semantic change

Positive sources doctrine is part of a decidedly normative construction of legitimate order that spins off from ideas of sovereignty. Taking a step back and looking at the times that shaped our ideas about legitimate authority helps to clarify the momentum of legitimation that is nested in the concept of sovereignty. Such an angle also points to one of the main challenges to consent-based theories of legitimacy in international law; namely, that once a norm is spelled out and set in place, it changes by way of interpretation and thus moves away from its source. This section takes a brief detour via the ideas of French revolutionaries in order to pursue a two-fold aim: to clarify the normative framework of which sources doctrine forms part and to capture the central problem of this construction that comes with semantic pragmatism and the 'linguistic turn'.

As is well known, the French Revolution established that sovereignty rests with the people and it corroborated a conception of sovereignty as a basis for

[49] But see among others Fastenrath, *Lücken*, 104–7.

[50] See, e.g., v Hoof, *Rethinking the Sources*, 171. Cf. in further detail below Chapter V, section B.1. It should be noted in passing that it might only on first sight be convenient to closely connect the question of what amounts to a source of law with what has an impact on the law. Competing conceptions of the relationship between norms and facts reverberate in this question.

[51] See in further detail below Chapter V, section B.1.

[52] See in further detail below Chapter V, section B.3.

legitimation. Sovereignty understood as the ultimate say about the exercise of all public power should rest with the people and the people are to decide about their own fate and government. What is less well known is that, at the same time, revolutionary thinkers developed a novel understanding with regard to the relationship between words and social or political change. Such change should be induced by conceptual anticipation, they suggested. The French revolutionaries and thinkers of the enlightenment saw their speeches and arguments as pioneering and anticipating what was yet to come about.[53] Denis Diderot developed a sophisticated understanding of the power of words throughout his work on the *Encyclopédie.* He was self-aware, and most likely correct in his belief, that his conceptual work provided an essential contribution to thinking the ideas that would carry the French Revolution. He eloquently expressed this thought in the auto-reflexive entry 'Encyclopédie' where he perceptively wrote that the language has to be fixed now in the spirit of the revolution so that it carries the revolution's ideas henceforth.[54]

Diderot put to use the power of a deliberately designed language in order to induce and bolster social and political change. This is one significant way in which interpretations can be understood as expressions of power. The French revolutionaries were engaged in a semantic struggle of shaping meanings to reach into the future.[55] When they recognized the power of words, they immediately saw their double-edged quality as forces towards both good and evil. If they were in a position to use them to their own ends, so could others, possibly turning their force against them. In an attempt to tie their might to revolutionary ideals, they advocated that '*les paroles nationales seront souverains de tous les souverains*'.[56] The meaning of sovereignty as ultimate authority is present in this statement just like its aspect of legitimation. Its ambiguity reflects the combination between power exercised by way of interpretation and the already present power of discursive structures that distribute the chances of interpretations to succeed.[57] The sovereign as a source of legitimacy should decide about the meaning of words. At the same time words should be sovereign, they should have the ultimate authority. With this statement words even gain personality. They are not *souveraines* (adjective) but *souverains* (noun). Words are the sovereign ruler—anthropomorphic, authoritative, and legitimate.

But there is an intricate tension between the fact that the words are *souverains*, on the one hand, and the fact that revolutionary thinkers tried to shape those same words so as to advance and buttress revolutionary ideas, on the other. This is the same tension that permeates the rule of law: law should be the sovereign ruler but

[53] R Koselleck, *Begriffsgeschichten* (Frankfurt am Main: Suhrkamp 2006), 298, with reference to B Schlieben-Lange, 'Die Französische Revolution und die Sprache' (1981) 41 *Zeitschrift für Literaturwissenschaft und Linguistik* 90–123.

[54] See Koselleck, *Begriffsgeschichten*, 299.

[55] R Koselleck, Begriffsgeschichte and Social History, in: *Futures Past. On the Semantics of Historical Time* (New York: Columbia University Press 1979), 75–93, 80.

[56] 'Abondance', in *Nouveau Dictionnaire Historique* (1791), quoted in Koselleck, *Begriffsgeschichten*, 300 (English: they advocated that 'national words will be sovereign of all the sovereigns').

[57] The relationship between actors and structures forms the subject of section B.2.b below.

depends in its application on the interpretation of concrete individuals who seek to bend it to their advantage.[58] It is also this tension that amounts to one of the main challenges to the normative framework underpinning sources doctrine. If international norms can change in the process of interpretation, then this process distances them from their source and, possibly, from the consent of those whom they govern. Notably, none other than the prime philosopher of the enlightenment, Immanuel Kant, argued long before the rise of legal realism that it is impossible to see the application of abstract concepts in concrete cases as an act of cognition in which their true content is recognized and made operative.[59] The use of words involves volition and judgement. In cases of legal dispute it is rather evident that interpretations are *decisions*. Decisions are choices between at least two alternatives and as such they defy the idea that they could be found or recognized.[60]

The authors of the *Enyclopédie* showed three key insights. They first of all recognized how words are powerful in the sense that they can constrain others in what they can say or do. They understood, second, that actors, just as they themselves were doing, fight about semantic content while they pursue their interests or convictions. They saw and expected meanings to shift in such semantic struggles. What matters then is who is influential and possibly dominates in such processes of semantic development. While the revolutionary thinkers coined *paroles nationales* when crafting the *Encyclopédie*, they realized that these words would take on a life of their own and would possibly escape their control. Keenly aware of the normative implications of semantic change, they thus argued, third, that meanings be tied back to the legitimating subject, the people. Powerful words should belong to them. But this last insight turned into a highly aspirational argument. The primary analytical question for any normative assessment is: Who has authority in semantic struggles?

3. From sources to communicative practice

Just as the *Encyclopédie* changed in the practice of semantic struggles, the contents of international legal commitments are subject to change enacted in practices of

58 See E H Carr, *The Twenty Years' Crisis 1919–1939* (New York: Harper Collins 1964 [1939]), 178 (quoting Chinese philosopher Hsun-tze: 'There are men who govern but there are no laws that govern.').

59 I Kant, *Critique of Pure Reason* (Cambridge: Cambridge University Press 1998), 267–77. Cf. M Koskenniemi, 'Constitutionalism as Mindset: Reflections on Kantian Themes About International Law and Globalization' (2007) 8 *Theoretical Inquiries in Law* 9–36.

60 Jacques Derrida and Niklas Luhmann have also forcefully made this point even if not all the consequences they draw are equally compelling, J Derrida, 'Force of Law. The Mystical Foundation of Authority' (1990) 11 *Cardozo Law Review* 919–1045; N Luhmann, *Das Recht der Gesellschaft* (Frankfurt am Main: Suhrkamp 1993), 308. It should be made clear that such a view on legal interpretation does not necessarily lead to *decisionism*. Decisions can still be meaningfully reasoned, scrutinized and processed. Cf. M Reisman, 'A Jurisprudence from the Perspective of the "Political Superior"' (1996) 23 *Northern Kentucky Law Review* 605–28, 608 (noting that '[o]ne of the functions of jurisprudence . . . in a democratic political system is to identify the points of choice in a legal system'); A Fischer-Lescano and R Christensen, 'Auctoritatis Interpositio. Die Dekonstruktion des Dezisionismus durch die Systemtheorie' (2005) 44 *Der Staat* 213–42.

interpretation. The making of international law is in significant parts a result of processes that cannot be convincingly captured in doctrines of sources. Sources picture lawmaking as a one-time act—ideally captured in the journalist's snapshot of state representatives signing an international treaty in festive environments.[61] In contrast to such a static view, the present theoretical perspective sets out to elucidate legal change in the dynamics of continuous norm-application. While Kant already hinted at the moment of creativity contained in applying abstract norms, the real theoretical break came with the 'linguistic turn' and semantic pragmatism.[62] They question the subtle assumption that the law can be fixed in sources and maintain instead that expressions do not have a meaning other than that attributed to them by their use.[63] In Wittgenstein's solemn observation, the best that can be done is to observe and find rules that describe the use of an expression. In attempting to find the meaning of a rule it is necessary to find the rule that explains the use of that rule.[64] The meaning of the explanatory rule is of course subject to the same fate so that one is caught in an infinite regress.[65] Only practice can help.

Already Hans Kelsen had forcefully critiqued orthodox judicial methodology for wanting to make believe that the act of interpretation is nothing but an act of understanding and clarification whereas it really depended on a choice—an act of will. In 1928 Kelsen competed against Heinrich Triepel on the topic of the nature and development of the constitutional judiciary. The occasion was the

[61] Only see the image of Anwar al-Sadat, Jimmy Carter, and Menachem Begin at the signing of the Egyptian-Israeli peace treaty in 1979 that adorns the cover of A Aust, *Modern Treaty Law and Practice* (Cambridge: Cambridge University Press 2007).

[62] On the notion of 'linguistic turn' with an apt sense for irony see R Rorty, Wittgenstein, Heidegger, and the Reification of Language, in: R Rorty (ed), *Essays on Heidegger and Others*, vol 2 (Cambridge: Cambridge Universtiy Press 1991), 50–65. The irony lies in the 'linguistic turn' coming to life in an attempt, as Rorty puts it, 'to keep philosophy an armchair discipline' (ibid., at 50)—in an attempt to investigate language as a 'mirror of nature' that ultimately came out to cut off access to nature unmediated by language. Also see his *Philosophy and the Mirror of Nature* (Princeton: Princeton University Press 1979). Rorty draws weighty consequences from the linguistic turn that extend to fundamental philosophical questions, in particular to epistemology. Even if one does not share the consequences he draws, the turn is yet pervasive because it has precisely transformed debates surrounding the relationship between expressions and whatever lies beyond expressions in the world or in our minds.

[63] Such semantic pragmatism in the wake of Wittgenstein can find considerable common ground. For a concise and accessible account see D M Patterson, 'Dworkin on the Semantics of Legal and Political Concepts' (2006) 26 *Oxford Journal of Legal Studies* 545–57 (inter alia specifying semantic pragmatism's main contentions and excluding a range of alleged implications that do not follow). Cf. D Canale and G Tuzet, 'On Legal Inferentialism. Toward a Pragmatics of Semantic Content in Legal Interpretation?' (2007) 20 *Ratio Juris* 32–44; M Winkler, 'Die normativität des Praktischen' (2009) *Juristenzeitung* 821–29.

[64] Wittgenstein, *Philosophical Investigations*, para 43. Also see S Krämer, *Sprache, Sprechakt, Kommunikation* (Frankfurt am Main: Suhrkamp 2001), 128.

[65] Kant's work already offers an early account of infinite regress when it comes to applying a general norm to concrete facts. See Kant, *Critique of Pure Reason*, 263 ('Now if [general logic] wanted to show generally how one ought to subsume under... rules, i.e., distinguish whether something stands under them or not, this could not happen except once again through a rule. But just because this is a rule, it would demand another instruction for the power of judgment, and so it becomes clear that... the power of judgment is a special talent that cannot be taught but only practiced.').

Staatsrechtslehrertagung in Vienna, the annual showdown of German-language public law scholars.[66] Kelsen famously argued that a categorical distinction between law-creation and law-application is untenable. Every act of law-application is also one of lawmaking.[67] The general and abstract norm cannot serve as a basis for recognizing what the concrete norm in the individual case must be. His contention that a norm derives its validity from another norm authorizing its creation is meant as a point on validity and precisely does not extend to the meaning of norms.[68] The foundational norm could never wholly determine the content (the meaning) of the norm that is based on it. His critique of methodological orthodoxy culminates in his sharp epitomizing statement that there is 'no imperative without an imperator'.[69] Kelsen had in effect pulled the rug from under traditional ideas of legal subsumption. The outer limits that mark the field of possible interpretations, the limits set by a kind of ordinary meaning of terms, may, according to Kelsen, be recognized in an act of scientific cognition by capable legal scholars; but true to the Kantian inspiration of his legal theory, the concrete meaning of a norm in the individually disputed case cannot be *discovered* but only *created*. He showed that the legal order only finds its concrete shape in processes of continuous application. While some fundamental differences certainly remain, this brings him in effect close to realist conceptions of the law.[70] Kelsen went a long way towards a communicative understanding of lawmaking but, also true to his Kantian inspiration, he maintained that able legal scholars could still in the abstract find the law in an act of cognition.[71] It is furthermore not clear whether he thought that the norm produced in the concrete application of the law would feed back onto the law in general.

While Kelsen might be read as having anticipated some of the challenges of the linguistic turn, a number of other approaches to international law have since better absorbed the critique of legal positivism's semantics—in particular those which, like Kelsen's theory, lean on sociological views of the law. It has been the particular strength of the New Haven School to offer a communicative approach to lawmaking. It elucidates the variety of actors engaged in lawmaking, but it obscures the logic of *legal* communication (a.). The theory of transnational legal processes has a slightly different focus but faces very similar problems (b.). Systems theory has also been path-breaking in its understanding of law as a system composed of self-referential communicative operations. It respects the intrinsic logic of the legal

[66] H Kelsen, *Wesen und Entwicklung der Staatsgerichtsbarkeit*, Veröffentlichungen der Vereinigung der Deutschen Staatsrechtslehrer, vol 5 (Berlin: Walter de Gruyter 1929).

[67] Ibid. Also see H Kelsen, *Reine Rechtslehre* (Leipzig: Deuticke 1934), 82–3 and 95. On this point Kelsen draws heavily on A Merkl, 'Das Doppelte Rechtantlitz' (1918) 47 *Juristische Blätter* 425.

[68] A Jakab, 'Probleme der Stufenbaulehre' (2005) 91 *Archiv für Rechts- und Sozialphilosophie* 333–65 (expounding the problems that arise from this bold distinction).

[69] H Kelsen, *General Theory of Norms* (Oxford: Clarendon 1991), 29.

[70] See H Dagan, 'The Realist Conception of Law' (2007) 57 *University of Toronto Law Journal* 607–60; H Kelsen, 'Eine "Realistische" und die Reine Rechtslehre' (1959) 10 *Österreichische Zeitschrift für öffentliches Recht* 1–25 (on the significant differences that Kelsen sees as distinguishing him from legal realism).

[71] Kelsen, *General Theory*, 44.

system but in order to achieve this gain, it forfeits its grasp on agency; that is, on any concrete actor (c.).

a) The New Haven School

The architects of a policy-oriented view on international law from New Haven were most outspoken about their disdain for thinking in terms of formal sources.[72] International law, Myres McDougal found, should be 'regarded not as mere rules but as a whole *process* of authoritative decisions in the world arena'.[73] Lawmaking neither ended nor started with sources. Seven phases of decision-making and execution were spelled out to help identify international law in the processes driven by power.[74] The early views cast on international law from New Haven were decidedly functional and endorsed a substantive overarching end towards which all efforts should be directed; namely, the protection of human dignity.[75] With this move away from positivism, the distinction between *lex lata* and *lex ferenda* became increasingly less important.[76] Doctrines of sources and references to Art. 38 ICJ Statute were replaced by a sociological view on what participants in legal discourse actually do—the focus shifted from sources to communication.

In his seminal article 'International Lawmaking: A Process of Communication' Michael Reisman argues that scholarly teachings and judgments had developed a myth—the myth that international law could be found by looking at what Art. 38 claims to be the sources of all law.[77] The model of positivism, he contends, is distorting precisely because it holds that law is made by the legislator.[78] Reisman maintains instead that international law emerges from the myriad of legal communications that a plethora of actors utter every day. In light of this observation, he develops a novel scheme, wholly unrelated to sources, that distinguishes legal from non-legal communications.[79] He maintains that sovereignty's lawmaking function

[72] See generally v Hoof, *Rethinking the Sources*, 39–44; Koskenniemi, *Gentle Civilizer of Nations*, 474–80.

[73] M S McDougal, *Studies in World Public Order* (New Haven: Yale University Press 1960), 169. Also see R Higgins, 'Policy Considerations and the International Judicial Process' (1968) 17 *International and Comparative Law Quarterly* 58–84, 58 ('international law is a continuing process of authoritative decisions'); B Cheng, Epilogue: On the Nature and Sources of International Law, in: *International Law: Teaching and Practice* (London: Stevens 1982), 203–33.

[74] M S McDougal, H D Lasswell, and J C Miller, *The Interpretation of Agreements and World Public Order* (New Haven, CT: Yale University Press 1967), 13–21.

[75] See M S McDougal, 'International Law, Power, and Policy: A Contemporary Conception' (1954) 82 *Recueil des Cours* 137–259; W M Reisman (ed), *Toward World Order and Human Dignity. Essays in Honor of Myres S. McDougal* (New York: Free Press 1976). It is interesting to note that this comes close to idealist positions in a natural law tradition, see v Hoof, *Rethinking the Sources*, 41.

[76] Higgins, *Problems & Process*, 10.

[77] M Reisman, 'International Lawmaking: A Process of Communication' (1981) 75 *American Society of International Law Proceedings* 101–20.

[78] Ibid., at 107.

[79] Ibid., at 108, drawing on a more detailed argument in M S McDougal and M Reisman, 'The Prescribing Function in World Constitutive Process: How International Law is Made' (1980) 6 *Yale Studies in World Public Order* 249–84.

may be found in all legal communications. International lawmaking is not a feature exclusively reserved for unitary sovereign states.[80] Reisman further finds that, given that the international legal process is no longer dominated by governments alone, newly generated legal norms can conflict with norms that others might find with a formalist look at traditional sources of the law. His process-oriented view of international law transcends formalism and claims to be in a position of granting humanitarian concerns, voiced by a wide range of actors in international political discourse, a legal status even if they conflict with norms that have a formal pedigree in the sources of law.[81] As in other sociological approaches to law, humanitarianism is construed as a social fact and constitutes a point of reference for normative judgment with certain autonomy from positive legal norms.[82]

b) Theory of transnational legal processes

The theory of transnational legal processes (TLP), a spin-off from New Haven, shares the critique of legal positivism and formalism. It does not look at formal sources of the law but at the dynamic and 'jurisgenerative' interactions among a multitude of actors.[83] But this approach does not share what may well be called the 'enlightenment confidence that science produces over time a stream of advances in knowledge, and the further conviction that if knowledge is properly put to the task of the realization of values, the results will lead inevitably to human betterment'.[84] In contrast to other voices from New Haven, TLP does not, at least not at first glimpse, put international law in the instrumental service of given goals. Its chief architect and proponent Harold Koh rather claims that transnational legal processes are themselves jurisgenerative and that it is the participation and interaction of the grand variety of non-state actors as well as the internalization of norms that ensures the normativity of the process.[85] It remains opaque why that should be the case. The main point of TLP appears to be its take on compliance theory.[86] As an approach to what international (or transnational) law is or where it can be found, it ranges from vague to simply mute.

Mary Ellen O'Connell has attempted to fill this theoretical gap within the framework of TLP. But in the end she comes around full cycle and embraces a functionalist perspective that she first strongly rejected. In the end she demands

[80] Reisman, 'Jurisprudence' 605–28.

[81] See for an illustrative example his legal justification of the NATO intervention in Kosovo, M Reisman, 'Unilateral Action and the Transformations of the World Constitutive Process: The special problem of humanitarian intervention' (2000) 11 *European Journal of International Law* 3–18.

[82] For a normative appraisal of this position see below Chapter V, section A.1.

[83] H H Koh, 'Transnational Legal Process' (1996) 75 *Nebraska Law Review* 181–207; it borrows the concept of 'jurisgenesis' from the work of Robert Cover, see R M Cover, 'Nomos and Narrative' (1983) 97 *Harvard Law Review* 4–68.

[84] R A Falk, 'Casting the Spell: The New Haven School of International Law' (1995) 104 *Yale Law Journal* 1991–2008, 2002, quoted in F Hanschmann, Theorie transnationaler Rechtsprozesse, in: S Buckel, R Christensen, and A Fischer-Lescano (eds), *Neue Theorien des Rechts* (Stuttgart: Lucius und Lucius 2009), 375–400, 384.

[85] Koh, 'Transnational Legal Process', 205.

[86] H H Koh, 'Bringing International Law Home' (1998) 35 *Houston Law Review* 623–81.

reaching out to society's values where treaties and customary rules do not fully support a desired outcome.[87] The strength of TLP after all seems to lie in its account of norm compliance; with at least one principal weakness, however. It suggests that the interaction between a variety of actors in a transnational legal process is jurisgenerative, and it contends at the same time that such processes account for norm compliance by way of internalization. Both propositions are probably true, but they stand in uneasy tension. Is it a given norm that is internalized or does this norm change in the process of internalization? Is it not a process that portrays law-creative features? The latter seems more plausible and fits with TLP's theoretical background but the thought is not taken any further.

Wayne Sandholtz picks up TLP as a theoretical frame in order to ask head-on how norms change. He arrives at a cyclic model in which disputes triggered by events generate debate that in turn changes norms.[88] This bodes well. Yet, again, TLP accounts primarily for processes of norm internalization rather than change. The law-creative aspect is nebulous to the extent that Sandholtz confines his observation to social norms because:

> International law, of course, has well-established rules for adding to or changing the stock of international legal norms: the sources of international law. New rules emerge and existing rules evolve through the formal process of treaty creation as well as through the development of customary law.[89]

How legal norms change is not even part of the question. It appears to be a lucky coincidence that at the end of each of his norm cycles governments signed a new treaty and thus the question did not arise with much force whether the legal norm had changed prior to that legislative act. In the last chapter Sandholtz ponders the question, however, whether, in light of the Iraq war and in view of arguments centred on the plundering of Iraqi museums, there now exists an obligation on the occupant to protect cultural property. He suggests that there is a consensus that carries this interpretation—'[w]hen a consensus emerges, the rule is altered.'[90] His book does not explore whether this also holds for legal rules. By his account, they only change through the formal channels offered by the sources of international law.

Paul Schiff Berman's approach may be read as a correction of this shortcoming. Berman highlights Robert Cover's work on jurisgenerative practices—that is continuous contestation among interpretative communities that 'do create law and do give meaning to law through their narratives and precepts'.[91] This opens the door

[87] M E O'Connell, 'New International Legal Process' (2004) 36 *Studies in Transnational Legal Policy* 79–107, 104.

[88] W Sandholtz, *Prohibiting Plunder: How Norms Change* (Oxford: Oxford University Press 2007). Cf. W Sandholtz and A Stone Sweet, Law, Politics, and International Governance, in: C Reus-Smit (ed), *The Politics of International Law* (Cambridge: Cambridge University Press 2004), 238–71; W Sandholtz and K Stiles, *International Norms and Cycles of Change* (Oxford: Oxford University Press 2009) (applying the cyclic model of norm change to a greater number of cases).

[89] Sandholtz, *Prohibiting Plunder*, 9.

[90] Ibid., at 262.

[91] P S Berman, 'A Pluralist Approach to International Law' (2007) 32 *Yale Journal of International Law* 301–29, quoting Cover, 'Nomos and Narrative', 40.

for sketching law as existing in numerous co-existing, competing, and overlapping normative universes. Cover did not himself engage in debates of legal pluralism but his work certainly lent itself in support of pluralist conceptions of law when he claimed that 'all collective behavior entailing systematic understandings of our commitments to future worlds [can lay] equal claim to the word "law"'.[92] Law is not tied to recognized sources but emerges from social interaction among a variety of actors, including multinational corporations, non-governmental organizations, international organizations, terrorist networks, media and, in special circumstances, individuals. There is no centralized process of lawmaking but multiple normative communities generate their own legal norms. The grand picture is one of global legal pluralism.[93] The focus then is not on semantic change of a given norm text but on the generation of new norms in complete detachment from avenues of formal lawmaking.

c) *Systems theory*

A quite similar picture of lawmaking in communicative processes has been drawn within the theoretical framework of systems theory.[94] It also absorbs the challenges of the linguistic turn but sets itself apart from policy-oriented jurisprudence by remaining bound to the intrinsic logic of the legal system. It finds that other external perspectives on legal practice tend to reduce such practice to the logics of other systems such as political, economic, or cultural systems with their respective logic. Legal practice then becomes indistinguishable.[95] In response, Niklas Luhmann saw law as a system within society, which is constituted by communications that operate with reference to the binary code of legal/illegal. This is their distinctive feature.[96]

One of systems theory's overarching propositions is that law is an autopoietic subsystem of society that encompasses all communications that contain claims about (il)legality.[97] The concept of autopoiesis is used to suggest that communications within a system can only operate by reference to communications of that same system—legal claims have to refer to legal claims in order to be valid legal claims.[98]

[92] R M Cover, 'The Folktales of Justice: Tales of Jurisdiction' (1985) 14 *Capital University Law Review* 179–203, 181.

[93] Berman, 'A Pluralist Approach'; also see P S Berman, 'Global Legal Pluralism' (2007) 80 *Southern California Law Review* 1155–237.

[94] On the similarities between TLP and systems theory, F Hanschmann, Theorie transnationaler Rechtsprozesse, in: S Buckel, R Christensen, and A Fischer-Lescano (eds), *Neue Theorien des Rechts* (Stuttgart: Lucius und Lucius 2009), 375–400.

[95] A Fischer-Lescano and G Teubner, 'Regime-Collisions: The Vain Search for Legal Unity in the Fragmentation of Global Law' (2004) 25 *Michigan Journal of International Law* 999–1045, 1003–4; Luhmann, *Das Recht der Gesellschaft*, 9–18.

[96] Ibid., especially at 61. On Luhmann's concept of law also see T Vesting, *Rechtstheorie* (München: Beck 2007), 57–71; R Dreier, 'Niklas Luhmanns Rechtsbegriff' (2002) 88 *Archiv für Rechts- und Sozialphilosophie* 305–22.

[97] Luhmann, *Recht der Gesellschaft*, chapter 2.

[98] Ibid., at 98; G Teubner, *Recht als autopoietisches System* (Frankfurt am Main: Suhrkamp 1989); T Vesting, 'Kein Anfang und kein Ende. Die Systemtheorie des Rechts als Herausforderung für

Legislative changes in the law can enter the legal system only by way of a 'structural coupling' between the political and legal system—in the domestic context this path is paved by the constitution.[99] In the international context this coupling portrays significantly different features and the chances of input from the political into the legal system are rather minimal.[100] There are two principal implications: first, international law evolves aloof from political-legislative input; second, since the functional and institutional differentiation of the political and legal system is only little advanced when compared with domestic contexts, communicative operations in international law tend to portray more elements that would usually belong to other systems—international legal argument would thus show more references to morality and politics, for instance.[101]

From the viewpoint of systems theory, the world society and global law are characterized by functional specializations rather than territorial delimitations. Leaning on Eugen Ehrlich's sociology of law, Gunther Teubner points towards 'Global Bukowina'—subsystems within the global society that create their own normative orders.[102] He argues that 'global law will grow mainly from the social peripheries, not from the political centres of nation-states and international institutions'.[103] In the outlook of systems theory, legal pluralism can be understood as the various communicative processes within particular social fields that operate according to the code of legal/illegal.[104] In such processes, the role and impact of non-state actors is of increasing importance. The communicative processes also fall into distinct sectors that are institutionally organized in various regimes and driven by particular rationalities.[105]

Rechtswissenschaft und Rechtsdogmatik' (2001) *JURA* 299–305. On the concept of autopoiesis also see N Luhmann, *Einführung in die Systemtheorie* (Heidelberg: Carl-Auer 2006), 109–18.

[99] Luhmann, *Recht der Gesellschaft*, chapter 9.

[100] Ibid., at 582; G Teubner, 'Global Bukowina': Legal Pluralism in the World Society, in: *Global Law Without a State* (Aldershot: Dartmouth 1997), 3–28, 6; Fischer-Lescano and Teubner, 'Regime-Collisions', 1014–17 (coining the notion of 'auto-constitutional regimes' in this regard).

[101] In other words, the legal system is not operationally closed. Luhmann, *Recht der Gesellschaft*, 157. One principal reason for this appears to be the relative absence of a system of compulsory international adjudication, something that has changed to some extent. On the contested borders between international law on the one hand, and morality and politics on the other, see M Neves, 'Grenzen der Autonomie des Rechts in einer asymmetrischen Weltgesellschaft' (2007) 93 *Archiv für Rechts- und Sozialphilosophie* 363–95; A Fischer-Lescano and P Liste, 'Völkerrechtspolitik. Zu Trennung und Verknüpfung von Politik und Recht der Weltgesellschaft' (2005) 12 *Zeitschrift für Internationale Beziehungen* 209–49. Also see D Kennedy, 'The Disciplines of International Law and Policy' (1999) 12 *Leiden Journal of International Law* 9–133.

[102] Teubner, Global Bukowina, 3–28 with reference to E Ehrlich, *Grundlegung der Soziologie des Rechts* (Berlin: Duncker & Humblot 1967), 390.

[103] Teubner, Global Bukowina, 7.

[104] Ibid., at 14.

[105] Fischer-Lescano and Teubner, 'Regime-Collisions'; G Teubner, 'Globale Zivilverfassungen: Alternativen zur staatszentrierten Verfassungstheorie' (2003) 63 *Zeitschrift für ausländisches öffentliches Recht und Völkerrecht* 1–28.

Thinking in terms of sources that carries ideas of political-legislative lawmaking gives way to a multiplicity of legal regimes arising out of self-organized social processes. It bears repeating that whether something is law or not can only be answered by observing the operations of the legal system. Understanding law as an operationally closed system of legal communications replaces answers to the question of legal validity that look at a norm's formal pedigree with the test of practice. Luhmann shows how the test for legal validity can only lie in the successful continuous connection from one communicative operation to another within the system.[106]

Approaches to lawmaking that build on jurisgenerative communicative acts have convincingly critiqued thinking about the origins of law in terms of sources. Yet, they suffer from either of two shortcomings. Approaches within the theoretical framework of systems theory find that views from New Haven have neglected the intrinsic logic of legal practice by subjecting interpretation in law to the logics of the political, economic, or cultural system. Conversely, systems theory has itself paid for recognizing legal practice as a distinct enterprise by losing an adequate grasp on the actual interpretative acts performed by living human beings. Either structural constraints (New Haven) or elements of agency (systems theory) have been largely lost. What remains lacking is a perspective that mediates between *agency* oblivious to the intrinsic logic of legal interpretation and *structure* oblivious to living actors.

B. Semantic struggles in the practice of legal interpretation

Systems theory has placed formal lawmaking by way of sources or in the form of 'legislation' at the periphery of the legal system. In its view, legal developments are not a matter of sources at all but, again fraught with imagery, a matter of evolution. While the concept of evolution might play a convincing role in explaining linguistic change, it bears considerable limitations for understanding legal change. Above all, it abstracts from agency and is oblivious to actual human practices. Interpreters speak the language of international law with the intention of seeking acceptance for their claims about the meaning of norms. It then seems only pertinent to focus more closely on the concrete communicative practices of individual actors. The concept of practice may carry an idea of agency while it remains mindful of structural constraints of legal interpretation (1.). A better conception of legal practice then paves the way for discussing freedom and constraint in the form and substance of legal interpretation (2.). While structural and semantic indeterminacy is tamed in concrete interpretative practice, which has to connect to the past in order to be convincing in the future, the question of how actors negotiate the content of their legal commitments compels closer analysis. Struggles about what the law means are sites for the exercise of power and authority (3.).

[106] Luhmann, *Recht der Gesellschaft*, 110.

1. Practice between agency and structure

a) From evolution to practice in law and language

With the conceptual move towards autopoiesis (the self-referential practice of the legal system) Luhmann had found a fitting response to the challenges that semantic pragmatism poses to legal positivism's thinking in terms of sources—as mentioned above, in the wake of Wittgenstein the question had been how it is possible to follow a rule if its interpretation always depends on another rule, and so forth. The answer Wittgenstein gave was that rule following is a matter of practice.[107] Practice here is used in a manner akin to habit or custom. It is a cultural phenomenon of almost natural quality—practitioners acquire the ability to follow a rule in processes of socialization.[108] An actor must have learned in practice what a rule means—she must have internalized the practice so as not to be in doubt about its meaning: 'I obey the rule blindly', Wittgenstein writes.[109] Interpretative acts that transform meanings evade closer scrutiny in such a praxeological conception of a rule. It may thus be deemed most fitting to think of norm change as a process of evolution. And it would then be the 'blind force of natural selection' that decides how norms change in international law.[110]

Luhmann goes to great lengths to formulate a theory of *legal evolution* and thus replaces the mystique of sources with yet another metaphor that is no less opaque and that no less distances the law from human action.[111] With the understanding of legal change as evolution he stands in good company.[112] It is intriguing that Hans Kelsen too opted for this imagery and developed an evolutionary theory of international law on the basis of an idea of 'biogenetic law'.[113] Scholarly literature

[107] Wittgenstein, *Philosophical Investigations*, para 202. Cf. C Taylor, To Follow a Rule... in: C Calhoun, E LiPuma, and M Postone (eds), *Bourdieu: Critical Perspectives* (Chicago: University of Chicago Press 1993), 45–60; B Bix, *Law, Language and Legal Determinacy* (Oxford: Oxford University Press 1993), 38–45.

[108] Wittgenstein shows right at the outset of his *Philosophical Investigations* that learning a language is not about explaining what an expression means but about drill and training, see para 208. Cf. Krämer, *Sprache, Sprechakt, Kommunikation,* 133.

[109] Wittgenstein, *Philosophical Investigations*, para 219.

[110] Luhmann, *Recht der Gesellschaft*, 239–96; Vesting, *Rechtstheorie*, 137–44; A Abegg, Evolutorische Rechtstheorie, in: S Buckel, R Christensen, and A Fischer-Lescano (eds), *Neue Theorien des Rechts* (Stuttgart: Lucius und Lucius 2009), 401–22.

[111] Compare the vivid narrative on the rise and fall of the 'natural science of law', R M Kiesow, *Das Naturgesetz des Rechts* (Frankfurt am Main: Suhrkamp 1997).

[112] It should be pointed out that Luhmann duly notes that thinking of legal change in terms of evolution only makes good sense if the legal system is operationally closed; that is, political operations do not have an immediate impact on legal communications. Luhmann, *Das Recht der Gesellschaft*, 257. This condition is at least as precarious in international law as it is in many domestic legal systems, see M Neves, 'Grenzen der Autonomie des Rechts in einer asymmetrischen Weltgesellschaft' (2007) 93 *Archiv für Rechts- und Sozialphilosophie* 363–95.

[113] H Kelsen, *Law and Peace in International Relations* (Cambridge, MA: Harvard University Press 1942), 148–9; cf. C Jabloner, 'Verrechtlichung und Rechtsdynamik' (1999) 54 *Zeitschrift für öffentliches Recht* 261–78. For the domesic context also see A Watson, *The Evolution of Law* (Oxford: Blackwell 1985), and for the use of evolutionary concepts in international relations theory see A Florini, 'The Evolution of International Norms' (1996) 40 *International Studies Quarterly* 363–89.

generally offers many uses of the concept of evolution.[114] Ian Sinclair for example found that 'the evolution of the law can be taken into account in interpreting certain terms in a treaty which are by their very nature expressed in such general terms as to lend themselves to an evolutionary interpretation'.[115]

Also judicial practice has warmly embraced this concept. Above all the European Court of Human Rights has accepted the *topos* of 'evolutive interpretation' as a common feature in its judgments.[116] The ICJ has spoken about the evolution of international law in a number of cases[117] and the WTO Appellate Body has found, for example, that the expression 'exhaustibly natural resources' is 'by definition, evolutionary'.[118] Also in *China—Publications and Audiovisual Products* the Panel held that China's schedule entry should be interpreted in an evolutionary fashion. In the appeal China then submitted that its scope of commitments could not be extended based on 'temporal variations in language'.[119] It failed with this claim and the Appellate Body simply stated that 'the terms used in China's GATS Schedule... [are] sufficiently generic that what they apply to may change over time'.[120] In short, it is rather common to understand developments in law and language as evolution.

Linguistic theory seems to readily support the conception of legal change in terms of evolution. The linguist Rudi Keller developed an evolutionary theory of language change and argued that language is an unintended by-product of a myriad of intentional actions—an 'object of the third kind', as he terms it.[121] For an

[114] See, e.g., A Anghie, 'The Evolution of International Law: Colonial and Postcolonial Realities' (2006) 27 *Third World Quarterly* 739–53; E Benvenisti and G W Downs, 'National Courts, Domestic Democracy, and the Evolution of International Law' (2009) 20 *European Journal of International Law* 59–72; R Kolb, 'Repères historiques dans l'évolution de l'occupation de guerre' (2007) *The Global Community* 65–102; N Schrijver, *The Evolution of Sustainable Development in International Law: Inception, Meaning and Status* (Leiden: Nijhoff 2008).

[115] I M Sinclair, *The Vienna Convention on the Law of Treaties* (Manchester: Manchester University Press 1984), 140.

[116] See, e.g., *Case of Bayatyan v Armenia*, 27 October 2009, para 63; *Case of Scoppola v Italy (No. 2)*, Grand Chamber, 17 September 2009, para 104; *Emonet and others v Switzerland*, 13 December 2007, paras 66 and 83. It should be noted, however, that the court has also repeatedly recalled that it 'cannot, by means of an evolutive interpretation, derive from these instruments a right that was not included therein at the outset. This is particularly so here, where the omission was deliberate.' *Case of Johnston and others v Ireland*, 18 December 1986, para 53. Cf. R Bernhardt, 'Evolutive Treaty Interpretation, Especially of the European Convention on Human Rights' (1999) 42 *German Yearbook of International Law* 11–25; G Malinverni, Il ruolo della Corte di Strasburgo nell'evoluzione della Convenzione europea di diritti dell'uomo, in: F Salerno (ed), *Il ruolo del giudice internazionale nell'evoluzione del diritto internazionale e communitario* (Padova: Cedam 1995), 125–42.

[117] *Aegean Sea Continental Shelf (Greece v Turkey)*, Judgment of 19 December 1978, ICJ Reports 3, para 77 (the court easily, though with an emphasis on the particularity of the convention under dispute, states that it 'hardly seems conceivable that in such a convention terms like "domestic jurisdiction" and "territorial status" were intended to have a fixed content regardless of the subsequent evolution of international law.'); *Case Concerning the Dispute Regarding Navigational and Related Rights (Costa Rica v Nicaragua)*, Judgment of 13 July 2009, para 65.

[118] Appellate Body Report, *United States—Import Prohibition of Certain Shrimp and Shrimp Like Products*, WT/DS58/AB/R, 6 November 1998, paras 127–131.

[119] Appellate Body Report, *China—Publications and Audiovisual Products*, WT/DS363/AB/R, 21 December 2009, para 47.

[120] Ibid., at para 396.

[121] R Keller, *Sprachwandel* (Tübingen: Francke 2003), 93.

evolutionary explanation to be adequate, he notes, three conditions have to be met: the process must not be analysed in light of a given goal (this precludes any talk of evolution towards something that has not yet come about[122]), it must be a cumulative process involving numerous individuals and knowing no single author, and the dynamics of the process must be based on a combination of variation and selection.[123] This fits well with central tenets of systems theory.[124] However, Keller is enormously cautious and notes with reference to his colleague Eugeniu Coşeriu that human sciences will eventually have to find their own concept to replace the term 'evolution'.[125] Coşeriu cautioned against the use of the concept and notably argued that nothing can impact language that does not pass through the speakers' freedom and intelligence.[126]

In sum, the competition between agency-centred and structural explanations flares up again in the discussion of the concept of evolution. Sure enough, no single interpretation can by and for itself be transformative—transformations in meaning hinge on acceptance within the community of interpreters. The concept of evolution highlights environmental (structural) conditions that drive selection processes and impact particular interpretations' chances of success. Yet, with this focus it blends out any bearing of actors on those same conditions. But actors in legal interpretation engage in semantic struggle with the decided interest of finding acceptance for their claims about the meaning of legal expressions and thus seek to influence what is considered (il)legal. In law, particular consequences attach to given expressions—e.g. once a person is a 'combatant' he may be detained until the end of hostilities.[127] Interpreters have an interest in the meaning of norms because the norms already contain a distribution of outcomes. Some actors possess immense resources that they are willing to put to use in semantic struggles in international law. Law, like language, is a social, not a natural product. While the concept of evolution recalls that no single act of interpretation generates meaning, it unduly abstracts from agency and from the politics at work within processes of change.[128] Max Weber wrote succinctly:

> The mere change of external conditions is . . . neither sufficient nor indispensible. Decisive is rather continuously novel *action*, which leads to semantic change of valid law or to the creation of new law.[129]

[122] Also Luhmann has aptly noted that the concept of evolution precludes predictions, *Recht der Gesellschaft*, 296. This fitting insight is certainly not widely heeded.

[123] Keller, *Sprachwandel*, 191–6.

[124] Luhmann, *Recht der Gesellschaft*, 277.

[125] E Coşeriu, *Synchronie, Diachronie und Geschichte. Das Problem des Sprachwandels* (München: 1974), 154.

[126] Ibid., at 169.

[127] I Venzke, 'Legal Contestation about "Enemy Combatants": On the Exercise of Power in Legal Interpretation' (2009) 5 *Journal of International Law & International Relations* 155–84.

[128] See below section B.3.

[129] M Weber, *Wirtschaft und Gesellschaft* (Paderborn: Voltmedia 2006 [1922]), 650 (German: 'Die bloße Änderung der äußeren Bedingungen ist . . . weder ausreichend noch unentbehrlich. Entscheidend ist vielmehr stets neuartiges *Handeln*, welches zu einem Bedeutungswandel von geltendem Recht oder zur Neuschaffung von Recht führt.').

On a very similar note, Rudolf von Jhering already critiqued Friedrich Carl von Savigny's historical school of law for its romantic idea that lawmaking unfolds in an inward process in analogy to language.[130] Von Jhering argued that such an analogy must be resolutely rejected. With regard to its political implications, he found that it contains one of the most calamitous heterodoxies: where man should act, and should act with a clear awareness of purpose and mobilizing all his power, this romantic idea consoles him with the suggestion that things work for themselves and that the best he can do is fold his hands in his lap and wait with confidence that the alleged 'original' sources slowly bring the law to the light of day bit by bit.[131] In order not to fall for such an error and not to snooze with a romanticized image of legal evolution on the mind, it is only pertinent to counterbalance the structural explanation by directing the spotlight at actual communicative practices and to show the actors behind them. A renewed conception of practice is well suited to do so.

Theoretical perspectives that give prime consideration to the concept of practice have long been mainly structuralist (and mainly Marxist). They have not combined a conception of practice with agency—their theoretical straightjacket would simply not allow this.[132] It was in particular Maurice Merleau-Ponty who brought life and agency into the concept of practice.[133] He conceived practice as historically situated speaking, thinking, and acting. Practice was not the embodiment of (material) structures but the acting of *living* persons.[134] This is an important change of perspective. It recognizes in principle the feedback that actors have on the structures that constitute and constrain their actions.

130 R v Jhering, *The Struggle for Law* (Chicago: Callaghan 1915), 7. On Savigny's idea of law, see M Kriele, *Theorie der Rechtsgewinnung. Entwickelt am Problem der Verfassungsinterpretation* (Berlin: Duncker & Humblot 1976), 67–84; A Dufour, 'Droit et langage dans l'École historique du Droit' (1974) 19 *Archives de philosophie du droit* 151–80.

131 v Jhering, *Struggle for Law*, 14–15 ('we are compelled decidedly to reject the parallel instituted by Savigny—a parallel which found universal favor so rapidly—between law on the one hand and language and art on the other. This doctrine is false, but not dangerous as a philosophical opinion. As a political maxim, however, it contains an error pregnant with the most ominous consequences imaginable, because it feeds man with hope where he should act, and act with a full and clear consciousness of the object aimed at, and with all his strength. It feeds him with the hope that things will take care of themselves, and that the best he can do is to fold his arms and confidently wait for what may gradually spring to light from that primitive source of all law called: the natural conviction of legal right').

132 See, however, the notable attempt at introducing agency into structures by M Hardt and A Negri, *Multitude. War and Democracy in the Age of Empire* (London: Penguin Books 2006) (drawing in particular on Judith Butler's work on transformative speech).

133 'Praxis', in *Handbuch Philosophischer Grundbegriffe*, vol II (München: Koesel 1973), 1131. For a renewed appreciation of the concept see T R Schatzki, Introduction: Practice Theory, in: T R Schatzki, K Knorr Cetina, and E von Savigny (eds), *The Practice Turn in Contemporary Theory* (London: Routledge 2001), 1–14.

134 M Merleau-Ponty, *Die Abenteuer der Dialektik* (Frankfurt am Main: Suhrkamp 1968), 62–3. Cf. Taylor, To Follow a Rule, 49 (on the commonalities between Merleau-Ponty and Wittgenstein with regard to their understanding of actors as engaged in practices—as beings who act in and on the world).

Pierre Bourdieu was still blunter in his critique of structuralist abstractions from agency: they blunder into the trap of equating what they see as objective observation (unburdened with dealings of living persons) with the view that actors themselves have of their practice.[135] Social actors tend to be ignored where they should rather be included as a constitutive element of the social world.[136] On the contrary, however, only taking account of practice without any critical detachment and understanding for structural predispositions would of course fall for the fallacies of an unbroken subjectivism: sociological insight would be impossible. In other words, factors that explain an actor's behaviour (its legal interpretations) should not be equated with the reasons actors themselves see for their actions. Bourdieu developed his sociology in an attempt to overcome this divide with the notion of a praxeological epistemology.[137] His sociology may be understood as analysis of the intrinsic logic of social actions embedded in structures. It remains bound to structuralist traditions but breaks with them in its focus on practice.

b) Co-constitutive actors and structures

Innovations in international relations theory lend further support to the concept of practice and confirm that it is well suited to advance our understanding of legal interpretation. A short sketch of key developments may suffice to prove the point. It can start with the discipline's critical moment when it (re-)discovered norms as a germane subject of analysis in the late 1970s. At that time, competing theoretical perspectives were designed in order to look at 'regimes', which were understood in Steven Krasner's influential terms as 'principles, norms, rules, and decision-making procedures around which actor expectations converge in a given issue-area'.[138]

In the slightly antiquated regime debate three groups of thought have competed with each other in their description and explanation of the world, each just a notch too myopic.[139] While this debate has been recast ad nauseam, it shows the starting point of important developments that lead to practice as a key concept to support

[135] M Schwingel, *Pierre Bourdieu* (Hamburg: Junius 1995), 52; P Bourdieu, *Sozialer Sinn. Kritik der theoretischen Vernunft* (Frankfurt am Main: Suhrkamp 1987), 56 (calling this move 'intellectualism'). Compare the juxtaposition of internal and external perspectives in legal scholarship, Hart, *Concept of Law*, 88–9.

[136] This critique may also be directed at strong variants of ideal political theory, R Geuss, *Philosophy & Real Politics* (New Jersey: Princeton University Press 2008).

[137] See his *Entwurf einer Theorie der Praxis* (Frankfurt am Main: Suhrkamp 1996). Of course the agency–structure divide reverberates in his concepts of 'habitus' and 'field'. For legal practice see P Bourdieu, 'The Force of Law: Toward a Sociology of the Juridical Field' (1987) 38 *Hastings Law Journal* 814–53; cf. M G Villegas, 'On Pierre Bourdieu's Legal Thought' (2004) 56–7 *Droit et Société* 57–71.

[138] S D Krasner, Structural Causes and Regime Consequences: Regimes as intervening variables, in: S D Krasner (ed), *International Regimes* (Ithaca, NY: Cornell University Press 1983), 1–21, 1. Cf. J G Ruggie, 'International Responses to Technology: Concepts and Trends' (1975) 29 *International Organization* 557–83, 570.

[139] The debates are well captured in Krasner, *International Regimes*; V Rittberger (ed), *Regime Theory and International Relations* (Oxford: Oxford University Press 1993); A Hasenclever, P Mayer, and V Rittberger, *Theories of International Regimes* (Cambridge: Cambridge University Press 1997); for an illustrative juxtaposition of 'rational' and 'reflexive' approaches in the regime debate, also see

an understanding of lawmaking by way of interpretation. Roughly, a first group of *realist* scholars denied that regimes could have any independent effect on state behaviour and argued that regimes are mere epiphenomenona—side effects of state action without any independent influence on decision-making.[140] The second group of *institutionalists* shared some of the ontological assumptions with realists, such as the strong emphasis on unitary states as actors who pursue given interests, but it set itself apart by explaining a genuine impact of institutions on state behaviour by way of changes in the structure of outcomes.[141] Finally, the group of *constructivists* argued that regimes bear on actors' behaviour by way of impacting their identities and preferences, thus developing a sociological-structuralist account that underlies actors' calculations.[142]

The entrenched debates have refined the arguments on all sides and, rather than digging deeper, some bridges were built. First, a concentration on the explanatory value of distinct theories, the recognition that one size does not fit all, and the elaboration of scope conditions have arranged competing approaches in a division of labour. While actor-centred rational choice explanations set in on the assumption of given preferences, constructivist approaches take a step back and look at the formation and change of such preferences.[143] Second, in the camp leaning towards rational-choice approaches, the concept of 'regime' has been largely replaced by that of 'institution'—encapsulating lessons learned from the regime debate.[144] The definition of institutions as 'the rules of the game in a society or [...] the humanly devised constraints that shape human interaction'[145] pays due regard to the fact that institutions are always both endogenous to actors' choice (they are shaped by

R O Keohane, *International Institutions and State Power: Essays in International Relations Theory* (Boulder: Westview Press 1989), chapter 7.

140 J J Mearsheimer, 'The False Promise of International Institutions' (1994) 19 *International Security* 5–49; J Sterling-Folker, Realist Global Governance: Revisiting *cave! hic dragones* and beyond, in: A D Ba and M J Hoffmann (eds), *Contending Perspectives on Global Governance* (London: Routledge 2005), 17–38.

141 L L Martin and B Simmons, 'Theories and Empirical Studies of International Institutions' (1998) 52 *International Organization* 729–57.

142 A Wendt, 'Constructing International Politics' (1995) 20 *International Security* 71–81.

143 K W Abbott, 'Toward a Richer Institutionalism for International Law and Policy' (2006) 1 *Journal of International Law & International Relations* 9–34; D Ambrosetti, 'Contre l'opposition 'intérêts *versus* normes'. Rivalités interétatiques et relations de cleintèle sous un prisme constructiviste' (2006) 37 *Études internationales* 525–46; J T Checkel, 'The Constructivist Turn in International Relations Theory' (1998) 50 *World Politics* 324–48 (already voicing the pertinent criticism that constructivism fails to explain where structures come from).

144 See A-M Slaughter, 'International Law and International Relations' (2000) 285 *Recueil des Cours* 13–249, 35–9. On early understandings of institution see Keohane, *International Institutions*, 163 (defining institutions as 'persistent and connected sets of rules (formal and informal) that prescribe behavioral roles, constrain activity, and shape expectations'); compare however Keohane's understanding *After Hegemony* (Princeton: Princeton University Press 1984), 246 ('institutions that facilitate cooperation do not mandate what governments must do; rather, they help governments pursue their own interests through cooperation'). Also see W Sandholtz and A Stone Sweet, Law, Politics, and International Governance, in: C Reus-Smit (ed), *The Politics of International Law* (Cambridge: Cambridge University Press 2004), 238–71, 239–44.

145 D C North, *Institutions, Institutional Change and Economic Performance* (Cambridge: Cambridge University Press 1990), 3.

actors) and exogenous (they have an independent effect on actors). They are product and constraint.[146] This development in the discipline of international relations lends strong support to a study of international law that centres on the transformative dimension of legal practice.

There are a number of concrete approaches that build on this renewed convergence of agency and structure.[147] It has found but one prominent expression in an 'actor-centred institutionalism', which understands institutions as products of interactions among intentional actors and maintains at the same time that these interactions are structured and shaped by the institutional settings.[148] Equipped with such an understanding of institutions, institutional change can be conceived as the interplay between intentional social action and institutional settings—shaped by and shaping social action.[149]

Constructivists in international relations theory, conversely, have preferred to talk of 'norms' rather than 'institutions' or 'regimes'. The focus has for some time been on compliance, which constructivists have explained by pointing to processes of socialization and internalization of a given norm.[150] In contrast to such *behaviourist* strands that look at the effect of *static* norms, *reflexive* approaches look at the effect of communicative practices on the *transformation* of norms. It is not the working of a given norm that is at issue but rather the change of norms in processes of contestation.[151] Anthony Giddens' classical argument figures as a source of inspiration. 'Structural properties of social systems' he maintained, 'are both the medium and the outcome of the practices that constitute those systems.'[152]

[146] D Snidal, 'Political Economy and International Institutions' (1996) 16 *International Review of Law and Economics* 121–37, 127. Also see A Héritier, *Explaining Institutional Change in Europe* (Oxford: Oxford University Press 2007), 5–7.

[147] For a pointed introduction into the problem see A Wendt, 'The Agent-Structure Problem in International Relations Theory' (1987) 41 *International Organization* 335–70.

[148] R Mayntz and F W Scharpf, Der Ansatz des akteurzentrierten Institutionalismus, in: R Mayntz and F W Scharpf (eds), *Steuerung und Selbstorganisation in staatsnahen Sektoren* (Frankfurt am Main: Campus 1995), 39–72; F W Scharpf, *Games Real Actors Play* (Boulder: Westview Press 1997). Cf. O Keck, 'Zur sozialen Konstruktion des Rational-Choice-Ansatzes. Einige Klarstellungen zur Rationalismus-Konstruktivismus-Debatte' (1997) 4 *Zeitschrift für Internationale Beziehungen* 139–51. See further S Oeter, Theorising the Global Legal Order—An Institutionalist Perspective, in: A Halpin and V Roeben (eds), *Theorising the Global Legal Order* (Oxford: Hart 2009), 61–83 (drawing on actor-centred institutionalism in a legal perspective).

[149] P Pierson, *Politics in Time* (Princeton: Princeton University Press 2004), 153–66; A Héritier, *Explaining Institutional Change in Europe* (Oxford: Oxford University Press 2007), 10–66.

[150] See, e.g., M Finnemore, 'Norms, Culture and World Politics: Insights from Sociology's Institutionalism' (1996) 50 *International Organization* 325–47; T Risse and K Sikkink, The Socialization of International Human Rights Norms into Domestic Practices: Introduction, in: T Risse, S C Ropp, and K Sikkink (eds), *The Power of Human Rights. International Norms and Domestic Change* (Cambridge: Cambridge University Press 1999), 1–38. This is where constructivist research and theories of transnational legal process meet.

[151] A Wiener, 'Contested Compliance: Interventions on the Normative Structure of World Politics' (2004) 10 *European Journal of International Relations* 189–234; A Wiener and U Puetter, 'The Quality of Norms is What Actors Make of It. Critical Constructivist Research on Norms' (2009) 5 *Journal of International Law & International Relations* 1–15.

[152] A Giddens, *Central Problems in Social Theory. Action, Structure and Contradiction in Social Analysis* (London: Macmillan 1979), 69. Cf. T J Berard, 'Rethinking Practices and Structures' (2005) 35 *Philosophy of the Social Sciences* 196–230.

In brief, norms and actors are co-constitutive.[153] As of late, also constructivist approaches have opened up to considerations of agency.[154] Here agency has entered theoretical approaches in the form of strategic construction which directs attention to interest and preference expressed in actors' descriptions of the world.[155]

Overall, the convergence of actors and structure in international relations theory leads to an emphasis of the concept of practice.[156] Moves from the by now classical regime debate to the concepts of institutions and norms eventually lead to the increasing recognition of a co-constitutive relationship between agents and structures. The discipline seems now to turn to practice as a concept that tries to capture these developments.[157] Practice can account for agency in the transformation of structures without neglecting the working of those same structures. For meaningful analyses it might be necessary to cut through this loop at one point in time and to look at one part of the equation. This book's focus on the semantic authority of international institutions is likely to err on the side of the actors. But it deliberately uses a nuanced understanding of practice that soaks up the lesson of long battles on the agency–structure divide in order to remain mindful of the other half of the equation.

There remains however a weak spot in political science research on norms that is akin to that of policy-oriented jurisprudence: it tends to neglect the particularities of *legal* discourse.[158] The following section thus sets out to develop a view of legal

153 A Wendt, *Social Theory of International Politics* (Cambridge: Cambridge University Press 2000), chapter 2.

154 F V Kratochwil, How do Norms Matter?, in: M Byers (ed), *The Role of Law in International Politics* (Oxford: Oxford University Press 2000), 35–68; A Wiener, Die Wende zum Dialog: Konstruktivistische Brückenstationen und ihre Zukunft, in: G Hellmann, K D Wolf, and M Zürn (eds), *Die neuen Internationalen Beziehungen* (Baden-Baden: Nomos 2003), 133–59.

155 M Finnemore and K Sikkink, 'International Norm Dynamics and Political Change' (1998) 52 *International Organization* 887–917; R A Payne, 'Persuasion, Frames and Norm Construction' (2001) 7 *European Journal of International Relations* 37–61.

156 In the same vein, see J Friedrichs and F Kratochwil, 'On Acting and Knowing: How Pragmatism Can Advance International Relations Research and Methodology' (2009) 63 *International Organization* 701–31; C Bueger and F Gadinger, 'Praktisch Gedacht! Praxistheoretischer Konstruktivismus in den Internationalen Beziehungen' (2008) 15 *Zeitschrift für Internationale Beziehungen* 273–302. Cf. the idea of communities of practice J Brunée and S Toope, *Legitimacy and Legality in International Law* (Cambridge: Cambridge University Press 2010), especially at 21–3 and 353; E Adler, Communities of Practice in International Relations, in: *Communitarian International Relations* (London: Routledge 2005), 3–28.

157 See P J Katzenstein and R Sil, Eclectic Theorizing in the Study and Practice of International Relations, in: C Reus-Smit and D Snidal (eds), *The Oxford Handbook of International Relations* (Oxford: Oxford University Press 2008), 109–30, 113 ('pragmatism may be considered an ideal-typical center'); C Navari, 'The Concept of Practice in the English School' (2011) 17 *European Journal of International Relations* 611–30; V Pouliot, 'The Logic of Practicality: A Theory of Practice of Security Communities' (2008) 62 *International Organization* 257–88. For a general introduction into the relatively new theoretical perspective of pragmatism in international relations also see G Hellmann, Pragmatismus, in: C Masala, F Sauer, and A Wilhelm (eds), *Handbuch der Internationalen Politik* (Berlin: Springer 2010), 148–81.

158 Notable exceptions to this general weakness include H Bull, *The Anarchical Society* (London: Macmillan 1977), 130 (conceiving international law as a practical activity based on the assumption that what is at issue is law and nothing else); N G Onuf, *World of Our Making: Rules and Rule in Social Theory and International Relations* (Columbia, SC: University of South Carolina Press 1989), 67;

interpretation that can accommodate the transformative moment of interpretative acts within the prevailing structures of the legal discourse.

2. On the form and substance of legal interpretation

> 'Faust: What is your name?
> Mephistopheles: The question seems but cheap
> From one who for the Word has such contempt,
> Who from all outward show is quite exempt
> And only into beings would delve deep.'

Participants in legal discourse invest considerable effort into supporting their claims about what the law is. This section first develops the argument that such contestation in law unfolds on the stabilizing ground of interpretative communities between the extremes of pure objectivity and pure subjectivity. Structural and semantic indeterminacy are usually limited in concrete practice (a.). It then turns to the form of legal interpretation, the rules of interpretation as well as the expectations concerning what interpretation is about that uphold the outward show of legal argument (b.). Finally, it discusses how actors engage in semantic struggles within this outward show and, in substance, negotiate and shift the content of legal commitments—how they make law by way of interpretation (c.).

a) Indeterminacy and contestability in legal interpretation

Locating international lawmaking in the practice of interpretation follows a shift from sources towards communicative practices provoked by the argument that legal norms do not have a meaning other than that attributed to them by their use. This move raises challenges with regard to the concept of law and as H L A Hart observed, '[l]egal theory has in this matter a curious history; for it is apt either to ignore or to exaggerate the indeterminacies of legal rules'.[159] In order not to add yet another twist to this curious history, the concept of practice mediates between unconstrained agency and determinative structures. Hart further suggests distinguishing a core of settled meanings from disputed meanings.[160] To this it is worth adding that a norm's settled meaning is not due to a stable connection between the word (expression) used and the thing or concept to which it refers.[161] Stable meaning is rather the result of the absence of dispute. While

Kratochwil, How do Norms Matter?, 35–68, 36 (noting that 'if we are interested in how norms matter, we must begin with the problem of praxis and draw from there the implications for both political and legal analysis'); Finnemore and Sikkink, 'International Norm Dynamics', 916.

[159] Hart, *Concept of Law*, 130. Also see S Cobb, 'A Critique of Critical Discourse Analysis: Deconstructing and Reconstructing the Role of Intention' (1994) 4 *Communication Theory* 132–52.

[160] Hart, *Concept of Law*, 120–8.

[161] The relationship between expression, meaning, and thing is classically portrayed in the semiotic triangle introduced by C K Ogden and I A Richards, *The Meaning of Meaning. A Study of the Influence of Language upon Thought and of the Science of Symbolism* (London: Routledge & Kegan 1972), 11.

there may sometimes be some plausibility to the recurrent argument that there is no dispute because the norm is clear, the direction of causality should usually be turned into the opposite. Most of the time the norm is clear because there is no dispute.

But how free or constrained is an interpreter in making claims about the law? In addition to arguments that relate to semantic pragmatism, David Kennedy has developed the complementary argument that international law is structurally indeterminate because it purports to bind the subjects who are at the same time the source of all law.[162] Martti Koskenniemi picked up this argument and meticulously showed how it plays out in concrete instances of applying a norm. He maintains that interpretations either rely on the consent of the sovereign state or else have to resort to an idea of substantive justice. In the first case, Koskenniemi argues, they are apologetic, the direction of argument is ascending or inductive. In the latter case they are utopian, the direction of argument is descending or deductive. International legal argument inescapably oscillates between these two poles and rarely comes to rest.[163]

Koskenniemi's thesis on the structural indeterminacy is for the most part not geared towards capturing change in the law that comes about by way of interpretation. On the face of it, change in the meaning of norms escapes a view on legal argument that concentrates on its oscillation between apology (references to substantive yardsticks of justice) and utopia (references to state consent). Indeed, no external yardstick can decide legal disputes. I take this to be part of the concept of contestation in the way Walter Bryce Gallie coined it: 'what I am claiming is that a certain piece of evidence or argument put forward by one side in an apparently endless dispute can be recognized to have a definite logical force, even by those whom it entirely fails to win over or convert to the side in question.'[164] Contestation is always a possibility. And yet, some interpretations are more likely to succeed than others.[165]

With some distance and hindsight, changes in interpretations' chances to succeed can be termed developments in international norms. In Martti Koskenniemi's work, the concepts of grammar and structural bias flank his indeterminacy argument to suggest that of course not every argument goes. There is a grammar

This still appears to be a useful illustration but must not be mistaken as tying the meaning of an expression to the thing it refers to; compare U Eco, *Einführung in die Semiotik* (München: Fink 2002), 69–74 (accusing Ogden and Richards for lending support to such a mistake).

162 D Kennedy, 'Theses about International Law Discourse' (1980) 23 *German Yearbook of International Law* 353–91. Cf. K Günther, 'The Pragmatic and Functional Indeterminacy of Law' (2011) 12 *German Law Journal* 407–29; N G Onuf, 'Do Rules Say What They Do? From Ordinary Language to International Law' (1985) 26 *Harvard International Law Journal* 385–410.

163 Koskenniemi, *From Apology to Utopia.*

164 W B Gallie, 'Essentially Contested Concepts' (1956) 56 *Proceedings of the Aristotelian Society* 167–98, 190.

165 See U Fastenrath, 'Relative Normativity in International Law' (1993) 4 *European Journal of International Law* 305–40, 336–8 (on the factors that influence an interpretation's chance to succeed).

that interpreters cannot escape and there is a structural bias deeply engrained in international law that channels attention and emphasis.[166] This goes a long way towards understanding interpretation as an exercise that rests on a choice which involves the preferences of the speaker and that is at the same time constrained by past practices. But it still says little about the interaction between actors, or interpreters, and the law, or the structure. It still merits closer analysis as to what those practical constraints on the possibility of contestation are, i.e. the particularities of *legal* discourse. They are of two kinds, relating to the form and the substance of interpretation.

First, the possibility of acceptance of interpretative claims in legal discourse is premised on an argument's qualification as a *legal* interpretative claim. Rules of interpretation and standards upheld by the legal profession prescribe how a legal argument has to be crafted.[167] More precisely, they prescribe how claims have to be argumentatively tied to authoritative reference points—this is more of a necessity than elegance.[168] Certainly, the rules of interpretation are themselves nothing but rules and subject to the same fate of interpretation.[169] Yet, interpretation in law is a distinct enterprise. Its particularity is upheld by a combination of moral choice, beliefs, ethos, and habit.[170]

A second way in which the possibility of contestation is practically limited lies in the fact that interpretations need to connect to the past uses of concepts. Concepts come with histories and already with some content that is carried along by past practices. Some interpretations may be plainly inconceivable and others may not even have the slightest chance of being accepted by other participants in relevant communities. Limitations set by interpretative communities take the ground between the pitfalls of objectivity (the plain meaning of the text) and pure

[166] Koskenniemi, *From Apology to Utopia*, 568 (suggesting that the grammar of international law organizes the production of legal arguments). Cf. M Koskenniemi, '"The Lady Doth Protest Too Much" Kosovo, and the Turn to Ethics in International Law' (2002) 65 *Modern Law Review* 159–75 (offering a concrete example of structural biases and doctrinal blind spots at work in international humanitarian law).

[167] J v Bernstorff, 'Sisyphus was an International Lawyer. On Martti Koskenniemi's "From Apology to Utopia" and the place of law in international politics.' (2006) 7 *German Law Journal* 1015–35, 1029 (arguing that the necessity of tying argumentative claims in a formal way to general legal expressions conveys law's intrinsic aspiration to formal equality); Kratochwil, How do Norms Matter?, 47. Similarly, but with distinct historical baggage, J Waldron, The Rule of Law as a Theatre of Debate, in: J Burley (ed), *Dworkin and his Critics* (Malden, MA: Blackwell Publishers 2004), 319–36.

[168] Cf. Lauterpacht, 'Restrictive Interpretation' (stating that 'it is elegant—and it inspires confidence—to give the garb of an established rule of interpretation to a conclusion reached as to the meaning . . . of a treaty.').

[169] Hart, *Concept of Law*, 126.

[170] J N Shklar, *Legalism* (Cambridge, MA: Harvard University Press 1964); E J Weinrib, 'Legal Formalism: On the Immanent Rationality of Law' (1988) 97 *Yale Law Journal* 949–1016; Bourdieu, 'The Force of Law'.

subjectivity (the unconstrained reading of the text).[171] Robert Brandom has perceptively argued that present interpreters are constrained both by past and future practices. They need to connect to the past in order to be understood and, if they want to be successful and wish to assert their authority, they need to consider in anticipation how their interpretations will be received.[172] In this sense, the development of the law is interstitial.[173] It stands between the past and the future.

When actors enter legal discourses, they enter a context that is already structured by past practices and perpetuated rules. In such concrete contexts, relevant structures may be understood as the already present distribution of a legal claim's chance to succeed in the practice of interpretation. Such structures are themselves products of action and represent an aggregate of various different factors that feed into action. They are also formed by legislation and the positive legal material. Not least, they are shaped by the shifting fortunes of general approaches to international law. Practical limits on the indeterminacy of law and on the theoretical possibility of contestability in legal interpretation point to the binding force of international law. In other words, grasping this constraint approaches the normativity of law. The following two sections expand on the form and substance of legal interpretation respectively.

b) The outward show: Legal argument and rules of interpretation

The legal argumentative form finds loose contours in a 'culture of formalism', a 'legal culture [that] compels a move away from one's idiosyncratic interests and preferences by insisting on their justification in terms of the historical practices'.[174] The culture of formalism emphasizes contestability and agency, on the one hand, and the particularities of legal discourse, on the other. It highlights the necessary translation of idiosyncratic positions into a legal form as an indispensable step that everyone has to take who wants to participate in legal discourse. And with this move, actors have to justify their claims in a context marked by legal concepts that have histories.[175]

171 Fish, *Doing What Comes Naturally*, 141–60.

172 R Brandom, 'Some Pragmatist Themes in Hegel's Idealism: Negotiation and Administration in Hegel's Account of the Structure and Content of Conceptual Norms' (1999) 7 *European Journal of Philosophy* 164–89, 181 (summarizing his thought when he writes that '[t]he current judge is held accountable to the tradition she inherits by the judges yet to come.'). Cf. R Christensen, Neo-Pragmatismus: Brandom, in: S Buckel, R Christensen, and A Fischer-Lescano (eds), *Neue Theorien des Rechts* (Stuttgart: Lucius und Lucius 2009), 239–62.

173 See the famous words of Judge Oliver Wendell Holmes in his dissent in *Southern Pacific Co. v Jensen*, 244 US 205 (1917), 221 ('I recognize without hesitation that judges do and must legislate, but they can do so only interstitially').

174 M Koskenniemi, 'The Place of Law in Collective Security' (1996) 17 *Michigan Journal of International Law* 455, 478; Koskenniemi, *The Gentle Civilizer of Nations*, 494 and 596.

175 Venzke, 'Legal Contestation' (offering a concrete analysis of how this works out in the practice of arguing about 'enemy combatants').

The rules of interpretation that actors have to follow in legal discourse are more precisely spelled out for treaty interpretation in the VCLT that provides the widely accepted standard on how treaties should be interpreted.[176] They are the point of reference for discussing what counts as legal interpretation and what does not. No matter which reasons or motivations drive an interpretation, it needs to be couched within the argumentative standards contoured by the rules of interpretation. Article 31(1) VCLT postulates:

> A treaty shall be interpreted in good faith in accordance with the ordinary meaning to be given to the terms of the treaty in their context and in the light of its object and purpose.

The text's ordinary meaning is the starting point of interpretation. In its early years the ICJ has held that

> the first duty of a tribunal which is called upon to interpret and apply provisions of a treaty, is to endeavour to give effect to them in their natural and ordinary meaning in the context in which they occur.[177]

The courts' statement testifies to a common understanding of interpretation as a matter of looking closely at the ordinary meaning of the law as the first natural starting point—the *word* is in the beginning of interpretation. Above all judges, who have compelling reasons for portraying their interpretations as purely rule-based and objective, have embraced the VCLT to focus on the ordinary meaning of texts in settling disputes before them. The WTO Appellate Body in particular has pursued this strategy in its early years to such an extent that it was even seen to be inflicted by a 'textual fetish'.[178] In the hard-fought and seminal *United States–Shrimp* case, the Appellate Body for example criticized the panel for not having followed the international law rules of interpretation and underscored that '[a] treaty interpreter must begin with, and focus upon, the text of the particular provision to be interpreted'.[179] The hermeneutics of different judges and different institutions certainly diverges, but by and large they have sought to find a solid basis for their decisions in the ordinary text of the treaty they are called upon to apply. The form of argument thus strongly suggests that *words* themselves would give away the answer to disputes about their interpretation.[180]

[176] Cf. J-F Lévesque, 'Traités de Verre: Réflexions sur l'interprétation' (2006) 19 *Revue Québécoise de droit international* 53–78 (offering a reconstruction of the rules of interpretation in view of developments in the theory of language).

[177] *Competence of the General Assembly for the Admission of a State to the United Nations*, Advisory Opinion of 3 March 1950, ICJ Reports 4, 8.

[178] D A Irwin and J H H Weiler, 'Measures Affecting the Cross-Border Supply of Gambling and Betting Services (DS 285)' (2008) 7 *World Trade Review* 71–113, 89–95. Cf. G Abi-Saab, The Appellate Body and Treaty Interpretation, in: G Sacerdoti, A Yanovich, and J Bohanes (eds), *The WTO at Ten* (Cambridge: Cambridge University Press 2006), 453–64; I van Damme, *Treaty Interpretation by the WTO Appellate Body* (Oxford: Oxford University Press 2009), 222–35.

[179] Appellate Body Report, *United States—Import Prohibition of Certain Shrimp and Shrimp Products*, WT/DS58/AB/R, 12 October 1998, para 114.

[180] In closer detail see I Venzke, 'The Role of International Courts as Interpreters and Developers of the Law: Working out the Jurisgenerative Practice of Interpretation' (2012) 34 *Loyola of Los Angeles International and Comparative Law Review* 119–51.

Scholarly doctrine also generally upholds the assumption that the text itself could distinguish permissible from impermissible interpretations. In a slightly antiquated, venerable, and still influential approach to interpretation in international law, Alexander Orakhelashvili first portrays the rules of interpretation as rock-solid guides to interpretation and then opines that they serve the aim of 'deduc[ing] the meaning exactly of what has been consented to and agreed'.[181] In their contribution on Art. 31 in the recent commentary on the VCLT, Jean-Marc Sorel and Valérie Boré-Eveno contend that interpretation is of fundamental importance because it results in 'releasing [*dégager*] the exact meaning and the content of the rule of law that is applicable to a given situation'.[182] Such belief shapes the form of interpretation.[183] On this account, rules of interpretation firmly assign interpretation its place within the confines of what is permissible by the text of the norm.[184] Interpretation could concretize the law, maybe, but surely not make it—lawmaking would be beyond the permissible.[185] This view seems to hold even for Robert Kolb who has developed a fresh look at doctrine by drawing on studies in hermeneutics and who decidedly breaks with some of the more mythical and outdated semantic assumptions.[186] But all the same he sticks to classical hermeneutics and argues that interpreters must not fill the text with anything that it does not already contain.[187] If the meaning of words is contested, their *sense* provides the yardstick for judgment.[188] And if that did not resolve the issue, then resorting to the *force* behind the treaty should guide interpretation. Either way, interpretation would,

[181] A Orakhelashvili, *The Interpretation of Acts and Rules in Public International Law* (Oxford: Oxford University Press 2008), 286. Cf. M Waibel, 'Demystifying the Art of Interpretation (Review Essay)' (2011) 22 *European Journal of International Law* 571–88, 583.

[182] J-M Sorel and V Boré-Eveno, Article 31, in: O Corten and P Klein (eds), *The Vienna Conventions on the Law of Treaties: A Commentary* (Oxford: Oxford University Press 2011), 804–37, 806.

[183] If one lets go of this belief, as one should, this would neither render interpretative struggles nonsensical, nor would it fundamentally shatter the form of interpretation. Norm text would still be authoritative reference points and rules of interpretations would guarantee possibilities of critique. Cf. A v Bogdandy and I Venzke, 'In Whose Name? An Investigation of International Courts' Public Authority and its Democratic Justification' (2012) 23 *European Journal of International Law* 7–41, 15–16.

[184] Further examples abound. See, e.g., R K Gardiner, *Treaty Interpretation* (Oxford: Oxford University Press 2008), 87. Cf. the classic statement by Sir Gerald Fitzmaurice: 'texts must be interpreted as they stand, and, prima facie, without reference to extraneous factors', G S Fitzmaurice, 'The Law and Procedure of the International Court of Justice. Treaty Interpretation and Other Treaty Points' (1957) 33 *British Yearbook of International Law* 203–93, 212.

[185] Note that Hersch Lauterpacht and Hans Wehberg, like others, use 'clarification' and 'development' of the law synonymously. See with further references Venzke, 'Role of International Courts'.

[186] For instance, he finds it staggering not to see creativity in interpretation and sensibly suggests that interpretation develops the law. R Kolb, *Interprétation et création du droit international. Esquisse d'une herméneutique juridique moderne pour le droit international public* (Brussels: Bruylant 2006), 103–22.

[187] Ibid., at 412–13. It might be possible to read this passage of the book as engaging in the perspective of the judge; but a certain tension or disconnect between internal and external perspectives on the practice of interpretation still seems to run through Kolb's treatise.

[188] Cf. U Linderfalk, *On the Interpretation of Treaties* (Dordrecht: Springer 2007), 43.

at the most, amount to a clarification of the law, but not to lawmaking. Its task and nature are—in whatever way this might be done best—to find the will of the parties, of consenting unitary states.[189] Interpretation should give effect to the *force* that lies behind the law and that heaved it into existence. Such is the legacy of an overwhelming strand in legal doctrine rooted in the classical liberalist thinking of international law. In the opinion of the ICJ just quoted above, the court continued to argue that

> [i]f... the words in their natural and ordinary meaning are ambiguous or lead to an unreasonable result, then, and then only, must the Court, by resort to other methods of interpretation, seek to ascertain what the parties did mean when they used these words.[190]

This understanding of interpretation in international law and the argumentative form it demands have been challenged from the vantage point of competing paradigms. Just what is the force behind the law, and what interpretation is about, has been subject to foundational debate and, arguably, to some change. To note but briefly, the centrality of human rights, the general prohibition of the use of force, supranational elements in the Charter of the United Nations, and the rise of international criminal law can be seen as the most evident manifestations of a transformation in the international legal order ever since the Holocaust and the Second World War. In the words of Jürgen Habermas it has 'marked the beginning of the end of international law as a law of states'.[191]

Such transformations have also left marks on the form of interpretation.[192] They can be read as expressing interests or values of an international community or, which is related, as advancing the constitutionalization of international law.[193] If a document like the UN Charter is read as a constitution, less emphasis would probably be based on the original will of the parties and static-subjective approaches to interpretation would have to give

[189] See above Chapter I. Cf. G Fitzmaurice, 'Vae Victis or Woe to the Negotiator! Your Treaty or our "Interpretation" of it?' (1971) 65 *American Journal of International Law* 358–73 (critiquing McDougal's argument thoroughly); D J Bederman, *Classical Canons: Rhetoric, Classicism and Treaty Interpretation* (Aldershot: Ashgate 2001), 192–200 (on the formative jurisprudence of the PCIJ on this matter).

[190] *Competence of the General Assembly for the Admission of a State to the United Nations*, Advisory Opinion of 3 March 1950, (1950) ICJ Reports 4, p 8.

[191] See J Habermas, *The Divided West* (Cambridge: Polity Press 2006), 158–9; P-M Dupuy, 'L'unité de l'ordre juridique international' (2002) 297 *Recueil des Cours* 9–490, 414–18; W G Friedmann, *The Changing Structure of International Law* (New York: Columbia University Press 1964), 60–74 (prominently juxtaposing a traditional law of coexistence with a modern law of co-operation); J H H Weiler, 'The Geology of International Law—Governance, Democracy and Legitimacy' (2004) 64 *Zeitschrift für ausländisches öffentliches Recht und Völkerrecht* 547–62 (on the structural transformation of international law beyond a shift to human rights and criminal law).

[192] See B Simma, 'From Bilateralism to Community Interest in International Law' (1994) 250 *Recueil des Cours* 221–384; C Tomuschat, 'International Law: Ensuring the Survival of Mankind on the Eve of a New Century' (2001) 281 *Recueil des Cours* 13–438. Cf. Kolb, *Interprétation et création*, 920–6.

[193] For overviews of constitutionalist approaches see T Kleinlein, *Konstitutionalisierung im Völkerrecht* (Berlin: Springer 2012), especially 76–99. Cf. M Payandeh, *Internationales Gemeinschaftsrecht* (Heidelberg: Springer 2010), 509–12; J Klabbers, Law-making and Constitutionalism, in: J Klabbers, A Peters, and G Ulfstein (eds), *The Constitutionalization of International Law* (Oxford: Oxford University Press 2009), 81–125; A L Paulus, *Die internationale Gemeinschaft im Völkerrecht* (München: Beck 2001), 3.

way to an 'evolutionary' way of interpretation that is responsive to the dynamics and incompleteness of any constitution.[194]

In short, the understanding of international law as a system of contractual obligations among sovereign and equal states has been complemented by an increasingly strong community paradigm that makes international law the handmaiden of community values with repercussions for the form of legal argument.[195] Benedict Kingsbury observes an increasing publicness of international law in this regard. With the concept of publicness he refers precisely to

> the claim of law to stand in the name of the whole society and to speak to that whole society even when any particular rule may in fact be addressed to narrower groups. I argue that this quality is increasingly part of the concept of international law, and that this quality is having a transformative effect on the sources of international law, reducing the significance of voluntarism, bilaterality and opposability, and increasing the significance of generality, solidarity and the integration of international law into a conception of world public order.[196]

Sure enough, interests of the community do not create law out of thin air, but when the words or sense of the law are contested, interests of the community or the public may also be a reference point in legal interpretation. Understandings of interpretation might thus vary among different institutions and according to what it is that is interpreted—ranging from a bilateral treaty establishing specific (maybe technical) obligations all the way to the Charter of the United Nations.[197] There is flux in the outward show of interpretation and from the vantage point of competing paradigms of international law one might think of it in various ways. But on the whole, this flux does not detract from the fact that anyone who enters a legal discourse needs to present his or her argument precisely as a *legal* claim in a way that is roughly outlined by the rules of interpretation.

What any of the approaches has anyway in common is that it sees interpretation as finding something. The outward show of interpretation not only suggests that interpreters are constrained by how they have to craft their argument but also by its substance. They not only need to couch their claims within the form of legal argument but also seem to be constrained by what they find; namely, by the text

[194] B Fassbender, 'The United Nations Charter as Constitution of the International Community' (1998) 36 *Columbia Journal of Transnational Law* 529–619, 595; R S J Macdonald, The United Nations Charter: Constitution or Contract? in: R S J Macdonald and D M Johnston (eds), *The Structure and Process of International Law* (Dordrecht: Nijhoff 1986), 889–912.

[195] For the field of international criminal law, see, e.g., M Kuhli and K Günther, 'Judicial Lawmaking, Discourse Theory, and the ICTY on Belligerent Reprisals' (2011) 12 *German Law Journal* 1261–78.

[196] B Kingsbury, International Law as Inter-Public Law, in: H Richardson and M Williams (eds), *Moral Universalism and Pluralism* (New York: New York University Press 2009), 167–204, 174. Cf. B Kingsbury and Donaldson, From Bilateralism to Publicness in International Law, in: U Fastenrath, R Geiger, D-E Khan, A Paulus, S von Schorlemer, and C Vedder (eds), *From Bilateralism to Community Interest. Essays in Honour of Bruno Simma* (Oxford: Oxford University Press 2011), 79–89.

[197] Cf. Bederman, *Classical Canons*, 4; C Brölmann, 'Law-Making Treaties: Form and Function in International Law' (2005) 74 *Nordic Journal of International Law* 383–404.

they are called upon to interpret and its meaning. What interpreters find could tell whether they were right or wrong. Interpreters could be judged (in)correct on the basis of the contents of their interpretations. But the present theoretical view on the practice of legal interpretation turns this understanding around and contends that interpretations contribute to creating what they find. How is a constraint beyond the form of legal argument all the same possible?

c) *The content of legal commitments*

The form of legal interpretation ties interpreters to norm texts. What is permitted in interpretation—what amounts to (in)correct use of texts or possibly other reference points—is shifting in response to the strength of competing general paradigms of international law. While the practice of interpretation unfolds on the stabilizing ground of interpretative communities, there remains a fundamental question: How can we understand interpretation as constrained by rules if it is that same practice that creates the rules? This question after all also extends to the rules of interpretation themselves.

The challenge is articulated clearly by John Austin who encapsulates what is at stake in legal interpretation: 'there can hardly be any longer a possibility of not seeing that stating is performing an act', he writes.[198] This act portrays itself as legal practice—as a practice of interpretation in law.[199] To illustrate his argument, Austin coins the concept of performative speech, by which he refers to communicative utterances that change the world.[200] The worn example is the utterance of the words 'I do', which in the right context may create the bond of marriage. In a clever move, Austin tries to come up with distinctions that separate such creative *performative* speech acts from simple *constative* acts like 'this is an apple'.[201] If an interpreter only engaged in constative acts of the kind 'this is what the law is', then he or she could possibly withdraw from any charge of lawmaking. Austin suggests, however, that this is simply not possible.[202] It is impossible to use legal norms without interpretation and to thus perform an act.[203] He ultimately comes to the conclusion that every attempt at distinguishing performative from constative acts

[198] J L Austin, *How to Do Things with Words* (Oxford: Oxford University Press 1979 [1962]), 139.

[199] Ronald Dworkin has pioneered this thought in legal theory. See, for instance, R Dworkin, 'Law as Interpretation' (1982) 60 *Critical Inquiry* 179–200. I cannot discuss his theory head-on. The main reasons why it does not gain a more prominent place in this book relate to its semantics and to its use of ideal theory. On these points of critique see Patterson, 'Dworkin on the Semantics of Legal and Political Concepts' 545–57 (on the problematic semantic assumptions); J Habermas, *Faktizität und Geltung* (Frankfurt am Main: Suhrkamp 1992), 258–74 (on the theory's alleged solipsism); Geuss, *Philosophy* (on the downsides of strong variants of ideal theory more generally).

[200] Austin, *Things with Words*, 138–39.

[201] Ibid., at 140–1.

[202] Ibid., at 141.

[203] Luhmann, *Recht der Gesellschaft*, 256.

fails because it is impossible to withhold from interpreting even simple objects like apples, let alone complex things like the law.[204] Austin thus lets this distinction collapse, thereby adding on to the strand of thinking that follows from the linguistic turn and its proposition that communicative practices shapes meanings.[205]

Judicial interpretations that present themselves as declaring what the law really is contribute to its creation. Austin, a companion of H L A Hart at Oxford, wrote that '[o]f all people, jurists should be best aware of the true sense of affairs . . . [y]et they succumb to their own timorous fiction, that a statement of "the law" is a statement of fact'.[206] Quite the contrary, a statement of the law forms part of lawmaking. While travelling further on this theoretical path, the present theoretical perspective on the practice of interpretation understands successful legal interpretative acts as contributing to the creation of what they find. But it also sees that the law that is interpreted has a history and for any interpretation to be successful it has to find the acceptance of other actors in the community of interpreters.

The tension between words that constrain and speakers that shape the meaning of words has received prime attention in the theory and philosophy of language. An episode of the British comic character Humpty Dumpty in which he discusses semantics with Alice has become a famous reference in this regard:

> 'I don't know what you mean by "glory",' Alice said.
> Humpty Dumpty smiled contemptuously. 'Of course you don't – till I tell you. I meant "there's a nice knock-down argument for you!"'
> 'But "glory" doesn't mean "a nice knock-down argument",' Alice objected.
> 'When I use a word,' Humpty Dumpty said, in a rather a scornful tone, 'it means just what I choose it to mean—neither more nor less.'
> 'The question is,' said Alice, 'whether you *can* make words mean so many different things.'
> 'The question is,' said Humpty Dumpty, 'which is to be master—that's all.'[207]

The treatment of this passage in semantic theory has produced competing answers to the question where meaning comes from. These answers immediately bear on how interpretations can possibly be constrained. On a first account, words have a meaning that is independent from concrete instances of communication, or at least they do not quickly respond to the will or intentions of particular speakers. On a second account, only the concrete use of words shapes their meanings and this use translates the intentions of speakers into meanings.[208] As of late, also from the point of view of semantic theory, the concept of communicative *practice* mediates

[204] Austin, *Things with Words*, 142–3; Krämer, *Sprache, Sprechakt, Kommunikation*, 135–53; Fish, *Doing What Comes Naturally*, 488–91.

[205] See Austin, *Things with Words*, 138–9.

[206] Ibid., at 4.

[207] L Carroll, *Through the Looking-Glass, and What Alice Found There* (Raleigh, NC: Hayes Barton Press 1872), 72.

[208] See J Liptow, *Regel und Interpretation* (Weilerswist: Velbrück 2004), 205–7.

between these two answers and undermines the assumption that they are alternatives at all. The thought of Donald Davidson and, more recently, of Robert Brandom have been the driving forces behind this development.[209]

Brandom combines his approach to overcoming these alternatives with an appreciation of normativity in language. While his treatment of the subject dives deep into theoretical philosophy, it ultimately surfaces with straightforward support on how to understand the practical generation of legal normativity in (international) law—lawmaking through interpretation, in other words. At the outset, Brandom takes up the Kantian as well as Hegelian view that human judgement and action are distinct from other things in that humans are responsible for them.[210] In Brandom's understanding, judgements and actions are '*commitments* that are subject to a certain kind of normative assessment, as correct or incorrect'.[211] Normativity as a sense of obligation about how one should act, how one should interpret legal texts, he continues to clarify, is brought into the world by our normative attitudes. With enlightened thought, normativity does not come down on earth from a higher authority but it is part of our own making. In the classical liberalist view, we would be ready to accept a constraint on our action because we have endorsed or acknowledged this constraint as binding:

> [R]ules get their normative force, come to govern our doings, only in virtue of our own attitudes. One is genuinely responsible only for that for which one *takes* responsibility; one is genuinely committed only to that to which one has committed oneself.[212]

At the same time, it would be implausible to talk of a rule as a constraint if actors could freely dispose of the content of a rule. They would then not be bound by it in any meaningful way.[213] The nearby answer would be to distinguish between placing a rule into existence and applying it at a later point in time. This would be the answer given by orthodox legal positivism. But semantic pragmatism challenges precisely this distinction. The question persists: How is it possible to follow a rule that is only instituted by the practice of rule following?[214]

[209] D Davidson, Convention and Communication, in: *Inquiries into Truth and Interpretation*, (Oxford: Oxford University Press 2001 [1984]), 265–96; R Brandom, *Articulating Reasons: An Introduction to Inferentialism* (Cambridge, MA: Harvard University Press 2000). Cf. Liptow, *Regel und Interpretation*, 218–47.

[210] Brandom, 'Pragmatist Themes', 165–6.

[211] Ibid., at 165. For international lawyers it is interesting to note that on an earlier occasion Brandom referred to Samuel Pufendorf in support of this same idea, R Brandom, *Making it Explicit* (Cambridge: Harvard University Press 1998), 45–6, with reference to S Pufendorf, *De Jure Naturae et Gentium (On the Law of Nature and of Nations)*, vol 1 (Oxford: Clarendon Press 1934 [1672]), § 2.

[212] Brandom, 'Pragmatist Themes', 171.

[213] Ibid.

[214] This is one of the principal questions that pervades Wittgenstein's *Philosophical Investigations*, see above notes 64–67. It has since created an abundant amount of literature, see the seminal treatment in S A Kripke, *Wittgenstein on Rules and Private Language* Harvard University Press 1982), as well as the overview provided by Taylor, To Follow a Rule.

The response that Brandom offers is strikingly straightforward and appealing to any (international) lawyer. Once an actor has consented to a rule, she has committed herself in relation to others to using certain expressions. The actual content of that commitment, the meaning of the expressions, is consequently the product of a process of 'negotiation' with others.

> [T]he boundaries around what one has and has not committed oneself to by using a particular concept (and what is and is not a correct application of it) are determined by a process of *negotiation* among actual attitudes of application and assessments of application.[215]

This argument for now leaves a number of open questions. With regard to the origins of normativity it is above all interesting to further focus on which grounds may form a basis for the assessment that an application of a norm (that the use of an expression or an interpretative act in international law) was (in)correct. Brandom rightly and perceptively suggests that this assessment can only be part of the communicative practice itself. In this practice, applications of a concept in the present have to connect to the past in a way that convinces future applications. In order to illustrate the point, he resorts to a case-law model of communication in which '[t]he current judge is held accountable to the tradition she inherits by the judges yet to come'.[216] Contents of commitments gain shape and develop in this process of 'negotiation'; that is, in the practice of demanding and giving reasons for or against a particular application of a concept (a particular interpretation of an international norm).

With a view to developing a theoretical perspective that is attuned to changes in the law by way of interpretation—in particular under the impact of international institutions—the ensuing task would be to look more closely at this process of negotiating content. Who is influential in this process? The working of actors' interests and preferences—how they try to influence semantic content—would be of key interest. Humpty Dumpty claimed to be able to choose what 'glory' means if only he was 'to be the master, that's all'. He not only stirred discussion in semantic theory, but he also made a claim to exercise power or authority.

3. Power and authority in semantic struggles

If the master determines meaning, interpretations could well be understood as acts of power. Such an understanding could build on a strong but marginalized tradition while renewed emphasis on the politics of legal interpretation might add further clarity (a.). Building on a distinction between politics as a means to an

215 Brandom, 'Pragmatist Themes', 173.

216 Ibid., at 181. For a concise introduction and summary see Liptow, *Regel und Interpretation*, 220–6; Christensen, Neo-Pragmatismus, 239–62; Winkler, 'Normativität des Praktischen', 821–9.

end and a process of contesting normative reasons then leads to the observation that actors frequently seek to find acceptance for their preferred interpretations by trying to induce a belief in the rightness of the claims they make. If they succeed, interpretations would then be hegemonic (b.). But the possibility of genuine agreement can after all not be ruled out categorically and the concept of authority is thus better suited than notions of power to capture how communicative lawmaking hinges on the general acceptance of interpretative claims. What matters primarily in processes of negotiating the contents of legal commitments is an actor's semantic authority (c.).

a) Power, rhetoric, and politics in legal interpretation

Understanding successful interpretations as acts of power would usefully highlight how actors seek to tap law's force to their advantage. Successful interpretations have the faculty to create as well as the ability to control. Already the French revolutionaries tried to create a language that would carry their ideas into the future and they sought to implement meanings so as to ensure that their aims would live long.[217] Such an understanding of interpretations could build on a definition of power as 'the production, in and through social relations, of effects that shape the capacities of actors to determine their own circumstances and fate'.[218] If an interpretation becomes an accepted statement about what the law is, others have to struggle against it. If an actor manages to implement new reference points in legal argument that are aligned with its interest, others face an uphill battle.[219]

I suggest picturing the practice of legal interpretation as semantic struggles in which actors craft legal interpretations in an attempt to implement meanings of legal expressions that are aligned with their convictions or interests.[220] Success in interpretation translates into 'winning' a semantic struggle in a particular instance by finding acceptance for one's use of legal expressions. Linguist Dietrich Busse aptly notes that '[t]he "winner" of a semantic struggle has succeeded in establishing his or her own rule-of-use as the linguistic norm for the linguistic community'.[221]

[217] See above section A.2.

[218] M Barnett and R Duvall, Power in Global Governance, in: M Barnett and R Duvall (eds), *Power in Global Governance* (Cambridge: Cambridge University Press 2005), 1–32, 3, slightly amending the definition offered by J Scott, *Power* (Cambridge: Polity Press 2001), 1–2.

[219] Venzke, 'Legal Contestation'.

[220] On the concept of semantic struggle in a historical as well as linguistic perspective see Koselleck, Begriffsgeschichte and Social History, 75–93, 80; D Busse, Semantic Strategies as a Means of Politics: Linguistic approaches to the analysis of 'semantic stugles', in: P Ahonen (ed), *Tracing the Semiotic Boundaries of Politics* (Berlin: de Gruyter 1993), 121–8. On the related idea of semantic *fights* see R Christensen and M Sokolowski, Recht als Einsatz im Semantischen Kampf, in: E Felder (ed), *Semantische Kämpfe. Macht und Sprache in den Wissenschaften* (Berlin: de Gruyter 2006), 353–71.

[221] Busse, Semantic Strategies, 122–3. Cf. J Combacau and S Sur, *Droit international public* (Paris: Montchrestien 2010), 172 ('Les controverses relatives à l'interprétation ne seraient pas si vives si elles ne traduisaient pas une lutte pour la maîtrise du système juridique, qui fait du processus interprétatif une variante de la lutte pour le droit.').

Participants in legal discourse craft claims about (il)legality, seek to bend the payoffs distributed by international law, and wish to tap law's symbolic power.[222] Power as a vector of sovereignty thus extends to the ability to shape meanings. Carl Schmitt enigmatically noted that 'whoever has true power is able to determine the content of concepts and words. *Caesar dominus et supra grammaticam.* (Caesar is also lord over grammar.)'[223] This observation, or at least fascination, about the power of words cuts across the political spectrum. The French revolutionary thinkers—precisely in fear of what Schmitt pithily brought to the point—argued that words should belong to the nation and thus attempted to tie the power of words to the power of the people, rather than any other master.[224]

Examining power in interpretations has an even longer tradition. The Roman rhetorician Quintilianus already acknowledged his debt to Cicero as well as to Aristotle's *Art of Rhetoric* and developed a technique of description that aligns the image arising from a description with the interest of the speaker or writer.[225] This thought has received continuous appreciation across the breadth of social sciences. In social and political theory generally, strategies of representation as well as the phenomenon of how power is enacted in descriptions have drawn increasing attention.[226] Also international relations scholars have stressed the power of persuasion and emphasized strategic elements in the construction of social reality.[227] The notion of semantic struggle captures precisely this thought. Writing on 'Semantic strategies as a means of politics', Busse pertinently found that

> the semantic possibilities of linguistic signs correspond to the form of reality, or the view towards reality, admitted by society. Politicians and political agencies that desire to influence the publicly accepted view of political reality will try to dominate the linguistic possibilities within the discourse of politics. Thus language (especially the semantics of political terminology) becomes a means of political action: the so called 'semantic struggles' arise.[228]

This observation holds true all the same for legal terminology. Legal scholarship doctrine, with the impetus of providing guidance for legal practice, has been less

[222] Bourdieu, 'The Force of Law', 838 (arguing that '[l]aw is the quintessential form of the symbolic power of naming that creates the things named...It confers upon the reality which arises from its classificatory operations the maximum permanence.').

[223] Quoted in C Mouffe, *On the Political* (London: Routledge 2005), 87.

[224] See above note 207.

[225] Q Skinner, 'Rhetoric and Conceptual Change' (1999) 3 *Finnish Yearbook of Political Thought* 60–72. Such insights have also fed the so-called 'New Rhetoric'. See C Perelman, *Logique Juridique. Nouvelle Rhétorique* (Paris: Dalloz 2001); P Goodrich, *Legal Discourse: Studies in Linguistics, Rhetoric, and Legal Analysis* (New York: St Martin's 1987), chapter 5.

[226] E Laclau, *Emancipation(s)* (New York: Verso 1996), 83–104; K Palonen, *Quentin Skinner: History, Politics, Rhetoric* (Cambridge: Polity 2003), 133–72.

[227] Payne, 'Persuasion'; R R Krebs and P T Jackson, 'Twisting Tongues and Twisting Arms: The Power of Political Rhetoric' (2007) 13 *European Journal of International Relations* 35–66; Finnemore and Sikkink, 'International Norm Dynamics' (speaking of 'coercive constructivism').

[228] Busse, Semantic Strategies, 121.

inclined to entertain the thought that interpretations can also be acts of power.[229] As of late however, legal scholars of different *couleur* have chimed in with voices suggesting that legal interpretations depend on a political choice. In light of theoretical or practical indeterminacy (or ambiguity, at any rate) with regard to the meaning of a norm, it is suggested that the interpreter cannot escape a decision between at least two alternative meanings. This choice has then pervasively but evasively been termed 'political'.[230] What does political mean in this context?[231]

Politics may first be seen as a technique for arriving at a given aim. This is the way it is used most frequently. It denotes the manoeuvres and ruses that strategic actors employ while aiming at given objectives. With the possession of power reigning above all other competing targets of political action, politics may be understood as striving for the possession of power.[232] Second, politics may also refer to matters of practical philosophy.[233] It is the space in which individuals contest competing conceptions of a good life. Politics then extends to the question of which goals actors should strive for.[234]

Legal interpretations are political in both ways. They are crafted in such a way as to arrive at a given aim—to have others accept claims about (il)legality while such acceptance may be the result of a variety of motives. Acceptance as a matter of fact should not be confused with acceptability which is a concept of political philosophy; nor is the acceptance of an interpretation always normatively meaningful.[235] Actors might see themselves simply materially forced to accept an interpretation, they might see an interpretation neatly coinciding with their interests, or they might perceive it to be the morally right legal interpretation. Frequently, actors in legal discourse seek acceptance for their interpretations by inducing a belief in the rightness of the interpretation they endorse.

[229] Notable exceptions of realist and critical legal scholars include the work of Robert Cover who vividly pictures legal interpretations as a form of violence because they set out to kill alternative meanings. R M Cover, 'Violence and the Word' (1986) 95 *Yale Law Journal* 1601–30. With the idea of contestability spelled out above, however, speaking of the killing of meanings appears to be misleading as no death would be permanent. Interpretations are contestable, even those of very authoritative actors.

[230] M Koskenniemi, 'The Politics of International Law' (1990) 1 *European Journal of International Law* 4–32. Cf. H Ruiz Fabri, Drawing a Line of Equilibrium in a Complex World, in: G Sacerdoti, A Yanovich, and J Bohanes (eds), *The WTO at Ten* (Cambridge: Cambridge University Press 2006), 125–42, 135 (noting that 'every interpretation involves a choice and every choice is, by necessity, a political one').

[231] Cf. C Schmitt, *Der Begriff des Politischen* (Berlin: Duncker & Humblot 1963), 31–2 (observing that politics is a very charged notion—a '*Kampfbegriff*').

[232] M Weber, Politik als Beruf (1919), in: *Gesammelte Politische Schriften* (Tübingen: Mohr 1971), 506; M Horkheimer, *Anfänge der bürgerlichen Geschichtsphilosophie* (Frankfurt am Main: Fischer 1971 [1930]), 12 ('Der Inbegriff der Wege, die dazu führen, und der Maßnahmen, die der Aufrechterhaltung [der Herrschaft von Menschen über Menschen] dienen, heißt Politik').

[233] H Kelsen, *Allgemeine Staatslehre* (Berlin: Springer 1925), 27–8; (distinguishing between 'politics-as-ethics' and 'politics-as-technique'). Cf. M Zamboni, *Law and Politics. A Dilemma for Contemporary Legal Theory* (Heidelberg: Springer 2007), 23–5; E Vollrath, *Was ist das Politische? Eine Theorie des Politischen und seiner Wahrnehmung* (Würzburg: Könighausen & Neumann 2003).

[234] See O Höffe, Einführung in Aristoteles' *Politik*, in: O Höffe (ed), *Aristoteles. Politik* (Berlin: Akademie Verlag 2001), 5–19, 13–16. In International Relations such an understanding has been cherished by the English School. See Carr, *The Twenty Years' Crisis*, 5 (maintaining that 'political science is the science not only of what is, but also of what ought to be').

[235] For a more detailed normative assessment see below Chapter V, section A.3.b.

b) Hegemony, universality, and agreement

The understanding of interpretation as an act of seeking acceptance for a claim about meaning by inducing a belief in the rightness of the claim demands closer scrutiny. Against the backdrop of this thought, it may be a small further step towards thinking of all legal interpretations as hegemonic—echoing Koskenniemi's observation that:

> [i]ntentional actors routinely challenge each other by invoking legal rules and principles on which they have projected meanings that support their preferences and counteract their opponents. [...] To think of this struggle as *hegemonic* is to understand that the objective of the contestants is to make their partial view of that meaning appear as the total view, their preferences seem like the *universal preference*.[236]

The concept of hegemony makes the distinction between politics as a technique of gaining or maintaining power and its normative side of debating ways of living a good life collapse: power is exercised by making others believe in the rightness of interpretations.[237] On the premise that there is no external yardstick that can decide disputes about the meaning of (legal) expressions, any meaning would be a function of power relations. Chantal Mouffe made the point overtly clear when she wrote that 'power is constitutive of the social because the social could not exist without the power relations through which it is given shape'.[238] And 'since power relations are constitutive of the social, every order is by necessity a hegemonic order.'[239] This reasoning has of course multiple implications and assumptions. Something like true agreement—agreement in the absence of power and inspired by normative reasons—would be dismissed as downright impossible. It seems as if after the death of God as an authority for legitimate order, the later death of the subject in post-modern theory left only power as a constitutive building block for social order.[240] But the spirited critique of metaphysics and of moral naturalisms rests on the assumption that moral values or rationality do not exist—an assumption that itself ironically requires impossible metaphysical insight.

236 M Koskenniemi, 'International Law and Hegemony: A Reconfiguration' (2004) 17 *Cambridge Review of International Affairs* 197–218, 199.

237 Cf. R W Cox, 'Gramsci, Hegemony and International Relations: An Essay in Method' (1983) 12 *Millennium* 162–75; A Fischer-Lescano and S Buckel, 'Gramsci Reconsidered. Hegemony in Global Law' (2009) 22 *Leiden Journal of International Law* 437–54; Carr, *The Twenty Years' Crisis*, 80 (arguing that a claim to a shared international morality can amount to an 'ingenious moral device invoked, in perfect sincerity, by privileged groups in order to justify and maintain their dominant position').

238 Mouffe, *On the Political*, 18.

239 Ibid., at 106.

240 From the wealth of literature on this issue, see in particular M Foucault, Two Lectures, in: C Gordon (ed), *Power/Knowledge* (New York: Pantheon Books 1980), 78–108; M Foucault, Afterword: The Subject and Power, in: H L Dreyfus and P Rabinow (eds), *Michel Foucault: Beyond Structualism and Hermeneutics* (Chicago: University of Chicago Press 1983), 208–26; J-F Lyotard, *The Postmodern Condition* (Minneapolis: University of Minnesota Press 1984). Cf. M Merleau-Ponty, Everywhere and Nowhere, in: *Signs* (Evanston: Northwesteren University Press 1964), 126–58, 153 ('Subjectivity was not waiting for philosophers.... They constructed, created it.... And what they have done must perhaps be undone.').

In contrast to such a thread of categorical critique, the present perspective on the practice of legal interpretation endorses a semantic pragmatism that does not outright defy moral realism or the presence of rationality. It neither categorically rejects the view that international law might express universal preferences, nor does it mock every narrative of progress. It entails a less far-reaching claim and only follows from the absence of 'uncontroversial and well-developed methods for thinking about morality'.[241] The distinction between hegemonic interpretations and those interpretations that meet acceptance motivated by normative reasons cannot be ruled out in principle. At the same time, a fixed standpoint for distinguishing one from the other is not available.[242] What politics means depends on the concrete communicative practice that vacillates between persuasion as an expression of power and conviction as an expression of true agreement. In view of this impasse, the concept of authority is ultimately better suited than power for understanding semantic struggles in law.

c) *Semantic authority and legal normativity*

Picturing disputes about what the law means as semantic struggles highlights how actors make interpretative claims that are aligned with their interests or convictions. It is this interpretative practice that shifts the contents of legal commitments, generates meaning, and that makes international law. In order for actors to be successful in this struggle for the law, they need to find acceptance for their interpretations and frequently they seek to induce a belief in the rightness of the claim they make. Successful interpretations might thus be understood as expressions of power in the sense that they influence what the law means and thus shape others in the determination of their own circumstances and fate.

But such an understanding ultimately belies the fact that actors can accept interpretations out of genuine agreement. Discussing the hegemonic structuring of belief and social interaction has pointed out how power relations might constitute—or at least influence—understandings of what is right. Such an approach has significant purchase and goes a long way. But its rejection of something like genuine agreement ultimately seems to rest on a metaphysical claim about the non-existence of universal morality. Such a claim would be as difficult as its inverse, declaring the existence of universal morality. The present theoretical perspective on the practice of interpretation is agnostic in this regard. It makes but a minimal commitment. What genuine agreement does imply and require is a minimal residual element of subjectivity. Taking such a requirement on board is a shaky position, but for a book that aims to analyse how actors develop the law in the practice of interpretation, it should not come as a surprise. Throwing this element

[241] T Nagel, *The Last Word* (Oxford: Oxford University Press 1997), 102.

[242] J Habermas, *Theorie und Praxis* (Frankfurt am Main: Suhrkamp 1971), 45; R Forst, *Das Recht auf Rechtfertigung. Elemente einer konstruktivistischen Theorie der Gerechtigkeit*, (Frankfurt am Main: Suhrkamp 2007), 354–7 (suggesting that the distinction will itself have to be part of an inclusive political process). For a more fervent argument on the constitutive relationship between ethics and politics see R Geuss, *Outside Ethics* (New Jersey: Princeton University Press 2005).

overboard would lead to the kind of exclusively structural analysis that the concept of practice tries to overcome. Actors can agree and accept the interpretive claims of others in a way that expresses their autonomous choice. An understanding of interpretations as acts that constrain others cuts this point short. It is a different matter that not every actor's acceptance might be required for semantic change. Even vocal resistance by some might be glossed over. But because the development of international norms by way of interpretation generally relies on acceptance, it might be better to understand interpretations as acts of authority rather than power.

Unlike exercising power at the point of a gun, legal interpretation seeks to induce acceptance by way of argument or persuasion.[243] The practice of interpretation develops the law and thus shapes the capacities of actors to determine their own circumstances and fate. It is powerful. But an actor's capacity to influence processes of communicative lawmaking hinges on their authority.

It is rather obvious that different actors who negotiate the content of legal commitments have different chances of finding acceptance. Acceptance is a function not only of the content of the claim that is being made or of the interests and convictions of the accepting actor, but also of the author of the claim. What I say as a scholar about the law has, when compared to a report by the WTO Appellate Body, for instance, of course relatively little or, which is more likely, no influence on what the law means. What matters in legal interpretative practice is *semantic authority*.

By semantic authority I refer to an actor's capacity to influence and shape meanings as well as the ability to establish its communications as authoritative reference points in legal discourse. Not only does an actor with authority influence the meaning of given norm texts, but its communications structure the space of contestation. Guidelines issued by the UNHCR and, even more so, reports of adjudicators in the WTO form part of the very subject of legal discourse. Their communications become reference points in later legal argument so that distinctions between interpretations, on the one hand, and what was to be interpreted, on the other, start to blur. Actors in the WTO may come to fight about the meaning of precedents just as they contest the meaning of norm texts that have passed through the traditional sources of international law. Such semantic authority increases an actor's capacity to create and its faculty to control—to make law and to constrain by way of law.

To have authority is distinct from having power in that it implies a certain degree of deferred judgement on part of others.[244] It feeds on social legitimacy—on the general belief of society, which upholds that one should do what the authority says. Such authority can be the product of many different contributing factors. Mechanisms of explicit delegation—conferring legal competence on an actor to do

[243] L V Prott, 'Argumentation in International Law' (1991) *Argumentation* 299–310.

[244] Certain types of power can do that too, but it is characteristic for authority. M Barnett and M Finnemore, The Power of Liberal International Organizations, in: M Barnett and R Duvall (eds), *Power in Global Governance* (Cambridge: Cambridge University Press 2005), 161–84, 170–72. Cf. H Arendt, What is Authority, in: *Between Past and Future* (London: Penguin Books 2006), 91–141, 92–3.

something—are certainly a primary one. But there are other factors that lie in the characteristics and behaviour of the actor such as its expertise or, roughly, moral appeal. Robert Brandom is ready to recognize that authority matters in the practice of negotiating the content of legal commitments. He emphasizes how an interpreter who has interpreted correctly in the past gains certain credit for the future. In Brandom's terms, the interpreter has a higher balance on her 'deontic scorekeeping account'.[245] Experience feeds confidence.

I notably take authority to be a phenomenon that can be justified as well as unjustified. As a capacity to develop international norms by way of interpretation and to establish communications as authoritative reference points in legal discourse, an emphasis on semantic authority redirects considerations of legitimation. It is a primary step in approaching normative problems and does not by itself identify legitimatory problems or offer their solution.

Focusing on authority in the practice of interpretation has another significant advantage. It opens up perspectives on the origins and transformations of legal normativity. It helps in comprehending mixtures of constraint and freedom in interpretation. I have argued earlier that in law the act of committing to a norm, typically the act of legislation or, paradigmatically in international law, the signing and ratification of a treaty, is of central importance. This act of consent has significant normative force. But semantic pragmatism points to the fact that this is not (and cannot be) the whole story. When meaning is less of a fixed attribute of words and more a product of the practice of interpretation, legal normativity becomes part of that practice. Understanding interpretative practice as the expression of power alone would run into the difficulty of being unable to account for why actors *should* follow rules thus generated. Normativity comes into the world by virtue of our attitudes.[246] Authority takes those attitudes on board.

There might be general characteristics of the process of interpretation that render it more or less appealing, normatively.[247] But questions of legitimacy would above all have to connect to the actors who exercise authority in this practice. Analytically, the primary question still is: Who has authority in semantic struggles for the law?

C. Actors in the practice of interpretation

There is an impressive magnitude of participants in international legal discourse. This section introduces actors that have for some time carried on a dismal existence in the overburdening shadow of the unitary state. It first points briefly to the role of private norm entrepreneurs such as legal scholars and NGOs as actors who usually enjoy very little semantic authority in communicative lawmaking. But exceptions

245 Brandom, *Making it Explicit*, chapter 8.
246 Brandom, 'Pragmatist Themes', 171.
247 See in detail below Chapter V.

apply and, notably, private actors can try to tap the authority of others (1.). It then dismantles the state as an actor in legal practice in international law to bring to light how its parts act autonomously as participants in legal discourse with some authority (2.). It finally introduces international bureaucracies as well as international courts and tribunals as independent actors who, sometimes at least, enjoy significant semantic authority—the focus of this book. International institutions frequently show the capacity to develop the law by way of their practice and to establish their communications as authoritative reference points in legal discourse (3.).

1. Private norm entrepreneurs

It is one of the well-known curiosities of international law that Art. 38(1)(d) ICJ Statute refers to 'teachings of the most highly qualified publicists of the various nations, as subsidiary means for the determination of rules of law'.[248] Scholars play an important role in international legal discourse. Among other things, they discuss judicial decisions and suggest where courts might have reasoned unconvincingly and where a different interpretation should have prevailed, they comment on events and developments, engage in critique, make normative propositions, and they teach law. Many legal scholars are also dedicated to developing doctrinal constructions that systematize a part or the whole of international law and thus give meaning to norm texts.[249] On an even more distanced but practically not less relevant theoretical level it is the orienting and framing by theory which provides guidance for interpretation.[250] But by and large, any individual scholar's semantic authority is at best marginal.

Scholars and practitioners gain more force when they act collectively and by way of institutions that enjoy some authority.[251] For example they contribute to communicative lawmaking in the International Law Commission (ILC) which, according to Article 2 ILC of its statute, shall consist of 'persons of recognized competence in international law' and which is tasked with 'the progressive development of international law'.[252] Leading scholars of the field have left a mark on

[248] Remember that the article is the product of legal scholars, Skouteris, Force of a Doctrine, 69–80.

[249] E Benvenisti, 'The Conception of International Law as a Legal System' (2008) 50 *German Yearbook of International Law* 393–405; Jennings, 'What is International Law?', 88. Cf. Oscar Schachter, 'The Invisible College of International Lawyers' (1977) 72 *Northwestern University Law Review* 217–26; David Kennedy, 'The Politics of the Invisible College: International Governance and the Politics of Expertise' (2001) 5 *European Human Rights Law Review* 463–97.

[250] See T S Kuhn, *The Structure of Scientific Revolutions* (Chicago: University of Chicago Press 1996), 113 (contending that 'a paradigm is prerequisite to perception itself').

[251] S E Goddard, 'Brokering Change: Networks and entrepreneurs in international politics' (2009) 1 *International Theory* 249–81.

[252] According to Art. 13(1) UNC '[t]he General Assembly shall initiate studies and make recommendations for the purpose of... encouraging the progressive development of international law and its codifications.' In 1947 the General Assembly delegated this matter to the ILC, UNGA res 174 (II), 21 November 1947. Cf. Y-L Liang, 'The General Assembly and the Progressive Development and Codification of International Law' (1948) 42 *American Journal of International Law* 66–97.

international law by way of their actions in the Commission—the concept of *jus cogens*, for instance, was above all a scholarly idea before it made its way through the ILC via the VCLT into legal practice and ultimately into the jurisprudence of the ICJ.[253] Also the law on state responsibility is inseparably interwoven with the work of its first and last Special Rapporteurs: Roberto Ago and James Crawford. Hersch Lauterpacht, after his two years as a member of the ILC (1952–1954), even went so far as to suggest that the Commission's exercise of codification is, in essence, a legislative matter.[254] In line with the practice of legal discourse, however, it seems more fitting to understand it as creative interpretation. The Institut de Droit International and the International Law Association, though not linked to any international organization and not publicly mandated, pursue a task similar to that of the ILC.

Next to individual interpreters,the role of NGOs is usually seen in formalized procedures that result in new norm texts. Private norm entrepreneurs and transnational advocacy networks, a common thread goes, have given rise to a number of international treaties and have increased their effectiveness and implementation.[255] The codification processes leading to the Kyoto Protocol,[256] to the Ottawa Treaty banning anti-personnel landmines,[257] and to the Rome Statute of the International Criminal Court,[258] serve as prime examples for the drafting of provisions marked by substantial NGO participation.[259] Andreas Fischer-Lescano, conversely, has highlighted the law-creative side of legal communications among actors of civil society outside any institutionalized fora of legislation.[260]

253 A Orakhelashvili, *Peremptory Norms in International Law* (Oxford: Oxford University Press 2006), 8; L Grosse, 'Racines historiques et fondements contemporains des normes impératives (Jus cogens) dans la théorie et la pratique du droit international' (1995) 73 *Revue de droit international, de sciences diplomatiques et politiques* 225–50; K Zemanek, The Metamorphosis of *Jus Cogens*: From an Institution of Treaty Law to the Bedrock of the International Legal Order, in: E Cannizzaro (ed), *The Law of Treaties Beyond the Vienna Convention* (Oxford: Oxford University Press 2011), 381–409. For the concept's arrival in judicial practice, see *Armed Activities on the Territory of the Congo* (New Application: 2002), Jurisdiction of the Court and Admissibility of the Application, Judgment of 3 February 2006, ICJ Reports 1, at paras 64 and 125. Cf. A Bianchi, 'Human Rights and the Magic of Jus Cogens' (2008) 19 *European Journal of International Law* 491–508, 501–5.

254 H Lauterpacht, 'Codification and Development of International Law' (1955) 49 *American Journal of Economics and Sociology* 16–43, 29; M Koskenniemi, 'International Legislation Today: Limits and Possibilities' (2005) 23 *Wisconsin International Law Journal* 61–92, 69–71.

255 E A Nadelmann, 'Global Prohibition Regimes: The Evolution of Norms in International Society' (1990) 44 *International Organization* 479–526, 482; M E Keck and K Sikkink, *Activists Beyond Borders. Advocacy Networks in International Politics* (Ithaca, NY: Cornell University Press 1998); J Kelley, 'Assessing the Complex Evolution of Norms: The Rise of International Election Monitoring' (2008) 62 *International Organization* 221–55.

256 Kyoto Protocol to the United Nations Framework Convention on Climate Change, 11 December 1997.

257 Convention on the Prohibition of the Use, Stockpiling, Production and Transfer of Anti-Personnel Mines and on their Destruction, 1 March 1999. See K Anderson, 'The Ottawa Convention Banning Landmines, the Role of International Non-Governmental Organizations and the Idea of International Civil Society' (2000) 11 *European Journal of International Law* 91–120.

258 Rome Statute of the International Criminal Court, 1 July 2002.

259 Cf. A Zimmermann and R Hofmann (eds), *Unity and Diversity in International Law* (Berlin: Duncker & Humblot 2006); Boyle and Chinkin, *The Making of International Law*, 41–66.

260 A Fischer-Lescano, *Globalverfassung. Die Geltungsbegründung der Menschenrechte* (Weilerswist: Velbrück Wissenschaft 2005).

Less attention has however been paid to NGOs' participation in the interpretation of given norm texts whereas also NGOs throw their weight into struggles about what the law means and thereby partake in its making. They frequently participate in domestic and international judicial proceedings—for example by way of submitting *amicus curiae* briefs—and at times they pursue litigation strategies to find further authoritative acceptance for their interpretations by courts. Among other things they are potent actors behind large amounts of human rights litigation. Their involvement in international semantic struggles nicely shows how actors can seek the authority of others in communicative lawmaking.

Lastly, it might be suggested that the interpretative acts of any world citizen might bear on the meaning of international norms, just as long as they are loud enough. Christian Tomuschat notably finds that 'discourse on issues of international law must [. . .] be couched in language that allows everyone affected by its operation to make its voice heard'.[261] It is unlikely that an individual's claim would be heard if it is not voiced in specific settings or carried by the general public and a (global) media. Individual voices might however trigger broader action in civil society that could possibly ride the wave of a *colère publique mondiale*.[262] Social platforms on the Internet may certainly play a facilitating role. But by and large, the interpretative claims crafted by private norm entrepreneurs need the backing of public or institutional actors to be noticeable.

2. The disaggregated state

It is one of the remaining hypostatizations of the state that it has the capacity to act. And if it is not the state that acts as a person, then it is its head or its organs.[263] Quite frequently, however, actions of specific state organs may only be linked back to 'the state' at a far stretch and looking at them as independent actors might be much more convincing. In fact, institutions and individuals forming part of all branches of government can and do engage as actors in the interpretation of international law.[264] Rather than acting on behalf of 'their' state, those distinct actors might align themselves according to sectoral interests in order to act on the international level, seeking to conclude international commitments and thus to gain advantage in competition on the domestic level.[265] What is more, domestic

261 C Tomuschat, 'International Law: Ensuring the Survival of Mankind on the Eve of a New Century' (2001) 281 *Recueil des Cours* 13–438, 28.

262 Fischer-Lescano, *Globalverfassung*, 68, with reference to Émile Durkheim.

263 See R Koselleck, Staat und Souveränität III, in: O Brunner, W Conze, and R Koselleck (eds), *Geschichtliche Grundbegriffe*, vol VI (Stuttgart: Klett-Cotta 1990), 25–64, 26.

264 A-M Slaughter, *A New World Order* (Princeton: Princeton University Press 2004), 12–15; C Möllers, 'Transnationale Behördenkooperation. Verfassungs- und völkerrechtliche Probleme transnationaler administrativer Standardsetzung' (2005) 65 *Zeitschrift für ausländisches öffentliches Recht und Völkerrecht* 351–89.

265 On the dynamics at the interplay between the international and domestic level see E Benvenisti, 'Exit and Voice in the Age of Globalization' (1999) 98 *Michigan Law Review* 167–213; R D Putnam, 'Diplomacy and Domestic Politics: The Logic of Two-Level Games' (1988) 42 *International Organization* 427–60. On alignments along sectoral lines see A Fischer-Lescano and G Teubner, *Regime-Kollisionen. Zur Fragmentierung des globalen Rechts* (Frankfurt am Main: Suhrkamp 2006).

actors can play a supportive and facilitative role in relation to the authority of international institutions. Guidelines of the UNHCR turn out to be authoritative in virtue of the way they are treated in domestic courts, for example.[266]

The fact that other domestic actors line up to challenge the lead role of official governmental representatives does not cast into doubt that the latter retain a strong role to play in international legal discourse. They interpret and argue with international law in litigation, in policy statements, in media comments, and in many other fora.[267]

But apart from legislatures that sometimes step up as actors on the international level by way of signalling what they believe to be permitted or prohibited by international law, it is most of all the impact of domestic courts that merits emphasis.

They have become more significant and self-confident actors in the practice of interpreting international law.[268] In some fields of international law, a number of domestic courts of different states have formed what Eyal Benvenisti has termed a 'united, coordinated judicial front'.[269] Already in 1929 Hersch Lauterpacht suggested that domestic courts' impact on the development of international law is widely underestimated, and he showed how they play a crucial part in 'creating general rules of customary international law [and in] developing the substance of international law'.[270] George Scelle later made the prominent argument that domestic organs also act as organs of the international community in a *dédoublement fonctionnel*, an idea that resonates with Richard Falk's suggestion that

> the decentralized quality of international law places a special burden upon all legal institutions at the national level. Domestic courts are agents of a developing international legal order, as well as servants of various national interests [. . .].[271]

But the phenomenon of domestic judicial cooperation that Benvenisti describes is relatively new. As he notes, '[i]t demonstrates yet again the consequences of the "disaggregated state," as both the national government and the national court seek foreign allies in their quest to balance each other out.'[272] In many scenarios

[266] See below Chapter III.

[267] Reisman, 'Process of Communication', 107–10.

[268] A Nollkaemper, *National Courts and the International Rule of Law* (Oxford: Oxford University Press 2011), 6–10; K F Gärditz, 'Die Legitimation der Justiz zur Völkerrechtsfortbildung' (2008) 47 *Der Staat* 381–409; E Benvenisti, 'Reclaiming Democracy: The Strategic Uses of Foreign and International Law by National Courts' (2008) 102 *American Journal of International Law* 241–74.

[269] Ibid., at 249.

[270] H Lauterpacht, 'Decisions of Municipal Courts as a Source of International Law' (1929) 10 *British Yearbook of International Law* 65–95, 92.

[271] R A Falk, *The Role of Domestic Courts in the International Legal Order* (Syracuse: Syracuse University Press 1964), 65; G Scelle, Le Phénomène Juridique du Dédoublement Fonctionnel, in: W Schätzel and H J Schlochauer (eds), *Rechtsfragen Internationaler Organisation. Festschrift für Hans Wehberg* (Frankfurt am Main: Klostermann 1956), 324–42.

[272] Benvenisti, 'Reclaiming Democracy', 44.

domestic courts act independently and, contrary to what the construction of the state as an actor may suggest, they compete with other domestic actors. Oftentimes domestic courts do not say what the head of state thinks.

Domestic courts do not merely implement or enforce international law but their practice has a transformative momentum. In recent years, their role has become more visible and their mutual exchange has increased, enough at least for Anne-Marie Slaughter to find types of 'transjudicial communication' that reflect 'judicial autonomy; a reliance on persuasive authority; and a sense of common judicial identity and enterprise'.[273] The impact of domestic courts on international law also caught the attention of the Institut de Droit International. Its resolution on 'The Activities of National Judges and the International Relations of their State' passed in 1993 reads like a manifesto on the international agency of domestic judiciaries.[274] It may suffice to point to the resolution's first article stating that '[n]ational courts should be empowered by their domestic legal order to interpret and apply international law with full independence'. The autonomy of domestic courts, their transnational relations, and a shared legal ethos all suggest looking at domestic courts as independent actors in international legal discourse rather than keeping them locked away in the black box of the unitary state. They have had a considerable say in shaping the meaning of international norms.

3. International institutions: Bureaucracies and judicial bodies

Sidelined for long on the periphery of political relevance or nurtured by a number of overpowering states, many international institutions now live strong lives of their own and engage in international legal practice with significant repercussions. Even after the argument made headway that institutions do matter, research still continued to be dominated by the question of why rational actors (unitary states) set up international institutions in the first place. This left international institutions' qualities as actors largely in the dark. In legal scholarship it was the spell of the normative construction of sources doctrine that compelled onlookers to tie the actions of international institutions to the constitutive treaty. As with specific state actors, it may often be more plausible and illuminating to look at international actors not as agents under the tutelage of their creators but as independent participants in legal discourse.[275] Many fields of international law are now marked

[273] A-M Slaughter, 'A Typology of Transjudicial Communication' (1994) 29 *University of Richmond Law Review* 99–137, 102. Also see Slaughter, *A New World Order*, 65–103. A Reinisch, The International Relations of National Courts: A Discourse on International Law Norms on Jurisdictional and Enforcement Immunity, in: A Reinisch and U Kriebaum (eds), *The Law of International Relations—Liber Amicorum Hanspeter Neuhold* (Utrecht: Eleven 2007), 289–309, 309 (concluding that 'in the long run, national courts will increasingly shape international law through their transnational exchanges.').

[274] Institut de Droit International, 'The Activities of National Judges and the International Relations of their State' (1993-I) 65 *Annuaire de l'Institut de Droit International* 328–444.

[275] This is fleshed out in more detail at the beginning of Chapters III and IV.

by the presence of international organizations or less formal international institutions. While international organizations have been around for some time, they have increased in number as well as impact.

Notably, actors within international institutions have interpreted their statute or mandate so as to increase the scope and impact of their actions—a phenomenon frequently termed mission creep.[276] The growth of the UNHCR tells an illuminating story in this regard. With innovative interpretative moves the secretariat and strong High Commissioners were successful in broadening the scope and substance of their actions.[277] Legal doctrine has played its role in accompanying the autonomous agency of those actors, above all with the notions of implied or even inherent powers.[278] The ICJ walks the borderlines. Its Advisory Opinion on *Reparations for Injuries* found that an international organization 'must be deemed to have those powers which, though not expressly provided in the Charter, are conferred upon it by necessary implication as being essential to the performance of its duties'.[279]

As subjects of international law, international organizations may be authors of new treaties or they may pass legal acts creating new norms.[280] The present focus however falls on their authority in the interpretative practice centred on given norm texts. But at the same time it is true that their interpretations frequently do more than contributing to changes of meaning. Their communications also create new reference points for legal discourse. Chapter III illustrates the argument with a focus on the UNHCR and its impact on the interpretation of its own Statute as well as on the meaning of the 1951 Convention relating to the Status of Refugees. Once it became evident that no new treaty text would be forthcoming, UNHCR invested its efforts into bending the meaning of given texts to meet its convictions and preferences. For that purpose it crafted a number of interpretative documents that other actors then also used as reference points to support their claims about what international refugee law means.

The semantic authority of international judicial institutions is in many cases still greater when compared to bureaucracies.[281] Over the past years, international judicial institutions have grown in quantity as well as quality.[282] Many international courts and judges do not only see themselves as arbiters deciding between the concrete parties but also as actors in the deliberate development of the international

[276] D G Hawkins and W Jacoby, How Agents Matter, in: D G Hawkins, D A Lake, D L Nielson, and M J Tierney (eds), *Delegation and Agency in International Organizations* (Cambridge: Cambridge University Press 2006), 199–228, 206–7; E B Haas, *Beyond the Nation-state* (Stanford: Stanford University Press 1964), 90–2.

[277] See below Chapter III, section B.

[278] See J Klabbers, *An Introduction to International Institutional Law* (Cambridge: Cambridge University Press 2009), 66–9.

[279] *Reparation for Injuries Suffered in the Service of the United Nations*, Advisory Opinion of 11 April 1949, ICJ Reports 174, 182.

[280] J E Alvarez, *International Organizations as Law-Makers* (Oxford: Oxford University Press 2005), 273–91.

[281] See in closer detail Venzke, 'Role of International Courts'.

[282] See below Chapter IV, section A.1.

legal system.[283] Even if they focus on the resolution of the concrete dispute at hand, they can hardly avoid contributing to the making of international law. In many fields, international courts and tribunals have become significant lawmakers.[284]

To see the development of international law in judicial practice is most interesting because the foundation of courts' authority usually precludes them from openly pushing for change. Their sociological legitimacy rests on others' belief that they apply the law and do not make it. The decisions of judges are shielded by an outward show of judicial technique.[285] Judith Shklar argued that the expectations about what judges (or courts) do and the basis of their authority and reputation set in place a self-reinforcing legalism that involves all the tricks in the book in order to tie the interpretation to what was already established and accepted. This is no mask for anything, she further clarifies, but part of a judicial ethos that leads judges to fear little more than the reproach of engaging in legislation rather than interpretation.[286] In spite of the outward show of legal argument, a court's interpretation, like any other actor's interpretation, contributes to the creation of what it finds. Courts' semantic authority makes it even more likely—in fact it is the default position of the legal system—that they find acceptance with their interpretations.

International judicial institutions shift meanings and can establish their own interpretations as new reference points for legal discourse. The working of precedents is key in their contribution to the making of international law. In many fields, participants in legal discourse can simply not avoid relating their argument to earlier judicial decisions. They are expected to do so. This constellation makes semantic struggles in the context of judicial proceedings one of the main sites where interpretation makes international law. Chapter IV develops the argument and analysis further in the context of the GATT/WTO and shows how judicial practice made the general exceptions in international trade law that are spelled out in Art. XX GATT.

[283] Explicit testimony to such a self-understanding may even be found in the field of investment arbitration which, due to its decentralized institutional setup, may count as an unlikely case. See, e.g., *Saipem S.p.A. v The People's Republic of Bangladesh*, ICSID Case No ARB/05/7, Award of 30 June 2009, para 80 ('it [the tribunal] has a duty to seek to contribute to the harmonious development of investment law and thereby to meet the legitimate expectations of the community of States and investors towards certainty of the rule of law'). Cf. Y Shany, 'No Longer a Weak Department of Power? Reflections on the Emergence of a New International Judiciary' (2009) 20 *European Journal of International Law* 73–91.

[284] Armin von Bogdandy and Ingo Venzke (eds), 'Beyond Dispute: International Judicial Institutions as Lawmakers' Special Issue (2011) 12 *German Law Journal* 979–1370.

[285] Shklar, *Legalism*, 10–11; N Luhmann, *Legitimation durch Verfahren* (Frankfurt am Main: Suhrkamp 1983), see especially at 108; Bourdieu, 'The Force of Law', 828.

[286] Shklar, *Legalism*, 10–11. Cf. P Weil, 'Le droit international en quête de son identité' (1992) 237 *Recueil des Cours* 9–370, 143 ('[l]orsque le juge énonce une règle qu'il crée en même temps qu'il l'énonce, il la présentera comme une règle coutumière préexistante qu'il fait semblant de constater.').

III

UNHCR and the Making of Refugee Law

The project of international law has always and for good reasons been closely intertwined with moves towards international institutions.[1] International institutions should take the passion out of conflictuous international politics, curb self-serving interpretations of the law by contracting parties, and pursue mutual or global goals. They should function as technical creatures and, frequently, in the name of the international community. With such aspirations, the increase in international institutions and their prominent place in global governance processes may well be viewed as the long overdue realization of a lasting hope. International institutions are not only the venue where representatives of unitary state are crowded around large conference tables and occasionally put together a new legal document that oftentimes lacks real bite. They are also autonomous actors in international relations with differing degrees of authority and, sometimes at least, with remarkable repercussions on the making of international law through communicative practice. Jan Klabbers evocatively opens his *Introduction to International Institutional Law* with an epigram from Mary Shelley's *Frankenstein*: 'You are my creator, but I am your master; obey!'[2]

This chapter and the following one focus on international institutions as actors in the making of international law by way of interpretation. While the present chapter concentrates on international bureaucracies and specifically on UNHCR, the following chapter is centred on international judicial institutions and specifically on adjudication in the GATT/WTO. A number of prominent examples elucidating semantic change under the auspices of international institutions are easily to hand. The notable change in the meaning of 'threat to peace' (Art. 39 UNC) serves as a well-known case in point. This qualification provides the threshold for any Security Council actions under Chapter VII UNC. Only if a situation at least qualifies as a threat to peace may the Security Council make use of its coercive powers.[3] While it was rather evident throughout the early decades of the United Nations that only international military action could amount to a threat to peace, the Security Council has since pushed towards a more encompassing meaning of

[1] D Kennedy, 'The Move to Institutions' (1987) 8 *Cardozo Law Review* 841–988.

[2] J Klabbers, *An Introduction to International Institutional Law* (Cambridge: Cambridge University Press 2009).

[3] M Bothe, Les Limites des Pouvoirs du Conseil de Sécurité, in: R-J Dupuy (ed), *The Development of the Role of the Security Council* (Dordrecht: Kluwer 1993), 67–82, 68. Cf. J E Alvarez, *International Organizations as Law-Makers* (Oxford: Oxford University Press 2005), 169–83.

Art. 39 and has successfully enlarged its room for manoeuvre.[4] By now it stands rather undisputed that situations of gross violations of human rights within one country could meet the threshold of Art. 39 even if there is no physical international nexus.[5] The British delegation recently even placed climate change on the agenda and treated it as a phenomenon that could constitute a threat to peace. While some speakers voiced scepticism about this topic's nexus with peace and security, maybe weary that the Security Council might eventually wield its coercive Chapter VII powers to tackle this issue, the link between climate change and peace does not actually seem to be all that far-fetched.[6]

United Nations peace-keeping operations serve as another renowned example. Their legal anchoring stretched the provisions delimiting the powers of the Security Council, the General Assembly, and the Secretary-General; and yet, their legal basis no longer stands in question.[7] A very striking and prominent semantic shift has also taken place with regard to the meaning of Art. 27(3) UNC, providing that decisions on non-procedural Security Council matters shall be taken 'by an affirmative vote of nine members including the concurring votes of the permanent members'. In 1946 the Soviet delegate abstained from a decision and the decision's legality was challenged on this ground. In later practice, however, there remained little doubt that taking a decision with an abstention does not stand in tension with Art. 27(3) UNC. Most commentators have argued that this is within the permissible bounds of the wording of the Charter.[8] The ICJ too has favoured such an interpretation of Art. 27(3) UNC—stretching the meaning of 'concurrent vote' but steering away from yet more slippery slopes of reasoning and avoiding raising the charge of treaty violation.[9]

It might well be objected that the Security Council had little influence on these semantic developments as an actor in its own right and that changes rather relate to the interests of powerful states. If anything, the Council would be a tool in the

[4] Cf. E de Wet, *The Chapter VII Powers of the United Nations Security Council* (Oxford: Hart 2004), 133–77 (showing this transformation in detail; curiously, however, discussing these shifts under the heading of *limitations* to the Security Council's actions); P H Kooijmans, The Enlargement of the Concept 'Threat to the Peace', in: R-J Dupuy (ed), *The Development of the Role of the Security Council* (Dordrecht: Kluwer 1993), 111–21.

[5] J Frowein and N Krisch, Article 39, in: B Simma (ed), *The Charter of the United Nations: A Commentary* (Oxford: Oxford University Press 2002), 717–29, Mns 16–25.

[6] Meeting Coverage, SC/9000, 27 April 2007, Security Council holds first-ever debate on impact of climate change on peace, security, hearing over 50 speakers, available at <http://www.un.org/News/Press/docs/2007/sc9000.doc.htm>.

[7] M Bothe, Peace-keeping, in: B Simma (ed), *The Charter of the United Nations: A Commentary* (Oxford: Oxford University Press 2002), 648–700; *Certain Expenses of the United Nations (Article 17, paragraph 2, of the Charter)*, Advisory Opinion of 20 July 1962, (1962) ICJ Reports 151 (setting aside most of the doubts of peace-keeping operations' legal basis in the UNC).

[8] B Simma, S Brunner and H-P Kaul, Article 27, in: B Simma (ed), *The Charter of the United Nations: A Commentary* (Oxford: Oxford University Press 2002), 476–523, Mns 46–60 (investing quite some effort in reconciling this practice with the text of the Charter).

[9] *Legal Consequences for States of the Continuing Presence of South Africa in Namibia (South West Africa) notwithstanding Security Council Resolution 276 (1970)*, Advisory Opinion of 21 June 1971, (1971) ICJ Reports 16, para 22. Cf. T M Franck, *Recourse to Force: State Action against Threats and Armed Attacks* (Cambridge: Cambridge University Press 2002), 7–8; J Klabbers, *The Concept of Treaty in International Law* (The Hague: Kluwer 1996), 16.

hands of some of its members but certainly not a grown master subjecting them to obedience. There is a looming danger in portraying parts of international institutions as autonomous actors because the resulting picture might disguise the real power relations at work.[10] Mindful of such dangers, the present chapter all the same seeks to highlight the authority of international bureaucracies in communicative lawmaking.

Examples from organizations other than the UN illustrate semantic changes of sometimes amazing creativity just as well. It is particularly noteworthy that treaties, above all those setting up international organizations, sometimes link the interpretation of their own provisions to instruments of other institutions. Such instruments of other institutions thus gain legal normativity in the process in which they are used. For example, the Codex Alimentarius Commission, a joint venture of the Food and Agricultural Organization (FAO) and World Health Organization (WHO), has developed a standard, the 'Codex Alimentarius', that was then used in order to determine the permissible levels of protection in the international trade of goods within the framework of the WTO. The Agreement on Sanitary and Phytosanitary Measures (SPS Agreement) as well as the Agreement on Technical Barriers to Trade (TBT Agreement) explicitly refer to instruments adopted by bodies such as the Codex Alimentarius Commission or by other bodies in the more amorphous 'international standardization community'.[11] Another case in point are WTO Schedules that adapt to changes in the Harmonized System, which offers a nomenclature for all traded goods and is maintained by the World Customs Organization (WCO).[12] Turning to another field of law, the International Maritime Organization (IMO) interprets and spells out the 'rules and standards' relating to the pollution of vessels that are part of Art. 211 United Nations Convention on the Law of the Sea (UNCLOS). In fact, UNCLOS repeatedly refers to 'competent international organization(s)' in order to further specify its provisions.[13] All these

[10] Of course the opposite, blending out the agency of international institutions altogether, may be equally misguided. It might just as well overlook actors and actions that should be subjected to critical discussion. See, for instance, T Piiparinen, 'The Rise and Fall of Bureaucratic Rationalization: Exploring the Possibilities and Limitations of the UN Secretariat in Conflict Prevention' (2008) 14 *European Journal of International Relations* 697–724.

[11] This term is used in Art. 1(2) TBT Agreement. Cf. R A Pereira, 'Why Would International Administrative Activity Be Any Less Legitimate?—A Study of the Codex Alimentarius Commission' (2008) 9 *German Law Journal* 1693–718; R Howse, A New Device for Creating International Legal Normativity: The WTO Technical Barriers to Trade Agreement and 'International Standards', in: C Joerges and E-U Petersmann (eds), *Constitutionalism, Multilevel Trade Governance and Social Regulation* (Oxford: Hart 2006), 383–95.

[12] I Feichtner, 'The Administration of the Vocabulary of International Trade: The Adaptation of WTO Schedules to Changes in the Harmonized System' (2008) 9 *German Law Journal* 1481–511.

[13] UNCLOS mentions 'competent international institution(s)' a total of 82 times. Links to other international institutions are particularly strong in the field of maritime environment and safety of navigation; cf. S Trevisanut, La convention des Nations Unies sur le droit de la mer et le droit de l'environnement: développement intrasystémique et renvoi intersystémique, in: H Ruiz Fabri and L Gradoni (eds), *La Circulation des Concepts Juridiques* (Paris: Société de législation comparée 2009), 397–426; B Vukas, Generally Accepted International Rules and Standards, in: A H Soons (ed), *Implementation of the Law of the Sea Convention through International Institutions* (Honolulu: The Law of the Sea Institute 1990), 405–21.

examples show how the semantic content of treaty commitments is negotiated in a context that gives international institutions a very powerful say. The examples also indicate that international institutions not only influence the development of given norm texts, but their communications structure the space of interpretation and offer new reference points in legal discourse.

The concept of 'institution' refers above all to rather loose structures of governance. In international relations parlance it inherits some lessons learned from the debates on regimes, but for present purposes it is still over-inclusive.[14] In order to capture agency in interpretation it is necessary to be more specific as well as nuanced and to differentiate between bureaucracies, on the one hand, and international courts and tribunals, on the other. This chapter elucidates the qualities of international bureaucracies as participants in the practice of interpretation with a focus on UNHCR. Against the backdrop of a strong realist tradition in international relations theory, it introduces international bureaucracies as autonomous actors. They can draw on delegated authority from member states and they may tap into further resources of authority: the aura of non-political technocrats working for human betterment, the dynamism of a dedicated or at least experienced civil staff, and resources of knowledge and expertise. International bureaucracies have developed capacities for action that have made them increasingly significant actors in lawmaking on the stage of international legal interpretation (A.).

There are two main dimensions to UNHCR's interpretative struggles that are closely related but should better be kept apart. The first concerns UNHCR's claims about the meaning of its own Statute. It mainly relates to what 'international protection' means and who qualifies to receive it. While at the outset of its life it was understood that at the most UNHCR was to provide quasi-consular protection to a rather narrow group of refugees, by the time it was 50 years old it had grown to be the world's chief international agency providing humanitarian assistance to a host of people in need. Building on the force of humanitarian imperatives, UNHCR succeeded in restructuring the debate surrounding the meaning of its Statute: its competence is no longer triggered by the definition of refugee, so it seems, but by an individual's need for assistance and ultimately for protection (B.).

The second dimension of UNHCR's participation in negotiating the content of commitments relates to the definition of refugee spelled out in the 1951 Geneva Convention Relating to the Status of Refugees. UNHCR has relied on its function of supervising the implementation of the Convention in order to develop weighty interpretations of the law and to intervene in seminal cases, thereby directing semantic developments. When new challenges arose to which the Convention appeared to offer insufficient answers and at the same time no new treaty appeared to be forthcoming that could ease the concerns, UNHCR vested considerable efforts into shifting the interpretation of the Convention in order to meet the exigencies of new refugee situations (C.). In conclusion, I will briefly summarize and tentatively discuss the significant semantic change of UNHCR's Statute and of the 1951 Convention with a broader outlook (D.).

[14] See above Chapter II, section B.1.b.

A. International bureaucracies as actors in legal discourse

International bureaucracies are autonomous actors in processes of legal interpretation. To a varying degree, they gain and enjoy semantic authority in struggles over what the law says. Their actions are oftentimes removed from the intentions and control of their creators and they engage in subject matters not formerly within their reach. Their factual impact remains frequently underestimated and little consolation can, in principle, be found in the contention that they merely seek effective implementation of global goals. In some cases, a yawning gap unfolds between the mechanisms of control, ways and means of contesting the influence of bureaucracies on the one hand, and their actual exercise of power, on the other.

Research in international relations long provided only a rather nebulous view on international organizations and less formal institutions because its focus rested on the question of *why* international organizations exist and persist.[15] The effect of regimes was constantly challenged on realist premises: they are an academic fad that distracts from the analysis of underlying power structures and institutions have arguably no independent effect on state behaviour, so the argument went.[16] The question of what international organizations actually do, a conception of international organizations as actors as well as an understanding and explanation of their actions, has been largely overshadowed by the more fundamental theoretical entanglement on *whether* they matter at all. Scholarship in international relations has been, so to speak, driving with a rear-view mirror pointed at those primary questions at the beginning of the road.[17] This has certainly benefited the understanding of international organizations but has also come at a regrettable loss. Most importantly, this focus has left international organizations and less formal institutions as actors in a dead angle from which they have only slowly emerged to attract some attention.[18]

This chapter offers an understanding of UNHCR as a bureaucracy and it thereby elucidates UNHCR's sources of autonomy and authority. It also highlights common mechanisms to which international bureaucracies resort in the exercise of

[15] J J Mearsheimer, 'The False Promise of International Institutions' (1994) 19 *International Security* 5–49; B Verbeek, International organizations. The ugly duckling of international relations theory?, in: B Reinalda and B Verbeek (eds), *Autonomous Policy Making by International Organizations* (London: Routledge 1998), 11–26; L L Martin and B Simmons, 'Theories and Empirical Studies of International Institutions' (1998) 52 *International Organization* 729–57.

[16] S Strange, Cave! Hic Dragones: A Critique of Regime Analysis, in: S D Krasner (ed), *International Regimes* (Ithaca, NY: Cornell University Press 1983), 337–54; J Sterling-Folker, Realist global governance: Revisiting *cave! hic dragones* and beyond, in: A D Ba and M J Hoffmann (eds), *Contending Perspectives on Global Governance. Coherence, Contestation and World Order* (London: Routledge 2005), 17–38.

[17] A Wendt, 'Driving with the Rearview Mirror: On the Rational Science of Institutional Design' (2001) 55 *International Organization* 1019–49.

[18] See generally T Benner, S Mergenthaler, and P Rotmann, 'Internationale Bürokratien und Organisationslernen. Konturen einer Forschungsagenda' (2009) 16 *Zeitschrift für Internationale Beziehungen* 203–36; I Venzke, 'International Bureaucracies in a Political Science Perspective—Agency, Authority and International Institutional Law' (2008) 9 *German Law Journal* 1401–28.

authority. In order to fully grasp their autonomous actions, it is necessary to direct the gaze away from the rear-view mirror focused on international institutions' embryonic stages under the tutelage of (dominant) constituent members. International institutions have grown up. Attention should be given to the perimeters of their action, the sources of their autonomy and to *how* they act. In short, even if it were still doubtful that international organizations do matter, it is not a bad idea to also scrutinize them as actors. Otherwise they might emerge from the dead angle of research agendas to suddenly claim obedience. With due regard to methodological challenges, empirical research has largely defied at least the unqualified argument that regimes are generally without teeth—mere epiphenomena of state action.[19] The so-called regime debate has been taken over by research agendas focusing on the institutions and norms and a number of accounts have since attempted to set the record straight.[20]

The aim of this section is to corroborate the thesis that, apart from *instruments* in the hand of one or a number of powerful actors or *arenas* for decision-making, international bureaucracies are also autonomous *actors* in the practice of interpretation in international law.[21] An affirmative argument on *whether* institutions matter compels an argument on *why* and *how* they matter. Such argument rests on two broad and interrelated lines of reasoning. First, under rational choice premises it might simply be instrumental for principals to grant organizations a certain degree of autonomy—the focus thus lies on the rationale of principals for delegating authority to agents (1.). The second line of reasoning zooms in on the actor and dwells on the concept of international bureaucracies. It highlights their characteristic traits and emphasizes their strong repository of knowledge as well as expertise as a source of authority. It contends that, in addition to delegation, this authority is an important source of autonomy as well as a significant factor backing international organizations' position in struggles about the meaning of international norms (2).

1. Delegation from principals to agents

The most straightforward explanation for international bureaucracies' autonomy rests on the reasons principals might have for delegating authority to them. On the premise that actors act strategically—that is instrumentally rational in pursuit of

[19] Cf. R D Keohane and L L Martin, 'The Promise of Institutionalist Theory' (1995) 20 *International Security* 39–51; H Breitmeier, O R Young, and M Zürn, *Analyzing International Environmental Regimes: From Case Study to Database* (Cambridge, MA: The MIT Press 2006); S Bauer, 'Does Bureaucracy Really Matter? The Authority of Intergovernmental Treaty Secretariats in Global Environmental Politics' (2006) 6 *Global Environmental Politics* 24–49; F Biermann and B Siebenhüner (eds), *Managers of Global Change. The Influence of International Environmental Bureaucracies* (Cambridge, MA: MIT Press 2009).

[20] Notably among others, F V Kratochwil and J G Ruggie, 'International Organization: A state of art and an art of the state' (1986) 40 *International Organization* 753–75; B A Simmons and L L Martin, International Organizations and Institutions, in: W Carlsnaes, T Risse, and B A Simmons (eds), *Handbook of International Relations* (London: Sage Publications 2002), 192–211. See above Chapter II, section B.1.b.

[21] C Archer, *International Organizations* (London: Routledge 2001), 68–87 (for the understanding of IOs as instruments, arenas, and actors).

given interests—several explanations can be offered as to why principals delegate authority to bureaucracies. More precisely, the main premise translates into the contention that contracting states (principals) delegate authority to international bureaucracies (agents) and tolerate a certain degree of autonomy of the agent when they expect instrumental gains. In their rational choice analysis of delegation, Hawkins *et al.* define delegation as a 'conditional grant of authority from a *principal* to an *agent*'.[22] They further claim that '[a]ll delegation is premised upon the division of labor and gains from specialization'.[23] Principals delegate authority and allow for a margin of autonomy of an agent in order to carry out a task in a way that is more efficient or effective when compared with the principals themselves carrying out this task. Gains from specialization are likely to be greatest when the task performed by the agent is frequent, repetitive, and when it requires specific expertise or knowledge.[24]

International agents play a particularly important role in overcoming problems of coordination and in the enforcement of agreements. Bearing again in mind that principals usually have incentives to cheat on their commitments, delegating the authority to monitor and possibly to enforce the terms of an agreement to an agent increases the credibility of commitments and makes cooperation more likely.[25] Also prime functions of UNHCR can be explained as a form of delegated authority on the basis of this reasoning. It is entrusted with the task of supervising and, to some extent, enforcing international commitments. Its Statute and Art. 35 Refugee Convention endow it with a supervisory function and its role includes preventing contracting states from unilaterally projecting their preferences onto the definition of refugee.[26] It counteracts parties' self-serving interpretations. Walter Kälin has forcefully argued that one of UNHCR's crucial functions lies in overcoming

[22] D G Hawkins, D A Lake, D L Nielson, and M J Tierney, Delegation under Anarchy: States, international organizations, and principal-agent theory, in: D G Hawkins, D A Lake, D L Nielson, and M J Tierney (eds), *Delegation and Agency in International Organizations* (Cambridge: Cambridge University Press 2006), 3–38, 7. Cf. C A Bradley and J G Kelley, 'The Concept of International Delegation' (2008) 71 *Law and Contemporary Problems* 1–36, 3 (defining international delegation 'as a grant of authority by two or more states to an international body to make decisions or take actions').

[23] Hawkins et al., Delegation under Anarchy, at 13.

[24] Ibid., at 13–15; K W Abbott and D Snidal, 'Why States Act through Formal International Organizations' (1998) 42 *Journal of Conflict Resolution* 3–32, 9–16. Cf. B Koremenos, 'When, What and Why Do States Choose to Delegate?' (2008) 71 *Law and Contemporary Problems* 151–92.

[25] Hawkins et al., Delegation under Anarchy, 18–19; A T Guzman, 'The Design of International Agreements' (2005) 16 *European Journal of International Law* 579–612; B Koremenos, C Lipson, and D Snidal, 'The Rational Design of International Institutions' (2001) 55 *International Organization* 761–99.

[26] E J Lentini, 'The Definition of Refugees in International Law: Proposals for the Future' (1985) 5 *Boston College Third World Law Journal* 183–98, 195 (showing how national interests impact competing interpretations of the refugee convention and suggesting that, given 'the problem of ensuring consistent and impartial application of the existing definition', this task 'should involve enforcement or decision-making by a regional or international organization.').

collective action problems among states. If one state were to introduce higher thresholds for refugee status, others would face a greater share of the problem.[27]

Adjudication is a distinct way of delegating enforcement to an agent.[28] Principals invest a third party with the authority of deciding on future conflicts over the terms of an agreement. The multiplication of international courts and tribunals is one of the most distinctive characteristics in the development of the international legal order over the past two decades. Their impact in international legal practice will be the focus of the following chapter on adjudication in the GATT/WTO.

Principals might further have an interest in entrusting an agent to set the agenda and to thereby overcome stalemates in negotiations. Secretariats can formally or informally take up this role. For instance, the WTO likes to portray itself as a purely member-driven organization.[29] According to its constitutive agreement, it shall only provide a common institutional framework.[30] The secretariat may facilitate negotiation rounds but formally has no proactive role to play. However, a closer look reveals that at times the secretariat does become active, though cautiously and in acquiescence with at least some member states. It impacts the course of events and influences substantive decisions.[31] In a persistent stalemate during the Uruguay Round, for example, the secretariat came to draft a text which was in line with the prevalent objectives of the organization, provided the reference point in discussions, and in effect crucially channelled the outcome.[32] The Dispute Settlement Understanding (DSU) also formally provides that the Secretariat propose panellists to the parties to a dispute.[33] Should the parties object and with compelling reasons not come to an agreement within 20 days, then the Director General determines the

27 W Kälin, Supervising the 1951 Convention Relating to the Status of Refugees: Article 35 and beyond, in: E Feller, V Türk, and F Nicholson (eds), *Refugee Protection in International Law: UNHCR's Global Consultations on International Protection* (Cambridge: Cambridge University Press 2003), 613–66. Kälin is quick to add, however, that UNHCR falls short of fulfilling this role satisfactorily and unfolds a detailed argument for reforming its monitoring and enforcement mechanisms. Cf. M Zieck, *UNHCR's Parallel Universe: Marking the Contours of a Problem* (Amsterdam: Amsterdam University Press 2010) (on the structural and practical conditions that undermine UNHCR's supervisory function).

28 Hawkins et al., Delegation under Anarchy, 17; K Alter 'Delegating to International Courts: Self-Binding vs. Other-Binding Delegation' (2008) 38 *Law and Contemporary Problems* 37–76.

29 For example, the WTO deals with '10 common misunderstandings about the WTO' on its website. The first misunderstanding it wants to rectify is: '1. The WTO does NOT tell governments what to do. The WTO does not tell governments how to conduct their trade policies. Rather, it's a "member-driven" organization.' <http://www.wto.org/english/thewto_e/whatis_e/10mis_e/10m01_e.htm>.

30 Art. II(1) WTO Agreement.

31 For the GATT/WTO Secretariat see in closer detail below Chapter IV, section A.3.

32 Y-C Xu and P M Weller, *The Governance of World Trade. International civil servants and GATT/WTO* (Cheltenham: Elgar 2004), 264–5; E-U Petersmann, From 'Member-driven Governance' to Constitutionally Limited 'Multi-level Governance' in the WTO, in: G Sacerdoti, A Yanovich, and J Bohanes (eds), *The WTO at Ten* (Cambridge: Cambridge University Press 2006), 86–110.

33 Art. 8(6) DSU.

composition of the panel.[34] In doing so the Director General enjoys discretion and is likely to further the objectives of the organization.[35]

UNHCR plays a considerable role in setting the agenda of the Executive Committee (ExCom)—its advisory body that is formally a subsidiary organ of the ECOSOC and made up of government representatives. Only on the face of it does ExCom resemble an intergovernmental body where state delegates are in charge. It usually acts upon the initiative and with strong guidance of the High Commissioner. What is more, ExCom meetings themselves are oftentimes not decisive because critical questions are settled in informal meetings beforehand, or during the sessions of the Standing Committee, which would again be under the influence of the UNHCR bureaucracy.[36] These mechanisms do not take away from the fact that state representatives do exercise control in ExCom and notably have the power of the purse.

Delegating authority to international organizations may furthermore be explained with regard to domestic political processes. An incentive for political players to delegate authority may lie in their interest in creating commitments that cement policy decisions by placing them outside the reach of any new majority.[37] They may also seek international commitments in order to outplay domestic competitors on the national level.[38] Delegation to an international agent may furthermore serve to engage in action, which would be perceived as illegitimate if it was undertaken unilaterally by the domestic actor.[39] Even more critical is such action on the international level that would not only appear illegitimate in bilateral relations but would simply be illegal if it was to be undertaken by the principal itself.[40]

[34] Art. 8(7) DSU.

[35] A v Bogdandy, 'Law and Politics in the WTO—Strategies to Cope with a Deficient Relationship' (2001) 5 *Max Planck Yearbook of United Nations Law* 609–73, 615–16; J H H Weiler, 'The Rule of Lawyers and the Ethos of Diplomats. Reflections on the Internal and External Legitimacy of WTO Dispute Settlement' (2001) 35 *Journal of World Trade* 191–207, 202–6.

[36] On these dynamics see G Loescher, A Betts, and J Milner, *The United Nations High Commissioner for Refugees (UNHCR)* (New York: Routledge 2008), 73–9.

[37] E Benvenisti, 'Exit and Voice in the Age of Globalization' (1999) 98 *Michigan Law Review* 167–213; K W Abbott and D Snidal, 'Hard and Soft Law in International Governance' (2000) 54 *International Organization* 421–56, 439.

[38] R D Putnam, 'Diplomacy and Domestic Politics: The Logic of Two-Level Games' (1988) 42 *International Organization* 427–60; H V Milner, *Interests, Institutions, and Information* (Princeton: Princeton University Press 1997), 33; X Dai, *International Insitutions and National Policies* (Cambridge: Cambridge University Press 2007), 27.

[39] Abbott and Snidal, 'Why States Act through Formal International Organizations', 18 (calling this political strategy 'laundering'). It looks more legitimate, for instance, if the International Financial Institutions link loans to the achievement of domestic reforms in the target country when compared with the imposition of conditionality by one state in relation to another—in particular if the colonial past taints their bilateral relationship or if the more powerful state seeks direct political influence.

[40] Placing individuals on the consolidated list of terrorist suspects administered by the Al Qaeda and Taliban Sanctions Committee, a subsidiary organ of the UN Security Council, may serve as a case in point. This listing has immediate consequences for this individual, including the freezing of his or her financial assets, and is usually not subject to judicial review or minimal procedural guarantees. See C A Feinäugle, 'The UN Security Council Al-Qaida and Taliban Sanctions Committee: Emerging Principles of International Institutional Law for the Protection of Individuals?' (2008) 9 *German Law Journal* 1513–39. See also J d'Aspremont, 'Abuse of the Legal Personality of International

Arguably, some states have delegated the determination of refugee status to UNHCR in order to rid themselves of 'unpleasant work'.[41]

An agent can only then sensibly be called autonomous if its actions cannot be reduced to the interests of its principals.[42] And only then does it possibly exercise authority. The fact that delegation is a *conditional* grant of authority does not imply that the international bureaucracy necessarily does what principals want or had expected. The concept of 'agency slack' captures actions by the agent that are undesired by the principal.[43] And little in modelling the relations between contracting states and international bureaucracies in terms of principal–agent theory suggests that the agent actually does what the principal wanted; with the caveat that principals might change their calculations in light of lessons learned from frustrated expectations about agents' actions. Hawkins *et al.* are quick to add in their model of delegated authority that agents of course do 'pursue their own interests strategically'.[44] Also Robert Cox and Harold Jacobson already pointed out in their early study of 1973 that

> [r]egardless of the rigidity of their charters, . . . once international organizations are established, in many instances they evolve in ways that could not have been foreseen by their founders. [. . .] Thus, once established, organizations take on a life of their own and develop their own inner dynamics.[45]

In order to support the view of UNHCR and other international institutions as rather independent actors whose actions cannot simply be reduced to instrumental delegation and possibly exceed or even contravene the interests and intentions of principals, it is helpful to develop a complementary account that zooms in on *how* they exercise authority—an account that focuses on the agent as an actor rather than an instrument in the hands of its principals alone.

Organizations and the Responsibility of Member States' (2007) 4 *International Organization Law Review* 91–119.

[41] Cf. M Smrkolj, 'International Bureaucracies and Individualized Decision-Making: An Example of UNHCR's Refuge Status Determination' (2008) 9 *German Law Journal* 1779–803. Also see V Türk and E Eyster, 'Strengthening Accountability in UNHCR' (2010) 22 *International Journal of Refugee Law* 159–72, (implicitly acknowledging the problem of weaker procedural guarantees at the international level).

[42] B Koremenos, C Lipson, and D Snidal, 'The Rational Design of International Institutions' (2001) 55 *International Organization* 761–99; Guzman, 'The Design of International Agreements'; Y Z Haftel and A Thompson, 'The Independence of International Organizations: Concept and Applications' (2006) 50 *Journal of Conflict Resolution* 253–75; 255–7 (maintaining that a difference in interest between principals and agents is a constitutive element of international organizations' independence).

[43] Hawkins et al., Delegation under Anarchy, 8.

[44] Ibid., at 5.

[45] R W Cox and H K Jacobson, *The Anatomy of Influence. Decision Making in International Organization* (New Haven, CT: Yale University Press 1973), 7.

2. The authority of international bureaucracies

Drawing attention to the agents and their characteristics in exercising authority further contributes to understanding their room for manoeuvre. Conceptualizing agents as international bureaucracies brings to light sources of their autonomy that relate to characteristic traits of bureaucracies: above all, their apparent rational-legal form of administration, their civil staff, and their knowledge as well as expertise. All these general characteristics find strong expression in the concrete case of UNHCR.

Max Weber developed the concept of bureaucracy as a strong analytical tool.[46] By his account, bureaucracies are a distinct organizational form. They exercise authority in a larger organizational and normative structure, which usually presents itself as an apparent rational-legal process of administration and that fosters the belief in the rightness of the authority exercised. Furthermore, they are staffed with civil servants who are mostly seen to be objective technocrats. Michael Barnett and Martha Finnemore convincingly define authority as 'the ability of one actor to use institutional and discursive resources to induce deference from others'.[47] Authority is, following Weber, legitimated domination and it involves some element of consent.[48] This fits well with an understanding of semantic authority as an actor's capacity to influence and shape meanings as well as the ability to establish its communications as authoritative reference points in legal discourse. In short, a further source of autonomy can be located, apart from deliberate delegation, in bureaucracies' authority that stems from their characteristic traits.

At first glance, the conceptualization of international agents as bureaucracies arguably supports the idea that they are well-behaved and exclusively act in the service of their principals. Bordering on simplicity it might be suggested that as parts of the executive they execute what they are told to do. The idea of depoliticized international institutions that implement the political agreements of constituent members, or possibly act in the general interest, already figured prominently in the functionalist account of international integration developed by David Mitrany. Mitrany suggested that states delegate authority to functional organs in pursuit of mutual or global goals. His work was among the first to highlight the agency and impact of institutions with functionally defined tasks. Not unlike most

[46] M Weber, *Wirtschaft und Gesellschaft* (Paderborn: Voltmedia 2006 [1922]), 1046–92. Compare J P Olsen, 'Maybe it is Time to Rediscover Bureaucracies' (2006) 16 *Journal of Public Administration Research and Theory* 1–24 (defending the use of bureaucracy as an *Idealtypus*); E B Haas, *Beyond the Nation-state. Functionalism and international organization* (Stanford: Stanford University Press 1964), 96 (calling for caution in this regard).

[47] M Barnett and M Finnemore, *Rules for the World. International Organizations in Global Politics* (Ithaca, NY: Cornell University Press 2004), 5. Cf. C A Cutler, V Haufler, and T Porter, The Contours and Significance of Private Authority in International Affairs, in: C A Cutler, V Haufler, and T Porter (eds), *Private Authority and International Affairs* (Albany, NY: State University of New York Press 1999), 333–76, 334 (arguing that authority 'involves a surrendering of individual judgment, an acceptance of its dictates based not on the merits of any particular pronouncement but on a belief in the rightness of the authority of itself').

[48] Barnett and Finnemore, *Rules for the World*, 29.

of the explanations offered in response to why principals might delegate authority, Mitrany's functionalism rests on the belief in a separation of practical issues that are aimed at implementing uncontentious welfare goals, on the one hand, and political activities, on the other.[49] The expansion of technical issues and the contraction of areas for politics would then lead to a true world community.[50]

Mitrany's functionalism portrays an astonishing submission to a technological rationality. At a critical juncture in his argument, he writes for instance that functional agencies move on 'shaped not by any theory of political self-determination of the parties, but by the technological self-determination of each of the matters involved'.[51] His fundamental distinction between political (read 'conflictuous/bad') and non-political (read 'technical/good') is yet more doubtful. It is plausible in some particular cases at best, and in any case it is most contingent and vulnerable.[52] It also seems that it is not the nature of things that separates them into *political* and *non-political* issues but the absence of strong interests that makes them look less conflictuous—just as a dispute about what the law says usually does not depend on its language, but on the presence of diverging interests or convictions. The question of what is political is one of subjective assessment in the eyes of the beholder rather than one of content or issue area.[53] In spite of much room for critique, functionalism does point to a very important source of international bureaucracies' authority: the perception that shared or global goals are pursued effectively and efficiently. From this action and perception, international bureaucracies can scrounge significant moral authority—a particularly strong variant of social legitimacy fed on beliefs about what is right.[54]

In order to understand international bureaucracies as actors in broader governance processes and as participants in international legal discourse, it is furthermore insightful to look at another characteristic trait: their staff of civil servants. Arguments relating to international bureaucracies' civil servants have a long tradition but have for some time stood in isolation from the debate on international institutions'

[49] D Mitrany, *A Working Peace System. An argument for the functional development of international organization* (London: Royal Institute of International Affairs 1943), 19–24.

[50] D Mitrany, *The Functional Theory of Politics* (London: London School of Economics & Political Science 1975), 113–22; cf. Haas, *Beyond the Nation-state*, 6.

[51] Mitrany, *Functional Theory of Politics*, 250–1.

[52] R D Keohane, 'The Functional Theory of Politics by David Mitrany (Book Review)' (1978) 72 *American Political Science Review* 805–6; Haas, *Beyond the Nation-state*, 88.

[53] C Schmitt, *Der Begriff des Politischen* (Berlin: Duncker & Humblot 1963), 26–7. Also see above Chapter II, section B.2.c.

[54] This statement is of course not affected by considerations about whether such authority is good or justified. See Barnett and Finnemore, *Rules for the World*, 21–2; T Risse, Transnational Governance and Legitimacy, in: A Benz and Y Papadopoulos (eds), *Governance and Democracy: Comparing National, European and International Experiences* (London: Routledge 2006), 179–99, 188; D Kennedy, *The Dark Sides of Virtue. Reassessing International Humanitarianism* (Princeton: Princeton University Press 2004), 111–46.

autonomy and authority.[55] Only recently have they come to impact international relations scholarship.[56] Functionalist accounts of regional and international integration have always stressed the role of an institution's staff. They have maintained that individual loyalties are created by the functions an individual carries out. Even if civil servants are sent by national governments or selected on the basis of a national quota, the transfer of functions that comes with taking up a position in an international organization can produce a shift in loyalty.[57] This functionalist argument found further support in sociologically informed accounts that point to the individual socialization processes of bureaucrats.[58]

The law of many international institutions contains a provision similar to Art. 100 UNC which provides that the 'Secretary-General and the staff shall not seek or receive instructions from any government or from any other authority external to the Organization. They shall refrain from any action which might reflect on their position as international officials responsible only to the organization.'[59] The second paragraph says that member states should refrain from seeking influence on the Secretary-General and the staff. While practice generally contravenes the latter provision, most accounts of practitioners do point to an international staff dedicated to organizational goals, though in tension with influence by member states.[60] UNHCR's Statute provides that the High Commissioner appoints his or

[55] See E F Ranshofen-Wertheimer, *The International Secretariat. A Great Experiment in International Administration* (Washington, DC: Carnegie Endowment for International Peace 1945), 239–46 (reflecting on his experience at the League of Nations and providing a detailed account on the work of its secretariat and the code of international officials); A Sweetser, 'The World's Civil Service' (1945) 30 *Iowa Law Review* 478–89, 478 (pointing out that '[o]ne of the most important but least discussed elements of the general international organization on which the world's hopes are now focussed will center around the kind and type of international staff which will constitute its permanent service.'). Also see M Bedjaoui, *Fonction Publique Internationale et Influences Nationales* (London: Stevens 1958); G Langrod, *La fonction publique internationale. Sa genèse, son essence, son evolution* (Leyden: Sythoff 1963); T G Weiss, *International Bureaucracy. An analysis of the operation of functional and global international secretariats* (Lexington, MA: Lexington Books 1975); A Plantey and F Loriot, *Fonction publique internationale. Organisations mondiales et européennes* (Paris: CNRS Éd. 2005); J Mathiason, *Invisible Governance. International Secretariats in World Politics* (Bloomfield, CT: Kumarian 2007).

[56] Cf. A Liese and S Weinlich, Die Rolle von Verwaltungsstäben internationaler Organisationen. Lücken, Tücken und Konturen eines (neuen) Forschungsgebiets., in: J Bogumil, W Jann, and F Nullmeier (eds), *Politik und Verwaltung. PVS-Sonderheft 37* (Wiesbaden: VS Verlag für Sozialwissenschaften 2006), 491–525, 500–10; T Benner, S Mergenthaler, and P Rotmann, 'Internationale Bürokratien und Organisationslernen. Konturen einer Forschungsagenda' (2009) 16 *Zeitschrift für Internationale Beziehungen* 203–36.

[57] Haas, *Beyond the Nation-state*, 22.

[58] A I Johnston, 'Treating International Institutions as Social Environments' (2001) 45 *International Studies Quarterly* 487–515; M Finnemore, 'Norms, Culture and World Politics: Insights from Sociology's Institutionalism' (1996) 50 *International Organization* 325–47.

[59] See, e.g., Art. 8(2) FAO Constitution; Art. 6(4) WTO Agreement; Art. 4 Section V IBDR Articles of Agreement; Art. 11 Convention on the Organisation for Economic Co-operation and Development.

[60] Cf. K T Paschke, UNO von innen—die Besonderheiten einer multinationalen Bürokratie, in: S v Schorlemer (ed), *Praxishandbuch UNO. Die Vereinten Nationen im Lichte globaler Herausforderungen* (Berlin, Heidelberg: Springer 2003), 553–67, 565–6; R S Jordan, 'Truly' International Bureaucracies: Real or Imagined?, in: L S Finkelstein (ed), *Politics in the United Nations System* (Durham: Duke University Press 1988), 424–45.

her staff, that '[s]uch staff shall be chosen from persons devoted to the purposes of the Office of the High Commissioner', and that conditions of employment follow the practice in the UN.[61] UNHCR is the only UN agency that publishes its staff surveys and prides itself on the dedication and commitment shown by its employees.[62]

It might be a step too optimistic to picture the staff of international civil servants as whole-heartedly dedicated to organizational goals beyond the reach of their respective national governments. The extent to which a dedicated civil service exists and how it relates to the balance between autonomy and the impact by other actors cannot be specified generally but must be examined in each particular case.[63] However, the dynamic and *esprit de corps* of bureaucracies' civil staff as well as the person heading a bureaucracy are likely to have an influence on the autonomy and authority of international bureaucracies.[64] This certainly holds true for UNHCR, which has been marked by the leadership and political activism of its High Commissioners.[65]

It is of prime significance for international bureaucracies' autonomy, authority, and for their agency in the practice of interpretation that they oftentimes command considerable knowledge and expertise. They have a decisive role in defining specific problems to be solved and on the construction of social reality more generally.[66] International bureaucracies' authority gives them a strong influence on perception. To be clear, exercising power by way of impacting social construction is one of the most effective mechanisms. Constructivists who still recall the early up-hill battle against the fortified belief that all that mattered was material, have continuously stressed, and rightly so, the power of ideas and the reality of social constructions.[67] Social action is based on knowledge, views of the world as well as normative and causal convictions. To impact knowledge is to impact the social construction of reality and to thereby influence actors' behaviour.[68] This is old news. But it needs to be served afresh in order to appreciate international bureaucracies' semantic authority in negotiating the contents of legal commitments. Max Weber already pointed out in 1922 that 'bureaucratic

[61] Para 15 UNHCR Statute.

[62] See, e.g., Standing Committee, Organizational Development and Management, 44th Meeting, 5 March 2009 (summarizing the results of the Global Staff Survey of 2008).

[63] Liese and Weinlich, Die Rolle von Verwaltungsstäben, 514–18.

[64] Cf. R W Cox, 'The Executive Head: An Essay on Leadership in International Organization' (1969) 23 *International Organization* 205–30.

[65] G Loescher, *The UNHCR and World Politics. A Perilous Path* (Oxford: Oxford University Press 2006).

[66] Cf. E B Haas, *When Knowledge is Power. Three models of change in international organizations* (Berkeley: University of California Press 1990).

[67] A Wendt, 'Anarchy is What States Make of It: The Social Construction of Power Politics' (1992) 46 *International Organization* 391–425.

[68] See the early account by J G Ruggie, 'International Responses to Technology: Concepts and Trends' (1975) 29 *International Organization* 557–83, 569–70.

administration means: exercise of authority by way of *knowledge*: that is its specifically rational and fundamental character'.[69]

Comparative advantage in knowledge is a specifically powerful asset in semantic struggles over what the law says. I suggested earlier that such struggles unfold on the stabilizing grounds of interpretative communities.[70] Appreciating international bureaucracies' grip on knowledge draws attention to their influence on the social construction of reality. Linked with interpretative communities are more foundational epistemic communities—a concept coined by Peter Haas as 'a network of professionals with recognized expertise and competence in a particular domain and an authoritative claim to policy-relevant knowledge within that domain or issue area.'[71] The demand for expert knowledge is particularly high when problems are complex and goals uncertain.[72] This is the specific realm of bureaucratic authority.[73] Empirical studies have shown bureaucracies' impact in this regard with a focus on how they influence beliefs or consensual knowledge. They support the proposition that 'scientific knowledge will create a consensual basis for the recognition of new cause/effect links which had not been recognized before'.[74] Such a view should be complemented with a grasp on how actors try to find acceptance for their propositions generally, or for their claims about what the law says specifically, by way of seeking to induce a belief in the rightness of their positions. This would draw attention to exercises of power and to power relations possibly embedded in what looks like consensual knowledge.[75] In this vein, it has been observed that, in pursuing their objectives, international bureaucracies have strategically interpreted their mandates, cooperated with third parties and buffered information, manoeuvred between competing interests among constituent members as well as third parties, and have in effect grown in size and impact.[76] Bureaucracies use asymmetries of knowledge to their advantage or at least in line with their interests or convictions—no bad intentions needed.

In sum then, international bureaucracies' influence in the development of international norms by way of interpretation rests not only on delegated authority, but to a large extent also on their perceived expertise and knowledge. They enjoy

[69] Weber, *Wirtschaft und Gesellschaft*, 226 ('Die bürokratische Verwaltung bedeutet: Herrschaft kraft *Wissen*: dies ist ihr spezifisch rationaler Grundcharakter.').

[70] See above Chapter II, section B.

[71] P M Haas, 'Epistemic Communities and International Policy Coordination' (1992) 46 *International Organization* 1–35, 3.

[72] Cf. P M Haas, 'Epistemic Communities and International Policy Coordination' (1992) 46 *International Organization* 1–35, 12.

[73] Barnett and Finnemore, *Rules for the World*, 24–5 (noting that bureaucracies' command over expertise and knowledge increases their autonomy and authority).

[74] E B Haas, 'Is there a Hole in the Whole? Knowledge, Technology, Interdependence, and the Construction of International Regimes' (1975) 29 *International Organization.* 827–76, 858–9. Also see H Breitmeier, 'Die Output-orientierte Legitimität des globalen Regierens. Empirische Befunde aus der quantitativen Erforschung internationaler Umweltregime' (2006) 13 *Zeitschrift für Internationale Beziehungen* 39–74.

[75] See above Chapter II, section B.3 on hegemony and universal agreement in semantic struggles.

[76] On these strategies compare M Barnett and L Coleman, 'Designing Police: Interpol and the Study of Change in International Organizations' (2005) 49 *International Studies Quarterly* 593–620.

semantic authority because of such assets. Thus the International Labour Organization (ILO) for example found that the most effective means of promoting labour standards lies in strategies of promotion and persuasion. It has sought to develop international standards not so much by way of pushing for the ratification of conventions but by way of persuasion. Erika de Wet observed that its strategy 'rest[s] on the assumption that increased awareness, knowledge and expertise are the critical pathways for changing government policies and behaviours'.[77] This holds true for UNHCR just as well. Rather than pushing for new universal treaty instruments, UNHCR has chosen to use its semantic authority in developing the law by way of interpretation.[78] It offers a prime example of an international bureaucracy, which acts autonomously in processes of international communicative lawmaking.

Governments have entrusted UNHCR among other things with the task of providing international protection on behalf of refugees and specifically endowed it with a supervisory function with regard to the 1951 Refugee Convention. Once in place, UNHCR has considerably grown in size and it has thrown its authority into struggles about what its Statute allows it to do as well as what the Convention means. So there are two dimensions to its interpretative practice that will be subject to closer analysis. First, the semantic change of its own Statute (B.), and second, the interpretation of the Refugee Convention (C.).

But before entering into such analysis, the sociological understanding of UNHCR as a bureaucracy should be briefly complemented by a legal perspective. It should be clarified above all that UNHCR is not itself an international organization but part of the UN. It was not set up by an international treaty but by a Resolution of the General Assembly.[79] At the same time, state parties to the 1951 Refugee Convention have entrusted UNHCR with a supervising function according to Art. 35 of the Convention.[80]

B. The expansion of UNHCR's Statute

In retrospect, the life of UNHCR reads like an amazing success story. Starting out in 1950 on the shaky basis of a Statute that was subject to renewal after three years and only provided for very narrow competences, UNHCR has come to be the world's main international agency to provide humanitarian assistance. At the time

[77] E de Wet, 'Governance through Promotion and Persuasion: The 1998 ILO Declaration on Fundamental Principles and Rights at Work' (2009) 9 *German Law Journal* 1429–51, 1450. See further V P Nanda, The Role of International Organizations in Non-contractual Lawmaking, in: R Wolfrum and V Röben (eds), *Developments of International Law in Treaty Making* (Heidelberg: Springer 2005), 157–70.

[78] The Convention Plus initiative might be seen as such an attempt, but it is better captured as a process that interprets given provisions.

[79] UNGA res 428 (V), 14 December 1950. See below section B.1.

[80] United Nations Convention relating to the Status of Refugees, 28 July 1951.

of its creation, it was composed of 35 employees and had a budget of $300,000.[81] Now UNHCR commands a budget of $3.59 billion for 2012 and employs 7,685 staff members working in 126 countries.[82] UNHCR was awarded the Nobel Peace Prize in 1954 and 1981 for its actions on behalf of refugees, it has massed together vast resources of knowledge and expertise, and it has successfully built up an aura of moral authority.

According to para 1 UNHCR Statute, it 'shall assume the function of providing international protection, under the auspices of the United Nations, to *refugees who fall within the scope of the present Statute* and of seeking permanent solutions for the problem of refugees'. UNHCR's core function, it is commonly agreed, is international protection on behalf of refugees.[83] For a long time, and quite sensibly so, the way to determine UNHCR's competence was to first establish whether a person qualified as a refugee. This qualification, if positive, would then open up the way towards mechanisms of international protection that are spelled out in more detail in para 8 UNHCR Statute. Both crucial elements in this formula—the meaning of 'refugee' and of 'international protection'—as well as the structure of reasoning—have undergone remarkable developments in the practice of interpretation over time.

Over the past years, the meaning of refugee, in the sense of the Statute, has changed with a shift in the pattern of interpretation: it is less the definition of refugee which determines who qualifies as a refugee than a person's need for international protection which has come to make him or her a refugee. The meaning of international protection has also undergone a considerable shift. It is no longer a kind of surrogate quasi-consular legal protection, but it may entail a variety of mechanisms of procedural and material assistance. UNHCR's politics have been key in inducing these semantic changes and transformations in argumentative patterns. In this process it has gained considerably in power and authority. UNHCR has itself changed remarkably not only in size, but also in substance and function.[84] It has become the United Nation's lead humanitarian agency that administers large refugee camps in the field and portrays grown features of a surrogate state.[85]

[81] M Zieck, *UNHCR's Worldwide Presence in the Field* (Nijmegen: Wolf Legal Publishers 2006), 38–41; D Gallagher, 'The Evolution of the International Refugee System' (1989) 23 *International Migration Review* 579–98 at 580; E Feller and A Klug, Refugees, United Nations High Commissioner (UNHCR), in: R Wolfrum (ed), *MPEPIL* (Oxford: Oxford University Press 2007), Mn 3.

[82] For the current figures see <http://www.unhcr.org/pages/49c3646c14.html> (last visited 20 December 2011).

[83] Kälin, Supervising the 1951 Convention, 619–20.

[84] On the transformations generally, see G Loescher, *The UNHCR and World Politics. A Perilous Path* (Oxford: Oxford University Press 2006); M Zieck, *UNHCR and Voluntary Repatriation of Refugees: A Legal Analysis* (Dordrecht: Kluwer 1997), 79–100.

[85] A Slaughter and J Crisp, 'A Surrogate State? The role of UNHCR in protracted refugee situations' (2009) New Issues in Refugee Research, Research Paper No 168, UNHCR. Cf. M Barnett, Humanitarianism, Paternalism, and the UNHCR, in: A Betts and G Loescher (eds), *Refugees in International Relations* (Oxford: Oxford University Press 2010), 105–32; M Agier, *Aux bords du monde, les refugiés* (Paris: Flammarion 2002).

UNHCR did not go this way alone. Other UN organs have played a major role in developing the meaning of its Statute. By virtue of paras 3 and 4 of its Statute, UNHCR is obliged to follow directives issued by the General Assembly, the Economic and Cultural Council (ECOSOC), as well as ECOSOC's Advisory Committee on Refugees[86] which later became the Executive Committee of the High Commissioner's Programme (ExCom).[87] Also Western donor countries used their leverage, above all their funding policies, to bend UNHCR's actions to meet their interests. Looking at outside influences, it is true that legal developments and semantic changes can to some extent be traced back to Western states' interest in containing refugee flows where they occur so that these states would not face mass influxes of forced migrants—thus shifting emphasis from international protection and resettlement to material assistance and humanitarian aid.[88]

UNHCR is certainly embedded in a context that crowds together many different actors with distinct agendas. They all pull and tug on its actions and engage in semantic struggles about the meaning of its Statute. The expansion of its mandate has taken place within this interplay of interests. It may be observed, however, that UNHCR could successfully manoeuvre between competing coalitions.[89] In this section, I place emphasis on UNHCR as an actor in the practice of interpretation. Speaking of its interpretative *practice* should recall that its interpretation of legal norms takes place between actor-centred politics and prevalent discursive structures.

UNHCR's semantic struggle centred on its Statute took off against the background of refugee protection at the time of the League of Nations and was informed by experiences made with regard to its immediate predecessor, the International Refugee Organizations (IRO). This background has fed the expectations and concerns pervading the negotiations that lead up to UNHCR (1.). UNHCR's early steps were rather timid and indeed primarily focused on international legal protection of refugees within Europe (2.). New refugee situations challenged prevalent meanings of 'refugee' as well as 'international protection' and UNHCR pushed the interpretation of its Statute to carry its actions. It complemented its

[86] Cf. Economic and Social Council Resolution 393 (XIII), 10 September 1951 (establishing the Advisory Committee on Refugees).

[87] UNGA res 1166 (XII), 26 November 1957; Economic and Social Council Resolution 672 (XXV), 30 April 1958. Before it also figured as United Nations Refugee Fund (UNREF), see Executive Committee, Economic and Social Council Resolution 565 (XIX), 31 March 1955; UNGA res 832 (IX), 21 October 1954.

[88] T A Aleinikoff, 'State-Centered Refugee Law: From Resettlement to Containment' (1992–1993) 14 *Michigan Journal of International Law* 120–38; S Kanako, 'Genuine Protection of International Refugees: A Study of the Influence of Western States on the Mandate of the UNHCR' (2003–2004) 11 *Asian Yearbook of International Law* 89–121; T Krever, '"Mopping-up": UNHCR, Neutrality and Non-Refoulement since the Cold War' (2011) 11 *Chinese Journal of International Law* 587–608.

[89] M Moussalli, The Evolving Functions of the Office of the High Commissioner for Refugees, in: V Gowlland and K Samson (eds), *Problems and Prospects of Refugee Law* (Geneva: The Graduate Institute of International Studies 1992), 81–103, 91.

legal protection with material assistance and the definition of refugee started to be overtaken by the prima facie assessments of the need for assistance (3.). International protection later lost most of its once prevalent meaning and came to be used synonymously with humanitarian aid. Now 'refugees' in the sense of the Statute are, by and large, those individuals who have been forcefully uprooted, who cannot be expected to return to their place of original residence, and who are thus in need of international protection (4.).

1. Expectations and concerns

The emergence of an international refugee definition came hand in hand with the first international responses to large-scale situations of forcefully displaced persons.[90] Repercussions of the Bolshevik Revolution of 1917 drove about 800,000 Russian refugees out of their homes and scattered them across Europe. On top of that, the Bolshevik government decreed in 1921 that Russians living abroad or who had left Russia after 7 November 1917 without official authorization would lose their Russian citizenship. Most of them would, in effect, be rendered stateless.[91] Following the gathering of representatives of non-governmental relief organizations in Geneva in 1921, Gustav Ador, then president of the International Committee of the Red Cross (ICRC), addressed the League of Nations with the suggestion that a Commissioner for Refugees be appointed 'to define the status of Russian refugees, to secure their repatriation or their employment outside Russia, and to coordinate measures for their assistance'.[92] The League's Council followed Mr Ador's appeal and on 20 August 1921 appointed Fridtjof Nansen as 'High Commissioner on behalf of the League in connection with the problem of Russian refugees in Europe'.[93] Support was forthcoming chiefly because state representatives were increasingly concerned with the destabilizing effect that migration flows were starting to have. Some diplomats were also keen on levelling the charge of political persecution against communist Russia.[94]

[90] It was only with the spread of nationalism and growing concerns about the control of the population within nation states that the phenomenon of refugees gave rise to legal challenges in a way that still structures current debates. J C Hathaway, 'The Evolution of Refugee Status in International Law: 1920–1950' (1984) 33 *International and Comparative Law Quarterly* 348–80, 248–9; D Kennedy, 'International Refugee Protection' (1986) 8 *Human Rights Quarterly* 1–69, 22–5; L Barnett, 'Global Governance and the Evolution of the International Refugee Regime' (2002) 14 *International Journal of Refugee Law* 238–62, 239.

[91] W Czapliński and P Šturma, 'La responsabilité des Etats pour les flux de réfugiés provoqués par eux' (1994) 40 *Annuaire Français de Droit International* 156–69; Hathaway, 'Evolution of Refugee Status', 350–2; L W Holborn, *Refugees. A Problem of Our Time* (Metuchen: Scarecrow Press 1975), 4–6.

[92] Citation reproduced in Holborn, *Refugees*, 5–6.

[93] L W Holborn, *Refugees. A Problem of Our Time* (Metuchen: Scarecrow Press 1975), 7; D Kugelmann, Refugees, League of Nations Offices, in: R Wolfrum (ed), *MPEPIL* (Oxford: Oxford University Press 2007), Mn 2.

[94] Barnett and Finnemore, *Rules for the World*, 77.

Prior to his appointment, Fridtjof Nansen had already acted on behalf of the League and was very successful in the repatriation of German and Austrian prisoners of war from Siberia. He enjoyed the confidence of many governments including Russia.[95] It was clear to him that the amelioration of the situation of refugees was in many ways premised on their legal status—any long-term solution could only be pursued once their special status was recognized. In July 1922 he convinced state representatives that Russian refugees should be given a specific certificate of identity (known as the 'Nansen Passport') that, though not on an equal footing with a real passport, opened up some of the most critical barriers for refugees on their way to finding a new home and employment.[96] This was an important precedent. Only two years later, the same arrangement was extended to Armenian refugees and in the following years to Assyrians, Assyro-Chaldeans, Rutheans, Montenegrins, Jews, Turks, and Hungarians.[97] The personal figure of Mr Nansen has inspired many of his successors.[98] He was a typical international civil servant walking the edges of international advocacy and governmental support while finding balance in a strong personality, leadership, and political strategy.

Even if the arrangements to issue identity certificates did not contain any definition of the term 'refugee', they did share common elements: at issue were individuals outside their country of origin and without the legal protection of their own state.[99] The principal task of the High Commissioner was to step up to the role of the former sovereign—the country of citizenship—and to offer some of its administrative functions; above all, to provide official documents of identification as a necessary first step for other responses and processes to set in. Refugees were individuals without *de facto* or *de jure* protection of their former government and the High Commissioner resumed such a role in a quasi-consular capacity.[100] These were the concerns and settings that structured the debate in the early years of the League of Nations and that have lived on to inform the role and functions of UNHCR.[101] It is noteworthy that the preoccupation with the definition of refugee centred on the lack of protection and was detached from the underlying causes. The fact that someone was outside their country of origin and without protection of a government was a sufficient condition for determining refugee status.[102]

With the lead up to the Second World War, this preoccupation shifted slightly towards a refugee definition reflecting a more social understanding of the phenomenon

[95] Ibid.; Holborn, *Refugees*, 6.

[96] Ibid., at 9; C M Skran, Historical Development of International Refugee Law, in: A Zimmermann (ed), *The 1951 Convention Relating to the Status of Refugees and its 1967 Protocol: A Commentary* (Oxford: Oxford University Press 2011), 3–36 Mns 22–27.

[97] Hathaway, 'Evolution of Refugee Status', 352–7.

[98] C Lewis, 'UNHCR's Contribution to the Development of International Refugee Law: Its Foundations and Evolution' (2005) 17 *International Journal of Refugee Law* 67–90, 74.

[99] Hathaway, 'Evolution of Refugee Status', 359.

[100] Holborn, *Refugees*, 10.

[101] Cf. S B Young, 'Between Sovereigns: A Reexamination of the Refugee's Status' (1982) 3 *Michigan Yearbook of International Legal Studies* 339–72.

[102] G S Goodwin-Gill, *The Refugee in International Law* (Oxford: Clarendon Press 1983), 2.

and taking into account the causes and contexts of refugee flows.[103] At the dawn of the new world order that would emerge with the end of the war, the concept of refugee again accommodated a shift in emphasis. For many actors, the essential characteristic of a refugee came to be the fundamental incompatibility between the individual and his or her government.[104] Debates leading to the creation of UNHCR were marked by strong positions that advocated an individualist approach to the refugee definition. Refugee status and international protection, they argued, should be understood as a means of facilitating movement across borders for those in search of personal freedom.[105] With such an outlook, the debate was inevitably enmeshed in the mounting confrontations that would characterize the Cold War.

Ideological confrontations projected onto the definition of refugees had already posed a serious challenge for the way any international body was to deal with refugees and displaced persons. In its first session, the UN General Assembly passed Resolution 8(1) which set the loose parameters and provided that any international body attending to the issue would act so that no refugee or displaced person expressing 'valid objections to returning to their countries of origin' shall be compelled to return.[106] At the same time it encouraged such an organization to assist in every way their early return to their country of origin. While these elements may seem logical and complementary (no involuntary return when there are indeed valid objections and otherwise assist in return), they also testify to competing preferences among state representatives. The international body that would take up the task was the International Refugee Organization (IRO) established in the same year of 1946.[107] IRO's Convention then contained a very detailed definition of refugee that turned around the question of whether the individual could express 'valid objections' to returning to his or her country of origin.[108] It went on to

[103] Hathaway, 'Evolution of Refugee Status', 367. This understanding emerged first with the Saar crisis. The Treaty of Versailles mandated the League of Nations with administrating the territory and when its administration came to an end, a referendum decided on the fate of the territory. A majority voted for a union with Germany and in response approximately 3,300 inhabitants fled to neighbouring France and Luxembourg in 1935, largely because they were either opposed to the German government or feared repression. The League accepted its responsibility and provided international protection even if in most cases there were in fact no problems with the inhabitants' international legal status. Ibid., at 361–2 and 368.

[104] A Grahl-Madsen, *The Status of Refugees in International Law*, vol 1 (Leyden: Sijthoff 1966), 74.

[105] J G Stoessinger, *The Refugee and the World Community* (Minneapolis: University of Minnesota Press 1956), 71–6.

[106] UNGA res 8 (I), 12 February 1946.

[107] The IRO practically took over most of the functions of the Intergovernmental Committee on Refugees (1938–1947) and of the United Nations Relief and Rehabilitation Administration (UNRRA) that had been established in the interim. See UNGA res 62(1), 15 December 1946 (adopting the Constitution of the International Refugee Organization and Agreement on Interim Measures in Respect of Refugees and Displaced Persons). Cf. Zieck, *Presence in the Field*, 17–24; Moussalli, Evolving Functions, 83–4.

[108] Part I(A)(1) and (C)(1) IRO Convention. Note that the Convention defines 'displaced persons' separately in Part I(B) and then stipulates the conditions under which both refugees and displaced persons become the concern of the organization.

provide that such valid objections could be the fear of persecution relating to the individual's race, religion, nationality, or political opinion.[109] The Convention thus explicitly recognized the right of refugees not to be returned to their country of origin against their will and, for the first time, linked the refugee definition to a fear of persecution. For these reasons it faced strong criticism by a number of state representatives grouped around the Soviet Union. One of the arguments they voiced in opposition to this understanding unmistakably reflects the rising ideological tensions. Liberal democracies, they maintained, should not be permitted to harbour emigrated enemies of the regime.[110]

The Soviet Union never joined the IRO Convention and in face of its opposition, only 18 states became members. Nevertheless, by mid-1947 the IRO Convention contained the only available definition of refugee. Remarkably, the Soviet Union's defeat in the struggle about what 'refugee' should mean and its subsequent withdrawal from international discussions on that matter did not effectively prevent the definition from developing further. Withdrawal is usually not an option in semantic struggles and is tantamount to defeat. The IRO definition was put into practice in a large number of cases in which the organization decided whether an individual qualified as a refugee and was thus eligible to receive protection and assistance. The IRO had established eligibility boards in most field offices that were charged with taking such decisions. Applicants could even challenge a finding against them in front of a Review Board for Eligibility Appeals.[111] Such practice created a massive amount of precedents, developed a more lenient standard of status assessment, and informed debates leading to the creation of UNHCR and to the 1951 Refugee Convention.[112]

IRO was only set up for three years and when it soon became evident that it was unable to complete its task in time, the IRO Director-General suggested that its work be taken over by a successor organization.[113] 1.25 million refugees were still scattered across Europe by the end of 1950.[114] One critical aspect of the deliberations with regard to a new agency concerned the selection of the future High Commissioner for Refugees because the selection process would have direct repercussions on the Commissioner's strength, prestige, and authority in international interpretative practice. It was ultimately the view according to which the

[109] Part I(C)(1)(a)(i) IRO Convention. Cf. Stoessinger, *Refugee and the World Community*, 85–8.

[110] The Soviet delegate, Mr Soldatov, argued that from UN assistance should be excluded 'not only those who, during the war, fought actively on the side of the enemy against the people and government of their own country, but all those other traitors who are refusing to return home to serve their country together with their fellow citizens'. Quoted J C Hathaway, *The Law of Refugee Status* (Toronto: Butterworths 1991), 7.

[111] G Melander, International Refugee Organization (IRO), in: R Wolfrum (ed), *MPEPIL* (Oxford: Oxford University Press 2007), Mn 5.

[112] Ibid., Mn 16; J Vernant, *The Refugee in the Post-war World* (London: Allen & Unwin 1953), 33–8.

[113] Holborn, *Refugees*, 36–8.

[114] Barnett, 'Evolution of the International Refugee Regime', 245.

High Commissioner be elected by the GA upon the nomination of the Secretary-General that prevailed.[115] According to the French delegate, Mr Rochefort, this 'would show that the United Nations had full confidence in him and would be of immeasurable value to him in his negotiations with Governments'.[116] Procedures nourish social legitimacy and semantic authority.[117]

There was lasting disagreement with regard to the lifespan of the new organization. The resulting compromise stated that its mandate would need to be renewed by a decision of the GA every three years. Delegates' expectations on this matter diverged but most believed that a positive decision to that effect would eventually be taken.[118] With hindsight, it appears difficult to imagine that this might simply not have been the case. But in its first years, UNHCR suffered serious threats of financial starvation and blatant neglect. It faced continuous resistance from the Soviet Union and also the US favoured other agencies that were more responsive to its foreign policy goals.[119] Had it not been for a $3 million grant from the Ford Foundation in 1952, UNHCR would have hardly survived its early years.[120]

One of the most decisive as well as divisive issues in setting up UNHCR was unsurprisingly the delineation of the High Commissioner's competences, which of course hinged on the definition of 'refugee'.[121] State representatives were divided to the extent that the British delegate eventually found approval for his suggestion of separating negotiations on a statute delimiting the competences of the new international agency, on the one hand, and a convention that would be directed toward state action, on the other. While agreement for broader action was forthcoming for a future High Commissioner, reluctance prevailed with regard to legal obligations directed at states.[122] In the end, however, the defining characteristics of a refugee were to be almost identical in both documents. But interpretations have increasingly diverged and it has thus become customary to distinguish between statute (or mandate) refugees and convention refugees.

[115] Para 13 UNHCR Statute; Holborn, *Refugees*, 66–7.

[116] Statement by the Representative of France, UN doc A/C.3/SR.262, 14 November 1949; quoted in Lewis, 'UNHCR's Contribution to the Development', 74.

[117] N Luhmann, *Legitimation durch Verfahren* (Frankfurt am Main: Suhrkamp 1983), 20–6.

[118] Holborn, *Refugees*, 67–8.

[119] Barnett and Finnemore, *Rules for the World*, 86.

[120] Gallagher, 'Evolution of the International Refugee System', 582; Loescher, *UNHCR and World Politics*, 67.

[121] Holborn, *Refugees*, 73–5; J Sztucki, Who is a Refugee? The Convention definition: universal or obsolete?, in: F Nicholson and P Twomey (eds), *Refugee Rights and Realities: Evolving international concepts and regimes* (Cambridge: Cambridge University Press 1999), 55–80, 55.

[122] Holborn, *Refugees*, 80–1.

In December 1950 the General Assembly adopted the Statute of the United Nations High Commissioner for Refugees and a conference of plenipotentiaries adopted the United Nations Convention relating to the Status of Refugees on 28 July 1951.[123] According to para 6 (A) of the Statute and Art. 1 (A) of the Convention a refugee is defined as any person who,

> owing to well-founded fear of being persecuted for reasons of race, religion, nationality, membership of a particular social group or political opinion, is outside the country of his nationality and is unable or, owing to such fear, is unwilling to avail himself of the protection of that country; or who, not having a nationality and being outside the country of his former habitual residence as a result of such events, is unable or, owing to such fear, is unwilling to return to it.

One difference between the Statute and the Convention is that the latter confined its definition of refugees to those persons who had fled as a result of events occurring before January 1951. Signatories of the Convention could further specify that they understood this limitation to refer to events occurring in Europe. Both limitations were lifted by the 1967 Protocol relating to the Status of Refugees.[124] It should also be mentioned that the Statute, in contrast to the Convention, does not spell out 'membership of a particular social group' as a ground for persecution. This difference has proved to have no practical significance.[125]

2. International protection and humble beginnings

UNHCR was not off to a very promising start. With a rather narrow mandate and little security that it would not be discontinued after its first three years, sidelined by the US and enmeshed in the confrontations of the Cold War, it looked as if it could do very little to help the individual needs of refugees. Many state representatives at the United Nations understood UNHCR's main function of providing international protection to mean that the new agency would, at the most, take up a quasi-consular role to provide legal protection on behalf of refugees. It was to bridge the gap in which refugees could no longer avail themselves of the protection of their former government and did not yet have a new legal standing in the territory subject to the jurisdiction of the new sovereign.[126] Paragraph 8 UNHCR Statute refers to its functions and suggests that its role might be even more limited than that, only relating to a kind of international supervision of states' actions dealing with refugees.[127] When deliberations on UNHCR's Statute at the UN drew to an

[123] See UNGA res 428 (V), 14 December 1950 (the Statute of the UNHCR is annexed to this resolution); 1951 Convention relating to the Status of Refugees (opened for signature 28 July 1951, entered into force 22 April 1954) 189 UNTS 150.

[124] 606 UNTS 267.

[125] G S Goodwin-Gill and J McAdam, *The Refugee in International Law* (Oxford: Oxford University Press 2007), 36.

[126] Barnett and Finnemore, *Rules for the World*, 82.

[127] Para 8 UNHCR Statute states:

> 'The High Commissioner shall provide for the protection of refugees falling under the competence of his Office by: (a) Promoting the conclusion and ratification of international conventions for the protection of refugees, supervising their application and proposing amend-

end, the French delegate observed that the assumption appears to be that actual protection of refugees would be provided by governments while the High Commissioner would merely carry out functions 'of a higher direction, liaison and control service'.[128] International protection was thought to be a very limited and mainly coordinative thing that was premised on an individual's qualification as refugee. Once an individual met the legal definition, he or she evidently required international protection and UNHCR was to provide it.[129]

A broader mandate might have involved greater burden sharing among the countries as well as entrusting the international agency with providing material assistance. But state representatives arguing in favour of such a mandate could not succeed. Mrs Roosevelt argued on behalf of the US that the UN was essentially a deliberative forum and should not be pushed into becoming an international relief agency.[130] The view she expressed ultimately prevailed and UNHCR was given no direct operational capacity of extending material assistance. Paragraph 9 UNHCR Statute merely expresses a meagre compromise by stating that '[t]he High Commissioner shall engage in such additional activities, including repatriation and resettlement, as the General Assembly may determine, within the limits of the resources placed at his disposal'. As concerns financial resources and assistance to refugees, para 10 provides further that

> [t]he High Commissioner shall administer any funds, public or private, which he receives for assistance to refugees, and shall distribute them among the private and, as appropriate, public agencies which he deems best qualified to administer such assistance. . . . The High Commissioner shall not appeal to Governments for funds or make a general appeal, without the prior approval of the General Assembly.

On the face of it, the task and competence delegated to UNHCR are confined to the administration of funds that it may occasionally receive. Rather than getting involved in material assistance, the High Commissioner should pass on any fund to those other public and private actors that already provide material assistance to refugees.

ments thereto; (b) Promoting through special agreements with Governments the execution of any measures calculated to improve the situation of refugees and to reduce the number requiring protection; (c) Assisting governmental and private efforts to promote voluntary repatriation or assimilation within new national communities; (d) Promoting the admission of refugees, not excluding those in the most destitute categories, to the territories of States; (e) Endeavouring to obtain permission for refugees to transfer their assets and especially those necessary for their resettlement; (f) Obtaining from Governments information concerning the number and conditions of refugees in their territories and the laws and regulations concerning them; (g) Keeping in close touch with the Governments and inter-governmental organizations concerned; (h) Establishing contact in such manner as he may think best with private organizations dealing with refugee questions; (i) Facilitating the co-ordination of the efforts of private organizations concerned with the welfare of refugees.'

[128] Holborn, *Refugees*, 100, citing GA (IV), Third Committee, Official Records, p 105.

[129] Barnett and Finnemore, *Rules for the World*, 82; Loescher, Betts, Milner, *The United Nations High Commissioner for Refugees*, 17–19.

[130] Holborn, *Refugees*, 68–72.

State representatives would continue to project divergent expectations and preferences onto UNHCR's Statute. Changes in its meaning, however, have been largely the product of advocacy by the new international agency. UNHCR's first High Commissioner, Gerrit J van Heuven Goedhart (1951–1956), showed strong leadership and dedication—a prime example of how leadership can make a difference in the life of an international institution.[131] Mr van Heuven Goedhart had chaired the GA's Third Committee during its critical meetings centred on the drafting of the Statute in 1950, and he was thus very well acquainted with the governments' interests and sensibilities. While catering to governments' concerns, he interpreted UNHCR's Statute in a way that would give the agency more room to manoeuvre, and at times he took a bold stance appealing to the needs of refugees. He masterfully thrived on the moral impetus of his arguments and invoked sentiments of justice in his legal rhetoric.[132]

The main targets of his interpretations were the meaning of international protection and the individualistic definition of refugees. From the outset, the High Commissioner and his staff interpreted international protection in a decisively broader manner when compared to the opinions that many delegates voiced during the negotiations leading to the Statute. High Commissioner van Heuven Goedhart maintained in 1954: 'It is clear that the international protection for which my office is responsible is wider than the legal and political protection with which previous international organizations concerned with refugees were charged.'[133] UNHCR's staff would argue that limited legal protection would be nothing without material assistance. If states insisted that material assistance was not one of UNHCR's functions and beyond its scope of competences, they reasoned, this would simply be out of step with UNHCR's purpose of responding to the needs of refugees.[134] UNHCR pushed the direction of legal argument so that the focus would first of all fall on the needs of the refugees and then on the meaning of the Statute. By its account, UNHCR's provisions on competences would mean whatever was necessary for meeting the demands of its mission. From the outset the High Commissioner has also consistently argued that the list of functions contained in para 8 of its Statute was certainly not exhaustive.[135]

Apart from the meaning of international protection, a second key point of controversy concerned the very individualistic definition of refugee spelled out in para 6. In the deliberations at the United Nations many state delegates expressed dissatisfaction with the detailed and elaborate procedures that the IRO had practised in order to establish eligibility. This was not only considered too 'legalistic' but also too costly in terms of the financial resources spent and the civil servants involved. While the IRO had required a considerable body of trained eligibility

[131] Cf. Cox, 'The Executive Head'.

[132] See Holborn, *Refugees*, 93.

[133] Quoted in M Barnett and M Finnemore, *Rules for the World. International Organizations in Global Politics* (Ithaca, NY: Cornell University Press 2004), 82.

[134] Barnett and Finnemore, *Rules for the World*, 82–3.

[135] Holborn, *Refugees*, 98–9.

experts, UNHCR was to be a much smaller institution and should thus apply a much simpler definition of refugee.[136] This expectation is not reflected in para 6 but does find expression in para 2, which provides that '[t]he work of the High Commissioner... shall relate, as a rule, to groups and categories of refugees'. This instruction is at some odds with the individualistic refugee definition delineating UNHCR's competence *ratione personae*.[137] Was UNHCR to provide international protection for persons that came within its competence because of their membership in a group that prima facie is made up of refugees, or would the individual person have to be qualified as a refugee? The High Commissioner and its staff could use such tensions and ambiguities to broaden their competences. This may very well be illustrated with reference to the refugee crisis in the wake of the Hungarian Revolution of 1956. In the context of this crisis, UNHCR could already turn the argumentative pattern half way around: rather than formally testing whether an individual falls within the definition of refugee, the first argumentative step would be to instrumentally ask whether an individual is in need of protection.

3. Material assistance, good offices, and displaced persons

When Soviet forces quashed the Hungarian Revolution in the fall of 1956 and marched into Budapest, about 200,000 individuals fled to neighbouring Austria and triggered one of the major refugee crises since the Second World War. The Red Cross and the Austrian army set up refugee tents and UNHCR willingly responded to Austria's formal request for assistance, embracing the opportunity to assert its competence in this case and to step up to assist refugees. The Hungarian refugee crisis provided ample proof in support of the argument that refugee flows would be a recurrent phenomenon right about the time that UNHCR's mandate would need to be renewed for a third time in 1958.

There were, however, two obstacles to UNHCR's action on behalf of Hungarian refugees.[138] First, even if its Statute contained neither a temporal nor a geographic limitation with regard to the question of which refugees would fall within its competence, the 1951 Convention did only apply to those who had become refugees 'as a result of events occurring before 1 January 1951'. Upon acceding to the Convention some states had further specified that they took this to refer to 'events having occurred in Europe'. Acting on behalf of Hungarian refugees, UNHCR would thus have to find a way of dealing with such limitations. Second, given the massive flow of refugees and urgency of the situation, a case-by-case assessment of refugee status—as would be required in light of the rather detailed and individualistic refugee definition, including, for instance, an assessment of a particular individual's fear of persecution—seemed neither warranted nor feasible.

[136] Holborn, *Refugees*, 77.

[137] F Schnyder, 'Les aspects juridiques actuels du problème des réfugiés' (1965) 114 *Recueil des Cours* 341–450, 396–7.

[138] Holborn, *Refugees*, 419–33.

The new High Commissioner, Auguste Lindt (1957–1960), mastered both obstacles with strikingly innovative interpretations of UNHCR's Statute. With the onset of the crisis, UNHCR had informed the UN Secretary-General about the situation and started to respond to Austria's request to assist Hungarian refugees. Only after the fact did the GA endorse UNHCR's actions in spite of fierce opposition by the Soviet Union.[139] What is more, the GA called upon governments to contribute to UNHCR's efforts and named it lead agency to coordinate humanitarian assistance.[140] In January 1957 Auguste Lindt argued in front of the GA with a slight stretch that the events, which formed part of the Soviet dominion over Eastern Europe, were a product of the Second World War and the refugee flow was thus related to events in Europe before 1 January 1951. Personal competence in situations like these, he claimed further, could be assessed for the group of persons fleeing from Soviet repression and would not need to relate to every person individually.[141]

Despite the fact that these truly original interpretations were a far cry from what state delegates might have had in mind when they voted on the Statute, and notwithstanding that Lindt's claims could barely connect to how its wording used to be understood, the High Commissioner did find acceptance for his interpretations and set an important precedent for subsequent action.[142] This was a strong indication of, and boost for, UNHCR's semantic authority. It was indicative of its authority because an actor requires more strength to bridge a greater distance to past understandings.[143] It was reinforcing because such success forms part of the experience that shapes other actors' confidence and expectations.[144]

UNHCR had to overcome even higher legal and political barriers on its way to assisting individuals who fled communist rule in China to seek refuge in Hong Kong. Difficulties arose from the fact that the Taiwanese government of Chiang Kai-shek was internationally still considered representative of the whole of China as well as from Great Britain's caution not to provoke a crisis in its relations with mainland China by labelling the individuals who fled Mao's government 'refugees'. Such a label would have unmistakably implied a charge of persecution that it did not want to raise. While these events could more easily be related to events occurring before 1 January 1951, they certainly did not occur in Europe. UNHCR

139 UNGA res 1129 (XI), 21 November 1956.

140 Barnett and Finnemore, *Rules for the World*, 87.

141 Ibid., Gallagher, 'Evolution of the International Refugee System', 582.

142 L Gordenker, *Refugees in International Politics* (London: Croom Helm 1987), 35; Gallagher, 'Evolution of the International Refugee System', 582.

143 See U Fastenrath, 'Relative Normativity in International Law' (1993) 4 *European Journal of International Law* 305–40, 336 ('The greater the deviation from the general linguistic convention, the greater will be the degree of authority required to ensure its acceptance.').

144 See Luhmann, *Legitimation durch Verfahren*, 33.

and the GA again worked out an innovative solution to overcome the constraints set by prevalent meanings of the Statute and by the political sentiments of some states. In November 1957 the GA 'authorize[d] the United Nations High Commissioner for Refugees to use his good offices to encourage arrangements for contributions'.[145] It was evident to all actors involved that the people to be assisted did not easily fall within the definition of refugee. The GA simply recognized 'that the problem is such as to be of concern to the international community'.[146] UNHCR's competence followed suit.

The notion of 'good offices' would become a standard modus of UNHCR's engagement. It expanded its scope of activity in three ways. First, UNHCR could assist refugees who were not formally part of its competence *ratione personae*. Second, it allowed assistance without establishing that individuals feared persecution from their own government. And third, the notion entailed that UNHCR would provide material assistance rather than legal protection.[147] While UNHCR's function might once have been thought to rest with international protection in the narrow sense of quasi-consular services, the needs of Hungarian refugees in Austria and Chinese refugees in Hong Kong pushed it towards material assistance.[148] As High Commissioner Felix Schnyder (1961–1965) could point out a little later, the notion of good offices in effect reconciled the imperative of relating to groups in para 2 with the individualistic refugee definition of para 6.[149] It furthermore provided a bluntly pragmatic solution to assisting refugees who did not easily come within the terms of the Refugee Convention or UNHCR's Statute.[150] Thriving on the fact that the GA had recognized that the problem of Chinese refugees in Hong Kong is such 'as to be of concern to the international community', UNHCR contributed to the transformation of argumentative patterns relating to its competence. It was increasingly less an individual's qualification as refugee that entitled him or her to UNHCR's international assistance or protection, but rather the individual's need of assistance or protection made him or her a refugee.

145 UNGA res 1167 (XII), 26 November 1957. The GA again reaffirmed its commitment and UNHCR's lead role in assisting Chinese refugees in Hong Kong in UNGA res 1784(XVII), 7 December 1962.

146 UNGA res 1167 (XII), 26 November 1957.

147 V Türk, *Das Flüchtlingshochkommissariat der Vereinten Nationen (UNHCR)* (Berlin: Duncker und Humblot 1992), 298–300; Goodwin-Gill and McAdam, *The Refugee in International Law*, 24.

148 Gallagher, 'Evolution of the International Refugee System', 594; Holborn, *Refugees*, 434–50.

149 Compare the observation of High Commissioner Sadruddin Aga Khan (1966–1977), who juxtaposed 'human' and 'legalistic' approaches, S Aga Khan, 'Legal Problems Relating to Refugees and Displaced Persons' (1976) 149 *Recueil des Cours* 287–352, 339 (stating that '[a] concept of collective prima facie eligibility, prompted by events, thus gradually took shape. It departed from the individualist concept linked to the definition of the term "refugee" in the Statute and Convention, and progressed towards a more pragmatic and human rather than legalistic approach to the refugee problem').

150 Moussalli, Evolving Functions, 94–6; Goodwin-Gill and McAdam, *The Refugee in International Law*, 23–4.

The Hungarian precedent proved invaluable in approaching another most decisive and transformative incident in UNHCR's early years: the assistance rendered on behalf of people who fled the Algerian War of Independence and sought refuge in neighbouring Morocco and Tunisia. By May 1957 about 85,000 refugees had settled in Tunisia leading the Tunisian government to ask UNHCR for assistance. Auguste Lindt sensed that this provided a crucial challenge and opportunity. Would UNHCR stick to what many governments thought to be its main function—that is, resolve the refugee problem in Europe—or should it take the chance and also get involved in refugee protection and assistance in the developing world? Lindt advocated a broader range of actions drawing force from a humanitarian vantage point. He maintained that there is simply no reason why one should be more important than the other. He also feared charges of discrimination against non-Europeans and accusations of Western patronage. In pursuing his preferences, Auguste Lindt had to overcome stern French opposition to UNHCR's action on behalf of Algerian refugees. But the urgency of the matter and the force of arguments worked in Lindt's favour and opened UNHCR's way towards material assistance.[151] Lindt could count moral authority on his side.

1959 was World Refugee Year. The GA endorsed UNHCR's actions on behalf of Algerian refugees in Morocco and Tunisia, passed a resolution praising UNHCR for its role in alleviating the hardships faced by refugees, and called for states' support of its efforts.[152] It then expressly authorized the High Commissioner 'in respect of refugees who do not come within the competence of the United Nations, to use his good offices in the transition of contributions designed to provide assistance to these refugees'.[153] This was a strong moment of success for UNHCR's advocacy within the UN System. Notably, due to the pressure of France, a colonial power in Morocco and Tunisia until 1956 and embroiled in a war in Algeria since 1954, the resolution did not specify the refugees who would thus be eligible to receive assistance and left wide discretion to the agency.

Within a decade, UNHCR had turned into the principal international agency offering material assistance with ample room for manoeuvre. The tight constraints on providing material assistance were lifted, the High Commissioner could appeal for funds without asking the GA for prior approval, and he could independently administer an emergency fund that was at his sole discretion. From the outset of his term, High Commissioner Felix Schnyder made it known that he would use his good offices to provide assistance to refugees outside Europe and to those that would not squarely meet the more precise refugee definition.[154] He buttressed the wide interpretations of UNHCR's Statute and mandate with moral claims and

[151] Barnett and Finnemore, *Rules for the World*, 89; Loescher, *UNHCR and World Politics*, 24.
[152] Cf. Schnyder, 'Les aspects juridiques', 354–6.
[153] UNGA res 1388, 1389, and 1399 (XIV), 20 November 1959.
[154] Loescher, *UNHCR and World Politics*, 106–10.

humanitarian imperatives.[155] From the end of the 1950s he turned UNHCR's attention steadily towards refugee crises in the developing world. In so doing, he could gain the support of the GA that was increasingly influenced by the preferences of newly independent states. The GA repeatedly backed UNHCR's actions and started to make UNHCR the lead agency in control of emergency situations with massive refugee flows.[156]

While the GA routinely distinguished between refugees within the competence of UNHCR's Statute, on the one hand, and those to whom the concept of good offices could be applied (for some time also known as non-statutory refugees), on the other, it is remarkable that it eventually glossed over this distinction and started to use 'refugee' as a generic term to denote both statutory and non-statutory refugees.[157] Upon receiving UNHCR's annual report and hearing its High Commissioner, UNGA res 2039 (XX) of 7 December 1965 simply

> requests the United Nations High Commissioner for Refugees to pursue his efforts with a view to ensuring an adequate international protection of refugees and to provide satisfactory permanent solutions to the problems affecting the various groups of refugees within his competence....[158]

The former distinction had disappeared and the expression 'refugee' was used in a novel way. This was not a slip of the pen but part of UNHCR's political strategy. Refugees outside its competence and under the umbrella of its good offices came to be part of its competence, not by amending the Statute or changing the black letter definition of refugees, but by way of a subtler semantic shift.

Once the concept of good offices had faded away, the expression of 'displaced persons' made its first appearance. While its use is quite chequered in practice, it may well be understood as a tool for slowly grinding down one of the most solid cornerstones of the international legal system generally, and a strong limitation to UNHCR's scope of activity in particular. UNHCR's actions were confined to what is *inter-national*; that is, part of the relations between sovereign states. State sovereignty and the persistent sanctity of states' internal affairs (its *domaine reservé*) have long permeated the international legal system. They find but one expression in the conception of international protection as a substitute and quasi-consular

[155] Barnett and Finnemore, *Rules for the World*, 90–1.

[156] In its session on 18 December 1969, for instance, it passed resolutions endorsing UNHCR's assistance on behalf of Algerian Refugees in Morocco and Tunisia and on behalf of Angolan Refugees in Congo as well as a resolution of general support backing the UNHCR's report to the GA. UNGA res 1871, 1872, and 1873 (XVI), 18 December 1961.

[157] Aga Khan, 'Legal Problems', 338–47.

[158] First operational clause. In UNGA res 1673 (XVI), 18 December 1961, para 1, the GA still distinguished between refugees and those to whom UNHCR extends its good offices but did not reiterate that the latter 'do not come within the competence of the United Nations', as it used to do previously, e.g. UNGA res 1499 (XV), 5 December 1960. Cf. Türk, *Flüchtlingshochkommissariat*, 282–3; P Macalister-Smith, 'International Humanitarian Assistance for Refugees: Law and Practice' (1985) 15 *Indian Journal of International Law* 365–85, 374.

activity. It has been a decisive element in the definition of refugee that a person crossed an international border. Only then could international protection and assistance set in. Throughout the 1970s, a number of situations made it more and more evident that people who fled to a place of safety *within* a country might face the same needs and hardships as those who had crossed an international frontier. Non-international armed conflicts started to account for an increasing part of forced displacement. The UNHCR and other UN bodies then started to speak of 'displaced persons' and provided assistance within such persons' countries.[159]

In 1972 the ECOSOC promoted the voluntary repatriation of refugees to Sudan and extended the measures of rehabilitation and assistance to 'persons displaced within the country'.[160] In the same year the GA followed suit and endorsed UNHCR's actions 'in the relief, rehabilitation and resettlement of Sudanese refugees coming from abroad and other displaced persons'.[161] The term 'displaced persons' was used to refer to those Sudanese who were not refugees precisely because they had not crossed an international border. Yet they should receive UNHCR's assistance. In 1975 the GA—retrospectively, as usual—sanctioned UNHCR's assistance to 'Indo-Chinese displaced persons' that the agency rendered inside Laos and Vietnam.[162] Guy Goodwin-Gill and Jane MacAdam summarize that

> [t]he 'displaced persons' category, with its foundations in humanitarian necessity, was the natural successor to the 'good offices' approach; in its time, 'good offices' had accommodated the need for *prima facie* eligibility, while 'displaced persons' came in to describe UNHCR action on the ground – providing humanitarian assistance to those displaced within divided countries....[163]

For UNHCR, these situations again formed the background for semantic struggles about the terms of its competences. In his report to the General Assembly in 1976, High Commissioner Sadruddin Aga Khan (1966–1977) commented on the general developments in UNHCR's assistance activities in Asia and spoke of 'displaced persons who face problems analogous to those of refugees'.[164] The ECOSOC went along and *'[c]ommend[ed]* the United Nations High Commissioner for Refugees for his efforts on behalf of refugees and displaced persons, victims of man-made disasters, requiring urgent humanitarian assistance'.[165] Further adding

159 Cf. Goodwin-Gill and McAdam, *The Refugee in International Law*, 481–9.

160 ECOSOC res 1655 (LII), 1 June 1972; cf. I C Jackson, *The Refugee Concept in Group Situations* (The Hague: Nijhoff 1999), 229–35.

161 UNGA res 2958 (XXVII), 12 December 1972, third operative clause.

162 UNGA res 3455 (XXX), 9 December 1975; cf. Moussalli, Evolving Functions, 96–7.

163 Goodwin-Gill and McAdam, *The Refugee in International Law*, 27.

164 UN High Commissioner for Refugees, *Report of the United Nations High Commissioner for Refugees*, 1 January 1976, A/31/12, para 170.

165 UN Economic and Social Council (ECOSOC), *Report of the United Nations High Commissioner for Refugees*, 2 August 1976, E/RES/2011 (LXI).

to the inflation of expressions and concepts, ExCom first spoke of 'asylum seekers' who had left their country in small boats but a little later saw no obstacles to speaking of the problem of *refugees* from Indo-China, thus once more glossing over differences and speaking generically of refugees in a way that included externally displaced persons analogous to those of refugees.[166] While the refugee definition spelled out in the UNHCR Statute was again used to include categories of individuals not formerly within its reach, its precise contours continue to be contested in view of the problem of internally displaced persons (IDPs).[167]

4. Humanitarian aid and voluntary repatriation

Under the direction of Sadruddin Aga Khan, UNHCR successfully positioned itself as the UN's leading humanitarian institution. It found itself in increasing competition with the Office of the United Nations Disaster Relief Coordinator (UNDRO), founded in 1971 and later turned into the Office for the Coordination of Humanitarian Affairs (OCHA), but could effectively fend off attempts to be merged into UNDRO's structures. The United Nations had grown considerably and new international agencies as well as non-governmental organizations providing humanitarian assistance had mushroomed. Sadruddin could gain the confidence of Kurt Waldheim, UN Secretary-General from 1972 to 1981, who repeatedly entrusted him with heading UN humanitarian relief programmes and with serving as a focal point in emergency situations.[168] In 1976 the ECOSOC sanctioned UNHCR's leading role and expanded competences in humanitarian relief actions when it requested the High Commissioner 'to continue his activities . . . to alleviate the suffering of all those of concern to his Office' and identified such persons of concern to be 'refugees and displaced persons, victims of man-made disasters, requiring urgent humanitarian assistance'.[169]

UNHCR's financial and human resources rose with its tasks. Its budget of $300,000 in 1950 amounted to $8.3 million in 1970 and $69 million in 1974. Its expenditures for assistance operations grew thirty-fold between 1966 and

[166] UN doc A/AC.96/534, para 87(3); UN doc A/AC.96/549, para 36(b). Cf. Goodwin-Gill and McAdam, *The Refugee in International Law*, 28; Barnett, 'Evolution of the International Refugee Regime', 248; V Türk, The Role of UNHCR in the Development of International Refugee Law, in: F Nicholson and P Twomey (eds), *Refugee Rights and Realities: Evolving international concepts and regimes* (Cambridge: Cambridge University Press 1999), 153–74, 155.

[167] G S Pelláthy, The Evolving Definitions of IDPs and Links to Ethnic Cleansing in Europe, in: S B Várdy and T H Tooley (eds), *Ethnic Cleansing in 20th-century Europe* (Boulder: Columbia University Press, 2003), 757–72; G Citroni, La giurisprudenza di due corti regionali dei diritti umani in tema di spollati interni, in: I Papanicolopulu and T Scovazzi (eds), *Conflitti armati e situazioni di emergenza: la risposta del diritto internazionale* (Milan: Giuffrè 2007), 93–141.

[168] Loescher, *UNHCR and World Politics*, 150–60.

[169] ECOSOC res 2011 (LXI), 2 August 1976.

1975.[170] By the mid-1970s, UNHCR had turned into the internationally leading humanitarian relief organization and it could look back at its humble origins with a glare of surprise or cunning satisfaction. Throughout the following years, UNHCR would strengthen its global role and become further involved in humanitarian missions. In the five years until 1980 its budget further multiplied more than sevenfold, now amounting to $510 million, and its staff more than doubled during that time.[171]

The swelling tides of forced migrants throughout the 1980s, financial burdens as well as shifts in the preferences of Western asylum and donor countries led UNHCR towards a path that it has continued to tread until the present day, seeking new opportunities and fields of action. An increasing refugee population that looked more and more as if it was there to stay made UNHCR focus more on the causes of refugee flows and on repatriating refugees—maybe the lesser evil—as the preferred permanent solution. It also became more involved in broader humanitarian aid efforts of the UN.

In light of protracted refugee situations in the developing world and increasing pressure from donor countries, UNHCR started to develop what Michael Barnett and Martha Finnemore have termed a 'repatriation culture'—a culture that took shape together with a shift in the preferred solution to refugee problems from resettlement to repatriation.[172] While in principle it makes good sense to repatriate where such repatriation is voluntary and clearly possible, such a culture grew so strong that in some cases it allegedly accommodated violations of refugee rights, thus contradicting the terms of the mandate and its primary object and purpose. Already in 1980 ExCom had '[r]ecognized that voluntary repatriation constitutes generally, and in particular when a country accedes to independence, the most appropriate solution for refugee problems'.[173] Faced with a huge refugee population, High Commissioner Jean-Pierre Hocké (1986–1989) regarded repatriation as the only viable solution and started vigorously to promote the return of refugees, even if the situation from which they had fled was still precarious at best.[174] This shift in emphasis was also responsive to the interests of donor countries pushing UNHCR to quick and economically efficient solutions. The policy of repatriation, however, took on a life of its own and persisted even in situations in which there was no governmental pressure. It would form part of the strategy of the international institution in some isolation from external factors.[175] This holds

[170] Loescher, *UNHCR and World Politics*, 31.

[171] Feller and Klug, Refugees, Mn 7.

[172] Barnett and Finnemore, *Rules for the World*, 93–118.

[173] UN High Commissioner for Refugees, *Voluntary Repatriation*, 16 October 1980, No 18 (XXXI).

[174] See Zieck *UNHCR and Voluntary Repatriation*, 438–43.

[175] B S Chimni, 'The Meaning of Words and the Role of UNHCR in Voluntary Repatriation' (1993) 5 *International Journal of Refugee Law* 442–60. Cf. Moussalli, Evolving Functions, 98–100;

true in spite of tight constraints on UNHCR's actions that do exist and (Western) states' persistent reluctance to receive refugees as part of resettlement programmes.

Overall, the cases in which repatriation allegedly violated refugee rights might be exceptional.[176] But they are indicative of an organizational practice and routine, which guides international action and which can possibly turn pathological. The practice of repatriations of Rohingyan refugees from Bangladesh to Burma serves as a case in point.[177] In this context, there was no financial pressure to push towards a solution of the refugee situation by way of repatriation but quite to the contrary UNHCR retained a budgetary surplus for this matter. Nor did Bangladesh push for a return of Rohingyan refugees to Burma in a way that would have impeded UNHCR from pursuing other alternatives. And yet, even if conditions in Burma had not changed or even deteriorated, UNHCR carried out repatriations of Rohingyan refugees in tension with the principle that repatriation must be 'voluntary'.[178] Barnett and Finnemore summarize:

> [The repatriation] culture shifted the operational meaning of 'voluntary' so that the voice that counted was the agency's and not the refugees'. It also shifted the meaning of 'protection' so that the ultimate form of protection was defined as getting refugees home as soon as possible.[179]

Apart from shifts towards a preference on repatriation and changes in the meaning of 'voluntary', the growing refugee population also facilitated UNHCR's further expansion into providing humanitarian aid. A large fraction of the refugees that could be attributed to wars were connected to processes of decolonization and to the end of the Cold War. UNHCR thus came to be involved in broader humanitarian responses, under the umbrella of the UN, that targeted underlying causes.

The most significant factor UNHCR would have to cope with, however, was increasing ethnic conflicts and the massive population flows that ethnic strife quite inevitably entails.[180] The disintegration of Yugoslavia is a case in point. It produced the largest refugee crisis in Europe since the Second World War and engaged

E Khiddu-Makubuya, Voluntary Repatriation by Force: The case of Rwandan refugees in Uganda, in: H Adelman (ed), *African refugees. Development Aid and Repatriation* (Boulder: Westview Press 1994), 143–58.

[176] See Zieck, *UNHCR and Voluntary Repatriation*.

[177] For the following see Barnett and Finnemore, *Rules for the World*, 105–18; Loescher, *UNHCR and World Politics*, 224–5.

[178] Paras 1 and 8(c) UNHCR Statute.

[179] Barnett and Finnemore, *Rules for the World*, 75.

[180] I Salehyan and K S Gleditsch, 'Refugees and the Spread of Civil War' (2006) 60 *International Organization* 335–66. Other constellations, such as the exodus of Kurds from northern Iraq in 1991, add to the matrix of scenarios. See Zieck, *UNHCR and Voluntary Repatriation*, 171–88.

UNHCR as part of a broader response of the UN as well as NATO.[181] The UN Secretary-General asked UNHCR to coordinate humanitarian action and made it the lead agency in the Yugoslav crisis, thus supporting a significant broadening of UNHCR's mandate.[182] This development has been met with wholehearted approval while critical voices suggest that UNHCR is ill-equipped to lead humanitarian action and should rather concentrate on its core mandate of international protection for refugees.[183] Its core function might also be undermined by an increasing politicization and militarization of refugee protection.[184]

The militarization of refugee protection and assistance has grown to be an increasing problem for UNHCR in its extended role of managing refugee camps and providing humanitarian aid in crisis situations. This was most evident in the case of Rwandan refugees after the genocide and during the following civil war. Many of the refugee camps were in the firm control of the former Rwandese government and harboured people who were actively involved in the genocide.[185] This is only one facet of the intricacies emerging from UNHCR's increased entanglement in humanitarian assistance operations. In spite of the apparent problems, in September 2006 the Inter-Agency Standing Committee (IASC)[186] assigned UNHCR the lead role for protection, shelter, and camp management on behalf of IDPs. It is thus 'likely that UNHCR's involvement with non-refugee emergencies will continue to grow, representing one of the most significant evolutions in the interpretation of UNHCR's mandate'.[187]

In sum, there has been considerable development in what both 'refugee' and 'international protection' mean in UNHCR's Statute. Volker Türk, Director of International Protection, now emphasizes that an extended use of 'refugee' has successively been backed by the General Assembly that first reluctantly employed

[181] See UNSC res 688, 5 April 1991 (on the situation between Iraq and Kuwait); UNSC res 1244, 10 June 1999 (on the deployment of international civil and security presences in Kosovo).

[182] S A Cunliffe and M C Pugh, UNHCR as Leader in Humanitarian Assistance: Triumph of politics over law?, in: F Nicholson and P Twomey (eds), *Refugee Rights and Realities: Evolving international concepts and regimes* (Cambridge: Cambridge University Press 1999), 175–99, 175–88; Barnett, 'Evolution of the International Refugee Regime', 240.

[183] For a welcoming embrace of these developments see T G Weiss and A Pasić, 'Reinventing UNHCR: Enterprising Humanitarians in the Former Yugoslavia' (1997) 3 *Global Governance* 41. Critical nuances may inter alia be found in M Barutciski, 'A Critical View on UNHCR's Mandate Dilemmas' (2002) 14 *International Journal of Refugee Law* 365–81; Krever, 'UNHCR, Neutrality and Non-Refoulement'. UNHCR itself is surely well aware of the difficulties of providing humanitarian aid in the midst of conflict, see UNHCR, Note on International Protection, 7 September 1994, A/AC.96/830, para 2.

[184] Cunliffe and Pugh, Leader in Humanitarian Assistance; Loescher, *UNHCR and World Politics*, 214–16 and 223–4.

[185] K Wagner, 'UNHCR's Involvement in the Great Lakes Refugee Crisis' (2009) 21 *Pace International Law Review* 365–86; R Muggah (ed), *No Refuge: The crisis of refugee militarization in Africa* (London: Zed 2006).

[186] IASC was established by the GA in 1991 and aimed at the coordination of humanitarian assistance among UN agencies, UNGA res 46/182, 19 December 1991.

[187] G Loescher, A Betts, and J Milner, *The United Nations High Commissioner for Refugees (UNHCR)* (New York: Routledge 2008), 68.

distinct expressions ('people who left their countries in small boats', 'displaced persons', 'persons who face problems analogous to those of refugees') and eventually started referring to those categories of persons as 'refugees'. He finds that '[a]n analysis of these resolutions leads to the conclusion that activities, which were originally outside UNHCR's mandate, are later integrated into the omnibus resolution'.[188] Against the background of recent legal practice he then offers an exemplary statement on what may now be considered a refugee: 'The term "refugee"... covers all persons who are outside their country of origin for reasons of feared persecution, armed conflict, generalised violence, foreign aggression or other circumstances which have seriously disturbed public order, and who, as a result, require international protection.'[189] The argumentative pattern has turned full circle: it is not the definition spelled out in the Statute which tells who is a refugee, but the need of assistance which does so. Every person in need of UNHCR's international protection seems to qualify as a refugee.[190]

The meaning of 'international protection', UNHCR's main function, has been the second major target of interpretation and has likewise undergone considerable change. As Walter Kälin summarizes:

> International protection on behalf of refugees is UNHCR's core function. It has evolved from a surrogate for consular and diplomatic protection of refugees who can no longer enjoy such protection by their country of origin into a broader concept that includes protection not only of rights provided for by the 1951 Convention and the 1967 Protocol but also of refugees' human rights in general.[191]

UNHCR has also started to engage in a whole host of activities that are only covered by its international protection function at some stretch. Usually not even an attempt is made any longer to place them within the legal provisions on international protection, but they are rather discussed in terms of material assistance and humanitarian aid. UNHCR's Note on International Protection of 2000 evocatively and glaringly stated that 'the nature and content of UNHCR's international protection function has come under increasing scrutiny. The Office is frequently asked what its international protection mandate actually entails.'[192] This is indeed a good question.

[188] Türk, Role of UNHCR, 154–5.

[189] Ibid., at 155.

[190] Note that the new Resettlement Handbook is slightly more circumspect and defines as refugees under the broader definition of its protection mandate, any individual 'outside their country of origin or habitual residence and unable to return there owing to serious and indiscriminate threats to life, physical integrity or freedom resulting from generalized violence or events seriously disturbing public order'. UNHCR Resettlement Handbook, 4 July 2011, p 81.

[191] Kälin, Supervising the 1951 Convention, 619–20.

[192] UNHCR, Note on International Protection, 7 July 2000, A/AC.96/930, para 4.

C. UNHCR and the meaning of the Convention

Next to developments in the scope and meaning of UNHCR's Statute, this chapter's main focus lies on semantic struggles with regard to the refugee definition contained in the 1951 Refugee Convention. UNHCR acknowledges that, even if its Statute and the Convention contain almost identical black letter definitions, its mandate is ultimately broader than the Convention.[193] But it aims to broaden the latter in view of semantic changes in its own Statute and in light of developments of its mandate. Türk illustratively writes that '[i]n UNHCR's view, an appropriately liberal interpretation, in the dynamic spirit of international law, of the Geneva Convention criteria would mean that a large number of persons falling within UNHCR's competence could—and indeed should—be considered Convention refugees'.[194] And in fact, while some suggest distinguishing the two, other commentators do not and the remarkable expansion of who qualifies as a refugee and thus qualifies to receive UNHCR's international protection (or, who needs international protection and thus qualifies as a refugee) might then come to bear on the Convention.[195]

Sure enough the development of the Convention has not quite taken the route of the UNHCR Statute. On the whole, states could to some extent prevent the expansion of the personal scope of UNHCR's activities going hand in hand with an extended meaning of 'refugee' in terms of the Convention. UNHCR wishes that this was otherwise but knows that it is not. Still, it has been successful in inducing changes by way of interpretation in some key elements of the refugee definition. In particular, it has sharpened a number of activities that form part of its supervisory function for this purpose (1.) For example, it has contributed to shifting the meaning of both 'persecution' and 'membership of a particular social group' to better accommodate its convictions and interests (2.). As an actor with semantic authority, it has subtly influenced the contents of the legal commitments that states entered into as parties to the Refugee Convention.

[193] See, e.g., UNHCR Resettlement Handbook, 4 July 2011, pp 80–1; UNHCR, Note on International Protection, 7 September 1994, A/AC.96/830, para 21.

[194] Türk, Role of UNHCR, 156. Cf. G S Goodwin-Gill, The Search for One, True Meaning . . . , in: G S Goodwin-Gill and H Lambert (eds), *The Limits of Transnational Law: Refugee Law, Policy Harmonization and Judicial Dialogue in the European Union* (Cambridge: Cambridge University Press 2010), 204–37, 239.

[195] Barnett, 'Evolution of the International Refugee Regime', 248 (noting that '[a]lthough the Convention definition itself was not changed to accommodate new refugee flows, in actual practice UNHCR applied an expanded definition to deal with the larger refugee movements of the 1970s in Cambodia, Laos, and Vietnam'). There are however significant limits to such a possible spill-over stemming from both the legal framework and political conditions. See Zieck, *UNHCR's Parallel Universe*.

1. UNHCR's role in developing the Convention

With new refugee flows ever since the Hungarian crisis, it soon became evident that the refugee definition put together against the background of the Second World War is out of touch with actual needs. It was further rather apparent that no new treaty text would be forthcoming to react to the concerns, at least not on a universal level.[196] UNHCR has thus thrown a lot of its weight into changing the meaning of the Convention. As Jerzy Sztucki points out: 'regional instruments provide an extended concept or definition of "refugee", whereas UNHCR's position is that of extensive interpretation of the Convention definition.'[197] Also Guy Goodwin-Gill noted that '[t]he inadequacies of the refugee definition are both procedural and substantive... and only *forced interpretations* can even begin to cope with the protection needs of women, children, or those fleeing civil war or generalized violence'.[198]

UNHCR has grown to be a weighty actor in the practice of interpretation with regard to the refugee definition of the 1951 Convention and has convincingly linked its authority in this regard to its supervisory function. Its struggle for broader interpretations of the term 'refugee' thus builds on an expanded understanding of what its supervisory function actually entails (a.). As a participant in legal discourse, UNHCR has offered a variety of documents that purport to clarify refugee law and that structure the space of interpretative practice (b.). It has also proven to be a very promising avenue for UNHCR to exert its influence in the making of refugee law by intervening in court proceedings, to aim at finding recognition for interpretative claims in judicial decisions, and to thus leech on to the semantic authority of other actors (c.).

a) UNHCR's supervisory function

The list of functions spelled out in para 8 UNHCR Statute is headed by UNHCR's task of '[p]romoting the conclusion and ratification of international conventions for the protection of refugees, supervising their application and proposing amendments thereto'.[199] The office shall further provide protection for refugees by '[o]btaining

[196] Noteworthy regional developments include the 1969 Convention on the Specific Aspects of Refugee Problems in Africa; the 1984 Cartagena Declaration on Refugees; the Asian-African Consultative Committee's 1966 Bangkok Principles on Status and Treatment of Refugees and the 2001 Principles concerning Admission and Treatment of Aliens; and, for the European context, Directive 2011/95/EU of the European Parliament and of the Council of 13 December 2011 on Standards for the Qualification (recast); European Council Directive 2005/85/EC of 1 December 2005 on Minimum Standards on Procedures in Member States for Granting and Withdrawing Refugee Status; Council Directive 2003/9/EC of 27 January 2003 laying down minimum standards for the reception of asylum seekers; Council Directive 2001/55/EC of 20 July 2001 on Minimum Standards for Giving Temporary Protection.

[197] Sztucki, Who is a Refugee?, 63

[198] G S Goodwin-Gill, 'Asylum: The Law and Politics of Change' (1995) 7 *International Journal of Refugee Law* 1–18, 8 (italics added).

[199] It may also be suggested that this function is derived from the General Assembly's task of 'encouraging the progressive development of international law and its codification' (Art. 13(1) UNC).

from Governments information concerning the number and conditions of refugees in their territories and the laws and regulations concerning them'.[200] The 1951 Convention relating to the Status of Refugees supports UNHCR's supervisory role by providing for modes of cooperation.[201]

When the General Assembly passed the Convention's final draft to be considered by a conference of plenipotentiaries, that draft included a noteworthy paragraph (F), which would in fact have vested the General Assembly with legislative powers.[202] It provided that 'Contracting States may agree to add to the definition of the term "refugee" contained in the present article persons in other categories, including such as may be recommended by the General Assembly'. Even if the General Assembly could not have changed the wording of the Convention, it could have changed contracting states' obligations by changing the scope of persons that qualify as refugees.[203]

Vesting the General Assembly with such powers struck many as a truly valiant move. State representatives were ultimately not ready to entrust the United Nations with such powers and deleted paragraph (F) from the Convention, wary that their commitments might change through the actions of an organ which escapes any individual member's control. The Final Act of the conference of plenipotentiaries then merely expressed the hope that the Convention 'will have value as an example exceeding its contractual scope and that all nations will be guided by it in granting so far as possible to persons in their territory as refugees and who would not be covered by the terms of the Convention, the treatment for which it provides'.[204] No international assembly would thus be responsible for expanding the scope of those who come under the heading of refugees. Such a decision remained a prerogative of states, or so it seemed.

In spite of the fact that the law stopped short of formally recognizing a legislative role of an international body, the Refugee Convention does recognize UNHCR's

C-A Fleischhauer, Article 13, in: B Simma (ed), *The Charter of the United Nations: A Commentary* (Oxford: Oxford University Press 2002), 298–317 (on the varieties of mechanisms and bodies that are linked to Art. 13(1) UNC, however with no special mention of the UNHCR).

200 Para 8(f) UNHCR Statute.

201 Art. 35 Refugee Convention. On the influence of UNHCR on the drafting of the Convention and specifically as it provides for cooperation with UNHCR, see M Zieck, Article 35 of the 1951 Convention/Article II of the 1967 Protocol, in: A Zimmermann (ed), *The 1951 Convention Relating to the Status of Refugees and its 1967 Protocol: A Commentary* (Oxford: Oxford University Press 2011), 1459–510, Mns 6–17.

202 UNGA res 439 (V), 14 December 1950.

203 P Kourula, *Broadening the Edges. Refugee definition and international protection revisited* (The Hague: Nijhoff 1997), 54–6. A similar mechanism was later used in the Convention on International Trade in Endangered Species of Wild Fauna and Flora (CITES), see J Brunnée, Reweaving the Fabric of International Law? Patterns of Consent in Environmental Framework Agreements, in: R Wolfrum and V Röben (eds), *Developments of International Law in Treaty Making* (Berlin: Springer 2005), 101–26.

204 Final Act of the 1951 United Nations Conference of Plenipotentiaries on the Status of Refugees and Stateless Persons, Part IV, Recommendation E, Collection, Vol I, p 37. Cf. P Weis, 'Le concept de réfugié en droit international' (1960) 87 *Journal du Droit International* 929–1001, 993–4.

supervisory function and its role in developing refugee law.[205] Its Art. 35(1) concerns the cooperation of national authorities with the United Nations. It specifies that

> [t]he Contracting States undertake to co-operate with the Office of the United Nations High Commissioner for Refugees, or any other agency of the United Nations which may succeed it, in the exercise of its functions, and shall in particular facilitate its duty of supervising the application of the provisions of this Convention.[206]

Paragraph 2 then continues to provide that state parties undertake to provide UNHCR with information and statistical data. But notably the purpose is 'to enable the Office of the high Commissioner... to make reports to the competent organs of the United Nations', not to facilitate supervision, as might lie near. In practice UNHCR has so far made little use of this provision to solicit information.[207] This has however not prevented UNHCR from harvesting and synthesizing legal practice on the domestic and international level and from thus using yet another source of authority. Moreover, it has used the anchoring of its supervisory function in paragraph 1 to successfully assert that UNHCR does not have to be invited to become involved in protection matters, for instance in domestic administrative or judicial proceedings.[208] Even if neither UNHCR nor the GA were vested with any kind of formal legislative powers, UNHCR's supervisory function would come to carry part of its contribution to the making of refugee law by way of interpretation.

Under the Convention there are three dimensions to UNHCR's role in legal practice. The first is most straightforward and relates to the production of new norm texts—'promoting the conclusion and ratification of international conventions for the protection of refugees'. On two occasions UNHCR was successful in pushing for the conclusion of new treaties. One was the 1957 Agreement on Refugee Seamen[209] and the other, more significantly, was the 1967 Protocol relating to the Status of Refugees.[210]

[205] V Türk, 'UNHCR's Supervisory Responsibility' (2001) 14 *Revue Québécoise de Droit International* 135–58, 139–41.

[206] Art. 35(1) Refugee Convention, Art. II of the 1967 Protocol. Note that municipal instruments can further support and facilitate UNHCR's supervisory function. See for instance Arts 7.2, 12.1(a), and 36 Directive 2011/95/EU of the European Parliament and of the Council of 13 December 2011 on Standards for the Qualification (recast); para 9 German Asylum Procedure Law (Asylverfahrensgesetz, AsylVfG).

[207] Zieck, Article 35, Mn 65.

[208] UNHCR, Note on International Protection, 7 July 2000, A/AC.96/930, para 71. See Kälin, Supervising the 1951 Convention, 623.

[209] 506 UNTS 125.

[210] 606 UNTS 267. Apart from this, UNHCR has formed part of the making of a number of regional treaties that are at times quite significant but fall outside the focus of this chapter, see Holborn, *Refugees*, 202–49; Goodwin-Gill and McAdam, *The Refugee in International Law*, 37–49.

UNHCR's role in the process geared towards the conclusion of a Protocol—that would inter alia delete the temporal and geographical limitations of the Convention—is not of focal interest but still worthy of note. In view of mounting refugee flows in Asia and Africa throughout the 1960s, in consideration of the fact that the Convention only applied to events that occurred before 1 January 1951, and bearing in mind that at least some contracting parties had submitted interpretative declarations confining the Convention's applicability to events having occurred in Europe, UNHCR increased its efforts in studying 'ways and means by which the personal scope of the 1951 Convention might be liberalized'.[211] It thus convened an international colloquium of experts of refugee law, drafted a background paper that would inform the discussions and then, in 1965, put together a first initial draft of the Protocol in light of the colloquium's report.[212] It modified the text in view of comments by governments and then passed the final draft on to the General Assembly via ECOSOC. The Protocol was thus not drafted and adopted in the course of a conference of plenipotentiaries but through a process of codification that was driven by UNHCR—in coordination with states, sure enough, but largely under its guidance.[213]

The Protocol removed the temporal as well as geographical limitations of the Convention and left the refugee definition otherwise unchanged.[214] It neither expanded the arguably narrow persecutory grounds nor did it increase the chances of individuals fleeing from developing countries to qualify as refugees. Ethnic strife, civil war, and other man-made or natural disasters were not explicitly included.[215] In any event, the 1967 Protocol was the last time that UNHCR could carve out a new textual legal basis of refugee law on a universal level.[216] Together with the GA and ECOSOC it has since repeatedly and quite habitually called for the ratification of instruments of protection but it has not again aimed at a new legal instrument. While there may be considerable dissatisfaction with the wording of the Convention at present and considerable divergence with regard to the interpretation of its provisions, there is after all a consensus that sets itself against reconsidering or reopening, so to speak, the positive law. The shared expectation appears to be that any new attempt is likely to weaken the law and would be doomed to lead to a

[211] UNHCR, Addendum to the Report of the United Nations High Commissioner for Refugees, UN doc A/5811/Rev.1/Add.1, 1965, para 33.

[212] Lewis, 'UNHCR's Contribution to the Development', 77.

[213] P Weis, 'The 1967 Protocol relating to the Status of Refugees and Some Questions of the Law of Treaties' (1967) 42 *British Yearbook of International Law* 39–70; Türk, Role of UNHCR, 162.

[214] Hathaway, *The Law of Refugee Status*, 10.

[215] A Grahl-Madsen, 'International Refugee Law Today and Tomorrow' (1982) 20 *Archiv des Völkerrechts* 411–67, 422.

[216] This leaves regional developments again aside, see above note 194.

common denominator below present standards of protection.[217] The idea is to better stick to what you have got, i.e. the 1951 Refugee Convention.

UNHCR thus turned out to be more active in the further development through interpretation of the law that is already out there. If the Convention could not realistically be updated to fit the needs of refugee protection and new treaty law was not forthcoming, UNHCR would need to make the best of it and interpret the Convention according to its interests and convictions.[218] The other two dimensions of UNHCR's role in the making of refugee law do not relate to the production of new texts, but to legal developments by way of interpretation. The driving interest in how norms develop in interpretative practice places these dimensions at the centre of attention. The second dimension of UNHCR's role in the making of refugee law relates to its pushing for particular interpretations of the definition (b.). UNHCR's advocacy and pointed interventions in court proceedings make up a third dimension (c.).

b) Providing interpretative guidance: Making law by clarifying it

After the failure of the UN Conference on Territorial Asylum in 1976 and with constant tensions between governments creating great obstacles to any attempt at laying down new international refugee law, UNHCR shifted more attention towards the strategic interpretation of international norms.[219] In this endeavour it could work in tandem with ExCom and, to a lesser extent, with the GA. In 1982 ExCom '[w]elcomed . . . the efforts undertaken by the High Commissioner to promote a wider understanding of international refugee law [and] urged the continued development and elaboration of refugee law in response to the new and changing humanitarian and other problems of refugees and asylum-seekers'.[220] On another occasion ExCom encouraged UNHCR to further advance the legal framework for international protection in particular by 'exploring the development

[217] J A C Gonzaga, The Role of the United Nations High Commissioner for Refugees and the Refugee Definition, in: S Kneebone (ed), *The Refugees Convention 50 Years On. Globalization and International Law* (Aldershot: Ashgate 2003), 223–50, 250 (noting that '[t]he UNHCR is concerned that if the Convention is reopened for the purpose of reforming it, the likelihood that it will be replaced by anything approaching its value is remote.'). Disenchantment in striving for new conventions was fuelled by the failure to find support for a Convention on Territorial Asylum in 1976, see A Grahl-Madsen, *Territorial Asylum* (Stockholm: Almqvist & Wiksell International 1980), 64; Türk, Role of UNHCR, 163–4.

[218] Consider also the practice in the framework of country specific cooperation agreements that incorporate the UNHCR Statute, the Convention, and the Protocol as a material basis. See Zieck, *Presence in the Field*, 264–9.

[219] Lewis, 'UNHCR's Contribution to the Development', 78; Sztucki, Who is a Refugee?, 62–3.

[220] ExCom, General Conclusion on International Protection, No 25 (XXXIII), 20 October 1982, lit (i).

of guiding principles'.[221] In this way, UNHCR was to contribute to the development of the international refugee law that was already spelled out. Apart from backing UNHCR's role in the making of international refugee law, ExCom has itself contributed to the semantic change of some of the terms contained in the Refugee Convention, in particular of those terms marking the definition of refugees.

In 1975 ExCom created the Sub-Committee of the Whole on International Protection and endowed it with the task of studying problems in refugee protection in more detail.[222] The sub-committee's results have since usually been adopted as Conclusions on International Protection by ExCom and occasionally received further support by ECOSOC and the GA. Despite the fact that, on the face of it, ExCom has only an advisory role to play upon UNHCR's request, its annual conclusions have had an important standard-setting effect.[223] When existing treaty law appeared to be increasingly ill-equipped for attending to the needs of refugees and advances for a new treaty would have been plainly futile, UNHCR, together with ExCom, turned to vesting interests and convictions in claims about the meaning of the Convention and its Protocol.[224] The Conclusions on International Protection represent particularly authoritative statements in the semantic struggle over what international refugee law means.

At first glimpse, ExCom indeed looks like an inter-governmental forum where state representatives are in charge.[225] But such a view unduly blends out the considerable influence the UNHCR secretariat exerts on the process of the drafting of the Conclusions. UNHCR sets the agenda, writes background papers, and prepares initial texts for the negotiators—all of which has time and again proven to have critical influence on the outcomes.[226] All critical points are introduced and settled in the Standing Committee that complements the Committee on the Whole. ExCom only steps in at the very end and usually gives its blessing without much discussion to whatever was agreed upon before.

[221] ExCom, General Conclusion on International Protection, No 81 (XLVIII), 17 October 1997, lit (p). Cf. Lewis, 'UNHCR's Contribution to the Development', 82 (with further references).

[222] Türk, *Flüchtlingshochkommissariat*, 105–9.

[223] UNGA res 1166 (XII), 26 November 1957 (setting out ExCom's madate); Türk, Role of UNHCR, 164–5.

[224] J Sztucki, 'The Conclusions on the International Protection of Refugees Adopted by the Executive Committee of the UNHCR Programme' (1989) 1 *International Journal of Refugee Law* 285–318.

[225] Türk, *Flüchtlingshochkommissariat*, 101–11.

[226] Cf. M A Pollack, 'Delegation, Agency, and Agenda Setting in the European Community' (1997) 51 *International Organization* 99–134; R Hudec, The Role of the GATT Secretariat in the Evolution of the WTO Dispute Settlement Procedure, in: J Bhagwati and M Hirsch (eds), *The Uruguay Round and Beyond: Essays in Honour of Arthur Dunkel* (Heidelberg: Springer 1998), 101–20.

Apart from ExCom's Conclusions, UNHCR has crafted a number of documents that develop existing treaty law by way of interpretation. They range from the very foundational Handbook on Procedures and Criteria for Determining Refugee Status via Guidelines on International Protection to more specific Protection Guidelines and Guidance Notes. All these documents are interpretations of international refugee law and form part of the practice of interpretation that shapes the meaning of the relevant provisions. In their outward show they portray themselves as clarifications of the law. They usually state that

> [t]hrough analyzing international legal principles, jurisprudence and other relevant materials, these Guidance Notes seek to clarify applicable law and legal standards with the aim of providing guidance in the particular thematic area concerned.... When related to refugee status determination, the Guidance Notes supplement and should be read in conjunction with the relevant Guidelines on International Protection.[227]

But also interpretations that vest themselves as clarifications come with varying degrees of innovation and creativity. Next to Guidance Notes, a number of other documents mounting an authoritative interpretative claim have emerged from UNHCR's Global Consultations on International Protection—a process initiated on the occasion of the Convention's 50th anniversary, geared towards reaffirming the centrality of the Convention, and aimed at finding acceptance for interpretations that fit with UNHCR's convictions and interests. This process has so far been UNHCR's most significant assertion of authority in semantic disputes over provisions pertaining to the protection of refugees.[228] One of the principal outputs have been a number of new Guidelines on International Protection that take up topical issues and throw UNHCR's weight behind specific interpretations. The first such guideline dates from 2002 and speaks on 'Gender-Related Persecution Within the Context of Article 1A(2) of the 1951 Convention and/or its 1967 Protocol Relating to the Status of Refugees'.[229] The most recent one of December 2009 concerns 'Child Asylum Claims under Articles 1(A)2 and 1(F)'.[230]

[227] This sort of disclaimer usually precedes Guidelines and Guidance Notes, see, e.g., UNHCR, Guidelines on International Protection No. 8: Child Asylum Claims under Articles 1(A)2 and 1(F) of the 1951 Convention and/or 1967 Protocol relating to the Status of Refugees, 22 December 2009, HCR/GIP/09/08; UNHCR, Guidance Note on Refugee Claims Relating to Sexual Orientation and Gender Identity, 21 November 2008.

[228] ExCom, Conclusion on International Protection, No 90 (LII), 5 October 2001, lit (g); UNGA res 137, A/RES/56/137, 15 February 2002. E Feller, V Türk, and F Nicholson (eds), *Refugee Protection in International Law: UNHCR's global consultations on international protection* (Cambridge: Cambridge University Press 2003). Since 2002 the process of consultations that formed part of the Global Consultations are continued with the Agenda for Protection, A/AC.96/965/Add.1, 26 June 2002. Cf. V Chetail (ed), *La Convention de Genève du 8 juillet 1951 relative au statut des réfugiés 50 ans après. Bilan et perspectives* (Bruxelles: Bruylant 2001).

[229] UNHCR, Guidelines on International Protection No. 1: Gender-Related Persecution Within the Context of Article 1A(2) of the 1951 Convention and/or its 1967 Protocol Relating to the Status of Refugees, 7 May 2002, HCR/GIP/02/01.

[230] UNHCR, Guidelines on International Protection No. 8: Child Asylum Claims under Articles 1 (A)2 and 1(F) of the 1951 Convention and/or 1967 Protocol relating to the Status of Refugees, 22 December 2009, HCR/GIP/09/08. In addition, UNHCR has published numerous other reference

It appears to be widely accepted that ExCom's General Conclusions and other forms of directives are binding for UNHCR, at least when they are endorsed by the ECOSOC or the General Assembly.[231] It stands disputed, however, whether its interpretative documents such as the Handbook or Guidelines are binding as part of UNHCR's internal law. In any event, it is beyond doubt that they have a strong practical significance. In particular UNHCR staff carrying out refugee status determinations in the field will resort to such documents for guidance and comfort.[232] It is again beyond doubt that such documents are not binding on states. But this does not exhaust the issue of their standing in the practice of interpretation and their influence in processes of communicative lawmaking. UNHCR claims semantic authority and enjoys such authority in the eyes of others.

Domestic courts and other domestic institutions deciding whether an individual qualifies as a refugee have continuously reiterated that UNHCR's interpretations are not binding.[233] And yet such institutions have repeatedly relied on Art. 35 Refugee Convention to support their resort to UNHCR's statements on the law.[234] In *Khalif Mohamed Abdi*, for instance, the English Court of Appeal looked at Art. 35 to argue that UNHCR should be considered 'a source of assistance and information'.[235] Lord Justice Brown of the English High Court quoted UNHCR Guidelines on the Detention of Asylum Seekers and stated that '[h]aving regard to Article 35(1) of the Convention, it seems to me that such Guidelines should be accorded considerable weight'.[236] Blurring the distinction between a source of law and its interpretation, Lord Lloyd of Berwick mysteriously stated that the Handbook is an 'important source of law (though it does not have the force

documents such as thematic guidelines or training manuals. See <http://www.unhcr.org/refworld/type.html>.

231 Para 3 UNCR Statute. Cf. Feller and Klug, Refugees, Mn 24; Sztucki, 'Conclusions on the International Protection'; Türk, *Flüchtlingshochkommissariat*, 102–9.

232 See Smrkolj, 'UNHCR's Refuge Status Determination'.

233 Kälin, Supervising the 1951 Convention, 625–7 (offering a review of pertinent domestic jurisprudence). See, e.g., Lord Bridge of Harwich in *R v Secretary of State for the Home Department, ex parte Bugdaycay*, House of Lords, 19 February 1987, [1987] 1 All ER 940, (stating with regard to the UNHCR Handbook and Conclusions of ExCom that 'it is, as it seems to me, neither necessary nor desirable that this House should attempt to interpret an instrument of this character which is of no binding force either in municipal or international law.').

234 There is a considerable amount of jurisprudence in this regard that may be accessed at UNHCR's database *Refworld*, <http://www.unhcr.org/refworld/>. Cf. J McAdam, Interpretation of the 1951 Convention, in: A Zimmermann (ed), *The 1951 Convention Relating to the Status of Refugees and its 1967 Protocol: A Commentary* (Oxford: Oxford University Press 2011), 75–115, Mn 111 (noting that '[s]uperior courts have generally been supportive of UNHCR's views').

235 *Secretary of State for the Home Department v Khalif Mohamed Abdi*, English Court of Appeal (Civil Division), 20 April 1994, [1994] ImmAR402, Gibson LJ.

236 *R v UxbridgeMagistrates' Court and Another, ex parte Adimi*, English High Court (Divisional Court), 29 July 1999, Brown LJ [1999] ImmAR560, [1999] 4 All ER 520.

of law itself)'.[237] Lord Steyn summarizes aptly: that 'UNHCR plays a critical role in the application of the Refugee Convention.... It is not surprising therefore that the UNHCR Handbook, although not binding on states, has high persuasive authority, and is much relied on by domestic courts and tribunals.'[238] The House of Lords' treatment of the *Fournah* case is replete with extensive arguments building on and relating to UNHCR's interpretative guidelines.[239]

Other domestic courts are similarly embracing. The US Supreme Court stressed that the Handbook had no force of law, but found that it 'provides significant guidance in construing the Protocol, to which Congress sought to conform. It has been widely considered useful in giving content to the obligations that the Protocol establishes.'[240] The New Zealand Refugee Status Appeals Authority argued that it related its reasoning to UNHCR's interpretations due to their 'considerable persuasive authority'.[241] When the High Court of Australia was squarely confronted with pronouncing on the standing of UNHCR's interpretations 2006, it asked whether

> in answering the issues in this appeal, should this Court pay any regard to the submissions offered to it by and on behalf of the UNHCR? In construing the Convention and provisions of the Act referring to the Convention, should the Court take into account opinions expressed in the UNHCR Handbook, Guidelines and reports of expert meetings concerning the meaning of the Convention and its intended operation?[242]

The Minister for Immigration and Multicultural and Indigenous Affairs had expressed misgivings about the use of UNHCR documents in adjudication. But Judge Kirby rejected such concerns and opined that

> [t]his Court has frequently resorted to the UNHCR Guidelines and the Handbook in construing and applying the Convention. This has been done because of the expertise of the UNHCR in the application of the Convention... In effect, in deciding cases such as the present, national courts are exercising a species of international jurisdiction. The more

237 *T v Secretary of State for the Home Department*, House of Lords, 22 May 1996, [1996] 2 All ER 865.

238 *R v Secretary of State for the Home Department, ex parte Adan and Aitseguer*, 19 December 2000, [2001] 2 AC 477 (UK), 516, 520.

239 *Secretary of State for the Home Department v Fornah*, House of Lords, 18 October 2006, [2006] UKHL 46. Consider further that Lord Bingham opined that the UNHCR Handbook is an 'important source of guidance' *Sepet and Bulbul v Secretary of State for the Home Department*, 20 March 2003, [2003] UKHL 15, para 12.

240 *Immigration and Naturalization Service v Cardoza-Fonseca*, US Supreme Court, 480 US 421, 107 S Ct 1207, 9 March 1987; reaffirmed in *Immigration and Naturalization Service v Juan Anibal Aguirre-Aguirre*, US Supreme Court, 526 US 415, 119 S Ct 1439, 3 May 1999.

241 *Re S.A.*, Refugee Appeal No 1/92, New Zealand, Refugee Status Appeals Authority, 30 April 1992, available at <http://www.refugee.org.nz/rsaa/text/docs/1-92.htm>.

242 *Minister for Immigration and Multicultural and Indigenous Affairs v QAAH of 2004*, High Court of Australia, 15 November 2006, [2006] HCA 53, J Kirby, para 65. In the present case UNHCR also intervened as *amicus curiae*, see *Outline of submissions on behalf of the Office of the United Nations High Commissioner for Refugees (as Amicus Curiae)*, 8 June 2006, available at <http://www.unhcr.org/refworld/docid/4b614d092.html>.

assistance courts can receive from the relevant international agencies, in discharging such international functions, the better.[243]

In lieu of a comprehensive overview of how other actors contribute to the authority of UNHCR's Handbook or Guidelines, these examples from domestic practice are offered in support of UNHCR's standing as an actor with semantic authority in the making of refugee law by way of interpretation. Apart from delegation and characteristic traits of bureaucracies such as rational administration or expertise, authority is the product of a dynamic practice and past experiences. UNHCR can use the past in trying to influence the future. Specifically, it can try to use the authority of other actors such as courts.

c) *Supervising, intervening, and the authority of others*

Apart from crafting documents that should generally guide interpretations, concrete instances of pointed interventions on the part of UNHCR may not only work to the benefit of the individual(s) concerned, they also leave their mark on the development of international refugee law. UNHCR has relied on its supervisory role carved into its Statute and supported by Art. 35 Refugee Convention in order to intervene in concrete cases pending before domestic, supranational, and international institutions. Its action has taken the form of verbal representations to governments and written propositions in administrative and court proceedings. The results reached in each case tend to have notable repercussions, as precedents with respective jurisdictions, but also generally as influential past practice. Being aware of the potential of other institutions' semantic authority, UNHCR intervenes as *amicus curiae*, seeks to influence outcomes and to find recognition of its interpretative claims in jurisprudence that then contributes to the making of refugee law.

Türk sees it as a crucial element of UNHCR's supervision 'to influence state practice by providing guidance on the eligibility of certain groups of refugees and by advising the authorities, courts and other bodies, on the interpretation and practical application of the provisions of the international refugee instruments'. He continues to point out that 'UNHCR's involvement in precedent-setting cases, including through submissions to courts, has also often resulted in positive developments in a number of countries'.[244]

In 2003, ExCom looked back at the results of UNHCR's Global Consultations process and its effects on international refugee law.[245] It noted that

[243] *Minister for Immigration and Multicultural and Indigenous Affairs v QAAH of 2004*, High Court of Australia, 15 November 2006, [2006] HCA 53, J Kirby, paras 76–78. Cf. M Kirby, 'Transnational Judicial Dialogue, Internationalisation of Law and Australian Judges' (2008) 9 *Melbourne Journal of International Law* 171.

[244] Türk, 'UNHCR's Supervisory Responsibility', 148.

[245] UNHCR, Note on International Protection, 2 July 2003, A/AC.96/975, paras 40–54.

[a]micus curiae briefs and court submissions represented valuable tools to promote the proper interpretation of national and international refugee law. During the reporting period, such interventions resulted in judgments improving access to full reception benefits, ruling out detention solely on the grounds of absence of documentation, increasing recognition that persecution by non-State actors as well as gender-related persecution should be considered under the 1951 Convention.[246]

There is again a multitude of cases in which UNHCR has intervened—a total of 120 submissions until December 2011.[247] UNHCR's reasoning and its claim to authority follows the pattern illustrated by way of example in its *amicus curiae* submission in the case of *Doe v Holder, Attorney General* before the United States Court of Appeals for the Seventh Circuit.[248] At the outset, UNHCR recalls the statutory basis of its supervisory function that is backed by Art. 35 Refugee Convention as well as Art. II Protocol and affirms that its 'primary purpose is to safeguard the rights and well-being of refugees'.[249] It then supports the authority of its interpretations in the following manner:

The views of UNHCR are informed by over 55 years of experience supervising the treaty-based system of refugee protection established by the international community.... It has twice received the Nobel Peace Prize, in 1954 and 1981, for its work on behalf of refugees. UNHCR's interpretation of the provisions of the 1951 Convention and its 1967 Protocol are both authoritative and integral to promoting consistency in the global regime for the protection of refugees.[250]

UNHCR tends to invest substantive effort in cases that are likely to have precedential effects and that may shift argumentative burdens in interpretative practice centred on the Refugee Convention. In the case at hand, it 'anticipates that the decision in this case may influence the manner in which the authorities of other countries apply the refugee definition'.[251] It welcomed the fact that the Board of Immigration Appeals, from where the case had moved to the Court of Appeals, had cited its guidelines but laments that it did so completely inaccurately. It thus seems that even if the board could apparently not really rely on UNHCR's interpretation in its support, it nevertheless felt that it had to relate to it.

UNHCR has recognized the mounting influence that domestic jurisprudence may have on international refugee law and it tries to leech on to such dynamics both through claiming authority of its interpretations of the law and, specifically, by intervening in court proceedings to find acceptance for its claims. Domestic

[246] Ibid., at para 45.

[247] Information kindly offered by Cornelius Wouters, Senior Refugee Law Advisor, Division of International Protection, UNHCR. Cf. <http://www.unhcr.org/refworld/type/AMICUS.html>.

[248] UNHCR, *Doe v Holder, Attorney General: Brief of the United Nations High Commissioner for Refugees as Amicus Curiae in Support of Petitioner*, 13 November 2009, available at <http://www.unhcr.org/refworld/docid/4b03eb182.html>.

[249] Ibid., at 1.

[250] Ibid., at 2.

[251] Ibid., at 3.

courts speak across borders, knit ties among one another, and influence the development of the law. UNHCR jumps on the bandwagon in the communicative making of refugee law. Refugee law serves as a prime example of judicial cooperation.[252] The International Association of Refugee Law Judges[253] enables and promotes judicial dialogue and so do very well administered databases of pertinent case law such as *Refworld* run by UNHCR[254] or the *Refugee Caselaw Site* at the University of Michigan Law School.[255] These are powerful tools in shaping the law.

UNHCR's interventions might have an even greater effect on the meaning of international refugee law if they can influence interpretations rendered by certain international courts or the supranational Court of Justice of the European Union (CJEU). Not many international institutions have pronounced on the Refugee Convention. They rather speak on refuge rights under other instruments. The Inter-American Court of Human Rights (IACtHR) has only occasionally done so but the European Court of Human Rights (ECtHR) has indeed developed a considerable body of jurisprudence centred on Art. 3 ECHR prohibiting torture and, by interpretative extension, also protects against *refoulement*.[256] UNHCR has repeatedly been admitted to intervene in ECtHR proceedings and further contributed through informal channels such as by sending a letter to the court.[257] UNHCR recently for the first time played a role in proceedings before the CJEU—an avenue supported by legislative instruments in European asylum law which stresses that Member States shall fulfil their obligations under EU law in conformity with the Refugee Convention.[258]

252 E Benvenisti, 'Reclaiming Democracy: The Strategic Uses of Foreign and International Law by National Courts' (2008) 102 *American Journal of International Law* 241–74, 261–7.

253 <http://www.iarlj.org>.

254 <http://www.unhcr.org/refworld/>.

255 <http://refugeecaselaw.org/>.

256 Consider the recent prominent case of *M.S.S. v Belgium and Greece*, Judgment of the Grand Chamber of 21 January 2011. UNHCR submitted an intervention in this case, available at <http://www.unhcr.org/refworld/docid/4c19e7512.html>.

257 See, e.g., UNHCR, *Letter to the European Court of Human Rights on forced returns to Iraq*, 9 November 2010. Cf. K Zwaan, *UNHCR and the European Asylum Law* (Nijmegen: Wolf 2005), 41.

258 See, e.g., UNHCR, *Statement on religious persecution and the interpretation of Article 9(1) of the EU Qualification Directive*, 17 June 2011, (issued in the context of two references for a preliminary ruling to the Court of Justice of the European Union (CJEU) from the Bundesverwaltungsgericht (Germany) lodged on 18 February and 2 March 2011—*Federal Republic of Germany v Y* (Case C-71/11) and *Federal Republic of Germany v Z* (Case C-99/11)); UNHCR, *Statement on the reception conditions of asylum-seekers under the Dublin procedure*, 1 August 2011, C-179/11 (issued in the context of a reference for a preliminary ruling addressed to Court of Justice of the European Union by the French Council of State lodged on 18 April 2011—*CIMADE and GISTI v Ministry of the Interior* (Case C-179/11)). The relevant legislative instruments are Directive 2011/95/EU of the European Parliament and of the Council of 13 December 2011, Council Directive 2004/83/EC of 29 April 2004 and Council Directive 2005/85/EC of 1 December 2005. When the CJEU interprets the Refugee Convention, or Council Directives purporting to implement international obligations, its authority and the fact that its judgments are immediately translated into all 23 official languages of the EU are likely to increase the weight of its decisions. Cf. J Kumin, UNHCR, the EU and Refugees, in: J Wouters, F Hoffmeister, and T Ruys (eds), *The United Nations and the European Union: An ever stronger partnership* (The Hague: T.M.C. Asser Press 2006), 171–82; Zwaan, *UNHCR and the European Asylum Law*, 13–15. Already in 2003 the European Commission stated in a communication to the Parliament and the Council that UNHCR could intervene in such cases before domestic courts

While UNHCR seeks to influence the development of refugee law by way of crafting documents that claim to authoritatively clarify the law, it also intervenes in concrete cases—drawing on its documents of interpretative guidance and seeking to find acceptance for its claims. It asserts its authority as a weighty participant in semantic struggles over what the Refugee Convention means and at the same time seeks the authority of other institutions, above all of domestic courts. It then harvests domestic jurisprudence, makes it accessible, and uses it again in crafting new general interpretative guidance. It asserts its authority and uses the authority of others. How does this work with regard to concrete elements of the refugee definition?

2. Semantic change at work: Shifting elements in the meaning of 'refugee'

In pushing for developments in the definition of refugee that is spelled out in the Convention, UNHCR could above all build on developments in human rights law. Almost all elements of the definition have been subject to change. Moreover, there is considerable dispute with regard to the burden of proof that has to be met in establishing refugee status. It used to be not uncommon, for example, to demand *clear probability* as an objective test for finding that fear of persecution was well founded. Now it looks as if a more lenient standard of a *balance of probability* should be decisive.[259] The development of two parts of the refugee definition will serve as concrete examples: the meaning of 'persecution' (a.) and the meaning of 'membership of a particular social group' (b.).

a) Persecution and its agents

It is one critical element in the definition of 'refugee' that a person is 'persecuted'. The concept of persecution is of relatively recent origin and only came to form part of the vernacular of international law with the new beginnings after the Second World War. It may be recalled that the IRO Convention spoke of 'valid objections to returning' to the country of origin and its Annex named persecution as an example of such a valid objection.[260] This was the first time that 'persecution' entered the determination of who qualifies as a refugee.[261] It then made its way into Art. 14(1) Universal Declaration of Human Rights proclaiming that '[e]veryone has the right to seek and to enjoy in other countries asylum from persecution'. Both UNHCR Statute and the Refugee Convention include persecution as an element of

that lead to preliminary ruling proceedings and that involve the application of the Geneva Convention, see COM (2003) 152 final, Brussels, 26 March 2003, *Communication from the Commission to the Council and the European Parliament on the common asylum policy and the Agenda for protection*, p 8.

[259] For an overview see Goodwin-Gill and McAdam, *The Refugee in International Law*, 54–60.

[260] See above note 107.

[261] Grahl-Madsen, *Status of Refugees*, 188–9.

the refugee definition without describing it any further. At the time of drafting, it appeared to be generally accepted that at least a threat to life or freedom constitutes persecution. This also follows quite easily from a systematic reading of the Convention whose Arts 31 and 33 speak of individuals whose life or freedom was, or would be, threatened.[262]

Beyond this minimal common denominator, there has always been strong disagreement. On the one hand, Paul Weiss, one of the chief lawyers at UNHCR and at the time on his way to becoming one of the leading experts, argued in 1960 that, apart from threats to life or liberty, any 'other measure in disregard to human dignity may also constitute persecution'.[263] His interpretation of persecution already brings the concept close to the human rights discourse. In a similar vein, Jacques Vernant had argued that persecution meant 'severe measures and sanctions of an arbitrary nature, incompatible with the principles set forth in the Universal Declaration of Human Rights'.[264] Vernant was quick to add that the UDHR 'merely enunciates certain principles solemnly proclaimed by the General Assembly'. But still, the principles could acquire legal bite in finding out what persecution means. In contrast to these rather encompassing interpretations, others, like Karl Friedrich Zink, have argued that only threats to an individual's life or liberty may amount to persecution. Other (legal) interests do not qualify in an assessment of whether an individual is persecuted in the sense of the refugee definition.[265] While such restrictive interpretative claims could still build on some domestic jurisprudence, they faced an increasingly hard time.[266] The question of what persecution is became closely linked with the vibrant human rights discourse and its innovations. Emphasis shifted from the interests of the country of asylum to the human rights of the refugee.[267]

UNHCR pushed for this move seeking the support of ExCom. It successively placed persecution into formulations that recall themes of human rights law. While persecution stood alone as a legal concept forming part of the refugee definition, it was later qualified more specifically.[268] In Conclusion No 73 of 1993, for instance, ExCom was adamant to establish that sexual violence is a form of

[262] M Bettati, *L'asile politique en question. Un statut pour les réfugiés* (Paris: Presses Universitaires de France 1985), 10; J-Y Carlier, Et Genève sera... La définition du réfugié: Bilan et perspectives, in: V Chetail (ed), *La Convention de Genève du 8 juillet 1951 relative au statut des réfugiés 50 ans après* (Bruxelles: Bruylant 2001), 63–89, 67.

[263] Weis, 'Le concept de réfugié, 970.

[264] Vernant, *The Refugee in the Post-War World*, 8.

[265] K F Zink, Zur Bestimmung des Begriffs 'Verfolgung' im Sinne des Abkommens vom 28. Juli 1951 über die Rechtsstellung der Flüchtlinge, in: M Kornrumpf (ed), *Zweites Internationales Asyl-Colloquium* (Köln: Heymanns 1965), 115–22, 121.

[266] Vernant, *The Refugee in the Post-War World*, 193–4.

[267] F Franz, Die Wandlung des Asylrechts vom Souveränitätsrecht des Staates zum Freiheitsrecht des Einzelnen, in: M Kornrumpf (ed), *Zweites Internationales Asyl-Colloquium* (Köln: Heymanns 1965), 133–9.

[268] UNHCR provides a compilation of all of ExCom's Conclusions on International Protection up to the year 2004, available at <http://www.unhcr.org/41b041534.html>.

persecution.[269] And ever since, it has repeatedly mentioned that the refugee definition includes 'persecution through sexual violence or other gender-related persecution'.[270] As of late, ExCom has shown an even wider understanding of persecution by placing the concept side by side with 'generalized violence and violations of human rights which continue to cause and perpetuate displacement within and beyond national borders'.[271] Also, the UNHCR Handbook for Determining Refugee Status links the concept of persecution to 'serious violations of human rights'.[272]

Developments in human rights law itself have offered support. The 1984 UN Convention against Torture (CAT)[273] has had strong repercussions on the meaning of persecution. It is safe to say that by the time the CAT entered into force in 1987, the prevalent reference point for determining persecution had shifted from 'life and liberty' to the 'prohibition of cruel, inhuman, or degrading treatment or punishment'.[274] Finding what persecution means, Guy Goodwin-Gill and Jane McAdam summarize, 'requires the general notion of persecution to be related to developments within the broad field of human rights'.[275] Such developments, they conclude, take the concept of persecution far beyond the grounds spelled out in the Refugee Convention.[276] This is also the position taken in Art. 9 EU Qualification Directive—a legislative instrument that feeds back into international legal discourse like domestic court proceedings. It provides that

> acts of persecution within the meaning of article 1 A of the Geneva Convention must:
> (a) be sufficiently serious by their nature or repetition as to constitute a severe violation of basic human rights, in particular the rights from which derogation cannot be made under Article 15(2) of the European Convention for the Protection of Human Rights and Fundamental Freedoms; or
> (b) be an accumulation of various measures, including violations of human rights which is sufficiently severe as to affect an individual in a similar manner as mentioned in (a).[277]

[269] ExCom, Conclusion No 73 (XLIV) Refugee Protection and Sexual Violence, (1993).

[270] See, e.g., Conclusion No 77 (XLVI) General (1995), lit (g); Conclusion No 79 (XLVII) General (1996), lit o; Conclusion No 71 (XLVII) General (1997), lit t.

[271] Conclusion No 99 (LV) General (2004), lit l.

[272] UNHCR, Handbook for Determining Refugee Status (1992), para 51.

[273] Convention against Torture and Other Cruel, Inhuman or Degrading Treatment or Punishment, 1465 UNTS 85; adopted by UNGA res A/39/51, 10 December 1984.

[274] This formulation forms part of Art. 16 CAT; Art. 7 ICCPR; Art. 3 ECHR; Art. 5 ACHR; Art. 5 ACHPR, and Art. 8 ArabCHR.

[275] Goodwin-Gill and McAdam, *The Refugee in International Law*, 91.

[276] Ibid., at 93.

[277] Council Directive 2004/83/EC of 29 April 2004 on minimum standards for the qualification and status of third country nationals or stateless persons as refugees or as persons who otherwise need international protection and the content of the protection granted, 30 September 2004, pp 12–23. UNHCR commented in detail on the Directive and its application in its response to the Commission's Green Paper on a Common Asylum System, see UNHCR, Response to the European Commission's Green Paper on the Future Common European Asylum System (2007). The Directive has now been recast and modified by Directive 2011/95/EU of the European Parliament and of the Council of 13 December 2011.

Related to the question of *which* acts or situations count as persecution is the question of *whose* acts can possibly amount to persecution in the sense of the refugee definition. Does persecution only relate to agents of the state or also to non-state actors?[278] The Refugee Convention is silent on the issue. For some time the predominant interpretation in domestic jurisprudence and scholarship has been that only persecution on the part of state authorities would qualify in the sense of the Refugee Convention. A Bavarian Administrative Court stirred up much attention when it handed down a judgment on the matter in 1961. There it unmistakably held that 'persecution in the sense of the [Geneva Convention] must as a matter of principle emanate from a state, or the state must knowingly tolerate it'.[279] This interpretation pervaded subsequent jurisprudence, above all in Germany but also beyond. On this basis Atle Grahl-Madsen, among other scholars, tied the concept of persecution to 'acts or circumstances for which the government (or, in appropriate cases, the ruling party) is responsible, that is, ... acts committed by the government (or the party) or organs at its disposal, or behaviour tolerated by the government in such a way as to leave the victims virtually unprotected by the agencies of the State'.[280] The view gained currency that simple incapacity would also suffice—in the words of the German Federal Administrative Court:

> It is necessary to recognize that there needs to be a connection... between the act of persecution and the organization of the state. It is possible to think of cases, in which persecution does not emanate from the state itself, nor would it be knowingly tolerated by it, but in which for other reasons the state is unable to provide necessary protection.[281]

From the perspective of the individual, it does make obvious sense to treat refugees persecuted by non-state agents in the same way as those fleeing from state action; after all, they may be just as destitute.[282] UNHCR has therefore persistently maintained that the decisive point is that the refugee is in need of international protection whoever the agent of persecution may be.[283] In its Note on Interna-

[278] Note that the term 'agent' is used in the legal discourse without suggesting that there is also a corresponding 'principal', as the use of the term in political science would suggest, see above note 22.

[279] Bayerisches Verwaltungsgericht Ansbach, Case 2377–79 II/59 (17 January 1961), cited in Grahl-Madsen, *Status of Refugees*, 189 ('eine Verfolgung im Sinne der [Genfer Konvention] muss grundsätzlich vom Staate ausgehen bzw. von diesem bewusst geduldet werden').

[280] Grahl-Madsen, *Status of Refugees*, 189; Hathaway, *Law of Refugee Status*, 125–33.

[281] *Rundberg et al. v Bundesrepublik Deutschland*, 1C 118.62, 1 June 1965 ('[es] ist zu berücksichtigen, dass zwischen dem Verfolgungstatbestand und der staatlichen Organisation des Landes ... ein Zusammenhang bestehen muss. Es sind Fälle der Verfolgung denkbar, die zwar nicht vom Staate selbst ausgehen, auch von diesem nicht bewusst geduldet werden, aber in denen aus anderen Gründen der Staat nicht den notwendigen Schutz gewähren kann'). Curiously, the website of the Federal Administrative is only available in German but for one exception. On the first page there is a link in English to 'Decisions in Asylum and Immigration Law'—indicating the importance for judicial dialogue in this field of the law. See <http://www.bverwg.de>.

[282] Grahl-Madsen, *Status of Refugees*, 191.

[283] See already UNHCR, Handbook for Determining Refugee Status (1992), para 65. The position is contested in European Law, see Art. 7 Council Directive 2004/83/EC of 29 April 2004;

tional Protection of 1994, it recognized that non-state persecution accounts for an increasingly large share of the refugee flows and argued strongly that from the perspective of the refugee it makes no difference who the author of persecution is. UNHCR follows a pervasive argumentative pattern in its reasoning that appeals to common sense and moral sensibilities. The starting point is the protection of refugees and in consequence, persecution must be interpreted broadly.[284] The same rhetoric is put to use in its detailed study on 'The International Protection of Refugees: Interpreting Article 1 of the 1951 Convention Relating to the Status of Refugees':

> In UNHCR's view, the source of the feared harm is of little, if any, relevance to the finding whether persecution has occurred, or is likely to occur. It is axiomatic that the purpose and objective of the 1951 Convention is to ensure the protection of refugees. There is certainly nothing in the text of the Article that suggests the source of the feared harm is in any way determinative of that issue. UNHCR has consistently argued, therefore, that the concerns of well-foundedness of fear, of an actual or potential harm which is serious enough to amount to persecution, for a reason enumerated in the Convention are the most relevant considerations.[285]

UNHCR has taken this view into legal practice, for instance as *amicus curiae* and in submissions to governmental agencies.[286] Also where it did not intervene, UNHCR's position has formed a strong reference point in legal practice. In *AE and FE v Secretary of State for the Home Department*, the UK Court of Appeals for England and Wales, for example, engaged at length with the interpretation offered by UNHCR on this matter.[287]

The issue of which agents qualify in the assessment of persecution is closely related to the question of whether individuals fleeing from civil war may qualify as refugees. In such situations the ruling government has evidently lost control over at least part of its territory. Leaving the agents of persecution aside, does general violence qualify as a ground of persecution? Walter Kälin, former Representative of the Secretary-General on the human rights of internally displaced persons, suggested that the way forward is to progressively adapt the refugee definition to new challenges. He offers a well-argued answer in the affirmative. Kälin also portrays a recurrent and intriguing trick in semantic struggles; namely, defaming others as being political while declaring that one's own interpretation rests on the purity and beauty of the law.[288] He is honest about it but a sense of irony is hard to avoid:

cf. the commentary by Kay Hailbronner and Simone Alt in Kay Hailbronner (ed), *EU Immigration and Asylum Law—Commentary* (München, Beck 2010), 1047–8.

[284] UNHCR, Note on International Protection, 7 September 1994, A/AC.96/830, para 22.

[285] UNHCR, The International Protection of Refugees: Interpreting Article 1 of the 1951 Convention Relating to the Status of Refugees, April 2001, para 19.

[286] See for instance its submission *In the Matter of Michelle Thomas et al.*, 25 January 2007, available at <http://www.unhcr.org/refworld/docid/45c34c244.html>.

[287] *AE and FE v Secretary of State for the Home Department*, United Kingdom, Court of Appeal (England and Wales), 16 July 2003, [2003] EWCA Civ 1032, para 34.

[288] Cf. C Schmitt, *The Concept of the Political* (Chicago: Chicago University Press 1996), 21 (noting that 'designating the adversary as political and oneself as nonpolitical (i.e., scientific, just, objective, neutral. etc.) is in actuality a typical and unusually intensive way of pursuing politics.').

> [T]he decision to choose a restrictive interpretation is, basically, a political one. In contrast, an interpretation affording more protection to victims of persecution in the context of civil war and similar situations is one based upon convincing legal arguments if it attempts to get refugee law back into the mainstream of international law.[289]

b) Reasons for persecution: The social group

Apart from the meaning of persecution, each of the stated reasons for persecution in the refugee definition—race, religion, nationality, membership of a particular social group, and political opinion—has to some extent been transformed in the practice of interpretation. Developments in human rights law have again left their mark. With regard to race, for instance, UNHCR and other actors in the practice of interpretation could build on the impact of the 1966 Convention on the Elimination of All Forms of Racial Discrimination, which provides in Art. 1 that

> the term 'racial discrimination' shall mean any distinction, exclusion, restriction or preference based on race, colour, descent, or national or ethnic origin which has the purpose or effect of nullifying or impairing the recognition, enjoyment or exercise, on an equal footing, of human rights and fundamental freedoms in the political, economic, social, cultural or any other field of public life.

This interpretation of racial discrimination has swooped into the interpretation of the refugee definition and of 'race' as a reason for persecution.[290] What race is and how to find out who belongs to a race has further been detailed in the jurisprudence of international criminal tribunals, specifically with reference to the elements of genocide.[291]

It has also come to be a widely accepted interpretation that 'political opinion' should be understood in relation to developments in human rights law.[292] In particular, interpretations of Art. 18 International Covenant on Civil and Political Rights (ICCPR) reverberate in discussions on refugee status and the UNHCR Handbook clearly links the interpretation of 'political opinion' with international norms on freedom of thought, conscience, and religion. The interplay and mutual support between UNHCR's interpretations and domestic jurisprudence further corroborate the convergence between human rights norms and the meaning of 'political opinion'.[293] By way of example, the following analysis concentrates on

289 W Kälin, 'Refugees and Civil Wars: Only a Matter of Interpretation?' (1991) 3 *International Journal of Refugee Law* 435–51, 451.

290 Cf. Goodwin-Gill and McAdam, *The Refugee in International Law*, 70–1.

291 A number of seminal cases have become reference points in legal argument, see in particular *Prosecutor v Jelisic,* Case No IT-95-10-A, 5 July 2001; *Prosecutor v Krstic*, Case No IT-98-33-T, 2 August 2001; *Prosecutor v Akayesu,* Case No ICTR-96-4-T, 2 September 1998. For earlier developments compare G Verdirame, 'The Genocide Definition in the Jurisprudence of the AdHoc Tribunals' (2000) 49 *International and Comparative Law Quarterly* 578–98.

292 Goodwin-Gill and McAdam, *The Refugee in International Law*, 87 (with further references to jurisprudence).

293 K Musalo, 'Claims for Protection based on Religion or Belief' (2004) 16 *International Journal of Refugee Law* 165–226.

illustrating changes in the interpretation of 'membership of a particular social group' and on the workings of UNHCR's semantic authority in accommodating such shifts. More precisely, it emphasizes the growing acceptance of claims that 'social group' includes women and people of certain sexual orientation.[294]

'[M]embership of a particular social group' as a ground of persecution was introduced into the refugee definition without much discussion at a very late stage during the conference of plenipotentiaries. It was part of a proposition by the Swedish delegate who argued that there may well be considerable overlap with other reasons for persecution, but 'membership of a particular social group' should be included in order to prevent gaps.[295] The intent of the framers has since been subject to unremitting contestation. Some have argued that 'membership' was supposed to cover particular groups targeted by communist rulers and others have suggested a very purposive interpretation that '[t]he "social group" category was meant to be a catch-all which could include all the bases for and types of persecution which an imaginative despot might conjure up'.[296] Since little guidance can be found in the *travaux préparatoires*, what drafters intended is up for conjecture. If anything, it is safe to assume that their intentions were not uniform. Goodwin-Gill and McAdam observe that it is simply not clear 'whether the notion of "social group" was expected or intended to apply generally to then unrecognized groups facing new forms of persecution. The answer to that question will never be found, but there is no reason in principle why this ground, like others, should not be progressively developed.'[297] The text, not the intentions, is after all the primary reference point.[298] This was also the point of view taken by Lord Hoffmann of the House of Lords:

> It is plausibly suggested that the delegates may have had in mind persecutions in Communist countries of people who were stigmatised as members of the bourgeoisie. But the concept of a social group is a general one and its meaning cannot be confined to those social groups which the framers of the Convention may have had in mind. In choosing to use the general term 'particular social group' rather than an enumeration of specific social groups, the framers of the Convention were in my opinion intending to include whatever groups might be regarded as coming within the antidiscriminatory objectives of the Convention.[299]

[294] See J Fitzpatrick, 'Revitalizing the 1951 Convention' (1996) 9 *Harvard Human Rights Journal* 229–53, 239.

[295] Grahl-Madsen, *Status of Refugees*, 219.

[296] A C Helton, 'Persecution on Account of Membership in a Social Group As a Basis for Refugee Status' (1983) 15 *Columbia Human Rights Law Review* 39–68, 45.

[297] Goodwin-Gill and McAdam, *The Refugee in International Law*, 74.

[298] See R Bernhardt, *Die Auslegung völkerrechtlicher Verträge. Insbesondere in der neueren Rechtsprechung internationaler Gerichte* (Heidelberg: Heymann 1963), 132. Cf. my account of the discussions leading up to the VCLT in Chapter I.

[299] *Islam v Secretary of State for the Home Department; R v Immigration Appeal Tribunal and Another, ex parte Shah*, House of Lords, 25 March 1999, at p 15.

For some time, membership of a particular social group did not figure prominently in legal debates; and if it did, it usually referred to parts of the society targeted by socialist rulers. UNHCR was rather quick, however, to notice the specific needs of refugee women and already in 1985 advanced the 'interpretation that women-asylum seekers who face harsh or inhuman treatment due to their having transgressed social mores of the society in which they live may be considered as a "particular social group" within the meaning of Article 1A(2)'.[300] In the seminal judgment of the House of Lords in *Islam* and *Shah*, UNHCR had intervened to give effect to its position. It contributed to convincing the House of Lords to recognize women as a particular social group and to understand domestic violence as persecution because the decisive issue is that victims cannot avail themselves of the protection of their state.[301]

Once again, UNHCR and other interpreters reached out for the human rights discourse in support of their interpretations.[302] In so doing they could build on the bold support rendered by the Supreme Court of Canada arguing that '[i]n distilling the contents of the head of "particular social group", account should be taken of the general underlying themes of the defence of human rights and anti-discrimination that form the basis for the international refugee protection initiative'.[303] It was in the field of human rights that feminist critique had succeeded in shaking the public/private distinction and in pushing domestic violence onto the agenda. UNHCR picked up the issue and brought its weight to bear on the interpretation of the Refugee Convention.

It may be recalled that the largest undertaking to this effect were UNHCR's Global Consultations on International Protection that aimed at aligning the interpretation of the Refugee Convention with current challenges. The principal outcome of this process was UNHCR's Guidelines on International Protection, each stating that they are 'intended to provide legal interpretative guidance'. The first two guidelines both received the blessing of an expert meeting in San Remo in 2001 and were released in May 2002. They both dealt with the topical issue of gender-based persecution and the interpretation of 'membership of a particular social group'.[304] The meaning of the law was in particular flux in this regard, and an authoritative statement promised to have considerable influence on

300 ExCom Conclusion No 39, Refugees, Women and International Protection (1985). This is not to say that UNHCR staff and structures have been immune from critique that points out how claims by refugee women are disadvantaged. See E Copeland, A Rare Opening in the Wall: The Growing Recognition of Gender-Based Persecution, in: N Steiner, M Gibney, and G Loescher (eds), *Problems of Protection. The UNHCR, refugees, and human rights*, (New York: Routledge 2003), 101–15.

301 G S Goodwin-Gill, 'Judicial Reasoning and "Social Group" after *Islam* and *Shah*' (1999) 11 *International Journal of Refugee Law* 537–43; S Kirvan, 'Women and Asylum: A Particular Social Group' (1999) 7 *Feminist Legal Studies* 333–42.

302 Art. 2 UDHR, Art. 2 ICCPR and Art. 2 ICESCR all prohibit discrimination of any kind.

303 *Canada (Attorney General) v Ward*, Supreme Court of Canada, 30 June 1993, [1993] 2 SCR 689.

304 UNHCR, Guidelines on International Protection No. 1: Gender-Related Persecution within the context of Article 1A(2) of the 1951 Convention and/or its 1967 Protocol relating to the Status of Refugees, 7 May 2002, HCR/GIP/02/01; UNHCR, Guidelines on International Protection No. 2: 'Membership of a Particular Social Group' Within the Context of Article 1A(2) of the 1951

future semantic developments. Both documents seek the support of the human rights discourse and rely on its momentum in order to work towards innovation in refugee law.

When faced with the issue of whether women having a well founded fear of being subjected to female genital mutilation can qualify as refugees, the House of Lords readily turned to UNHCR's Guidelines in interpreting 'membership of a particular social group'.[305] All the Law Lords engaged with UNHCR's interpretations and they all, by and large, followed UNHCR's interpretive claims. Lord Bingham of Cornhill stated: '[i]t appears to me that the *UNHCR Guidelines*, clearly based on a careful reading of the international authorities, provide a very accurate and helpful distillation of their effect.'[306] Also Lord Hale of Richmond approvingly quoted the Guidelines at length and went on to point out the remarkable development that the meaning of 'social group' had undergone over time.[307] This is not a singular case. In many contexts, interpreters now have very good chances to succeed in their interpretation that women constitute a 'social group'.[308] The disappointment that some scholars voice with regard to the fact that contracting states are so reluctant to include 'gender' as a sixth reason for persecution may actually have little justification if one bears in mind that the meaning of 'social group' has significantly expanded.[309] A lot has changed in the law, even if the text remains as it was carved into the 1951 Refugee Convention.

D. Conclusions: Change and contexts

Over the years, UNHCR has become a hefty actor in the making of refugee law through communicative practice. It has strategically interpreted its Statute to enlarge its scope of action. It has in particular used its semantic authority to contribute to shifts in the meaning of the refugee definition and in the content of 'international protection'. Notably, it has successfully transformed the debate surrounding its competences from a more rigorous interpretation of the refugee definition as a first step in determining its competence to a more sweeping assessment of the needs of individuals. Should an individual need UNHCR's international protection, the argument now seems to go, he or she should be considered a refugee and should thus fall within UNHCR's personal competence of the agency. The need for protection tells what the refugee definition means. In this

Convention and/or its 1967 Protocol Relating to the Status of Refugees, 7 May 2002, HCR/GIP/02/02.

305 *Secretary of State for the Home Department v Fornah*, House of Lords, 18 October 2006, [2006] UKHL 46.

306 Ibid., at para 15.

307 Ibid., at paras 84–85.

308 Cf. R Errera, The Concept of Membership of a Particular Social Group in Refugee Law, in: P-M Dupuy, B Fassbender, M N Shaw, and K P Sommermann (eds), *Völkerrecht als Wertordnung: Festschrift für Christian Tomuschat* (Kehl: Engel 2006), 133–51.

309 Copeland, The Growing Recognition of Gender-Based Persecution.

transformation, UNHCR could invoke the undeniable plight of persons subject to forced displacement. It could build on its moral authority—the perception that it advocates a good cause. Such rhetoric has also left its mark on the outward show of legal argument. Close references to the legal text have faced the reproach of being too 'legalistic'. The more appealing arguments were those that broke out of apparently rigid formalism and called upon the needs of refugees. Shifts in the personal scope of UNHCR's competences have been paralleled by changes in UNHCR's protection function that developed from a kind of quasi-consular legal protection into a broad array of forms of material assistance and humanitarian aid.

Apart from a considerable expansion of its Statute, UNHCR has worked towards developing the 1951 Refugee Convention. Its advocacy in this regard is premised on a wide interpretation of its Statute in the first place. UNHCR has built on its supervisory function in order to foster its position in its semantic struggle centred on the Convention. On this basis, it has crafted a number of documents that unfold legal interpretations with a considerable impact on the development of legal normativity. It has also increasingly intervened in administrative proceedings and, above all, in cases before domestic courts in order to bend the law to meet its interests and convictions. It could, for example, contribute to a considerable shift in what 'persecution' means and in how 'membership of a particular social group' is interpreted. In support of its interpretative claims, UNHCR has put to use the force of the human rights discourse.[310] It rather successfully sought the momentum of human rights to direct developments in the meaning of refugee law. Its success in this regard thrives on and reflects elements of a structural transformation of international legal discourse more generally, by and large cautiously and unsteadily shifting emphasis from state consent to the interests of individuals.[311]

It merits emphasis that UNHCR has frequently sought recognition for its interpretations in court proceedings while it tried to use the authority of other actors. In tandem with UNHCR, domestic courts have displayed considerable influence on the meaning of the Refugee Convention.[312] As Eyal Benvenisti has shown, international refugee law provides a prime example of how domestic courts engage in a dialogue, which builds up opposition to states' executives.[313] Domestic courts act as independent participants in international legal contestation and they have come to provide crucial fora for UNHCR to bring its authority to bear on the

310 Cf. J v Bernstorff, 'The Changing Fortunes of the Universal Declaration of Human Rights: Genesis and Symbolic Dimensions of the Turn to Rights in International Law' (2008) 19 *European Journal of International Law* 903–24 (on the force and potential of the human rights discourse more generally).

311 On such shifts in the outward show of legal argument see above Chapter II, section B.

312 Barnett, 'Evolution of the International Refugee Regime', 261 (maintaining that '[i]n order for UNHCR to be of significant value as an operational refugee regime, it must retain support from domestic courts while enhancing its own supervisory capacities').

313 Benvenisti, 'Reclaiming Democracy'.

meaning of international norms pertaining to the protection of refugees. The authority of domestic courts can in turn help the struggle of UNHCR.

In conclusion, it is instructive to recall the context of UNHCR's role in the making of international refugee law. It should first be remembered that its participation in international legal discourse and the impact of its interpretative practice on the development of international norms is unique in some ways but certainly not exceptional on a more general note. There are numerous other international bureaucracies that have shaped international law in their fields, at times competing on the same subject matter. In the field of migration, for example, UNHCR stands next to the convictions and interests pursued by the International Organization for Migration (IOM). Also the International Labour Organization (ILO) and even the World Trade Organization (WTO) have something to say on parts of the subject.[314] The legal practice of many international organizations is likely to have an increasing impact on how international norms change in communicative practices.

It furthermore bears repeating that the autonomy of international bureaucracies implies that their actions cannot be reduced to the will of other constituencies—be it individual governments, states in their collective, or a constituency like refugees. With regard to the development of UNHCR's international protection function and its involvement in humanitarian aid operations in the broader UN framework, often coupled with military deployments, it has already been pointed out that this might in fact turn out to draw resources and attention away from its traditional task of providing permanent solutions to refugees by way of resettlement.[315] UNHCR's recurrent appeal to the interests of refugees does not of necessity mean that its actions and interpretations actually work to their advantage. The development of UNHCR's Statute is also driven by its own interests and convictions; organizational expansion may well be one prominent target of action.[316]

Changes in the meaning of 'international protection' and in who qualifies as a refugee, it should be borne in mind, also unfold in relation to other (international) norms. It is probably the most blatant imperfection that the considerable dynamism in large parts of international refugee law is at severe odds with the absence of

[314] J Bast, Das Demokratiedefizit fragmentierter Internationalisierung, in: H Brunkhorst (ed), *Demokratie in der Weltgesellschaft. Soziale Welt Sonderband 18* (Baden-Baden: Nomos 2009), 177–85.

[315] Gallagher, 'Evolution of the International Refugee System', 596; T Krever, '"Mopping-up": UNHCR, Neutrality and Non-Refoulement since the Cold War' (2011) 11 *Chinese Journal of International Law* 587–608, 608 ('A provisional balance sheet of the post-Cold War period suggests the past two decades have been a prelude to a new era of relations in which UNHCR increasingly plays handmaid to the interests of States—not vulnerable individuals.').

[316] Loescher, Betts, Milner, *The United Nations High Commissioner for Refugees*, 129 (noting that '[a]t times, organizational expansion has been in the interests of the Office's leadership and bureaucracy.... In particular, the expansion of the organization during the 1990s into areas such as emergency relief and IDP protection may have brought prestige, additional funding and new jobs, but this might have been in tension with the fulfilment of the Office's core mandate').

significant developments in the rather static law on asylum.[317] David Kennedy blames patterns of the legal discourse prevailing at UNHCR for part of the problem that international refugee protection has arguably become so egregiously detached from the real issue of inducing states to grant asylum. UNHCR has quite successfully pushed for strengthening the principle of *non-refoulement* according to which a refugee may not be returned to a place where he or she would again fear persecution.[318] But it has largely washed its hands of the issue of asylum. Asylum has been seen as part of the nasty domestic political business whereas UNHCR walks in the pure beauty of law on the international level.[319]

Lastly, UNHCR's and other international bureaucracies' actions are embedded in contexts of interpretative practice that know many other participants. They all pull and tug on UNHCR's actions and on the meaning of international norms. Domestic governments and in part also legislatures, above all in the political West, tend to employ narrow interpretations of 'refugee'. They have created alternative categories of individuals who would be granted temporary permission but no access to the privileges of refugees. Such temporary solutions are above all common in cases of mass influx and have been endorsed by UNHCR itself as early as 1994.[320] There are a number of drawbacks with this development. Above all, it falls short of the protection standards for refugees and it might well be that those who would readily meet the refugee definition even in a very narrow interpretation do not receive the treatment and assistance states are obliged to render. It may in fact establish a parallel regime in which many individuals are worse off.[321] In the wake of the Bosnian humanitarian crisis of the late 1990s, UNHCR went along with how states granted subsidiary and temporary protection to the group of Bosnian displaced persons. Some have persuasively suggested that it thereby acted against its mission because the group included individuals who would have easily qualified as refugees and should thus have received a higher level of protection.[322] While the group concept first extended protection and UNHCR's scope of action in the

[317] Goodwin-Gill, 'Asylum', 9.

[318] UNHCR has early on asserted that the rule on *non-refoulement* is part of customary international law. See UNHCR, The Principle of Non-Refoulement as a Norm of Customary International Law: Response to the Questions Posed to UNHCR by the Federal Constitutional Court of the Federal Republic of Germany in Cases 2 BvR 1938/93, 2 BvR 1953/93, 2 BvR 1954/93, 31 January 1994, para 3. Cf. E Lauterpacht and D Bethlehem, The Scope and Content of the Principle of Non-Refoulement: Opinion, in: E Feller, V Türk, and F Nicholson (eds), *Refugee Protection in International Law: UNHCR's Global Consultations on International Protection* (Cambridge: Cambridge University Press 2003), 87–177; S Trevisanut, 'The Principle of Non-Refoulement at Sea and the Effectiveness of Asylum Protection' (2008) 12 *Max Planck Yearbook of United Nations Law* 205–46; M d Heijer, *Europe and Extraterritorial Asylum* (Oxford: Hart 2012), 120–41.

[319] Kennedy, 'International Refugee Protection'.

[320] UNHCR, Note on International Protection, 7 September 1994, A/AC.96/830, paras 45–51; also see UNHCR, Providing International Protection including through Complementary Forms of Protection, EC/55/SC/CRP.16, 2 June 2005.

[321] In detail see J Fitzpatrick, 'Temporary Protection of Refugees: Elements of a Formalized Regime' (2000) 94 *American Journal of International Law* 279–306.

[322] J Fitzpatrick, 'The End of Protection: Legal Standards for Cessation of Refugee Status and Withdrawal of Temporary Protection' (1999) 13 *Georgetown Immigration Law Journal* 343–81.

Hungarian crisis, it may now work so as to curtail protection. This only shows how UNHCR's semantic struggle with regard to the meaning of 'refugee' takes place in competition with other participants in international legal contestation.

Even if developments in the Refugee Convention are limited by powerful interventions of governments, it is nevertheless correct that 'it would hardly be permissible for a state to seek to avoid its obligations . . . by ignoring the development of the refugee concept in state and international organization practice'.[323] In the middle of all gains and drawbacks, in the room for manoeuvre between autonomy and constraint, UNHCR's semantic struggles are there to stay for better and in some cases possibly for worse.

[323] Goodwin-Gill, *The Refugee in International Law*, 18–19.

IV

Adjudication in the GATT/WTO: Making General Exceptions in Trade Law

In cases of uncertainty about what a norm means, courts promise clarification. Parties to the proceedings fight about the meaning of norms and seek to find acceptance for their interpretations—authoritative recognition for claims about (il)legality, that is. Before court, each side to a dispute invokes the law for its position and adjudicators then decide what the law really means. In international law, for a long time there were few avenues that would lead to international adjudication—few international courts, little adjudicatory practice, and almost no compulsory jurisdiction. That has changed, at least in some fields of international law. The creation of new and the increasing use of existing international courts has been one of the most significant developments in the international legal order of the past two decades.[1]

New judicial institutions have been created and others expanded. In 1992 the Security Council set up the ICTY and in 1994 the ICTR, in 1994 also the United Nations Convention on the Law of the Sea (UNCLOS) entered into force and paved the way for the International Tribunal for the Law of the Sea (ITLOS) to take off, in 1995 the Marrakesh Agreement created the WTO and with it established compulsory adjudication in international trade law, in 1998 the European Commission of Human Rights was abolished and all cases come directly before the ECtHR, and in 2002 the Rome Statute set up the ICC which lately put its power to the test with the arrest warrants for Sudanese President Umar al-Bashir as well as former Libyan leader Muammar Ghadaffi and his son Saif al Islam. The Project on International Courts and Tribunals now lists a total of 125 institutions with competences to decide legal questions in a judicial manner. Some of the creatures assembled in this compilation may indeed have little impact and may even suffer a dismal and peripheral existence at the margins of the international legal order. And

[1] R Y Jennings, 'The Proliferation of Adjudicatory Bodies: Dangers and Possible Answers' (1995) *ASIL Bulletin* 2, 2, (speaking of a 'quiet revolution' in international law); C P R Romano, 'The Proliferation of International Judicial Bodies: The Pieces of the Puzzle' (1999) 31 *NYU Journal of International Law & Politics* 709–51, 709, (observing that 'the enormous expansion and transformation of the international judiciary as the single most important development of the post-Cold War age.'). I use 'court' in a broad way to include different kinds of judicial institutions including those that usually go by such names as 'tribunal' or 'panel'. Cf. C P R Romano, 'A Taxonomy of International Rule of Law Institutions' (2011) 2 *Journal of International Dispute Settlement* 241–77.

yet, empirical analysis suggests that international courts do play an increasingly significant role and should probably move closer to the centre of attention.[2]

The quantitative development has gone hand in hand with a shift in quality. By and large, international courts have surpassed their traditional role of successfully settling disputes in concrete cases. Instead they frequently direct their clout at expanding the reach of the international law by way of judicial practice. As Yuval Shany observed, many international courts are 'no longer a weak department of power'.[3] They do not simply find the law that is out there and aim at the successful resolution of individual disputes. They also deliberately aim at influencing the development of international norms by way of their interpretative practice. Even if such intent were absent, the effect would still persist. Judicial lawmaking is an inevitable byproduct in the practice of interpretation by institutions with a certain degree of semantic authority. As such, it ranges across the spectrum of old and new judicial institutions.[4]

In the WTO specifically, judicial lawmaking has attracted considerable attention. Whatever its normative appraisal, adjudicatory practice has as a matter of fact developed some of trade law's cardinal norms and principles. It has generated new legal normativity, structured the space in which actors craft their interpretations, and, in short, it has changed the law. John Jackson, one of the leading scholars in the field, opines that

> [t]here are some important lessons in the GATT/WTO story... Perhaps the most significant lesson is that human institutions inevitably evolve and change, and concepts which ignore that, such as concepts which try to cling to 'original intent of draftspersons,' or some inclination to disparage or deny the validity of some of these evolutions and changes, could be damaging to the broader purposes of the institutions.[5]

There are numerous examples of how norms develop and change their meaning in international trade law. One might for instance think of Art. XXIII GATT

[2] A Helmedach, Uneinheitliche Judizialisierung der internationalen Streitbeilegung: Empirische Ergebnisse, in: B Zangl (ed), *Auf dem Weg zu internationaler Rechtsherrschaft? Streitbeilegung zwischen Politik und Recht* (Frankfurt am Main: Campus 2009), 267–93; B Zangl, Das Entstehen internationaler Rechtstaatlichkeit?, in: S Leibfried and M Zürn (eds), *Transformationen des Staates?* (Frankfurt am Main: Suhrkamp 2006), 123–50; K J Alter, 'Delegating to International Courts: Self-Binding vs. Other-Binding Delegation' (2008) 38 *Law and Contemporary Problems* 37–76. From a more legal perspective see Romano, 'Proliferation of International Judicial Bodies'; J E Alvarez, 'The New Dispute Settlers: (Half) Truths and Consequences' (2003) 38 *Texas International Law Journal* 405–44; T Treves, Judicial Lawmaking in an Era of 'Proliferation' of International Courts and Tribunals: Development or Fragmentation of International Law?, in: R Wolfrum and V Röben (eds), *Developments of International Law in Treaty Making* (Berlin: Springer 2005), 587–620; K Oellers-Frahm, 'Multiplication of International Courts and Tribunals and Conflicting Jurisdiction: Problems and possible solutions' (2001) 5 *Max Planck Yearbook of United Nations Law* 67–104.

[3] Y Shany, 'No Longer a Weak Department of Power? Reflections on the Emergence of a New International Judiciary' (2009) 20 *European Journal of International Law* 73–91.

[4] See A v Bogdandy and I Venzke (eds), 'Beyond Dispute: International Judicial Institutions as Lawmakers' Special Issue (2011) 12 *German Law Journal* 979–1370.

[5] J H Jackson, *Sovereignty, the WTO and Changing Fundamentals of International Law* (Cambridge: Cambridge University Press 2006), 82.

stipulating that a member may file a complaint if it 'consider[s] that any benefit accruing to it directly or indirectly under this Agreement is being nullified or impaired'. This used to mean that it is neither sufficient nor necessary to find a breach of obligation. Jurisprudence would hold that any harm in trade would qualify that 'could not reasonably have been anticipated' at the time when concessions were negotiated. The test was one akin to something like 'legitimate expectations', known from contract law.[6] In a landslide shift in the early 60s, a panel then established that a violation of the GATT would be considered a 'prima facie nullification or impairment' in the sense of Art. XXIII.[7] In practice, this interpretation grew to build up the almost irrefutable presumption that any violation would also be a nullification or impairment. The GATT panel in *Oil Fee* later cemented this interpretation by reasoning that a finding of nullification or impairment derives practically *ipso facto* from a violation of the GATT. As Jackson observes, the meaning of Art. XXIII was thus 'brought almost full circle by the evolutionary case-by-case process' of adjudication.[8]

The development of norms through adjudicatory practice is certainly not confined to the context of the WTO.[9] The ICTY and ICTR have shaped the meaning of many elements of international criminal law by way of their practice.[10] A system of bilateral investment treaties stands under the spell of precedents set by arbitration tribunals,[11] and whoever wishes to find out what the ECHR means will need to look at the ECtHR's jurisprudence (or at a commentary that does the work

[6] Working Party Report, *The Australian Subsidy on Ammonium Sulphate*, GATT/CP.4/39, adopted 3 April 1950, BISD II/188; GATT Panel Report, *Treatment by Germany of Imports of Sardines*, G/26, adopted 31 October 1952, BISD 1S/53.

[7] GATT Panel Report, *Uruguayan Recourse to Article XXIII, L/1923*, adopted 16 November 1962, BISD 11S/95.

[8] Jackson, *Changing Fundamentals*, 143 (also noting that '[t]he *Oil Fee* case may perhaps be a high-water mark in this regard, since it arguably reverses the treaty language'). See GATT Panel Report, *United States—Taxes on Petroleum and Certain Imported Substances*, L/6175, adopted 17 June 1987, BISD 34S/136 (known as the *Oil Fee* or as the *Superfund* case). Cf. A Davies, 'The DSU Artilce 3.8 Presumption That an Infringement Constitutes a *Prima Facie* Case of Nullification or Impairment: When Does it Operate and Why?' (2010) 13 *Journal of International Economic Law* 181–204, 186–95 (in further detail tracing the origins of the presumption that a GATT violation constitutes a nullification or impairment).

[9] A v Bogdandy and I Venzke, 'Beyond Dispute: International Judicial Institutions as Lawmakers' (2011) 12 *German Law Journal* 979–1004. Cf. F Salerno (ed), *Il ruolo del giudice internazionale nell'evoluzione del diritto internazionale e comunitario* (Padova: Cedam 1995).

[10] M Kuhli and K Günther, 'Judicial Lawmaking, Discourse Theory, and the ICTY on Belligerent Reprisals' (2011) 12 *German Law Journal* 1261–78; M Swart, 'Judicial Lawmaking at the Ad Hoc Tribunals: the Creative Use of the Sources of International Law and "Adventurous Interpretation"' (2010) 70 *Zeitschrift für ausländisches öffentliches Recht und Völkerrecht* 459–86; A M Danner, 'When Courts Make Law: How the International Criminal Tribunals Recast the Laws of War' (2006) 59 *Vanderbilt Law Review* 1–65; C Greenwood, 'The Development of International Humanitarian Law by the International Criminal Tribunal for the Former Yugoslavia' (1998) 2 *Max Planck Yearbook of United Nations Law* 97–140.

[11] S W Schill, 'System-Building in Investment Treaty Arbitration and Lawmaking' (2011) 12 *German Law Journal* 1083–110.

instead).[12] Other regional human rights courts have been just as active.[13] As part of sectoral regimes, international courts tend to project their particular perspective onto the law—maybe even with a missionary fervour.[14] Some judicial institutions have even been created precisely for the purpose of lawmaking. The International Centre for the Settlement of Investment Disputes (ICSID), for example, by and large goes back to the initiative of the then General Counsel of the World Bank Aron Broches who, in the face of failed multilateral negotiations about the applicable substantive law, advanced the programmatic formula 'procedure before substance'. The substance would, he maintained, follow quite naturally in the practice of adjudication.[15] And so it did, deeply imbued in the functionally tailored perspective of the investment protection regime.[16]

This chapter focuses on the agency of GATT/WTO adjudicators in developing the provisions on general exceptions in Art. XX GATT. The practice of adjudication has not only contributed to semantic changes of the provisions. But judicial precedents have also generated new reference points in legal argument and the authority of precedents has generated new legal normativity. The chapter first introduces international courts as actors in international legal discourse and suggests that they have come to wield increasing power in the development of international norms. In particular, judicial precedents weigh strongly in semantic disputes about what international norms mean. The GATT/WTO context portrays a number of particular features with regard to lawmaking by adjudicators' interpretative practice (A.).

The next two sections analyse concrete developments in the general exceptions of international trade law and point to changes in the institutional context that have nurtured the authority of adjudicators. In the era of the GATT, case-law set up a standard that made it very difficult to justify a policy on the basis of general exceptions. Faced with increasing challenges of policies aiming at the pursuit of

[12] R Bernhardt, Rechtsfortbildung durch den Europäischen Gerichtshof für Menschenrechte, in: S Breitenmoser and L Wildhaber (eds), *Human Rights, Democracy and the Rule of Law. Liber amicorum Luzius Wildhaber* (Zürich and St. Gallen: Dike 2007), 91–101; G Malinverni, Il ruolo della Corte di Strasburgo nell'evoluzione della Convenzione europea di diritti dell'uomo, in: F Salerno (ed), *Il ruolo del giudice internazionale nell'evoluzione del diritto internazionale e communitario* (Padova: Cedam 1995), 125–42; M Fyrnys, 'Expanding Competences by Judicial Lawmaking: The Pilot Judgment Procedure of the European Court of Human Rights' (2011) 12 *German Law Journal* 1231–60.

[13] C Binder, 'Towards a Latin American Constitutional Court? The Jurisprudence of the Inter-American Court of Human Rights with special Focus on Amnesties' (2010) 12 *German Law Journal* 1203–29.

[14] M Koskenniemi and P Leino, 'Fragmentation of International Law? Postmodern Anxieties' (2002) 15 *Leiden Journal of International Law* 553–79. Cf. R G Teitel and R Howse, 'Cross-Judging: Tribunalization in a fragmented but interconnected global order' (2009) 41 *NYU Journal of International Law & Politics* 959–90.

[15] R Dolzer and C Schreuer, *Principles of International Investment Law* (Oxford: Oxford Universtiy Press 2008), 18–19.

[16] The necessity defense may serve as a case in point, see W Burke-White, 'The Argentine Financial Crisis: State Liability Under BITs and the Legitimacy of the ICSID System' (2008) 3 *Asian Journal of WTO & International Health Law and Policy* 199–234; S W Schill, 'International Investment Law and the Host State's Power to Handle Economic Crises. Comment on the ICSID decision in LG& E v. Argentina' (2007) 24 *Journal of International Arbitration* 265–86.

non-trade objectives, adjudicators raised another barrier in a tone of existentialist angst: measures aimed at subject matters outside the member state's jurisdiction were on the whole hardly justifiable (B.).

A lot has changed since the dawn of the WTO. While the new Appellate Body engaged at length with the precedents set by previous panels, it first tore down the so-called 'territorial limitation', lowered the threshold slightly but significantly, and then built up a rich body of jurisprudence with regard to general exceptions that introduces requirements of balancing into the legal analysis. What the new standard means remains thoroughly contested. Little doubt remains, however, that the Appellate Body has in effect come to reign over the intersection between trade objectives and other public policy concerns in the WTO (C.).

The conclusion emphasizes the powerful spell of precedents in international trade law and dwells on the observation that the practice of legal interpretation centred on Art. XX has actually turned into a discourse about what adjudicators can legitimately do in a system of multi-level governance (D.).

A. International adjudicators as actors in legal discourse

Over the past two decades, a number of international courts have entered the stage of international legal discourse with new qualities.[17] A shift in ethos has to some extent accompanied their increase in number and in business. While they once primarily formulated their self-understanding in light of the primary objective of ensuring peace by way of successful inter-party dispute settlement, they now lean towards the deliberate development of international law by way of interpretation.[18] Neither international courts nor their agency in lawmaking are entirely new phenomena. Hopes for a lasting international peace have long been vested in an international judiciary that should actively engage in the development of international law. 'More growth of international law through international decisions!' was Hans Wehberg's illustrative slogan that encapsulates much of the spirit of the interwar period.[19] The project of international peace has traditionally informed the understanding of international courts' functions (1.). New international courts have in large part superseded their traditional role of effectively settling disputes in the service of international peace to engage in judicial lawmaking—with deliberate intention, or as a matter of inevitable fact. In the practice of interpretation courts take an outstanding position. They usually have an extraordinary impact on the development of the law due to the working of precedents (2.). The rise of the

[17] In this section, I draw on A v Bogdandy and I Venzke, 'In Whose Name? An Investigation of International Courts' Public Authority and its Democratic Justification' (2012) 23 *European Journal of International Law* 7–41.

[18] Self-understandings are seldom made explicit but are all the same nested in judicial hermeneutics and reasoning. Among the more outspoken instances, consider by way of example *Saipem S.p.A. v The People's Republic of Bangladesh*, ICSID Case No ARB/05/7, Award, 30 June 2009, paras 89–90.

[19] H Wehberg, *Das Problem eines internationalen Staatengerichtshofes* (München: Duncker & Humblot 1912), 11 ('Mehr Fortbildung des Völkerrechts durch internationale Entscheidungen!').

adjudicatory bodies within the GATT/WTO context provides a fitting example while it portrays a number of specific features (3.).

1. Historiography: Longing for international adjudication

The creation of a strong international judiciary was a central demand of various peace movements throughout the nineteenth century.[20] Also many progressive international lawyers pushed this goal. The Institut de Droit International, founded in Ghent in 1873, invested its efforts in promoting the development of international arbitration ever since its early beginnings and formulated draft procedures for international arbitration.[21] The International Law Association, founded in the same year, dedicated itself to the same project. At its very first meeting, it adopted a resolution confirming its conviction that arbitration is 'le moyen essentiellement juste, raisonnable, et même obligatoire, pour les nations, de terminer les différends internationaux'.[22] Similarly, the Interparliamentary Union, created in 1889, was committed to working towards the peaceful settlement of disputes and put together a 'Draft for the Organization of a Permanent Court of Arbitration' that would actually come to serve as a reference point in discussions at the First Hague Peace Conference of 1899.[23] In short, the development of the international judiciary at the beginning of the twentieth century is hard to imagine without the impulses of the peace movement and the political commitment of prominent international lawyers.

However, it was Tsar Nicholas II of Russia who, in 1898, surprised everyone with his invitation to an international conference that would pursue the goal of giving effect to the grand idea of world peace and making it triumph over all elements of strife and mischief.[24] At first the focus of the conference was supposed to lie on issues of disarmament. But as the conference drew nearer, the emphasis shifted towards international adjudication. The aim of disarmament, the argument went, could only be met if states did not resort to war when conflicts between them escalated but rather turned to judicial dispute settlement. Laying down the foundations for such a path towards the peaceful resolution of disputes then became the

[20] H Wehberg, *Die internationale Friedensbewegung*, Staatsbürgerbibliothek Heft 22, (Mönchengladbach: Volksvereins-Verlag 1911); H Lammasch, Die Lehre von der Schiedsgerichtsbarkeit in ihrem ganzen Umfange, in: F Stier-Somlo (ed), *Handbuch des Völkerrechts*, vol 5 (Stuttgart: Kohlhammer 1914), 36–7.

[21] Institut de Droit International, 'Projet de règlement pour la procédure arbitrale internationale', Session de La Haye, 1875, available at <http://www.idi-iil.org/idiF/resolutionsF/1875_haye_01_fr.pdf>.

[22] Quoted in C Denfeld, *Hans Wehberg (1885–1962). Die Organisation der Staatengemeinschaft* (Baden-Baden: Nomos 2008), 115.

[23] A H Fried, *Handbuch der Friedensbewegung* (Wien: Verlag der Österreichischen Friedensgesellschaft 1905), 262–5; R P Anand, *International Courts and Contemporary Conflicts* (New York: Asia Publishing House 1974), 27; J H Ralston, *International Arbitration from Athens to Locarno*, (Stanford, CA: Stanford University Press 1929), 140.

[24] Fried, *Friedensbewegung*, 163; J B Scott, *The Hague Peace Conferences of 1899 and 1907* (Baltimore: Johns Hopkins 1909), 736–7.

central task of the 1899 Peace Conference in The Hague. In spite of its sobering results, the conference entered the historiography of international adjudication as a milestone on the way towards a permanent international court.[25]

In the wake of the First Peace Conference, the project of international adjudication found considerable support within the US administration. Theodore Roosevelt and both of his ministers of state, John Hay and Elihu Root, were ardent supporters of judicial dispute settlement at the international level. Roosevelt also took the initiative that led to the Second Hague Peace Conference of 1907, even if he left the formal invitation to Tsar Nicholas II. In a few aspects the second conference surpassed the results of 1899, but it could not achieve the creation of a truly permanent international court. One of the main points of controversy related to the independence of the court and the election of its judges. European great powers argued that international dispute settlement is in essence part of the political domain and naturally unsuited for judicial resolution. They maintained that a strong political influence should also be felt in the judicial process.[26] In this vein, Friedrich von Martens, the chief Russian delegate to both Peace Conferences and arbitrator in very high demand in his time, argued that international arbitration was merely concerned with successfully disposing of a dispute. He was of the opinion that judicial reasoning is only of subordinate importance for this purpose.[27] On the contrary, Elihu Root placed his hopes on the logic of the law and relied on the pacifying tongue of legal argument. He drew a close analogy to the US Supreme Court and argued that only independent judges and their impartial resolution of conflicts could gain the confidence of the parties: 'What we need for the further development of arbitration is the substitution of judicial action for diplomatic action, the substitution of judicial sense of responsibility for diplomatic sense of responsibility.'[28]

Even though the project of a permanent court had suffered repeated setbacks, many international lawyers felt vindicated by the Hague Peace Conferences in their quest for international dispute resolution and continued to pursue this project with renewed vigour.[29] In Germany, for example, Hans Wehberg crafted a remarkable critique of case-specific arbitration that, in his view, was attached too closely to the logic of politics. It is indispensable, he maintained, that a permanent international

[25] D D Caron, 'War and International Adjudication: Reflections on the 1899 Peace Conference' (2000) 94 *American Journal of International Law* 4–30; Anand, *International Courts*, 33.

[26] P Zorn, *Die beiden Haager Friedenskonferenzen von 1899 und 1907* (Stuttgart: Kohlhammer 1914); cf. C H Brower II, 'The Functions and Limits of Arbitration and Judicial Settlement Under Private and Public International Law' (2008) 18 *Duke Journal of International and Comparative Law* 259–309.

[27] H Wehberg, 'Friedrich von Martens und die Haager Friedenskonferenzen' (1910) 20 *Zeitschrift für internationales Recht* 343–57.

[28] 'President on Peace', *New York Daily Tribune*, 16 April 1907, p 4.

[29] See for instance W Schücking (ed), *Das Werk vom Haag* (München: Duncker & Humblot 1912); W Schücking, Die Organisation der Welt, in: W v Calker (ed), *Staatsrechtliche Abhandlungen. Festgabe für Paul Laband zum 50. Jahrestage der Doktor-Promotion* (Tübingen: Mohr 1908), 533–617. Also see F Bodendiek, *Walther Schückings Konzeption der internationalen Ordnung. Dogmatische Strukturen und ideengeschichtliche Bedeutung* (Berlin: Duncker & Humblot 2001).

court be set up in order to prevent states from invoking violations of their legal rights as pretexts for war. Wehberg continued to argue that arbitral awards are wholly unsuited to achieve this effect because they cannot build on, nor contribute to, the clarity of the generally applicable law. Arbitration also typically fell short of standards of legal reasoning that were absolutely necessary for international adjudication to fulfil its promise. For Wehberg, the way towards world peace inevitably led via a permanent international court. When he enthusiastically demanded 'more development of international law by international decisions',[30] he offered a characteristic legitimatory narrative of international courts: international courts are the handmaidens of peace.

Aspirations to a permanent international court were finally met after the First World War when the Permanent International Court of Justice (PCIJ) was erected in 1920 within the new institutional framework of the League of Nations.[31] Many scholars and commentators cheerfully praised this as an epochal event.[32] James Brown Scott illustratively expressed his relief in the *American Journal of International Law*: 'We should . . . fall upon our knees and thank God that the hope of ages is in process of realization.'[33] Also Nicolas Politis welcomed the new court as 'l'avènement d'une ère nouvelle dans la civilisation mondiale'.[34]

A number of international lawyers on both sides of the Atlantic projected their hopes onto the young PCIJ and complemented its work with doctrinal, theoretical, and philosophical works. Manley O Hudson succeeded in developing a remarkable plan for an international order of peace that focused on a strong international judiciary. His monograph *Progress in International Organization* (1932) theoretically backed up and conceptually framed his programmatic article *The Permanent Court of International Justice—An Indispensable First Step* (1923).[35]

After some first and shy steps, the court seemed as if it might actually live up to high expectations. Hersch Lauterpacht could already look back on a rich body of case-law in his *The Development of International Law by the Permanent Court of International Justice* of 1934 and highlighted the lawmaking side of the court's judicial practice. Like Hudson, Lauterpacht maintained that judge-made law was an inevitable feature of every legally constituted community. There is no exception on the international level in this regard.[36] Unlike Hudson, however, he did not see

[30] Wehberg, *Staatengerichtshofes*, 11 ('Mehr Fortbildung des Völkerrechts durch internationale Entscheidungen!').

[31] On the regional level it was only predated by the Central American Court of Justice that lived for ten years starting in 1908.

[32] O Spiermann, *International Legal Argument in the Permanent Court of International Justice. The rise of the international judiciary* (Cambridge: Cambridge University Press 2005), 14–23.

[33] J B Scott, 'A Permanent Court of International Justice (Editorial Comment)' (1921) 15 *American Journal of International Law* 53–5, 55; M Koskenniemi, The Ideology of International Adjudication and the 1907 Hague Conference, in: Y Daudet (ed), *Topicality of the 1907 Hague Conference, the Second Peace Conference* (Leiden: Nijhoff 2008), 127–52.

[34] N Politis, *La justice internationale* (Paris: Hachette 1924), 182.

[35] M O Hudson, *Progress in International Organization* (Littleton: Rothman 1981 [1932]); M O Hudson, 'The Permanent Court of International Justice—An Indispensable First Step' (1923) 108 *American Academy of Political And Social Science, Annals* 188–92.

[36] H Lauterpacht, *The Development of International Law by the Permanent Court of International Justice* (London: Longmans Green 1934), chapter III.

the project of a strong international judiciary as part of a bigger package that would eventually also include a centralized international legislative body or even a kind of world government. It merits emphasis that Hudson and others pictured the centralization of the judiciary as a first step towards an international political order with a centralized legislative organ.[37] This latter approach was particularly dominant in Germany where Immanuel Kant's *Perpetual Peace* was dusted off and served as a theoretical foundation for blueprints of international order.[38]

A little later, it was Hans Kelsen who advanced the Kantian peace project with all his astonishing acuity. Kelsen saw no alternative to ensuring international peace by way of international law and universal compulsory international adjudication.[39] In his account, the continuous centralization of state powers and the institutional separation of legislation and law-application are part of the natural evolution of law. It is simply the tide of things, Kelsen observed, that law-application is centralized first and that the legislature lags behind.[40] In order to gain lasting international peace, states would have to obligatorily subject their differences to the compulsory jurisdiction of a permanent international court.[41] Kelsen developed this argument looking back at the ignominious demise of the League of Nations, boldly facing the Second World War, and looking ahead to the design of the post-war order. It had been the critical error in the construction of the League, he argued, that the Council and not the Permanent Court was the most powerful organ. Every decision in the Council had to be taken with unanimity and no member could thus be bound against its will. Only decision-making processes in international courts were not shackled by the principle of unanimity and the road to an international order in the service of peace therefore had to go via universal compulsory adjudication.[42] The lack of a functional legislature does not weigh against this path because the natural evolution of the law proceeds without a centralized legislative body—the law is a product of agreement and habits, themselves usually products of judicial practice.[43] As soon as a central and

[37] Koskenniemi, Ideology of International Adjudication.

[38] Bodendiek, *Walther Schückings*, 117 and 179–82. With regard to the peace movement, without explicit reference to Kant but very much in his style, see Fried, *Friedensbewegung*, 20–2. Compare, however, Lammasch, Schiedsgerichtsbarkeit, 37 (calling the references to Kant's project of perpetual peace 'mere decoration').

[39] J v Bernstorff, *Der Glaube an das universale Recht. Zur Völkerrechtstheorie Hans Kelsens und seiner Schüler* (Baden-Baden: Nomos 2001), 169; D Zolo, 'Hans Kelsen: International Peace through International Law' (1998) 9 *European Journal of International Law* 306–24.

[40] H Kelsen, *Law and Peace in International Relations* (Cambridge, MA: Harvard University Press 1942), 146–8; C Jabloner, 'Verrechtlichung und Rechtsdynamik' (1999) 54 *Zeitschrift für öffentliches Recht* 261–78.

[41] Kelsen, *Law and Peace*, 150.

[42] H Kelsen, 'International Peace-By Court or Government?' (1941) 46 *The American Journal of Sociology* 571–81.

[43] Kelsen, *Law and Peace*, 161–3.

universally competent international judiciary exists, it continuously develops the law in constant legal practice and adapts it to prevailing needs.[44]

A historiography of the international judiciary shows that the conception of international courts as actors in the development of the law has been a rather common theme in international legal thinking. José Alvarez observes that 'the notion that international judges are charged only with applying pre-existing law seems laughable'.[45] And yet, remnants of the bygone thought that any court's role lies in nothing other than the recognition of the law still overshadow courts agency to some extent.[46] The theoretical perspective on the practice of interpretation set out above endeavours to contrast this thinking with a focus on the politics of interpretation. Extending this perspective onto courts as actors in international legal discourse merits a special note of vindication.

2. Judicial decisions and precedents

No actor other than courts has succeeded to such a large degree in portraying its interpretations to stand unsoiled and above the dirty business of politics. Even if the metaphor describing judges as the 'bouche de la loi' no longer—if ever—directs the thought on what they actually do, the understanding is still ubiquitous that judges find the right decision in the individual case by looking at the relevant norms in the context of the legal system.[47] Max Weber, himself a lawyer and close companion of Georg Jellinek, one of the key figures in continental legal thinking, wrote that case-law shows what is valid law in a way that follows compelling logical deduction or that is bound by conventional schemata of judicial thinking.[48] Most certainly, few courts would contradict this view on their practice but might rather be inclined to do everything to sustain it. What is more, this understanding forms an intricate part of a prevailing and self-reinforcing judicial ethos: judges apply the law, the law is the source of their authority, and whenever the perception grows that this is not what they are doing, they face critique. Also the rules of legal discourse might convey the premise that judges can and hopefully do find the law. The law is the reference

[44] H Kelsen, 'Compulsory Ajudication of International Disputes' (1943) 37 *American Journal of International Law* 397–406.

[45] J E Alvarez, *International Organizations as Law-Makers* (Oxford: Oxford University Press 2005), 523.

[46] On persistent myths in the field of adjudication see in detail I Venzke, 'The Role of International Courts as Interpreters and Developers of the Law: Working out the Jurisgenerative Practice of Interpretation' (2012) 34 *Loyola of Los Angeles International and Comparative Law Review* 119–51.

[47] J Lege, Was Juristen wiklich tun. Jurisprudential Realism, in: W Brugger, U Neumann, and S Kirste (eds), *Rechtsphilosophie im 21. Jahrhundert* (Frankfurt am Main: Suhrkamp 2008), 207–33, 216; R Christensen and H Kudlich, *Theorie richterlichen Begründens* (Berlin: Duncker und Humblot 2001), 26.

[48] M Weber, Wissenschaft als Beruf (1917/19), in: H Baier (ed), *Max Weber Gesamtausgabe*, vol 17 (Tübingen: Mohr Siebeck 1992), 95 ('die Jurisprudenz . . . stellt fest, was nach den Regeln des teils zwingend logisch, teils durch konventionell gegebene Schemata gebundenen, juristischen Denkens gilt.'). Cf. A. Somek, 'The Indelible Science of Law' (2009) 7 *International Journal of Constitutional Law* 424–41, 440.

point for all contestants and the judges must justify their decision by reference to the existing law.[49] In prototypical fashion, the ICJ stressed that 'the Court, as a court of law, cannot render judgment *sub specie legis ferendae*, or anticipate the law before the legislator has laid it down'.[50] On the later occasion of its *Nuclear Weapons* Advisory Opinion it reiterated that it 'cannot legislate, and, in the circumstances of the present case, it is not called upon to do so. Rather its task is to engage in its normal judicial function of ascertaining the existence or otherwise of legal principles and rules applicable to the threat or use of nuclear weapons.'[51] In short, the self-portrait of the judiciary as an institution for finding the right meaning of the law does inform the understanding of what it actually does.[52]

The persistence of this understanding is surprising, not only because of ages of realist critique, but also because ever since Kant's *Critique* it has no longer been possible to claim that decisions in concrete situations can be deduced from abstract concepts.[53] Since the end of the nineteenth century, legal theory has wrestled with the repercussions of this thought.[54] It is Hans Kelsen's neo-Kantian critique that stands out in formulating the consequences in this regard. The linguistic turn and the advancement of semantic pragmatism later further corroborate the point: there is no escaping interpretation and interpretations take part in the construction of meaning.[55]

The law-creative side of courts' decisions has two closely intertwined dimensions. One centres on the particular case and on lawmaking in the dispute between the parties.[56] This is reflected in the doctrine of *res judicata*, the law spoken in the individual case and binding only between the immediate parties.[57] The other

[49] In a theoretically solid fashion, however, a defence of a deductive mode of reasoning cannot build on an elusive belief in the determinative content of abstract concepts but would instead be based on the need for justification and for providing prerequisites of meaningful critique. In other words, judicial reasoning is concerned with *justifying* a decision and not with *finding* it. On 'the reasons for reasons' see v Bogdandy and Venzke, 'In Whose Name?', 15–16. Cf. U Neumann, Theorie der juristischen Argumentation, in: W Brugger, U Neumann, and S Kirste (eds), *Rechtsphilosophie im 21. Jahrhundert* (Frankfurt am Main: Suhrkamp 2008), 233–60.

[50] *Fisheries Jurisdiction (Great Britain and Northern Ireland v Iceland)*, Judgment of 25 July 1974, (1974) ICJ Reports 3, para 53.

[51] *Legality of the Threat or Use of Nuclear Weapons*, Advisory Opinion of 8 July 1996, ICJ Reports 226, para 18.

[52] P Bourdieu, 'The Force of Law: Toward a Sociology of the Juridical Field' (1987) 38 *Hastings Law Journal* 814–53, 820; N Luhmann, *Legitimation durch Verfahren* (Frankfurt am Main: Suhrkamp 1983), 16; N Luhmann, *Das Recht der Gesellschaft* (Frankfurt am Main: Suhrkamp 1993), 308.

[53] I Kant, *Kritik der Reinen Vernunft* (Frankfurt am Main: Suhrkamp 1974 [1781]), 183–94 (A 131–48); cf. M Koskenniemi, 'Constitutionalism as Mindset: Reflections on Kantian Themes About International Law and Globalization' (2007) 8 *Theoretical Inquiries in Law* 9–36.

[54] J Habermas, *Faktizität und Geltung* (Frankfurt am Main: Suhrkamp 1992), 238–72; also see R Ogorek, *Richterkönig oder Subsumtionsautomat?* (Frankfurt am Main: Klostermann 1986) (for a detailed recollection of how this thought has been dealt with).

[55] See in detail above Chapter II, sections A.3 and B.

[56] F Müller, Richterrecht—rechtstheoretisch formuliert, in: *Richterliche Rechtsfortbildung, Festschrift der Juristischen Fakultät der Universität Heidelberg* (Heidelberg: 1986), 65–84, 78–9.

[57] I Scobbie, 'Res Judicata, Precedent, and the International Court: A Preliminary Sketch' (1999) 20 *Australian Yearbook of International Law* 299–318.

dimension goes beyond the individual dispute.[58] A judicial judgment, the decision as well as its justification, may amount to an important argument in subsequent legal practice.[59] Courts that publish their decisions and justifications also engage in broader processes of legal discourse—both with the decision's justification (*ratio decidendi*) as well as with everything said on the side (*obiter dictum*).[60] Many judgments even appear to be candidly geared towards providing an authoritative reference point for future discourse by crafting general and abstract formulations.

To be sure, categorically marking the lawmaking momentum vested in the justification of legal decisions as an undue expansion of competences and as a usurpation of power by politicized courts would be plainly short-sighted. Judicial lawmaking is a quite inevitable part of adjudication and justifying a decision is even a legal requirement.[61] The alternative, refraining from justifying decisions or from making them public, might possibly weaken the jurisgenerative dimension of adjudicatory practice. But it would be tantamount to a Pyrrhic victory. The larger legal discourse could then no longer function as a mechanism of control and critique. Also legal certainty would be sacrificed. The reasoning that carries legal decisions is part of judicial legitimation and very different legal theories share the understanding that the stabilization of normative expectations is a chief function of the law.[62] An international court that neglects this function falls short of one of its central tasks. Judicial lawmaking then is not a sort of nuisance resulting from a dysfunction but quite to the contrary part of the normal business of courts.

International courts are particularly influential actors in the practice of interpretation because of the operation of their decisions as precedents. Precedents play a key role in how international courts develop the law and generate legal normativity. Of course doctrine strikes a different tone—it is a trite commonplace that international law knows no *stare decisis* rule, that judgments are binding only *inter partes*,[63] and that Art. 38(1)(d) ICJ Statute mentions judicial decisions only as subsidiary

[58] v Bogdandy and Venzke, 'Beyond Dispute?'.

[59] Christensen and Kudlich, *Theorie richterlichen Begründens*; C Kirchner, Zur konsequentialistischen Interpretationsmethode, in: T Eger, J Bigus, C Ott, and G v Wangenheim (eds), *Internationalisierung des Rechts und seine ökonomische Analyse* (Wiesbaden: Gabler 2008), 37–49, 39.

[60] M Jacob, 'Precedents: Lawmaking Through International Adjudication' (2011) 12 *German Law Journal* 1005–32. Cf. M Shahabuddeen, *Precedent in the World Court* (Cambridge: Cambridge University Press 1996), 76–83; S W Schill, *The Multilateralization of International Investment Law* (Cambridge: Cambridge University Press 2009), 321–61; A Höland, 'Wie wirkt Rechtsprechung?' (2009) 30 *Zeitschrift für Rechtssoziologie* 23–46 (offering an account of precedents in the German and European legal systems).

[61] See, e.g., Art. 56(1) ICJ Statute. Cf. A Ross, *Theorie der Rechtsquellen* (Leipzig: Deuticke 1929), 283; M Kriele, *Theorie der Rechtsgewinnung. Entwickelt am Problem der Verfassungsinterpretation* (Berlin: Duncker & Humblot 1976), 167–71.

[62] Habermas, *Faktizität und Geltung*, 516; Luhmann, *Recht der Gesellschaft*, 151. Cf. A v Bogdandy and I Venzke, 'On the Democratic Legitimation of International Judicial Lawmaking' (2011) 12 *German Law Journal* 1341–70, 1344–9.

[63] R Bernhardt, Article 59, in: A Zimmermann, C Tomuschat, and K Oellers-Frahm (eds), *The Statute of the International Court of Justice: A Commentary* (Oxford: Oxford University Press 2006), 1231–51.

means of interpretation, as a *Rechtserkenntnisquelle* (source for recognizing the law) and not a *Rechtsquelle* (a source of law). Good reasons may speak in favour of this distinction in doctrine, but it does overshadow the actual workings of precedents. As a matter of fact, in many judgments precedents amount to influential arguments and actors in legal interpretation wrangle about the meaning of previous decisions just as they fight about the meaning of treaty texts. In most practical circumstances, interpreters cannot escape the discussion of case-law. Judicial decisions significantly redistribute argumentative burdens and courts are expected to decide consistently or, if they deviate from precious jurisprudence, to give reasons for why that is.[64] It is another matter that international courts frequently do not live up to these expectations. There is both a force as a matter of fact as well as an attitude that interpretation should relate to relevant earlier decisions. The working of precedents underlies international courts' remarkably strong semantic authority in international legal discourse.[65]

Courts have continuously and for a long time stressed the significance of precedents and have thus contributed to their authority. Already in the *Mavrommatis* case the PCIJ found that it had 'no reason to depart from a construction which clearly flows from the previous judgments the reasoning of which it still regards as sound'.[66] In his thorough analysis of the PCIJ, Ole Spiermann has shown that the court portrayed an increasing inclination to actively engage in the development of international law—the working of precedents was crucial in this endeavour.[67] The semantic authority of international judicial institutions and international judicial lawmaking are thus certainly not new phenomenona, but they have lately gained increasing magnitude.

3. The GATT/WTO context

Adjudication displays a number of particular features in the context of the GATT/WTO. The institutional development of this context is a superb illustration of institutional growth (or mission creep) that connects to the preceding chapter on the agency of international organizations. Its story has been told many times: after the Second World War it was evident that economic recovery would only be possible with a novel expansion of international trade, the prospects of which

[64] G Abi-Saab, Les sources du droit international: Essai de déconstruction, in: M Rama-Montaldo (ed), *El derecho internacional en un mundo en transformación. Liber amicorum en homenaje al Profesor Eduardo Jiménez de Aréchaga*, vol 1 (Montevideo: Fundación de Cultura Universitaria 1994), 29–49; A E Boyle and C M Chinkin, *The Making of International Law* (Oxford: Oxford University Press 2007), 267.

[65] Cf. R M Cover, 'Violence and the Word' (1986) 95 *Yale Law Journal* 1601–30 (submitting with a challenging and problematic drasticity that judges are murderers because they kill alternative meanings); Jacob, 'Precedents' (on the working of precedents more generally).

[66] *Case of Readaptation of the Mavrommatis Jerusalem Concessions*, Jurisdiction, 10 October 1927, PCIJ Series A, No 11, para 43. Cf. Shahabuddeen, *Precedent*, 16–29.

[67] Spiermann, *Permanent Court of International Justice*, 394.

were hampered by outstandingly high tariffs and by a tight network of quantitative restrictions, or quotas. To overcome these trade barriers, governments, partly driven by the United States and the United Kingdom, negotiated the GATT—a multilateral trade agreement whose basic idea it was to centre all foreign trade policies on tariffs, to control all other forms of non-tariff barriers to trade, and to then successively lower tariffs in continuous negotiations that would lead to legally binding commitments on tariff rates for each country, drawn together in the schedules of concessions. The GATT was meant to form part of an International Trade Organization (ITO) that never came into existence and until 1995 the GATT of 1947 was applied provisionally.[68]

The GATT only contains vague dispute settlement procedures. By and large, Art. XXIII on nullification and impairment indicates that a member, whose benefits under the agreement might be impaired or nullified, consults with the member(s) in question and, should this not lead to satisfactory results, refers the matter to the contracting parties. The member whose benefits are found to be impaired or nullified may withdraw equivalent concessions. The mechanism thus rests on reciprocity. Its procedure resorts to consultation and hinges on negotiation—a long way from anything that resembles court-like proceedings. In Robert Hudec's fitting words, '[i]t was a diplomat's legal order. At least, that is the way it started out.'[69] After all, the GATT was to be institutionally embedded within the ITO, only that the ITO never came about.

Over the years, the GATT developed features that made it look and work very much like any other international organization in spite of its defects at birth. The GATT secretariat took a crucial role in this development, in particular with regard to the dispute settlement mechanism. At its inception, the GATT was run and characterized by the same diplomats who had negotiated the GATT, they represented the parties, and also staffed the small secretariat. On their own initiative, they developed the now well-known panel procedure for dealing with disputes, which has since advanced to be one of trade law's flagships. A legal dispute is referred to a panel of three or five independent panellists, usually GATT delegates from neutral countries selected by the parties or the secretariat. The panel deals with competing claims in written and oral submissions, deliberates *in camera*, usually receives advice from the GATT secretariat, and renders a report containing a justified legal decision on the matters under dispute. This report is itself without

[68] R Hudec, *Enforcing International Trade Law. The Evolution of the Modern GATT Legal System* (Salem, NH: Butterworth Legal Publishers 1993), 4–5; J H Jackson, *The World Trade Organization: Constitution and Jurisprudence* (London: Royal Institute of International Affairs 1998), 16–18; P v d Bossche, *The Law and Policy of the World Trade Organization* (Cambridge: Cambridge University Press 2008), 78–81. It should be noted, however, that the GATT of 1947 was modified with the Final Act of the Uruguay Round in 1994. The changes are not of concern for the present purposes.

[69] Hudec, *International Trade Law*, 7. In detail also see R Hudec, 'The GATT Legal System: A Diplomat's Jurisprudence' (1970) 4 *Journal of World Trade* 615; J H Jackson, 'The Case of the World Trade Organization' (2008) 84 *International Affairs* 437–54 (speaking of a transition from negotiation or a diplomacy-oriented approach towards a rules-oriented approach).

binding force and may be adopted, or not, by the Council made up of all contracting parties.

There has been considerable development in each of these steps. Most importantly, consensus decisions were necessary at decisive points in the process, meaning that every member, including any disputing party, could block the process from moving on—a requirement that has gradually eroded.[70] Most significantly, the process, once dominated by GATT diplomats and trade experts, has increasingly come under the influence of trained lawyers. With this shift in personnel, the characteristic reasoning also moved towards judicial technique.[71] The creation of a legal division within the GATT secretariat in the early 1980s is of great importance in this regard and has had a lasting impact on the adjudicating bodies. Starting in the mid-1980s it would regularly draft panel reports, work towards consistency, and contribute to a legal mode of dispute settlement.[72] Institutional growth in the GATT thus largely equalled a more professionally legal mode of working with disputes.[73]

With the Marrakesh Agreement setting up the WTO in 1995, the new appeal mechanism in adjudication would come with a most crucial shift in patterns of reasoning. Suffice it for now to point out that the Appellate Body (AB) has had an immense impact on the practice of interpretation in international trade law.[74] Three aspects stand out. First, the Appellate Body as an institution as well as the work of its individual members has further buttressed the transformation of discourse within the GATT/WTO context towards a legal mode of argument. One of the principal manifestations is, second, how the new adjudicators have embraced the VCLT in their first decisions as the rules of the game. Third, the appellate mechanism has critically fostered the impact of precedents in the practice of interpretation. The weight the AB explicitly attaches to its previous reports almost makes a mockery out of suggestions that reports have no legal effects beyond the parties to the dispute. The systemic impact of adjudication upon trade law in general has thus come to be commonly recognized among relevant actors. In the discussion of one of the first AB reports in the Dispute Settlement Body, the minutes of the meeting record the words of the Brazilian representative:

[70] W Benedek, *Die Rechtsordnung des GATT aus völkerrechtlicher Sicht* (Graz: Springer 1990), 232–6; Hudec, *International Trade Law*, 9.

[71] M Nettesheim, 'Von der Verhandlungsdiplomatie zur internationalen Wirtschaftsordnung: Zur Entwicklung des internationalen Wirtschaftsrechts' (2000) 19 *Jahrbuch für Neue Politische Ökonomie* 48–76; J H H Weiler, 'The Rule of Lawyers and the Ethos of Diplomats. Reflections on the Internal and External Legitimacy of WTO Dispute Settlement' (2001) 35 *Journal of World Trade* 191–207; R Howse, 'From Politics to Technocracy—and Back Again: The Fate of the Multilateral Trading Regime' (2002) 96 *American Journal of International Law* 94–117.

[72] E-U Petersmann, *The GATT/WTO Dispute Settlement System: International Law, International Organizations and Dispute Settlement* (London: Kluwer 1997), 85.

[73] Nettesheim, 'Verhandlungsdiplomatie', 54–6 (treating both phenomena under the heading of institutionalization).

[74] Cf. below section C.

> [i]t was well-known that in practice any decision of a panel or the Appellate Body with regard to a specific case would go beyond such a specific case. Although no binding precedents had been created, the findings and conclusions of panels and the Appellate Body adopted by the DSB had created expectations concerning future interpretations of the DSU and the WTO Agreement. Therefore, in light of these systemic implications of decisions and recommendations pertaining to a specific case, Brazil wished to state its position with regard to certain findings of the Appellate Body.[75]

In sum, over the course of institutional development within the GATT/WTO the body of jurisprudence has gained an increasing momentum. I shall now turn to the more detailed analysis of semantic change in Art. XX GATT. For this purpose, it is helpful to place general exceptions into their context within the GATT and to elaborate in little more detail what stirs up semantic disputes on this matter.

B. Article XX in the era of the GATT

1. General exceptions: A general prologue

Public policy considerations such as the protection of human, animal, or plant life have long served as the rationale and justification for trade restrictive policies.[76] In 1906 state representatives met in Berne in order to prohibit the international trading of matches produced with and containing poisonous white phosphorus. Countries that had taken the lead in banning white phosphorus in their production processes pushed for a far-reaching import ban. Their industries had already moved to more costly alternative substances and now suffered a disadvantage in price competition.[77] The mixture between trade objectives and other concerns like workers' health protection is easy to see in this example: the ban on white phosphorus was pushed with reference to health concerns by those who also sought to level out competitive disadvantages.[78] A treaty of 1911 on seal hunting serves as another case in point. It obliged its members to prohibit the importation of sealskins produced in violation of that treaty.[79] There are numerous further examples of trade restrictions aimed at public concerns like health or environmental protection. Before the rise of free trade agreements, however, the trade implications of such policies did not usually give rise to knotty legal questions.

[75] Dispute Settlement Body, Minutes of the Meeting held on 6 November 1998, WT/DSB/M/50, p 12 (the meeting concerned the adoption of the Appellate Body Report in *United States—Shrimp*).

[76] In the following sections I specifically draw on I Venzke, 'Making General Exceptions: The Spell of Precedents in Developing Art. XX into Standards for Domestic Regulatory Policy' (2011) 12 *German Law Journal* 1111–40.

[77] S Charnovitz, 'Exploring the Environmental Exceptions in GATT Article XX' (1991) 25 *Journal of World Trade* 37–55, 39; B E Lowe, *The International Protection of Labor* (New York: Macmillan 1921), 142–4.

[78] Ibid.

[79] Charnovitz, 'Environmental Exception', 39. An issue that has not faded, see *EC—Seal Products I*, DS400 & 401, panels established on 25 March and 21 April 2011 respectively.

The first significant attempt at a multilateral trade agreement was taken within the framework of the League of Nations in 1927. The International Convention for the Abolition of Import and Export Prohibitions and Restrictions aimed high, tried to abolish quantitative restrictions, and sought to reduce tariffs within six months.[80] According to Art. 5, 'vital interests' should still be protected. The Convention never took off, not least due to the heavy burdens of the economic downturn of the late 1920s, which proffered protectionism as the nearby answer to boarding economic problems.[81] Notably, the League's Economic Committee observed that there had been a long-established international practice on public policy exceptions, which are regarded as indispensable and as not contravening the aims of free trade.[82] The 1927 Convention made an important qualification in this regard and specified that exceptions should 'not be applied in a manner as to constitute a means of arbitrary discrimination between foreign countries where the same conditions prevail, or a disguised restriction on international trade' (Art. 4). This wording made its way through a number of negotiations into the 1947 General Agreement on Tariffs and Trade (GATT).[83]

Article XX GATT reads:

> Subject to the requirement that such measures are not applied in a manner which would constitute a means of arbitrary or unjustifiable discrimination between countries where the same conditions prevail, or a disguised restriction on international trade, nothing in this Agreement shall be construed to prevent the adoption or enforcement by any contracting party of measures:
>
> (a) necessary to protect public morals;
> (b) necessary to protect human, animal or plant life or health; . . .
> (d) necessary to secure compliance with laws or regulations which are not inconsistent with the provisions of this Agreement, including those relating to customs enforcement, the enforcement of monopolies operated under paragraph 4 of Article II and Article XVII, the protection of patents, trade marks and copyrights, and the prevention of deceptive practices; . . .
> (g) relating to the conservation of exhaustible natural resources if such measures are made effective in conjunction with restrictions on domestic production or consumption; . . . .

This article on general exceptions stands in close relationship with other GATT provisions, above all those giving expression to the principle of non-discrimination.

80 Convention for the Abolition of Import and Export Prohibitions and Restrictions, 8 November 1927, reproduced in (1931) 25 *American Journal of International Law*, Supplement: Official Documents, 121–45.

81 D A Irwin, P C Mavroidis and A O Sykes, *The Genesis of the GATT* (Cambridge: Cambridge University Press 2008), 5.

82 Charnovitz, 'Environmental Exceptions', 41, quoting League Doc C.E.I, 222, p 21.

83 Irwin, Mavroidis, and Sykes, *Genesis*, 162–4; P Ala'i, 'Free Trade or Sustainable Development? An Analysis of the WTO Appellate Body's Shift to a More Balanced Approach to Trade Liberalization' (1998) 14 *American University International Law Review* 1129–71, 1132–6.

The necessary basics are that Art. XX comes into play in practice as a justification of trade restrictions that would otherwise amount to a violation of the GATT. Measures that come under Art. XX normally aim at non-trade objectives and need justification because they conflict with the general prohibition of quantitative restrictions (Art. XI), with the prohibition of discrimination between like products whose imports are still restricted in quantitative terms (Art. XIII), or where the measures conflict with the obligation to provide national treatment with regard to internal taxation and regulation (Art. III).[84] For Art. XX to become relevant there needs to be an inconsistency in the first place. While there is room for considering a policy's aim already at this stage of the legal analysis (with the possible effect of finding that there is no violation),[85] trade restrictive measures that aim at other public policy considerations are typically found to be in prima facie violation of the GATT and are accordingly addressed under Art. XX. Before turning to the analysis of developments in Art. XX, the interpretation of Art. III is key and a place of no less interesting semantic struggles.

Article III reads:

1. The contracting parties recognize that internal taxes and other internal charges, and laws, regulations and requirements affecting the internal sale, offering for sale, purchase, transportation, distribution or use of products, and internal quantitative regulations requiring the mixture, processing or use of products in specified amounts or proportions, should not be applied to imported or domestic products so as to afford protection to domestic production.
2. The products of the territory of any contracting party imported into the territory of any other contracting party shall not be subject, directly or indirectly, to internal taxes or other internal charges of any kind in excess of those applied, directly or indirectly, to like domestic products. Moreover, no contracting party shall otherwise apply internal taxes or other internal charges to imported or domestic products in a manner contrary to the principles set forth in paragraph 1.

...

4. The products of the territory of any contracting party imported into the territory of any other contracting party shall be accorded treatment no less favourable than that accorded to like products of national origin in respect of all laws, regulations and requirements affecting their internal sale, offering for sale, purchase, transportation, distribution or use. The provisions of this paragraph shall not prevent the application of differential internal transportation charges which are based exclusively on the economic operation of the means of transport and not on the nationality of the product.

[84] J H H Weiler, Law, Culture, and Values in the WTO—Gazing into the Crystal Ball, in: D L Bethlehem, D RcRae, R Neufeld, and I Van Damme (eds), *The Oxford Handbook of International Trade Law* (Oxford: Oxford University Press 2009), 749–72, 758.

[85] I have deliberately tried to leave aside the considerable jurisprudence and commentary on the well-known intricacies in determining 'likeness' as much as the subject permits.

And *ad* Art. III(2) (part of Annex I GATT) explains that

> [a] tax conforming to the requirements of the first sentence of paragraph 2 would be considered to be inconsistent with the provisions of the second sentence only in cases where competition was involved between, on the one hand, the taxed product and, on the other hand, a directly competitive or substitutable product which was not similarly taxed.

Determining whether a policy is in breach of Art. III inescapably runs into some complex and fundamental discussions of trade law, including the meaning of 'like product' and of 'so as to afford protection'. Joseph Weiler pertinently observed that 'the material and conceptual contours of the discipline of national treatment not only remain contested but are, par excellence, the creature of legal discourse'. He goes on to note that they are 'the most telling examples of the law of the WTO as reflecting and constituting the deepest ontological issues of the system'.[86]

For the present context and with regard to the intersection of trade objectives with other public policy considerations, it is helpful to point out that a policy's aim may be considered at three stages in the legal analysis.[87] It may first come into play in the comparison of imported products with domestic products—in the determination of whether the products are like or whether they are directly competitive or substitutable products.[88] A first thing to note is that the meaning of 'like' can plausibly differ within the GATT and also within Art. III itself.[89] The interpretation of Art. III in the GATT era then shows that already in the comparison of the imported with the domestic products the 'aim and effect' of the policy under scrutiny could be considered.[90] A difference in treatment between two products that share very similar characteristics as well as similar attributes on the market could not amount to discrimination in the sense of the national treatment rule because the difference in treatment did not aim to provide an advantage for domestic products. The Appellate Body later clearly rejected the view that intent may indicate whether products are like and common wisdom at present holds that

[86] Weiler, Crystal Ball, 758.

[87] Ibid., at 765–6; J Wouters and B De Meester, *The World Trade Organization. A Legal and Institutional Analysis* (Antwerp: Intersentia 2007), 52–4.

[88] For illustrative and illuminating contributions in the plethora of scholarly literature on the issue of 'likeness' in this regard see D K Tarullo, 'Logic, Myth, and the International Economic Order' (1985) 26 *Harvard International Law Journal* 533–52; R Howse and D Regan, 'The Product/Process Distinction—An Illusory Basis for Disciplining "Unilateralism" in Trade Policy' (2000) 11 *European Journal of International Law* 249–89; H Horn and J H H Weiler, 'EC–Asbestos European Communities—Measures Affecting Asbestos and Asbestos-Containing Products' (2004) 3 *World Trade Review* 129–51.

[89] It is easy to see that this could not be otherwise because then a contracting party could transform a tax measure into internal regulations in order to come under a more lenient standard, Appellate Body Report, *European Communities—Measures Affecting Asbestos and Products Containing Asbestos*, WT/DS135/AB/R, 12 March 2001, para 99.

[90] GATT Panel Report, *United States—Taxes on Petroleum and Certain Imported Substances*, L/6175, adopted 17 June 1987, BISD 34S/136, para 5.1.9; GATT Panel Report, *United States—Measures Affecting Alcoholic and Malt Beverages*, DS23/R, adopted 19 June 1992, BISD 39S/206, para 5.74. See the seminal piece by R Hudec, 'GATT/WTO Constraints on National Regulation. Requiem for an "Aim and Effects" Test' (1998) 32 *International Lawyer* 619–49.

two products' likeness is to be determined in the market place by the use of a number of indicators.[91] Aim and effect no longer seem to matter in determining 'likeness'. But there still appears to be much room for contesting this position. The best help for this comes from the Appellate Body itself; namely, from its report in *EC—Asbestos* where it reversed the panel's interpretation that France's import ban on asbestos and products containing asbestos violates the national treatment requirement of Art. III(4). It held that asbestos, and products containing asbestos, and the closest substitute, cellulose and glass fibres, are unlike products. It did so by placing emphasis on the 'well-known, life-threatening, health risks posed by asbestos fibres', thus silently suggesting that the bygone aim and effect test could render products unlike.[92] But ultimately the Appellate Body tied the test of likeness again back to the market place, i.e. to consumers' tastes and habits.[93] Thus even if in the end the comparison of the two products' market behaviour was decisive for determining likeness, the Appellate Body's reasoning goes in the direction of contemplating a regulation's objective in examining the relationship between two products.

At this point it is worth mentioning that it also remains questionable whether a differentiation can in principle only be based on physical characteristics of the product or if it can also extend to the product's production and process method (PPM). This issue has drawn great attention ever since the *Tuna—Dolphin I* panel held 'that Article III covers only measures affecting products *as such*'.[94] According to this interpretation, only differences that leave their mark on a certain product may render it unlike another. Differences in the PPMs alone, e.g. in tuna fishing techniques would not suffice. This has been affirmed in *Tuna—Dolphin II* and in most cases thereafter, certainly not without heavy critique.[95] In the WTO era, the Appellate Body has so far left the issue open. Some have advocated that integrating public policy considerations at this point of the legal analysis rather than another might be an elegant and preferable solution.[96] The WTO secretariat also appears to

[91] Appellate Body Report, *Japan—Taxes on Alcoholic Beverages*, WT/DS8, 10 & 11/AB/R, 4 October 1996, pp 18–19; cf. H Horn and P C Mavroidis, 'Still Hazy after All These Years: The Interpretation of National Treatment in the GATT/WTO Case-law on Tax Discrimination' (2004) 15 *European Journal of International Law* 39–69.

[92] Appellate Body Report, *European Communities—Measures Affecting Asbestos and Products Containing Asbestos*, WT/DS135/AB/R, 12 March 2001, para 172.

[93] Ibid., at, para 130. In this report the Appellate Body also noted that determination of likeness needs to take place on a case-by-case basis thus leaving ample room for manoeuvre (at paras 101–102); cf. Appellate Body Report, *Japan—Taxes on Alcoholic Beverages*, WT/DS8, 10 & 11/AB/R, 4 October 1996, p 21.

[94] GATT Panel Report, *United States—Restrictions on Imports of Tuna*, DS21/R, 3 September 1991, unadopted, BISD 39S/155, para 5.11 (italics added).

[95] *United States—Restrictions on Imports of Tuna*, DS29/R, 16 June 1994, unadopted, para 5.8; S Charnovitz, 'The Law of Environmental "PPMs" in the WTO: Debunking the Myth of Illegality' (2002) 27 *Yale Journal of International Law* 59–110; Howse and Regan, 'Product/Process Distinction'.

[96] Weiler, Crystal Ball, 766–72.

suggest that this might be a good way to go in its Report on Trade and Climate Change, a joint product with the UNEP secretariat. In its view, for example, border tax adjustments for otherwise identical products might not be considered discriminatory if they relate to the carbon emissions accumulated during production processes.[97]

This first stage in the legal analysis at which public policy considerations may come into play (in the determination of likeness) is closely intertwined with a second step in which a policy's aim may be taken into account: the analysis of products' treatment and whether they are treated differently 'so as to afford protection' as it is spelled out in Art. III(1). Controversies not only turn on this qualification's meaning but also on its status for the interpretation of the other paragraphs—only *ad* Art. III(2) links the second paragraph's second sentence directly to the first paragraph. It is most interesting to see that in *Japan—Alcoholic Beverages II* the US had in all matters of practical consequence won the case and yet appealed the panel decision because it did not agree with the panel's reasoning on this issue.[98] The appeal in this case may well be seen as yet another straightforward recognition of the fact that judicial decisions and their reasoning have repercussions beyond the individual case. The US criticized the panel's isolated treatment of Art. III(2) and maintained that the first paragraph is an integral part of the context and must inform the reading of the second paragraph as well. Therefore, the US continued to argue, the panel erred in determining 'likeness' purely on the basis of physical characteristics and in not considering the policy under scrutiny (the Japanese tax scheme on alcoholic beverages). The US complained that the panel did not explore whether Japan really discriminated so as to afford protection.[99]

The argument developed by the US mingles the first and second steps. The question is clear nevertheless: does the intention behind the regulation matter in the analysis of legality under Art. III? The Appellate Body said that it does not, in a way. It starts out its examination of 'so as to afford protection' with the blunt statement that '[t]his is not an issue of intent'.[100] And yet, it continues to argue that Art. III compels a 'comprehensive and objective analysis of the structure and application of the measure in question on domestic as compared to imported products' and that it is thus possible to 'examine objectively the underlying criteria' even though the 'aim of a measure may not be easily ascertained'.[101] This does seem to come close to an objective test to *infer* the regulator's intention.[102] A finding of dissimilar treatment of like products would then be a necessary but not sufficient

[97] WTO-UNEP Report, Trade and Climate Change (2009), 107.

[98] Appellate Body Report, *Japan—Alcoholic Beverages II*, WT/DS8, 10 & 11/AB/R, pp 4–6.

[99] Ibid., at pp 4–5.

[100] Ibid., at p 27.

[101] Ibid., at p 29.

[102] Horn and Mavroidis, 'Still Hazy', also see Panel Report, *Mexico—Taxes on Soft Drinks*, WT/DS308/R, 7 October 2005, para 8.91 (noting that 'the declared intention of legislators and regulators of a Member adopting the measure should not be totally disregarded').

condition for discrimination. A determination of (il)legality would still hinge on whether it is applied 'so as to afford protection to domestic products'.[103]

If the aim of a measure could not be brought into legal consideration either in the determination of the relationship between two products (their 'likeness' or that they are directly competitive and substitutable) or in the qualification of 'so as to afford protection', it might finally come into play in the third step: the analysis of a justification by way of general exceptions of Art. XX. This has come to be the place where competing aims, trade objectives, and other public policy considerations, are usually dealt with. Having placed Art. XX into its legal context, I will also briefly place it in its broader social context which explains why the interpretation of Art. XX has come to be an issue and why it had remained dormant for some time.

Potential conflicts between trade and other policy considerations have for some time slumbered beneath an agreed upon borderline separating normal trade policies from policies that struck everyone as unjustified and abnormal—an understanding that John Ruggie famously termed 'embedded liberalism'.[104] Trade liberalization would be embedded in the usual working of the interventionist welfare state and this context would provide the preconditions for GATT experts to follow a narrow focus on trade liberalization. At the end of the day, the argument went, everybody would be better off and issues of redistribution would be managed by the welfare state.[105] Within the group of GATT trade experts, shared understandings of an embedded liberalism were transformed into an economic free trade ideology that became increasingly detached from the preconditions under which its arguments did actually work.[106] With the political shift towards deregulatory economic policy at the end of the 1970s, spearheaded by Ronald Reagan and Margaret Thatcher, the consensus among the contracting parties over what was appropriate intervention in contrast to an illegitimate barrier to free trade broke away and GATT disputes mounted.[107]

As a general thread, GATT panels sought to argue along lines drawn in the past and manifestly wished to isolate trade objectives from other policy concerns. While the number of disputes surged, the old ethos of GATT trade experts and an *esprit de corps* retained its grasp on the interpretation of the law. Robert Howse observes that 'one of the crucial functions of the insider network was to maintain continuity of

[103] Appellate Body Report, *Japan—Alcoholic Beverages II*, WT/DS8, 10 & 11/AB/R, pp 30–1.

[104] J G Ruggie, 'International Regimes, Transactions, and Change: Embedded Liberalism in the Postwar Economic Order' (1982) 36 *International Organization* 379–415. Also see his seminal J G Ruggie, 'International Responses to Technology: Concepts and Trends' (1975) 29 *International Organization* 557–83.

[105] Weiler, 'Rule of Lawyers', 194–5; Howse, 'Politics/Technocracy', 99.

[106] Howse, 'Politics/Technocracy', 99.

[107] Hudec, *International Trade Law*; D Bodansky and J C Lawrence, Trade and Environment, in: D L Bethlehem, D McRae, R Neufeld, and I Van Damme (eds), *The Oxford Handbook of International Trade Law* (Oxford: Oxford University Press 2009), 505–38, 508–13.

meaning . . . with respect to treaty interpretation'.[108] The insider network figured as an interpretative community and also worked to sustain insulation from seemingly disturbing outside perspectives. It has been rather successful in this regard by creating and maintaining a very high threshold for policies to be justifiable under Art. XX and by trying to create what has been termed a territorial limitation.

2. The creation of a high threshold

Since the early 1980s, a number of policies that did not fit with established patterns hit the GATT dispute settlement system and its community. They put into question the prevailing understanding that trade objectives are fully compatible with other policy concerns and do not give rise to conflicts that could not be managed by the GATT system. Such disputes for instance challenged domestic regulations, which conditioned market access on the fulfilment of certain criteria by the exporter or the exporter's country. Some early cases were rather obvious attempts by governments to disguise and justify protectionist trade restrictions, others were less clear.

The *United States—Tuna* dispute provides an illustrative example of what is at issue. It also takes a first small step in the direction of what would eventually become a thick body of case-law giving meaning to Art. XX.[109] Canada filed a complaint against actions taken by the US government prohibiting imports of albacore tuna and related products from Canada. The context of events showed that the US took such action in response to the seizure of 19 fishing vessels and the arrest by Canadian authorities of a number of US fishermen that, according to Canada, had fished illegally within 200 miles of its West Coast and thus under its fisheries jurisdiction. The US contested this view of the facts and the legal implications.[110] The trade law dispute was but one aspect of a broader quarrel between the two countries about jurisdictional delimitation and the panel underlined that it did not pronounce on that issue but would confine itself solely to examining the actions in light of the GATT provisions.[111] Without much difficulty, the panel found the embargo on imports to be in violation of the prohibition of quantitative restrictions (Art. XI).[112] This was an easy task and did not yield any surprises. In fact, the parties had already agreed to lift the import ban by the time the panel made its decision. Yet, they also agreed that the panel should continue its work to decide the crucial question 'whether or not a contracting party should have the right to disregard obligations under the GATT in order to use trade measures to bring bilateral pressure to bear on non-trade issues'.[113] This was the question that has pervaded significant parts of GATT/WTO adjudication in the following decades.

108 Howse, 'Politics/Technocracy', 108.

109 GATT Panel Report, *United States—Prohibition of Imports of Tuna and Tuna Products from Canada*, L/5198, adopted 22 February 1982, BISD 29S/91.

110 Ibid., at para 2.1.

111 Ibid., at para 4.1.

112 Ibid., at para 4.15.

113 Ibid., at para 3.4.

The US argued in the case at hand that its import ban was based on the Fishery Conservation and Management Act of 1976 (inter alia aiming at the conservation of tuna stocks) and that it was justified under Art. XX(g). The Act of 1976 provided that an embargo on imports should be the reaction to the seizure of ships that were fishing in waters not recognized by the US to be under any state's jurisdiction. Canada maintained that the Act as well as its sanctioning mechanism were the product of pressure by the US tuna industry and aimed at deterring Canada and other states from enforcing domestic laws that are detrimental to the US tuna industry's commercial interests.[114] In the present dispute, the action was plainly not motivated by conserving tuna stock but just one move in the more complex fisheries squabble. The panel pointed to the telling fact that the US did not subject domestic production or consumption to restrictions equivalent to those projected onto other states. It also found that the US did not subject other species of tuna that are equally under threat of over-exploitation to similar protective regulations. In view of these considerations, the violation of Art. XI could not be justified under Art. XX(g)—a straightforward model case.[115]

The panel left open, in principle, what it itself highlighted to be the critical question: can market entry be conditioned by policies pursuing non-trade objectives? The disputing parties had notably referred this question to the panel in spite of the fact that the dispute had already been settled. However, the panel apparently did not see itself as being up to the task of answering such a legal question with significant repercussions. It confined itself to pointing out the rather evident fact that the US policy did not really pursue the aim of conserving the livestock of tuna and thus left open the more principled question.

Arguably, the panel's analysis of whether the US policy did actually pursue its stated aim suggests that these kinds of policies are at least not categorically excluded from the scope of Art. XX. This is how Canada a little later read the report in its defence in *Herring and Salmon*—the landmark case on Art. XX(g) and on what it means that a policy has to be '*related to* the conservation of exhaustible natural resources'. The case again involved the US next to Canada in a dispute concerning fisheries, but this time in reversed roles. In *Herring and Salmon* the US claimed that the Canadian prohibition on the exportation of certain unprocessed salmon and unprocessed herring was inconsistent with the GATT and Canada in turn sought to justify its policy with reference to Art. XX(g).[116] Canada considered the panel report in *United States—Tuna* to be a direct precedent and claimed that the panel had erected a four-pronged test: (1) the measure must not be applied in a manner which would constitute a means of arbitrary or unjustifiable discrimination, (2) it must not be a disguised restriction on international trade, (3) it must relate to the conservation of exhaustible natural resources, and (4) it must be made effective in

[114] Ibid., at para 3.15 [115] Ibid., at para 4.9.

[116] GATT Panel Report, *Canada—Measures Affecting Exports of Unprocessed Herring and Salmon*, L/6268, adopted 22 March 1988, BISD 35S/98. Canada also argued that the measure did not amount to a violation because of the exceptions provided for in XI:2(b) GATT. This was clearly to no avail. Ibid., at paras 4.2–4.3.

conjunction with restrictions on domestic production or consumption.[117] Canada maintained that the export prohibition was in place to allow for a precise catch control indispensable for managing the stock, that the measure met all parts of the test, and that that was all there was to it. Notably, it stressed that the provisions of Article XX(g) only required it to demonstrate that its measures *related to* conservation, not that they were 'essential' or even 'necessary'.[118]

The United States hit the weak spot in the line of defence by pointing out that the export prohibition itself does little to protect the vulnerable stocks and that other measures were available for an accurate catch control—Canada did in fact use alternative measures that were a lot less trade restrictive for other species. The United States was also able to produce a report of the Canadian Department of Fisheries and Oceans stating that the export restrictions were in place for the purpose of 'promoting jobs for Canadians (by increasing the amount of processing done in Canada)'.[119]

The panel saw the task before it to lie in the interpretation of 'related to' in Art. XX(g). It found that the text does not state how trade measures have to be related to the aim of conservation, contrasted paragraph (g) with other paragraphs, and came to the conclusion that measures for the conservation of exhaustible resources may possibly be justified even if they are not strictly necessary or essential.[120] In its decisive move, however, it said that the requirement that the measure must be 'primarily aimed at' the conservation of exhaustible natural resources was to be considered as 'relating to' conservation within the meaning of Article XX(g).[121] It did not hint at any authority or offer any reasoning that might support its interpretation. Examining whether Canada's export prohibition on certain unprocessed salmon and unprocessed herring primarily aimed at the conservation of exhaustible natural resources, the panel had an easy time finding that this was not the case. It placed the weight of its conclusion on the fact that there were alternative means available that Canada could have employed. The fact that Canada did not do so with regard to certain herring and salmon stocks is proof of ulterior motives, i.e. the protection of employment within the fish processing industry.[122] The panel looked neither into Canada's legislative history nor into the decision-making process leading to the export prohibition but relied on what may be termed an objective test of primary intent.[123]

The panel's invention of a 'primarily aimed at' standard has had much appeal and a lasting impact. With *Herring and Salmon* the panel successfully established its new standard as a reference point in legal discourse, overlying the treaty text. Subsequent legal interpretation centred on whether a measure was 'primarily aimed at' the conservation of exhaustible natural resources as if the treaty text

[117] Ibid., at para 3.24. [118] Ibid., at para 3.13.
[119] Ibid., at para 3.11. [120] Ibid., at para 4.5.
[121] Ibid., at para 4.6. [122] Ibid., at para 4.7.
[123] See Charnovitz, 'Environmental Exceptions', 50–1; M J Trebilcock and R Howse, *The Regulation of International Trade* (London: Routledge 2005), 516–18.

had been forgotten. A reference point in interpretation would no longer be 'related to' but the panel's precedent.

In the immediate follow-up, a panel under the Canada–US Free Trade Agreement, which incorporates Art. XX GATT by reference, was set up to examine whether Canada's move away from an export prohibition towards a landing requirement for all salmon and herring caught on its West Coast (the requirement that they be first brought onto land in Canada) could now be justified on the basis of Art. XX(g).[124] The US and Canada both referred right away to 'primarily aimed at' as the relevant standard for the case.[125] The panel then did recall the treaty text and went on to interpret it along the lines of the *Herring and Salmon* precedent, quoting the latter at length and finding that a measure has to be 'primarily aimed at the conservation of an exhaustible natural resource to be considered as relating to'.[126] On this basis it found Canada's new policy to be an unjustified trade restriction because there were alternative measures available to Canada that it could have employed to meet the aim of conserving fish stocks. In short, there would have been less trade restrictive alternatives.[127] An analysis of whether the measure employed is least trade restrictive establishes whether it is 'primarily aimed at' so that 'related to' is now used to mean 'least trade restrictive'.

It might be suggested that these decisions on the interpretation of Art. XX(g) are only binding between the identical parties to both disputes; after all, they so far only involved Canada and the US. This would miss the effect that interpretations with authority have on the law and it falls short of capturing what actually happens in the practice of legal discourse. The panel in *United States—Gasoline*, one of the first within the WTO context, dealt with a complaint by Brazil and Venezuela against the United States involving Art. XX(g) and, again, the panel quotes at length from *Herring and Salmon* to conclude that 'the less favourable baseline establishments methods at issue in this case were not primarily aimed at the conservation of natural resources'.[128] It thus confirmed that the relevant issue was to interpret 'primarily aimed at' and further corroborated the view that this requires a measure to be the least trade restrictive. In *United States—Gasoline* the panel was overruled on this point on appeal, but also the Appellate Body goes to great lengths in its treatment of the *Herring and Salmon* precedent to note that the formerly prevalent interpretation used to effectively level out any differences between 'related to' and 'necessary' as it is mentioned in other paragraphs of Art. XX.[129] The AB then continued to deliberately reject this interpretation with considerable argumentative force—thereby confirming that this had been the law as it stood before its decision.

[124] *In the Matter of Canada's Landing Requirement for Pacific Coast Salmon and Herring*, Final Report, 16 October 1989.
[125] Ibid., at paras 5.03–5.04.
[126] Ibid., at paras 7.04–7.05.
[127] Ibid., at paras 7.04–7.11 and 7.38.
[128] Panel Report, *United States—Gasoline*, WT/DS2/R, 29 January 1996, para 6.40.
[129] Appellate Body Report, *United States—Gasoline*, WT/DS2/AB/R, 29 April 1996, p 16.

Suggesting that judicial decisions are only binding *inter partes* is at severe odds with large chunks of legal practice, just as saying that international law knows no system of precedents. Participants in the practice of interpretation do not generally even make such doctrinal arguments but rather fight about the meaning of earlier decisions—regardless of whether they were parties to the dispute—just as they base their claims on treaty provisions.

This is equally evident in the communicative practice that developed the meaning of 'necessary'. The defining showdown took place in the dispute between the European Commission and the United States on the application of Section 337 of the US Tariff Act of 1930 that subjects foreign products to distinct procedures. In the eyes of the EC this constituted a violation of the national treatment rule in Art. III GATT and was not justifiable under Art. XX(d). The decisive point of controversy was vested in interpretative claims about the meaning of 'necessary' in Art. XX(d). Every party seemed to argue against the background of their own legal system.[130] The EC argued that no measure could be justified unless it was the least trade restrictive measure available.[131] The US maintained to the contrary that such a requirement could not be read into the GATT and all that was required was that the measures meet a more lenient rational basis standard.[132] The panel noted this difference and in the same breath bluntly stated that 'necessary' in Art. XX(d) compels a least restrictive trade measure test:

> It was clear to the Panel that a contracting party cannot justify a measure inconsistent with another GATT provision as 'necessary' in terms of Article XX(d) if an alternative measure which it could reasonably be expected to employ and which is not inconsistent with other GATT provisions is available to it. By the same token, in cases where a measure consistent with other GATT provisions is not reasonably available, a contracting party is bound to use, among the measures reasonably available to it, that which entails the least degree of inconsistency with other GATT provisions.[133]

Maybe the issue was that clear to the panel because its president was Pierre Pescatore, a former Judge at the European Court of Justice who was of course well familiar with the standard of review advanced by the EC.

The US, however, could turn around and use the case it had just lost in its complaint against Thailand's restrictions and internal taxes on imported cigarettes. The panel in *Thai Cigarettes* found these restrictions to be GATT inconsistent and not justified under Art. XX(b) precisely because alternative measures were available that could have met Thailand's public health concerns. It held that 'import restrictions imposed by Thailand could be considered to be "necessary" in terms of Article XX(b) only if there were no alternative measure consistent with the General Agreement, or less inconsistent with it, which Thailand could reasonably

[130] A Stone Sweet and J Mathews, 'Proportionality Balancing and Global Constitutionalism' (2008) 47 *Columbia Journal of Transnational Law* 73–165, 157–9.

[131] GATT Panel Report, *United States Section 337 of the Tariff Act of 1930*, L/6439, adopted 7 November 1989, BISD 36S/345, para 3.60.

[132] Ibid., at para 3.59.

[133] Ibid., at para 5.26.

be expected to employ to achieve its health policy objectives'.[134] For example, the panel continued, Thailand could have examined the quality of foreign cigarettes, or it could have enacted a number of consumer warning mechanisms, public information campaigns, and requirements such as a complete disclosure of ingredients coupled with a ban on unhealthy substances.[135]

The panel's reasoning is remarkably determined by the objective of corroborating a high categorical standard that saves the GATT system from protectionist policies which might otherwise enter via Art. XX. According to its categorical pronouncement, the existence of an alternative that is less trade restrictive and reasonably available suffices to render a measure unnecessary. It merits emphasis that this general statement then formed the reference point in legal discourse according to which the legality of the measure at hand was analysed. Also, the panel did not consider the practical consequences of its findings, namely that alternative measures could entail insurmountable administrative or financial obstacles for Thailand.

Upon Thailand's request, the panel had called for a submission by the World Health Organization (WHO) on the issue but basically ignored it in its decisive steps of reasoning. The WHO in principle supported Thailand's measures and suggested that alternatives would be unduly burdensome and risky. It opined that Thailand's regulations were in line with the recommendations developed by the WHO Expert Committee on 'Smoking Control Strategies in Developing Countries' and further argued that due account must be given to Thailand's actual capabilities.[136] But this did not sway the panel.

Lastly, it is worth highlighting that the panel did not pick up the argument the US had submitted on the chapeau of Art. XX; namely, that a measure under the general exceptions provision must not be a disguised restriction of international trade.[137] This might have been a more appropriate basis for anchoring the judgment in the norm text. But previous panels had already put the narrow focus on the word 'necessary'.

Over time, GATT panels dealt with a number of disputes that juxtaposed trade objectives with other public policy considerations and they managed to maintain GATT in rather splendid isolation. They did so by creating a standard for regulators that was very difficult to meet.[138] For a measure to be 'necessary', or even if it was only to 'relate to' another legitimate aim, it had to be the least trade restrictive measure reasonably available. What might seem reasonable in the eyes of

[134] GATT Panel Report, *Thailand—Restrictions on Importation of and Internal Taxes on Cigarettes*, DS10/R, adopted 7 November 1990, BISD 37S/200, at para 75.

[135] Ibid., at para 77.

[136] Ibid., at paras 55–56.

[137] Ibid., at para 22.

[138] Cf. D C Esty, *Greening the GATT. Trade, environment, and the future* (Washington, DC: Institute for International Economics 1994); Ala'i, 'Free Trade or Sustainable Development?', 1137 (noting that 'the traditional analysis of the provisions of Article XX by the GATT panels made [the burden of proof on the party invoking an Article XX exception] a difficult, if not impossible, burden to meet.').

the GATT panel in *Thai Cigarettes* might in fact be an insurmountable burden for Thailand to overcome. In the making of this interpretation of general exceptions, panels reasoned along functionalist lines and stressed trade objectives. How this rhetoric played out in legal practice may further be shown in the analysis of another way in which panels sought to save the GATT system from policy considerations with a trade-distortive potential: the practice of adjudication arguably created a territorial limitation on the scope of the general exceptions.

3. A territorial limitation?

Disputes at the intersections between trade law and non-trade public policy aims grew in prominence in the early 1990s, fuelled by the panel reports in the *Tuna—Dolphin* cases. At issue were US policies conditioning market access for tuna exporters and aiming at the protection of dolphins. In *Tuna—Dolphin I* Mexico complained against the US prohibition of imports of tuna harvested in a way that, according to the US, posed an exceedingly high risk to dolphins.[139] The panel found the import prohibition to be in violation of Art. XI GATT and not justified under Art. XX(b) or (g).[140] Picking up the arguments of the parties, it saw the crucial question to be 'whether Article XX(b) covers measures necessary to protect human, animal or plant life or health *outside the jurisdiction* of the contracting party taking the measure'.[141] Mexico had submitted that the justification advanced by the US would require a concept of extraterritoriality to be inserted into Art. XX and that the panel was in no position to do so. Nothing in the agreement, it claimed, entitled the US to subject production methods within Mexico's jurisdiction to US legislation.[142] The concept of extraterritoriality was used to refer to the fact that policies aimed at subject matters beyond the jurisdiction of the respective polity. The US argued in contrast to Mexico that nothing about its legislation conditioning market access was 'extraterritorial'. It rather maintained that it was quite natural that domestic trade measures had effects outside the contracting party's territory.[143]

The panel noted that the text of Art. XX does not provide an answer to the question before it and it thus turned to the drafting history and the purpose of the provision (from the *word* to its *sense* and then to its *force*). It purported to see in the drafting process that the provisions were only meant to allow the protection of human, animal, and plant life that are under an importing country's jurisdiction.[144] The panel then expressed its apocalyptic angst:

139 GATT Panel Report, *United States—Restrictions on Imports of Tuna*, DS21/R, 3 September 1991, unadopted, BISD 39S/155.

140 One issue that has to be sidestepped here but which is of crucial significance generally is the delineation of Art. XI dealing with quantitative restrictions from Art. III concerning internal regulations.

141 GATT Panel Report, *United States—Restrictions on Imports of Tuna*, DS21/R, 3 September 1991, unadopted, BISD 39S/155, para 5.25 (italics added).

142 Ibid., at paras 3.31 and 3.58.

143 Ibid., at para 3.49.

144 Ibid., at para 5.26.

> The Panel considered that if the broad interpretation of Article XX(b) suggested by the United States were accepted, each contracting party could unilaterally determine the life or health protection policies from which other contracting parties could not deviate without jeopardizing their rights under the General Agreement. The General Agreement would then no longer constitute a multilateral framework for trade among all contracting parties but would provide legal security only in respect of trade between a limited number of contracting parties with identical internal regulations.[145]

If members could unilaterally prohibit imports on the basis of the conditions under which the products have been produced, the panel argued, the multilateral trade regime would ultimately collapse. The US could thus not justify its policy under Art. XX(b)—nor, for the same reason, under subparagraph (g).

The panel could have stopped here. Instead it proceeded to cultivate and strengthen the jurisprudence on the relationship between the concrete policy and the stated aim. Even if an extraterritorial protection were permitted, the import prohibition would still not be justified because it was not 'necessary'. With reference to *Thai Cigarettes*, the panel found that a reasonable alternative was available; namely, negotiating international cooperative agreements. The panel even raised the threshold a notch: it required that the US 'had exhausted all options reasonably available to it to pursue its dolphin protection objectives through measures consistent with the General Agreement' for its policy to qualify as a necessary exception.[146] And as concerns subparagraph (g), with reference to *Herring and Salmon*, the measure did not primarily aim at the conservation of natural resources, for the same reason as it was not necessary under subparagraph (b).[147] The panel's reasoning as to whether the policy was 'necessary' or 'related to' appears to be a superfluous second basis of illegality after finding that extraterritorial policies are generally excluded. The panel did not however lose the opportunity to support its finding also on these grounds. Remarkably, this GATT decision of 1991 is closely interwoven with a number of precedents—referenced in 45 footnotes on its 40 pages. The practice of interpretation was already deeply embedded in a thick structure of adjudicatory practice that directed all actors' interpretations.

The report in *Tuna—Dolphin I* was heavily criticized by environmentalists and sternly defended by the GATT secretariat. The latter acted in an effort to successfully keep non-trade issues from interfering with trade law. On the occasion of the 1992 Rio Summit of the United Nations Conference on Environment and Development the secretariat had crafted a report on trade and environment stressing the point that trade liberalization only has negative environmental consequences in the absence of governmental action—thus testifying to trade experts' trust in the regulatory capacity of the state.[148] What is more, it then focused on the looming

145 Ibid., at para 5.27. 146 Ibid., at para 5.28.

147 Ibid., at paras 5.31–5.33.

148 B Kingsbury, 'The Tuna-Dolphin Controversy, the World Trade Organization, and the Liberal Project to Reconceptualize International Law' (1994) 5 *Yearbook of International Environmental Law* 1, 6; also compare the evocative 1971 report of the GATT secretariat in this regard, GATT Secretariat, GATT Studies in International Trade, No 1, Industrial Pollution Control and International Trade (1971).

threat of protectionism and spoke out strongly against unilaterally conditioning market access by regulations that invoke public policy considerations in their justification. It even went on to consider the threat that might arise in case protectionists and environmentalists came together.[149] The report categorically argued against unilateral measures and echoed the critical question that the early panel in *United States—Tuna* had ducked: 'whether or not a contracting party should have the right to disregard obligations under the GATT in order to use trade measures to bring bilateral pressure to bear on non-trade issues.'[150] The secretariat held such measures to be unacceptable because they 'dictate changes in environmental policies of other nations'. It found the solution to lie in multilateral standards, thus attempting to free itself and the GATT system from the burden of giving further thought to this issue. With this argument, the secretariat also tried to reject the mounting criticism by playing the ball, with the help of the reasoning in *Tuna—Dolphin I*, to the political-legislative process.[151] For the time being at least, it did in fact establish that trade was trump.

This bottom line constituted the major point for critique.[152] Above all environmentalists argued along the lines of the US that there was nothing extraterritorial about the regulations under scrutiny.[153] Others went further and demanded that GATT law open up to other policy considerations on the basis of Art. XX. Some already argued that panels should explicitly balance trade objectives against other aims.[154] Many commentators found good reasons in the panel's decision and vested their hopes in political processes to correct the issues.[155] However, political agreement was not forthcoming and the controversy instead continued to make its way into GATT adjudication. International trade norms on this issue continued to be primarily formed in the practice of interpretation.

In *Tuna—Dolphin II*, the European Communities challenged the US import prohibition of tuna as well as the intermediary nation embargo which was supposed to prevent the import prohibition being circumvented by passing tuna through a third country. The US required that a third country, not itself harvesting tuna but

[149] GATT Studies in International Trade, No 1, Industrial Pollution Control and International Trade (1971).

[150] GATT Panel Report, *United States—Prohibition of Imports of Tuna and Tuna Products from Canada*, L/5198, adopted 22 February 1982, BISD 29S/91, para 3.4.

[151] GATT Secretarial, Trade and the Environment (1992).

[152] For an analytical overview over see Kingsbury, 'The Tuna-Dolphin Controversy'.

[153] S Charnovitz, 'GATT and the Environment: Examining the Issues' (1992) 4 *International Environmental Affairs* 203–33.

[154] J L Dunoff, 'Reconciling International Trade with Preservation of the Global Commons: Can We Prosper and Protect' (1992) 49 *Washington & Lee Law Review* 1407–54.

[155] A v Bogdandy, 'Internationaler Handel und nationaler Umweltschutz: Eine Abgrenzung im Lichte des GATT' (1992) *Europäische Zeitschrift für Wirtschaftsrecht* 243–7, 247 (noting that GATT adjudicators lacked the authority for balancing competing interests); J H Jackson, 'World Trade Rules and Environmental Policies: Congruence or Conflict' (1992) 49 *Washington & Lee Law Review* 1227–78 (finding a possible solution to lie in the waiver procedure). On this latter suggestion also see I Feichtner, 'The Waiver Power of the WTO: Opening the WTO for Political Debate on the Reconciliation of Public Interests' (2009) 20 *European Journal of International Law* 615–45.

importing and then exporting tuna, had to have a primary embargo itself or it would otherwise be subject to the US import prohibition. The panel observed that the parties, clearly under the spell of *Tuna—Dolphin I* report, had placed great emphasis on the question of whether a policy could aim beyond a contracting state's territorial jurisdiction. In contrast to *Tuna—Dolphin I*, the panel could not find support in the drafting history for the conclusion that there was a categorical jurisdictional limitation.[156] Nor does general international law impede states from pursuing aims outside its territorial jurisdiction by internal regulation, so the panel found.[157] This was an important and lasting change in the interpretation of Art. XX. But it was immediately called into question.

The panel proceeded by examining whether the measures were 'relating to' or 'necessary' and here it again gave much weight to considerations of jurisdiction. Echoing *Tuna—Dolphin I*, it found that the GATT would no longer serve as a multilateral framework for trade among the contracting parties if trade access were to depend on the internal regulations of the exporter and whether or not they conformed to the demands of the importing country.[158] At this juncture, it again held the matter of jurisdiction to be the decisive issue and found that a member could not force others to change policies within their own jurisdiction. The panel reasoned that such trade measures could simply not be primarily aimed at the conservation of exhaustible natural resources, nor could they be considered necessary for the protection of animal life or health in the sense of Art XX(b).[159] The panel in effect upheld a territorial limitation but shifted its place into an analysis of primary intention.

The reception of *Tuna—Dolphin II* was predictable and fell along the lines drawn in the reactions to *Tuna—Dolphin I*. Much has been made of whether the treatment of the crucial question in terms of extraterritorial jurisdiction was actually adequate.[160] Be that as it may, it is hard to deny that it is a valid question to ask 'whether or not a contracting party should have the right to disregard obligations under the GATT in order to use trade measures to bring bilateral pressure to bear on non-trade issues'.[161] The panel in *Tuna—Dolphin II* again suggested that the

[156] GATT Panel Report, *United States—Restrictions on Imports of Tuna*, DS29/R, 16 June 1994, unadopted, para 5.20.

[157] Ibid., at para 5.17.

[158] Ibid., at para 5.26.

[159] Ibid., at paras 5.27 and 5.38–5.39.

[160] Howse and Regan, 'Product/Process Distinction', 274 (arguing in the negative: 'process-based distinctions do not directly regulate any behaviour occurring outside the border.... [N]othing that has happened outside the border attracts, by itself, any criminal or civil sanction.'); L Bartels, 'Article XX of GATT and the Problem of Extraterritorial Jurisdiction. The Case of Trade Measures for the Protection of Human Rights' (2002) 36 *Journal of World Trade* 353–403, 377, (arguing to the contrary that that the 'mere existence of legislation can amount to an international wrong regardless of whether the legislation is enforced'). Also see W Meng, *Extraterritoriale Jurisdiktion im öffentlichen Wirtschaftsrecht* (Heidelberg: Springer 1994), (embracing the concept of extraterritoriality).

[161] GATT Panel Report, *United States—Prohibition of Imports of Tuna and Tuna Products from Canada*, L/5198, adopted 22 February 1982, BISD 29S/91, at para 3.4.

question's resolution should be pursued in political-legislative processes and noted too in this vein that the relationship between environmental and trade measures was now to be considered in the negotiations leading to the creation of the WTO.[162] Notably, the contracting parties adopted neither *Tuna—Dolphin* decision. And yet, both panel reports had repercussions that were felt strongly at the inception of the WTO. They tangibly redistributed argumentative burdens and shaped legal discourse.[163]

C. Article XX in the era of the WTO

Semantic changes in the wake of the transformative years surrounding the inception of the WTO in 1995 are once more closely intertwined with institutional reforms. In particular, the working of precedents has come to be of increased significance in view of the dynamics unfolding in a dispute settlement mechanism with appellate review (1.). GATT precedents still directed actors' arguments on Art. XX in the early WTO cases but were forcefully redirected by the new Appellate Body, both with regard to the threshold that policies have to meet in order to be justifiable on the basis of general exceptions as well as with regard to such policies' territorial scope (2.). Interpretative claims of the adjudicatory bodies have then once more focused on the meaning of 'necessary' while the key issue has been whether assessing the necessity of a policy implies a proportionality test and what such a test would actually entail (3.).

1. Institutional changes and the working of precedents

Both *Tuna—Dolphin* cases had pointed to the political-legislative process as the appropriate venue for resolving tensions between trade obligations and other areas of public policy. In particular, environmental objectives began to take the form of legal obligations so that actual legal conflict started to be a real possibility. The negotiations in the Uruguay Round leading up to the Marrakesh Summit of April 1994 were thus burdened with specifying the provisions on general exceptions and with guiding adjudicators on the still daunting question relating to the intersection between trade objectives and other public policy concerns.

With strong leadership on the part of the US and in light of considerable dissatisfaction with how the GATT panels had handled non-trade concerns, negotiators attempted to resolve the controversy by enacting new legal provisions on the issue. Little agreement could however be reached and protracted disagreement only allowed for a rather general and laudatory 'Decision on Trade and Environment' which states that '[t]here should not be, nor need be, any policy

[162] GATT Panel Report, *United States—Restrictions on Imports of Tuna*, DS29/R, 16 June 1994, unadopted, at para 5.34.

[163] D Driesen, 'What is Free Trade? The real issue lurking behind the trade and environment debate' (2001) 41 *Virginia Journal of International Law* 279–368, 306.

contradiction between upholding and safeguarding an open, non-discriminatory and equitable multilateral trading system on the one hand, and acting for the protection of the environment, and the promotion of sustainable development on the other'.[164] This was of course of little help as disputes arising from contradictions had already been plaguing GATT panels for some time. The task of finding a remedy was delegated to the newly established Committee on Trade and Environment (CTE). The CTE first discussed ambitious reforms of Art. XX but has so far not been able to secure even a modest consensus on the interpretation of general exceptions, let alone an interpretative statement or even a reform of the treaty text.[165] Thus, the task again largely fell on the adjudicators.

Non-trade concerns did, however, find their way into the preamble of the WTO agreement providing that trade relations 'should be conducted with a view to raising standards of living, ... while allowing for the optimal use of the world's resources in accordance with the objective of sustainable development, seeking both to protect and preserve the environment and to enhance the means for doing so in a manner consistent with their respective needs and concerns at different levels of economic development'. This wording became an important reference point in legal discourse ever since the Appellate Body took its first decisive steps.

Furthermore, a number of additional agreements could be reached, some of which might have repercussions on what Art. XX means. The Agreement on Sanitary and Phytosanitary Measures (SPS Agreement) notably provides in its Art. 2(4) that '[s]anitary or phytosanitary measures which conform to the relevant provisions of this Agreement shall be presumed to be in accordance with the obligations of the Members under the provisions of GATT 1994 which relate to the use of sanitary or phytosanitary measures, in particular the provisions of Article XX(b)'. Also the Agreement on Technical Barriers to Trade (TBT Agreement) may be of relevance with regard to the meaning of Art. XX even if it does not contain any similar express reference.

When it comes to the topic of trade and environment, legislative change has thus overall been at best modest. Most importantly, Art. XX GATT has remained as it stood. Major changes did however occur with regard to the institutional structure and the dispute settlement mechanism.[166] The GATT era had been marked by an intriguing pattern of institutional growth and by increasingly sophisticated dispute settlement procedures. Now the detailed Dispute Settlement Understanding

[164] <http://www.wto.org/english/tratop_e/envir_e/issu5_e.htm>.

[165] The Doha Declaration invested the CTE with a renewed mandate, Doha Ministerial Declaration, WT/MIN(01)/DEC/1, 20 November 2001, at paras 31–33. Again, little progress could be made. Cf. Trebilcock and Howse, *International Trade*, 545–8. What the CTE indeed does is to pass notes on Art. XX that summarize the pertinent case-law and pay close lip-service to judicial reports. They barely add a single word of genuine assessment or direction, see, e.g., Committee on Trade and Environment, GATT/WTO Dispute Settlement Practice relating to GATT Article XX, paras (b), (d) and (g), Note by the Secretariat, WT/CTE/W/203, 8 March 2002.

[166] See generally E-U Petersmann, 'The Transformation of the World Trading System through the 1994 Agreement Establishing the World Trade Organization' (1995) 6 *European Journal of International Law* 161–221.

(DSU) formalized previous practices and introduced a number of further innovations. One of the principal novelties was the possibility for appellate review. A number of indicators suggest that the new Appellate Body was supposed and expected to have but a limited role. It might in fact have looked like a not so significant by-product of the whole package deal. According to a proposal by the European Communities the Appellate Body would only come to act if the panel report was 'erroneous or incomplete'.[167] Canada saw its role in correcting 'fundamentally flawed decisions' and also the US thought that the new body would only review 'extraordinary cases'.[168] The contracting parties apparently thought that appellate review would be so limited that its seven members, a relatively small number anyway, would only need to be employed part-time and could be paid in addition for actual working days.[169]

From the day of its creation, however, the Appellate Body has grown from an 'afterthought to a centrepiece' as now Appellate Body member Peter van den Bossche summarized.[170] Van den Bossche makes out six reasons for the AB's rise to success: first, its composition of mostly international lawyers who had general legal training and who were not excessively focused on *trade* law; second, its Working Procedures and the implementation of the principle of collegiality; third, the AB's reliance on the VCLT and on the norm text as a starting point of legal interpretation; fourth, the frequent recourse to appellate review—in the first two years following the establishment of the AB *every* panel report was appealed; fifth, the building up of persuasive authority and a consistent body of case-law; and sixth, the appropriate balance struck between trade objectives and other public policy goals in its jurisprudence.[171]

The institutional changes brought about by the Marrakesh Agreement and the DSU included a number of elements that aimed at strengthening the enforcement of commitments. This aim inevitably implied that the adjudicative bodies would enjoy greater autonomy and authority in relation to the contacting parties.[172] A crucial element was the change from a consensus requirement in the adoption

[167] P v d Bossche, From Afterthought to Centrepiece: The WTO Appellate Body and its Rise to Prominence in the World Trading System, in: G Sacerdoti, A Yanovich, and J Bohanes (eds), *The WTO at Ten: The Contribution of the Dispute Settlement System* (Cambridge: Cambridge University Press 2006), 289–325, 292–3.

[168] Ibid.

[169] Dispute Settlement Body, Establishment of the Appellate Body, 19 June 1995, decision adopted on 10 February 1995, WT/DSB/1, paras 11–12.

[170] P v d Bossche, From Afterthought to Centrepiece: The WTO Appellate Body and its Rise to Prominence in the World Trading System, in: G Sacerdoti, A Yanovich, and J Bohanes (eds), *The WTO at Ten: The Contribution of the Dispute Settlement System* (Cambridge: Cambridge University Press 2006), 289–325. See further H Ruiz Fabri, 'Le juge de l'OMC: Ombres et lumières d'une figure judiciaire singulière' (2006) 110 *Revue Générale de Droit International Public* 39–83.

[171] P v d Bossche, From Afterthought to Centrepiece: The WTO Appellate Body and its Rise to Prominence in the World Trading System, in: G Sacerdoti, A Yanovich, and J Bohanes (eds), *The WTO at Ten: The Contribution of the Dispute Settlement System* (Cambridge: Cambridge University Press 2006), 289–325, 300–25.

[172] Cf. E A Posner and J C Yoo, 'Judicial Independence in International Tribunals' (2005) 93 *California Law Review* 1–74 (making the skewed and empirically dubious claim that independent courts are less effective); compare the critique by A-M Slaughter and L R Helfer, 'Why States Create

of the panel and Appellate Body reports to a negative consensus rule. A consensus would now be required in order to reject a report. In all practical circumstances this amounts to automatic adoption with a lasting effect on the relationship between adjudication and political-legislative control.[173]

State representatives have thus sought to limit the lawmaking dimension of judicial interpretation by tying the adjudicators to their consent in a number of ways. An outstanding manifestation of anxiety that the adjudicators might not always live up to their ideal role of finding the law that is present in the applicable treaties can be found in the intriguing Art. 3(2) DSU. It stipulates that recommendations and rulings of the DSB 'cannot add to or diminish the rights and obligations provided in the covered agreements'.[174] This provision was apparently so dear to the contracting parties that they reiterated this wording *verbatim* in Art. 19(2) DSU. It has figured as a reference point in panel proceedings and in the discussion of reports to buttress an actor's claim that the panel or AB transgresses its legal function and engages in lawmaking. While empirically speculative, it may well be suggested that this provision has done little to work against the phenomenon of judicial lawmaking. It is hard to see what more it does than to restate the adjudicators' task of applying the law. In particular, it does not affect the working of case-law in developing meaning or, more generally, communicative practices from making law.

Article 3(2) DSU also provides that '[t]he dispute settlement of the WTO is a central element in providing security and predictability to the multilateral trading system'. In its early steps in *Japan—Alcoholic Beverages II* the Appellate Body leaned on this provision to argue that reports, even if they do not amount to binding precedents, 'create legitimate expectations among WTO Members, and, therefore, should be taken into account where they are relevant to any dispute'.[175] The Appellate Body went on to concur with the panel that unadopted reports have no legal status in the GATT/WTO system—bear in mind, however, that also adopted reports do not have anything that could sensibly be termed a legal status—but 'a panel could nevertheless find useful guidance in the reasoning of an unadopted panel report that it considered to be relevant.'[176] The Appellate

International Tribunals: A Response to Professors Posner and Yoo' (2005) 93 *California Law Review* 899–956.

[173] A v Bogdandy, 'Law and Politics in the WTO—Strategies to Cope with a Deficient Relationship' (2001) 5 *Max Planck Yearbook of United Nations Law* 609–73; J E Alvarez, 'The New Dispute Settlers: (Half) Truths and Consequences' (2003) 38 *Texas International Law Journal* 405–44; L Bartels, 'The Separation of Powers in the WTO: How to Avoid Judicial Activism?' (2004) 53 *International and Comparative Law Quarterly* 861–95; P Eeckhout, 'The Scales of Trade—Reflections on the Growth and Functions of the WTO Adjudicative Branch' (2010) 13 *Journal of International Economic Law* 3–26.

[174] See J Klabbers, 'On Rationalism in Politics: Interpretation of Treaties and the World Trade Organization' (2005) 74 *Nordic Journal of International Law* 405–28.

[175] Appellate Body Report, *Japan—Taxes on Alcoholic Beverages* WT/DS8, 10 & 11/AB/R, 4 October 1996, pp 14–15.

[176] Ibid., at p 15, quoting Panel Report, *Japan—Taxes on Alcoholic Beverages*, WT/DS8, 10 & 11/R, 11 July 1996, at para 6.10.

Body's take on the working of precedents underscores that a precedent's quality of being binding or not is not determinative of its authority in legal discourse.

Considerable evidence for the authority of precedents already stems from the GATT era. The proceedings in the *Oilseeds* case provide a most interesting illustration. The disputing parties and the panel all argued with reference to the *Canned Fruit* report, which had not only remained unadopted due to the EC's objections but was even withdrawn from the GATT Council's agenda on behalf of the US as part of the final settlement.[177] The fact that all parties and the adjudicators in *Oilseeds* nevertheless fought vehemently about its meaning is a strong indication for the power of precedents in trade law and for the thought that much of the impact of judicial decisions depends on their authority or, better put, on the authority that can be made of it, rather than its 'legal status'. Participants in legal discourse do not usually even put forward the argument that earlier decisions are not binding or that they are not bound by them, but they rather try to distinguish them or, even more so, struggle over their meaning.

As of late, the Appellate Body has furthered the authority of its reports as decisive reference points for panel proceedings. To a large extent this dynamic has unfolded in the context of disputes over 'zeroing', a method for calculating anti-dumping duties.[178] It appears to be rather evident from the negotiating history of the Anti-Dumping Agreement (ADA) that the WTO members could not come to an agreement over the legality of zeroing. In a last minute compromise, they added Art. 17(6)(ii) to the ADA testifying to their disagreement: 'Where the panel finds that a relevant provision of the Agreement admits of more than one permissible interpretation, the panel shall find the authorities' measure to be in conformity with the Agreement if it rests upon one of those permissible interpretations.'[179]

A lot could be made out of the assumptions and understandings of interpretation lingering behind this wording.[180] In the present context it is worth highlighting that panels have recurrently found that nothing prohibits zeroing while the Appellate Body has consistently reversed panel reports on this matter. The AB eventually boldly backed the authority of its decision. In *United States—Oil Country Tubular Goods Sunset Review* it already went beyond its position in *Japan—Alcoholic Beverages II*

[177] Hudec, *International Trade Law*, 265.

[178] Cf. J Gomula, 'Precedential Effect of WTO Decisions: Note on the Zeroing Cases' (2008) 1 *The Global Community: Yearbook of International Law and Jurisprudence* 295–317.

[179] Art. 17(6)(ii) was introduced upon the advocacy of the United States. At the time it was inserted into the agreement, the issue of zeroing was one of the big unresolved issues and, while the provision does not explicitly refer to zeroing, the US is not too far off when it relies on the article as evidence of disagreement over precisely this issue. See Appellate Body Report, *United States—Final Anti-Dumping Measures on Stainless Steel from Mexico*, WT/DS344/AB/R, 30 April 2008, para 39 (on the US submission in this regard). Cf. D McRae, Treaty Interpretation by the WTO Appellate Body: The Conundrum of Article 17(6) of the WTO Antidumping Agreement, in: E Cannizzaro (ed), *The Law of Treaties Beyond the Vienna Convention* (Oxford: Oxford University Press 2011), 164–85.

[180] On the Appellate Body's take on its relation to the VCLT, see especially Appellate Body Report, *United States—Anti-Dumping Measures on Certain Hot-Rolled Steel Products from Japan*, WT/DS184/AB/R, 24 July 2001, para 59; Appellate Body Report, *United States—Continued Existence and Application of Zeroing Methodology*, WT/DS350/AB/R, 4 February 2009, para 312.

and found that it is not only appropriate for panels to follow AB jurisprudence but that it would even be expected that they do so.[181] In a renewed appeal on issues of zeroing, in *United States—Stainless Steel (Mexico)*, the AB then recalled that the WTO Members have repeatedly stressed the importance of consistency and stability in interpretation. The AB emphasized that its findings are clarifications of the law and, as such, are not limited to the specific case. It strongly criticized the panel:

> We are deeply concerned about the Panel's decision to depart from well-established Appellate Body jurisprudence clarifying the interpretation of the same legal issues. The Panel's approach has serious implications for the proper functioning of the WTO dispute settlement system . . . .[182]

The EC had joined the proceedings as a third party and attempted to push the argument even further. It argued that the AB should make it unambiguously clear that the panels are not only expected but also obliged to follow the AB's findings. The EC argued that failing to do so would be in violation of the panel's obligations under Art. 11 DSU to conduct an 'objective assessment' of the matter before it.[183] The AB did not go that far. But it did create a lingering threat by suggesting that disregard for its precedents might actually amount to a panel's failure to properly exercise its judicial function.[184]

What has already been shown in the practice of legal argumentation with regard to Art. XX throughout the GATT era now appears but evident: GATT/WTO judicial practice has created a body of precedent that strongly bears on what international trade law really is. The working of precedents sustains adjudicators' high degree of semantic authority in the making of law by way of interpretation and participants in legal discourse can simply not escape the discussion of previous decisions. Interpreters are forced to do so as a matter of fact while practice also portrays a sense that they should relate their arguments to precedents. How does the process of legal development by way of interpretation unfold with regard to the general exceptions of Art. XX GATT in the era of the WTO?

2. A new beginning with the Appellate Body

The very first case that came before a panel within the brand new WTO institutional framework promptly played public policy concern against trade objectives.

[181] Appellate Body Report, *United States—Sunset Reviews of Anti-Dumping Measures on Oil Country Tubular Goods from Argentina*, WT/DS268/AB/R, 17 December 2004, para 188.

[182] Appellate Body Report, *United States—Final Anti-Dumping Measures on Stainless Steel from Mexico*, WT/DS344/AB/R, 30 April 2008, para 162. Also see Appellate Body Report, *United States—Continued Existence and Application of Zeroing Methodology*, WT/DS350/AB/R, 4 February 2009, paras 362–365; Appellate Body Report, *United States—Measures Relating to Shrimp from Thailand*, WT/DS343/AB/R, 16 July 2008 (concerning both issues of zeroing and a justification based on Art. XX(d)).

[183] Appellate Body Report, *United States—Final Anti-Dumping Measures on Stainless Steel from Mexico*, WT/DS344/AB/R, 30 April 2008, para 58.

[184] Ibid., at para 162.

In *United States—Gasoline*, Brazil and Venezuela complained about US measures in the implementation of its 1990 Clean Air Act. The US required foreign exporters of gasoline to meet certain compositional and performance specifications so that pollution from gasoline combustion would not exceed the levels of 1990. The Clean Air Act established baselines of pollution levels for this purpose. A cause of complaint was that the methods for setting up the baselines differed for domestic and foreign refiners in quite evident violation of Art. III(4) GATT.

Treading the path set in GATT jurisprudence, the panel held that the measures imposed on foreign producers of gasoline could neither be justified under Art. XX(b) nor under Art. XX(g). It found that there was a less trade restrictive alternative reasonably available so that the measures taken were not necessary in the sense of Art. XX(b).[185] With *Herring and Salmon* it argued that 'relating to' in Art. XX(b) means 'primarily aimed at' and that primary intent can be inferred from the fact of whether the measure was least trade restrictive—thus, again, in effect levelling out any difference between the standards.[186] With regard to both justifications the panel noted that finding the measure not to be least trade restrictive exhausts the issue. It was thus not necessary to examine the legality of the measures further under the chapeau of Art. XX. The panel's reasoning had by now become an easy exercise. At the time, it was a predictable statement of the law.

The US appealed and the Appellate Body's decision then demonstrated a remarkable shift in the practice of interpretation and marked the direction of legal developments to come. The AB redirected crucial steps in this easy exercise with a fresh look at the text and with a fresh general outlook. The aura of a new beginning still did not elevate its reasoning above the discussion of precedents. Its agency remained embedded in the structures of legal practice and its arguments testify to the strong spell exerted by earlier decisions. The AB concentrated on the justification by way of Art. XX(g) and criticized the panel's use of *Herring and Salmon*, observing that the prevalent interpretation of 'related to' had been that measures must be 'primarily aimed at' the stated legitimate objective and continued to point out that this had led to a least restrictive trade test as part of establishing primary intent. Such an interpretation was indeed carried by constant jurisprudence. The AB saw itself forced to engage with this interpretation, took up the challenge head on, and managed to get out of this deadlock. How did it do so?

The AB found the prevalent interpretation of Art. XX(g) to be in violation of the Vienna Convention on the Law of Treaties (VCLT) because it disregarded the difference in wording between the paragraphs.[187] It is interesting that none of the disputing parties had questioned that 'related to' means 'primarily aimed at'—this seems to have already been beyond doubt even if, as the AB highlights, 'the phrase "primarily aimed at" is not treaty language and was not designed as a simple litmus

[185] Panel Report, *United States—Gasoline*, WT/DS2/R, 29 January 1996, at para 6.28.

[186] Ibid., at para 6.40.

[187] Appellate Body Report, *United States—Gasoline*, WT/DS2/AB/R, 29 April 1996 (adopted 20 May 1996), pp 16–17.

test for inclusion or exclusion from Art. XX(g)'.[188] Nonetheless, and with some uneasiness, the AB continued to examine whether the measures at issue were 'primarily aimed at' the conversation of exhaustible natural resources, using this wording for a more lenient standard. It concluded that the measures taken may qualify under paragraph (g) and overturned the panel on this point. It thus broke with precedents but connected to them. It continued to use the expression 'primarily aimed at' but used it with a different meaning.

The AB then turned to the chapeau of Art. XX whose main purpose it found to lie in preventing the abuse of exceptions.[189] It argued and stressed that Art. XX requires a two-tiered analysis: first of the measure at issue and whether it falls into the purview of one of the paragraphs (a) to (j), and second a further appraisal of whether the same measure is needed under the requirements set out in the chapeau. In the second step it is no longer the content of the specific measure, thus the Appellate Body, but the manner in which it is applied that is decisive.[190] Moreover, the panel had applied the necessity test as it was developed in *Section 337* and *Thai Cigarettes*; namely, that 'a contracting party is bound to use, among the measures reasonably available to it, that which entails the least degree of inconsistency with other GATT provisions'.[191] The Appellate Body now suggested that in applying this test, the panel unduly mingled questions of justification with questions of what would have been permissible under Art. III(4) GATT. At the stage of justification, the AB argued, the legal analysis must be centred on Art. XX. The panel (and its predecessors) had violated the general rule of interpretation providing that interpretation gives effect to all the terms of the treaties. With reference to the ICJ's *Corfu Channel* and *Territorial Dispute* judgments the AB stressed that it could not adopt an interpretation that would reduce the whole Art. XX to redundancy or inutility.[192] With this reasoning the AB also firmly positioned itself as partaking in the general international law discourse.

In the case at hand, the AB found the US regulation for foreign refiners of gasoline to amount to an unjustified discrimination because the US did not show why its concerns could not have been resolved by international cooperation, nor did it make an effort to enter into such cooperation before putting its regulatory system in place. The measure was also a disguised restriction of trade because

188 Ibid., at p 19.

189 Ibid., at p 22.

190 Ibid., at p 22. Note that in many concrete cases the distinction between the two is oftentimes far from evident. Compare R Wolfrum, Article XX GATT 1994, General Exceptions [Chapeau], in: R Wolfrum, P-T Stoll, and K Kaiser (eds), *Max Planck Commentaries on World Trade Law, vol 2 (WTO—institutions and dispute settlement)* (Leiden: Nijhoff 2006), 66–79, Mns 8–12.

191 Panel Report, *United States—Gasoline*, WT/DS2/R, 29 January 1996, para 6.24, referencing GATT Panel Report, *United States Section 337 of the Tariff Act of 1930*, L/6439, adopted 7 November 1989, BISD 36S/345.

192 Appellate Body Report, *United States—Gasoline*, WT/DS2/AB/R, 29 April 1996, p 23; referencing *Corfu Channel Case (United Kingdom of Great Britain and Northern Ireland v Albania)*, 9 April 1949, (1949) ICJ Reports 4, p 24; *Territorial Dispute Case (Libyan Arab Jamahiriya v Chad)*, 3 February 1994, (1994) ICJ Reports 6, p 23.

foreign producers had to bear avoidable costs as a result of the regulation that domestic producers did not have to suffer.

The shift in emphasis from the individual paragraphs to the chapeau in examining whether a measure may be justified by Art. XX has come with a significant change in the possibilities for future development. The panels' jurisprudence had reached a dead end, categorically brushing aside any policy measure that was not least trade restrictive. On the basis of the chapeau, the AB now opened up a new chapter of jurisprudence, connecting with the past but setting off in a different direction. It is also in this first report in *United States—Gasoline* that the AB expands the outlook for the interpretation of trade law beyond the narrow functionalist lines that had confined previous practice. The GATT is not, the AB noted *en passant* and with considerable repercussions, 'to be read in clinical isolation from public international law'.[193] This statement has come to be of immediate relevance in the AB's second decisive redirection of legal argument with regard to Art. XX at the inception of the WTO. After it had developed the interpretation of the threshold that a measure has to meet in order to be justifiable, it turned to the still pending question that came under the heading of 'extraterritoriality'.

United States—Shrimp was concerned with US import restrictions on shrimp and shrimp products. The US required that shrimp be harvested in a way not exceedingly harmful for sea turtles. Only then could they be imported. This case resembled *Tuna—Dolphin I* in almost all relevant elements. It is most remarkable, however, that despite the fact that neither *Tuna—Dolphin* report had been adopted, all parties as well as the panel argued precisely against the background of these reports. In both GATT cases, the US had maintained that there was nothing extraterritorial about its protection of dolphins beyond its territory by way of internal regulation. Nor does Art. XX, in the view of the US, exclude the justification of such measures even if they were termed 'extraterritorial'. Notably, the US did not attempt to argue that the dolphins were under its jurisdiction but rather that 'dolphin roamed the seas and were therefore common resources within the jurisdiction of no one contracting party'.[194] Under the impact of the *Tuna—Dolphin* reports' focus on issues of jurisdiction and in light of the discourse on 'extraterritoriality', the US now thought it safer to add that sea turtles 'regularly spent part of their lives in waters subject to US jurisdiction'.[195]

In its legal analysis, the panel does not recognize this shift in argument and poorly conflates the claim to a jurisdictional link with the suggestion that sea turtles are a shared global resource.[196] The panel is wholly unimpressed with the AB's

[193] Appellate Body Report, *United States—Gasoline*, WT/DS2/AB/R, 29 April 1996, p 17.

[194] GATT Panel Report, *United States—Restrictions on Imports of Tuna*, DS21/R, 3 September 1991, unadopted, BISD 39S/155, para 3.23.

[195] Panel Report, *United States—Import Prohibition of Certain Shrimp and Shrimp Products*, WB/DS58/R, 15 May 1998, para 3.36. Cf. Bartels, 'Extraterritorial Jurisdiction', 386–7.

[196] Panel Report, *United States—Import Prohibition of Certain Shrimp and Shrimp Products*, WB/DS58/R, 15 May 1998, para 7.53.

report in *United States—Gasoline* and follows the argumentative pattern carved out in GATT jurisprudence. It resumes the apocalyptic picture that had been drawn in the (unadopted) *Tuna—Dolphin I* panel report. If the US, or any other importing country, were allowed to require that importers meet regulatory standards that are set unilaterally, then the whole multilateral trading regime would be at risk. Trade would, it again argued, only be possible between a limited number of states with identical domestic regulation. Should the US measures be found justifiable under Art. XX, this would be the end of a free trade world. It is the very nature of the measures, the panel argued, that puts the multilateral trading system at risk.[197] The only repercussion that *United States—Gasoline* had on the panel's reasoning is that it now tied it analysis to the chapeau of Art. XX, but evidently it saw the chapeau as just another reference point for its ready-made reasoning.[198]

In its momentous *United States—Shrimp* report the Appellate Body overturned the panel's and its GATT predecessors' categorical argument that unilateral internal regulation for non-trade purposes and negative implications for free trade would in every case mean the end of the free trade world. It redirected the practice of interpretation and established a lasting precedent on how to deal with justifications on the basis of Art. XX. The US had argued on appeal that the panel judged the legality of its measures on the basis of whether they constituted a 'threat to the multilateral trading system'. It maintained that this test has no basis in the text of the GATT and, leaning on Art. 3.2 DSU, it argued that it diminishes contracting parties' rights under Art. XX.[199] The US was successful with this argument. Mirroring its report in *United States—Gasoline*, the AB criticized the fact that the panel had not followed the international law rules of interpretation and again underscored that the first task of the interpreter is to examine the ordinary meaning of the words of a treaty.[200] Contrary to the panel's reasoning, the chapeau cannot serve as a basis for excluding a whole range of policies and according to the Appellate Body it rather speaks of the *manner* in which policies are applied. Textual and contextual evidence indicates that the purpose of Art. XX is not to safeguard a functioning multilateral trading system but rather the abuse of exceptions, the AB argued. Therefore, again reiterating its finding in *United States—Gasoline*, it first had to be established whether the policy falls within the purview of one of the paragraphs and, secondly, whether the manner in which it is applied amounts to an abuse.[201]

The AB could have confined itself to precisely this programme. There is little doubt that the measures did in principle qualify under paragraph (g). The decisive issue then was whether they conformed to the demands of the chapeau. The Appellate Body's legal analysis at this stage is remarkably strong and the fortress of GATT jurisprudence and its legacy embedded in the panel reports crumble under its impact. The AB found that the purpose of a measure could not be

[197] Ibid., at paras 7.55 and 7.60.

[198] Ibid., at paras 7.31–7.62.

[199] Appellate Body Report, *United States—Import Prohibition of Certain Shrimp and Shrimp Products*, WB/DS58/AB/R, 12 October 1998, para 10.

[200] Ibid., at para 114.

[201] Ibid., at paras 116, 117, and 121.

invoked so as to categorically exclude a whole range of measures from the purview of Art. XX; the chapeau rather deals with the manner in which the policy is applied in order to separate illegitimate protectionism from justifiable measures.[202] The AB noted that neither Art. XX nor WTO law in general can be read so as to give effect to overarching trade objectives pushing aside all other considerations. It cited ample evidence from the Uruguay negotiations, the preamble to the WTO Agreement, and the Decision on Trade and Environment in support of its claim.[203] At the case at hand, however, the Appellate Body found that the US policies amounted to an unjustifiable discrimination of international trade because the US had failed to negotiate seriously with the complainants.[204] It was also an arbitrary discrimination because of the regulations' rigidity and inflexibility. The implementation of the regulations also lacked transparency and procedural fairness.[205]

The Appellate Body did, however, take a further step that it couched between these two parts of its legal analysis. It argued that measures seeking justification under Art. XX will in most practical circumstances be measures 'conditioning access to a member's domestic market on whether exporting Members comply with, or adopt, a policy or policies unilaterally prescribed by the importing Member'. It did not explicitly reference the unadopted *Tuna—Dolphin* panel reports but they are clearly the target of its reasoning. To argue that such 'extraterritorial' features make measures a priori incapable of justification under Art. XX, the Appellate Body held, would render 'most, if not all, the specific exceptions of Art. XX inutile, a result abhorrent to the principles of interpretation we are bound to apply'.[206] However, a little later the Appellate Body stated that it does 'not pass upon the question of whether there is an implied jurisdictional limitation in Article XX(g), and if so, the nature or extent of that limitation'.[207] In the case at hand it could rely on the sufficient territorial nexus between sea turtles and the US. The AB did however line up all the arguments that were necessary to eventually 'overrule' the GATT reports on this issue.

The findings on the principled scope of Art. XX were not precisely necessary in overturning the panel, they mark a stark departure from the traditional take on the issue, and interestingly form the centre of controversy in a request for surveillance according to Art. 21(5) DSU. In this second shot at challenging US measures in the implementation of the findings in *United States—Shrimp*, the claimant, Malaysia, again emphasized the unilateral nature of the US regulations conditioning market access and argued that such measures quite inevitably result in arbitrary or unjustified

202 Ibid., at para 149.

203 Ibid., at paras 152–154. Cf. R Howse, 'The Appellate Body Rulings in the Shrimp/Turtle case. A new legal baseline for the trade and environment debate' (2002) 27 *Columbia Journal of Environmental Law* 491–521, 509–10.

204 Appellate Body Report, *United States—Import Prohibition of Certain Shrimp and Shrimp Products*, WB/DS58/AB/R, 12 October 1998, paras 161–176.

205 Ibid., at paras 177–184.

206 Ibid., at para 121.

207 Ibid., at para 133. Cf. R Wolfrum, Article XX GATT 1994, General Exceptions [Chapeau], in: R Wolfrum, P-T Stoll, and K Kaiser (eds), *Max Planck Commentaries on World Trade Law*, vol 2 (Leiden: Nijhoff 2006), 66–79, Mns 34–44.

discrimination, recalling the apocalyptic scenario of the end of the free trade world. The panel rejected this claim closely along the lines of the AB report. Malaysia appealed and also noted that the panel had unduly relied on the AB report rather than its own objective assessment of the matter. It argued further that the AB's findings to the effect that unilateral measures such as those by the US were not a priori excluded from the scope of Art. XX were only *dicta*.

With regard to the preliminary question of whether the panel dutifully fulfilled its obligation under Arts 11 and 21(5) DSU or unduly relied on the AB report, it is interesting to note that the argument made by Malaysia centred not on an analysis of the DSU, but on the precedent set in *Canada—Aircraft (21.5)*.[208] While Malaysia tried to diminish the force of an earlier decision it evidently saw no better support for doing so than with the help of another earlier decision. The AB rejected Malaysia's appeal on this point and confirmed the reasoning of the panel.[209]

With regard to the scope of Art. XX and the status of the AB's findings in this matter, the AB then emphatically stated that its original findings were not *dicta* but that they rather expressed principles central to its ruling. It continued:

> The reasoning in our Report in *United States—Shrimp* on which the Panel relied was not *dicta*; it was essential to our ruling. The Panel was right to use it, and right to rely on it. Nor are we surprised that the Panel made frequent references to our Report in *United States—Shrimp*. Indeed, we would have expected the Panel to do so. The Panel had, necessarily, to consider our views on this subject, as we had overruled certain aspects of the findings of the original panel on this issue and, more important, had provided interpretative guidance for future panels, such as the Panel in this case.[210]

The 'territorial limitation' that had come to be part of interpretative practice since *Tuna—Dolphin I* had been challenged by a general statement in *United States—Shrimp* which was not precisely necessary for deciding the case and was later elevated in *United States—Shrimp (21.5)* to form an essential part of the AB's original ruling.[211] This is an intriguing pattern of politics in interpretation: a general statement may at first not be subject to much criticism because it is not decisive and may at a later stage be invoked as a basis for judgments of (il)legality. This could be both cunning technique or unforeseen effect. Either way, the pattern has worked in another decisive step that will come up shortly: *EC—Asbestos*.[212]

Before that, a further creative argumentative figure in the Appellate Body's report deserves to be highlighted; namely, the AB created some freedom for itself with the technique of 'completing the analysis'. While Art. 17(6) DSU confines appeals to

[208] Appellate Body Report, *Canada—Measures Affecting the Export of Civilian Aircraft (Article 21.5)*, WT/DS70/AB/R, 21 July 2000.

[209] Appellate Body Report, *United States—Import Prohibition of Certain Shrimp and Shrimp Products (Article 21.5)*, WB/DS58/AB/R, 22 October 2001, paras 84–99.

[210] Appellate Body Report, *United States—Import Prohibition of Certain Shrimp and Shrimp Products (Article 21.5)*, WB/DS58/AB/R, 22 October 2001, para 138.

[211] Trebilcock and Howse, *International Trade*, 532.

[212] Appellate Body Report, *European Communities—Measures Affecting Asbestos and Products Containing Asbestos*, WT/DS135/AB/R, 12 March 2001.

'issues of law covered in the panel reports and legal interpretations developed by the panel', the AB has used the technique of 'completing the analysis' to widen these limitations. Quite sensibly it had maintained in *EC—Poultry* that 'the reversal of a panel's finding on a legal issue may require us to make a finding on a legal issue which was not addressed by the panel'.[213] Under the heading of 'completing the analysis' the AB has since frequently continued its reasoning, sometimes with significant repercussions on future interpretations of WTO law. Also in *United States—Shrimp* it could have said a lot less if it had not completed the analysis.

One last feature that merits being highlighted in the seminal *United States—Shrimp* report is that the parties to the dispute fought about whether sea turtles are 'exhaustible natural resources' at all and it is in this context that the Appellate Body first spelled out its idea of evolutionary interpretation. It noted that 'the generic term "natural resources" in Article XX(g) is not "static" in its content or reference but is rather "by definition, evolutionary"'.[214] It went on to cite other new legal instruments that make references to natural resources and suggests that the meaning of para (g) has to evolve with broader developments in international law. It did so with reference to the ICJ's *Namibia* Advisory Opinion where the court stated that some concepts embodied in a treaty are 'by definition, evolutionary' and that their 'interpretation cannot remain unaffected by the subsequent development of law . . . '.[215] 'Moreover,' the ICJ continued, 'an international instrument has to be interpreted and applied within the framework of the entire legal system prevailing at the time of the interpretation.'[216] With this reference, the Appellate Body again placed the practice of interpretation in trade law within the broader international law context. The figure of evolutionary interpretation has since flared up time and again; lately it was a hotly disputed topic in *China—Publications and Audiovisual Products* where China complained on appeal that the panel had changed the meaning of the schedules to which it had committed itself.[217] In a rather *nonchalant* manner the AB intriguingly stated that 'we consider that the terms used in China's GATS Schedule ("sound recording" and "distribution") are sufficiently generic that what they apply to may change over time'.[218]

[213] Appellate Body Report, *European Communities—Measures Affecting the Importation of Certain Poultry Products*, WT/DS69/AB/R, 13 July 1998, (adopted 23 July 1998), para 156. Remember that the Appellate Body does not have the possibility of remanding a case to the panel. Cf. J P Trachtman, 'The World Trading System, the International Legal System and Multilevel Choice' (2006) 12 *European Law Journal* 469–85.

[214] Appellate Body Report, *United States—Import Prohibition of Certain Shrimp and Shrimp Products*, WB/DS58/AB/R, 12 October 1998, para 130.

[215] *Legal Consequences for States of the Continuing Presence of South Africa in Namibia (South West Africa) notwithstanding Security Council Resolution 276 (1970)*, Advisory Opinion of 21 June 1971, ICJ Reports 16, p 31. See also *Aegean Sea Continental Shelf (Greece v Turkey)*, Judgment of 19 December 1978, ICJ Reports 3, paras 76–77.

[216] Ibid.

[217] Appellate Body Report, *China—Measures Affecting Trading Rights and Distribution Services for Certain Publications and Audiovisual Entertainment Products*, WT/DS363/AB/R, 21 December 2009, para 47.

[218] Ibid., at para 369. Cf. Panel Report, *European Communities and its Member States—Tariff Treatment of Certain Information Technology Products*, WT/DS375, 376 & 377/R, 16 August 2010 (At issue was again the interpretation of concession commitments in view of technological progress. The

The institutional changes and the creation of the Appellate Body have truly marked a new beginning in legal practice with regard to Art. XX. While the panels in *United States—Gasoline* and *United States—Shrimp* testified to the lasting legacy of the old insider network, the new Appellate Body and its members engaged in incrementally transformative legal practice. Most importantly, they redirected legal argument from an exclusive focus on the paragraphs of Art. XX to a two-tiered analysis that would first examine whether a measure could in principle qualify under one of the paragraphs and then proceed to analyse whether the manner in which it is applied conforms with the requirements of the chapeau. With this move, the Appellate Body took a more considerate stance on environmental concerns as well as other public policy considerations. Rather than effectively establishing that trade is trump, it opened up avenues for member states to rely on general exceptions. At the same time, the Appellate Body opened up new ways for strengthening their own authority. As a bottom line, José Alvarez notes, '[n]either the WTO's admirers nor its detractors within the environmental community can deny that the *Shrimp/Turtle* Appellate Body has given a whole new layer of meaning to the bare text of article XX of the GATT.'[219] Of course this meaning is subject to continuous contestation.

3. Proportionality, interpretation, and legitimacy

Arguably, the new layer of meaning with which the practice of interpretation has now coated the text of Art. XX has come to demand that policies pursuing legitimate non-trade objectives be proportionate (a.). The Appellate Body does indeed seem to have further increased its powers by claiming that it needs to balance competing interests in order to assess whether a measure can be justified on the basis of general exceptions. What this balancing actually entails and whether it demands a fully-fledged proportionality test is a hotly disputed issue (b.). It is most striking that, with the advancement of the theme of proportionality, the discourse on Art. XX on the whole turned into a discourse about what WTO adjudicators can legitimately do. This question involves, above all, considerations about their role in a system of multilevel governance (c.).

a) Proportionality

In *United States—Gasoline* and *United States—Shrimp* the Appellate Body saw its task with regard to the chapeau of Art. XX to lie in examining whether measures were 'applied reasonably, with due regard both to the legal duties of the party

panel here found that it was unnecessary 'to resort to any form of evolutionary interpretation of the terms, in light of our conclusion on the ordinary meaning of the terms.' Quote at footnote 807).

[219] Alvarez, *International Organizations*, 472.

claiming the exception and the legal rights of the other parties concerned'.[220] In the latter report it specified that

> [t]he chapeau of Article XX is, in fact, but one expression of the principle of good faith. This principle, at once a general principle of law and a general principle of international law, controls the exercise of rights by states. One application of this general principle, the application widely known as the doctrine of *abus de droit*, prohibits the abusive exercise of a state's rights and enjoins that whenever the assertion of a right 'impinges on the field covered by [a] treaty obligation, it must be exercised bona fide, that is to say, reasonably.'[221]

Here the report quotes Bin Cheng who elaborated that '[a] reasonable and bona fide exercise of a right . . . is one which is appropriate and necessary for the purpose of the right'.[222] The Appellate Body immediately went on to state that

> [t]he task of interpreting and applying the chapeau is, hence, essentially the delicate one of locating and marking out a line of equilibrium between the right of a Member to invoke an exception under Article XX and the rights of the other Members under varying substantive provisions. . . . The location of the line of equilibrium, as expressed in the chapeau, is not fixed and unchanging; the line moves as the kind and the shape of the measures at stake vary and as the facts making up specific cases differ.[223]

Even though the report links its reasoning to the principle of good faith and the doctrine of abuse of rights, its language closely resembles a description of what would be required in the application of the principle of proportionality.[224] In light of the Appellate Body's pioneering treatment of the chapeau some commentators at the time saw the advent of proportionality in international trade law. Be it in praise or dismay, they stressed that proportionality analysis would now provide the standard for WTO adjudicators when assessing justifications.[225]

220 Appellate Body Report, *United States—Standards for Reformulated and Conventional Gasoline*, WT/DS2/AB/R, 29 April 1996, p 22; Appellate Body Report, *United States—Import Prohibition of Certain Shrimp and Shrimp Products*, WB/DS58/AB/R, 12 October 1998, para 151.

221 Ibid., at para 158.

222 B Cheng, *General Principles of Law as Applied by International Courts and Tribunals* (London: Stevens 1953), 125.

223 Appellate Body Report, *United States—Import Prohibition of Certain Shrimp and Shrimp Products*, WB/DS58/AB/R, 12 October 1998, para 159.

224 See M Byers, 'Abuse of Rights: An Old Principle, A New Age' (2002) 47 *McGill Law Journal* 389–431. On the distinction between the two concepts of abuse of right and proportionality that should probably not be glossed over too easily see, for instance, the discussion on the interpretation of former Art. 30 TEC by J Neumann and E Türk, 'Necessity Revisited: Proportionality in World Trade Organization law after Korea-Beef, EC-Asbestos and EC-Sardines' (2003) 37 *Journal of World Trade* 199–233, 205–6.

225 M Hilf, 'Power, Rules and Principles—which orientation for WTO/GATT law?' (2001) 4 *Journal of International Economic Law* 111–30, 121; J P Trachtman, 'The Domain of WTO Dispute Resolution' (1999) 40 *Harvard International Law Journal* 333–78, 362–4. Cautioning against such a step, R Howse and K Nicolaïdis, Legitimacy and Global Governance: Why Constitutionalizing the WTO is a Step Too Far, in: R B Porter, P Sauve, A Subramian, and A B Zampetti (eds), *Efficiency, Equity, Legitimacy and Governance: The Multilateral Trading System at the Millenium* (Washington: Brookings 2001), 227–52; v Bogdandy, 'Law and Politics in the WTO'.

Sure enough, proportionality analysis in law is used in distinct ways and thus comes with different meanings. A shared focus of its uses might lie in its reference to a balance to be struck between competing rights or interests. It may be well thought of as an analytical structure for striking such balance.[226] Its origin could well be traced back to practices in the German legal system where it over time gained a considerable degree of sophistication in court jurisprudence, legal doctrine, and legal theory.[227] Interestingly, the German Basic Law does not spell out the principle of proportionality explicitly but the Federal Constitutional Court has shaped it as an unwritten constitutional principle in its practice with reference to the concepts of the *Rechtsstaat* and fundamental rights.[228] According to the jurisprudence of the court, the principle of proportionality demands four steps in the legal evaluation of a certain measure: first, the measure must pursue a *legitimate aim (legitimer Zweck)*; second, it must be suitable or *effective* (*geeignet*) for the achievement of the stated objective; third, it must be *necessary* (*erforderlich*), which means that no less restrictive or less intrusive alternative is available; fourth, it must be *appropriate* (*angemessen*) for the achievement of the aim. This last element, also termed proportionality *stricto sensu*,[229] demands a weighing and balancing of competing interests with the possible result that a measure may be found illegal because it imposes an undue disadvantage even if no alternative was available that could achieve the stated objective to the same extent.[230]

The four-pronged proportionality analysis may be considered one of the major contributions of German legal thinking to European law. The jurisprudence of the ECJ established proportionality as a general principle of European law in the 1970s and has frequently applied it since with a meaning very much in line with its use in the German legal system.[231] Proportionality also made its way into European

[226] M Kumm, 'Constitutional Rights as Principles: On the Structure and Domain of Constitutional Justice' (2004) 2 *International Journal of Constitutional Law* 574–96.

[227] E Grabitz, 'Der Grundsatz der Verhältnismäßigkeit in der Rechtsprechung des Bundesverfassungsgerichts' (1973) 98 *Archiv des öffentlichen Rechts* 568–616 (on the formative years of the jurisprudence of the German Federal Constitutional Court); B Schlink, *Abwägung im Verfassungsrecht* (Berlin: Duncker & Humblot 1976); B Schlink, Der Grundsatz der Verhältnismäßigkeit, in: P Badura and H Dreier (eds), *Festschrift 50 Jahre Bundesverfassungsgericht* (Tübingen: Mohr Siebeck 2001), 445–65; R Alexy, *Theorie der Grundrechte*, (Frankfurt am Main: Suhrkamp 1994). Cf. M Hilf and S Puth, The Principle of Proportionality on its Way into WTO/GATT Law, in: A v Bogdandy, P C Mavroidis and Y Mény (eds), *European Integration and International Co-ordination* (The Hague: Kluwer 2002), 199–218, 200–2 (striking a link between these domestic practices and the Appellate Body's reasoning in *United States—Gasoline* and *United States—Shrimp*).

[228] German Constitutional Court, *Wencker*, 15 December 1965, 19 BVerfG 342, p 349 (finding that proportionality analysis follows directly from the nature of fundamental rights—'aus dem Wesen der Grundrechte selbst'); German Constitutional Court, *Zweckentfremdung von Wohnraum*, 4 February 1975, 38 BVerfG 348, p 368 (tying proportionality analysis to the principle of the *Rechtsstaat*).

[229] Not only to avoid theoretical squabbles about something like a 'strict sense' at this point, but also to avoid confusion by using the same expression for the whole test as well as its last element, I do not adopt that terminology but rather speak of 'appropriateness'.

[230] For an illustrative example from domestic constitutional law with a critical view on the negative repercussions of balancing, see J v Bernstorff, 'Pflichtenkollision und Menschenwürdegarantie: Zum Vorrang staatlicher Achtungspflichten im Normbereich von Art. 1 GG' (2008) 47 *Der Staat* 21–40.

[231] Case 174/82, *Sandoz* (1983) ECR 2445, para 18; Joined cases C-13/91 and C-113/91, *Debus* (1992) ECR I-3617, para 16; cf. J H H Weiler, Epilogue: Towards a Common Law of International

human rights law by way of the jurisprudence of the ECtHR. The court has for example interpreted the qualification that restrictions placed on Arts 8–11 ECHR must be 'necessary in a democratic society' to mean that the 'measure employed must be proportionate to the legitimate aim pursued'.[232] With slightly different features, the principle also appears prominently in the laws of armed conflict[233] and in the right to self-defence.[234] Note also that with regard to countermeasures, Art. 51 ILC Draft Articles on State Responsibility stipulates a general rule of proportionality: 'Countermeasures must be commensurate with the injury suffered, taking into account the gravity of the internationally wrongful act and the rights in question.'[235]

In view of this summary sketch of proportionality's track record it might not be surprising if it also found its way into international trade law. Treaty provisions and jurisprudence have been read in this light and sure enough, in *United States—Cotton Yarn*, proportionality did make its first appearance in the context of the WTO. In this case dealing with transitional safeguard remedies against certain imports under the Agreement on Textiles and Clothing (ATC), the Appellate Body read the conditions for attributing damages under Art. 6(4) ATC as an expression of the principle of proportionality and found support for its interpretation in the general international law on countermeasures.[236] It also tied its reasoning to Art. 22 (4) DSU providing that 'the suspension of concessions or other obligations authorized by the DSB shall be equivalent to the level of the nullification or impairment', thus suggesting that the principle of proportionality generally informs the law of countermeasures within the WTO.[237] The Agreement on Subsidies and Countervailing Measures (SCM Agreement) provides further support and guidance for this

Trade, in: J H H Weiler (ed), *The EU, the WTO and the NAFTA. Towards a common law of international trade?* (Oxford: Oxford University Press 2000), 201–32 (juxtaposing developments in European law with international trade law).

232 From the abundance of jurisprudence on this issue, see *Case of Gillow v The United Kingdom*, 24 November 1986, paras 55 and 120. Cf. J Frowein, Vorbemerkungen zu Art. 8–11, in: J Frowein and W Peukert (eds), *EMRK-Kommentar* (Kehl am Rhein: N.P. Engel 2009), 279–86, 284–86.

233 For a clear-cut expression of proportionality see Art. 51(5)(b) Protocol Additional to the Geneva Conventions of 12 August 1949 (Protocol I), 8 June 1977 (prohibiting 'an attack which may be expected to cause incidental loss of civilian life, injury to civilians, damage to civilian objects, or a combination thereof, which would be excessive in relation to the concrete and direct military advantage anticipated'). Cf. C Pilloud and Y Sandoz, *Commentary on the Additional Protocols of 8 June 1977 to the Geneva Conventions of 12 August 1949* (Geneva: Nijhoff 1987), 625–6.

234 *Military and Paramilitary Activities in and Against Nicaragua (Nicaragua v United States Of America)*, Judgment of 27 June 1986, ICJ Reports 14, para 176 (noting that the UN Charter 'does not contain any specific rule whereby self-defence would warrant only measures which are proportional to the armed attack and necessary to respond to it' but finding that this is 'a rule well established in customary international law.'). Also see *Legality of the Threat or Use of Nuclear Weapons*, Advisory Opinion of 8 July 1996, ICJ Reports 226, paras 41 and 46. Cf. M Krugmann, *Der Grundsatz der Verhältnismäßigkeit im Völkerrecht* (Berlin: Duncker & Humblot 2004); E Cannizzaro, *Il principio della proporzionalità nell'ordinamento internazionale* (Milano: Giuffrè 2000).

235 Also see *Gabčíkovo-Nagymaros Project (Hungary v Slovakia)*, Judgment of 25 September 1997, ICJ Reports 7, para 85.

236 Appellate Body Report, *United States—Transitional Safeguard Measure on Combed Cotton Yarn from Pakistan*, WT/DS192/AB/R, 8 October 2001, paras 120 and 122.

237 Ibid., at para 120.

position. But neither Art. 4(10) SCM Agreement, taken in support of proportionality analysis, nor the Agreement generally state the objective of countermeasures, thus leaving considerable discretion to the adjudicators on how to actually apply the test.[238] Even if its contours remain blurred, proportionality analysis has become a common feature in the trade law on countermeasures.[239]

Does this also hold true for the interpretation of Art. XX?[240] Has the Appellate Body introduced proportionality analysis into its analysis of general exceptions? This remains thoroughly debated by all actors involved. The material for contestation on this issue and shades of contingent answers again stem from judicial practice where the Appellate Body's report in *Korea—Beef* provides the main reference point.

b) The contested meaning of 'necessary'

The Appellate Body interpreted the term 'necessary' for the first time in *Korea—Beef* and its interpretation has provided contestants with ample ammunition to buttress their divergent claims ever since. The AB got off to a surprising start when it stressed that its task was to apply the ordinary meaning of the term and for that purpose turned to two standard dictionaries.[241] This is not only surprising because the meaning of 'necessary' had been thoroughly disputed by the parties who would then hardly be convinced by the authority of a dictionary with regard to the question of what 'necessary' really means. It is also surprising because the Appellate Body immediately afterwards rejected the definitions it had found in the dictionaries and came up with its own shot at the meaning. In its view, measures are necessary when they indispensable. But also measures which are not wholly indispensable may still be necessary.[242] Little if anything was gained by such a start. The Appellate Body went on to state in a key passage that

> a treaty interpreter assessing a measure claimed to be necessary to secure compliance of a WTO-consistent law or regulation may, in appropriate cases, take into account the relative importance of the common interests or values that the law or regulation to be enforced is intended to protect. The more vital or important those common interests or values are, the

[238] T Sebastian, 'World Trade Organization Remedies and the Assessment of Proportionality: Equivalence and Appropriateness' (2007) 48 *Harvard International Law Journal* 337–82, 344 (noting that 'significant parts of the law relating to WTO remedies must, by necessity, emerge from arbitral rulings rather than negotiated treaty text').

[239] See Appellate Body Report, *United States—Definitive Safeguard Measures on Imports of Circular Welded Carbon Quality Line Pipe from Korea*, WT/DS202/AB/R, 15 February 2002, paras 257–259. Cf. A D Mitchell, 'Proportionality and Remedies in WTO Disputes' (2006) 17 *European Journal of International Law* 985–1008.

[240] See A Desmedt, 'Proportionality in WTO Law' (2001) 4 *Journal of International Economic Law* 441–80 (offering an overview and comparison of the fields of trade law where proportionality has or might become relevant).

[241] Appellate Body Report, *Korea—Measures Affecting Imports of Fresh, Chilled and Frozen Beef*, WT/DS161 & 169/AB/R, 11 December 2000, paras 159–160.

[242] Ibid., at para 161.

easier it would be to accept as 'necessary' a measure designed as an enforcement instrument.[243]

. . .

In sum, determination of whether a measure, which is not 'indispensable', may nevertheless be 'necessary' within the contemplation of Article XX(d), *involves in every case a process of weighing and balancing* a series of factors which prominently include the contribution made by the compliance measure to the enforcement of the law or regulation at issue, the importance of the common interests or values protected by that law or regulation, and the accompanying impact of the law or regulation on imports or exports.[244]

The AB then candidly asserted that this interpretation is supported by the *United States—Section 337* precedent. It maintained that its demand for a process of weighing and balancing corresponds to the well-established qualification that an alternative measure be 'reasonably available'.[245] This is surely a far stretch and a bold claim. If nothing else it testifies to the Appellate Body's endeavour to connect its actions to precedents and to thus instantiate new meanings within discursive structures.

Korea had argued on appeal that the panel erred in introducing a consistency requirement into Art. XX, i.e. that a member must pursue a certain level of protection consistently. The Appellate Body found that consistency is indeed no requirement of Art. XX. Nor had the panel actually argued this, according to the AB. 'It is not open to doubt,' the Appellate Body continued, 'that Members of the WTO have the right to determine for themselves the level of enforcement of their WTO-consistent laws and regulations.'[246] It then went on to deal with the question of whether Korea could have reasonably been expected to employ an alternative measure 'to achieve the *same* result'.[247] It concurred with the panel that Korea's measures were 'a disproportionate measure not necessary to secure compliance with the Korean law against deceptive practices'.[248] In a final step, it pointed to the administrative costs that alternatives might imply and found that these would not be extraordinary. The Appellate Body thus concluded that a less trade restrictive measure was reasonably available and Korea's measures were thus not necessary in the sense of Art. XX(d).

Any further elaboration on the Appellate Body's reasoning is doomed to be imbued by one interpretation or another of what the Appellate Body actually did. This also holds true when discussing what the Appellate Body itself did with its reasoning in later cases. Has *Korea—Beef* introduced a fully-fledged proportionality analysis into the concept of necessity where it appears in Art. XX? Does Art. XX require that benefits achieved for a legitimate public policy aim are proportionate to the costs in terms of trade restrictions? Opinions diverge. One observation that could hardly be refuted is that there would be a manifest tension between the

[243] Ibid., at para 162. [244] Ibid., at para 164, (italics added). [245] Ibid., at para 166.
[246] Ibid., at para 176. [247] Ibid., at para 178, (italics added).
[248] Ibid., at para 179, referencing Panel Report, *Korea—Measures Affecting Imports of Fresh, Chilled and Frozen Beef*, WT/DS161 & 169/R, 31 July 2000, para 675.

requirements of a proportionality analysis and the categorical statement that members are free to choose their own level of protection. In contrast to a test demanding that the measure be least trade restrictive, a fully fledged proportionality analysis would demand in a fourth step that the measure be *appropriate (angemessen)*; that is, the measure's costs in trade restrictions must not be excessive to the benefits for the public policy aim. A measure might then be found unjustifiable even if there was no alternative to meet the member's level of protection. In other words, the interest of trade liberalization (the interest of other members in marked access) might *outweigh* another member's interest in health protection, for instance.[249] It is certainly hard to see how this would not stand in tension to the credo that a member state is free to choose its own level of protection.

In its immediate follow-up to *Korea—Beef*, the Appellate Body had to deal with a complaint by Canada against France's import ban on asbestos. Throughout the report in *EC—Asbestos*, it stressed the importance of health protection. It did so first in its remarkable finding that asbestos and the French substitute, cellulose and glass fibres, were unlike products.[250] This would have resolved the issue of legality. Only if a measure is discriminatory and therefore in prima facie violation of the GATT would it be in need of justification by way of Art. XX. The Appellate Body went on, however, to engage in an analysis of the general exceptions and extended its interpretation of 'necessity' to subparagraph (b). It reiterated the central passages of *Korea—Beef*, reproducing the tension between the observation that the more vital or important the public policy aims are the easier it would be to accept as 'necessary' a measure designed to achieve those ends, on the one hand, and the credo that the decisive question is whether there is an alternative measure that would achieve the *same* end and that is less restrictive of trade, on the other hand.[251] In *EC—Asbestos* the Appellate Body found that no other alternative could have met France's concern to the same extent thus making this case the first in which a member *could have* succeeded in justifying a policy by way of general exceptions. This finding was however not compelled by the case because the measure had already been found to be consistent with Art. III(4) and was therefore not even in need of justification. But with its pronouncements on Art. XX the AB did line up all the arguments in order to eventually find a measure to be justified by way of Art. XX.[252] This is the same pattern it had employed before in the *United States—Shrimp* saga in which previous *dicta* ultimately came to carry its decision.

[249] E Ruozzi, L'application du principe de proportionnalité en droit de l'Organisation Mondiale du Commerce, in: H Ruiz Fabri and L Gradoni (eds), *La Circulation des Concepts Juridiques* (Paris: Société de législation comparée 2009), 475–92, 475–80; D Regan, 'The Meaning of "Necessary" in GATT Article XX and GATS Article XIV: The myth of cost-benefit balancing' (2007) 6 *World Trade Review* 347–69, 347–53.

[250] Appellate Body Report, *European Communities—Measures Affecting Asbestos and Products Containing Asbestos*, WT/DS135/AB/R, 12 March 2001, paras 113–115 and 129–131. On the findings about the two products' 'likeness' see above note 92.

[251] Appellate Body Report, *European Communities—Measures Affecting Asbestos and Products Containing Asbestos*, WT/DS135/AB/R, 12 March 2001, para 172.

[252] Compare H Ruiz Fabri, Drawing a Line of Equilibrium in a Complex World, in: G Sacerdoti, A Yanovich, and J Bohanes (eds), *The WTO at Ten: The Contribution of the Dispute Settlement System*

In subsequent adjudicatory practice with regard to the term 'necessary' in Art. XX GATT, the Appellate Body has continued to reiterate its balancing test of *Korea—Beef* as well as the assertion that it is beyond doubt that members are free to choose their level of protection.[253] It was careful, however, not to include in its recital that an interpreter needs to 'take into account the relative importance of the common interests or values that the law or regulation to be enforced is intended to protect'.[254] In *Brazil—Retreaded Tyres* the EC had again strongly pushed for an outright proportionality test.[255] Also the Appellate Body was remarkably emphatic about the need to balance the importance of competing interests. It further fuelled controversy by coalescing a proportionality analysis with the requirement that the measure be least trade restrictive:

[I]n order to determine whether a measure is 'necessary' within the meaning of Article XX (b) of the GATT 1994, a panel must consider the relevant factors, particularly the importance of the interests or values at stake, the extent of the contribution to the achievement of the measure's objective, and its trade restrictiveness. If this analysis yields a preliminary conclusion that the measure is necessary, this result must be confirmed by comparing the measure with possible alternatives, which may be less trade restrictive while providing an equivalent contribution to the achievement of the objective. This comparison should be carried out in the light of the importance of the interests or values at stake. It is through this process that a panel determines whether a measure is necessary.[256]

It remains dubious whether the Appellate Body really means what it says or does what it says, i.e. whether it requires that measures under Art. XX can only be 'necessary' if they meet a fully-fledged proportionality test and whether it actually tests measures under this standard.[257] A range of different claims about what the

(Cambridge: Cambridge University Press 2006), 125–42, 141 (suggesting that this may be read as a signal sent by the judges that, once they get the chance, they would decide accordingly). The AB might also have intended to deter Canada from bringing the case again under the TBT Agreement. Cases have since increasingly shifted towards this basis, see the recent Appellate Body Report, *United States—Measures Affecting the Production and Sale of Clove Cigarettes*, WT/DS406/AB/R, 4 April 2012, paras 88–109 (noting that its analysis would be confined to the TBT Agreement and would not extend to Art. XX GATT).

[253] Appellate Body Report, *United States—Measures Affecting the Cross-Border Supply of Gambling and Betting Services*, WT/DS285/AB/R, 7 April 2005, paras 305–308 (involving Art. XIV GATS); Appellate Body Report, *Brazil—Measures Affecting Imports of Retreaded Tyres*, WT/DS332/AB/R, 3 December 2007, paras 176–183. Cf. F Ortino, 'Treaty Interpretation and the WTO Appellate Body Report in United States—Gambling: A critique' (2006) 9 *Journal of International Economic Law* 117–48.

[254] Appellate Body Report, *Korea—Measures Affecting Imports of Fresh, Chilled and Frozen Beef*, WT/DS161 & 169/AB/R, 11 December 2000, para 162. Even where parties to the dispute invoke this element of the *Korea—Beef* precedent, the Appellate Body did not again take it up. See Appellate Body Report, *Brazil—Measures Affecting Imports of Retreaded Tyres*, WT/DS332/AB/R, 3 December 2007, paras 24, 90, and 176–183.

[255] Appellate Body Report, *Brazil—Measures Affecting Imports of Retreaded Tyres*, WT/DS332/AB/R, 3 December 2007, para 137.

[256] Ibid., at para 178.

[257] It should also be noted that the SPS agreement might be interpreted so as to take away from the credo that members get to choose their own level of protection. It might indeed open up the way for examining a measure's appropriateness, see above all the interpretation of Art. 5(6) SPS Agreement in Appellate Body Report, *Japan—Measures Affecting the Importation of Apples*, WT/DS245/AB/R, 16

Appellate Body says or does and about what 'necessary' means are competing in legal discourse centred on its case-law. In scholarship this dispute explicitly extends to political and legal philosophy: the dispute about what 'necessary' means is largely carried out on the basis of whether adjudicators *should* engage in proportionality analysis.

c) Interpretation and legitimacy

The Appellate Body's words and deeds lend themselves to a wide spectrum of interpretations. Some argue that it has already engaged in proportionality analysis, others say it has not. Those who argue it has done so also believe that it should do so and those who say that it has not done so also argue that it should not do so—on both accounts the Appellate Body was right in what it did. More likely, however, the normative idea precedes the analysis of actual practice.[258] The issue appears to divide the community of scholarly commentators. One group claims that the Appellate Body balances the benefits of a certain measure for the achievement of a certain legitimate public policy goal against the cost of that measure in terms of reduced trade. Some had already sketched this path under the impact of the GATT decision in *Tuna—Dolphin I*,[259] others saw the advent of proportionality in the Appellate Body's first steps in *United States—Gasoline* and *United States—Shrimp*,[260] and finally the decision in *Korea—Beef* appeared to establish a straightforward test of appropriateness between measures aimed at public policy concerns and trade objectives.[261] Those who see a proportionality test at work also argue that the adjudicatory bodies within the WTO are right to examine a measure's appropriateness.

November 2003. Whether reasoning with regard to special agreements might spill over into the interpretation of Art. XX is much debated. See D J Neven and J H H Weiler, Japan—Measures Affecting the Importation of Apples: One Bad Apple?, in: H Horn and P C Mavroidis (eds), *The American Law Institute Reporters' Studies on WTO Case Law* (Cambridge: Cambridge University Press 2007), 850–79.

[258] The relationship between normative assessment and analysis of facts (if court jurisprudence or behaviour may be seen as facts) is of course much more complex than it could be discussed here. See only the by now classical *Positivismusstreit* summarized in T W Adorno, A Hans, R Dahrendorf, J Habermas, H Pilot, and K R Popper, *Der Positivismusstreit in der deutschen Soziologie* (Neuwied: Luchterhand 1969).

[259] Dunoff, 'International Trade and Global Commons' (1992).

[260] Hilf and Puth, Principle of Proportionality, 199.

[261] Ruozzi, Principe de proportionnalité, 480–4; G Marceau and J P Trachtman, 'The Technical Barriers to Trade Agreement, the Sanitary and Phytosanitary Measures Agreement, and the General Agreement on Tariffs and Trade: A map of the World Trade Organization law of domestic regulation of goods' (2002) 36 *Journal of World Trade* 811–81, 826–8, and 851–3; A-C Martineau, 'La technique du balancement par l'Organe d'appel de l'OMC (études de la justification dans les discours jurisdiques)' (2007) 123 *Revue du Droit Public* 991–1030, 1005–7; M Andenas and S Zleptnig, 'Proportionality: WTO Law in Comparative Perspective' (2007) 42 *Texas International Law Journal* 371–427, 408–16; Wouters and De Meester, *World Trade Organization*, 57–8.

A number of complementary reasons are offered in support of this suggestion. In a rational-choice perspective, balancing might be considered part of the task delegated to the courts (the agent) by the members (the principals).[262] A strong thread of constitutional doctrine and legal theory also holds balancing to be a quite natural dimension of legal reasoning and there is no apparent reason why this should be different in the context of the WTO. Authors tend to stress the rationalizing and constraining function that proportionality analysis in their view entails.[263] Balancing then tends to be linked to the constitutional qualities within the WTO.[264] Some commentators even suggest that 'the AB focuses on the balancing of competing rights, interests, and obligations as a pre-dominant feature within chapeau analysis'.[265] Also the WTO secretariat found in 2002 that '[i]t may be possible to say that there has been some evolution in the interpretation of the necessity requirement of Article XX(b) and (d). It has evolved from a least-trade restrictive approach to a less-trade restrictive one, supplemented with a proportionality test ("a process of weighing and balancing a series of factors").'[266] And the WTO's World Trade Report of 2005 embraces the jurisprudence on balancing in support of trade law's openness for non-trade public policy considerations—a good thing after all.[267]

In contrast, another group claims that the Appellate Body's rhetoric on balancing is misleading and it should not be taken to imply a proportionality test as it is known from domestic or European law.[268] They maintain that the Appellate Body respects, as it says it does, the regulative autonomy of its members and members' right to freely choose their level of protection. It does engage in a balancing exercise, but this balancing does not extend to the benefits of the measure for legitimate

[262] Trachtman, 'WTO Dispute Resolution', 362; Alter, Delegating to International Courts.

[263] Cf. Martineau, 'La technique du balancement', 1022–30.

[264] D Z Cass, *The Constitutionalization of the World Trade Organization. Legitimacy, Democracy, and Community in the International Trading System* (Oxford: Oxford University Press 2005), 34; E-U Petersmann, From 'Member-driven Governance' to Constitutionally Limited 'Multi-level Governance' in the WTO, in: G Sacerdoti, A Yanovich, and J Bohanes (eds), *The WTO at Ten: The Contribution of the Dispute Settlement System* (Cambridge: Cambridge University Press 2006), 86–110, 99–104.

[265] Andenas and Zleptnig, 'Proportionality', 414.

[266] Committee on Trade and Environment, GATT/WTO Dispute Settlement Practice relating to GATT Article XX, paragraphs (b), (d) and (g), Note by the Secretariat, WT/CTE/W/203, 8 March 2002, para 42.

[267] WTO Secretariat, World Trade Report 2005: Exploring the Links between Trade, Standards and the WTO (2005), 135–6.

[268] D Regan, 'The Meaning of "Necessary" in GATT Article XX and GATS Article XIV: The myth of cost-benefit balancing' (2007) 6 *World Trade Review* 347–69; P C Mavroidis, 'Trade and Environment after the Shrimps-Turtles Litigation' (2000) 34 *Journal of World Trade* 73–88, 79; B McGrady, 'Necessity Exceptions in WTO Law: Retreaded Tyres, Regulatory Purpose and Cumulative Regulatory Measures' (2009) 12 *Journal of International Economic Law* 153–73. Also see A Lang, 'Reflecting on Linkage: Cognitive and Institutional Change in the International Trading System' (2007) 70 *Modern Law Review* 523–50 (offering a thorough critique of the discourse around the 'trade-and...' topic and suggesting that it in effect entrenches the categorical preference for free trade objectives).

public policy aims. This would inevitably contradict a member's right to freely choose its level of protection. Balancing is part of examining whether an alternative measure is reasonably available that would be less trade restrictive and yet would meet the same level of protection.[269] Such an alternative measure might be more costly and this is where the Appellate Body engages in balancing the additional administrative or enforcement costs against the benefits in lesser trade restrictions. Such an analysis leaves the public policy interests of a measure untouched. Neither should the Appellate Body engage in examining the appropriateness of measures, such scholars argue, because it lacks a number of indispensable prerequisites for doing so. Above all, judicial interpretation is not embedded in a functionally equivalent institutional context when compared to domestic or European arenas.[270]

D. Conclusions: Adjudication, precedents, and legitimacy

GATT/WTO adjudicators have shaped and developed Art. XX GATT in their interpretative practice. While at one point in time an attempt at justifying trade restrictions by way of general exceptions was unlikely to succeed because of an exceedingly high threshold and because of the understanding that there was something like a territorial limitation built into Art. XX, such an attempt now faces fewer obstacles. GATT panels of the 1980s and 1990s coated the norm text with their interpretations and also established that a measure, in order to be justifiable, had to be least trade restrictive among reasonably available alternatives. This was the settled interpretation of measures that according to Art. XX need to be 'related to' or 'necessary' for the achievement of a legitimate policy objective. Jurisprudence had created a high threshold that was very difficult to meet. Hypothetical alternatives, if only they were less trade restrictive, sufficed to render a measure unjustified. Panels erected another barrier against what the insider network of trade experts perceived to be a threat to the multilateral trading system emanating from the challenge of policies aiming at non-trade objectives by claiming that there is territorial limitation for measures that could in principle be justified under Art. XX. Arguing with a palpable sense of existentialist angst, they feared that the multilateral trade regime would ultimately collapse if member states were able to condition market entry on process and production methods.

Now, under the tutelage of the Appellate Body, a two-tiered test prevails according to which a measure first has to come under one of the paragraphs, and, second, has to be implemented in a manner that does not violate the chapeau of

[269] See Panel Report, *Canada—Measures Relating to Exports of Wheat and Treatment of Imported Grain*, WT/DS276/R, 30 August 2004, para 6.226 (connecting proportionality analysis to the question of a reasonably available alternative).

[270] Neumann and Türk, 'Necessity Revisited'; Desmedt, 'Protionality', 475–6 (noting, however, that there are other places in WTO law, like the law on countermeasures, where proportionality may well have a role to play).

Art. XX; above all, it must not constitute 'arbitrary or unjustifiable discrimination' or constitute a 'disguised restriction on international trade'. It is now also safe to say that Art. XX does not limit legitimate objectives to policy goals that stay within the jurisdiction of individual states. Such significant developments in trade law have come about by way of interpretation. The practice of interpretation has made Art. XX. Uncertainties remain.

Legal argument now centres on questions of balancing, on what balancing and proportionality actually mean, and on how they relate to the regulatory autonomy of the contracting parties. The reference point in legal discourse is the Appellate Body's pronouncement that determining whether a measure is necessary 'involves in every case a process of weighing and balancing a series of factors which prominently include the contribution made by the compliance measure to the enforcement of the law or regulation at issue, the importance of the common interests or values protected by that law or regulation, and the accompanying impact of the law or regulation on imports or exports'.[271] What does it mean, for instance, that adjudicators should, or even must, take into account the importance of the values or interests of a policy?

Critical changes in the law have gone hand in hand with changes in the institutional setup of adjudication. The creation of the WTO with its DSU and the possibility of appellate review were of course most significant and consequential. In its first decisive steps, the new Appellate Body redirected processes of semantic change. It broke down, at least in part, the high barriers that GATT jurisprudence had erected against threats from the outside non-trade law world and placed its reasoning within the broader context of the international legal order. It critically contributed to a shift from political dispute resolution that followed the logics of diplomacy towards a legal mode of adjudication.

The task of negotiating how commitments to liberalized trade relate to non-trade public policy objectives has notably continued to fall on adjudicating bodies. While early panels played the ball to political processes, the political-legislative process has remained uninformative and unsupportive in this regard. Panels inter alia suggested that multilateral environmental standards should prevent unilateralism. They should curtail protectionism in disguise. But political negotiations have not resolved any of the key questions. The prospects of the climate change regime reinforce this view and suggest that unilateral action appears to be the only alternative. It might thus possibly again fall upon the Appellate Body to decide, for instance, whether, when, and how the competitive disadvantage which domestic producers bear because of taxes they must pay for carbon emissions, can be levelled out in relation to imported products.

The Appellate Body especially carried changes in the meaning of the GATT with the help of precedents whose force it increased itself. The power of precedents is clearly tangible while doctrine and treaty provisions strike a different tone. Even unadopted panel reports have figured prominently in subsequent legal practice.

[271] Appellate Body Report, *Korea—Measures Affecting Imports of Fresh, Chilled and Frozen Beef*, WT/DS161 & 169/AB/R, 11 December 2000, para 164.

Adjudicators frequently do engage with precedents at length and relate their arguments to previous decisions. They use previous reasoning to support their findings, highlight why the present case is different, or, where it is the same, why they differ. Arguing with precedents is a natural part of legal reasoning, just like arguing by way of analogy, for instance. After all, the expectation in law is that the same cases are treated alike.[272] Theoretical approaches of quite different pedigrees agree that one of law's principal functions is to stabilize normative expectations.[273] If a case is decided differently from a similar previous one, then this has to be explained. It is interesting to note that disputing parties do not usually counter a precedent invoked by the adversary by arguing that it is not binding, but by distinguishing it or by giving it a different spin in semantic struggles. Participants in legal discourse are forced to relate to precedents in order to succeed and they are expected to do so. The power of precedents lies at the core of international judicial institutions' semantic authority.

In addition to this general working of precedents, GATT/WTO adjudicators have explicitly strengthened the impact of their reports on subsequent legal practice. At an early stage, it may be recalled, the Appellate Body clarified that precedents, 'create legitimate expectations among WTO Members, and, therefore, should be taken into account where they are relevant to any dispute'.[274] And on another occasion it expressed its deep concern 'about the Panel's decision to depart from well-established Appellate Body jurisprudence clarifying the interpretation of the same legal issues'. It continued to threaten that, if future panels failed to follow suit, this might amount to a failure of its obligation to objectively assess the matter before it.[275] Under the impact of such high esteem for judicial decisions, actors in legal discourse cannot escape the force of precedents and have to engage with them in making their claims. Precedents redistribute argumentative burdens and heavily bear on an interpretation's chances of succeeding. This is common knowledge among the actors and explains the interest in the proceedings and the reasoning that adjudicators employ. Even if the outcome of a report might be shared, members still scrutinize and possibly challenge the reasoning in political bodies or on appeal because it feeds into later practice.[276] As happened in both *Japan—Alcoholic Beverages (II)* and *EC—Asbestos*, parties might appeal even if they had won the

[272] Jacob, 'Precedents'; M J Gerhardt, *The Power of Precedent* (Oxford: Oxford University Press 2008), 79.

[273] Habermas, *Faktizität und Geltung*, 516; Luhmann, *Recht der Gesellschaft*, 151.

[274] Appellate Body Report, *Japan—Taxes on Alcoholic Beverages*, WT/DS8, 10 & 11/AB/R, 4 October 1996, pp 14–15.

[275] Appellate Body Report, *United States—Continued Existence and Application of Zeroing Methodology*, WT/DS350/AB/R, 4 February 2009, paras 362–365.

[276] G Abi-Saab, The Appellate Body and Treaty Interpretation, in: G Sacerdoti, A Yanovich, and J Bohanes (eds), *The WTO at Ten: The Contribution of the Dispute Settlement System* (Cambridge: Cambridge University Press 2006), 453–64, 455.

case at first instance in all practical matters, precisely because they do not want to let a bad precedent stand.[277]

Such concern is not without reason. It is interesting to note that a number of decisive steps in the Appellate Body's development of the law have first been paved in *dicta*. It has made general statements that were not decisive to later build on its general pronouncements in decisive steps. This was the case in overturning what had come under the heading of a 'territorial limitation' in Art. XX. In *United States—Shrimp* the AB said that it does not share the view according to which a measure seeking to protect shared natural resources outside the jurisdiction of a member state ('extraterritorially', so to speak) renders the measure categorically unjustifiable. This had, however, been the interpretation used by GATT panels and was a position that many actors endorsed. The AB gave its opinion but eased opposition by saying that this was not decisive in the present case. It spoke and said that it remained silent. It would 'not pass upon the question of whether there is an implied jurisdictional limitation in Article XX(g), and if so, the nature or extent of that limitation'.[278] In the subsequent proceedings relating to the request for surveillance according to Art. 21(5) DSU, however, the AB then found that its pronouncement on the issue was not a mere *dictum* but the expression of a principle that carried its decision.

Again in *EC—Asbestos* it was not strictly necessary for the Appellate Body to discuss the justification of the import ban on products containing asbestos. And yet it developed a whole line of reasoning that could later be employed in support of a finding of (il)legality. One may also wonder in this regard about (and be wary of) the constant reiteration that adjudicators should, or must, take into consideration the importance of the value pursued in the process of balancing that is required for determining whether a measure is necessary. So far the AB has never said that the objective a member pursues is unimportant—but the arguments are out there and might, at one point in time, support the finding that a measure is not necessary because the trade restrictions are not proportionate to the importance of the goal pursued.

It has been suggested with good reasons that this should not happen. Adjudicators, many argue, do not have the authority to engage in a fully-fledged proportionality test, encroaching upon member state regulatory autonomy and contradicting the credo that members are free to choose their own level of protection. The balancing that might indeed be required does not extend to the importance of the goal, but rather to the costs of alternatives that are no less suited to meet the same level of protection. To the contrary, it could be argued that there is nothing odd about a fully-fledged proportionality test. Some even suggest that it is an expression of the constitutional quality of the WTO legal system.

277 Appellate Body Report, *Japan—Taxes on Alcoholic Beverages*, WT/DS8, 10 & 11/AB/R, 4 October 1996; Appellate Body Report, *European Communities—Measures Affecting Asbestos and Products Containing Asbestos*, WT/DS135/AB/R, 12 March 2001.

278 Appellate Body Report, *United States—Import Prohibition of Certain Shrimp and Shrimp Products*, WB/DS58/AB/R, 12 October 1998, para 133.

So far, it seems that in fact WTO adjudicators have not actually gone as far as to explicitly throw the importance of the goal itself into the process of balancing. They have rather allowed for more leeway on the part of member states by taking into consideration the cost of alternative measures that would be less trade restrictive.[279] It is remarkable in any event that the semantic struggle about what 'necessary' means has turned into a discourse about what adjudicators can legitimately do.[280] The search for meaning has come to be centred on questions of legitimacy in a system of multilevel governance.

In a summary overview it first of all merits emphasis that the spell of precedents in international trade law is neither all curse nor all cure. While it might distance the law from the reach of political legislation, a body of case-law aims at coherence and serves the imperatives of legal certainty and stability. The stabilization of legitimate expectations is a central function of law and judicial practice needs to be embedded in the past in order to instruct the future.

Second, the asymmetry between judicial lawmaking and politico-legislative processes is one of the decisive elements in the debate surrounding what adjudicators in the WTO can and cannot legitimately do. One way of taking away some of the legitimatory weight that international adjudicators need to shoulder in the WTO might lie in a strategy of reviewing the process that has led to a regulatory decision and to strengthen procedural elements in this process rather than to add to the substance of Art. XX. To illustrate the point: when trade measures are the result of a decision-making process that meets certain criteria, when it includes meaningful participation and reason-giving, then it might be presumed to be justified.[281] A complementary strategy would look at avenues of politicization that contribute to the creation and better use of fora in which judicial lawmaking may be politically embedded.[282]

Lastly, a particularly intricate issue concerns the repercussions of fragmentation. The isolation of trade law from non-trade objectives reached its problematic peak at the end of the GATT era with the *Tuna—Dolphin* cases. The Appellate Body has since done a lot to overcome this isolation and to open up to competing perspectives.[283] Apart from the extensive quarrels in terms of judicial methodology and possible confines placed on adjudicators by positive trade law, political considera-

[279] Cf. Trebilcock and Howse, *International Trade*, 543–4 (arguing that *Korea—Beef* did not introduce any additional requirement of proportionality into the adjudicators' assessment but rather opened up more leeway on the part of member state regulation and reversed the restrictive trend that took off with *Thai Cigarettes*).

[280] For an early argument to this effect, R Howse, Adjudicative Legitimacy and Treaty Interpretation in International Trade Law, in: J H H Weiler (ed), *The EU, the WTO and the NAFTA: Towards a Common Law of International Trade?* (Oxford: Oxford University Press 2000), 35–69.

[281] M Ioannidis, 'A Procedural Approach to the Legitimacy of International Adjudication: Developing Standards of Participation in WTO Law' (2011) 12 *German Law Journal* 1175–202; R B Stewart and M Ratton Sanchez Badin, 'The World Trade Organization and Global Administrative Law' (2011) 9 *International Journal of Constitutional Law* 556–86.

[282] I Feichtner, *The Law and Politics of WTO Waivers: Stability and Flexibility in Public International Law* (Cambridge: Cambridge University Press 2012).

[283] Cf. T Kleinlein, 'Establishing Elements of Pluralist Constitutionalism in International Law by Recourse to Formal Principles' (2011) 12 *German Law Journal* 1141–74.

tions about the wisdom and likely effects of the further introduction of non-trade objectives like environmental or human rights protection into the WTO system and adjudication persist and need to be explored in further detail.

There are many other elements to the legitimacy debate that are pertinent and that would need to be taken into account: considerations of due process, the use of *amicus curiae* briefs, and also more substantive considerations of what good has actually come out of judicial lawmaking, to name just a few. The point is that large parts of the legal dispute concerning what Art. XX means in its central elements can hardly be decoupled from considerations of legitimacy. The practice of the legal discourse testifies to how semantic struggles extend to debates about the legitimacy of international adjudication. The reign of the Appellate Body over general exceptions should be understood in the context of a scheme of multilevel governance. This demands above all due regard of the repercussions that interpretations have for the purposes of international law just as much as for municipal legal orders. The following chapters turn in closer detail to the normative implications that arise in the face of international institutions' semantic authority and in view of lawmaking by way of interpretation.

V

Creative Interpretations: Normative Twists

The analysis of interpretative practice has shown how interpretation generates meanings and develops norms. In this way, legal practice makes law—shaping meanings and providing new reference points for legal discourse. A closer look at changes enacted in practice has responded to a blind spot in the construction of sources doctrine and it has offered a complementary account on where international law comes from. International actors have taken centre stage and the outward show of their struggles about what norms mean has been subject to closer scrutiny. So far, I have mainly aimed at analysis and at a better understanding of legal practice in the international order. The preceding theoretical perspective and a detailed study of two concrete fields of law now paves the way for entertaining normative twists that connect to the phenomenon of lawmaking in the practice of interpretation. More precisely, what are the normative implications of international institutions' semantic authority in communicative lawmaking?

The task is set by the challenge that the development of international norms by way of interpretative practice poses for the prevalent positivist narrative of legitimacy in international law. According to such a narrative, international law is valid and binding because it rests on the consent of those unitary states that are subject to it. This idea persists in spite of all the qualifications it demands—including qualifications that have come with the rise of human rights law and international criminal law as well as with developments in philosophy and legal theory.[1] As part of the necessary context for normative discussions it may further be recalled that Martti Koskenniemi locates international law's structural indeterminacy at this classic liberal foundation of international law. If a subject cannot be bound against its will, then an interpretation that contradicts its will, he argues, has to resort to an idea of justice and it thereby turns into utopia.[2] Interpretations would then arguably have to invoke a competing narrative of legitimacy that connects to ideas of substantive justice and they could then in turn be challenged with reference to state consent. Legal argument is trapped between these two poles and constantly oscillates between apology and utopia. Against this backdrop, I have suggested looking at the practice that shapes and shifts the meaning of international norms, that structures the space for interpretation with

[1] See above Chapter II, section B.2.b.

[2] M Koskenniemi, *From Apology to Utopia. The Structure of International Legal Argument* (Cambridge: Cambridge University Press 2005), 59; also see above Chapter II, section B.2.a.

new relevant communications, and that generates legal normativity. In practice, interpretation and meaning are contingent but not arbitrary or indeterminate. Interpretation develops semantic content in incremental steps. Normative assessments of legal developments by way of interpretative practice will have to concentrate on this *locus* of international lawmaking that occupies the space between the norm texts and the law. It is here that practice negotiates the contents of commitments.

The space between the text and the law is of major significance because it accounts for some of the grand transformations that are taking place in the international legal order. Great changes in international law stand in stark contrast to relatively little new treaty text. Some of the changes are part of custom. But above all, changes in the law have come about by way of interpretation. Vaughan Lowe contemplated the *Politics of Lawmaking* and asked a decade ago: *Are the Method and Character of Norm Creation Changing?*[3] He argued that major developments in international law will not come on the level of legislation that passes through the channel of sources but by way of shifting interpretations of such material that is already out there.[4] Even if this view might be slightly too dismissive of past legislative developments and their future potential, it still persuasively points towards the space of interpretation as the place that accommodates major developments in international law. With developments in the semantic authority of international institutions, lawmaking in the space of interpretation becomes yet more interesting.

This chapter first considers assessments of legal developments that look at considerations of justice for guidance and that paint with rather broad strokes. While it is neither entirely convincing to whole-heartedly embrace semantic shifts and changes in legal normativity from the vantage point of narratives of progress, it is neither compelling to categorically understand them as the vile work of malevolent actors who seek domination and attempt to disguise their ulterior motives. Looking at the preconditions for an exchange of interpretative claims that renders such a process normatively meaningful appears to be more promising. Yet, not too much confidence should be placed on a concept of arguing that is overburdened with normative aspirations (A.).

The discussion of the bittersweet taste of justice in international legal discourse points towards two principal tasks for international law to take up. First, it functions to induce actors to translate their idiosyncratic positions into a workable language that channels dispute. Second, international law serves as a medium that justifies the exercise of authority. The chapter continues by focusing on this second aspect and sets out to test international law and its doctrine against the question of how they may contribute to the legitimation of international actors' semantic authority. It first underscores that at present there is a considerable dissonance

[3] V Lowe, The Politics of Law-Making: Are the Method and Character of Norm Creation Changing?, in: M Byers (ed), *The Role of Law in International Politics* (New York, Oxford: Oxford University Press 2000), 207–26.

[4] Ibid., at 212–13.

between processes of lawmaking in communicative practice and the normative construction of sources doctrine. A number of developments in legal doctrine may then be read as a response to this dissonance and as attempts to account for the actions of international institutions: the notion of 'soft law', subsequent practice in the sense of Art. 31(3)(b) VCLT, approaches that come with the field of global administrative law, and research centred on the exercise of international public authority (B.).

Even if these developments in international law and legal doctrine continued successfully, doubt would still persist that international law could always convincingly shoulder the burden of legitimating power exercised on the international level. Such doubt ultimately directs attention towards the interplay between levels of governance. While architectural reforms on each level of governance may improve the legitimatory input that actors can bring into the practice of interpretation in international law, the attitudes among actors who occupy the space between legal orders are of key importance. Interpretation should be informed by an actor's sense about its place in a grand normative pluriverse. It is a difficult and lasting endeavour to contribute to a recalibration between legal orders that proceeds on solid empirical grounds and that is at the same time informed by considerations of legitimate governance (C.).

A. The bittersweet taste of justice in legal discourse

Increased attention for the rhetoric that participants employ in semantic struggles for the law and understanding the creative character of interpretative practice shifts in emphasis. In such struggles, and within the loose contours of the outward show of legal argument drawn by the rules of interpretation, actors craft arguments as to why it is that others should accept their claims. Such arguments frequently do not follow the simple algorithm of legal subsumption and their form blurs the distinction between legal discourse and other types of argument. In many instances actors in the practice of legal interpretation seek to induce acceptance by way of what I wish to call a *rhetoric of justice*. They appeal to a sense of justice and seek to find acceptance for interpretations by inducing a belief in the rightness of their interpretations. Even if other participants might neither be determined to act on their belief of rightness, nor convinced by the rightness of an interpretative claim, they might still find it difficult to reject it because it resonates well with the opinion of peers or of relevant publics.

Such strands of argument usually do not clearly fall outside the scope of what is permitted in legal discourse. They especially overlap to some extent with teleological and systematic interpretations. It should also be pointed out that human rights as well as other legal provisions, which are typically understood as embodiments of considerations of justice, do of course form part of the law. Boundaries as to what is permitted in *legal* discourse shift with transformations in the outward show of legal interpretation and with changes in the understanding of what interpretation is about. The will of the parties and private-law analogies that read international treaties like contracts have been complemented by substantive values and community interests as reference points in legal argument.

This section develops normative appraisals of lawmaking in the practice of interpretation and of shifts in patterns of reasoning. It answers the blunt question of what good or bad has come out of the rhetoric of justice in the development of the law. To an uncritical extent this notably goes against the book's initial caveat that the question of *why* meanings change would not form part of its agenda. Arguments and assumptions on this matter do pervade normative assessments. Theoretical approaches diverge over their assessment of international law's history—the extent to which international law does in fact reflect aspirations of justice. Under the surface of competing approaches to internal law and its relationship with justice linger divergent judgements about the status quo of international law, its history, its achievements, and its future.[5] This section then resumes the idea that semantic historiography paves the way for refined normative appraisal. Changes in interpretations' chances to succeed are a fair proxy to understanding transformations in the structure of international society—'[g]rammar is a mirror of reality',[6] in Wittgenstein's words.

A historical view is inevitable and it is inevitably fraught with difficulties.[7] After the profound break of 1989/90 new windows of opportunity opened up for pushing agendas of international politics that had been put on hold. The prospect of new possibilities made some actors dust off old blueprints for a better world. Others distinguished what was in the past from whatever would be in the future; namely, a liberal and democratic world fulfilling humanitarian aspirations.[8] In this latter view, the bad past is pictured as a point of departure for a better future, a rhetorical and motivational device. It might amount to what Nietzsche has bitingly described as a 'monumental history' that fuels human action in the pursuit of progress, in contrast to a 'critical history' that judges and condemns.[9] Whereas the

[5] With this understanding and throughout this section I draw on J v Bernstorff and I Venzke, Ethos, Ethics and Morality in International Relations, in: R Wolfrum (ed), *MPEPIL* (Oxford: Oxford Universtiy Press 2011).

[6] Quoted in R Monk, *Ludwig Wittgenstein. The Duty of Genius* (London: Vintage 1991), 291. Cf. D Busse, Semantic Strategies as a Means of Politics: Linguistic approaches to the analysis of 'semantic stugles', in: P Ahonen (ed), *Tracing the Semiotic Boundaries of Politics* (Berlin: de Gruyter 1993), 121–8, 121 (noting that 'the semantic possibilities of linguistic signs correspond to the form of reality, or the view towards reality, admitted by society.').

[7] The rising interest in the history of international law highlights those difficulties very well. See R Lesaffer, International Law and Its History: The Story of an Unrequited Love, in: M C R Craven, M Fitzmaurice, and M Vogiatzi (eds), *Time, History and International Law* (Leiden: Nijhoff 2007), 27–42; G R Bandeira Galindo, 'Martti Koskenniemi and the Historiographical Turn in International Law' (2005) 16 *European Journal of International Law* 539–59; I J Hueck, 'The Discipline of the History of International Law—New Trends and Methods on the History of International Law' (2001) 3 *Journal of the History of International Law* 194–217.

[8] M Koskenniemi, 'Why History of International Law Today?' (2004) 4 *Rechtsgeschichte* 61–6; Lesaffer, International Law and Its History.

[9] F Nietzsche, *The Use and Abuse of History for Life* (New York: Cosimo 2006 [1873]). Compare J-F Lyotard, Memorandum der Legitimität, in: P Engelmann (ed), *Postmoderne und Dekonstruktion* (Stuttgart: Reclam 2004), 54–75 (similarly unfolding the uses of history has a motivational device for contemporary action).

former leans towards emphasis on emancipation and betterment, the latter concentrates on domination and is attuned to the potential evil vested in human beings, whether driven by good or bad faith.[10]

Historical narratives are frequently used to tell history in light of a given vantage point. It is interesting to note that political action in the present is frequently forced towards justifications that refer to the past. History, like international law, then becomes the site of yet another level of semantic disputes: actors struggle for authority over what the past means. History becomes significant in light of discourses in a moving present and its reading is subject to continuous contestation.[11] Also here a successful interpretation of the past can be an act of power. Milan Kundera perceptively writes to the point in his literary treatment of themes of totalitarian rule: 'The struggle of people against power is the struggle of memory against forgetting.'[12] Generally, such snags on the way towards the past suggest analysing communications in their social contexts over time.[13]

In order to understand and evaluate how the rhetoric of justice has played out in the practice of interpretation specifically, there are then three broad strands. A first strand embraces the development of norms and semantic change under the spell of narratives of progress and pictures changes as advents of justice (1.). Another strikes a sceptical note and emphasizes how the rhetoric of justice fosters domination and disguises ulterior motives (2.). Both of these strands can convincingly point to examples of legal developments in their support but neither can offer a firm basis for overarching assessment. Normative appraisals will hinge on concrete argumentative practices. If truth lies somewhere in the middle, a third strand might refine the argument by looking at the conditions under which argumentative processes are likely to lead to better outcomes. But the concept of arguing should ultimately not be overburdened with normative aspirations (3.).

1. Narratives of progress and advents of justice

A first broad strand of approaches embraces the rhetoric of justice as a benevolent force or expression of other forces working towards human betterment. It tends to

[10] Cf. T Skouteris, *The Notion of Progress in International Law Discourse* (The Hague: Asser 2010). On mythical narrations and narrations of emancipation generally see J-F Lyotard, *The Postmodern Condition: A Report on Knowledge* (Minneapolis: University of Minnesota Press 1984). Also consider the seminal piece by H White, 'The Question of Narrative in Contemporary Historical Theory' (1984) 23 *History and Theory* 1–33.

[11] Cf. R Koselleck, *Begriffsgeschichten* (Frankfurt am Main: Suhrkamp 2006), 18 (arguing that access to the past is always mediated by language—whatever happened beyond personal experience is only accessible via language with all the intricacies this involves).

[12] M Kundera, *Das Buch vom Lachen und Vergessen* (München: Carl Hanser 2004), 10 ('Der Kampf des Menschen gegen die Macht ist der Kampf des Gedächtnisses gegen das Vergessen.').

[13] Such is the undertaking of a conceptual or discourse history. The starring protagonists of such an approach are, among others, Reinhart Koselleck in Germany and Quentin Skinner in England. For an introduction see K Palonen, *Die Entzauberung der Begriffe* (Berlin: LIT Verlag 2003). Also see P Sarasin, Diskurstheorie und Geschichtswissenschaft, in: R Keller, A Hirseland, W Schneider, and W Viehöver (eds), *Handbuch Sozialwissenschaftliche Diskursanalyse*, vol 1 (Wiesbaden: Verlag für Sozialwissenschaften 2006), 55–83.

understand semantic changes as manifestations of an ongoing transformation of international society and its legal order. Legal development is told as a part of narratives of progress. According to this view, developments in the law by way of interpretation testify to the fact that, in spite of a repugnant prevalence of injustice, humanity slowly but more or less steadily progresses.[14]

There are numerous concrete examples that may be drawn upon in support of such an understanding and assessment. Changes in the meaning of the refugee definition may readily be offered as telling evidence. In the past, the meaning of what amounts to 'persecution' used to be confined to concrete threats to life and liberty. Also the qualification 'reasons of race, religion, nationality, membership of a particular social group or political opinion' was interpreted narrowly. Now it has come to be a standard proposition that violations of human rights may constitute persecution and human rights law has also informed the interpretation of what may amount to reasons of persecution. The structure of legal argument in this regard shows how human rights law pervades other fields of international law and how it promises to improve the situation of individuals in need. Also the increasing integration and harmonization between trade objectives and other public policy concerns like environmental protection in the context of the WTO may serve as a fitting case in point.

Further examples abound. In her analysis of recent developments in international law, Ruti Teitel sees change of such impressive magnitude that she speaks of a paradigm shift that consists in international law's increasing consideration for humanitarian values.[15] Antônio Augusto Cançado Trindade also shares such a perspective, among others, and now introduces it into practice as a judge at the ICJ.[16] This shift expresses changing beliefs about international law's normative foundation, abstracts from state consent, and turns to other subjects of the law, in particular persons and peoples.[17] The new international legal discourse is no longer preoccupied with the 'statist lexicon of national self-determination and state sovereignty'[18] but replete with references to notions of justice. Teitel writes that '[t]he transformed discourse is appropriate for contemporary globalizing politics because it complements the prevailing state-centred approach and its attention to the protection of state borders, with an approach that is predicated on alternative

[14] Cf. Skouteris, *The Notion of Progress*.

[15] R G Teitel, 'Humanity's Law: Rule of Law for the New Global Politics' (2002) 35 *Cornell International Law Journal* 355–87. Her argument is now spelled out in further detail in R G Teitel, *Humanity's Law* (New York: Oxford University Press 2011).

[16] A A Cançado Trindade, *International Law for Humankind: Towards a New Jus Gentium* (Leiden: Nijhoff 2010). From his opinions as an ICJ judge, see *Application of the International Convention on the Elimination of All Forms of Racial Discrimination (Georgia v Russian Federation)*, Preliminary Objections, Judgment of 1 April 2011, Dissenting Opinion of Judge Cançado Trinidade, paras 69–70 (arguing that in the interpretation of human rights treaties there has been 'a primacy of considerations of *ordre public*, of the collective guarantee exercised by all the States Parties, of the accomplishment of a common goal, superior to the individual interests of each Contracting Party').

[17] Teitel, 'Humanity's Law', 362–3.

[18] Ibid., at 370.

humanitarian concerns'.[19] The main thrust of the argument may be descriptive, but one can hardly miss a sense that this transformation is not only appropriate but also very welcome.[20]

a) Liberalisms, social facts, and constitutionalisms

While Teitel is cautious about her normative assessment, others are less guarded. Wayne Sandholtz' account of how norms change their meaning in processes of argumentation embraces a straightforward normative reading of the change that has in fact happened. He argues that there are three main factors that impact an argument's chance of winning: first, how much it is backed by powerful actors; second, how well it connects to precedents; and third, how it chimes with 'foundational metanorms of international society . . . that are at the core of the liberal Western tradition which is increasingly globalized'.[21] Such metanorms, Sandholtz writes, include equality, individual dignity, and the norm that international rules be applied universally. There is an uneasy tension within this statement between the universality of such norms—they belong to the international society—and their particular origin, the West. The observation that they are 'global*ized*' indicates direction and projection. Sandholtz recognizes this and observes that they oftentimes clash with other metanorms such as sovereignty and non-intervention. With regard to change in the laws of war, on humanitarian intervention, terrorism, asylum and refugee law, and self-determination, Sandholtz finds a broader underlying trend. All such developments are linked to 'the emergence of *the* liberal world'.[22]

His argument on how norms develop resonates well with other accounts in an overall liberal approach to international law. International law is above all viewed as handmaiden of a number of global goals. On this note, Anne-Marie Slaughter has offered an understanding of international law as a tool to be used in the endeavour of striving for a better world that is not only more peaceful and stable but is also marked by 'social and political justice, a measure of prosperity, and preservation of our environment'.[23] These goals are taken as a fact. Slaughter reiterates, faithful to the promise of new positivist (in the sense of social science methodology) liberal theory, that she does not endorse any particular set of normative propositions.[24] This element in her liberal theory may well be cast into doubt and it is a standard critique that normative preferences are embedded in particular perspectives.[25]

[19] Ibid., at 370.

[20] This is explicit and evident in Cançado Trindade, *International Law for Humankind*.

[21] W Sandholtz, *Prohibiting Plunder: How Norms Change* (Oxford: Oxford University Press 2007), 21 and 270.

[22] Ibid., at 270 (italics added).

[23] A-M Slaughter, 'A Liberal Theory of International Law' (2000) 94 *Proceedings of the American Society of International Law* 240–9, 241.

[24] Ibid., drawing on A Moravcsik, 'Taking Preferences Seriously a Liberal Theory of International Politics' (1997) 51 *International Organization* 513–53.

[25] C Reus-Smit, 'The Strange Death of Liberal International Theory' (2001) 12 *European Journal of International Law* 573–93.

In political philosophy one may then find liberal variants of ideal theory that is deliberately crafted to guide interpretation in international law. This is for instance the thrust of John Rawls' argument in *Law of Peoples*.[26] In other variants, the protection of human rights reigns supreme and should inform all legal practice. And in part, it looks as if it actually does. A growing number of scholarly contributions respond to a certain discontent with state-centred positivism by stressing the fundamental and all-pervasive aim of protecting human rights.[27] UNCHR could after all thrive on the force of the human rights discourse and use its impetus in pushing for semantic changes in the Refugee Convention. The ICJ has also at times explicitly referred to moral arguments at the margins of the legal discourse. In the *Corfu Channel Case*, for example, it based its legal findings on 'certain general and well-recognized principles, namely: elementary considerations of humanity'[28] and in *Armed Activities* it granted the imprimatur to the concept of *jus cogens*—which is of course a legal concept but loaded with overtones of morality.[29]

With their reference to given global goals and values, liberal approaches to understanding how international norms change their meaning overlap with sociological approaches that have informed contributions by the New Haven School. In their view, certain norms that give effect to moral values, above all human dignity, have gained a privileged status in a 'world public order' and should take precedence over other norms.[30] Michael Reisman maintains that human rights norms have acquired such an imperative character in the second half of the twentieth century that they overtake other norms like procedural rules set out in the UN Charter.[31] The notion of humanitarian intervention and changes in the law on the use of force are but one example that he welcomes. Humanitarianism is again construed as a social fact that may constitute a reference point in normative judgement and that offers guidance for legal practice at some distance from the black letters of conventional law.[32]

There is yet another strand of approaches that embraces a substantive backing of international law, its interpretation, and its change. In the early twentieth century

[26] J Rawls, *The Law of Peoples* (Cambridge, MA: Harvard University Press 1999); C Brown, 'The Construction of a "Realistic Utopia": John Rawls and International Political Theory' (2002) 28 *Review of International Studies* 5–21.

[27] See, e.g., F R Tesón, *Humanitarian Intervention. An Inquiry into Law and Morality* (Ardsley, NY: Transnational Publishers 2005); A Buchanan, *Justice, Legitimacy, and Self-Determination: Moral Foundations for International Law* (New York: Oxford University Press 2004), 53–9.

[28] *Corfu Channel Case (United Kingdom of Great Britain and Northern Ireland v Albania)*, Judgment of 9 April 1949, ICJ Reports 4, p 22.

[29] *Armed Activities on the Territory of the Congo* (New Application: 2002), Jurisdiction of the Court and Admissibility of the Application, Judgment of 3 February 2006, ICJ Reports 1, at paras 64 and 125.

[30] M S McDougal, H D Lasswell, and L-C Chen, *Human Rights and World Public Order* (New Haven, CT: Yale University Press 1980), 367–73; M S McDougal, *Studies in World Public Order* (New Haven, CT: Yale University Press 1960).

[31] M Reisman, 'Unilateral Action and the Transformations of the World Constitutive Process: The special problem of humanitarian intervention' (2000) 11 *European Journal of International Law* 3–18

[32] Ibid.

Hersch Lauterpacht and Alfred Verdross were two of the most influential proponents of a theoretical connection between international law and remnants of natural law. Both were influenced by Hans Kelsen at the beginning of their academic careers and later distanced themselves from him precisely because of his moral agnosticism. Hersch Lauterpacht conceded that natural justice is in fact frequently invoked to disguise selfish interests. But he maintained that this was not sufficient reason for dispensing with natural justice altogether. He suggested instead that '[w]e would rather err in the pursuit of a good life for all than glory in the secure infallibility of moral indifference'.[33] In Lauterpacht's understanding, natural justice always remains in the background of the positive legal order, even if only subconsciously playing its vital part through filling gaps and directing legal development towards an enlightened individualism.[34]

Alfred Verdross took direct recourse to the writings of the Spanish late-scholastic writers Francisco de Vitoria and Francisco Suarez, who had promoted a construction of international law based on Christian religious principles. For him the binding nature of international law was based on the divine idea of humankind ('Menschheit') as a unity composed of individual states. In order to explore the nature of international law, Verdross deemed it necessary to recognize that the divine idea of humankind lies at the basis of the international order. The legal practice of states, he maintained, should be read as an expression of this idea.[35] Verdross also was the first modern international lawyer who advocated the concept of a constitution of the international legal order that was made up of its most fundamental laws.[36] Constructing a certain body of norms as a constitution quite evidently informs what is at issue in interpretation and directs the development of other norms.[37]

This strand of thinking has more recently resurfaced in a number of constitutionalisms in international law that connect to the idea of an international community and contend that a set of fundamental values or principles have acquired, or are about to acquire, a constitutional status.[38] Constitutionalist approaches oftentimes

[33] H Lauterpacht, Kelsen's Pure Science of Law, in: *Collected Papers*, vol 2 (Cambridge: Cambridge University Press 1975), 404–30, 418–19.

[34] See H Lauterpacht, 'The Grotian Tradition in International Law' (1946) 23 *British Yearbook of International Law* 1–53.

[35] A Verdross, Die allgemeinen Rechtsgrundsätze des Völkerrechts, in: A Verdross (ed), *Gesellschaft, Staat und Recht. Festschrift für Hans Kelsen* (Wien: Springer 1931), 354–65, 358.

[36] A Verdross, *Die Verfassung der Völkerrechtsgemeinschaft* (Wien: Springer 1926). Cf. T Kleinlein, *Konstitutionalisierung im Völkerrecht: Konstruktion und Elemente einer idealistischen Völkerrechtslehre* (Berlin: Springer 2012), 207.

[37] C Tomuschat, 'International Law: Ensuring the Survival of Mankind on the Eve of a New Century' (2001) 281 *Recueil des Cours* 13–438 (arguing that certain foundational norms at heart of the international legal order—above all those qualifying as *jus cogens*—emerge as a constitution).

[38] This is a common denominator of quite distinct constitutionalisms. See B Fassbender, 'The United Nations Charter as Constitution of the International Community' (1998) 36 *Columbia Journal of Transnational Law* 529–619; J Frowein, 'Konstitutionalisierung des Völkerrechts' (2000) 39 *Berichte der Deutschen Gesellschaft für Völkerrecht* 427–48; E de Wet, 'The International Constitutional Order' (2006) 55 *International and Comparative Law Quarterly* 51–76; S Kadelbach and T Kleinlein,

suggest that the current world order is based on a priority of values that informs a hierarchy of international legal norms; thereby they promote a constitutionalism, which does not necessarily presuppose an institutional backing of the respective constitutional norms.[39] Even if one does not buy into this theoretical framework, it is quite possible to observe that *jus cogens* guides the development of international law and works most successfully on the level of interpretation in the dynamic change of how international norms are interpreted, and in interpretation made.[40]

Some of the affirmatory accounts of semantic change in international law (broadly, liberalism, sociological jurisprudence, and constitutionalisms) are worlds apart. But they do share the view that benevolent forces of justice have driven the development of international norms by way of interpretation. As an explanation of why change happens the way it does, they can claim considerable plausibility. The human rights discourse has sloshed over into many fields of international law and has guided law's general development. It is hard to deny that this is indeed the case. It is easier to doubt the normative conclusions drawn from this observation. At times it is also difficult to avoid the impression that the force of normative conviction unduly imbues descriptions of what actually happens, maybe even to the extent that explanations unduly blend out other considerations and factors of explanation. Protagonists with a realist and sceptical leaning have articulated a strong categorical critique to which I shall turn immediately. On a prior and more pointed note, the normative conclusions and the underlying understanding of international law and interpretation already face a number of problems.

b) Instrumentalism, finitude, and kitsch

Approaches that embrace the rhetoric of justice tend to share an essentially instrumental or managerial understanding of international law. International law, legal interpretation, and even international organizations are the handmaidens of given global goals, universal values, or community interests—be it in the particular variants of liberalism, sociological legal process, or from the point of view of a substantive constitutionalism. Some approaches even portray a palpable disdain for the formal sources of international law as a result of their fixation on what lies behind the law. Slaughter and others are candid about this when they tellingly paraphrase Carl von Clausewitz and write that 'law is a continuation of political

'International Law—a Constitution for Mankind? An Attempt at a Re-appraisal with an Analysis of Constitutional Principles' (2007) 50 *German Yearbook of International Law* 303–48 (setting out to distinguish themselves from more value-laden and substantive constitutionalisms by way of reconstructing foundational norms as general principles that can be taken from international practice); cf. A L Paulus, The International Legal System as a Constitution, in: J L Dunoff and J P Trachtman (eds), *Ruling the World? Constitutionalism, International Law, and Global Governance* (Cambridge: Cambridge University Press 2009), 69–111.

[39] A Bianchi, 'Human Rights and the Magic of Jus Cogens' (2008) 19 *European Journal of International Law* 491–508.

[40] C Focarelli, 'Diniego dell'immunita giurisdizionale degli Stati stranieri per crimini, jus cogens e dinamica del diritto internazionale' (2008) 91 *Rivista di diritto internazionale* 738–57.

intercourse, with the addition of other means'.[41] It may be recalled that for Clausewitz it was impossible to think about the means without the goal. Never, he clarified, could the means be conceived without the ends.[42] One of the main problems in this strand of entertaining normative twists of international legal developments by way of interpretation is its postulation of global goals, universal values, or community interests that are themselves little scrutinized.[43] And even if they were to be taken as given reference points in discourse, their content would still hinge on what actors make out of them in processes of performative practice. It is then notable that concrete actors are usually conspicuously absent in narratives about progress as they are concerned with the interpretative making of international law and its transformations.

It then turns out that the assumption of a precise fixed point for normative action bears considerable resemblance with the doubtful proposition of an end of history in which all competing narratives and value conflicts are glossed over by substantive (liberal) convictions.[44] Hedley Bull already epitomized such a strand of critique when he spoke of 'premature global solidarism'.[45] He argued that excessive belief in the already existing normative substance, which binds people and peoples together, might lead to unwarranted action because it unduly blends out the persistence of value conflict and power imbalances.[46] The understanding of interpretation as semantic struggle and a focus on how authority is exercised in interpretation also spurs the thought that even if truly universal goals or values were out there, their implementation would yet again depend on the acts of concrete individual interpreters. And even if interpreters were to act in a sincere rather than cynical fashion, they could not escape historical and contextual contingency, the social embeddedness of their actions, and the boundedness in their reasoning.[47] In short, actors cannot overcome their concrete finitude.

It is fitting to close the discussion of this strand of appraising legal developments in international law by returning to Wayne Sandholtz' view on norm change. Sandholtz illustrates his argument with regard to the laws of war on the prohibition of plunder and tells the reader that this is due to his love for art. It is precisely art,

[41] K W Abbott, R D Keohane, A Moravcsik, A-M Slaughter, and D Snidal, 'The Concept of Legalization' (2000) 54 *International Organization* 401–19, 419.

[42] C v Clausewitz, *Vom Kriege* (Reinbeck: Rowohlt 2006), 22 ('die politische Absicht ist der Zweck, der Krieg ist das Mittel, und niemals kann das Mittel ohne Zweck gedacht werden.').

[43] M Finnemore and S Toope, 'Alternatives to "Legalization": Richer Views of Law and Politics' (2001) 55 *International Organization* 743–58; N Krisch, 'Amerikanische Hegemone und liberale Revolution im Völkerrecht' (2004) 43 *Der Staat* 267–97; M Koskenniemi, 'Global Governance and Public International Law' (2004) 37 *Kritische Justiz* 241–54, 251 (stating that 'the governance mindset is itself a form of mythical thinking, a thinking that believes that *behind* law's form there is—accessible to all of us—a blueprint of a better world').

[44] See already S Marks, 'The End of History? Reflections on Some International Legal Theses' (1997) 8 *European Journal of International Law* 449–77.

[45] See A Hurrell, The State of International Society, in: R Little and J Williams (eds), *The Anarchical Society in a Globalised World* (Basingstoke: Palgrave 2006), 191–215, 197, and 212.

[46] A Hurrell, *On Global Order. Power, Values and the Constitution of International Society* (Oxford: Oxford University Press 2007), 55 (carving out this prominent thread in Bulls' *œuvre*).

[47] J Habermas, Does the Constitutionalization of International Law Still have a chance?, in: *The Divided West* (Cambridge: Polity Press 2006), 115–93.

however, that over the past century has come to embrace the thought of creative and constructive interpretation. Umberto Eco demonstrates that the poetics of the open work of art seek to induce interpretative acts of deliberate freedom on the part of the spectator.[48] When analysing norm change by way of interpretation it might be worthwhile to appraise the creativity of interpretations that rests on choices at the intersection between agency and structure. As a work of art, the picture of *the* liberal world might otherwise end up looking like kitsch.[49]

2. Scepticism and realism

A second broad strand of approaches to explaining and appraising how the practice of interpretation under the spell of international institutions makes international law is marked by deep scepticism about postulations of global goals and about invocations of justice in international legal discourse. These approaches very much doubt the actual explanatory force of arguments leaning on the benevolent force of justice, its work towards progress, and its benign impact on how law changes by way of interpretation.

They can just as well offer numerous examples in support of their position. UNHCR has for example frequently appealed to sentiments of justice, in particular the humanitarian needs of refugees, but has mostly strayed away from fundamental issues of asylum. It may be suggested that its rhetoric of justice might have changed refugee law while states remain largely unconstrained in their decision whether or not to provide asylum or to offer space for third country resettlement. Also the extension of UNHCR actions into administering refugee camps and providing humanitarian assistance might quite plausibly be read as a development that helps to keep refugees away from the borders of the political West and distracts from the fact that states are increasingly less inclined to provide refuge. Changes in Art. XX GATT might have their dark sides just as well. Greater credit paid to public policy considerations as justifications for trade restrictions may disguise protectionism and it might be seen to undermine trade benefits on the part of developing countries.[50]

Some legal scholars have developed a critical historical perspective and contend that one of the primary effects of justice rhetoric in the past has been to accommodate European imperialism.[51] They argue that it has formed international law to play a concomitant role in legitimizing the cruellest atrocities in the context of colonialism. For example they point to categories embedded in the law that have divided the (European) self from the (barbarian) other. The concept of humanity, they point out, has been reserved for what was European while others

[48] U Eco, *The Open Work* (Cambridge, MA: Harvard University Press 1989).

[49] Cf. M Koskenniemi, 'International Law in Europe between Tradition and Renewal' (2005) 16 *European Journal of International Law* 113–24.

[50] See A Cosbey, The Trade, Investment and Environment Interface, in: S R Khan (ed), *Trade and Environment: Difficult Policy Choices at the Interface* (London: Zen Books 2002), 7–16.

[51] A Anghie, *Imperialism, Sovereignty, and the Making of International Law* (Cambridge: Cambridge University Press 2005); B S Chimni, 'The Past, Present and Future of International Law. A critical third world approach' (2007) *Melbourne Journal of International Law* 499–515.

are 'humanized' in acts of subjugation.[52] Authors of such critiques are quick to add that their accounts of norm change claim continuous relevance by providing a critical yardstick for contemporary projects and developments. Colonialism is not only a thing of the past but reverberates in many contested issues of our day.[53] Critiques of territorial administration as an extension of the League of Nations' mandate system, that was imbued with the mission of civilizing the uncivilized, spring to mind.[54] Also semantic changes in the law of occupation offer ample food for thought. Article 43 of the 1907 Hague Regulations used to oblige the occupant to respect the laws and institutions in force in the country unless he was 'absolutely prevented'. In the past only his military security could qualify but now also claims to human rights can justify disregard for existing laws and institutions, thus giving considerable discretion to the occupant.[55]

a) Scepticism in international law

Approaches in legal scholarship that are marked by a tangible scepticism about the use of justice rhetoric in international legal discourse have oftentimes drawn inspiration from both Hans Kelsen and Carl Schmitt. Both otherwise antagonistic scholars voiced radical critiques of the use of justice rhetoric in legal discourse and laid bare its ideological instrumentalization.[56] It is noteworthy that they argued on the basis of radically opposed conceptions of law and politics but shared the critical intuition that arguments of justice are often abused to conceal ulterior political motives.[57] For Kelsen, arguing about justice rather than law was to move from what could be objective, or at least scrutinized in the mode of science, to shaky foundations of subjectivism.[58] This was one of his general threads of argument and he

[52] A Anghie, 'The Evolution of International Law: Colonial and Postcolonial Realities' (2006) 27 *Third World Quarterly* 739–53 (examining the actual working of the concept of humanity in the writings of Francisco de Victoria and in the context of the Spanish conquest of America); cf. A Orford, A Jurisprudence of the Limit, in: A Orford (ed), *International Law and its Others* (Cambridge: Cambridge University Press 2006), 1–33. For an illustrative scholarly argument in the context of the Berlin Conference of 1884–1885 see F de Martens, 'La Conférence du Congo à Berlin et la Politique Coloniale des États modernes' (1886) XVIII *Revue de Droit International et de Législation Comparée* 244.

[53] See G Simpson, *Great Powers and Outlaw States. Unequal Sovereigns in the International Legal Order* (Cambridge: Cambridge University Press 2004), 319–51.

[54] R Paris, 'International peacebuilding and the "mission civilisatrice"' (2002) 28 *Review of International Studies* 637; R Wilde, *International Territorial Administration: How the Truseeship and the Civilizing Mission Never Went Away* (Oxford: Oxford University Press 2008), 364–72.

[55] See A M Gross, 'Human Proportions: Are Human Rights the Emperor's New Clothes of the International Law of Occupation?' (2007) 18 *European Journal of International Law* 1–35; N Bhuta, 'The Antinomies of Transformative Occupation' (2005) 16 *European Journal of International Law* 721–40.

[56] H Kelsen, *Introduction to the Problems of Legal Theory* (Oxford: Clarendon Press 1992), 15–19; H Kelsen, What is Justice?, in: *What is Justice? Justice, Law, and Politics in the Mirror of Science* (Berkeley: University of Carlifornia Press 1971), 1–24; C Schmitt, *The Concept of the Political* (Chicago: Chicago University Press 1996), especially at 67.

[57] See v Bernstorff and Venzke, Ethos, Ethics and Morality, Mn. 6.

[58] Kelsen, What is Justice?, 1–24.

sharpened it specifically with regard to international legal discourse. He opined that on the international plane antagonistic politics, an overwhelming plurality of interests, and contradicting claims as to what justice requires would make it even worse to leave the relatively stable ground of the law for rickety moral grounds.[59]

Although with different sensibilities, Carl Schmitt was equally sceptical about references to justice and invocations of humanity in international legal discourse. He brought his critique to the point in the well-known statement which he adopted from Pierre-Joseph Proudhon: '[W]hoever invokes humanity wants to cheat.'[60] In his *Concept of the Political* Schmitt sees a close connection between political violence and moral claims. He observed that states attempt to wage wars in the name of humanity in order to justify political violence. By invoking terms such as 'humanity', the political opponent is rendered an outlaw standing outside humanity and outside the law. Claims to universal values can be used to justify violence of a particularly extreme nature by drawing a moral boundary between oneself and the political 'enemy'.[61] This insight did not stop Schmitt from intensively collaborating with the Nazi government in the first years of their rule in Germany or to uncritically chime in with some of their blunt claims to speak in the name of humanity.

In a Neo-Schmittean account of international political processes, Chantal Mouffe has recently lent a strong voice to the claim that invocations of justice and consensus can lead to the strongest forms of domination.[62] As I have discussed above, she argues that every order is based on constitutive power relations and is therefore by necessity hegemonic.[63] Even if her argument could ultimately not convince, the work of Carl Schmitt is analytically powerful and has inspired a number of strong critiques of political and legal rhetoric in the 'war on terror', for instance, as well as critical responses to the resurfacing concept of 'just war'.[64]

Kelsen and Schmitt both exposed the abusive use of humanitarian arguments and claims to justice in international legal discourse. Their thought has inspired normative appraisals of the rhetoric of justice ever since. Martti Koskenniemi is for example greatly indebted to their thinking and shares the view that the rhetoric of justice undermines the formality of legal discourse.[65] And in a bleaker outlook on the vices of virtuous humanitarianism, David Kennedy has uncovered the dark

[59] H Kelsen, 'The Essential Conditions of International Justice' (1941) 35 *Proceedings of the American Society of International Law* 70–86, 71.

[60] Schmitt, *The Political*, 54.

[61] Ibid., at 67; C Schmitt, *Die Wendung zum diskriminierenden Kriegsbegriff* (Berlin: Duncker und Humblot 1938). Cf. C Brown, From Humanized War to Humanitarian Intervention: Carl Schmitt's Critique of the Just War Tradition, in: L Odysseos (ed), *The International Political Thought of Carl Schmitt: Terror, Liberal War and the Crisis of Global Order* (London: Routledge 2007), 56–69.

[62] C Mouffe, *On the Political* (London: Routledge 2005).

[63] See above Chapter II, section B.3.

[64] W E Scheuerman, 'Carl Schmitt and the Road to Abu Ghraib' (2006) *Constellations* 108–24; W Rasch, 'A Just War? Or Just a War?: Schmitt, Habermas, and the Cosmopolitan Orthodoxy' (2000) 21 *Cardozo Law Review* 1665–84.

[65] M Koskenniemi, '"The Lady Doth Protest Too Much" Kosovo, and the Turn to Ethics in International Law' (2002) 65 *Modern Law Review* 159–75; M Koskenniemi, 'The Fate of Public International Law: Between Technique and Politics' (2007) 70 *Modern Law Review* 1–30.

sides of the humanitarian project. Kennedy argues that the human rights vocabulary strengthens the tendency of international lawyers to concern themselves with constitutional questions of the regime itself rather than with questions of distribution in the broader society. He highlights that human rights can and have been abused to legitimate war, religious oppression, and other repressive projects. In view of how humanitarian endeavours have gone wrong, he demands a 'pragmatic reassessment of our most sacred humanitarian commitments, tactics and tools'.[66] Humanitarian fervour appears to be a powerful source pushing for betterment that may in effect do more harm than good.[67]

In an assessment of the development of refugee law under the influence of the UNHCR, Tor Krever engages in a critical analysis and comes to the bleak conclusion that 'the past two decades have been a prelude to a new era of relations in which UNHCR increasingly plays handmaid to the interests of States—not vulnerable individuals'.[68] The enmeshment of UNHCR in humanitarian aid or peacekeeping operations, its management of refugee camps, as well as the administration of voluntary repatriation have stirred similar critiques.[69] Humanity or substantive notions of justice have been a less prominent *topos* in legal discourse and adjudication pertaining to international trade law. But also here one may caution with good reasons against granting human rights a more prominent and influential standing.[70] Or one could draw attention more generally to what has not happened within the WTO framework—to effectively liberalize trade in agricultural products, for instance—or point to the fact that non-economic interests such as environmental protection are not backed by institutional mechanisms similarly powerful to those in the field of economic interactions.[71]

With regard to its normative appraisal, approaches in this second strand of scepticism in international law do not necessarily hold that nothing good can ever come out of justice rhetoric and its accommodation of semantic change in

66 D Kennedy, *The Dark Sides of Virtue. Reassessing International Humanitarianism* (Princeton, NJ: Princeton University Press 2004), 35. With an apt sense of the exercise of power by way of semantics also see D Kennedy, *Of War and Law* (Princeton: Princeton University Press 2006) (noting inter alia at p 122 that fighting war extends to communicating the war; precisely, that '[d]efining the battlefield is not only a matter of deployed force, or privileging killing; it is also a rhetorical claim.').

67 Cf. G Best, *War and Law since 1945* (Oxford: Clarendon Press 1994), 238 (concluding as part of a less engaged analysis that 'the word "humanitarian" has come to carry a slippery mixture of meanings and applications which facilitate ambiguous and manipulative uses').

68 T Krever, '"Mopping-up": UNHCR, Neutrality and Non-Refoulement since the Cold War' (2011) 11 *Chinese Journal of International Law* 587–608, 608.

69 See above Chapter III, section B.4.

70 See the debate between Ernst-Ulrich Petersmann, arguing in favour of including human rights considerations more prominently in the WTO, and Robert Howse, cautioning against such a move, E-U Petersmann, 'Time for a United Nations "Global Compact" for Integrating Human Rights into the Law of Worldwide Organizations: Lessons from European Integration' (2002) 13 *European Journal of International Law* 621–50; R Howse, 'Human Rights in the WTO: Whose Rights, What Humanity? Comment on Petersmann' (2002) 13 *European Journal of International Law* 651–9.

71 Koskenniemi, *From Apology to Utopia*, 600–14 (on a structural basis entrenched in international law and legal discourse); B Kingsbury, International Courts: Uneven Judicialization in Global Order, in: J Crawford and M Koskenniemi (eds), *Cambridge Companion to International Law* (Cambridge: Cambridge University Press 2011), 202–28.

international law. They rather point to the many instances where cynicism has prevailed or where sincerity has yet led to detrimental outcomes. More than a motivational device, a cause for action or change, humanity would be a vehicle that cloaks and accommodates action springing from self-interested and other considerations. The rhetoric of justice offers but hollow words while change and legal developments really respond to shifts in power relations.

b) Realism in international relations

At its outset in the United States, the discipline of international relations was heavily influenced by Carl Schmitt's and Hans Kelsen's concerns and controversies, above all by way of German émigré Hans Morgenthau whose work provides one of the early cornerstones of the initially consuming realist paradigm in international relations scholarship.[72] Morgenthau endorsed a scientific conception of politics that finds the laws governing politics in human nature and viewed the rhetoric of justice as a simple distraction. It was beside the point. 'International politics, like all politics,' he maintained, 'is a struggle for power.'[73] To invoke moral arguments in semantic struggles over what the law means is really one strategy among many others employed by actors in order to get what they want. Morgenthau said little on the question of normative assessment. If anything, his work reflects scepticism and moral agnosticism.[74]

Claims to global goals, humanitarian imperatives, or considerations of justice are but a reflection of actors' tendency to identify particular preferences with concepts that are said to be universal. In the traditional realist strand of thought, constraints on state action could only derive from a community of interests or from a balance of power. Where there is neither, the enterprise of international law is doomed to failure. In order to pursue ambitious aims, such as peace, it is necessary to work with the societal forces and with struggles for power that pervade political action. Morgenthau cautioned that one should beware any 'attempt to exorcise social evils by the indefatigable repetition of magic formulae'.[75] The hollow words of international legal argument and in particular interpretations that lean on appeals to justice tend to distract from prudent reasoning which rather needs to focus on actors' interests as the perennial standard by which political action has to be judged.[76]

[72] M Koskenniemi, *The Gentle Civilizer of Nations* (Cambridge: Cambridge University Press 2001), 413–80.

[73] H J Morgenthau, *Politics Among Nations the Struggle for Power and Peace* (New York: Knopf 1949), 13.

[74] Note that Morgenthau wrote his *Habilitation* with Hans Kelsen and Paul Guggenheim in Geneva. See J v Bernstorff, *The Public International Law Theory of Hans Kelsen: Believing in Universal Law* (Cambridge: Cambridge University Press 2010), 257; O Jütersonke, *Morgenthau, Law and Realism* (Cambridge: Cambridge University Press 2010), 75–104.

[75] H J Morgenthau, 'Positivism, Functionalism and International Law' (1940) 34 *American Journal of International Law* 261–84, 260.

[76] H J Morgenthau, *In Defense of the National Interest: A Critical Examination of American Foreign Policy* (New York: Knopf 1951), 242. Cf. Jütersonke, *Morgenthau*, 160.

Neo-realist accounts have placed emphasis on the anarchic character of international relations and explained the unmediated struggle for power by the absence of central enforcement mechanisms, thus largely replacing Morgenthau's classical anthropological basis of realism.[77] Yet more recent realist approaches are still united in their disdain for international law or justice rhetoric. They do not credit international law or universal values with any explanatory force. Social or legal institutions, the argument goes, are mere epiphenomena of state action without any effect and at the most distractions for imprudent actors. The explanation of the development of international norms they could actually offer would relate to shifts in underlying power structures. But bearing in mind the futility of wasting much thought on international norms, it is really none of their concern.[78] They follow Morgenthau's creed that one should not be fooled by the talk of law and justice.[79]

Already on the eve of the Second World War and a few years before Morgenthau, Edward Hallett Carr argued that the rhetoric of justice tends to disguise the pursuit of self-interest and often turns out entrenching structures of domination.[80] His analysis may best be understood against the background of an increasing incongruence between the belief in the working of the League of Nations, on the one hand, and an analysis of actual events, such as the Japanese invasion of Manchuria in 1931, on the other.[81] Carr set out a discerning critique of the then predominant liberal research agenda. He claimed that the dismantling of the League testified to the inadequacy of pure aspiration as the basis for a science of international politics. According to Carr '[t]he exposure of the real basis of the professedly abstract principles commonly invoked in international politics is the most damning and most convincing part of the realist indictment of utopianism'.[82] He did not argue that actors are never guided by considerations of justice, but rather, and this is a common thread of realist approaches, that the principles actors do commonly invoke as principles of justice are not principles at all but reflections

[77] John Herz, another émigré from the Weimar Republic, prominently spelled out the idea of a security dilemma in international relations that prevails in the absence of centralized enforcement, see J H Herz, *Political Realism and Political Idealism. A Study in Theories and Realities* (Chicago: University of Chicago Press 1951). Cf. K N Waltz, *Man, the State, and War* (New York: Columbia University Press 1959).

[78] J L Goldsmith and E A Posner, *The Limits of International Law* (Oxford: Oxford University Press 2005), 13 and 167–84; E A Posner, *The Perils of Global Legalism* (Chicago: University of Chicago Press 2009). For a succinct critique see R Howse and R G Teitel, 'Beyond Compliance: Rethinking Why International Law Really Matters' (2011) 2 *Global Policy* 127–36.

[79] Like many truly great thinkers, Morgenthau was much more nuanced than what has been made out of his take on realism. See C Brown, 'The Twilight of International Morality'? Hans J. Morgenthau and Carl Schmitt on the end of the Jus Publicum Europaeum, in: M C Williams (ed), *Realism Reconsidered: The Legacy of Hans Morgenthau in International Relations* (Oxford: Oxford University Press 2007), 42–61; S Dellavalle, The Necessity of International Law Against the A-normativity of Neo-Conservative Thought, in: R Miller and R Bratspies (eds), *Progress in International Law* (Leiden: Martinus Nijhoff 2008), 95–118.

[80] E H Carr, *The Twenty Years' Crisis 1919–1939* (New York: Harper Collins 1964 [1939]), 75–85.

[81] Carr was reviewing the page proofs of his book right on the brink of the Second World War in September of 1939. See his preface to the first edition in ibid., at ix.

[82] Ibid., at 87.

of self-interest. Rhetoric of justice serves to conceal self-interested action and something like international morality is likely to be the product of dominant groups that have succeeded in aligning a sense of what is right and good with their interests and views.[83] In a claim to a shared international morality, Carr saw an 'ingenious moral device invoked, in perfect sincerity, by privileged groups in order to justify and maintain their dominant position'.[84]

It is one of the beauties of Carr's indictment of lofty liberalism that he draws attention to the limits of realism just as well. According to Carr, realism does not usually offer a good account of the springs of action, a grasp of why it is that actors are inspired to do something, motivated, and dedicated. The force of ideas is stronger than what realists make of them, he argued. And not least, Carr uncovered that realism is replete with normative preferences for which it can offer no explanation.[85] While conceding that international law and legal practice quite inevitably appeal to a sense of right that prevails in the respective community, it can, according to Carr, neither be reduced to moralism, nor to the mere exercise of power. 'Law, like politics,' he writes, 'is a meeting place for ethics and power.'[86]

Carr has inspired broad stands of realist challenges to justice rhetoric but walked the lines between an all-too-poor realism and the naïveté that tends to beset some narratives of progress. The English School in international relations theory has continued to tread these lines and made Carr its founding father.[87] In particular Hedley Bull, next in the pedigree of the school, pioneered a conception of international society (a society of states) as being based on a minimum of certain common interests and common values.[88] States consider themselves bound by a common set of rules, Bull maintained, that are aimed at a minimal conception of order as a precondition for coexistence.[89] This thin pluralist international society, he continued to argue, finds a basis in reality—precarious and threatened, but nevertheless real. It allows that, in addition to rules of prudence or experience, morality and international law may have an independent effect on state decisions. With his theoretical approach, Bull claimed to occupy a middle ground between realist and liberalist conceptions and offered first hints of a refined concept of practice for the discipline.[90]

For Bull the primary mechanisms to account for such a possible impact of international norms are processes of socialization in continuous interaction and communication. In his analysis, Bull could only find the acceptance of minimal standards of coexistence in such practice. But he did express the hope that there

[83] Ibid., at 80–5. [84] Ibid., at 80. [85] Ibid., at 89–94. [86] Ibid., at 178.

[87] Cf. R Little, 'The English School's Contribution to the Study of International Relations' (2000) 6 *European Journal of International Relations* 395–422.

[88] See C Brown, 'World Society and the English School: An "International Society" Perspective on World Society' (2001) 7 *European Journal of International Relations* 434.

[89] H Bull, *The Anarchical Society. A Study of Order in World Politics* (London: Macmillan 1977), 17 and 42.

[90] C Navari, 'The Concept of Practice in the English School' (2011) 17 *European Journal of International Relations* 611–30. See above (Chapter II, section B.1.b).

would eventually be a strong 'embedded cosmopolitanism'.[91] It is embedded in the sense that it must start from an analysis of real practices and be mindful of contextual constraints. Otherwise conceptions of global order might unduly endorse a 'premature global solidarism'—i.e., the claim that certain values and interests are universal which in fact find no basis in reality.[92] Such an assertion would therefore be prone to contributing to the projection of a particular *Weltanschauung* onto the world at large.

3. The practice of interpretation and communicative action

The development of international norms, aided and abetted by the rhetoric of justice, is neither all cure nor all curse. Bearing in mind abundant examples of how changes have formed part of shaping or perpetuating patterns of injustice severely limits the level of confidence that narratives of progress can plausibly sustain. On the contrary, resignation and fatalism are just as ill-advised. They unduly defy potentials for betterment and paint the change that has happened in colours that are all too bleak. Fatalism also excuses inaction where action in the face of blatant injustice would be imperative.

While idealist approaches trying to explain and assess semantic change as well as deeper transformations in the international legal order usually abstract from any concrete actor, realist approaches zoom in on concrete actors and look at anthropological or structural conditions for action. The notion of communicative action situates itself between these two competing paradigms and focuses on the actions of socially embedded actors.[93] In so doing, it seeks to explain and to provide a foundation for legitimate order that is situated in inter-subjectivity. For an assessment of international lawmaking by way of interpretation it might harbour great potential because it connects so distinctively to argumentative processes.

a) Preconditions and process

Andrew Hurrell has developed a view *On Global Order* that responds to the downside of both realist and liberal views on semantic change in international law. He argues perceptively that a realist picture is likely to exaggerate the extent of conflict and is unable to respond to moral demands induced by pressing contemporary challenges. A liberal picture, on the contrary, tends to underestimate the

[91] Bull, *Anarchical Society*. Cf. J M Almeida, Hedley Bull, 'Embedded Cosmopolitanism', and the Pluralist-Solidarist Debate, in: R Little and J Williams (eds), *The Anarchical Society in a Globalized World* (Basingstoke: Palgrave Macmillan 2006), 51–72.

[92] Hurrell, *On Global Order*, 55.

[93] Cf. J Habermas, *Between Facts and Norms: Contributions to a Discourse Theory of Law and Democracy* (Cambridge, MA: MIT Press 1997), 174–23 (introducing communicative action in legal discourse against a critique of both realist non-normativity and strong patterns of powerless idealization).

extent of value conflict and the impact of power relations, he argues.[94] Given this tension, it is necessary to reconsider and investigate preconditions for pursuing justice globally.[95] Hurrell is quick to add that Bull's conception of a thin pluralist international society can no longer satisfy. Global challenges of our day inevitably demand broader avenues for international action. It is now necessary to identify substantive collective goals and policies as well as to create institutionalized structures of governance to implement them.[96]

A third path opens up between headily taking the rhetoric of justice at face value and categorically rejecting it on the face of it. This third strand of approaches dwells on the bittersweet taste of justice in international legal discourse, seeks to tap its potential, and ponders the preconditions to make sure that it does not turn sour. Hurrell fleshes out what this way may look like and identifies three preconditions for pursuing justice globally. First, arguments have to be morally accessible which translates into the need for a shared vocabulary that allows argumentative exchange. Second, international institutions are essential in providing the means for debate, to secure stable implementation, and to carry the potential for a progressive development of a global moral community. Third and finally, pursuing justice globally demands effective institutions and political capacities for action—that is the ability of individuals and representatives of collective actors to participate in international discourse, specifically including otherwise disadvantaged actors. This last precondition entails a demand for distributive justice.[97]

Notably, international law is crucial in meeting these prerequisites and it provides the mechanisms for maintaining and developing an international society. International law is neither reduced to the working of politics in the sense of strategic action aimed at maintaining or increasing power, nor is it reduced to a mere instrument in the pursuit of given global goals or in the implementation of given universal values. International law rather contributes to the preconditions for political processes that are aimed at identifying goals and values as well as at arriving at concrete decisions in their implementation. The normative assessment of semantic change in international norms can then not rest on an outside perspective. Nor can it find decisive orientation in considerations of substantive justice.[98] Finding such orientation may be possible in some clear cases, but usually the identification of global goals and their implementation would have to be part of a political process that satisfies certain preconditions.

[94] Hurrell, *On Global Order*, chapter 2 (introducing the realist understanding of global (dis-)order and its limits) and chapter 3 (conversely discussing the idealist or liberalist view of the world and its shortcomings).

[95] Hurrell, *On Global Order*, at 298.

[96] Ibid., at 308–14.

[97] Ibid., at 298–318. One may add that this would also entail the demand of democratic domestic governance, but Hurrell does not speak on this issue. See in detail on this point N Petersen, *Demokratie als teleologisches Prinzip* (Heidelberg: Springer 2009).

[98] See already Carr, *The Twenty Years' Crisis*, 21 (maintaining that 'the search for ethical norms outside politics is doomed to frustration').

On this note, progress remains a prospect at the vanishing point of political processes and such processes hinge on a legal framework to maintain their promise.[99]

This third line of thinking strongly resembles the *œuvre* of Jürgen Habermas.[100] Habermas has critiqued unilateral assertions about what it is that justice demands as 'hegemonic liberalism'.[101] He suggests that such unilateralism leads to a dead-end because in concrete cases even a benevolent hegemon could not know what would be good for others. Beyond a minimal pragmatic consensus in the form of fundamental human rights and minimal guarantees for coexistence, morality can only be the aim of an inclusive deliberative process in which actors can reason for and against normative propositions. The ethical foundation of a unilateral assertion with regard to universal values necessarily remains deficient.[102] But the minimal pragmatic consensus is just as much in need of interpretation. It is not self-explanatory and more often than not it is contested. Even where a minimal basis does exist, where it is indeed shared, it is so narrow that it can barely guide concrete action. Processes of global governance tend to go well beyond this slim foundation and struggle to find a legitimate foundation or a link with legitimating political processes.

Habermas further develops an idea of constitutionalism in international law that does not straightforwardly build on universal values but rather asks for the necessary preconditions for a cooperative and discursive mode of dealing with normative disagreement.[103] Fundamental prerequisites are the prohibition of the use of force as well as the protection of human rights. They find their foundation in their constitutive function for such a discourse.[104] Habermas' approach locates part of the normativity of decisions taken in the processes of arguing among concrete and socially embedded individuals. One of its great merits is that it responds precisely to the problems of positivism provoked by semantic pragmatism and the linguistic turn. It attempts to bridge liberal positions that rely primarily on abstract, not contextualized human reason, on the one hand, and communitarian approaches

[99] Hurrell embraces legal positivism's core intuition in this regard, namely, 'that, in an international society characterized by deep and fundamental value conflict and by the constant difficulty of managing unequal power, a viable and stable international legal order must be built around shared processes and procedures, accepted understandings of legal sources, and a commitment to diplomatic negotiation and dialogue.' Hurrell, *On Global Order*, 312–13.

[100] Jürgen Habermas' thought permeates parts of Hurell's book, Hurrell, *On Global Order*, see especially at 315.

[101] Habermas, The Constitutionalization of International Law, 183–5.

[102] Ibid. Also see M Koskenniemi, 'Perceptions of Justice: Walls and Bridges Between Europe and the United States' (2004) 64 *Zeitschrift für ausländisches öffentliches Recht und Völkerrecht* 305.

[103] Habermas, The Constitutionalization of International Law.

[104] J Habermas, *Die postnationale Konstellation* (Frankfurt am Main: Suhrkamp 1998), 162–9; S Kadelbach, *Zwingendes Völkerrecht* (Berlin: Duncker & Humblot 1992). What Habermas finds as necessary preconditions in his normative theory resemble closely what Hedley Bull had found as social facts in international society.

that are centred on actual community processes, on the other. One of the chief roles for international law is to safeguard and promote the preconditions that are necessary for this process to be normatively meaningful.[105] How can the practice of arguing contribute to the legitimation of interpretations?

b) Communicative action

There is one particular strand of thought that further investigates whether and how processes of international legal argument may contribute to the legitimation of norm development and semantic change by way of interpretation. It builds on Habermas' concept of communicative action that wishes to tap into the rationality that is nested in intersubjective communicative practice, and it sees in processes of argumentation themselves, to the extent that they show certain qualities, a source of legitimation. This strand of thought could be of critical importance for a normative assessment of lawmaking by way of interpretation because it draws attention to potentials for legitimation that are immanent in the practice of arguing. In contrast to approaches that either cling to a substantive conception of justice or avow their deep-seated scepticism, this third strand centres on the practice of interpretation itself. In this view, the legitimacy of outcomes is also (note, not exclusively so) part of the process of arguing.

Drawing on the theory of communicative action, some scholars have suggested dealing with concerns about the legitimacy of global governance by focusing on contexts of deliberation and by improving the conditions under which processes of arguing can generate better outcomes.[106] When it comes to *legal* argument, a closer look at the theory of communicative action is specifically warranted because the legal form of argument provides some of the conditions under which the logic of arguing can set in. Robert Alexy, Klaus Günther, and then Jürgen Habermas have shown how the theory of communicative action may be cast into a theory of legal discourse.[107] On a preliminary and introductory note: What are communicative action and its theory?

105 See J Habermas, *Faktizität und Geltung* (Frankfurt am Main: Suhrkamp 1992), 238–91; cf. A v Bogdandy and S Dellavalle, 'Universalism Renewed: Habermas' Theory of International Order in Light of Competing Paradigms' (2009) 10 *German Law Journal* 5–29.

106 J Steffek, 'The Legitimation of International Governance: A Discourse Approach' (2003) 9 *European Journal of International Relations* 249–76 (which suggests shifting some emphasis from considerations of democratic deficits in international governance towards the potential of justificatory discourses); T Risse, Transnational Governance and Legitimacy, in: A Benz and Y Papadopoulos (eds), *Governance and Democracy: Comparing National, European and International Experiences* (London and New York: Routledge 2006), 179–99 (showing the constraints on what internal and external accountability can achieve and suggesting, with due caution, that public transparency and deliberative governance processes might play a compensatory role).

107 R Alexy, *Theorie der juristischen Argumentation* (Frankfurt am Main: Suhrkamp 1991); K Günther, 'Ein normativer Begriff der Kohärenz. Für eine Theorie der juristischen Argumentation' (1989) 20 *Rechtstheorie* 163–90; Habermas, *Faktizität und Geltung*, 272–91. Also see U Neumann, Theorie der juristischen Argumentation, in: W Brugger, U Neumann, and S Kirste (eds), *Rechtsphilosophie im 21. Jahrhundert* (Frankfurt am Main: Suhrkamp 2008), 233–60 (juxtaposing the use of the concept of communication in Habermas' theory of judicial discourse with its use in systems theory).

The theory of communicative action draws on a concept of arguing that is rich in content. Arguing offers an avenue for arriving at normatively superior outcomes, ideally at a communicative consensus that reflects true agreement. In his *Theory of Communicative Action*, Jürgen Habermas locates rationality (reason to believe in progress, dim as it may be, and anchor for the project of modernity) in intersubjective processes of communication.[108] Claims about meaning and truth are translated into validity claims in language that have to be validated in processes of communicative action. With this approach Habermas responds to the linguistic turn in semantics and epistemology that defies any attempt to decide about these claims with references to the outer world.[109] This merits further explanation.

Habermas introduces communicative action in contradistinction to strategic action—a mode in which actors pursue given interests and cunningly seek to make their own preferences prevail.[110] Strategic action corresponds to the view on legal interpretation as political in the sense that actors try to bend the law to their advantage. Communicative action is a different mode of social action, a different way of using interpretations. Communicative action aims at understanding and it builds on the assumption that speakers in a deliberative setting yield to the force of the better argument. It is not just a lofty ideal, proponents of the theory quickly add. Sometimes also strategic actors would be inclined to shift to a communicative modus in order to reach gains that they would otherwise forgo. The logic of arguing does not require actors to be genuinely motivated by seeking the truth or by finding out how a norm should best be interpreted. It could well be that they act strategically but are then caught in the process of arguing which they could only escape at a certain cost. At times actors can only realize certain objectives—have others accept an interpretative claim about what the law says, for instance—if they are willing to enter a mode of communicative action.[111] Thomas Risse called this 'argumentative self- entrapment'.[112]

Finding acceptance for a legal interpretation is indeed a very good case in point. According to the theory of communicative action, actors must first understand each other in order to find acceptance for their interpretative claims. All understanding, Habermas clarifies, is premised on acceptance. And most importantly, acceptance is not just a brute fact but it is normatively meaningful. It expresses the belief that a speech act is valid. If an actor doubts the validity of another actor's speech act, she

[108] See his introduction to the challenge in J Habermas, *The Theory of Communicative Action* vol 1 (Boston: Beacon Press 1984), 1–42.

[109] J Habermas, Zur Kritik der Bedeutungstheorie, in: *Nachmetaphysisches Denken: Philosophische Aufsätze* (Frankfurt am Main: Suhrkamp 1988), 105–35, 124; J Habermas, Handlungen, Sprechakte, sprachlich vermittelte Interaktionen und Lebenswelt, in: *Nachmetaphysisches Denken: Philosophische Aufsätze* (Frankfurt am Main: Suhrkamp 1988), 63–104, 80 ('Nach dieser epistemischen Wende der Wahrheitssemantik kann die Frage der Geltung eines Satzes nicht mehr als eine vom Kommunikationsvorgang losgelöste Frage des objektiven Verhältnisses von Sprache und Welt betrachtet werden.').

[110] J Habermas, *The Theory of Communicative Action*, vol 2 (Boston: Beacon Press 1987), chapter V.

[111] H Müller, 'Arguing, Bargaining and All That: Communicative Action, Rationalist Theory and the Logic of Appropriateness in International Relations' (2004) 10 *European Journal of International Relations* 395–435, 404–8.

[112] T Risse, '"Let's Argue!": Communicative Action in World Politics' (2000) 54 *International Organization* 1–39, 23.

might challenge its validity claims. Only if the actor is then willing to respond and engage in a process of arguing, could she succeed in finding acceptance for her interpretation. According to Habermas and others, each speech act contains three validity claims: that the act is true (*truth*), that it is morally right (*rightness*), and that it is truthful in the sense that the actor is not lying and acts sincerely (*sincerity*).[113] Habermas defines 'argument' as a justification that motivates others to accept a speech act's claim to validity.[114]

It bears repeating that Habermas' theory of communicative action does not doubt that actors do frequently act strategically, that they may lie and speak to further their interests. The decisive point is that for any strategically desired effect to set in, actors first need to understand each other.[115] It is also quite clear that an actor may understand the speech act of another actor without accepting that it is valid—she understands but does not agree. According to Habermas this is only possible, however, because at one prior point in time there was an understanding about what words at issue mean and this understanding, at least, rests on normative acceptance. Strategic action, he argues, is only possible because there was prior communicative action in which actors accepted what a certain expression means. This is a very delicate part of the theory and critical when it comes to normative assessments of semantic change. Habermas writes:

> In manifestly strategic action, illocutionarily disempowered speech acts, in order to be comprehensible, continue to be related to the meaning that they owe to a prior, well-rehearsed linguistic use which originally aimed at communication.[116]

An expression's meaning then always results from a situation of communicative action. In these situations, speakers do not—well, *cannot*—exercise power with their speech because acceptance leans on validity and validity excludes categories of strategy. Influences and factors that work towards acceptance may run through other channels (the barrel of a gun, for instance), but not through language itself.[117]

[113] Habermas, *Communicative Action*, vol 1, 273–338.

[114] Habermas, *Faktizität und Geltung*, 276 ('Argumente sind Gründe, die einen mit konstativen oder regulativen Sprechakten erhobenen Geltungsanspruch unter Diskursbedingungen einlösen und damit Argumentationsteilnehmer rational dazu bewegen, entsprechende deskriptive oder normative Aussagen als gültig zu akzeptieren.').

[115] There is a further distinction at play here between dimensions of speech acts: the *locutionary* dimension relates to the act itself, its utterances or signs (if it is written down), the *illocutionary* dimension relates to the meaning of the speech act, and the *perlocutionary* dimension relates to the effect that the speaker wanted to achieve with the speech act. The contention is that perlocutionary effects of a speech act are premised on illocutionary success. Habermas develops these dimensions of speech acts leaning on John Austin and John Searle. Habermas, *Communicative Action*, vol 1, 277. For the use of this distinction in international relations theory also see F V Kratochwil, *Rules, Norms and Decisions: On the Conditions of Practical and Legal Reasoning in International Relations and Domestic Affairs* (Cambridge: Cambridge University Press 1989), 27–30.

[116] Habermas, Kritik der Bedeutungstheorie, 135 ('Im manifest strategischen Handeln bleiben illokutionär entkräftete Sprechakte, wenn sie verständlich sein sollen, auf die Bedeutung bezogen, die sie einer vorgängig, eingespielten, originär verständigungsorientierten Sprachverwendung verdanken.').

[117] Habermas, Handlungen, Sprechakte, Lebenswelt, 69.

This has far-reaching consequences with regard to the development of international law by way of interpretative practice. If Habermas' argument is right, this means that changes in the meaning of international norms can only be brought about in a communicative mode of action. And if this were so, there would be few, if any, concerns about exercising power or authority by way of interpretation.

c) Theoretical and practical problems

The theory of communicative action would offer great guidance for entertaining normative twists of lawmaking by way of interpretation in international law. Alas, there are good reasons for second thoughts. Some problems are theoretical and others practical.

On a theoretical note, there is room to question the assumption that actors in disagreement about what an expression means may resort to a mode of communicative action and settle their differences in a deliberative discourse. Leaving aside the question whether they may be inclined to do so, actors who challenge each other's validity claims would have to rely on a language that already exists. Validity is judged against a language that was produced in prior communicative actions.[118] Communicative action is a rare phenomenon and is used as an ideal in Habermas' theory. But his theory also takes this ideal and makes it a prerequisite for any communication—again, strategic action is only possible on the basis of prior communicative action.[119] Can and should the rare exception be taken as the prototype of communication?[120] In linguistic theory, it may be added, there are many alternative accounts that explain how communication can work without any (prior) agreement about the use of an expression.[121] Actors in disagreement could

[118] Habermas is straightforward in this regard when he speaks of communicative action as the original mode of action (*Originalmodus*) that comes prior to all other modes of action and that can only live parasitically, J Habermas, *Theorie des kommunikativen Handelns* (Frankfurt am Main: Suhrkamp 1995 [1981]), 388; in English: Habermas, *Communicative Action*, vol 1, 288.

[119] J Habermas, Was heißt Universalpragmatik, in: *Vorstudien und Ergänzungen zur Theorie des kommunikativen Handelns* (Frankfurt am Main: Suhrkamp 1984), 353–440, translated in J Habermas, What is Universal Pragmatics? (1976), in: M Cooke (ed), *On the Pragmatics of Communication* (MIT Press 1998), 21–104 (dealing with the tension between the construction of an ideal and its status as a prerequisite in reality). For a less modest ideal theory that abstracts from considerations of concrete acceptance and rather takes off into the lofty sphere of the pure *ought*, see K-O Apel, Faktische Anerkennung oder einsehbar notwendige Anerkennung? Beruht der Ansatz der transzendentalpragmatischen Diskursethik auf einem intellektualistischen Fehlschluss?, in: K-O Apel and R Pozzo (eds), *Zur Rekonstruktion der praktischen Philosophie. Gedenkschrift für Karl-Heinz Ilting* (Stuttgart-Bad Cannstatt: Frommann-Holzboog 1990), 67–123.

[120] S Krämer, *Sprache, Sprechakt, Kommunikation* (Frankfurt am Main: Suhrkamp 2001), 89–90 and 103–5.

[121] This holds true for all those positions that Krämer places beyond the fallacies of intellectualizing language and communication—a charge she also raises against Habermas: Krämer, *Sprache, Sprechakt, Kommunikation*, chapters 7–13; for a more pointed argument on this issue also see S Krämer, Sprache und Sprechen oder: Wie sinnvoll ist die Unterscheidung zwischen einem Schema und seinem Gebrauch?, in: S Krämer and E König (eds), *Gibt es eine Sprache hinter dem Sprechen?* (Frankfurt am Main: Suhrkamp 2002), 97–125. Donald Davidson, among others, has for example offered an account of how communication is possible with less far reaching assumptions about the

not actually settle their disagreement against the background of an already existing language but would make up this language as they went along. One critical consequence would be that this process is again open to the exercise of power.[122] The stable ground of an existing language, which levels out power imbalances and contributes to better outcomes, breaks away. Actors and their strategies again step to the forefront. What matters then is the capacity of actors to influence and shape meanings as well as the ability to establish their communications as authoritative reference points in legal discourse. What matters is their semantic authority.[123]

Practical considerations may sway further doubts about the theory of communicative action. Above all, they foster concerns that may spring from the postulation of an ideal that is conspicuous by its absence. To some extent this is a lame accusation because it is part of the ideal that reality does not usually live up to it. But if it rarely ever does and the ideal is nevertheless taken as a prototype that explains reality, second thoughts might well arise.

Proponents of putting the idea of communicative action to use in the context of international relations have responded to critiques of the theory's practical worth with empirical evidence. They have combed though reality in search of communicative action and some of the instances they have found do indeed point to limits of alternative theoretical accounts.[124] Their explanations continue to be challenged in modified rationalist accounts and the controversy about which accounts are more plausible has not yet produced any clear victories or defeats.[125]

capacities of language. He understands communication as a process of continuous mutual interpretation and highlights the creative dimension of every act of communication. With his provoking statement that '[t]here is no such thing as a language, not if a language is anything like what many philosophers and linguists have supposed' he has fuelled an extensive debate which is collected in E Lepore (ed), *Truth and Interpretation: Perspectives on the Philosophy of Donald Davidson* (Oxford: Basil Blackwell 1986). The quotation is taken from *A Nice Derangement of Epitaphs*, reprinted ibid., 433–46, at 446. To be clear, also Davidson's account does not render it implausible to speak of 'a language'. The main point of caution is directed against overburdening language with functions it cannot provide.

[122] An actor's status is thus taken into consideration in Robert Brandom's Neo-Pragmatist theory, see above Chapter II, section B. Compare M Winkler, 'Die normativität des Praktischen' (2009) *Juristenzeitung* 821–9; J Liptow, *Regel und Interpretation. Eine Untersuchung zur sozialen Struktur sprachlicher Praxis* (Weilerswist: Velbrück 2004) (also drawing on Brandom and focusing on social structures rather than actors in linguistic practice).

[123] See above Chapter II, sections A.2 and B.3.

[124] N Deitelhoff and H Müller, 'Theoretical Paradise—Empirically Lost? Arguing with Habermas' (2005) 31 *Review of International Studies* 167–79; C Ulbert and T Risse, 'Deliberately Changing the Discourse: What Does Make Arguing Effective?' (2005) 40 *Acta Politica* 351–67; H Müller, Internationale Verhandlungen, Argumente und Verständigungshandeln. Verteidigung, Befunde, Warnung, in: P Niesen and B Herborth (eds), *Anarchie der kommunikativen Freiheit. Jürgen Habermas und die Theorie der internationalen Politik* (Frankfurt am Main: Suhrkamp 2007), 199–223; N Deitelhoff, *Überzeugung in der Politik. Grundzüge einer Diskurstheorie internationalen Regierens* (Frankfurt am Main: Suhrkamp 2006) (offering a detailed analysis of the negotiations leading up to the establishment of the International Criminal Court on the basis of a discourse theoretical model).

[125] O Keck, 'Zur sozialen Konstruktion des Rational-Choice-Ansatzes. Einige Klarstellungen zur Rationalismus-Konstruktivismus-Debatte' (1997) 4 *Zeitschrift für Internationale Beziehungen* 139–51;

While this dispute continues, it may still be asked what normative consequences could possibly be based on processes of communicative action. The underlying premise of those who project communicative theory from the context of democratic polities onto the level of international relations appears to be that processes of arguing provide a significant source of legitimation because they permit actors to challenge validity claims and to arrive at normatively meaningful acceptance. Power recedes into the background. This is only possible, however, if one buys into the implicit linguistic assumptions that face a whole host of critiques.[126] Since these grounds are shaky, it may be better not to place too much legitimatory weight on processes of arguing. To be sure, such scepticism or hesitation does not emasculate international law's role in providing part of the preconditions for pursuing justice globally. Indeed, Habermas himself has been rather reluctant to embrace the use of his theory of communicative action for the study of international relations and he does not draw on these theoretical premises in support of his argument for the centrality of international law in international politics.[127]

By way of overall conclusion on the use of justice rhetoric in the practice of interpretation, it may be summarized that a first broad group of scholars understands universally shared values or social facts to lay the foundation of international law. These foundations provide guidance for its development by way of interpretation and they are the ultimate yardsticks for any normative assessment. Such universals form the spine of a normative order that aims at effective governance to safeguard and promote global goals. These approaches are rejected, or at least modified, by a second broad group of scholars who direct attention towards persistent normative conflicts, rather unmediated power relations, and towards the snares on the way to just action. They tend to caution against the imposition of particular interests or particular moral convictions in the guise of claims to justice. They see clearly the danger that the law falls prey to hegemonic projects in the way it is shaped in its interpretation.

C Grobe, 'The Power of Words: Argumentative Persuasion in International Negotiations' (2010) 16 *European Journal of International Relations* 5–29.

[126] Risse, 'Let's Argue!', 16–19 (rejecting Foucault's idea of how power relations are reflected in a consensus by pointing to processes of verifying speech acts; thus denying, as Habermasian communicative theory indeed does, that language itself expresses power relations).

[127] J Habermas, 'Concluding Comments on Empirical Approaches to Deliberative Politics' (2005) 40 *Acta Politica* 384–92; J Habermas, 'Eine politische Verfassung für die pluralistische Weltgesellschaft' (2005) 38 *Kritische Justiz* 222–47; J Habermas, Konstitutionalisierung des Völkerrechts und die Legitimationsprobleme einer verfassten Weltgesellschaft, in: W Brugger, U Neumann, and S Kirste (eds), *Rechtsphilosophie im 21. Jahrhundert* (Frankfurt: Suhrkamp 2008), 360–96; J Habermas, *Zur Verfassung Europas—Ein Essay* (Berlin: Suhrkamp 2011). Compare v Bogdandy and Dellavalle, 'Universalism Renewed' (looking at some of the possible links that might exist between Habermas' conception of international order and his communicative theory; to the extent that it is possible to make out such links, they relate, as the theory of communicative action originally did, to an intersubjective foundation of legitimate order rather than a logic of arguing in international relations).

A third group of approaches carves out preconditions for just action and places emphasis on processes of arguing. On the basis of the theory of communicative action, the practice of interpretation could itself provide a strong source of legitimation. Only this basis appears to shake and partially crumble under closer scrutiny. The critique does not take away from the common denominator that unites approaches in this third group. They see in international law a necessary means to allow and facilitate the pursuit of justice. International law helps to circumvent evident pitfalls on the way to just action. It translates idiosyncratic positions into a workable language that allows and channels dispute.[128] This is also the confidence that remains for Martti Koskenniemi after he has stripped the international legal enterprise from much of its inflated normative aspiration. He suggests on the penultimate page of his reissued *From Apology to Utopia* that '[w]hatever historical baggage, including bad faith, such culture [of formalism] entails, its ideals include those of accountability, equality, reciprocity and transparency, and it comes to us with an embedded vocabulary of (formal) rights'.[129] The crucial insight that emerges from the discussion of this third group of approaches is that international law plays an important role in curbing the negative repercussions of power imbalances and in offering a language that allows meaningful argument in a world characterized by an irreducible plurality of convictions, interests, and beliefs. Sure enough, there is an element of violence in international law as a universal language, both in its form as well as in the history of its vocabulary. And still it is without convincing alternative.

B. The centrality of law: Dissonances and developments in legal doctrine

The discussion of approaches that engross the idea of justice has pointed to the centrality of international law. International law opens up spaces in which particular normative convictions and political projects can compete. This moves the discussion of semantic change and normative twists from elevated places of political philosophy and social theory into the realm of international law and its doctrine—much to the delight of the international lawyer. This move follows from the thought that competing values and power imbalances demand a legal order that allows conflictuous tension to be translated into legal argument.[130]

[128] Cf. F V Kratochwil, How do Norms Matter?, in: M Byers (ed), *The Role of Law in International Politics: Essays in International Relations and International Law* (Oxford, New York: Oxford University Press 2000), 35–68, 47.

[129] Koskenniemi, *From Apology to Utopia*, 616.

[130] Compare A v Bogdandy, 'Constitutionalism in International Law: Comment on a Proposal from Germany' (2006) 47 *Harvard International Law Journal* 223–42, 227 (maintaining that 'social theory and political philosophy . . . have never proved able to lead the debate on "right or wrong" more effectively than the established paths of legal reasoning.'). Cf. B Kingsbury, 'Legal Positivism as Normative Politics. International society, balance of power and Lassa Oppenheim's positive international law' (2002) 13 *European Journal of International Law* 401–36.

The place of semantic struggles for the law is also the site where actors generate legal normativity and contribute to the making of international law. In the interpretative practice that moves the law, the impact of some actors is particularly noteworthy. While the argumentative process harbours a legitimatory potential, it does not by itself conclude normative assessments.[131] The process of making international law by way of interpretation knows some actors that are more influential than others. Those who enjoy a higher degree of semantic authority have a palpably stronger impact on what the law is. Over the past decades, international institutions, both bureaucracies and judicial bodies, have built up significant authority that increases the force of their claims.

For some time international bureaucracies and judicial institutions have scrounged moral authority from the goals they pursued, from their expertise, or from the default assumption that all they do is to apply the law. They could thrive on a perception that they serve noble causes and thereby evaded closer scrutiny. Even if such a perception was vindicated and functional narratives of legitimacy were made plausible, they would still be insufficient in the same way in which justice does not provide stable ground for assessing the normative twists of legal change. This is where a second key function of international law comes in. In addition to translating claims into a workable language for carrying out conflicts, international law functions as a medium that can justify the exercise of authority. While neither substantive reference points of justice nor the process of arguing itself settle the blunt question of what good or bad has come out of the interpretative practice that makes international law, the semantic authority of specific actors offers a focal point for analysis and reaction.

International law and its doctrine should be tested against the question of how they contribute to the legitimation of international actors' semantic authority. To be clear, international law is seen from two different angles at this point. First it is the target of semantic struggles and a medium through which powerful actors exercise authority. Second, it is a medium that can be used to justify authority, both by argumentatively tying powerful actors to authoritative reference points and by offering procedures, or an institutional framework more generally, that allows for meaningful input and contestation.

This section now tests international law with regard to its function of contributing to the legitimation of international institutions' authority and it examines recent developments in legal doctrine in this regard. The exercise of authority has to first of all be captured in legal discourse for law to possibly take up its task of justifying authority.

This question and endeavour may seem odd and at the same time strikingly traditional. It may seem odd because it asks for mechanisms to justify something that after all portrays itself as interpretation. Even on the basis of the contention that interpretation can amount to an exercise of authority that contributes to the generation of legal normativity it may still be odd because the present section now

[131] To be clear, Habermas would not pretend otherwise. See J Habermas, 'Concluding Comments on Empirical Approaches to Deliberative Politics' (2005) 40 *Acta Politica* 384–92.

places this observation within the discussion of legal doctrine and thus connects to the internal point of view of legal practice itself. Such an internal point of view does not mean, however, that it cannot absorb or reflect external observations. It is certainly possible and even inevitable that it does.[132]

Examining international law in the present outlook at the same time connects to a long tradition in law and legal thinking. First of all, the sources of international law have always been primarily part of a normative construction. They hold up the idea that international law should be law because its subjects have given their consent. If dissonances between this idea and actual processes of lawmaking increase, the persuasiveness of sources doctrine suffers on this point. The concern for a normative anchor and a more specific democratic liberal ethos then direct attention towards the sites where practice generates legal normativity and prompts the question of how authoritative actors can relate to the consent of those governed.

There are three main developments in legal doctrine that respond to the semantic authority of international actors and their influence in the making of international law. In their attempt to capture the authority that is exercised in the space of legal practice, they meet international law's function as a medium for the legitimation of such authority to varying degrees. The notion of 'soft law' is probably the most prominent manifestation of dissonances between acts that have legal effect and acts that fall within the purview of sources. Due to conceptual hazards and political drawbacks, however, it is of little help in strengthening international law's aspiration to legitimize and constrain power (1.). A more promising avenue opens up with the rules of interpretation and in particular with the notion of subsequent practice in the sense of Art. 31(3)(b) VCLT. There remains considerable uncertainty, however, *what* amounts to practice and *whose* practice counts. There is significant room for doctrinal development, but also some pitfalls on the way (2.). Modes of thought that come with the field of global administrative law and with research centred on the exercise of international public authority eventually shift the emphasis away from sources and push for methodological innovation (3.). The fate of these developments will above all hinge on one of the biggest challenges for international legal thinking: the adaptation of international law and its doctrine to the post-national constellation that fundamentally challenges ideas about the legitimation of authority.

1. The appeal and futility of soft law

The notion of soft law is one of the most prominent manifestations of dissonances in international legal doctrine. Ever since it first appeared on the horizon of international legal law, it has brought with it foundational challenges for the

[132] K Günther, 'Legal Pluralism or Uniform Concept of Law?' (2008) 5 *No Foundations: Journal of Extreme Legal Positivism* 5–21 (discussing the interaction between internal and external perspectives on the law). The distinction has emanated with force from H L A Hart, *The Concept of Law* (Oxford: Oxford University Press 1997 [1961]), 89. Also see A v Bogdandy, P Dann, and M Goldmann, 'Developing the Publicness of Public International Law: Towards a Legal Framework for Global Governance Activities' (2008) 9 *German Law Journal* 1375–400, 1386–90.

discipline.[133] By and large, soft law first had to defend its existence and to find a place within the legal order throughout the 1970s, then it had to fend off conceptual challenges in the 80s, and eventually it has been marked by a kind of functionalism ever since the 90s. With this last move, discussions have shifted from examining the idea of soft law in terms of sources towards an emphasis on its place in compliance and processes of global governance.[134]

The phenomenon of soft law is above all a response to the observation that certain legal communications that are not legally binding and do not neatly fit into Art. 38 ICJ Statute nevertheless have legal effects and, which is the typical structure of the argument, *therefore* they should be taken into account.[135] Some even define soft law explicitly *ex negativo* as those things that have certain legal effects but are outside the scope of Art. 38 ICJ Statute.[136] Alan Boyle writes that 'the term "soft law" is simply a convenient description for a variety of non-legally binding instruments used in contemporary international relations by States and international organizations'.[137] There is general agreement that it refers to non-binding norms but apart from that there is little more common ground. Definitions are highly elusive and have so far failed to pin down the idea of soft law.[138] Most of all, it remains obscure how non-binding norms that form part of the law should be distinguished from any other kind of non-binding norms, social mores, for instance.[139]

Nor does the concept of soft law add to the explanation of reality. Actors in international legal practice do maintain a distinction in how they deal with soft law as compared to hard law; at the latest when it comes to questions of domestic

[133] For early accounts on the fundamental challenges that the phenomenon of soft law poses to international legal thinking, see O Schachter, 'The Twilight Existence of Nonbinding International Agreements' (1977) 71 *American Journal of International Law* 296–304; P-M Eisemann, 'Le Gentlemen's agreement comme source du droit international' (1979) 106 *Journal du Droit International* 326–48.

[134] J Klabbers, 'Reflections on Soft International Law in a Privatized World' (2005) 16 *Finnish Yearbook of International Law* 313–28, 314–16. Especially in the field of environmental law soft law mechanisms have gained a prominent place, J Klabbers, 'Redundancy of Soft Law' (1996) 65 *Nordic Journal of International Law* 167–82.

[135] See H Hillenberg, 'A Fresh Look at Soft Law' (1999) 10 *European Journal of International Law* 499–515. It is a different thing altogether to use the concept of soft law to refer to instruments that are all the same binding but are soft in content; that this, they contain provisions which are particularly vague. See J d'Aspremont, 'Softness in International Law: A Self-Serving Quest for New Legal Materials' (2008) 19 *European Journal of International Law* 1075–93, 1081–8 (discussing the distinction between *soft instrumentum* and *soft negotium* that forms part of positivist thinking). On the relationship between form, specifically bindingness, and substance also see K Raustiala, 'Form and Substance in International Agreements' (2005) 99 *American Journal of International Law* 581–614 (arguing that in a payoff between strong commitments and strong content, non-binding pledges may be more promising than clear legal obligations).

[136] F Francioni, International 'Soft Law': A Contemporary Assessment, in: V Lowe and M Fitzmaurice (eds), *Fifty Years of the International Court of Justice. Essays in Honour of Sir Robert Jennings* (Cambridge: Cambidge University Press 1996), 167–80, 168.

[137] A Boyle, Soft Law in International Law-Making, in: M D Evans (ed), *International Law* (Oxford: Oxford University Press 2006), 141–57, 142.

[138] Ibid., at 142–3 (trying to answer the question of what soft law is but implicitly admitting to failure by simply pointing to a number of examples).

[139] Klabbers, 'Redundancy of Soft Law' (for a most pointed critique of attempts at distinguishing soft *law* from other kinds of norms).

implementation.[140] In the end the question is still decisive whether a norm can support findings of (il)legality or not. Domestic courts treat UNHCR Guidance Notes as interpretations of the Refugee Convention. The Convention and not the Guidance Note carries their finding of (il)legality.

Intricacies of definition set aside, many scholars and other actors in international legal discourse see soft law as a much needed response to the apparently deficient modes of traditional lawmaking that are shackled by sources doctrine. Commentators tend to stress soft law's flexibility and its effectiveness. They point to the many advantages over treaty law including greater flexibility and a larger number of participating state representatives who are willing to consent to non-binding agreements rather than clear obligations.[141] Treaty regimes, to the contrary, frequently leave out some important actors and might be scattered by reservations.[142] From this point of view, soft law should be embraced as a phenomenon that benevolently pushes the development of international law while circumventing the drawbacks of traditional modes of lawmaking.

Christine Chinkin illustratively argues in this vein that soft law responds to the need for more dynamism in international lawmaking. She recalls soft law's first prominent appearance in the context of decolonization when newly independent countries gained the upper hand in the General Assembly and pushed for a New International Economic Order as well as a right to development. General Assembly resolutions were one of the first things that came to be discussed under the heading soft law.[143] These origins of the concept indicate that soft law frequently forms part of a programme for the progressive development of the law.[144] Chinkin summarizes that

> the international legal order is an evolving one that requires a wide range of modalities for change and development, especially into new subject areas. The participants within the decentralized legal system . . . must draw upon the entire continuum of mechanisms ranging from the traditional international legal forms to the soft law instruments. While this process inevitably causes normative confusion and uncertainty in terms of the traditional sources of

140 C Redgwell, International Soft Law and Globalization, in: B Barton, L K Barrera-Hernández, A R Lucas, and A Rønne (eds), *Regulating Energy and Natural Resources* (Oxford: Oxford University Press 2006), 89–107, 106. For analyses on how domestic courts relate to diverse international legal instruments. See B Kingsbury, International Law as Inter-Public Law, in: H Richardson and M Williams (eds), *Moral Universalism and Pluralism* (New York: New York University Press 2009), 167–204; A Aust, Domestic Consequences of Non-Treaty (Non-Conventional) Law-Making, in: R Wolfrum and V Röben (eds), *Developments of International Law in Treaty Making* (Heidelberg: Springer 2005), 487–96.

141 Cf. Raustiala, 'Form and Substance in International Agreements'; cf. J J Kirton and M J Trebilcock (eds), *Hard Choices, Soft Law: Voluntary Standards in Global Trade, Environment and Social Governance* (Aldershot: Ashgate 2004); D Shelton (ed), *Commitment and Compliance. The Role of Non-Binding Norms in the International Legal System* (Oxford: Oxford University Press 2000).

142 Boyle, Soft Law in International Law-Making, 143–8.

143 C M Chinkin, 'The Challenge of Soft Law: Development and Change in International Law' (1989) 38 *International and Comparative Law Quarterly* 850–66, 851–2.

144 Ibid.

international law, it is probably the inevitable consequence of unresolved pressures for change in international law.[145]

This opinion expresses a widely shared view on what international soft law is and what it is for.[146] Catherine Redgwell further adds that international soft law has increased in prominence precisely because of the forceful impact of international institutions in processes of international legal discourse.[147]

UN General Assembly resolutions that interpret the Statute of the UNHCR and expand its mandate as well as documents issued by the UNHCR itself would amount to prime examples of soft law. UNHCR pushed the development of refugee law by way of soft law and adopted new legal instruments such as a number of Guidance Notes when it was evident that there was little hope that existing treaty law would be revised. Conventional refugee law is indeed hard to change and attempts at introducing changes by way of binding documents could rightly be expected to have little chance of success. Important actors would not have signed on to renewed legal obligations. Soft law then appeared as a good way to go forward.[148]

The thought vested in the idea of soft law is that whatever has legal effects should be considered as law. Soft law has expanded the scope of international law and notably the scope of what falls within the competence of international lawyers.[149] It could then be suggested that it offers a fitting response to dissonances between doctrines of sources and jurisgenerative legal practice. But apart from the conceptual hazards it also suffers from political drawbacks that ultimately render it unconstructive. Besides, it might even turn out to be detrimental to international law's function as a medium contributing to the justification of public authority.

It may well be cautioned that in its interplay with hard law, soft law might actually have the effect of softening what has already been legally binding.[150] Even more fundamentally strikes the critique that soft law is frequently as effective as binding law but does not live up to similar procedural thresholds in its making. Most commentators, whatever their normative appraisal of the matter, agree that

[145] Ibid., at 866.

[146] D Shelton, Introduction: Law, Non-Law and the Problem of 'Soft Law', in: D Shelton (ed), *Commitment and Compliance* (Oxford: Oxford University Press 2000), 1–19; K W Abbott and D Snidal, 'Hard and Soft Law in International Governance' (2000) 54 *International Organization* 421–56; P-M Dupuy, 'Soft Law and the International Law of the Environment' (1991) 12 *Michigan Journal of International Law* 420–35.

[147] Redgwell, International Soft Law and Globalization, 98 (referring to the 'rise of international institutions as vehicles for less formal mechanisms of norm-creation, adaptation and change' as the first reason for soft law's prominence).

[148] It is a bit unusual to discuss judicial decisions under the heading of soft law, but doing so would not be without precedent. J E Alvarez, *International Organizations as Law-Makers* (Oxford: Oxford University Press 2005), 502–9 (discussing both a variety of different legal instruments issued by international organizations and decisions rendered by (quasi-) judicial institutions under the rubric of soft law).

[149] d'Aspremont, 'Softness in International Law'.

[150] M v Engelhardt, 'Opportunities and Challenges of a Soft Law Track to Economic and Social Rights—The Case of the Voluntary Guidelines on the Right to Food' (2009) 42 *Verfassung und Recht in Übersee* 502–25.

soft law is at times very effective and does influence the behaviour of governments as well as other actors in the international legal order. In fact, those who are inclined to welcome soft law mechanisms tend to argue that this is precisely its beauty. Soft law complements other legally binding mechanisms in the process of global governance which is geared towards the enforcement of community interests or global goals.[151] The downside is, however, that soft law cannot claim the pedigree of sources doctrine in support of its authority. Put drastically: effectiveness replaces consent as a normative foundation. Those who have recognized this hitch are inclined to follow the argument along the lines of Alan Boyle. '[S]oft law in its various forms can of course be abused,' he argues, 'but so can most legal forms, and it has generally been more helpful to the process of international lawmaking than objectionable.'[152] This rule of thumb assessment of legitimacy neglects international law's function as a medium of legitimation, and without offering a convincing alternative it brushes aside the after all powerful idea that law should be because it flows from the consent of those subject to it.

Jan Klabbers fittingly attributed a 'cavalier attitude' to this position.[153] Such a rule of thumb appraisal of the benefits of soft law is generally not concerned with formal rule systems, nor does it take the normative import of sources doctrine seriously. It knows what is right and wrong and then adjusts actions and normative assessments accordingly. It is instrumentalist, overlooks actors' concrete finitude, and borders on kitsch.[154]

Even if one does not wish to place too much emphasis on the legitimatory dimension that relates to law's formal pedigree, scepticism about soft law's desirability might be centred precisely on what others see as its prime advantage; namely, its flexibility and the fact that it does not have to meet high thresholds of formal consent.[155] This might also render soft instruments more prone to unilateral projections of power. Klabbers concludes that '[s]oft law, in the end, is but one emanation of a broader trend: it is the handmaiden of the increasing deformalization of global politics'.[156] And deformalization is frequently a strategy of the more powerful to overcome formalist hurdles in the exercise of power.[157] Rather than

[151] See above note 145.

[152] Boyle, Soft Law in International Law-Making, 156.

[153] Klabbers, 'Reflections on Soft International Law', 314.

[154] See above Chapter V, section A.1.b.

[155] A v Bogdandy, Lawmaking by International Organizations. Some Thoughts on Non-Binding Instruments and Democratic Legitimacy, in: R Wolfrum and V Röben (eds), *Developments of International Law in Treaty Making* (Heidelberg: Springer 2005), 171–82.

[156] Klabbers, 'Reflections on Soft International Law', 327.

[157] N Krisch, 'International Law in Times of Hegemony: Unequal Power and the Shaping of the International Legal Order' (2005) 16 *European Journal of International Law* 369–408, 391–2 (using trends towards soft law as an illustration of how more powerful actors seek to reshape the legal order); Koskenniemi, 'Global Governance and Public International Law', 243; Koskenniemi, 'The Fate of Public International Law', 9–15; J Klabbers, 'Undesirability of Soft Law' (1998) 67 *Nordic Journal of International Law* 381–92 (arguing this point in the context of the European Union).

strengthening international law's function as a medium for the legitimation of international institutions' authority, the notion of soft law is rather vulnerable to ending up undermining this same function. It threatens to replace consent, or at least participation, with effectiveness as a normative yardstick. The effective pursuit of specific goals is critically important, sure enough. Inaction might at times be worse than action in dubious legal form or with shaky procedural legitimacy. But this is a slippery slope that is also very narrow. It does not offer a view on struggles for power or on normative conflicts.[158] Generally, not too much confidence should be placed even in the 'enlightened ruler'.

2. Intertemporal law and subsequent practice: Shortening the leash?

The notion of soft law has inflated and expanded the concept of law in an attempt to take acts of international institutions better into account. It in fact elevates those acts into the realm of law but unduly neglects the normative import of sources doctrine replacing consent and participation with effectiveness and adjunct functional narratives of legitimacy. It largely fails when tested against international law's function as a medium of legitimating international authority. The flipside of such an attempt would be to tie interpretations of international institutions closer to the will of the parties as presumably expressed in the norm that forms the focal point of interpretation. A first prominent doctrinal notion to speak on how to interpret treaties with the passing of time is that of intertemporal law. It turns out to be enigmatic and of little help. More promising is the road of looking at subsequent practice in interpretation in the sense of Art. 31(3)(b) VCLT.

To note but briefly, it might be suggested that an interpreter stick to the rule of intertemporal law when interpreting a treaty.[159] The notion is however strikingly hollow because it is either interpreted so as to require a kind of original intentionalism,[160] or it simply states that the legality of an action should be assessed with regard to the law valid at the time of such action while implying that of course the

[158] I have developed a more elaborate account and critique of such functionalist arguments in I Venzke, 'International Bureaucracies in a Political Science Perspective—Agency, Authority and International Institutional Law' (2008) 9 *German Law Journal* 1401–28, 1416–23.

[159] In the famous words of Judge Max Huber in the *Islas of Palmas* arbitration of 1928, 'a juridical fact must be appreciated in the light of the law contemporary with it, and not of the law in force at the time when the dispute in regard to it arises or falls to be settled'. And further: 'As regards the question which of different legal systems prevailing at successive periods is to be applied in a particular case (the so-called inter-temporal law), a distinction must be made between the creation of rights and the existence of rights. The same principle which subjects the acts creative of a right to the law in force at the time the right arises, demands that the existence of the right, in other words its continued manifestation, shall follow the conditions required by the evolution of law.' *Island of Palmas Case (Netherlands v United States of America)*, 4 April 1928 (1928) 2 Reports of International Arbitral Awards 829, 845.

[160] Cf. R Higgins, Some Observations on the Inter-Temporal Rule in International Law, in: J Makarczyk (ed), *Theory of International Law at the Threshold of the 21st Century* (The Hague: Kluwer Law International 1996), 173–82, 174 (arguing that this use would also completely blend out the need for dynamism in treaty interpretation); M Kotzur, Intertemporal Law, in: R Wolfrum (ed), *MPEPIL* (Oxford: Oxford Universtiy Press 2008), Mn 6 (neither adopting such an interpretation as his).

law is not the same at all times.[161] The *Institut de Droit International* sought to push the doctrine of intertemporal law to new prominence for little apparent reason or merit in 1975. It merely concluded that in interpreting a treaty it is necessary 'de tenir compte de ce double impératif de l'évolution et de la sécurité'.[162] Sure, but beyond stating the uncontroversial the doctrine is of little help. It either says nothing about how to interpret the law at any given time, or it weakly and faintly accommodates an unappealing original intentionalism. It therefore only seldom appears in judicial practice and when it does, it might even give rise to more questions and problems than it is supposed to answer or solve.

The *Arbitration Regarding the Iron Rhine ('Ijzeren Rijn') Railway*, faced with interpreting the Treaty of Separation of 1839 between Belgium and the Netherlands, notably preferred an 'evolutive interpretation, which would ensure an application of the treaty that would be effective in terms of its object and purpose... to a strict application of the intertemporal rule'.[163] While slightly unclear, the tribunal seems to suggest that following the intertemporal rule 'strictly' would require arguing more closely along the lines of parties' intentions. The tribunal then went on to approvingly quote the ICJ's statement in *Gabčíkovo-Nagymaros* where the court had found that the treaty at issue 'is not static, and is open to adapt to emerging norms of international law'.[164] The award in *Iron Rhine* ultimately illustrates how the decisive question still looms large. How precisely could such processes of 'evolution' or 'adaptation' be captured in the rules of interpretation?

In the *Case Concerning the Dispute Regarding Navigational and Related Rights*, the ICJ had to decide the semantic dispute between Costa Rica and Nicaragua over the 1858 Treaty of Limits. The treaty secured rights for Costa Rica to use the San Juan River, which first runs through Nicaragua and then forms the border between the

[161] U Linderfalk, 'The Application of International Legal Norms over Time: The Second Branch of Intertemporal Law' (2011) 58 *Netherlands International Law Review* 147–72, 151 (arguing that there is simply one basic principle vested in this doctrine: 'an action or a factual state of affairs must be assessed in the light of the law which is contemporary with it').

[162] Institut de Droit International, *Le problème intertemporel en droit international public*; (1975), available at <http://www.idi-iil.org/idiF/resolutionsF/1975_wies_01_fr.pdf>; G E d Nascimento e Silva, 'Le Facteur Temps et les Traités' (1977) 154 *Recueil des Cours* 215–97, 265–6. The matter was discussed with similarly reticent outcomes in the International Law Commission's (ILC) work on the law of treaties and then again in the study group on fragmentation. See ILC, *Yearbook*, vol 2 (1966), p 222 para 16; ILC, Report of the Study Group on Fragmentation, Official Records of the General Assembly Fifty-seventh Session, Supplement No 10 (A/60/10) p 250, para 475. Cf. G Nolte, Between Contemporaneous and Evolutive Interpretation: The Use of 'Subsequent Practice' in the Judgment of the International Court of Justice Concerning the Case of Costa Rica v. Nicaragua (2009), in: H P Hestermeyer, D König, N Matz-Lück, V Röben, A Seibert-Fohr, P-T Stoll, and S Vöneky (eds), *Coexistence, Cooperation and Solidarity*, vol II (Leiden: Martinus Nijhoff 2011), 1675–84, 1678.

[163] *Arbitration Regarding the Iron Rhine ('Ijzeren Rijn') Railway (Belgium v The Netherlands)*, Award of 24 May 2005, para 80. Cf. C Djeffal, 'The Iron Rhine Case—A Treaty's Journey from Peace to Sustainable Development' (2011) 71 *Zeitschrift für ausländisches öffentliches Recht und Völkerrecht* 569–86, 579.

[164] *Gabčíkovo-Nagymaros Project (Hungary v Slovakia)*, Judgment of 25 September 1997, (1997) ICJ Reports 7, para 112.

two countries, for 'libre navegación ... con objetos de comercio'.[165] Nicaragua claimed that the term 'commerce' should be attributed the meaning it had at the time the treaty was concluded. In its view, this would give effect to the intention of the parties and, after all, determining intent is the main task in the work of interpretation.[166] In a remarkable move as to how a treaty's meaning may shift over time, the court rejected Nicaragua's interpretation and its statement on methodology with it. It found that the meaning of the treaty did change and that this new meaning was decisive for the dispute.

The court offered two lines of reasoning in support of its conclusion. First, it argued that semantic change was itself intended by the parties already at the time of conclusion of the treaty, or that this can at least safely be presumed. The court nourished this strand of reasoning with its *Aegean Sea Continental Shelf* precedent where it found the expression 'the territorial status of Greece' to be a 'generic term' in whose interpretation 'the presumption necessarily arises that its meaning was intended to follow the evolution of the law and to correspond with the meaning attached to the expression by the law in force at any given time'. '[I]t hardly seems conceivable', the court continued, 'that in such a convention terms like "domestic jurisdiction" and "territorial status" were intended to have a fixed content regardless of the subsequent evolution of international law'.[167] With the force of this precedent the ICJ then held in the *Dispute Regarding Navigational and Related Rights* that

> where the parties have used generic terms in a treaty, the parties necessarily having been aware that the meaning of the terms was likely to evolve over time, and where the treaty has been entered into for a very long period or is 'of continuing duration', the parties must be presumed, as a general rule, to have intended those terms to have an evolving meaning.[168]

The court placed great stress on the link between what international law is and the prevalent narrative of legitimacy that connects to state consent. The necessary presumption that parties must have intended the meaning of a treaty to change as it did falls only slightly short of assuming that parties were clairvoyant at the moment of a treaty's conclusion.[169] It is also unclear what 'generic terms' are, or at least how the court uses this notion. In any event it seems to be a slightly hazy

[165] *Case Concerning the Dispute Regarding Navigational and Related Rights (Costa Rica v Nicaragua)*, Judgment of 13 July 2009 (the court takes 'free navigation ... for the purposes of commerce' as the English translation of the Spanish treaty text, ibid., at para 56).

[166] Ibid., at para 58. On a side note it may further be pointed out that Nicaragua inter alia tried to buttress its claim by arguing that the treaty establishes a limitation to its sovereignty and should therefore be interpreted narrowly. The idea that flares up here is the slightly quaint maxim of *in dubio mitius*. With remarkably little effort the court straightforwardly rejects this argument. Ibid., at para 48.

[167] *Aegean Sea Continental Shelf (Greece v Turkey)*, Judgment of 19 December 1978, ICJ Reports 3, para 77.

[168] *Case Concerning the Dispute Regarding Navigational and Related Rights (Costa Rica v Nicaragua)*, Judgment of 13 July 2009, para 66.

[169] Compare the, more guarded, argument by Judge ad hoc Guillaume in *Case Concerning the Dispute Regarding Navigational and Related Rights (Costa Rica v Nicaragua)*, Judgment of 13 July 2009, Declaration by Judge ad hoc Guillaume, para 15 ('In most cases parties to a treaty do not explicitly state in it whether they intend to fix for all time the meaning of the terms employed or whether they wish to allow the meaning to evolve. As a result, recourse must be had to presumptions.').

category whose content is subject to change. What might certainly happen is that something deemed specific and precise at one time, later turns out to be 'generic' and therefore subject to evolution.[170]

The court only briefly mentioned the second and probably more promising line of reasoning in support of its finding. It pointed to Art. 31(3)(b) VCLT which demands that in interpretation '[t]here shall be taken into account, together with the context... (b) any subsequent practice in the application of the treaty which established the agreement of the parties regarding its interpretation'. In the opinion of the court, subsequent practice can result in a departure from the original intentions.[171] While the first line of reasoning—evolutive interpretation due to semantic change—primarily enters on the wording of the treaty and on parties' intentions at the time of the treaty's conclusion, arguments based on subsequent practice seek a more stable ground by looking at renewed manifestations of agreement.

The court did not explore this latter avenue any further, much to the dismay of Judges Skotnikov and Guillaume who expressed their dissatisfaction with how the court comes up with an evolutive interpretation, which in their opinion pays insufficient regard to considerations of the intent of the parties and to elements that may indicate changes in their intention.[172] Depending on the circumstances of the case and on pragmatic considerations such as the availability of empirical material, looking at subsequent practice might indeed frequently turn out to be less speculative than conjecturing about what parties had to foretell at the time of a treaty's conclusion.

As of late, the rule in Art. 31(3)(b) has also made prominent appearances in WTO adjudication.[173] In its early report in *Japan—Alcoholic Beverages II* the Appellate Body maintained, overruling the panel on this point, that its judicial decisions within its framework do not amount to subsequent practice. The Appellate Body saw the main reason for this in the fact that the drafters of the WTO

170 That has arguably happened with regard to WTO member's schedule commitments, see Appellate Body Report, *China—Measures Affecting Trading Rights and Distribution Services for Certain Publications and Audiovisual Entertainment Products*, 21 December 2009, WT/DS363/AB/R, para 396; cf. Panel Report, *European Communities and its Member States—Tariff Treatment of Certain Information Technology Products*, WT/DS375, 376 & 377/R, 16 August 2010, paras 7.596–7.600. Also note that the tribunal in *Iron Rhine* did ultimately not consider the terms it had to apply to be 'conceptual or generic'. It rather found 'new technological developments relating to the operation and capacity of the railway' to be at issue and primarily relied on the principle of effectiveness in support of its evolutive approach, paras 80–84.

171 *Case Concerning the Dispute Regarding Navigational and Related Rights (Costa Rica v Nicaragua)*, Judgment of 13 July 2009, at para 64.

172 Ibid. Separate Opinion by Judge Skotnikov (para 6) and Declaration by Judge Guillaume (paras 9–15). Cf. R K Gardiner, *Treaty Interpretation* (Oxford: Oxford University Press 2008), 242–3 (on the distinction between subsequent practice and evolutive interpretation).

173 I v Damme, *Treaty Interpretation by the WTO Appellate Body* (Oxford: Oxford University Press 2009), 338–46; A M Feldman, 'Evolving Treaty Obligations: A Proposal for Analyzing Subsequent Practice Derived from WTO Dispute Settlement' (2009) 41 *NYU Journal of International Law & Politics* 655–706; G Nolte, Subsequent Practice as a Means of Interpretation in the Jurisprudence of the Appellate Body, in: E Cannizzaro (ed), *The Law of Treaties Beyond the Vienna Convention* (Oxford: Oxford University Press 2011), 138–44.

Agreement had reserved the competence of rendering authoritative interpretations for the Ministerial Conference and the General Council—Art. IX:2 WTO Agreement states that '[t]he Ministerial Conference and the General Council shall have the exclusive authority to adopt interpretations of this Agreement and of the Multilateral Trade Agreements'.[174] In contrast, the more recent report in *EC—Chicken Cuts* marks a significant shift away from this restriction on the working of subsequent practice in interpretation. The Appellate Body now argues that it 'fail[s] to see how the express authorization in the *WTO Agreement* for Members to adopt interpretations of WTO provisions... would impinge upon recourse to subsequent practice as a tool of treaty interpretation under Article 31(3)(b) of the *Vienna Convention*'.[175] In the same breath, it cautions that an interpretation with reference to subsequent practice should not be taken lightly 'because the interpretation of a treaty provision on the basis of subsequent practice is binding on all parties to the treaty, including those that have not actually engaged in such practice'.[176]

The path towards finding shifts in meaning by way of looking at subsequent practice in the sense of Art. 31(3)(b) VCLT might thus come with a mighty increase in the power of international courts. It possibly fuels and fosters their influence in international lawmaking by way of interpretation because they have another tool that allows them to push for change. 'Subsequent practice' comes to life in their interpretations. The notion is possibly conducive to interpretations that are more distanced from the texts and the parties' intentions; possibly more so than it actually ties interpretations to these foundations. But at the same time, it might offer a more solid basis for interpretation when compared with speculations about what parties might originally have intended when the terms of their commitments to evolve. Tying evolutive interpretation back to the will of the parties oftentimes implies a tenuous stretch and may leave international interpreters with yet more discretion.[177] How the response to the semantic authority of international institutions offered by the use of subsequent practice in interpretation plays out depends among other things on the level of scrutiny that it permits and sustains—whether it develops into a doctrine that does actually argumentatively constrain international interpreters. The doctrine is in flux and ultimately seems to face key questions about the foundation of international order.

[174] Appellate Body Report, *Japan—Taxes on Alcoholic Beverages*, WT/DS8, 10 & 11/AB/R, 4 October 1996, pp 12–13. At the same the Appellate Body did stress that the '[a]dopted panel reports are an important part of the GATT *acquis*. They are often considered by subsequent panels. They create legitimate expectations among WTO Members, and, therefore, should be taken into account where they are relevant to any dispute.' Ibid., at p 14. See in detail above Chapter IV, section B.1.

[175] Appellate Body Report, *European Communities—Customs Classification of Frozen Boneless Chicken Cuts*, WT/DS286/AB/R, 12 September 2005, para 273.

[176] Ibid.

[177] See Nolte, Between Contemporaneous and Evolutive Interpretation, 1683–4 (arguing that subsequent practice can play both an enabling as well as a limiting role).

It stands first of all in question, what exactly amounts to subsequent practice. To further investigate the issue, it is helpful to juxtapose 'subsequent *practice*' in Art. 31(3)(b) with Art. 31(3)(a) VCLT providing that 'there shall be taken into account . . . any subsequent *agreement* between the parties regarding the interpretation of the treaty or the application of its provisions'. The scope of these two paragraphs is not identical but certain circumstances may well come under both headings. With regard to *lit.* (a), instances in which a specific body has the explicit competence to authoritatively interpret a treaty—like the Ministerial Conference and the General Council according to Art. IX:2 WTO Agreement—are rather straightforward.[178] It is also generally agreed that the outward form is not decisive as long as there really is 'agreement'.[179] But such a proposition immediately begs the question of how we find agreement if we do not know what it looks like. It is undisputed, finally, that subsequent agreement can be less than a new treaty.[180]

The doctrinal debate on subsequent practice in *lit.* (b) is still more intricate.[181] To be clear, at issue here is subsequent practice as a doctrinal notion in the sense of the VCLT—it is not to be confused with the concept practice as it has been coined in this book's theoretical perspective. The common understanding in jurisprudence and scholarly literature is that practice in the sense of Art. 31(3)(b) VCLT has to be 'concordant, common and consistent'.[182] Beyond that there is considerable

[178] R K Gardiner, *Treaty Interpretation* (Oxford: Oxford University Press 2008), 117. Cf. van Damme, *Treaty Interpretation*, 346–50 (on the WTO jurisprudence with regard to the application of Art. 31(3)(a) VCLT).

[179] M K Yasseen, 'L'interprétation des traités d'après la Convention de Vienne sur le droit des traités' (1976) 151 *Recueil des Cours* 1–114, 44–7; Gardiner, *Treaty Interpretation*, 216–25; U Linderfalk, *On the Interpretation of Treaties. The Modern International Law as Expressed in the 1969 Vienna Convention on the Law of Treaties* (Dordrecht: Springer 2007), 162.

[180] See above note 140.

[181] D Simon, *L'Interprétation judiciaire des traités d'organisations internationales* (Paris: Pedone 1981), 378–84; Yasseen, 'L'interprétation des traités', 47–52; Gardiner, *Treaty Interpretation*, 225–49; Linderfalk, *Interpretation of Treaties*, 165–77.

[182] I M Sinclair, *The Vienna Convention on the Law of Treaties* (Manchester: Manchester University Press 1984), 137 (noting that '[t]he value and significance of subsequent practice will naturally depend on the extent to which it is concordant, common and consistent'), referencing Yasseen, 'L'interprétation des traités', 48 (stating that '[l]a pratique ultérieure doit donc être concordante, commune et d'une certaine constance.'). This qualification of subsequent practice has been taken up in WTO jurisprudence, see Appellate Body Report, *Japan—Taxes on Alcoholic Beverages*, WT/DS8, 10 & 11/AB/R, 4 October 1996, p 13; Appellate Body Report, *Chile—Price Band System and Safeguard Measures Relating to Certain Agricultural Products*, WT/DS207/AB/R, 23 September 2002, para 214; Appellate Body Report, *United States—Measures Affecting the Cross-Border Supply of Gambling and Betting Services*, WT/DS285/AB/R, 7 April 2005, paras 191–192; Appellate Body Report, *European Communities—Customs Classification of Frozen Boneless Chicken Cuts*, WT/DS286/AB/R, 12 September 2005, paras 256–258. Note, however, that so far, the Appellate Body has never based its interpretation on Art. 31(3)(b). In all cases where subsequent practice could have possibly been a factor in interpretation, it dismissed its relevance for one reason or another—usually the decisive issue was that the practice did not qualify as establishing the agreement of the parties regarding the treaty's interpretation. See A M Feldman, 'Evolving Treaty Obligations: A Proposal for Analyzing Subsequent Practice Derived from WTO Dispute Settlement' (2009) 41 *NYU Journal of International Law & Politics* 655–706,

uncertainty as to whether subsequent practice is really only about *interpretation* or if it can actually *modify* a treaty. Views further compete on *what* counts as practice and *whose* practice counts.

From the external perspective that has driven the analysis of how the practice of interpretation makes international law, specifically its building block of semantic pragmatism, it is particularly intriguing how doctrine and rules of interpretation deal with the question of whether subsequent practice can actually modify a treaty. Some stress that the issue is interpretation in contrast to modification and that the difference is analogous to the distinction between a declaratory act and a constitutive act. While interpretation uncovers what is out there, modification places something new into the world.[183] Special provisions for amending a treaty usually serve as a further argument in support of the view that a treaty cannot be modified by way of interpretation. The distinction between an interpretative declaration and a reservation to a treaty works in the same way. With reservations a government 'purports to exclude or modify the legal effect of certain provisions of the treaty' (Art. 2(1)(d) VCLT). An interpretative declaration, to the contrary, does not amount to a modification of the treaty but, in the words of the ILC, it is 'a unilateral statement... made by a State or by an international organization whereby that State or that organization purports to *specify or clarify* the meaning or scope attributed by the declarant to a treaty or to certain of its provisions'.[184]

Those who stress that subsequent practice functions on the level of interpretation rather than modification can point to the fact that Art. 38 of the ILC draft on the law of treaties faced the opposition of a considerable number of state representatives and was ultimately not included in the VCLT—the only article of the ILC draft that was deleted in its entirety.[185] It was titled '[m]odification of treaties by subsequent practice' and provided that '[a] treaty may be modified by subsequent practice in the application of the treaty establishing the agreement of the parties to modify its provisions'.[186] State representatives who opposed draft Art. 38 argued among other things that modification would have to pass through formal amend-

676, and 681–95. The ICJ has been more vague and a bit less prolific on the issue, see *Case Concerning Kasikili/Sedudu Island (Botswana v Namibia)*, Judgment of 13 December 1999, ICJ Reports 1045, paras 49–50 (quoting the ILC on 'subsequent practice' and recalling its jurisprudence on the matter); *Legal Consequences for States of the Continuing Presence of South Africa in Namibia (South West Africa) notwithstanding Security Council Resolution 276 (1970)*, Advisory Opinion of 21 June 1971, ICJ Reports 16, para 22 (stating that members of the Security Council have 'consistently and uniformly interpreted the practice of voluntary abstention by a permanent member as not constituting a bar to the adoption of resolutions'); *Certain Expenses of the United Nations (Article 17, paragraph 2, of the Charter)*, Advisory Opinion of 20 July 1962, ICJ Reports 151, p 160 (stating that '[i]t is a consistent practice of the General Assembly to include in the annual budget resolutions, provision for expenses relating to the maintenance of international peace and security').

[183] d Nascimento e Silva, 'Le Facteur Temps', 269.

[184] ILC, Report of the 59th Session 2007 (A/62/10), p 48 (italics added). Cf. M Heymann, *Einseitige Interpretationserklärungen zu multilateralen Verträgen* (Berlin: Duncker & Humblot 2005).

[185] W Karl, *Vertrag und spätere Praxis im Völkerrecht. Zum Einfluß der Praxis auf Inhalt und Bestand völkerrechtlicher Verträge* (Berlin: Springer 1983), 291–2.

[186] ILC, Yearbook, vol II (1966), p 236.

ment procedures. It was also pointed out that the article would be problematic from the perspective of domestic law and treaty application, in particular with regard to meeting constitutional demands of parliamentary ratification.[187]

Few would however assert that *interpretation* could be easily told apart from *modification*. In the commentaries on the ILC draft articles on the law of treaties, Sir Humphrey Waldock, already wrote that 'if the interpretation adopted by the parties diverges, as sometimes happens, from the natural and ordinary meaning of the terms, there may be a blurring of the line between the interpretation and the amendment of a treaty by subsequent practice'.[188] Others then claimed that it is next to impossible to distinguish one from the other, or at least to formulate such a distinction in general terms. It is for instance a central contention in Wolfram Karl's meticulous treatment of the matter that it is not possible to draw a clear and categorical borderline between interpretation and modification.[189] Karl and others also contend that rejecting draft Art. 38 was ill-conceived and that its rule in any event already formed part of customary international law.[190] Even if they do not accept a categorical distinction in principle, they still draw practical consequences from a distinction between interpretation and modification.[191] For example, they maintain that the threshold of consent is higher if subsequent practice is taken to amount to a modification rather than an interpretation. The latter demands more scrutiny and widespread agreement whereas for the former the silence of some parties to the treaty is not a big issue; after all, the practice of some states is only taken in support of an interpretation of what already exists.[192]

As a bottom line, subsequent practice can develop a treaty in a way that stops short of modifications that require formal amendment. The space in between—precisely the space of negotiating the content of legal commitments in the practice of interpretation—is nebulous from the point of view of legal doctrine. This does not surprise as legal doctrine continues to grapple with repercussions of the theoretical insight that it is impossible not to interpret and that interpretation contributes to creating what it finds.[193]

Apart from the question of whether subsequent practice can actually modify a treaty, views compete as to *what* counts as practice and *whose* practice counts. The scope of actors whose practice comes into consideration seems to have expanded.

[187] Karl, *Vertrag und spätere Praxis*, 294.

[188] ILC, Yearbook, *Third Report on the Law of Treaties*, vol 2 (1964), p 60, para 25.

[189] Karl, *Vertrag und spätere Praxis*, 3.

[190] Ibid., at 292–3; Feldman, 'Evolving Treaty Obligations', 671–2 (arguing that concerns about draft Art. 38 were misguided because, after all, agreement among the parties would still be required).

[191] Karl, *Vertrag und spätere Praxis*, 40–6.

[192] See for instance J-P Cot, 'La Conduite subséquente des Parties à un traité' (1966) 70 *Revue Générale de Droit International Public* 632–66, 645 (arguing that practice from a single state only may suffice in the sense of Art. 31(3)(b) if it is merely indicative of the will of the parties).

[193] See above Chapter II, section A.3.

In view of the increasing number and scope of participants in international legal discourse, this would on first sight be only plausible. While international law was once more centred on the practice of (high-ranking) members of the executive, now also other domestic actors, in particular domestic courts, and especially international organizations come into consideration.[194] The interpretative practice of international bureaucracies and international judicial institutions would then be captured as subsequent practice in the sense of Art. 31(3)(b) VCLT.[195] In such an approach, the acts of international organizations itself counts as practice. The doctrine of subsequent practice would then no longer offer a flipside argument in comparison to soft law by trying to tie international action to the consent of the parties, but it would, like soft law, elevate international practices to a stronger standing.

Such an approach would not be without support from legal practice. The ICJ looked for example at reports and resolutions of the World Health Organization (WHO) as 'subsequent practice' in the sense of Art. 31(3)(b) in its advisory opinion in *Legality of the Use by a State of Nuclear Weapons in Armed Conflict.*[196] And the WTO panel in *Japan—Alcoholic Beverages II* has attempted to qualify panel reports as subsequent practice.[197]

Expanding the concept of subsequent practice to international actors should be weighed carefully. In the advisory opinion just mentioned, the ICJ affirmed that the objective of constitutive instruments of international organizations 'is to create new subjects of law endowed with a certain autonomy, to which the parties entrust the task of realizing common goals'.[198] The court recognized the autonomy of international organizations and tried to thrive on a narrative of functional legitimacy. But as an assessment of the bittersweet taste of justice in legal discourse has shown, one-sided narratives of progress cannot convince. The semantic authority of international institutions requires a principled justification that leans on international law's legitimating function. What does this mean for the doctrine of subsequent practice?

First of all, expanding the concept of subsequent practice to include the practice of international institutions—the practice of autonomous actors in their own right—would be unexpected because Art. 31(3)(b) takes subsequent practice to establish an 'agreement between the parties'. Understanding acts of international

[194] A Nollkaemper, *National Courts and the International Rule of Law* (Oxford: Oxford University Press 2011), 271 (referring inter alia to the judgment in *Kristić* and how the ICTY grouped jurisprudence from the ICTR as well as state practice, 'notably through... national courts', together in its account of subsequent practice, *Prosecutor v Jelisić*, Judgment of 14 December 1999, ICTY-95-10-T, para 61).

[195] Karl, *Vertrag und spätere Praxis*, 114–17 and 170–1.

[196] *Legality of the Use by a State of Nuclear Weapons in Armed Conflict*, Advisory Opinion of 8 July 1996, ICJ Reports 66, paras 19–27.

[197] Panel Report, *Japan—Taxes on Alcoholic Beverages*, WT/DS8, 10 & 11/R, 11 July 1996, paras 6.8–6.10.

[198] *Legality of the Use by a State of Nuclear Weapons in Armed Conflict*, Advisory Opinion, 8 July 1996, ICJ Reports 66, para 19.

bureaucracies and even more so of judicial institutions as establishing an agreement between parties is rather curious. How could a judgment that authoritatively decides a *dispute* between two parties plausibly be taken to establish their agreement?

It is quite a different thing to use the subsequent practice of state actors in the interpretation of a treaty, including in contexts of adjudication. The judgment would not itself be taken as subsequent practice but as a proxy for the practice of state organs. This distinction, if taken seriously, comes with different argumentative demands. Taking international interpretations as a proxy for state action and using the concept of subsequent practice so as to tie the development of international law to renewed moments of state consent, is the primary focus of the project on *Treaties over Time* as it was included in the International Law Commission's programme of work in 2008.[199] In its argument on why the Commission should consider the topic, the proposal crafted by the study group's chairperson Georg Nolte observes that there is relatively little research and even less clarity on these means of interpretation.[200] What is more, subsequent agreements and practice are not always well documented.[201] The topic is furthermore of mounting importance because treaties are coming of age, mechanisms for amendment are burdensome and, notably, there is an 'increasing tendency of international courts to interpret treaties in a purpose-oriented and objective manner'.[202] The proposal maintains that, as time goes by, treaties have to adapt because otherwise they might no longer correspond to the intentions of the parties—subsequent agreement and practice should be explored as the preferable mechanisms of accommodating processes of change. It also implies that this way might be preferable to the alternative of purposive or even 'evolutionary' interpretation. It wants to investigate subsequent agreement and practice and develop a repository of such practice because '[w]ithout such guidance, judicial bodies might too easily identify what they consider to be the object and purpose of a treaty, thereby possibly overlooking the continuing role of States in treaty interpretation'.[203]

In sum, there are two avenues by way of which the notion of subsequent practice in the sense of Art. 31(3)(b) VCLT could help capture the practice of international institutions and its impact on the development of international law. One is to expand the concept to cover the practice of international institutions—be they bureaucracies like the UNHCR or judicial institutions in the WTO. This would place considerable stress on the wording of the article because it does after all speak of 'agreement between the parties'. It would appear to be rather unusual to understand the practice of autonomous actors to quite literally establish agreement

199 ILC, Report of the 60th Session 2008 (A/63/10), para 353; ILC, Report of the 63rd Session 2011 (A/66/10), p 284 (stating that there is tentative agreement among participating members of the commission that '[r]elevant subsequent practice can consist of acts of all State organs (executive, legislative, and judicial) which can be attributed to a State for the purpose of treaty interpretation . . . ').

200 ILC, Report of the 60th Session 2008 (A/63/10), pp 365–89 ('Annex A').

201 Ibid., at Annex A, para 13.

202 Ibid., at Annex A, paras 14–15.

203 Ibid., at Annex A, para 20.

between other actors. Such an avenue would be similar to the ideas of soft law in the way it elevates international practice to greater prominence and it invites critiques along similar lines. A second avenue is to confine the concept of subsequent practice to state actors and to use their input as guidance in interpretation. Such an approach places significant trust and confidence in the (international) interpreter that will after all bring such practice to life. If the doctrine of subsequent practice is indeed developed into a dense argumentative standard, it might have the potential of constraining international interpreters.[204] But conversely, pushing subsequent practice to greater prominence in treaty interpretation might also enlarge the discretion of international interpreters. It might then have the effect of actually reducing the impact that states have on what an international norm means. Given that the question of what amounts to meaningful subsequent practice and what does not is yet another strand of (largely) semantic struggle, international institutions' authority comes to bear on this question just as well.

The prospect of both avenues expanding the concept of subsequent practice in the sense of Art. 31(3)(b) VCLT will be decided at the intersections between the levels of governance. On the one hand, recognizing the practice of autonomous international actors as factors in interpretation might credit their well-founded claim to authority. On the other hand, tying the practice of international actors to the will of states alone—that is, to argue that only subsequent practice of the parties to a statutory treaty mattered—would rule out any such consideration. Where accountability gaps persist, there might indeed be second thoughts as to whether the actions of international actors should be credited as a reference point in legal argument, blessed as such by legal doctrine. But sometimes international action may also be a response to deficits that arise from ties with states that are too tight. The rules of interpretation, including the doctrine of subsequent practice, will need to develop in line with the justification of authority in a normative pluriverse in which state sovereignty is no longer the primary or even exclusive building block for legitimate order.

3. Global administrative law and international public authority

Two further approaches that react to the authority of international institutions are united in a partial rupture with traditional modes of legal thinking and notably take international institutions seriously as independent actors by not reducing their action, nor their justification, to the input of state actors alone. They in principle recognize international institutions' authority and push for innovation in order to invigorate international law in its function of providing a language for contestation and a mode of legitimation. The first is an approach that comes under the heading of global administrative law (GAL) and the second turns on the concept of international public authority (IPA).

[204] Also see v Damme, *Treaty Interpretation*, 338–46 (looking at subsequent practice as a mechanism for rebalancing the factors of interpretation in favour of state input).

Both GAL and research centred on IPA share the findings that resulted from the discussion of the bittersweet taste of justice in legal discourse. They take up the understanding that in most practical circumstances a shared language of international law is a necessary element in addressing concerns about legitimacy and they agree that a legal framework should help translate legitimacy concerns into legal arguments.[205] They further agree that discourses about legitimacy and legality are increasingly out of sync due to transformations in the patterns of governance. Both approaches are deliberately crafted so as to respond to the rise of global governance phenomena and their challenge for classical perspectives of international law. Against the backdrop of the mounting power of a plethora of actors and of processes that shape the conduct of political affairs in a way that is beyond the reach of unitary states, they seek to capture and conquer global governance phenomena in a legal vocabulary.[206] With this agenda they go beyond this contribution's more narrow focus on the exercise of authority by way of interpretation and, more pointedly, the semantic authority of international actors. The jurisgenerative practice of international bureaucracies and international judicial institutions is, however, a prime example of what comes under the heading of global governance. It may well be framed as administration or as public authority.

The GAL project has mainly been crafted as a response to growing accountability deficits in global governance processes. It is guided by the thought that much of global governance can be understood as administration and it defines global administrative law 'as comprising the mechanisms, principles, practices, and supporting social understandings that promote or otherwise affect the accountability of global administrative bodies'.[207] It thus extends its view beyond the purview of classical international law and aims at addressing the legitimacy of global governance phenomena by framing them as administrative action. This perspective, its proponents argue, has the potential of exposing legitimatory deficits and it may

[205] v Bogdandy, Dann, Goldmann, 'Developing the Publicness', 1380; M Goldmann, 'Inside Relative Normativity: From Sources to Standard Instruments for the Exercise of International Public Authority' (2008) 9 *German Law Journal* 1865–908, 1867–8 (embracing 'law's capacity to rationalize disagreement on questions of justice through the use of formalistic arguments about rights and obligations.'). I share the thrust of the argument, but would however play down the distribution of (ir)rationality between legal and other discourses, and add a word of caution about the blind spots of formalism, Venzke, 'International Bureaucracies'.

[206] B Kingsbury and N Krisch, 'Introduction: Global Governance and Global Administrative Law in the International Legal Order' (2006) 17 *European Journal of International Law* 1–13, 1 (stating at the outset that '[g]lobalization and the rise of global governance are transforming the structure of international law' and that 'much of this transformation takes place beneath the surface of the international legal order'); v Bogdandy, Dann, Goldmann, 'Developing the Publicness', 1375 (saying that they respond to the 'deep transformation in the conduct of public affairs epitomized by the term global governance'). On this transformation, cf. J H H Weiler, 'The Geology of International Law—Governance, Democracy and Legitimacy' (2004) 64 *Zeitschrift für ausländisches öffentliches Recht und Völkerrecht* 547–62.

[207] B Kingsbury, N Krisch, and R B Stewart, 'The Emergence of Global Administrative Law' (2005) 68 *Law and Contemporary Problems* 15–61, 17.

provide responses that stem from administrative law thinking. Principles of an administrative law character are introduced as a possible cure—principles of transparency, procedural participation, reasoned decision, and review. These procedural principles are complemented by substantive standards including proportionality, means-end rationality, avoidance of unnecessarily restrictive means, and legitimate expectations.[208]

To think of large parts of global governance as administration and to frame activities in terms of global administrative law is certainly a strong move laden with normative implications. Its proponents clearly flag that using administrative law terminology will stabilize global governance processes and might end up bestowing an air of legitimacy onto illegitimate exercises of power.[209] At the same time, its vocabulary and the principles that administrative law thinking employs may offer more pointed legal arguments for the critique of power. Protagonists within the project duly note that a number of factors, including questions of institutional design, will need to be fine-tuned so that the principles it holds dear do not end up contributing to undesirable outcomes—'[a]ccountability can dissipate effectiveness, participation can result in [capture] by special interests, transparency can mean populism triumphs over justice.'[210]

One of the GAL project's central elements is that it frames action that takes place in a rather amorphous 'global administrative space'.[211] This space transcends different levels of governance, degrades the distinction between the domestic and the international, and brings together public as well as private actors. Apart from an unsettled interplay with power relations and uncertainty about institutional design, the sweeping eradication of boundaries and a felt loss of clarity have been main points of critique.[212] Uneasiness about the use of 'law' in the GAL project and hesitation as to whether administrative law principles can be projected onto the international level where the 'administration' misses its conceptual neighbour 'legislation' have further stirred critical reactions.[213]

[208] Ibid., at 37–42.

[209] Ibid., at 27 ('On the one hand, casting global governance in administrative terms might lead to its stabilization and legitimation in ways that privilege current powerholders and reinforce the dominance of Northern and Western concepts of law and sound governance. On the other hand, it might also create a platform for critique.').

[210] Kingsbury and Krisch, 'Introduction', 4. Cf. B S Chimni, 'Co-Option and Resistance: Two Faces of Global Administrative Law' (2005) 37 *NYU Journal of International Law & Politics* 799–827, 805 (suggesting inter alia that the GAL project and its resort to procedural answers might end up justifying unjust substantive outcomes); S Marks, 'Naming Global Administrative Law' (2005) 37 *International Law and Politics* 995–1001.

[211] Kingsbury, Krisch, and Stewart, 'The Emergence of Global Administrative Law', 25–7.

[212] A v Bogdandy, 'General Principles of International Public Authority: Sketching a Research Field' (2008) 11 *German Law Journal* 1909–38, 1918–21.

[213] See A Somek, 'The Concept of "Law" in Global Administrative Law: A Reply to Benedict Kingsbury' (2009) 20 *European Journal of International Law* 985–95. Also compare J Borgumil, W Jann, and F Nullmeier, Perspektiven der politikwissenschaftlichen Verwaltungsforschung, in: J Borgumil, W Jann, and F Nullmeier (eds), *Politik und Verwaltung. PVS Sonderheft 37* (Wiesbaden:

Parts of a more elaborate critique have been developed from the perspective of research centred on the exercise of international public authority. Similar to the GAL project but with certain nuances, this second approach places great emphasis on promoting the publicness of public international law. Public law, it recalls, has the dual function of constituting as well as limiting public authority.[214] If public authority is understood as the capacity to unilaterally shape the legal and factual situation of others, then public law is precisely concerned with the tension between such authority and individual or collective freedom.[215] The development of international law by way of interpretation may well be captured as such public authority if only the actors of interpretation enjoy a certain standing. Actors with semantic authority condition other participants and subjects of the legal order in the exercise of their freedom by way of their interpretative practice.[216]

The dual function of public law may also be taken up by international law. It would appear only fitting to promote such an understanding of international law in view of the increasing exercise of power in processes of global governance that evades legal categories. At the moment, there is little that can be said about much of this power other than that it is not illegal. And yet it does frequently raise concerns about its legitimacy—'the discourse on legality is out of sync with the discourse on legitimacy.'[217] For public (international) law to fulfil its promise of constituting and constraining public authority, it is then necessary to (re-)align these discourses more closely.

Rather than postulating a *global* administrative space, however, research centred on IPA leans on *international* institutional law. It finds the differences between the levels of governance—their political institutions and mechanisms for generating legitimacy—to be too significant to discard the boundaries.[218] But how is it possible to expand international law in order to capture and conquer the exercise of authority that raises well-founded concerns about its legitimacy and still escapes legal terminology?

When it comes to international institutions generally, the answer might lie in a move from classical sources doctrine to standard instruments.[219] The idea is that

VS Verlag für Sozialwissenschaften 2006), 9–26, 18 (on the difficulties regarding a separation of powers on the international level).

[214] v Bogdandy, Dann, Goldmann, 'Developing the Publicness', 1380.

[215] Ibid., at 1376 (on the working of public law with regard to the tension between authority and freedom), and at 1381–2 (on the definition of public authority).

[216] A v Bogdandy and I Venzke, 'In Whose Name? An Investigation of International Courts' Public Authority and its Democratic Justification' (2012) 23 *European Journal of International Law* 7–41 (on the understanding of judicial interpretation as an exercise of public authority in closer detail).

[217] v Bogdandy, Dann, Goldmann, 'Developing the Publicness', 1389.

[218] v Bogdandy, 'General Principles', 1918–21.

[219] Goldmann, 'Inside Relative Normativity'.

certain parameters would be used to carve out a number of standard instruments that would then trigger legal regimes governing questions such as who is competent to adopt certain instruments, what the procedures are for their adoption, and whether they are subject to judicial review.[220] This shift towards standard instruments may be a response to the observation that neither the legal basis alone, nor nominal criteria (what something is called), can decide how to deal with a certain act. A critical point of departure is the expected effect that instruments may have in shaping the legal or factual situation of others.

To illustrate the point: at the moment there is little to say or do in terms of law about refugee status determinations carried out by UNHCR or the listing of terrorist suspects by the Security Council.[221] One might wonder about their legal basis but that is almost it. But searching for their legal basis would usually not exhaust the issues that are addressed as part of concerns about their legitimacy—shortcomings in the procedures that lead to such acts and limited judicial review, for instance. If one identifies these acts as international administrative decisions (a standard instrument), then it may be possible to develop a legal regime that governs procedures, effects, and review.[222] Also documents such as the UNHCR Guidance Notes fall between legal categories and their standardization may contribute to (international) public law's function of constituting and constraining public authority. It may further simply help legal practice in its handling of such legal communications. Thinking in terms of standard instruments is a promising approach that looks far into the future. A dialogue between scholars, politicians, civil society, and courts on different levels of governance would need to give shape and further detail to standard instruments and their legal regimes.[223]

When it comes to international judicial institutions, finding categories of standard instruments is not the primary issue; but here the procedural law of international courts and tribunals is of greater relevance. Responses to the exercise of public authority by judicial bodies would for instance need to look at how the judicial process relates to demands of publicness and transparency, to the possibilities of participation in the form of third party intervention or *amicus curiae* briefs.[224] Developing international law and its doctrine with regard to the

[220] A v Bogdandy, *Gubernative Rechtsetzung. Eine Neubestimmung der Rechtsetzung und des Regierungssystems unter dem Grundgesetz in der Perspektive gemeineuropäischer Dogmatik* (Tübingen: Mohr Siebeck 2000), 156–60; J Bast, *Grundbegriffe der Handlungsformen der EU. Entwickelt am Beschluss als praxisgenerierter Handlungsform des Unions- und Gemeinschaftsrechts* (Heidelberg: Springer 2006) (developing the doctrine of standard instruments in the context of the European Union).

[221] Cf. M Smrkolj, 'International Bureaucracies and Individualized Decision-Making: An Example of UNHCR's Refuge Status Determination' (2008) 9 *German Law Journal* 1779–1803; C A Feinäugle, 'The UN Security Council Al-Qaida and Taliban Sanctions Committee: Emerging Principles of International Institutional Law for the Protection of Individuals?' (2008) 9 *German Law Journal* 1513–39.

[222] Goldmann, 'Inside Relative Normativity', 1891.

[223] Ibid., at 1901.

[224] I Venzke, Antinomies and Change in International Dispute Settlement: An Exercise in Comparative Procedural Law, in: R Wolfrum and I Gätzschmann (eds), *International Dispute Settlement: Room for Innovations* (Heidelberg: Springer 2012 forthcoming).

jurisgenerative practice of international judiciaries would also include ways of further politicization of the regimes of which adjudicators form part. Reactions to the exercise of authority through adjudication could further look to the election of judges or arbitrators and legal doctrine could consider the repercussions that understanding the lawmaking dimension of interpretative practice has for the rules, methods, and expectations with regard to international adjudication.[225]

Even if GAL principles were to be implemented fully and institutional or procedural law was further advanced in reaction to the exercise of IPA, doubt would still remain whether the international legal order can always convincingly shoulder the burden of legitimating power on the international level and of keeping it in check. Both GAL and IPA come to terms with a kind of international public authority that cannot simply be reduced to the input of state actors—neither in a plausibly analytical perspective, nor in a normative theory. But they continue to stress the significant role of state actors in legitimating the exercise of authority beyond the state. They recognize distinct constituencies of political communities that overlap and sometimes conflict.[226]

Extending the legal vocabulary and legal processes in order to translate discourses about justice and legitimacy into legal discourse might end up embedding and perpetuating power imbalances and patterns of domination. Adjunct factors that complement public law's constitutive and constraining function, like a critical general public that nourishes normative discourses of a certain quality, are fragile on the international level. Persisting doubt as to the ability of international public law to fully live up to the function of legitimating the authority of international actors directs attention towards the potential of the municipal level of governance in relieving the international order from some of its legitimatory burden.

C. Evasive foundations: Semantic authority in a normative pluriverse

The theoretical perspective on semantic struggles in international law has brought to the fore how the practice of interpretation makes international law under the spell of international institutions' semantic authority. Its findings question the normative construction of sources doctrine and have led to a discussion of developments taking up the challenge. The increasing impact of international bureaucracies and judicial institutions has directed attention towards a public law conception of international law that places emphasis on its function of constituting

[225] A v Bogdandy and I Venzke, 'On the Democratic Legitimation of International Judicial Lawmaking' (2011) 12 *German Law Journal* 1341–70.

[226] N Krisch, 'The Pluralism of Global Administrative Law' (2006) 17 *European Journal of International Law* 247–78; v Bogdandy and Venzke, 'In Whose Name?', 39–41.

and constraining the exercise of authority. This concluding section develops further what responses to communicative lawmaking and to international institution's authority may look like.

In order to carry the ideas of the French Revolution into the future, the authors of the *Encyclopédie* had tried to design a language that would then constrain others in what they could say or do. Realizing however, that their work would inevitably be subject to semantic contestation, they feared that their project would be captured by their opponents and thus argued that the meaning of words be tied back to the legitimating subject. Words should be the sovereign arbiters with regard to all public authority exercised over the people.[227] But who really is 'sovereign' over what international law means and is the authority they exercise by way of interpretation well justified?

Sovereignty in the sense of a final say is ultimately evasive in a communicative perspective on international lawmaking where claims to finality are but one instance of an iterative process. When such claims do succeed they testify to an actor's semantic authority that is however not foundational, but established and sustained through interaction. While sovereignty in the sense of ultimate authority may indeed be better set aside, voices that happily join in with choruses praising the fact that the era of (state) sovereignty belongs to bygone times tend to be silent with regard to sovereignty's fate as a foundation for legitimate rule.[228] In law and legal doctrine, popular sovereignty and state sovereignty rarely aimed at factual description. The people in the domestic context, and the state in the international arena, have been the building blocks in normative conceptions of legitimate order.

In the postnational constellation, state sovereignty has now crumbled as the traditional building block for legitimate rule. This is not only so because sovereign states have lost their presumption of innocence.[229] But also because the postnational constellation is marked by an incongruence between the scope of individuals affected by decisions of a polity, on the one hand, and the scope of individuals assembled as the polity's constituency and thus possibly involved in its decision-making, on the other.[230] When the European Union for example conditions market access with regard to the ways in which a product is produced, this affects all producers outside the polity taking the decision. While such a constellation is in principle centuries old, interdependence has increased as a matter of fact and the normative argument in favour of taking into consideration

[227] See above Chapter II, section A.2.

[228] L Henkin, *International Law: Politics and Values* (The Hague: Kluwer 1995), 10 (arguing that 'for legal purposes at least, we might do well to relegate the term sovereignty to the shelf of history as a relic from an earlier era.'); S Oeter, Souveränität—ein überholtes Konzept?, in: H-J Cremer, T Griegerich, D Richter, and A Zimmermann (eds), *Tradition und Weltoffenheit des Rechts, Festschrift für Helmut Steinberger* (Berlin: Springer 2002), 259–90. See above Chapter II, section B.2.b.

[229] Habermas, The Constitutionalization of International Law, 115, 158; A Peters, 'Humanity as the A and Ω of Sovereignty' (2009) 20 *European Journal of International Law* 513–44.

[230] J Habermas, The Postnational Constellation and the Future of Democracy, in: M Pensky (ed), *The Postnational Constellation: Political Essays* (Cambridge: Polity Press 2001), 58–112, see especially at 76–84.

the effect on outsiders has hardened.[231] In this perspective then, international norms such as those in the framework of the WTO on the circumstances under which a polity may condition marked access level out a democratic deficit. They react to the exercise of power that would otherwise be projected unilaterally and unconstrained onto others.

While international law and the authority of international institutions are a response to legitimatory challenges in the postnational constellation, democratic processes of political will formation on the national level retain a potential for democratic legitimation that so far remains unmatched on the international level. Specifically social preconditions for legitimatory processes, such as a feeling of community and a relatively thick public sphere, are of higher quality within individual states when compared to the global space. This means first that international action needs to connect to the legitimatory potential of domestic democratic processes where they exist. Even if this comes with a number of practical and principled limitations to such a connection, it means secondly that domestic actors might have good arguments to resist international law, especially when taken away from a one-time act of consent by semantic developments carried in the practice of interpretation.

The consequence is that actors on each level of governance can frequently offer good arguments in terms of democratic legitimation for why their interpretation should prevail. There are other elements to legitimate rule and the concept of democracy is rather vague, at least at its borders and specifically with regard to international constellations. And yet, also in times of thorough transformations in processes of governance the idea of democracy remains the gold standard against which to assess the legitimacy of authority.[232]

This section first develops the argument that the question of who should have authority over the law and of which legal order prevails in case of conflict is very difficult, if indeed possible, to decide from the outside due to the lack of normative foundation (1.). It then suggests that on each level of governance it is possible to pursue more precise strategies as to how the legitimation of international lawmaking in processes of interpretation may be improved (2.). But architectural renovations will remain largely ineffective if they are not complemented by changes in the attitudes among the main individual and institutional actors that stand at the legal borders structuring a political system of multilateral governance. While little can be said about their actions from the outside other than that they should take into consideration the repercussions of their interpretations for

[231] The suggested trajectory of increasing interdependence is not steady over long periods of time, nor should it overshadow how trade has tied the world together in the past. But the process of globalization unfolding since the second half of the twentieth century, pushed by technological innovation, has all the same contributed to the fact that decisions in one part of the world are ever more strongly felt in another. Cf. R Findley and K H O'Rourke, *Power and Plenty: Trade, War, and the World Economy in the Second Millennium* (Princeton: Princeton University Press 2007); U Beck, *What Is Globalization?* (Cambridge: Polity Press 2000), 8–13.

[232] Habermas, *Zur Verfassung Europas*; N Krisch, *Beyond Constitutionalism. The Pluralist Structure of Postnational Law* (Oxford: Oxford University Press 2010), 264–8.

others, it could well be that their interaction gives meaning to doctrinal notions that function as modes for contesting and accommodating authority in a normative pluriverse (3.).

1. Principles of democracy and ultimate authority

In the wake of popular sovereignty, public law not only aspired to stand in the name of the whole community, but also transformed into a device that would give effect to the principles of individual and collective self-determination. In this tradition, public law constitutes and limits public power. It is both enabling and constraining. It legitimizes. The *democratic* state and its legal order formed a universe that ordered all normative concerns about public power. It gained its unity from one subject of legitimization: the people. While struggles between personal and popular sovereignty still reigned on the national level, the concept of state sovereignty entered the international plane where international law and its sources doctrine reproduced the idea that no subject should be legally bound without its consent. Classical liberalism in international law portrayed the state as an individual, state sovereignty came close to individual autonomy, and state consent has served as a normative foundation for international law ever since.[233]

The prevalent view at the time, and for a long time thereafter, has been that international law does not set up a public order at all. It governs horizontal relationships between publics, but it is not concerned with the vertical relationship between public power and those subjected to it.[234] It has been more akin to a private law of contracts than a public law of statutes.[235] I argued in Chapter II that one key question that troubled international legal thinking at this modern foundation was how international law could be binding in the absence of an overarching polity that centralizes the exercise of power. How could a state, source of all law, be bound by that same law? Answers revolved around ideas of legal commitment—a commitment once made would later have to be regarded as binding.[236] Of course there has always been the daunting intricacy of how to resolve a dispute about the content of commitments. It is this problem that is pushed further into the spotlight by the dynamics of lawmaking by way of interpretation. The practice of interpretation develops international law and thereby distances the law from its consensual basis. In such a constellation, it might then be increasingly more plausible that a

[233] G Simpson, 'Imagined consent: Democratic Liberalism in International Legal Theory' (1994) 15 *Australian Yearbook of International Law* 103–28. Koskenniemi, *From Apology to Utopia*, 256. See above Chapter II, section A.1.

[234] B Kingsbury, International Law as Inter-Public Law, in: H Richardson and M Williams (eds), *Moral Universalism and Pluralism* (New York: New York University Press 2009), 167–204.

[235] H Lauterpacht, *Private Law Sources and Analogies of International Law* (Hambden, Conn.: Archon Books 1970 [1927]), 53 and 82 (noting, however, that there are already elements of a public law type within the international legal order that are likely to increase in power in the future).

[236] See in particular G Jellinek, *Die Lehre von den Staatenverbindungen* (Wien: Alfred Hölder 1882) (developing the *Selbstverpflichtungslehre*, the doctrine of 'self-limitation'). Compare the critique in H Kelsen, *Hauptprobleme der Staatsrechtslehre* (Tübingen: Mohr 1923), 430–9.

contracting party has good arguments to back up its view that it never intended to make such a commitment and to thereby support its decision not to comply. Conversely, the dynamic development of the law and the interpretative claims of international actors might just as well be backed with persuasive arguments. Who should have the ultimate say?

Much speaks in favour of municipal constitutional organs, at least to the extent that they are part of a democratic system.[237] Democratic processes on the national level have a potential of generating legitimacy that is unmatched on the supra- or international level. The quality of the general public, the density of the discourse, the fine-tuning of democratic institutions and the significance of elections all indicate that the domestic level can back its claim to ultimate authority with the thickest possible threads of legitimation.[238] Also the convictions vested in domestic constitutions carry a lot of weight as expressions of ages of learning in political dispute and its resolution. All this then speaks in favour of strengthening the say that state representatives—and other domestic actors who can tap this source of legitimation— have in international legal contestation.

At the same time, however, the democratic legitimation that domestic polities can possibly generate is limited due to the external effects of their decisions. The incongruence between those who have a democratically meaningful say in the making of a policy, on the one hand, and those who are affected by it, on the other, is characteristic of the postnational constellation.[239] Processes of globalization increase interdependencies, water down national borders, and increase ruptures in the ties between those who exercise power and those who are affected.[240] International institutions, international law, and transnational political decision-making processes may then form an adequate response to the otherwise unilateral and unconstrained projection of power. For this reason it is unconvincing to see international authority which is not responsive to the input of individual states as inherently problematic.[241]

[237] A v Bogdandy, 'Pluralism, Direct Effect, and the Ultimate Say: On the relationship between international and domestic constitutional law' (2008) 6 *International Journal of Constitutional Law* 397–413.

[238] Habermas, *Zur Verfassung Europas*, 85.

[239] M Zürn, *Regieren jenseits des Nationalstaates: Globalisierung und Denationalisierung als Chance* (Frankfurt am Main: Suhrkamp 1998); Habermas, Postnational Constellation, 76–80.

[240] D Held, Democracy and Globalization, in: D Archibugi, D Held, and M Köhler (eds), *Re-Imagining Political Community: Studies in Cosmopolitan Democracy* (Cambridge: Polity Press 1998), 11–27; A v Bogdandy, 'Globalization and Europe: How to Square Democracy, Globalization, and International Law' (2004) 15 *European Journal of International Law* 885–906; G de Búrca, 'Developing Democracy Beyond the State' (2008) 46 *Columbia Journal of Transnational Law* 221–78.

[241] Such is generally the perspective of a holistic understanding of democracy that looks to nations for legitimation rather than individuals and that therefore stops at national borders. It is for instance the normative take of the much disputed rational choice analysis in J L Goldsmith and E A Posner, *The Limits of International Law* (Oxford: Oxford University Press 2005), 205–24. Cf. A v Bogdandy and S Dellavalle, Ad hostes docere—Zu den Ursprüngen und zur Präsenz partikularistisch-holistischen Denkens, in: A Fischer-Lescano, H-P Gasser, T Marauhn, and N Ronzitti (eds), *Frieden in Freiheit. Festschrift Bothe* (Baden-Baden: Nomos 2008), 847–63.

International actors can draw on the input of different domestic polities and sometimes they might even plausibly invoke the name of transnational or world citizens in support of their interpretations. Inter- and transnational action can then raise a claim to authority that rests on greater inclusiveness. The Doha TRIPS Declaration may serve as a case in point where WTO members and multiple non-governmental organizations, especially from the health industry and development-oriented NGOs, agreed on a reading of WTO law that would allow limitations on intellectual property rights for the purpose of opening up access to medicine.[242] Also UNHCR claims authority in its role of monitoring an agreement struck between states and it may further buttress its interpretation by claiming to give a voice to the constituency of refugees. Much thus speaks in favour of the proposition that international actors should have the ultimate say.[243] But this would be difficult to maintain categorically, in view of the relative strengths of domestic democratic processes and in view of persistent accountability gaps on the international level.

Answers to the question of who has, or should have, the ultimate say have frequently shown an unduly totalizing tendency. Either international or municipal actors would reign supreme. Depending on the status of international law in the respective municipal order, confrontations between actors would more often than not go hand in hand with a confrontation between legal orders. But neither side can ultimately convince when it raises a categorical claim. Because of the practical and principled advantages and disadvantages on both sides of the divide between international and municipal law, the question remains open. Sovereignty as highest authority evaporates in an analytical as well as a normative perspective in the interaction between levels of governance.[244] It is more pertinent to ask which actors have authority, how they exercise authority, whether it is sufficiently justified, and, if not, what can be done.

This foundational uncertainty is not unsatisfactory but rather desirable because in the postnational condition each level can in principle offer good arguments for why its interpretation should prevail. It is important to allocate authority in a formalized manner with the help of public law.[245] But spheres of competence intersect and it might be that actors on different levels of governance speak on the

[242] R Howse and K Nicolaïdis, Democracy without Sovereignty: The Global Vocation of Political Ethics, in: T Broude and Y Shany (eds), *The Shifting Allocation of Authority in International Law. Essays in Honour of Professor Ruth Lapidoth* (Oxford: Hart 2008), 163–92, 181.

[243] Cf. G R Bandeira Galindo, Revisiting Monism's Ethical Dimension, in: J Crawford and S Nouwen (eds), *Select Proceedings of the European Society of International Law* (Oxford: Hart 2012), 141–54.

[244] Compare the fitting updated definition of sovereignty offered by J L Cohen, Sovereignty in the Context of Globalization: A Constitutional Pluralist Perspective, in: S Besson and J Tasioulas (eds), *The Philosophy of International Law* (Oxford: Oxford University Press 2010), 261–81, 272 ('sovereignty is the unifying and self-identifying claim of a polity regarding the supremacy and autonomy of its legal order, the self-determination of its political system, and its status as the ultimate authority in its respective domain of jurisdiction and as an equal under international law.').

[245] The doctrine of competences plays a prominent role in this regard and probably bears unexplored potentials for further development, see A v Bogdandy and J Bast, The Federal Order of Competences, in: A v Bogdandy and J Bast (eds), *Principles of European Constitutional Law* (Oxford, München: Hart, Beck 2010), 275–307.

same issues and come to competing conclusions. It will then require a more nuanced and pointed analysis into the specific strengths of the respective claims, taking into account the democratic credentials of each actor, processes of decision-making and will-formation, respect for human rights, and also considerations of subsidiarity.[246] But elaborate normative frameworks for assessing competing claims to authority in a normative pluriverse are largely wanting.

This might be for a good reason. To settle potential conflict across levels of governance is impossible categorically and certainly difficult in concrete cases. There is usually no stable or sufficiently thick ground for deciding who should prevail—either in law or political theory.[247] Political theory is faced with multiple and overlapping constituencies that make reasonable claims to public autonomy.[248] And law does not seem to offer any meta-ordering between legal orders but appears to be rather speechless when two orders collide.[249] The process of European integration and developments in the understanding of how EU law relates to the law of member states teaches useful lessons in this regard. 'The EU System,' Robert Howse and Kalypso Nicolaïdis maintain, 'organises a dialogue between authorities rather than presenting a simple rule as to who prevails.'[250] At the present stage of European integration, the question of who has the ultimate say remains essentially unsettled—both the German Constitutional Court (and courts of other member states) as well as the European Court of Justice reserve the last word for themselves. Their competition has long been fought in terms of the competence to settle disputes between conflicting claims about who is ultimately competent—about who has the *Kompetenz-Kompetenz*—and it indeed teaches that ultimate authority dissolves in the interaction between equally assertive actors on different levels of governance.[251] Actors need to continuously put their semantic authority to the test.

246 M Kumm, The Cosmopolitan Turn in Constitutionalism: On the Relationship between Constitutionalism in and beyond the State, in: J L Dunoff and J P Trachtman (eds), *Ruling the World? Constitutionalism, International Law, and Global Governance* (Cambridge: Cambridge University Press 2009), 258–324.

247 Krisch, *Beyond Constitutionalism*, 89–107; Howse and Nicolaïdis, Democracy without Sovereignty, 167. Note that international law could of course give considerable deference to the domestic context and could thus organize a 'pluralism' under the supremacy of international law, an 'internal pluralism', as it were. See A Nollkaemper, Inside or Out: Two Types of International Legal Pluralism, in: J Klabbers and T Piiparinen (eds), *Normative Pluralism and International Law* (forthcoming 2012); N Walker, 'Beyond Boundary Disputes and Basic Grids: Mapping the Global Disorder of Normative Orders' (2008) 6 *International Journal of Constitutional Law* 373–96. Pluralism in such an approach is not about foundation but about content. Drawing boundaries of such pluralism would continue to be a troublesome challenge and it is doubtful whether the delimitation of 'permissible' content would not after all turn into foundational pluralism.

248 Krisch, *Beyond Constitutionalism*, 99–100 and 271–6.

249 Ibid., at 69–78 and 286 (arguing that the relationship between legal orders is not subject to legal regulation but rather of a political nature).

250 Howse and Nicolaïdis, Democracy without Sovereignty, 165.

251 M Kumm, 'Who is the Final Arbiter of Constitutionality in Europe? Three Conceptions of the Relationship Between the German Federal Constitutional Court and the European Court of Justice' (1999) 36 *Common Market Law Review* 351–86; M P Maduro, Contrapunctual Law: Europe's Constitutional Pluralism in Action, in: N Walker (ed), *Sovereignty in Transition* (Oxford: Hart 2003), 521; F C Mayer, Multilevel Constitutional Jurisdiction, in: A v Bogdandy and J Bast (eds),

While people established themselves as ultimate arbiters over public authority on the national level and implemented ideas of popular sovereignty, a parallel response to international authority would point to something like the sovereignty of world citizens. Grand designs of international order pondering such a revolutionary move tend to be vested in strong ideal theory that abstracts from real life necessities to such an extent that the desirability of the ideal is seriously damaged.[252] Such a move is neither forthcoming nor warranted. Different actors can draw legitimacy from different constituencies under different conditions and can then each offer good reasons for why their particular interpretations should prevail. This is the condition of a normative pluriverse.

2. Architectural renovation and institutional design

There are a number of avenues for improving the democratic legitimation of participants in international legal discourse by way of better institutional design. Much of the current institutional architecture still stands under the spell of the idea that everything going on beyond the confines of the state is carried by its consent. An analysis of how international norms develop in legal practice and an emphasis on the semantic authority of independent international actors has shown that this is not the case. Architectural reforms will therefore primarily need to aim at opening up spaces for contestation at the international level.[253] They need to go hand in hand with a better appreciation of what exactly the problems and challenges are from the perspective of democratic governance in and beyond the state. This section suggests in a tentative and summary fashion directions in which reactions to international institutions' semantic authority may proceed. Their stability and concrete shape very much depends on the specific institution and more empirical work is necessary in order to fully consider normative consequences.

Principles of European Constitutional Law (Oxford, Munich: Hart, Beck 2010), 299–339; D Halberstam, Local, Global, and Plural Constitutionalism: Europe Meets the World, in: J H H Weiler and G de Búrca (eds), *The Worlds of European Constitutionalism* (Cambridge: Cambridge University Press 2010), 150–201. It should be noted that the *champs de bataille* here extends to competing yardsticks for ultimate judgment (norms of different legal orders). But the lessons learned may all the same inform the understanding of disputes about the meaning of a given international norm. Compare N Krisch, 'The Open Architecture of European Human Rights Law' (2008) 71 *Modern Law Review* 183–216.

[252] O Höffe, *Demokratie im Zeitalter der Globalisierung* (München: Beck 1999), 320 (explicitly stating that it is not part of the realm of philosophical inquiry to address how it might actually be possible to prevent the dangers of a global Leviathan). Compare D Held, *Democracy and the Global Order* (Stanford: Stanford University Press 1995) (developing a more nuanced blueprint for a democratic international order but holding on tight to aspiration).

[253] Cf. N Fraser, *Scales of Justice. Reimagining Political Space in a Globalizing World* (New York: Columbia University Press 2009), 76–99.

To start on the domestic level, under standards of democratic legitimation a qualified role of the parliament is key.[254] Significant international treaties should be, and usually already are, subject to parliamentary ratification. While remnants of the idea that external affairs lie well in the hands of the executive still flare up in limitations to parliamentary participation, the continuing erosion between external (or 'foreign') and domestic politics should in principle go hand in hand with a bigger role for domestic parliaments.[255] In this line, they are for instance already given a more prominent role in European politics.[256] But there are a number of challenges to the legitimatory input that can possibly flow from parliamentary action, including from the ratification of treaties.

Notably, treaty texts are the outcome of diplomatic negotiations among executives that usually precede parliamentary procedures and domestic parliaments, with the exception of the US Congress, and tend to be rather deferential to the executive when compared with matters of domestic legislation.[257] The autonomy of governmental-administrative elites is considerably greater than in domestic political processes too, not least because international processes geared towards consensus require largely unconstrained actors.[258] Moreover, parliaments oftentimes lack information or knowledge. Overall, they remain sidelined.[259] It can also frequently be observed that interest groups and actors in the executive use contexts of multilevel governance to increase their power in relation to parliamentary bodies or to get an edge on competitors on the domestic level, thus further placing a strain on the potential of parliamentary legitimation of international treaties.[260]

These considerations extend to the legitimation of international law generally and not to its development through the practice of interpretation in particular. But

[254] Cf. E-W Böckenförde, Demokratie als Verfassungsprinzip, in: *Recht, Staat, Freiheit* (Frankfurt am Main: Suhrkamp 1991), 289–378, 322; P S Atiyah and R S Summers, *Form and Substance in Anglo-American Law* (Oxford: Clarendon 1987), 141. This discussion only pertains to countries with a democratic constitution. The legitimatory potential of the consent of authoritarian states could hardly count under standards of democratic legitimation, but it certainly does have certain merits. Cf. B Kingsbury, 'Sovereignty and Inequality' (1998) 9 *European Journal of International Law* 599–625.

[255] In detail, see R Wolfrum, Die Kontrolle der auswärtigen Gewalt, in: *Veröffentlichungen der Vereinigung der Deutschen Staatsrechtler*, vol 56 (Berlin: de Gruyter 1997), 38–66.

[256] See Arts 12 and 48 TEU; Arts 69, 70, 81, 352 TFEU; Protocol (No 1) on the Role of National Parliaments in the European Union. Cf C Callies, 'Nach dem Lissabon-Urteil des Bundesverfassungsgerichts: Parlamentarische Integrationsverantwortung auf europäischer und nationaler Ebene' (2010) 25 *Zeitschrift für Gesetzgebung* 1–34; A v Bogdandy, 'Parlamentarismus in Europa: eine Verfalls- oder Erfolgsgeschichte?' (2005) 130 *Archiv des öffentlichen Rechts* 445–64.

[257] P Dann, *Parlamente im Exekutivföderalismus: Eine Studie zum Verhältnis von föderaler Ordnung und parlamentarischer Demokratie in der Europäischen Union* (Berlin: Springer 2004), 294.

[258] E-W Böckenförde, Die Zukunft politischer Autonomie, in: *Recht, Staat, Freiheit* (Frankfurt am Main: Suhrkamp 1991), 103–26; M Zürn, *Regieren jenseits des Nationalstaates: Globalisierung und Denationalisierung als Chance* (Frankfurt am Main: Suhrkamp 1998), 233 and 347.

[259] For lessons from EU Law, see P Dann, The Political Institutions, in: A v Bogdandy and J Bast (eds), *Principles of European Constitutional Law* (Oxford, Munich: Hart, Beck 2010), 237–74, 267–9.

[260] R D Putnam, 'Diplomacy and Domestic Politics: The Logic of Two-Level Games' (1988) 42 *International Organization* 427–60. This holds just as well for the European context in relation to the international level, though the powers of the European Parliament are, even with changes under the Treaty of Lisbon, still more circumscribed. See D Curtin, *Executive Power in the European Union: Law, Practice, and Constitutionalism* (Oxford: Oxford University Press 2009), 260–5.

they are relevant nonetheless because an international interpreter does after all tap into the legitimation carried into the process of interpretation by the text of a provision.[261] From a more dynamic perspective specifically attuned to the challenges that come with legal change carried by interpretative practice, it is first of all critical that the increase in international institutions' semantic authority is not paralleled by developments in the political-legislative processes. Fields of international law that are marked by strong international bureaucracies or judicial bodies do not generally include functioning political legislatures. Once an international agreement is in place, it is thus largely withdrawn from the grasp of its makers unless they act through the prohibitively burdensome mechanism of treaty amendment. This profoundly changes the relationship between law and politics. By agreeing to an international treaty, the parliamentary majority of the moment cements its position and places it beyond reach of any later majority.[262] A later majority may in principle be able to exit a regime. But this can hardly be a sufficient escape hatch and, in any event, it frequently does not constitute a realistic option because the costs of exit are too high.[263] The legitimatory input flowing from domestic democratic processes into international interpretations suffers in consequence.

When exit is not a feasible option, the wish of actors to introduce their voice increases.[264] On the international level then, these observations point towards processes of politicization in the sense of opportunities for contesting ends as well as means within a given institutional arrangement rather than a brute and unconstrained struggle for power alone. International institutions should then not only be understood as instruments for the effective implementation of agreed-upon policies but also as arenas for debating and contesting goals and for channelling political conflict.[265] They are not only instrumental in managing common problems but are also sites for politics where actors argue about what should be—*agorae* in the Greek ideal of political spaces.[266]

[261] To be clear, also under premises of semantic pragmatism, the interpreter is of course tied to the text. It is just that the text itself does not tie the interpreter down but the practice of other interpreters does. See above Chapter II, section B.2.b.

[262] Abbott and Snidal, 'Hard and Soft Law'; J Goldstein, M Kahler, R D Keohane, and A-M Slaughter, 'Introduction: Legalization and World Politics' (2000) 54 *International Organization* 385–99.

[263] Although it does indeed remain a possibility. Consider for example Bolivia's as well as Venzuela's withdrawal from the ICSID Convention. See Bolivia Foreign Ministry, 'Letter Concerning Denunciation of ICSID Convention', 1 May 2007, 46 ILM (2007) 973; 'Gobierno Bolivariano denuncia convenio con Ciadi', 25 January 2012, <http://www.mre.gov.ve>.

[264] Cf. the classical explanatory framework of A O Hirschman, *Exit, Voice and Loyalty* (Cambridge: Harvard University Press 1970); J H H Weiler, 'The Transformation of Europe' (1991) 100 *Yale Law Journal* 2403–83; E Benvenisti, 'Exit and Voice in the Age of Globalization' (1999) 98 *Michigan Law Review* 167–213.

[265] Cf. D Dijkzeul and L Gordenker, Cures and Conclusions, in: D Dijkzeul and Y Beigbeder (eds), *Rethinking International Organizations. Pathology and Promise* (New York, NY: Berghahn 2003), 311–36; G D Ness and S R Brechin, 'Bridging the Gap: International Organizations as Organizations' (1988) 42 *International Organization* 245–73, 271.

[266] J Klabbers, The changing image of international organizations, in: J-M Coicaud and V Heiskane (eds), *The Legitimacy of International Organizations* (Tokyo: The United Nations University Press 2001), 221–55; Koskenniemi, 'Global Governance and Public International Law'.

Oftentimes such spaces do not exist at all. As a preliminary step and in line with its function as a medium both for channeling disputes as well as for legitimating the exercise of authority, international law would be used as material for constructing such spaces for political action. Such an endeavour resonates well with the conception of law as the city wall that protects the *polis* in Hannah Arendt's elaboration on 'the Greek solution':

> In their opinion, the lawmaker was like the builder of the city wall, someone who had to do and finish his work before political activity could begin.... Before men began to act, a definite space had to be secured and a structure built where all subsequent actions could take place, the space being the public realm of the *polis* and its structure the law; legislator and architect belonged in the same category.[267]

Where such structures for political action do already exist, they frequently need to be strengthened. Bearing in mind the limitations of state consent as a legitimatory foundation, drawing attention to the semantic authority of international institutions, pointing out asymmetries between powers in many international regimes ultimately directs attention towards opportunities for increased politicization. What such politicization might look like would again depend on the concrete regime and on the specific problems that do exist, if any. It could, for example, involve the better use of plenary bodies or parliamentary assemblies.[268] A push towards politicization would in any event have to overcome significant obstacles and be well balanced against considerations of effectiveness that are after all crucial even if by themselves insufficient. It is precisely the stalemates and inefficient decision-making in inclusive political bodies that have led to a 'flight from the plenary'.[269]

More specific architectural interventions might thus for principled as well as practical reasons be more promising than grand renovations of political processes. They could aim at giving effect to demands of transparency, means of review, reason giving, and facilities for increased participation.[270] There are a number of trends in the procedural law of international judicial institutions in particular that can be understood as a more definite response to adjudicators' semantic authority.[271] Three former WTO Director-Generals have pointedly recognized

[267] H Arendt, *The Human Condition* (Chicago: University of Chicago Press 1958), 194–5.

[268] v Bogdandy and Venzke, 'Democratic Legitimation'; I Feichtner, *The Law and Politics of WTO Waivers: Stability and Flexibility in Public International Law* (Cambridge: Cambridge University Press 2012), 332–5.

[269] J v Bernstorff, 'Procedures of Decision-Making and the Role of Law in International Institutions' (2008) 9 *German Law Journal* 1939–1964, 1946–7.

[270] Cf A Buchanan and R O Keohane, 'The Legitimacy of Global Governance Institutions' (2006) 20 *Ethics & International Affairs* 405–37; Kingsbury, Krisch, and Stewart, 'The Emergence of Global Administrative Law', 34–5; D Curtin and A Nollkaemper, 'Conceptualizing Accountability in International and European Law' (2005) 36 *Netherlands Yearbook of International Law* 3–20 (introducing a special issue on accountability in the international legal order).

[271] Venzke, Antinomies and Change.

the normative limits of legal change enacted in the practice of judicial interpretation. They complained that the organization is acutely threatened by member states' use of the dispute settlement procedures 'as a means of filling out gaps in the WTO system; first, where rules and disciplines have not been put in place, or, second, are the subject of differences of interpretation'.[272] Not least due to such input and in view of similar voices, the practice of dispute settlement in this field has opened up to demands for publicness and transparency, thus offering at least minimal conditions for critique and public discourse.[273] To allow for the submission of *amicus curiae* briefs would offer yet another way of recognizing and reacting to the authority of adjudicators.[274]

Any such developments and renovations need to swerve around a number of pitfalls such as giving a yet stronger voice to already dominant interest groups or leading to institutional lethargy. Effective international decision-making is indispensable as part of the responses to pressing global challenges. International institutions will continue to be torn between demands for more efficiency and effectiveness and the need for a qualified institutional framework for political contestation that can contribute to the democratic justification of their interpretations. But resistance to, or at least uneasiness about, international action eventually also impacts international institutions' semantic authority.[275] It could thus well be that patterns of interaction between actors on different levels of governance develop interface norms that both entrench authority perceived to be legitimate and undercut authority perceived to be illegitimate.[276]

3. Attitudes and interpretation at critical junctures

Reforms in institutional design need to be complemented by changes in the attitude of concrete individual and institutional actors who act on the borders of

[272] A Dunkel, P Sutherland, and R Ruggiero, 'Statement on the Multilateral Trading System' (2001), 1.

[273] See, e.g., Panel Report, *Canada—Continued Suspension of Obligations in the EC—Hormones Dispute*, WT/DS321/R, 31 March 2008, para 7.47. Appellate Body Report, *United States—Continued Existence and Application of Zeroing Methodology*, WT/DS350/AB/R, 4 February 2009, para 4.

[274] See R Howse, 'Membership and its Privileges: the WTO, Civil Society, and the Amicus Brief Controversy' (2003) 9 *European Law Journal* 496–510; P C Mavroidis, Amicus Curiae Briefs Before the WTO. Much Ado About Nothing, in: A v Bogdandy, Y Mény, and P C Mavroidis (eds), *European Integration and International Co-Ordination. Studies In Transnational Economic Law in Honour of Claus-Dieter Ehlermann* (The Hague: Kluwer 2002), 317–29; J v Bernstorff, Zivilgesellschaftliche Partizipation in Internationalen Organisationen: Form globaler Demokratie oder Baustein westlicher Expertenherrschaft?, in: H Brunkhorst (ed), *Demokratie in der Weltgesellschaft* (Baden-Baden: Nomos 2009), 277–302; P Nanz and J Steffek, Zivilgesellschaftliche Partizipation und die Demokratisierung internationalen Regierens, in: P Niesen and B Herborth (eds), *Anarchie der kommunikativen Freiheit* (Frankfurt am Main: Suhrkamp 2007), 87–110.

[275] M Zürn, 'Global Governance and Legitimacy Problems' (2004) 39 *Government and Opposition* 260–87 (pointing to concerns about legitimacy as a significant source of non-compliance). Conversely, Thomas Frank makes the prominent argument for a compliance pull stemming from the legitimacy of international law, T M Franck, *The Power of Legitimacy Among Nations* (Oxford: Oxford University Press 1990), especially at 193.

[276] Cf. Krisch, *Beyond Constitutionalism*, 285–96; E Benvenisti and G W Downs, 'Toward Global Checks and Balances' (2009) 20 *Constitutional Political Economy* 366–87.

legal orders and who feed into the space between competing levels of governance.[277] Such changes may in turn be facilitated and induced by incentives or by way of socialization. Understanding how legal interpretation is involved in accommodating and contesting authority in a normative pluriverse is a minimal and necessary starting point in this regard. Interpretation should be informed by an appreciation for the sources of legitimacy that competing actors can plausibly claim in support of their interpretations. International, supranational, as well as domestic actors should take into account the repercussions that interpretations have on different levels. The interplay between levels of governance can then constantly shape doctrinal concepts that accommodate the competition between spheres of authority. Some such concepts work primarily at the international level and others at the municipal level. While interaction unfolds primarily in everyday administrative practices, the main actors visibly shaping these concepts will most likely be courts.[278] Capturing and contributing to this process by way of scholarship would certainly be a lasting endeavour.[279] I shall try to offer first thoughts on relevant concepts and attempt to sketch directions in which further research might proceed.

From the perspective of the international level, standards of review are probably the most important mechanism for delineating spheres of authority.[280] The analysis of semantic change in Art. XX GATT has shown that disputes about what 'necessity' means have in fact turned into a dispute about what adjudicating bodies in the WTO can legitimately do. They primarily turn on the authority of adjudicators and on the effect of their practice with regard to the regulatory autonomy of members. Should WTO adjudicators engage in a fully-fledged proportionality test that throws the importance of the regulatory goal into the balance against

[277] A Hurrell, International Law and the Changing Constitution of International Society, in: M Byers (ed), *The Role of Law in International Politics* (Oxford: Oxford University Press 2000), 327–47, 346–7 (arguing that procedures are never the whole answer because actors engage with them on the basis of their attitudes); Howse and Nicolaïdis, Democracy without Sovereignty, 172 and 182 (contending that 'there is room for tinkering with the formal structures of decision-making, but the heart of the matter is else-where, in the behaviour of the relevant actors and in the beliefs, values and expectations that inspire them' and further arguing that it is impossible to find a stable allocation of sovereignty across the levels of governance—'[i]nstead, it is better to conceive of multi-level governance as a dynamic process: performance art rather than architecture.'); Cohen, Sovereignty in the Context of Globalization, 275–6 (arguing that what interpreters need to be reflexive about the repercussions of their communications and that this requires an '"internal attitude" towards global as well as domestic law and willingness to justify interpretations of global law in a universal rather than parochial terms.').

[278] Compare A Verdross, *Völkerrecht* (Wien: Springer 1950), 24–6 (speaking of courts as the '*Grenzorgane*' of a legal order).

[279] Cf. Y Shany, *Regulating Jurisdictional Relations Between National and International Courts* (Oxford: Oxford University Press 2007), 197–200; S Cassese, *When Legal Orders Collide: The Role of Courts* (Seville: Global Law Press 2010), 109–24; E D'Alterio, 'From Judicial Comity to Legal Comity: A judicial solution to global disorder?' (2011) 9 *International Journal of Constitutional Law* 394–424.

[280] Cf. A v Staden, 'Democratic Legitimacy of Review Beyond the State: The Need for an Appropriate Standard of Review' (2011) *Jean Monnet Working Paper* 10/11.

losses resulting from a restriction of liberalized trade? Or should they rather refrain from engaging in a fully-fledged proportionality analysis on the international level and defer to the value choice made by members on the importance of non-trade concerns?

How standards of review accommodate spheres of authority is again evident in a discourse that has started to emerge in the context of how ICSID tribunals should relate to domestic governance. Under the impact of private law analogies, the doctrine of legitimate expectations has figured prominently from the outset. But the recognition of how investment arbitration impacts on the room for manoeuvre of public actors on the municipal level has led to suggestions that maybe another standard would be more apt. The doctrine of a margin of appreciation or, once more, proportionality may come into consideration.[281] The very extensive body of research on judicial review in domestic constitutional and administrative law may offer ample inspiration for developing these notions further.[282]

From the perspective of the municipal level, domestic actors interpret and apply international or supranational law and as such they act as participants in international legal discourse. They can recognize and contribute to the authority of UNCHR guidelines, for example, or engage in interpretative practice themselves and thus contribute to the further development of international law.[283] But in case of conflict between international and domestic law, most domestic constitutional organs would choose the domestic legal order as a yardstick, at least to the extent that fundamental constitutional guarantees are concerned. The *Görgülü* judgment of the German Constitutional Court illustrates this well. On the one hand, the court argued that, in interpreting and applying the ECHR, domestic courts have to pay due regard to judgments rendered by the ECtHR.[284] But on the other hand, domestic organs retain the possibility of checking ECtHR judgments against the

[281] S W Schill and B Kingsbury, Public Law Concepts to Balance Investors' Rights with State Regulatory Actions in the Public Interest—The Concept of Proportionality, in: S W Schill (ed), *International Investment Law and Comparative Public Law* (Oxford: Oxford University Press 2010), 75–105.

[282] From the abundant literature that transcends many different legal systems, see M Jestaedt, *Grundrechtsentfaltung im Gesetz. Studien zur Interdependenz von Grundrechtsdogmatik und Rechtsgewinnungstheorie* (Tübingen: Mohr Siebeck 1999), 135–205, especially 174–86 (offering an argument in the context of German constitutional law that is akin to the present endeavour of assessing divisions of labour on the basis of plausible claims to authority); C Möllers, *Gewaltengliederung: Legitimation und Dogmatik im nationalen und internationalen Rechtsvergleich* (Tübingen: Mohr Siebeck 2005), 163–77 (offering a similar argument in German administrative law and a comparison with US-American legal doctrine); C R Sunstein and A Vermeule, 'Interpretation and institutions' (2003) 101 *Michigan Law Review* 885–951. Of course in the domestic context divisions of labour run across horizontal lines whereas the interplay between different levels of governance concerns a vertical relationship. But this does not mean that nothing could be learned from comparison, see D Halberstam, Local, Global, and Plural Constitutionalism: Europe Meets the World, in: J H H Weiler and G De Burca (eds), *The Worlds of European Constitutionalism* (Cambridge: Cambridge University Press 2010), 150–201.

[283] See above Chapter III, section C.3.

[284] BVerfG, 2 BvR 1481/04, 14 October 2004, para 68.

yardstick of fundamental constitutional principles, the court argued. And where there is incompatibility the domestic order prevails.[285]

This latter dimension to the court's reasoning on the intersection between European human rights law and domestic constitutional law has stirred the common critique that the constitutional court sent a wrong signal to other countries where effective human rights protection demands, even more so than in its own realm, that judgments of the ECtHR be followed without resistance and second-guesses. This was a prominent theme in the public dialogue between judges of the courts involved and the argument has hardened that domestic courts should take such systemic effects into consideration.[286] Nico Krisch has shown how this competition for ultimate authority is characteristic for the reception and working of the ECHR and human rights protection in Europe—not to be deplored but to be embraced as a process of contestation between competing constituencies over unsettled fundamentals.[287] Human rights related contestation centred on the ECHR or on the effect of Security Council sanctions against terror suspects fits this pattern just as well as disagreement about whether WTO members may legally prohibit the import of genetically modified organisms.[288]

Lessons of European integration are once more illuminating.[289] Competition between the ECJ and domestic courts suggests that ultimate authority evaporates in the interaction between levels of governance: The German Constitutional Court's *ultra vires* and identity reviews[290] stand against the ECJ's assertion of the

[285] Ibid., at paras 57–58. Such a constitutional check can even be detected in domestic constitutional orders that are in principle particularly friendly towards international law or towards the ECHR in particular. See Nollkaemper, *National Courts*, 280–96.

[286] This was for instance argued by Luzius Wildhaber, then president of the ECtHR, and by the German judge on the court, Georg Ress. For references to the public dialogue among judges see F Hoffmeister, 'Germany: Status of European Convention on Human Rights in domestic law' (2006) 4 *International Journal of Constitutional Law* 722–31, 729. Also in response to the *Lissabon* judgment of the German Constitutional Court (123 BVerfGE 267, 30 June 2009) it has been suggested that the court should take into consideration the repercussions that its interpretation has in the larger European legal space, see A v Bogdandy, 'Prinzipien der Rechtsfortbildung im Europäischen Rechtsraum. Überlegungen zum Lissabon-Urteil des BVerfG' (2010) 63 *Neue Juristische Wochenschrift* 1–5.

[287] N Krisch, 'The Open Architecture of European Human Rights Law' (2008) 71 *Modern Law Review* 183–216, 209–15.

[288] These are the main examples chosen for closer analysis in Krisch, *Beyond Constitutionalism*.

[289] Note that the argument is for comparison and possibly inspiration, not for emulation. Policy consequences would need to be checked against structural, institutional, and societal differences between the European and international space.

[290] The court first argued in 1974 that it would assert its jurisdiction and review European law against the yardstick of German core fundamental rights law as long as the European order does not secure fundamental rights in a way that lives up to the demands of the German Constitution (37 BVerfGE 271, 29 May 1974, *Solange I*). In 1986 the court then explicitly sanctioned the reverse formula stating that it would reserve its jurisdiction over acts of the Community as long as the ECJ sufficiently guarantees the protection of fundamental rights (in essence they must be comparable to those enshrined in the German Basic Law) against the exercise of public authority on the European level (73 BVerfGE 339, 22 October 1986, *Solange II*). The court now asserts its authority to judge acts of the European Union to be *ultra vires* against the standard of securing Germany's identity as a member state (123 BVerfGE 267, 30 June 2009, *Lissabon*).

supremacy of EU law and the ECJ's position as the ultimate arbiter.[291] The German Constitutional Court has liked to portray its relationship with the ECJ as one of cooperation[292] but now seems to have swayed towards the enigmatic concept of '*Europarechtsfreundlichkeit*', a general and rather amorphous 'friendliness towards European law'.[293] It sees itself in the role of a guardian for the possibilities of meaningful political processes, with slight etatistic overtones.[294] It communicates and claims authority for itself.

The ECJ might do something similar in relation to the international level. When the ECJ rejected the supremacy of Security Council resolutions in *Kadi*, it took a strictly dualist position and judged the EU Regulation (integrating the Security Council resolution *in verbatim*) against fundamental guarantees of the European legal order.[295] But it could itself have been guided by an adaptation of the German Constitutional Court's *Solange* jurisprudence in the sense that it would reserve the right to judge *international* actions against fundamentals of its *municipal* constitutional order as long as no sufficient guarantees are in place at the international level. It could thus send clearer signals when and under which conditions international action would meet acceptance and thereby play its part in pushing in that same direction.[296] Its contestation of international authority has all the same had some repercussions and induced improvements—albeit still insufficient—of individual rights of terror suspects subject to its sanctions regime.[297]

There are many more facets and prominent principles at work at this interplay between levels of governance. The doctrine of direct effect, the 'Charming Betsy' doctrine (the idea that domestic law should be interpreted in a way that is friendly towards international law)[298] and, last but not least, the principle of subsidiarity

[291] The well-known seminal judgments were Case 6/64, *Costa v ENEL* (1964) ECR 585, 593 (where the court first argued in support of the supremacy of European law); Case 106/77, *Amministrazione delle Finanze dello Stato v Simmenthal SpA* (1978) ECR 629 (adding that European law takes precedence over subsequent domestic legislation) and Case 11/70, *Internationale Handelsgesellschaft mbH v Einfuhr-und Vorratsstelle für Getreide und Futtermittel* (1970) ECR 1125 (asserting the supremacy of European law even in cases of conflict with fundamental rules of domestic constitutional law); Case 314/85, *Foto-Frost* (1987) ECR 4199 (holding that domestic courts cannot declare EU law to be invalid but rather need to submit the subject matter to the ECJ). See J H H Weiler, 'A Quiet Revolution: The European Court of Justice and its Interlocutors' (1994) 26 *Comparative Political Studies* 510–34; Mayer, Multilevel Constitutional Jurisdiction.

[292] This has been the tenor ever since its *Maastricht* Judgment, 89 BVerfGE 155, 12 October 1993.

[293] 123 BVerfGE 267, 30 June 2009, Mn 240.

[294] In its *Lissabon* judgment the court was torn with regard to the possibilities for democratic governance in the postnational constellation, see M Kottmann and C Wohlfahrt, 'Der gespaltene Wächter? Demokratie, Verfassungsidentität und Integrationsverantwortung im Lissabon-Urteil' (2009) 69 *Zeitschrift für ausländisches öffentliches Recht und Völkerrecht* 443–70.

[295] C-402 P, 415/05 P, *Kadi & Al Barakaat v Council & Commission* (2008) ECR I-6351, especially at paras 285–287.

[296] This argument was, apart from scholarly voices, also made by *Kadi* himself, see ibid., at para 256.

[297] T-85/09, *Kadi v Commission*, Judgment of the General Court (Seventh Chamber) of 30 September 2010, paras 171–188.

[298] *Murray v The Schooner Charming Betsy* (1804) 6 US (2 Cranch) 64 (arguing that where fairly possible, an act of Congress should be interpreted so as not to violate international law).

come to mind. All these doctrines accommodate authority across levels of governance and will gain meaning in dialogues and in competitive confrontations between levels of governance.

The attitude of the main institutional and individual actors acting at the borders between levels of governance remains crucial. They should take into consideration the consequences that their decisions have for actors in other polities and on other levels. They should consider their place in the grand scheme of things. This does not require a fixed idea about legitimate governance in the postnational constellation or a foundational scheme thick enough to always carry an answer to thorny questions about how a norm should be interpreted. But it demands that attitudes reflect a sensibility for the repercussions of interpretations in a grand normative pluriverse. This is aspirational. But there may be a more earthly motivational force at play as well. To the extent that actors meet the sentiment of others, they gain authority.

VI

Epilogue: In the End there is Eternity

Texts come to life in the practice of interpretation. The image of semantic struggles illustrates how actors shift the contents of commitments by way of their interpretations and the notion of semantic authority tries to capture actors' relative influence in such processes. This book's discussion of the normative implications of lawmaking through interpretative practice and of the increasingly prominent role of international actors on the stage of international legal discourse first focused more closely on the outward show and then tried to make more out of the process of arguing. In the end it has left actors with the suggestion that they be mindful of the repercussions of their actions in a grand normative pluriverse. With regard to a more determinative basis that would altogether carry and absorb the effects of interpretations, it has left them with little guidance. Interpreters enjoy varying degrees of freedom and need to assume responsibility for the choices they make. In other words, they have to live up to the commitments they make by using words in a certain way.[1] Their freedom is not bewildering but invigorating. The responsibility that rests on their shoulders does not need to tie them to the spot but it can be embedded in a context that allows a process of continuous contestation between different actors with different claims to authority. In the end there is eternity.

In the late nineteenth century, Rudolf von Jhering was first of all a representative and formidable craftsman of legal science. In the purity of a legal system, constructed on the basis of certain general legal concepts, legal norms added up to create a whole that could be discovered by the able legal professor. Abstract foundational legal concepts themselves gave birth to more concrete norms that in the end could be combined and narrowed down so as to yield the right answer. Reality did not figure in this abstract construction and was only subjected to the abstract law.[2] In December 1858, however, Jhering received a massive case file from the *Oberappellationsgericht* in Rostock and was asked to write an expert opinion. The case racked his brain. A trading company had sold a barrel of charcoal to one buyer and later, due to mismanagement, also to a second one. The ship carrying that barrel sank on its way to the second purchaser and now the trading company

[1] See above Chapter II, section B.

[2] Jhering's masterpiece in this tradition was the three volumes of R v Jhering, *Geist des römischen Rechts auf den verschiedenen Stufen seiner Entwicklung* (Leipzig: Breitkopf und Härtel 1866–1878).

claimed payments due for the barrel from both buyers, the first of whom now found himself in front of the court in Rostock.[3]

In the legal proceedings a scholarly article had played a prominent role, arguing that if a thing was sold twice and later destroyed by coincidence before it could be handed over to either of the purchasers, the payments could be claimed from both buying parties. The author of this article was Jhering himself. Nor could he now find any mistake in his earlier argument. But faced with the concrete case at hand, he was deeply troubled by its ultimate conclusion. His sense of justice told him that it would be wrong to have the first buyer pay the price because in any event he would never have received his purchase. Nor should the trading company be rewarded for its mismanagement. Cunningly, and without too much difficulty, Jhering distinguished the present case from his general argument and opined that the trading company's claim against the first buyer was not justified.

This incident did retain a bitter aftertaste. Jhering could not reconcile how his abstract argument could be impeccable and still yield an answer that was so at odds with his sense of what was just and right. If he could not rely on the logic of abstract constructions to produce good answers, then they were of no use. At the same time, he thought that the logic of legal argument was but hollow words if it simply couched the findings arrived at on the basis of little more than a gut feeling. Jhering suffered from this tension and grew sick of the whole legal enterprise for some time. He eventually recovered and distanced himself from his earlier belief in the beauty and purity of abstract conceptualism. He now turned to study precisely the processes that generated people's sense of what was right and with this interest he pioneered legal sociology. He now maintained that it was not bewildering that deduction from a system of abstract concepts could not reliably lead to right answers. Quite to the contrary it would be wrong and confusing to think that this was in fact possible. Jhering breathed new life and argued that concepts do not exist in isolation from reality but only take shape in concrete practice.[4] He directed his attention towards the actors and in his spirited *Der Kampf um's Recht (The Struggle for Law)* he described lawmaking mainly as a process of constant struggle between self-interested participants in legal practice. 'The idea of law,' he wrote, 'is an eternal Becoming.'[5] Invigorated, Jhering called for action.[6]

In the language of the law, actors strive for their convictions and interests. Understanding processes of interpretative practice offers critical distance and places the individual actor into the spotlight. Ernesto Laclau put the thought to the point when he wrote that

> the abandonment of aspiration to 'absolute' knowledge has exhilarating effects: on the one hand, human beings can recognize themselves as the true creators and no longer as the

[3] I write about this incident and Jhering's encounter with it on the basis of Michael Kunze, Die doppelt verkaufte Ladung Koks, in *Frankfurter Allgemeine Zeitung*, No 40, 17 February 2010, p N3.

[4] On Jhering's metamorphosis also see A Somek, 'Legal Formality and Freedom of Choice. A Moral Perspective on Jhering's Constructivism' (2002) 15 *Ratio Juris* 52–62.

[5] R v Jhering, *The Struggle for Law* (Chicago: Callaghan 1915) 13.

[6] Ibid., at 14–15. Cf. above Chapter II, section B.1.a.

passive recipients of a predetermined structure; on the other hand, as all social agents have to recognize their concrete finitude, nobody can aspire to be the true consciousness of the world. This opens the way to an endless interaction between various perspectives and makes ever more distant the possibility of any totalitarian dream.[7]

The open practice of legal interpretation stands against the reification of language and of grand concepts such as justice.[8] In this view, interpretation is understood as the battleground for disputes about what the law says. International law is not itself a cure that eases concerns about unwarranted exercises of power but rather a potential to be used. It is not innocent and transports patterns of violence in its history. But it offers a pacifying way of carrying out conflict.[9] To some extent it may level out power imbalances and its practice upholds an argumentative standard that allows for critique and scrutiny. Its formality is not only a façade that couches results arrived at by other means but the space where legal practice generates normativity. It constrains and legitimizes.

After Faust had faced Mephistopheles' mockery about how he could be so concerned with his name when actually he would delve deep only into beings, he paraphrased his question. 'Well now, who are you then?' Faust asked. And Mephistopheles replied that he was '[p]art of that Power which would/The Evil ever do, and ever does the Good'. It remains ambiguous what the power could be of which Mephistopheles is part. Would it yet be possible to reproduce the paradox when it comes to how the practice of interpretation develops international law?

Kant was torn on that question. He keenly argued that law works for the better even if all its subjects are devils. But this argument is confined to institutional settings in which 'the powers of each selfish inclination are so arranged in opposition that one moderates or destroys the ruinous effects of the other'.[10] As he saw it, only individual states could provide such conditions and in a world republic, despotism would reign supreme. Kant thus opted for a Federation of States, the institutional features of which he left extremely vague.[11]

His treatment of the matter shows that answers to the question of whether international lawmaking in the practice of interpretation works for better or worse will have to relate to the institutional contexts in which it takes place and to considerations of democratic legitimation. In the postnational condition, different constituencies enjoy legitimate authority and no single institutional blueprint is

[7] E Laclau, *Emancipation(s)* (New York: Verso 1996), 16–17.

[8] Cf. J v Bernstorff, *The Public International Law Theory of Hans Kelsen* (Cambridge: Cambridge University Press 2010), 271(on the symbol of the 'empty' legal form as a counter-hegemonic assumption); A Fischer-Lescano and R Christensen, 'Auctoritatis Interpositio. Die Dekonstruktion des Dezisionismus durch die Systemtheorie' (2005) 44 *Der Staat* 213–42, 231 (exposing the paradox of decisions in legal interpretation as never quite grasping what the law is and concluding on a positive note that the process of decision-making in law can be seen as an attempt to prevent the reification of justice by every trick in the book).

[9] Note the enigmatic motto of v Jhering, *The Struggle for Law*, 1 ('The end of the law is peace. The means to that end is war [*Kampf*]').

[10] I Kant, *Perpetual Peace: A Philosophical Sketch* (London: George Allen & Unwin 1917 [1795]), 30.

[11] Ibid.

available that assigns each actor its place. Actors are rather left to negotiate spheres of authority in their interchange and to reflect on the repercussions of their interpretations in a grand normative pluriverse. Guiding stars are so dim in this wide space that they may at best inform actors' sense of what is right and their sense of what they do not know. 'As for the philosophers,' Francis Bacon noted in *On the Advancement of Learning*, 'they make imaginary laws for imaginary commonwealths, and their discourses are as the stars, which give little light, because they are so high.'[12] It might thus be all the more necessary and rewarding to dive into the muddy business of concrete interpretative practice and to pursue a minimal ambition of informing practice about itself—to paint the larger picture, to show redistributive consequences, and to make alternative choices visible.

[12] F Bacon, On the Advancement of Learning (1605), quoted as an epigram in E H Carr, *The Twenty Years' Crisis 1919–1939* (New York: Harper Collins 1964 [1939]).

Bibliography

Abbott, Kenneth W, 'Toward a Richer Institutionalism for International Law and Policy' (2006) 1 *Journal of International Law & International Relations* 9–34.

——, 'Why States Act through Formal International Organizations' (1998) 42 *Journal of Conflict Resolution* 3–32.

—— and Duncan Snidal, 'Hard and Soft Law in International Governance' (2000) 54 *International Organization* 421–56.

——, Robert D Keohane, Andrew Moravcsik, Anne-Marie Slaughter, and Duncan Snidal, 'The Concept of Legalization' (2000) 54 *International Organization* 401–19.

Abegg, Andreas, Evolutorische Rechtstheorie, in: Sonja Buckel, Ralph Christensen and Andreas Fischer-Lescano (eds), *Neue Theorien des Rechts* (Stuttgart: Lucius und Lucius 2009), pp 401–22.

Abi-Saab, Georges, De la jurisprudence. Quelques réflexions sur son rôle dans le développement du droit international, in: *Hacia un nuevo orden internacional y europeo. Estudios en homenaje al profesor don Manuel Díez de Velasco* (Madrid: Tecnos 1993), pp 19–26.

——, Les sources du droit international: Essai de déconstruction, in: Manuel Rama-Montaldo (ed), *El derecho internacional en un mundo en transformación. Liber amicorum en homenaje al Profesor Eduardo Jiménez de Aréchaga*, vol 1 (Montevideo: Fundación de Cultura Universitaria 1994), pp 29–49.

——, The Appellate Body and Treaty Interpretation, in: Giorgio Sacerdoti, Alan Yanovich, and Jan Bohanes (eds), *The WTO at Ten: The Contribution of the Dispute Settlement System* (Cambridge: Cambridge University Press 2006), pp 453–64.

Adler, Emanuel, Communities of Practice in International Relations, in: *Communitarian International Relations: The Epistemic Foundations of International Relations* (London: Routledge 2005), pp 3–28.

Adorno, Theodor W, Albert Hans, Ralf Dahrendorf, Jürgen Habermas, Harald Pilot, and Karl R Popper, *Der Positivismusstreit in der deutschen Soziologie* (Neuwied: Luchterhand 1969).

Aga Khan, Sadruddin, 'Legal Problems Relating to Refugees and Displaced Persons' (1976) 149 *Recueil des Cours* 287–352.

Agier, Michel, *Aux bords du monde, les refugiés* (Paris: Flammarion 2002).

Ago, Roberto, 'Positive Law and International Law' (1957) 51 *American Journal of International Law* 691–753.

Akehurst, Michael, 'Custom as a Source of International Law' (1976) 47 *British Yearbook of International Law* 1–53.

——, 'Equity and General Principles of Law' (1976) 25 *International and Comparative Law Quarterly* 801–25.

Ala'i, Padideh, 'Free Trade or Sustainable Development? An Analysis of the WTO Appellate Body's Shift to a More Balanced Approach to Trade Liberalization' (1998) 14 *American University International Law Review* 1129–71.

Aleinikoff, T. Alexander, 'State-Centered Refugee Law: From Resettlement to Containment' (1992–1993) 14 *Michigan Journal of International Law* 120–38.

Alexy, Robert, *Theorie der juristischen Argumentation. Die Theorie des rationalen Diskurses als Theorie der juristischen Begründung* (Frankfurt am Main: Suhrkamp 1991).

——, *Theorie der Grundrechte* (Frankfurt am Main: Suhrkamp 1994).

Allott, Philip, 'The Concept of International Law' (1999) 10 *European Journal of International Law* 31–50.

Almeida, Joao M, Hedley Bull, 'Embedded Cosmopolitanism', and the Pluralist-Solidarist Debate, in: Richard Little and John Williams (eds), *The Anarchical Society in a Globalized World* (Basingstoke: Palgrave Macmillan 2006), pp 51–72.

Alter, Karen J, 'Delegating to International Courts: Self-Binding vs. Other-Binding Delegation' (2008) 38 *Law and Contemporary Problems* 37–76.

Alvarez, José E, 'The New Dispute Settlers: (Half) Truths and Consequences' (2003) 38 *Texas International Law Journal* 405–44.

——, *International Organizations as Law-Makers* (Oxford: Oxford University Press 2005).

Ambrosetti, David, 'Contre l'opposition "intérêts *versus* normes". Rivalités interétatiques et relations de cleintèle sous un prisme constructiviste' (2006) 37 *Études internationales* 525–46.

Anand, Ram Prakash, *International Courts and Contemporary Conflicts* (New York: Asia Publishing House 1974).

Andenas, Mads and Stefan Zleptnig, 'Proportionality: WTO Law in Comparative Perspective' (2007) 42 *Texas International Law Journal* 371–427.

Anderson, Kenneth, 'The Ottawa Convention Banning Landmines, the Role of International Non-Governmental Organizations and the Idea of International Civil Society' (2000) 11 *European Journal of International Law* 91–120.

Anghie, Antony, *Imperialism, Sovereignty, and the Making of International Law* (Cambridge: Cambridge University Press 2005).

——, 'The Evolution of International Law: Colonial and Postcolonial Realities' (2006) 27 *Third World Quarterly* 739–53.

Anscombe, Gertrude Elisabeth Margaret, *Intention* (Oxford: Blackwell 1967).

Anzilotti, Dionisio, *Corso di diritto internazionale* (Roma: Athenaeum 1923).

Apel, Karl-Otto, Faktische Anerkennung oder einsehbar notwendige Anerkennung? Beruht der Ansatz der transzendentalpragmatischen Diskursethik auf einem intellektualistischen Fehlschluss?, in: Karl-Otto Apel and Riccardo Pozzo (eds), *Zur Rekonstruktion der praktischen Philosophie. Gedenkschrift für Karl-Heinz Ilting* (Stuttgart-Bad Cannstatt: Frommann-Holzboog 1990), pp 67–123.

Archer, Clive, *International Organizations* (London: Routledge 2001).

Arendt, Hannah, *The Human Condition* (Chicago: University of Chicago Press 1958).

——, What is Authority, in: *Between Past and Future* (London: Penguin Books 2006), pp 91–141.

Atiyah, Patrick S and Robert Samuel Summers, *Form and Substance in Anglo-American Law* (Oxford: Clarendon 1987).

Aust, Anthony, Domestic Consequences of Non-Treaty (Non-Conventional) Law-Making, in: Rüdiger Wolfrum and Volker Röben (eds), *Developments of International Law in Treaty Making* (Heidelberg: Springer 2005), pp 487–96.

——, *Modern Treaty Law and Practice* (Cambridge: Cambridge University Press 2007).

Austin, John Langshaw, *How to Do Things with Words.* (Oxford: Oxford University Press 1979 [1962]).

Bandeira Galindo, George Rodrigo, 'Martti Koskenniemi and the Historiographical Turn in International Law' (2005) 16 *European Journal of International Law* 539–59.
——, Revisiting Monism's Ethical Dimension, in: James Crawford and Sarah Nouwen (eds), *Select Proceedings of the European Society of International Law* (Oxford: Hart 2012), pp 141–54.
Barnett, Laura, 'Global Governance and the Evolution of the International Refugee Regime' (2002) 14 *International Journal of Refugee Law* 238–62.
Barnett, Michael, Humanitarianism, Paternalism, and the UNHCR, in: Alexander Betts and Gil Loescher (eds), *Refugees in International Relations* (Oxford: Oxford University Press 2010), pp 105–32.
Barnett, Michael and Liv Coleman, 'Designing Police: Interpol and the Study of Change in International Organizations' (2005) 49 *International Studies Quarterly* 593–620.
Barnett, Michael and Raymond Duvall, Power in Global Governance, in: Michael Barnett and Raymond Duvall (eds), *Power in Global Governance* (Cambridge: Cambridge University Press 2005), pp 1–32.
Barnett, Michael and Martha Finnemore, The power of liberal international organizations, in: Michael Barnett and Raymond Duvall (eds), *Power in Global Governance* (Cambridge: Cambridge University Press 2005), pp 161–84.
Barnett, Michael and Martha Finnemore, *Rules for the World. International Organizations in Global Politics* (Ithaca, NY: Cornell University Press 2004).
Bartels, Lorand, 'Article XX of GATT and the Problem of Extraterritorial Jurisdiction. The Case of Trade Measures for the Protection of Human Rights' (2002) 36 *Journal of World Trade* 353–403.
——, 'The Separation of Powers in the WTO: How to Avoid Judicial Activism? ' (2004) 53 *International and Comparative Law Quarterly* 861–95.
Barutciski, Michael, 'A Critical View on UNHCR's Mandate Dilemmas' (2002) 14 *International Journal of Refugee Law* 365–81.
——, *Grundbegriffe der Handlungsformen der EU. Entwickelt am Beschluss als praxisgenerierter Handlungsform des Unions- und Gemeinschaftsrechts* (Heidelberg: Springer 2006).
Bast, Jürgen, Das Demokratiedefizit fragmentierter Internationalisierung, in: Hauke Brunkhorst (ed), *Demokratie in der Weltgesellschaft*. Soziale Welt Sonderband 18 (Baden-Baden: Nomos 2009), pp 177–85.
Bauer, Steffen, 'Does Bureaucracy Really Matter? The Authority of Intergovernmental Treaty Secretariats in Global Environmental Politics' (2006) 6 *Global Environmental Politics* 24–49.
Beck, Ulrich, *What Is Globalization?* (Cambridge: Polity Press 2000).
Bederman, David J, *Classical Canons: Rhetoric, Classicism and Treaty Interpretation* (Aldershot [u.a.]: Ashgate 2001).
Bedjaoui, Mohammed, *Fonction Publique Internationale et Influences Nationales* (London: Stevens 1958).
Benedek, Wolfgang, *Die Rechtsordnung des GATT aus völkerrechtlicher Sicht* (Graz: Springer 1990).
Benner, Thorsten, Stephan Mergenthaler, and Philipp Rotmann, 'Internationale Bürokratien und Organisationslernen. Konturen einer Forschungsagenda' (2009) 16 *Zeitschrift für Internationale Beziehungen* 203–36.

Bentham, Jeremy, *Principles of International Law*, vol 2 (Edinburgh: William Tait 1843 [1798]).

Benvenisti, Eyal, 'Exit and Voice in the Age of Globalization' (1999) 98 *Michigan Law Review* 167–213.

——, 'The Conception of International Law as a Legal System' (2008) 50 *German Yearbook of International Law* 393–405.

——, 'Reclaiming Democracy: The Strategic Uses of Foreign and International Law by National Courts' (2008) 102 *American Journal of International Law* 241–74.

—— and George W Downs, 'National Courts, Domestic Democracy, and the Evolution of International Law' (2009) 20 *European Journal of International Law* 59–72.

——, 'Toward Global Checks and Balances' (2009) 20 *Constitutional Political Economy* 366–87.

——, 'Prospects for the Increased Independence of International Tribunals' (2011) 12 *German Law Journal* 1057–82.

Berard, T J, 'Rethinking Practices and Structures' (2005) 35 *Philosophy of the Social Sciences* 196–230.

Berman, Paul Schiff, 'Global Legal Pluralism' (2007) 80 *Southern California Law Review* 1155–237.

——, 'A Pluralist Approach to International Law' (2007) 32 *Yale Journal of International Law* 301–29.

Bernhardt, Rudolf, *Die Auslegung völkerrechtlicher Verträge. Insbesondere in der neueren Rechtsprechung internationaler Gerichte* (Heidelberg: Heymann 1963).

——, 'Evolutive Treaty Interpretation, Especially of the European Convention on Human Rights' (1999) 42 *German Yearbook of International Law* 11–25.

——, Article 59, in: Andreas Zimmermann, Christian Tomuschat, and Karin Oellers-Frahm (eds), *The Statute of the International Court of Justice: A commentary* (Oxford: Oxford University Press 2006), pp 1231–51.

——, Rechtsfortbildung durch den Europäischen Gerichtshof für Menschenrechte, in: Stephan Breitenmoser and Luzius Wildhaber (eds), *Human Rights, Democracy and the Rule of Law. Liber amicorum Luzius Wildhaber* (Zürich and St. Gallen: Dike 2007), pp 91–101.

——, *Der Glaube an das universale Recht. Zur Völkerrechtstheorie Hans Kelsens und seiner Schüler* (Baden-Baden: Nomos 2001).

——, 'Sisyphus was an international lawyer. On Martti Koskenniemi's 'From Apology to Utopia' and the place of law in international politics' (2006) 7 *German Law Journal* 1015–35.

——, 'Pflichtenkollision und Menschenwürdegarantie: Zum Vorrang staatlicher Achtungspflichten im Normbereich von Art. 1 GG' (2008) 47 *Der Staat* 21–40.

——, 'Procedures of Decision-Making and the Role of Law in International Institutions' (2008) 9 *German Law Journal* 1939–64.

Bernstorff, Jochen von, 'The Changing Fortunes of the Universal Declaration of Human Rights: Genesis and Symbolic Dimensions of the Turn to Rights in International Law' (2008) 19 *European Journal of International Law* 903–24.

——, Zivilgesellschaftliche Partizipation in Internationalen Organisationen: Form globaler Demokratie oder Baustein westlicher Expertenherrschaft?, in: Hauke Brunkhorst (ed), *Demokratie in der Weltgesellschaft* (Baden-Baden: Nomos 2009), pp 277–302.

Bernstorff, Jochen von, *The Public International Law Theory of Hans Kelsen: Believing in Universal Law* (Cambridge: Cambridge University Press 2010).
—— and Ingo Venzke, Ethos, Ethics and Morality in International Relations, in: Rüdiger Wolfrum (ed), *MPEPIL* (Oxford: Oxford Universtiy Press 2011).
Best, Geoffrey, *War and Law since 1945* (Oxford: Clarendon Press 1994).
Bettati, Mario, *L'asile politique en question. Un statut pour les réfugiés* (Paris: Presses Universitaires de France 1985).
Bhuta, Nehal, 'The Antinomies of Transformative Occupation' (2005) 16 *European Journal of International Law* 721–40.
Bianchi, Andrea, 'Human Rights and the Magic of Jus Cogens' (2008) 19 *European Journal of International Law* 491–508.
Biermann, Frank and Bernd Siebenhüner (eds), *Managers of Global Change. The Influence of International Environmental Bureaucracies* (Cambridge, MA: MIT Press 2009).
Binder, Christina, 'Towards a Latin American Constitutional Court? The Jurisprudence of the Inter-American Court of Human Rights with special Focus on Amnesties' (2010) 12 *German Law Journal* 1203–29.
Bix, Brian, *Law, Language and Legal Determinacy* (Oxford: Oxford University Press 1993).
Böckenförde, Ernst-Wolfgang, Die Zukunft politischer Autonomie, in: *Recht, Staat, Freiheit* (Frankfurt am Main: Suhrkamp 1991), pp 103–26.
——, Demokratie als Verfassungsprinzip, in: *Recht, Staat, Freiheit* (Frankfurt am Main: Suhrkamp 1991), pp 289–378.
Bodansky, Daniel and Jessica C Lawrence, Trade and Environment, in: Daniel L Bethlehem, Donald McRae, Rodney Neufeld, and Isabelle Van Damme (eds), *The Oxford Handbook of International Trade Law* (Oxford: Oxford University Press 2009), pp 505–38.
Bodendiek, Frank, *Walther Schückings Konzeption der internationalen Ordnung. Dogmatische Strukturen und ideengeschichtliche Bedeutung* (Berlin: Duncker & Humblot 2001).
Bogdandy, Armin von, 'Internationaler Handel und nationaler Umweltschutz: Eine Abgrenzung im Lichte des GATT' (1992) *Europäische Zeitschrift für Wirtschaftsrecht* 243–47.
——, *Gubernative Rechtsetzung. Eine Neubestimmung der Rechtsetzung und des Regierungssystems unter dem Grundgesetz in der Perspektive gemeineuropäischer Dogmatik* (Tübingen: Mohr Siebeck 2000).
——, 'Law and Politics in the WTO—Strategies to Cope with a Deficient Relationship' (2001) 5 *Max Planck Yearbook of United Nations Law* 609–73.
——, 'Globalization and Europe: How to Square Democracy, Globalization, and International Law' (2004) 15 *European Journal of International Law* 885–906.
——, Lawmaking by International Organizations. Some Thoughts on Non-Binding Instruments and Democratic Legitimacy, in: Rüdiger Wolfrum and Volker Röben (eds), *Developments of International Law in Treaty Making* (Heidelberg: Springer 2005), pp 171–82.
——, 'Parlamentarismus in Europa: eine Verfalls- oder Erfolgsgeschichte?' (2005) 130 *Archiv des öffentlichen Rechts* 445–64.
——, 'Constitutionalism in International Law: Comment on a Proposal from Germany' (2006) 47 *Harvard International Law Journal* 223–42.

——, 'General Principles of International Public Authority: Sketching a Research Field' (2008) 11 *German Law Journal* 1909–38.

——, 'Pluralism, Direct Effect, and the Ultimate Say: On the relationship between international and domestic constitutional law' (2008) 6 *International Journal of Constitutional Law* 397–413.

——, 'Prinzipien der Rechtsfortbildung im Europäischen Rechtsraum. Überlegungen zum Lissabon-Urteil des BVerfG' (2010) 63 *Neue Juristische Wochenschrift* 1–5.

Bogdandy, Armin von and Jürgen Bast, The Federal Order of Competences, in: Armin von Bogdandy and Jürgen Bast (eds), *Principles of European Constitutional Law* (Oxford, Munich: Hart, Beck 2010), pp 275–307.

Bogdandy, Armin von and Sergio Dellavalle, Ad hostes docere—Zu den Ursprüngen und zur Präsenz partikularistisch-holistischen Denkens, in: Andreas Fischer-Lescano, Hans-Peter Gasser, Thilo Marauhn and Natalino Ronzitti (eds), *Frieden in Freiheit. Festschrift Bothe* (Baden-Baden: Nomos 2008), pp 847–63.

——, 'Universalism and Particularism as Paradigms of International Law' (2008) *IILJ Working Paper 2008/3*.

——, 'Universalism Renewed: Habermas' Theory of International Order in Light of Competing Paradigms' (2009) 10 *German Law Journal* 5–29.

Bogdandy, Armin von and Marc Jacob, The Judge as Law-Maker: Thoughts on Bruno Simma's Declaration in the Kosovo Opinion, in: Ulrich Fastenrath, Rudolf Geiger, Daniel-Erasmus Khan, Andreas Paulus, Sabine von Schorlemer and Christoph Vedder (eds), *From Bilateralism to Community Interest. Essays in Honour of Bruno Simma* (Oxford: Oxford University Press 2011), pp 809–24.

Bogdandy, Armin von and Ingo Venzke (eds), 'Beyond Dispute: International Judicial Institutions as Lawmakers' Special Issue (2011) 12 *German Law Journal* 979–1370.

Bogdandy, Armin von and Ingo Venzke, 'Beyond Dispute: International Judicial Institutions as Lawmakers' (2011) 12 *German Law Journal* 979–1004.

——, 'On the Democratic Legitimation of International Judicial Lawmaking' (2011) 12 *German Law Journal* 1341–70.

——, 'In Whose Name? An Investigation of International Courts' Public Authority and its Democratic Justification' (2012) 23 *European Journal of International Law* 7–41.

Bogdandy, Armin von, Philipp Dann, and Matthias Goldmann, 'Developing the Publicness of Public International Law: Towards a Legal Framework for Global Governance Activities' (2008) 9 *German Law Journal* 1375–400.

Boisson de Chazournes, Laurence, Qu'est-ce que la pratique en droit international?, in: Société Française pour le Droit International (ed), *La pratique et le droit international. Colloque de Genève* (Paris: Pedone 2004), pp 13–47.

Boldt, Hans, Staat und Souveränität IX-X, in: Otto Brunner, Werner Conze, and Reinhart Koselleck (eds), *Geschichtliche Grundbegriffe*, vol VI (Stuttgart: Klett-Cotta 1990), pp 129–54.

Borgumil, Jörg, Werner Jann, and Frank Nullmeier, Perspektiven der politikwissenschaftlichen Verwaltungsforschung, in: Jörg Borgumil, Werner Jann, and Frank Nullmeier (eds), *Politik und Verwaltung. PVS Sonderheft 37* (Wiesbaden: VS Verlag für Sozialwissenschaften 2006), pp 9–26.

Bos, Maarten, 'Recognized Manifestations of International Law—A New Theory of Sources' (1977) 19 *German Yearbook of International Law* 9–76.

Bos, Maarten, *A Methodology of International Law* (Amsterdam: North-Holland 1984).

Bossche, Peter van den, From Afterthought to Centrepiece: The WTO Appellate Body and its Rise to Prominence in the World Trading System, in: Giorgio Sacerdoti, Alan Yanovich, and Jan Bohanes (eds), *The WTO at Ten: The Contribution of the Dispute Settlement System* (Cambridge: Cambridge University Press 2006), pp 289–325.

——, *The Law and Policy of the World Trade Organization* (Cambridge: Cambridge University Press 2008).

Bothe, Michael, Les Limites des Pouvoirs du Conseil de Sécurité, in: René-Jean Dupuy (ed), *The Development of the Role of the Security Council* (Dordrecht: Kluwer 1993), pp 67–82.

——, Peace-keeping, in: Bruno Simma (ed), *The Charter of the United Nations: A Commentary* (Oxford: Oxford University Press 2002), pp 648–700.

Bourdieu, Pierre, *Sozialer Sinn. Kritik der theoretischen Vernunft* (Frankfurt am Main: Suhrkamp 1987).

——, 'The Force of Law: Toward a Sociology of the Juridical Field' (1987) 38 *Hastings Law Journal* 814–53.

——, *Entwurf einer Theorie der Praxis* (Frankfurt am Main: Suhrkamp 1996).

Bourdieu, Pierre and Loïc J D Wacquant, *An Invitation to Reflexive Sociology* (Chicago: University of Chicago Press 1992).

Boyle, Alan, Soft Law in International Law-Making, in: Malcom D. Evans (ed), *International Law* (Oxford: Oxford University Press 2006), pp 141–57.

Boyle, Alan E and Christine M Chinkin, *The Making of International Law* (Oxford: Oxford University Press 2007).

Bradley, Curtis A and Judith G Kelley, 'The Concept of International Delegation' (2008) 71 *Law and Contemporary Problems* 1–36.

Brandom, Robert, *Making it Explicit: Reasoning, Representing, and Discursive Commitment* (Cambridge, MA: Harvard University Press 1998).

——, 'Some Pragmatist Themes in Hegel's Idealism: Negotiation and Administration in Hegel's Account of the Structure and Content of Conceptual Norms' (1999) 7 *European Journal of Philosophy* 164–89.

——, *Articulating Reasons: An Introduction to Inferentialism* (Cambridge, MA: Harvard University Press 2000).

Breitmeier, Helmut, 'Die Output-orientierte Legitimität des globalen Regierens. Empirische Befunde aus der quantitativen Erforschung internationaler Umweltregime' (2006) 13 *Zeitschrift für Internationale Beziehungen* 39–74.

——, Oran R Young, and Michael Zürn, *Analyzing International Environmental Regimes: From Case Study to Database* (Cambridge, MA: The MIT Press 2006).

Brölmann, Catherine, 'Law-Making Treaties: Form and Function in International Law' (2005) 74 *Nordic Journal of International Law* 383–404.

Brower II, Charles H, 'The Functions and Limits of Arbitration and Judicial Settlement Under Private and Public International Law' (2008) 18 *Duke Journal of International and Comparative Law* 259–309.

Brown, Chester, 'The Inherent Powers of International Courts and Tribunals' (2005) 76 *British Yearbook of International Law* 195.

Brown, Chris, 'World Society and the English School: An "International Society" Perspective on World Society' (2001) 7 *European Journal of International Relations* 434.

——, 'The Construction of a "Realistic Utopia": John Rawls and International Political Theory' (2002) 28 *Review of International Studies* 5–21.

——, From Humanized War to Humanitarian Intervention: Carl Schmitt's Critique of the Just War Tradition, in: Louiza Odysseos (ed), *The International Political Thought of Carl Schmitt: Terror, Liberal War and the Crisis of Global Ord*er (London: Routledge 2007), pp 56–69.

——, 'The Twilight of International Morality'? Hans J. Morgenthau and Carl Schmitt on the end of the Jus Publicum Europaeum, in: Michael C. Williams (ed), *Realism Reconsidered: The Legacy of Hans Morgenthau in International Relations* (Oxford: Oxford University Press 2007), pp 42–61.

Brunée, Jutta and Stephen Toope, *Legitimacy and Legality in International Law: An Interactional Account* (Cambridge: Cambridge University Press 2010).

Bryde, Brun-Otto, *Verfassungsentwicklung. Stabilität und Dynamik im Verfassungsrecht der Bundesrepublik Deutschland* (Baden-Baden: Nomos 1982).

Buchanan, Allen, *Justice, Legitimacy, and Self-Determination: Moral Foundations for International Law* (New York: Oxford University Press 2004).

Buchanan, Allen and Robert O Keohane, 'The Legitimacy of Global Governance Institutions' (2006) 20 *Ethics & International Affairs* 405–37.

Bueger, Christian and Frank Gadinger, 'Praktisch Gedacht! Praxistheoretischer Konstruktivismus in den Internationalen Beziehungen' (2008) 15 *Zeitschrift für Internationale Beziehungen* 273–302.

Bull, Hedley, *The Anarchical Society. A Study of Order in World Politics* (London: Macmillan 1977).

Bulygin, Eugenio, Das Problem der Geltung bei Kelsen, in: Stanley L Paulson and Michael Stolleis (eds), *Hans Kelsen: Staatsrechtslehrer und Rechtstheoretiker des 20. Jahrhunderts* (Tübingen: Mohr Siebeck 2005), pp 80–95.

Burke-White, William, 'The Argentine Financial Crisis: State Liability Under BITs and the Legitimacy of the ICSID System' (2008) 3 *Asian Journal of WTO & International Health Law and Policy* 199–234.

Busse, Dietrich, Semantic Strategies as a Means of Politics: Linguistic approaches to the analysis of 'semantic stugles', in: Pertti Ahonen (ed), *Tracing the Semiotic Boundaries of Politics* (Berlin: de Gruyter 1993), pp 121–8.

—— and Wolfgang Teubert, Ist Diskurs ein sprachwissenschaftliches Objekt? Zur Methodenfrage der historischen Semantik, in: Dietrich Busse, Fritz Hermanns, and Wolfgang Teubert (eds), *Begriffsgeschichte und Diskursgeschichte* (Opladen: Westdeutscher Verlag 1994), pp 10–28.

Byers, Michael, 'Custom, Power, and the Power of Rules: Customary International Law from an Interdisciplinary Perspective' (1995) 17 *Michigan Journal of International Law* 109–80.

——, 'Abuse of Rights: An Old Principle, A New Age' (2002) 47 *McGill Law Journal* 389–431.

Callies, Christian, 'Nach dem Lissabon-Urteil des Bundesverfassungsgerichts: Parlamentarische Integrationsverantwortung auf europäischer und nationaler Ebene' (2010) 25 *Zeitschrift für Gesetzgebung* 1–34.

Canale, Damiano and Giovanni Tuzet, 'On Legal Inferentialism. Toward a Pragmatics of Semantic Content in Legal Interpretation?' (2007) 20 *Ratio Juris* 32–44.

Cançado Trindade, Antônio Augusto, *International Law for Humankind: Towards a New Jus Gentium* (Leiden: Nijhoff 2010).

Cannizzaro, Enzo, *Il principio della proporzionalità nell'ordinamento internazionale* (Milano: Giuffrè 2000).

Carlier, Jean-Yves, Et Genève sera... La définition du réfugié: Bilan et perspectives, in: Vincent Chetail (ed), *La Convention de Genève du 8 juillet 1951 relative au statut des réfugiés 50 ans après* (Bruxelles: Bruylant 2001), pp 63–89.

Caron, David D, 'War and International Adjudication: Reflections on the 1899 Peace Conference' (2000) 94 *American Journal of International Law* 4–30.

Carr, Edward Hallett, *The Twenty Years' Crisis 1919–1939: An Introduction to the Study of International Relations* (New York: Harper Collins 1964 [1939]).

Carroll, Lewis, *Through the Looking-Glass, and What Alice Found There* (Raleigh, NC: Hayes Barton Press 1872).

Carty, Anthony, *The Decay of International Law?* (Manchester: Manchester University Press 1986).

Cass, Deborah Z, *The Constitutionalization of the World Trade Organization. Legitimacy, Democracy, and Community in the International Trading System* (Oxford: Oxford University Press 2005).

Cassese, Sabino, *When Legal Orders Collide: The Role of Courts* (Seville: Global Law Press 2010).

Charnovitz, Steve, 'Exploring the Environmental Exceptions in GATT Article XX' (1991) 25 *Journal of World Trade* 37–55.

——, 'GATT and the Environment: Examining the Issues' (1992) 4 *International Environmental Affairs* 203–33.

——, 'The Law of Environmental "PPMs" in the WTO: Debunking the Myth of Illegality' (2002) 27 *Yale Journal of International Law* 59–110.

Cheng, Bin, *General Principles of Law as Applied by International Courts and Tribunals* (London: Stevens 1953).

——, Epilogue: On the Nature and Sources of International Law, in: *International Law: Teaching and Practice* (London: Stevens 1982), 203–33.

Chetail, Vincent (ed), *La Convention de Genève du 8 juillet 1951 relative au statut des réfugiés 50 ans après. Bilan et perspectives* (Bruxelles: Bruylant 2001).

Chimni, Bhupinder Singh, 'The Meaning of Words and the Role of UNHCR in Voluntary Repatriation' (1993) 5 *International Journal of Refugee Law* 442–60.

——, 'Co-Option and Resistance: Two Faces of Global Administrative Law' (2005) 37 *NYU Journal of International Law & Politics* 799–827.

——, 'The Past, Present and Future of International Law. A critical third world approach' (2007) 8(2) *Melbourne Journal of International Law* 499–515.

Chinkin, Christine M, 'The Challenge of Soft Law: Development and Change in International Law' (1989) 38 *International and Comparative Law Quarterly* 850–66.

Christensen, Ralph, Neo-Pragmatismus: Brandom, in: Sonja Buckel, Ralph Christensen and Andreas Fischer-Lescano (eds), *Neue Theorien des Rechts* (Stuttgart: Lucius und Lucius 2009), pp 239–62.

Christensen, Ralph, *Theorie richterlichen Begründens* (Berlin: Duncker und Humblot 2001).

Christensen, Ralph and Hans Kudlich, *Gesetzesbindung. Vom vertikalen zum horizontalen Verständnis* (Berlin: Duncker & Humblot 2008).

Christensen, Ralph and Michael Sokolowski, Recht als Einsatz im Semantischen Kampf, in: Ekkehard Felder (ed), *Semantische Kämpfe. Macht und Sprache in den Wissenschaften* (Berlin: de Gruyter 2006), pp 353–71.

Citroni, Gabriella, La giurisprudenza di due corti regionali dei diritti umani in tema di spollati interni, in: Irini Papanicolopulu and Tullio Scovazzi (eds), *Conflitti armati e situazioni di emergenza: la risposta del diritto internazionale* (Milan: Giuffrè 2007), pp 93–141.

Clausewitz, Carl von, *Vom Kriege* (Reinbeck: Rowohlt 2006).

Cobb, Sara, 'A Critique of Critical Discourse Analysis: Deconstructing and Reconstructing the Role of Intention' (1994) 4 *Communication Theory* 132–52.

Cohen, Felix S, 'Transcendental Nonsense and the Functional Approach' (1935) 35 *Columbia Law Review* 809–49.

Cohen, Jean L, 'Whose Sovereignty? Empire Versus International Law' (2004) 18 *Ethics & International Affairs* 1–24.

——, Sovereignty in the Context of Globalization: A Constitutional Pluralist Perspective, in: Samantha Besson and John Tasioulas (eds), *The Philosophy of International Law* (Oxford: Oxford University Press 2010), pp 261–81.

Collins, R, 'Constitutionalism as Liberal-Judicial Consciousness: Echoes from International Law's Past' (2009) 22 *Leiden Journal of International Law* 251–87.

Combacau, Jean and Serge Sur, *Droit international public* (Paris: Montchrestien 2010).

Copeland, Emily, A Rare Opening in the Wall: The Growing Recognition of Gender-Based Persecution, in: Niklaus Steiner, Mark Gibney, and Gil Loescher (eds), *Problems of Protection. The UNHCR, refugees, and human rights* (New York: Routledge 2003), pp 101–15.

Cosbey, Aaron, The Trade, Investment and Environment Interface, in: Shahrukh Rafi Khan (ed), *Trade and Environment: Difficult Policy Choices at the Interface* (London: Zen Books 2002), pp 7–16.

Coşeriu, Eugenio, *Synchronie, Diachronie und Geschichte. Das Problem des Sprachwandels* (München: Fink 1974).

Cot, Jean-Pierre, 'La Conduite subséquente des Parties à un traité' (1966) 70 *Revue Générale de Droit International Public* 632–66.

Cover, Robert M, 'Nomos and Narrative' (1983) 97 *Harvard Law Review* 4–68.

——, 'The Folktales of Justice: Tales of Jurisdiction' (1985) 14 *Capital University Law Review* 179–203.

——, 'Violence and the Word' (1986) 95 *Yale Law Journal* 1601–30.

Cox, Robert W, 'The Executive Head: An Essay on Leadership in International Organization' (1969) 23 *International Organization* 205–30.

——, 'Gramsci, Hegemony and International Relations: An Essay in Method' (1983) 12 *Millennium: Journal of International Studies* 162–75.

—— and Harold K Jacobson, *The Anatomy of Influence. Decision Making in International Organization* (New Haven, CT: Yale University Press 1973).

Croxton, Derek, 'The Peace of Westphalia of 1648 and the Origins of Sovereignty' (1999) 21 *International History Review* 569–91.

Cunliffe, S Alex and Michael C Pugh, UNHCR as leader in humanitarian assistance: triumph of politics over law?, in: Frances Nicholson and Patrick Twomey (eds), *Refugee*

Rights and Realities: Evolving international concepts and regimes (Cambridge: Cambridge University Press 1999), pp 175–99.

Curtin, Deirdre, *Executive Power in the European Union: Law, Practice, and Constitutionalism* (Oxford: Oxford University Press 2009).

—— and André Nollkaemper, 'Conceptualizing Accountability in International and European Law' (2005) 36 *Netherlands Yearbook of International Law* 3–20.

Cutler, Claire A, Virginia Haufler, and Tony Porter, The Contours and Significance of Private Authority in International Affairs, in: Claire A Cutler, Virginia Haufler, and Tony Porter (eds), *Private Authority and International Affairs* (Albany, NY: State University of New York Press 1999), pp 333–76.

Czapliński, Wladyslaw and Pavel Šturma, 'La responsabilité des Etats pour les flux de réfugiés provoqués par eux' (1994) 40 *Annuaire Français de Droit International* 156–69.

D'Alterio, Elisa, 'From Judicial Comity to Legal Comity: A judicial solution to global disorder?' (2011) 9 *International Journal of Constitutional Law* 394–424.

d'Aspremont, Jean, 'Abuse of the Legal Personality of International Organizations and the Responsibility of Member States' (2007) 4 *International Organization Law Review* 91–119.

——, 'Softness in International Law: A Self-Serving Quest for New Legal Materials' (2008) 19 *European Journal of International Law* 1075–93.

——, *Formalism and the Sources of International Law: A Theory of the Ascertainment of Legal Rules* (Oxford: Oxford University Press 2011).

—— and Frédéric Dopagne, 'Two Constitutionalisms in Europe: Pursuing an Articulation of the European and International Legal Orders' (2009) 69 *Zeitschrift für ausländisches öffentliches Recht und Völkerrecht* 939–78.

Dagan, Hanoch, 'The Realist Conception of Law' (2007) 57 *University of Toronto Law Journal* 607–60.

Dai, Xinyuan, *International Insitutions and National Policies* (Cambridge: Cambridge University Press 2007).

Dann, Philipp, *Parlamente im Exekutivföderalismus: Eine Studie zum Verhältnis von föderaler Ordnung und parlamentarischer Demokratie in der Europäischen Union* (Berlin: Springer 2004).

——, The Political Institutions, in: Armin von Bogdandy and Jürgen Bast (eds), *Principles of European Constitutional Law* (Oxford, Munich: Hart, Beck 2010), pp 237–74.

Danner, Allison Marston, 'When Courts Make Law: How the International Criminal Tribunals Recast the Laws of War' (2006) 59 *Vanderbilt Law Review* 1–65.

Davidson, David, Convention and Communication, in: *Inquiries into Truth and Interpretation* (Oxford: Oxford University Press 2001 [1984]), pp 265–96.

Davies, Arwel, 'The DSU Artilce 3.8 Presumption That an Infringement Constitutes a *Prima Facie* Case of Nullification or Impairment: When Does it Operate and Why?' (2010) 13 *Journal of International Economic Law* 181–204.

de Búrca, Gráinne 'Developing Democracy Beyond the State' (2008) 46 *Columbia Journal of Transnational Law* 221–78.

de Martens, Feodor, 'La Conférence du Congo à Berlin et la Politique Coloniale des États modernes' (1886) XVIII *Revue de Droit International et de Législation Comparée* 244.

de Wet, Erika, *The Chapter VII Powers of the United Nations Security Council* (Oxford: Hart 2004).

——, 'The International Constitutional Order' (2006) 55 *International and Comparative Law Quarterly* 51–76.

——, 'Governance through Promotion and Persuasion: The 1998 ILO Declaration on Fundamental Principles and Rights at Work' (2009) 9 *German Law Journal* 1429–51.

Degan, Vladimir-Đuro, *Sources of International Law* (The Hague: Nijhoff 1997).

Deitelhoff, Nicole, *Überzeugung in der Politik. Grundzüge einer Diskurstheorie internationalen Regierens* (Frankfurt am Main: Suhrkamp 2006).

—— and Harald Müller, 'Theoretical Paradise—Empirically Lost? Arguing with Habermas' (2005) 31 *Review of International Studies* 167–79.

Dellavalle, Sergio, The Necessity of International Law Against the A-normativity of Neo-Conservative Thought, in: Russell Miller and Rebecca Bratspies (eds), *Progress in International Law* (Leiden: Nijhoff 2008), pp 95–118.

Denfeld, Claudia, *Hans Wehberg (1885–1962). Die Organisation der Staatengemeinschaft* (Baden-Baden: Nomos 2008).

Derrida, Jacques, 'Force of Law. The Mystical Foundation of Authority' (1990) 11 *Cardozo Law Review* 919–1045.

Desmedt, Axel, 'Proportionality in WTO Law' (2001) 4 *Journal of International Economic Law* 441–80.

Destol, Chantal, 'Mythologies de l'international' (2006) *Politique Étrangère* 1075–83.

Dijkzeul, Dennis and Leon Gordenker, Cures and Conclusions, in: Dennis Dijkzeul and Yves Beigbeder (eds), *Rethinking International Organizations. Pathology and Promise* (New York: Berghahn 2003), pp 311–36.

Djeffal, Christian, 'The Iron Rhine Case—A Treaty's Journey from Peace to Sustainable Development' (2011) 71 *Zeitschrift für ausländisches öffentliches Recht und Völkerrecht* 569–86.

Dolzer, Rudolf and Christoph Schreuer, *Principles of International Investment Law* (Oxford: Oxford University Press 2008).

Dreier, Ralf, 'Niklas Luhmanns Rechtsbegriff' (2002) 88 *Archiv für Rechts- und Sozialphilosophie* 305–22.

Driesen, David, 'What is Free Trade? The real issue lurking behind the trade and environment debate' (2001) 41 *Virginia Journal of International Law* 279–368.

Dufour, Alfred, 'Droit et langage dans l'École historique du Droit' (1974) 19 *Archives de philosophie du droit* 151–80.

Duguit, Léon, *Le Droit Social, le Droit Individuel et la Transformation de l'État* (Paris: Alcan 1922).

Dunoff, Jeffrey L, 'Reconciling International Trade with Preservation of the Global Commons: Can We Prosper and Protect' (1992) 49 *Washington & Lee Law Review* 1407–54.

Dupuy, Pierre-Marie, 'Le juge et la règle générale' (1989) 93 *Revue Générale de Droit International Public* 569–98.

——, 'Soft Law and the International Law of the Environment' (1991) 12 *Michigan Journal of International Law* 420–35.

——, 'The Constitutional Dimension of the Charter of the United Nations Revisited' (1997) 1 *Max Planck Yearbook of United Nations Law* 1–33.

Dupuy, Pierre-Marie, 'L'unité de l'ordre juridique international' (2002) 297 *Recueil des Cours* 9–490.
Dworkin, Ronald, *Taking Rights Seriously* (London: Duckworth 1977).
——, 'Law as Interpretation' (1982) 60 *Critical Inquiry* 179–200.
Eco, Umberto, *The Open Work* (Cambridge, MA: Harvard University Press 1989).
——, *Einführung in die Semiotik* (München: Fink 2002).
Eeckhout, Piet, 'The Scales of Trade—Reflections on the Growth and Functions of the WTO Adjudicative Branch' (2010) 13 *Journal of International Economic Law* 3–26.
Ehrlich, Eugen, *Grundlegung der Soziologie des Rechts* (Berlin: Duncker & Humblot 1967).
Eisemann, Pierre-Marie, 'Le Gentlemen's agreement comme source du droit international' (1979) 106 *Journal du Droit International* 326–48.
Emiliou, Nicholas, *The Principle of Proportionality in European Law. A comparative study* (London: Kluwer 1996).
Engelhardt, Marie von, 'Opportunities and Challenges of a Soft Law Track to Economic and Social Rights—The Case of the Voluntary Guidelines on the Right to Food' (2009) 42 *Verfassung und Recht in Übersee* 502–25.
Errera, Roger, The Concept of Membership of a Particular Social Group in Refugee Law, in: Pierre-Marie Dupuy, Bardo Fassbender, Malcom N Shaw, and Karl P Sommermann (eds), *Völkerrecht als Wertordnung: Festschrift für Christian Tomuschat* (Kehl: Engel 2006), pp 133–51.
Esty, Daniel C, *Greening the GATT. Trade, environment, and the future* (Washington, DC: Institute for International Economics 1994).
Falk, Richard A, *The Role of Domestic Courts in the International Legal Order* (Syracuse: Syracuse University Press 1964).
——, 'Casting the Spell: The New Haven School of International Law' (1995) 104 *Yale Law Journal* 1991–2008.
Fassbender, Bardo, 'The United Nations Charter as Constitution of the International Community' (1998) 36 *Columbia Journal of Transnational Law* 529–619.
—— and Albert Bleckmann, Article 2(1), in: Bruno Simma (ed), *The Charter of the United Nations: A Commentary* (Oxford: Oxford University Press 2002), pp 68–91.
Fastenrath, Ulrich, *Lücken im Völkerrecht* (Berlin: Duncker und Humblot 1991).
——, 'Relative Normativity in International Law' (1993) 4 *European Journal of International Law* 305–40.
Feichtner, Isabel, 'The Administration of the Vocabulary of International Trade: The Adaptation of WTO Schedules to Changes in the Harmonized System' (2008) 9 *German Law Journal* 1481–511.
——, 'The Waiver Power of the WTO: Opening the WTO for Political Debate on the Reconciliation of Public Interests' (2009) 20 *European Journal of International Law* 615–45.
——, *The Law and Politics of WTO Waivers: Stability and Flexibility in Public International Law* (Cambridge: Cambridge University Press 2012).
Feinäugle, Clemens A, 'The UN Security Council Al-Qaida and Taliban Sanctions Committee: Emerging Principles of International Institutional Law for the Protection of Individuals?' (2008) 9 *German Law Journal* 1513–39.

Feldman, Alexander M, 'Evolving Treaty Obligations: A Proposal for Analyzing Subsequent Practice Derived from WTO Dispute Settlement' (2009) 41 *NYU Journal of International Law & Politics* 655–706.

Feller, Erika and Anja Klug, Refugees, United Nations High Commissioner (UNHCR), in: Rüdiger Wolfrum (ed), *MPEPIL* (Oxford: Oxford University Press 2007).

Feller, Erika, Volker Türk, and Frances Nicholson (eds), *Refugee Protection in International Law: UNHCR's global consultations on international protection* (Cambridge: Cambridge University Press 2003).

Findley, Ronald and Kevin H O'Rourke, *Power and Plenty: Trade, War, and the World Economy in the Second Millennium* (Princeton: Princeton University Press 2007).

Finnemore, Martha, 'Norms, Culture and World Politics: Insights from Sociology's Institutionalism' (1996) 50 *International Organization* 325–47.

—— and Kathryn Sikkink, 'International Norm Dynamics and Political Change' (1998) 52 *International Organization* 887–917.

—— and Stephen Toope, 'Alternatives to "Legalization": Richer Views of Law and Politics' (2001) 55 *International Organization* 743–58.

Fischer-Lescano, Andreas, *Globalverfassung. Die Geltungsbegründung der Menschenrechte* (Weilerswist: Velbrück Wissenschaft 2005).

—— and Sonja Buckel, 'Gramsci Reconsidered. Hegemony in Global Law' (2009) 22 *Leiden Journal of International Law* 437–54.

—— and Ralph Christensen, 'Auctoritatis Interpositio. Die Dekonstruktion des Dezisionismus durch die Systemtheorie' (2005) 44 *Der Staat* 213–42.

—— and Philip Liste, 'Völkerrechtspolitik. Zu Trennung und Verknüpfung von Politik und Recht der Weltgesellschaft' (2005) 12 *Zeitschrift für Internationale Beziehungen* 209–49.

—— and Gunther Teubner, 'Regime-Collisions: The Vain Search for Legal Unity in the Fragmentation of Global Law' (2004) 25 *Michigan Journal of International Law* 999–1045.

——, *Regime-Kollisionen. Zur Fragmentierung des globalen Rechts* (Frankfurt am Main: Suhrkamp 2006).

Fish, Stanley, *Doing What Comes Naturally. Change, Rhetoric, and the Practice of Theory in Literature and Legal Studies* (Durham: Duke University Press 1989).

Fitzmaurice, Gerald, 'Vae Victis or Woe to the Negotiator! Your Treaty or Our "Interpretation" of It?' (1971) 65 *American Journal of International Law* 358–73.

Fitzmaurice, Gerald Sir, 'The Law and Procedure of the International Court of Justice. Treaty Interpretation and Other Treaty Points' (1957) 33 *British Yearbook of International Law* 203–93.

Fitzmaurice, Malgosia A, 'Modifications to the Principle of Consent in Relation to Certain Treaty Obligations' (1997) 2 *Austrian Review of International and European Law* 275–317.

Fitzpatrick, Joan, 'Revitalizing the 1951 Convention' (1996) 9 *Harvard Human Rights Journal* 229–53.

——, 'The End of Protection: Legal Standards for Cessation of Refugee Status and Withdrawal of Temporary Protection' (1999) 13 *Georgetown Immigration Law Journal* 343–81.

Fitzpatrick, Joan, 'Temporary Protection of Refugees: Elements of a Formalized Regime' (2000) 94 *American Journal of International Law* 279–306.

Fleischhauer, Carl-August, Article 13, in: Bruno Simma (ed), *The Charter of the United Nations: A Commentary* (Oxford: Oxford University Press 2002), pp 298–317.

Florini, Ann, 'The Evolution of International Norms' (1996) 40 *International Studies Quarterly* 363–89.

Focarelli, Carlo, 'Diniego dell'immunita giurisdizionale degli Stati stranieri per crimini, jus cogens e dinamica del diritto internazionale' (2008) 91 *Rivista di diritto internazionale* 738–57.

Forst, Rainer, *Das Recht auf Rechtfertigung. Elemente einer konstruktivistischen Theorie der Gerechtigkeit* (Frankfurt am Main: Suhrkamp 2007).

——, *Discipline and Punishment* (London: Tavistock 1977).

——, Two Lectures, in: Colin Gordon (ed), *Power/Knowledge* (New York: Pantheon Books 1980), pp 78–108.

Foucault, Michel, Afterword: The Subject and Power, in: Hubert L Dreyfus and Paul Rabinow (eds), *Michel Foucault: Beyond Structualism and Hermeneutics* (Chicago: University of Chicago Press 1983), pp 208–26.

Francioni, Francesco, International 'Soft Law': A Contemporary Assessment, in: Vaughan Lowe and Malgosia Fitzmaurice (eds), *Fifty Years of the International Court of Justice. Essays in Honour of Sir Robert Jennings* (Cambridge: Cambidge University Press 1996), pp 167–80.

Franck, Thomas M, *The Power of Legitimacy Among Nations* (Oxford: Oxford University Press 1990).

——, *Recourse to Force: State Action against Threats and Armed Attacks* (Cambridge: Cambridge University Press 2002).

Franz, Fritz, Die Wandlung des Asylrechts vom Souveränitätsrecht des Staates zum Freiheitsrecht des Einzelnen, in: Martin Kornrumpf (ed), *Zweites Internationales Asyl-Colloquium* (Köln: Heymanns 1965), pp 133–9.

Fraser, Nancy, *Scales of Justice. Reimagining Political Space in a Globalizing World* (New York: Columbia University Press 2009).

Fried, Alfred H, *Handbuch der Friedensbewegung* (Wien: Verlag der Österreichischen Friedensgesellschaft 1905).

Friedmann, Wolfgang Gaston, *The Changing Structure of International Law* (New York: Columbia University Press 1964).

Friedrichs, Jörg and Friedrich Kratochwil, 'On Acting and Knowing: How Pragmatism Can Advance International Relations Research and Methodology' (2009) 63 *International Organization* 701–31.

Frowein, Jochen, 'Konstitutionalisierung des Völkerrechts' (2000) 39 *Berichte der Deutschen Gesellschaft für Völkerrecht* 427–48.

——, Vorbemerkungen zu Art. 8–11, in: Jochen Frowein and Wolfgang Peukert (eds), *EMRK-Kommentar* (Kehl am Rhein: N.P. Engel 2009), pp 279–86.

—— and Nico Krisch, Article 39, in: Bruno Simma (ed), *The Charter of the United Nations: A Commentary* (Oxford: Oxford University Press 2002), pp 717–29.

Fyrnys, Markus, 'Expanding Competences by Judicial Lawmaking: The Pilot Judgment Procedure of the European Court of Human Rights' (2011) 12 *German Law Journal* 1231–60.

Gallagher, Dennis, 'The Evolution of the International Refugee System' (1989) 23 *International Migration Review* 579–98.

Gallie, Walter Bryce, 'Essentially Contested Concepts' (1956) 56 *Proceedings of the Aristotelian Society* 167–98.

Gardiner, Richard K, *Treaty Interpretation* (Oxford: Oxford University Press 2008).

Gärditz, Klaus Ferdinand, 'Die Legitimation der Justiz zur Völkerrechtsfortbildung' (2008) 47 *Der Staat* 381–409.

Gerhardt, Michael J, *The Power of Precedent* (Oxford: Oxford University Press 2008).

Geuss, Raymond, *Outside Ethics* (New Jersey: Princeton University Press 2005).

——, *Philosophy & Real Politics* (New Jersey: Princeton University Press 2008).

Giddens, Anthony, *Central Problems in Social Theory. Action, Structure and Contradiction in Social Analysis* (London: Macmillan 1979).

Goddard, Stacie E, 'Brokering Change: Networks and entrepreneurs in international politics' (2009) 1 *International Theory* 249–81.

Goebel, Julius, *The Equality of States: A Study in the History of Law* (New York: Columbia University Press 1925).

Goldmann, Matthias, 'Inside Relative Normativity: From Sources to Standard Instruments for the Exercise of International Public Authority' (2008) 9 *German Law Journal* 1865–908.

Goldsmith, Jack L and Eric A Posner, *The Limits of International Law* (Oxford: Oxford University Press 2005).

Goldstein, Judith, Miles Kahler, Robert D Keohane, and Anne-Marie Slaughter, 'Introduction: Legalization and World Politics' (2000) 54 *International Organization* 385–99.

Gomula, Joanna, 'Precedential Effect of WTO Decisions: Note on the Zeroing Cases' (2008) 1 *The Global Community: Yearbook of International Law and Jurisprudence* 295–317.

Gonzaga, Jose Alvin C, The Role of the United Nations High Commissioner for Refugees and the Refugee Definition, in: Susan Kneebone (ed), *The Refugees Convention 50 Years on. Globalization and International Law* (Aldershot: Ashgate 2003), pp 223–50.

Goodrich, Peter, *Legal Discourse: Studies in Linguistics, Rhetoric, and Legal Analysis* (New York: St Martin's 1987).

Goodwin-Gill, Guy S, *The Refugee in International Law* (Oxford: Clarendon Press 1983).

——, 'Asylum: The Law and Politics of Change' (1995) 7 *International Journal of Refugee Law* 1–18.

——, 'Judicial Reasoning and "Social Group" after *Islam* and *Shah*' (1999) 11 *International Journal of Refugee Law* 537–43.

——, The Search for One, True Meaning…, in: Guy S Goodwin-Gill and H Lambert (eds), *The Limits of Transnational Law: Refugee Law, Policy Harmonization and Judicial Dialogue in the European Union* (Cambridge: Cambridge University Press 2010), pp 204–37.

—— and Jane McAdam, *The Refugee in International Law* (Oxford: Oxford University Press 2007).

Gordenker, Leon, *Refugees in International Politics* (London: Croom Helm 1987).

Grabitz, Eberhardt, 'Der Grundsatz der Verhältnismäßigkeit in der Rechtsprechung des Bundesverfassungsgerichts' (1973) 98 *Archiv des öffentlichen Rechts* 568–616.

Grahl-Madsen, Atle, *The Status of Refugees in International Law*, vol 1 (Leyden: Sijthoff 1966).
——, *Territorial Asylum* (Stockholm: Almqvist & Wiksell Internat. u.a. 1980).
——, 'International Refugee Law Today and Tomorrow' (1982) 20 *Archiv des Völkerrechts* 411–67.
Greenwood, Christopher, 'The Development of International Humanitarian Law by the International Criminal Tribunal for the Former Yugoslavia' (1998) 2 *Max Planck Yearbook of United Nations Law* 97–140.
Grewe, Wilhelm G, *The Epochs of International Law* (Berlin: de Gruyter 2000).
Grobe, Christian, 'The Power of Words: Argumentative Persuasion in International Negotiations' (2010) 16 *European Journal of International Relations* 5–29.
Gross, Aeyal M 'Human Proportions: Are Human Rights the Emperor's New Clothes of the International Law of Occupation?' (2007) 18 *European Journal of International Law* 1–35.
Grosse, Laurent, 'Racines historiques et fondements contemporains des normes impératives (Jus cogens) dans la the*i*orie et la pratique du droit international' (1995) 73 *Revue de droit international, de sciences diplomatiques et politiques* 225–50.
Guggenheim, Paul, Les Deux Eléments de la Coutume en Droit International, in: Charles Roussel (ed), *La Technique et les Principes du Droit Public—Etudes en l'Honneur de Georges Scelle* (Paris: LGDJ: 1950), pp 275–84.
——, 'Contribution à l'histoire des sources du droit des gens' (1958) 94 *Recueil des Cours* 5–82.
Günther, Klaus, 'Ein normativer Begriff der Kohärenz. Für eine Theorie der juristischen Argumentation' (1989) 20 *Rechtstheorie* 163–90.
——, 'Legal Pluralism or Uniform Concept of Law?' (2008) 5 *No Foundations: Journal of Extreme Legal Positivism* 5–21.
——, 'The Pragmatic and Functional Indeterminacy of Law' (2011) 12 *German Law Journal* 407–29.
Guzman, Andrew T, 'The Design of International Agreements' (2005) 16 *European Journal of International Law* 579–612.
Haas, Ernst B, *Beyond the Nation-state. Functionalism and international organization* (Stanford: Stanford University Press 1964).
——, 'Is there a Hole in the Whole? Knowledge, Technology, Interdependence, and the Construction of International Regimes' (1975) 29 *International Organization.* 827–76.
——, *When Knowledge is Power. Three models of change in international organizations* (Berkeley: University of California Press 1990).
Haas, Peter M, 'Epistemic Communities and International Policy Coordination' (1992) 46 *International Organization* 1–35.
Habermas, Jürgen, *Theorie und Praxis* (Frankfurt am Main: Suhrkamp 1971).
——, *Theorie des kommunikativen Handelns* (Frankfurt am Main: Suhrkamp 1995 [1981]).
——, *The Theory of Communicative Action*, vol 1 (Boston: Beacon Press 1984).
——, Was heißt Universalpragmatik, in: *Vorstudien und Ergänzungen zur Theorie des kommunikativen Handelns* (Frankfurt am Main: Suhrkamp 1984), pp 353–440.
——, *The Theory of Communicative Action*, vol 2 (Boston: Beacon Press 1987).

——, Handlungen, Sprechakte, sprachlich vermittelte Interaktionen und Lebenswelt, in: *Nachmetaphysisches Denken: Philosophische Aufsätze* (Frankfurt am Main: Suhrkamp 1988), pp 63–104.

——, Zur Kritik der Bedeutungstheorie, in: *Nachmetaphysisches Denken: Philosophische Aufsätze* (Frankfurt am Main: Suhrkamp 1988), pp 105–35.

——, *Faktizität und Geltung* (Frankfurt am Main: Suhrkamp 1992).

——, *Between Facts and Norms: Contributions to a Discourse Theory of Law and Democracy* (Cambridge, MA: MIT Press 1998).

——, *Die postnationale Konstellation* (Frankfurt am Main: Suhrkamp 1998).

——, What is Universal Pragmatics? (1976), in: Maeve Cooke (ed), *On the Pragmatics of Communication* (Cambridge, MA: MIT Press 1998), pp 21–104.

——, The Postnational Constellation and the Future of Democracy, in: Max Pensky (ed), *The Postnational Constellation: Political Essays* (Cambridge: Polity Press 2001), pp 58–112.

——, *Der gespaltene Westen* (Frankfurt am Main: Suhrkamp 2004).

——, 'Concluding Comments on Empirical Approaches to Deliberative Politics' (2005) 40 *Acta Politica* 384–92.

——, 'Eine politische Verfassung für die pluralistische Weltgesellschaft' (2005) 38 *Kritische Justiz* 222–47.

——, *The Divided West* (Cambridge: Polity Press 2006).

——, Does the Constitutionalization of International Law Still have a Chance?, in: *The Divided West* (Cambridge: Polity Press 2006), pp 115–93.

——, Konstitutionalisierung des Völkerrechts und die Legitimationsprobleme einer verfassten Weltgesellschaft, in: Winfried Brugger, Ulfried Neumann and Stephan Kirste (eds), *Rechtsphilosophie im 21. Jahrhundert* (Frankfurt am Main: Suhrkamp 2008), pp 360–96.

——, *Zur Verfassung Europas—Ein Essay* (Berlin: Suhrkamp 2011).

Haftel, Yoram Z and Alexander Thompson, 'The Independence of International Organizations: Concept and Applications' (2006) 50 *Journal of Conflict Resolution* 253–75.

Haggenmacher, P, 'La doctrine des deux éléments du droit coutumier dans la pactique de la Cour internationale' (1986) 90 *Revue Générale de Droit International Public* 5–126.

Halberstam, Daniel, Local, Global, and Plural Constitutionalism: Europe Meets the World, in: Joseph H H Weiler and Gráinne de Búrca (eds), *The Worlds of European Constitutionalism* (Cambridge: Cambridge University Press 2010), pp 150–201.

Hanschmann, Felix, Theorie transnationaler Rechtsprozesse, in: Sonja Buckel, Ralph Christensen and Andreas Fischer-Lescano (eds), *Neue Theorien des Rechts* (Stuttgart: Lucius und Lucius 2009), pp 375–400.

Hardt, Michael and Antonio Negri, *Empire* (Cambridge, MA: Harvard University Press 2002).

——, *Multitude. War and Democracy in the Age of Empire* (London: Penguin Books 2006).

Hart, Herbert Lionel Adolphus, *The Concept of Law* (Oxford: Oxford University Press 1997 [1961]).

——, 'Kelsen Visited' (1962) 10 *UCLA Law Review* 709–28.

Hasenclever, Andreas, Peter Mayer and Volker Rittberger, *Theories of International Regimes* (Cambridge: Cambridge University Press 1997).

Hathaway, James C, 'The Evolution of Refugee Status in International Law: 1920–1950' (1984) 33 *International and Comparative Law Quarterly* 348–80.
——, *The Law of Refugee Status* (Toronto: Butterworths 1991).
Hawkins, Darren G and Wade Jacoby, How Agents Matter, in: Darren G Hawkins, David A Lake, Daniel L Nielson, and Michael J Tierney (eds), *Delegation and Agency in International Organizations* (Cambridge: Cambridge University Press 2006), pp 199–228.
Hawkins, Darren G, David A Lake, Daniel L Nielson, and Michael J Tierney, Delegation under Anarchy: States, international organizations, and principal-agent theory, in: Darren G Hawkins, David A Lake, Daniel L Nielson, and Michael J Tierney (eds), *Delegation and Agency in International Organizations* (Cambridge: Cambridge University Press 2006), pp 3–38.
Hegel, Georg Wilhelm Friedrich, *Grundlinien der Philosophie des Rechts* (Frankfurt am Main: Suhrkamp 1986 [1821]).
Heijer, Maarten den, *Europe and Extraterritorial Asylum* (Oxford: Hart 2012).
Held, David, *Democracy and the Global Order. From the Modern State to Cosmopolitan Governance* (Stanford: Stanford University Press 1995).
——, Democracy and Globalization, in: Daniele Archibugi, David Held and Martin Köhler (eds), *Re-Imagining Political Community: Studies in Cosmopolitan Democracy* (Cambridge: Polity Press 1998), pp 11–27.
Hellmann, Gunther, Pragmatismus, in: Carlo Masala, Frank Sauer, and Andreas Wilhelm (eds), *Handbuch der Internationalen Politik* (Berlin: Springer 2010), pp 148–81.
Helmedach, Achim, Uneinheitliche Judizialisierung der internationalen Streitbeilegung: Empirische Ergebnisse, in: Bernhard Zangl (ed), *Auf dem Weg zu internationaler Rechtsherrschaft? Streitbeilegung zwischen Politik und Recht* (Frankfurt am Main: Campus 2009), pp 267–93.
Helton, Arthur C, 'Persecution on Account of Membership in a Social Group as a Basis for Refugee Status' (1983) 15 *Columbia Human Rights Law Review* 39–68.
Henkin, Louis, *International Law: Politics and Values* (The Hague: Kluwer 1995).
Héritier, Adrienne, *Explaining Institutional Change in Europe* (Oxford: Oxford University Press 2007).
Herz, John H, *Political Realism and Political Idealism. A Study in Theories and Realities* (Chicago: University of Chicago Press 1951).
Heymann, Monika, *Einseitige Interpretationserklärungen zu multilateralen Verträgen* (Berlin: Duncker & Humblot 2005).
Higgins, Rosalyn, 'Policy Considerations and the International Judicial Process' (1968) 17 *International and Comparative Law Quarterly* 58–84.
——, *Problems & Process. International Law and How We Use it* (Oxford: Oxford University Press 1994).
——, Some Observations on the Inter-Temporal Rule in International Law, in: Jerzy Makarczyk (ed), *Theory of International Law at the Threshold of the 21st Century. Essays in Honour of Krzysztof Skubiszewski* (The Hague: Kluwer Law International 1996), pp 173–82.
Hilf, Meinhard, 'Power, Rules and Principles—Which orientation for WTO/GATT law?' (2001) 4 *Journal of International Economic Law* 111–30.
—— and Sebastian Puth, The Principle of Proportionality on its Way into WTO/GATT Law, in: Armin von Bogdandy, Petros C Mavroidis, and Yves Mény (eds), *European*

Integration and International Co-ordination. Studies in transnational economic law in honour of Claus-Dieter Ehlermann (The Hague: Kluwer 2002), pp 199–218.

Hillenberg, Hartmut, 'A Fresh Look at Soft Law' (1999) 10 *European Journal of International Law* 499–515.

Hirschman, Albert O, *Exit, Voice and Loyalty* (Cambridge, MA: Harvard University Press 1970).

Höffe, Ottfried, *Demokratie im Zeitalter der Globalisierung* (München: Beck 1999).

——, Einführung in Aristoteles' *Politik*, in: Ottfried Höffe (ed), *Aristoteles. Politik* (Berlin: Akademie Verlag 2001), pp 5–19.

Hoffmeister, Frank, 'Germany: Status of European Convention on Human Rights in domestic law' (2006) 4 *International Journal of Constitutional Law* 722–31.

Höland, Armin, 'Wie wirkt Rechtsprechung?' (2009) 30 *Zeitschrift für Rechtssoziologie* 23–46.

Holborn, Louise Wilhelmine, *Refugees. A Problem of our Time* (Metuchen: Scarecrow Press 1975).

Hoof, Godefridus J H van, *Rethinking the Sources of International Law* (Deventer: Kluwer 1983).

Horkheimer, Max, *Anfänge der bürgerlichen Geschichtsphilosophie* (Frankfurt am Main: Fischer 1971 [1930]).

Horn, Henrik and Petros C Mavroidis, 'Still Hazy after All These Years: The Interpretation of National Treatment in the GATT/WTO Case-law on Tax Discrimination' (2004) 15 *European Journal of International Law* 39–69.

Horn, Henrik and Joseph H H Weiler, 'EC–Asbestos European Communities—Measures Affecting Asbestos and Asbestos-Containing Products' (2004) 3 *World Trade Review* 129–51.

Howse, Robert, Adjudicative Legitimacy and Treaty Interpretation in International Trade Law, in: Joseph H H Weiler (ed), *The EU, the WTO and the NAFTA: Towards a Common Law of International Trade?* (Oxford: Oxford University Press 2000), pp 35–69.

——, 'The Appellate Body Rulings in the Shrimp/Turtle Case. A new legal baseline for the trade and environment debate' (2002) 27 *Columbia Journal of Environmental Law* 491–521.

——, 'From Politics to Technocracy—and Back Again: The Fate of the Multilateral Trading Regime' (2002) 96 *American Journal of International Law* 94–117.

——, 'Human Rights in the WTO: Whose Rights, What Humanity? Comment on Petersmann' (2002) 13 *European Journal of International Law* 651–59.

——, 'Membership and its Privileges: the WTO, Civil Society, and the Amicus Brief Controversy' (2003) 9 *European Law Journal* 496–510.

——, 'Moving the WTO Forward—One Case at a Time' (2009) 42 *Cornell International Law Journal* 223–31.

——, A New Device for Creating International Legal Normativity: The WTO Technical Barriers to Trade Agreement and 'International Standards', in: Christian Joerges and Ernst-Ulrich Petersmann (eds), *Constitutionalism, Multilevel Trade Governance and Social Regulation* (Oxford: Hart 2006), pp 383–95.

—— and Kalypso Nicolaïdis, Legitimacy and Global Governance: Why Constitutionalizing the WTO is a Step Too Far, in: Roger B. Porter, Pierre Sauve, Arvind Subramian, and

Americo Beviglia Zampetti (eds), *Efficiency, Equity, Legitimacy and Governance: The Multilateral Trading System at the Millenium* (Washington: Brookings 2001), pp 227–52.

——, Democracy without Sovereignty: The Global Vocation of Political Ethics, in: Tomer Broude and Yuval Shany (eds), *The Shifting Allocation of Authority in International Law: Considering Sovereignty, Supremacy and Subsidiarity. Essays in Honour of Professor Ruth Lapidoth* (Oxford: Hart 2008), pp 163–92.

Howse, Robert and Donald Regan, 'The Product/Process Distinction—An Illusory Basis for Disciplining "Unilateralism" in Trade Policy' (2000) 11 *European Journal of International Law* 249–89.

Howse, Robert and Ruti G Teitel, 'Beyond Compliance: Rethinking Why International Law Really Matters' (2011) 2 *Global Policy* 127–36.

Hudec, Robert, 'The GATT Legal System: A Diplomat's Jurisprudence' (1970) 4 *Journal of World Trade* 615.

——, *Enforcing International Trade Law. The Evolution of the Modern GATT Legal System* (Salem, NH: Butterworth Legal Publishers 1993).

——, 'GATT/WTO Constraints on National Regulation. Requiem for an "Aim and Effects" Test' (1998) 32 *International Lawyer* 619–49.

——, The Role of the GATT Secretariat in the Evolution of the WTO Dispute Settlement Procedure, in: Jagdish Bhagwati and Mathias Hirsch (eds), *The Uruguay Round and Beyond: Essays in Honour of Arthur Dunkel* (Heidelberg: Springer 1998), pp 101–20.

Hudson, Manley O, 'The Permanent Court of International Justice—An Indispensable First Step' (1923) 108 *American Academy of Political And Social Science, Annals* 188–92.

——, *Progress in International Organization* (Littleton: Rothman 1981 [1932]).

Hueck, Ingo J, 'The Discipline of the History of International Law—New Trends and Methods on the History of International Law' (2001) 3 *Journal of the History of International Law* 194–217.

Hurrell, Andrew, International Law and the Changing Constitution of International Society, in: Michael Byers (ed), *The Role of Law in International Politics: Essays in International Relations and International Law* (Oxford, New York: Oxford University Press 2000), pp 327–47.

——, The State of International Society, in: Richard Little and John Williams (eds), *The Anarchical Society in a Globalised World* (Basingstoke: Palgrave Macmillan 2006), pp 191–215.

——, *On Global Order. Power, Values and the Constitution of International Society* (Oxford: Oxford University Press 2007).

International, Institut de Droit, 'The Activities of National Judges and the International Relations of their State' (1993-I) 65 *Annuaire de l'Institut de Droit International* 328–444.

Ioannidis, Michael, 'A Procedural Approach to the Legitimacy of International Adjudication: Developing Standards of Participation in WTO Law' (2011) 12 *German Law Journal* 1175–202.

Irwin, Douglas A, Petros C Mavroidis and Alan O Sykes, *The Genesis of the GATT* (Cambridge: Cambridge University Press 2008).

Irwin, Douglas A and Joseph H H Weiler, 'Measures Affecting the Cross-Border Supply of Gambling and Betting Services (DS 285)' (2008) 7 *World Trade Review* 71–113.

Jabloner, Clemens, 'Verrechtlichung und Rechtsdynamik' (1999) 54 *Zeitschrift für öffentliches Recht* 261–78.

Jackson, Ivor C, *The Refugee Concept in Group Situations* (The Hague: Nijhoff 1999).
Jackson, John H, 'World Trade Rules and Environmental Policies: Congruence or Conflict' (1992) 49 *Washington & Lee Law Review* 1227–78.
——, *The World Trade Organization: Constitution and Jurisprudence* (London: Royal Institute of International Affairs 1998).
——, *Sovereignty, the WTO and Changing Fundamentals of International Law* (Cambridge: Cambridge University Press 2006).
——, 'The Case of the World Trade Organization' (2008) 84 *International Affairs* 437–54.
Jacob, Marc, 'Precedents: Lawmaking Through International Adjudication' (2011) 12 *German Law Journal* 1005–32.
Jakab, András, 'Probleme der Stufenbaulehre' (2005) 91 *Archiv für Rechts- und Sozialphilosophie* 333–65.
Jellinek, Georg, *Die rechtliche Natur der Staatenverträge. Ein Beitrag zur juristischen Construction des Völkerrechts* (Wien: Hoelder 1880).
——, *Die Lehre von den Staatenverbindungen* (Wien: Alfred Hölder 1882).
Jennings, Robert Yewdall, 'What is International Law and How do we Tell it when we See it?' (1981) 37 *Schweizerisches Jahrbuch für Internationales Recht* 59–88.
——, 'The Proliferation of Adjudicatory Bodies: Dangers and Possible Answers' (1995) *ASIL Bulletin* 2.
Jestaedt, Matthias, *Grundrechtsentfaltung im Gesetz. Studien zur Interdependenz von Grundrechtsdogmatik und Rechtsgewinnungstheorie* (Tübingen: Mohr Siebeck 1999).
Jhering, Rudolf von, *Geist des römischen Rechts auf den verschiedenen Stufen seiner Entwicklung* (Leipzig: Breitkopf und Härtel 1866–78).
——, *Scherz und Ernst in der Jurisprudenz* (Leipzig: Breitkopf und Härtel 1884).
——, *Der Kampf um's Recht* (Frankfurt am Main: Klostermann 1948 [1913]).
——, *The Struggle for Law* (Chicago: Callaghan 1915).
Johnston, Alastair Iain, 'Treating International Institutions as Social Environments' (2001) 45 *International Studies Quarterly* 487–515.
Jordan, Robert S, 'Truly' International Bureaucracies: Real or Imagined?, in: Lawrence S Finkelstein (ed), *Politics in the United Nations System* (Durham: Duke University Press 1988), pp 424–45.
Juillard, Patrick, 'L'évolution des sources du droit des investissements' (1994) 250 *Recueil des Cours* 13–215.
Jütersonke, Oliver, *Morgenthau, Law and Realism* (Cambridge: Cambridge University Press 2010).
Kadelbach, Stefan, *Zwingendes Völkerrecht* (Berlin: Duncker & Humblot 1992).
——, 'Wandel und Kontinuitäten des Völkerrechts und seiner Theorie' (1997) *Archiv für Rechts- und Sozialphilosophie*, Beiheft 71, 178–93.
—— and Thomas Kleinlein, 'International Law—a Constitution for Mankind? An Attempt at a Re-appraisal with an Analysis of Constitutional Principles' (2007) 50 *German Yearbook of International Law* 303–48.
Kälin, Walter, 'Refugees and Civil Wars: Only a Matter of Interpretation?' (1991) 3 *International Journal of Refugee Law* 435–51.
——, Supervising the 1951 Convention Relating to the Status of Refugees: Article 35 and beyond, in: Erika Feller, Volker Türk and Frances Nicholson (eds), *Refugee Protection in*

International Law: UNHCR's Global Consultations on International Protection (Cambridge: Cambridge University Press 2003), pp 613–66.

Kanako, Sugiyama, 'Genuine Protection of International Refugees: A Study of the Influence of Western States on the Mandate of the UNHCR' (2003–2004) 11 *Asian Yearbook of International Law* 89–121.

Kant, Immanuel, *Perpetual Peace: A Philosophical Sketch* (London: George Allen & Unwin 1917 [1795]).

——, *Kritik der Reinen Vernunft* (Frankfurt am Main: Suhrkamp 1974 [1781]).

——, *Die Metaphysik der Sitten* (Frankfurt am Main: Surhkamp 1977 [1797]).

——, *Critique of Pure Reason* (Cambridge: Cambridge University Press 1998).

Karl, Wolfram, *Vertrag und spätere Praxis im Völkerrecht. Zum Einfluß der Praxis auf Inhalt und Bestand völkerrechtlicher Verträge* (Berlin: Springer 1983).

Katzenstein, Peter J and Rudra Sil, Eclectic Theorizing in the Study and Practice of International Relations, in: Christian Reus-Smit and Duncan Snidal (eds), *The Oxford Handbook of International Relations* (Oxford: Oxford University Press 2008), pp 109–30.

Keck, Margaret E and Kathryn Sikkink, *Activists Beyond Borders. Advocacy Networks in International Politics* (Ithaca, NY: Cornell University Press 1998).

Keck, Otto, 'Zur sozialen Konstruktion des Rational-Choice-Ansatzes. Einige Klarstellungen zur Rationalismus-Konstruktivismus-Debatte' (1997) 4 *Zeitschrift für Internationale Beziehungen* 139–51.

Keller, Reiner, Andreas Hirseland, Werner Schneider, and Willy Viehöver, Zur Aktualität sozialwissenschaftlicher Diskursanalyse—Eine Einführung, in: Reiner Keller, Andreas Hirseland, Werner Schneider and Willy Viehöver (eds), *Handbuch Sozialwissenschaftliche Diskursanalyse*, vol 1 (Wiesbaden: Verlag für Sozialwissenschaften 2006), pp 7–30.

Keller, Rudi, *Sprachwandel* (Tübingen: Francke 2003).

Kelley, Judith, 'Assessing the Complex Evolution of Norms: The Rise of International Election Monitoring' (2008) 62 *International Organization* 221–55.

Kelsen, Hans, *Das Problem der Souveränität und die Theorie des Völkerrechts* (Tübingen: Mohr 1920).

——, *Hauptprobleme der Staatsrechtslehre* (Tübingen: Mohr 1923).

——, *Allgemeine Staatslehre* (Berlin: Springer 1925).

——, *Wesen und Entwicklung der Staatsgerichtsbarkeit*, Veröffentlichungen der Vereinigung der Deutschen Staatsrechtslehrer, vol 5 (Berlin: de Gruyter 1929).

——, *Reine Rechtslehre. Einleitung in die rechtswissenschaftliche Problematik* (Leipzig: Deuticke 1934).

——, 'The Essential Conditions of International Justice' (1941) 35 *Proceedings of the American Society of International Law* 70–86.

——, 'International Peace-By Court or Government?' (1941) 46 *The American Journal of Sociology* 571–81.

——, *Law and Peace in International Relations* (Cambridge, MA: Harvard University Press 1942).

——, 'Compulsory Ajudication of International Disputes' (1943) 37 *American Journal of International Law* 397–406.

——, *General Theory of Law and State* (Cambridge, MA: Harvard University Press 1945).

——, 'Eine "Realistische" und die Reine Rechtslehre' (1959) 10 *Österreichische Zeitschrift für öffentliches Recht* 1–25.

——, *Pure Theory of Law* (Berkeley: UC Berkeley Press 1967).
——, What is Justice?, in: *What is Justice? Justice, Law, and Politics in the Mirror of Science* (Berkeley: University of Carlifornia Press 1971), pp 1–24.
——, *General Theory of Norms* (Oxford: Clarendon 1991).
——, *Introduction to the Problems of Legal Theory* (Oxford: Clarendon Press 1992).
Kennedy, David, 'Theses about International Law Discourse' (1980) 23 *German Yearbook of International Law* 353–91.
——, 'International Refugee Protection' (1986) 8 *Human Rights Quarterly* 1–69.
——, 'The Move to Institutions' (1987) 8 *Cardozo Law Review* 841–988.
——, 'The Disciplines of International Law and Policy' (1999) 12 *Leiden Journal of International Law,* 9–133.
——, 'The Politics of the Invisible College: International Governance and the Politics of Expertise' (2001) 5 *European Human Rights Law Review* 463–97.
——, *The Dark Sides of Virtue. Reassessing International Humanitarianism* (Princeton: Princeton University Press 2004).
——, *Of War and Law* (Princeton: Princeton University Press 2006).
Keohane, Robert O, 'The Functional Theory of Politics by David Mitrany (Book Review)' (1978) 72 *The American Political Science Review* 805–6.
——, *After Hegemony: Cooperation and Discord in the World Political Economy* (Princeton: Princeton University Press 1984).
——, *International Institutions and State Power: Essays in International Relations Theory* (Boulder: Westview Press 1989).
—— and Lisa L Martin, 'The Promise of Institutionalist Theory' (1995) 20 *International Security* 39–51.
Khiddu-Makubuya, Edward, Voluntary Repatriation by Force: the case of Rwandan refugees in Uganda, in: Howard Adelman (ed), *African Refugees. Development Aid and Repatriation* (Boulder: Westview Press 1994), pp 143–58.
Kiesow, Rainer Maria, *Das Naturgesetz des Rechts* (Frankfurt am Main: Suhrkamp 1997).
Kingsbury, Benedict, 'The Tuna-Dolphin Controversy, the World Trade Organization, and the Liberal Project to Reconceptualize International Law' (1994) 5 *Yearbook of International Environmental Law* 1–40.
——, 'Sovereignty and Inequality' (1998) 9 *European Journal of International Law* 599–625.
——, 'Legal Positivism as Normative Politics. International society, balance of power and Lassa Oppenheim's positive international law' (2002) 13 *European Journal of International Law* 401–36.
——, International Law as Inter-Public Law, in: H Richardson and M Williams (eds), *Moral Universalism and Pluralism* (New York: New York University Press 2009), pp 167–204.
——, International Courts: Uneven Judicialization in Global Order, in: James Crawford and Martti Koskenniemi (eds), *Cambridge Companion to International Law* (Cambridge: Cambridge University Press 2011), pp 202–28.
—— and Megan Donaldson, From Bilateralism to Publicness in International Law, in: Ulrich Fastenrath, Rudolf Geiger, Daniel-Erasmus Khan, Andreas Paulus, Sabine von Schorlemer, and Christoph Vedder (eds), *From Bilateralism to Community*

Interest. Essays in Honour of Bruno Simma (Oxford: Oxford University Press 2011), pp 79–89.

Kingsbury, Benedict and Nico Krisch, 'Introduction: Global Governance and Global Administrative Law in the International Legal Order' (2006) 17 *European Journal of International Law* 1–13.

Kingsbury, Benedict, Nico Krisch, and Richard B. Stewart, 'The Emergence of Global Administrative Law' (2005) 68 *Law and Contemporary Problems* 15–61.

Kirby, Michael, 'Transnational Judicial Dialogue, Internationalisation of Law and Australian Judges' (2008) 9 *Melbourne Journal of International Law* 171.

Kirchner, Christian, Zur konsequentialistischen Interpretationsmethode, in: Thomas Eger, Jochen Bigus, Claus Ott, and Georg von Wangenheim (eds), *Internationalisierung des Rechts und seine ökonomische Analyse* (Wiesbaden: Gabler 2008), pp 37–49.

Kirton, John J and Michael J Trebilcock (eds), *Hard Choices, Soft Law: Voluntary Standards in Global Trade, Environment and Social Governance* (Aldershot: Ashgate 2004).

Kirvan, Sue, 'Women and Asylum: A Particular Social Group' (1999) 7 *Feminist Legal Studies* 333–42.

Klabbers, Jan, *The Concept of Treaty in International Law* (The Hague: Kluwer 1996).

——, 'Redundancy of Soft Law' (1996) 65 *Nordic Journal of International Law* 167–82.

——, 'Undesirability of Soft Law' (1998) 67 *Nordic Journal of International Law* 381–92.

——, The Changing Image of International Organizations, in: Jean-Marc Coicaud and Veijo Heiskane (eds), *The Legitimacy of International Organizations* (Tokyo: The United Nations University Press 2001), pp 221–55.

——, 'International Legal Histories: The declining importance of *travaux préparatoires* in treaty interpretation?' (2003) 50 *Netherlands International Law Review* 267–88.

——, 'On Rationalism in Politics: Interpretation of Treaties and the World Trade Organization' (2005) 74 *Nordic Journal of International Law* 405–28.

——, 'Reflections on Soft International Law in a Privatized World' (2005) 16 *Finnish Yearbook of International Law* 313–28.

——, 'Two Concepts of International Organization' (2005) 2 *International Organization Law Review* 277–93.

——, *An Introduction to International Institutional Law* (Cambridge: Cambridge University Press 2009).

——, Law-making and Constitutionalism, in: Jan Klabbers, Anne Peters, and Geir Ulfstein (eds), *The Constitutionalization of International Law* (Oxford: Oxford University Press 2009), pp 81–125.

Kleinlein, Thomas, 'Establishing Elements of Pluralist Constitutionalism in International Law by Recourse to Formal Principles' (2011) 12 *German Law Journal* 1141–74.

——, *Konstitutionalisierung im Völkerrecht: Konstruktion und Elemente einer idealistischen Völkerrechtslehre* (Berlin: Springer 2012).

Koh, Hongju Harold, 'Transnational Legal Process' (1996) 75 *Nebraska Law Review* 181–207.

——, 'Bringing International Law Home' (1998) 35 *Houston Law Review* 623–81.

Kolb, Robert, *Interprétation et création du droit international. Esquisse d'une herméneutique juridique moderne pour le droit international public* (Brussels: Bruylant 2006).

——, 'Repères historiques dans l'évolution de l'occupation de guerre' (2007) *The Global Community: Yearbook of International Law and Jurisprudence* 65–102.

Kooijmans, Peter H, The Enlargement of the Concept 'Threat to the Peace', in: René-Jean Dupuy (ed), *The Development of the Role of the Security Council* (Dordrecht: Kluwer 1993), pp 111–21.

Koremenos, Barbara, 'When, What and Why Do States Choose to Delegate?' (2008) 71 *Law and Contemporary Problems* 151–92.

——, Charles Lipson and Duncan Snidal, 'The Rational Design of International Institutions' (2001) 55 *International Organization* 761–99.

Koselleck, Reinhart, Begriffsgeschichte and Social History, in: Futures Past. On the Semantics of Historical Time (New York: Columbia University Press 1979), pp 75–93.

——, Staat und Souveränität III, in: Otto Brunner, Werner Conze, and Reinhart Koselleck (eds), *Geschichtliche Grundbegriffe*, vol VI (Stuttgart: Klett-Cotta 1990), pp 25–64.

——, *Begriffsgeschichten* (Frankfurt am Main: Suhrkamp 2006).

Koskenniemi, Martti, 'General Principles: Reflexions on Constructivist Thinking in International Law' (1985) 18 *Oikeustiede-Jurisprudentia* 120–63.

——, 'The Politics of International Law' (1990) 1 *European Journal of International Law* 4–32.

——, 'The Place of Law in Collective Security' (1996) 17 *Michigan Journal of International Law* 455–90.

——, *The Gentle Civilizer of Nations* (Cambridge: Cambridge University Press 2001).

——, '"The Lady Doth Protest Too Much": Kosovo, and the Turn to Ethics in International Law' (2002) 65 *Modern Law Review* 159–75.

——, 'Global Governance and Public International Law' (2004) 37 *Kritische Justiz* 241–54.

——, 'International Law and Hegemony: A Reconfiguration' (2004) 17 *Cambridge Review of International Affairs* 197–218.

——, 'Perceptions of Justice: Walls and Bridges Between Europe and the United States' (2004) 64 *Zeitschrift für ausländisches öffentliches Recht und Völkerrecht* 305.

——, 'Why History of International Law Today?' (2004) 4 *Rechtsgeschichte* 61–66.

——, *From Apology to Utopia. The Structure of International Legal Argument* (Cambridge: Cambridge University Press 2005).

——, 'International Law in Europe between Tradition and Renewal' (2005) 16 *European Journal of International Law* 113–24.

——, 'International Legislation Today: Limits and Possibilities' (2005) 23 *Wisconsin International Law Journal* 61–92.

——, 'Constitutionalism as Mindset: Reflections on Kantian Themes About International Law and Globalization' (2007) 8 *Theoretical Inquiries in Law* 9–36.

——, 'The Fate of Public International Law: Between Technique and Politics' (2007) 70 *Modern Law Review* 1–30.

——, The Ideology of International Adjudication and the 1907 Hague Conference, in: Yves Daudet (ed), *Topicality of the 1907 Hague Conference, the Second Peace Conference* (Leiden: Nijhoff 2008), pp 127–52.

—— and Päivi Leino, 'Fragmentation of International Law? Postmodern Anxieties' (2002) 15 *Leiden Journal of International Law* 553–79.

Kottmann, Matthias and Christian Wohlfahrt, 'Der gespaltene Wächter? Demokratie, Verfassungsidentität und Integrationsverantwortung im Lissabon-Urteil' (2009) 69 *Zeitschrift für ausländisches öffentliches Recht und Völkerrecht* 443–70.

Kotzur, Markus, Intertemporal Law, in: Rüdiger Wolfrum (ed), *MPEPIL* (Oxford: Oxford Universtiy Press 2008),

Kourula, Pirkko, *Broadening the Edges. Refugee definition and international protection revisited* (The Hague: Nijhoff 1997).

Krämer, Sybille, *Sprache, Sprechakt, Kommunikation* (Frankfurt am Main: Suhrkamp 2001).

——, Sprache und Sprechen oder: Wie sinnvoll ist die Unterscheidung zwischen einem Schema und seinem Gebrauch?, in: Sybille Krämer and Ekkehard König (eds), *Gibt es eine Sprache hinter dem Sprechen?* (Frankfurt am Main: Suhrkamp 2002), pp 97–125.

Krasner, Stephen D (ed), *International Regimes* (Ithaca, NY: Cornell University Press 1983).

——, Structural Causes and Regime Consequences: Regimes as intervening variables, in: Stephen D Krasner (ed), *International Regimes* (Ithaca, NY: Cornell University Press 1983), pp 1–21.

Kratochwil, Friedrich V, *Rules, Norms and Decisions: On the Conditions of Practical and Legal Reasoning in International Relations and Domestic Affairs* (Cambridge: Cambridge University Press 1989).

——, How do Norms Matter?, in: Michael Byers (ed), *The Role of Law in International Politics: Essays in International Relations and International Law* (Oxford, New York: Oxford University Press 2000), pp 35–68.

—— and John Gerald Ruggie, 'International Organization: A state of art and an art of the state' (1986) 40 *International Organization* 753–75.

Krebs, Ronald R and Patrick Thaddeus Jackson, 'Twisting Tongues and Twisting Arms: The Power of Political Rhetoric' (2007) 13 *European Journal of International Relations* 35–66.

Krever, Tor, '"Mopping-up": UNHCR, Neutrality and Non-Refoulement since the Cold War' (2011) 11 *Chinese Journal of International Law* 587–608.

Kriele, Martin, *Theorie der Rechtsgewinnung. Entwickelt am Problem der Verfassungsinterpretation* (Berlin: Duncker & Humblot 1976).

Kripke, Saul A, *Wittgenstein on Rules and Private Language* (Cambridge, MA: Harvard University Press 1982).

Krisch, Nico, 'Amerikanische Hegemone und liberale Revolution im Völkerrecht' (2004) 43 *Der Staat* 267–97.

——, 'International Law in Times of Hegemony: Unequal Power and the Shaping of the International Legal Order' (2005) 16 *European Journal of International Law* 369–408.

——, 'The Pluralism of Global Administrative Law' (2006) 17 *European Journal of International Law* 247–78.

——, 'The Open Architecture of European Human Rights Law' (2008) 71 *Modern Law Review* 183–216.

——, *Beyond Constitutionalism. The Pluralist Structure of Postnational Law* (Oxford: Oxford University Press 2010).

Krugmann, Michael, *Der Grundsatz der Verhältnismäßigkeit im Völkerrecht* (Berlin: Duncker & Humblot 2004).

Kugelmann, Dieter, Refugees, League of Nations Offices, in: Rüdiger Wolfrum (ed), *MPEPIL* (Oxford: Oxford University Press 2007),

Kuhli, Milan and Klaus Günther, 'Judicial Lawmaking, Discourse Theory, and the ICTY on Belligerent Reprisals' (2011) 12 *German Law Journal* 1261–78.

Kuhn, Thomas S, *The Structure of Scientific Revolutions* (Chicago: University of Chicago Press 1996).

Kumin, Judith, UNHCR, the EU and Refugees, in: Jan Wouters, Frank Hoffmeister, and Tom Ruys (eds), *The United Nations and the European Union: An ever stronger partnership* (The Hague: T.M.C. Asser Press 2006), pp 171–82.

Kumm, Mattias, 'Who is the Final Arbiter of Constitutionality in Europe? Three Conceptions of the Relationship Between the German Federal Constitutional Court and the European Court of Justice' (1999) 36 *Common Market Law Review* 351–86.

——, 'Constitutional Rights as Principles: On the Structure and Domain of Constitutional Justice' (2004) 2 *International Journal of Constitutional Law* 574–96.

——, The Cosmopolitan Turn in Constitutionalism: On the Relationship between Constitutionalism in and beyond the State, in: Jeffrey L Dunoff and Joel P Trachtman (eds), *Ruling the World? Constitutionalism, International Law, and Global Governance* (Cambridge: Cambridge University Press 2009), pp 258–324.

Kundera, Milan, *Das Buch vom Lachen und Vergessen* (München: Carl Hanser 2004).

Kunz, Josef L, 'The Nature of Customary International Law' (1953) 47 *American Journal of International Law* 662–9.

Laclau, Ernesto, *Emancipation(s)* (New York: Verso 1996).

Lammasch, Heinrich, Die Lehre von der Schiedsgerichtsbarkeit in ihrem ganzen Umfange, in: Fritz Stier-Somlo (ed), *Handbuch des Völkerrechts*, vol 5 (Stuttgart: Kohlhammer 1914).

Lang, Andrew, 'Reflecting on Linkage: Cognitive and Institutional Change in the International Trading System' (2007) 70 *Modern Law Review* 523–50.

Langrod, Georges, *La fonction publique internationale. Sa genèse, son essence, son evolution* (Leyden: Sythoff 1963).

Laski, Harold Joseph, *The Foundations of Sovereignty* (New York: Harcourt, Brace and Company 1921).

Lauterpacht, Elihu and Daniel Bethlehem, The Scope and Content of the Principle of Non-Refoulement: Opinion, in: Erika Feller, Volker Türk, and Frances Nicholson (eds), *Refugee Protection in International Law: UNHCR's Global Consultations on International Protection* (Cambridge: Cambridge University Press 2003), pp 87–177.

Lauterpacht, Hersch, 'Decisions of Municipal Courts as a Source of International Law' (1929) 10 *British Yearbook of International Law* 65–95.

——, *The Development of International Law by the Permanent Court of International Justice* (London: Longmans Green 1934).

——, 'The Grotian Tradition in International Law' (1946) 23 *British Yearbook of International Law* 1–53.

——, 'Restrictive Interpretation and the Principle of Effectiveness in the Interpretation of Treaties' (1949) 26 *British Yearbook of International Law* 48–85.

——, 'De L'Interprétation des Traités: Rapport' (1950-II) 43 *Annuaire de l'Institut de Droit International* 366–460.

——, 'Codification and Development of International Law' (1955) 49 *American Journal of Economics and Sociology* 16–43.

——, *The Development of International Law by the International Court* (London: Stevens & Sons 1958).

——, *Private Law Sources and Analogies of International Law* (Hambden, CT: Archon Books 1970 [1927]).

Lauterpacht, Hersch, Kelsen's Pure Science of Law, in: *Collected Papers*, vol 2, (Cambridge: Cambridge Universtiy Press 1975), pp 404–30.

Leben, Charles, 'The Changing Structure of International Law Revisited. By Way of Introduction' (1997) 8 *European Journal of International Law* 399–408.

Lege, Joachim, Was Juristen wirklich tun. Jurisprudential Realism, in: Winfried Brugger, Ulfried Neumann, and Stephan Kirste (eds), *Rechtsphilosophie im 21. Jahrhundert* (Frankfurt am Main: Suhrkamp 2008), pp 207–33.

Lentini, E J, 'The Definition of Refugees in International Law: Proposals for the Future' (1985) 5 *Boston College Third World Law Journal* 183–98.

Lepore, Ernest (ed), *Truth and Interpretation: Perspectives on the Philosophy of Donald Davidson* (Oxford: Basil Blackwell 1986).

Lesaffer, Randall, International Law and Its History: The Story of an Unrequited Love, in: Matthew C R Craven, Malgosia Fitzmaurice, and Maria Vogiatzi (eds), *Time, History and International Law* (Leiden: Nijhoff 2007), pp 27–42.

Lévesque, Jean-François, 'Traités de Verre: Réflexions sur l'interprétation' (2006) 19 *Revue Québécoise de droit international* 53–78.

Lewis, Corinne, 'UNHCR's Contribution to the Development of International Refugee Law: Its Foundations and Evolution' (2005) 17 *International Journal of Refugee Law* 67–90.

Liang, Yuen-Li, 'The General Assembly and the Progressive Development and Codification of International Law' (1948) 42 *American Journal of International Law* 66–97.

Liese, Andrea and Silke Weinlich, Die Rolle von Verwaltungsstäben internationaler Organisationen. Lücken, Tücken und Konturen eines (neuen) Forschungsgebiets, in: Jörg Bogumil, Werner Jann, and Frank Nullmeier (eds), *Politik und Verwaltung. PVS-Sonderheft 37* (Wiesbaden: VS Verlag für Sozialwissenschaften 2006), pp 491–525.

Linderfalk, Ulf, *On the Interpretation of Treaties. The Modern International Law as Expressed in the 1969 Vienna Convention on the Law of Treaties* (Dordrecht: Springer 2007).

——, 'The Application of International Legal Norms over Time: The Second Branch of Intertemporal Law' (2011) 58 *Netherlands International Law Review* 147–72.

Liptow, Jasper, *Regel und Interpretation. Eine Untersuchung zur sozialen Struktur sprachlicher Praxis* (Weilerswist: Velbrück 2004).

Little, Richard, 'The English School's Contribution to the Study of International Relations' (2000) 6 *European Journal of International Relations* 395–422.

Loescher, Gil, *The UNHCR and World Politics. A Perilous Path* (Oxford: Oxford University Press 2006).

——, Alexander Betts, and James Milner, *The United Nations High Commissioner for Refugees (UNHCR). The Politics and Practice of Refugee Protection into the Twenty-First Century* (New York, NY: Routledge 2008).

Lowe, Boutelle Ellsworth, *The International Protection of Labor* (New York: Macmillan 1921).

Lowe, Vaughan, The Politics of Law-Making: Are the Method and Character of Norm Creation Changing?, in: Michael Byers (ed), *The Role of Law in International Politics* (New York, Oxford: Oxford University Press 2000), pp 207–26.

Luhmann, Niklas, 'Die Weltgesellschaft' (1971) 57 *Archiv für Rechts- und Sozialphilosophie* 1–35.

——, *Legitimation durch Verfahren* (Frankfurt am Main: Suhrkamp 1983).

——, *Das Recht der Gesellschaft* (Frankfurt am Main: Suhrkamp 1993).

——, *Einführung in die Systemtheorie* (Heidelberg: Carl-Auer 2006).

——, *Rechtssoziologie* (Wiesbaden: Verlag für Sozialwissenschaften 2008 [1972]).

Lyotard, Jean-François, *The Postmodern Condition: A Report on Knowledge* (Minneapolis: University of Minnesota Press 1984).

——, Memorandum der Legitimität, in: Peter Engelmann (ed), *Postmoderne und Dekonstruktion* (Stuttgart: Reclam 2004), pp 54–75.

Macalister-Smith, Peter, 'International Humanitarian Assistance for Refugees: Law and Practice' (1985) 15 *Indian Journal of International Law* 365–85.

Macdonald, Ronald St John, The United Nations Charter: Constitution or Contract?, in: Ronald St John Macdonald and Douglas M. Johnston (eds), *The Structure and Process of International Law: Essays in Legal Philosophy Doctrine and Theory* (Dodrecht: Nijhoff 1986), pp 889–912.

Maduro, Miguel Poiares, Contrapunctual Law: Europe's Constitutional Pluralism in Action, in: Neil Walker (ed), *Sovereignty in Transition* (Oxford: Hart 2003), pp 521–37.

Malinverni, Giorgio, Il ruolo della Corte di Strasburgo nell'evoluzione della Convenzione europea di diritti dell'uomo, in: Francesco Salerno (ed), *Il ruolo del giudice internazionale nell'evoluzione del diritto internazionale e communitario* (Padova: Cedam 1995), pp 125–42.

Marceau, Gabrielle and Joel P Trachtman, 'The Technical Barriers to Trade Agreement, the Sanitary and Phytosanitary Measures Agreement, and the General Agreement on Tariffs and Trade: A map of the World Trade Organization law of domestic regulation of goods' (2002) 36 *Journal of World Trade* 811–81.

Marks, Susan, 'The End of History? Reflections on Some International Legal Theses' (1997) 8 *European Journal of International Law* 449–77.

——, 'Naming Global Administrative Law' (2005) 37 *International Law and Politics* 995–1001.

Martin, Lisa L and Beth Simmons, 'Theories and Empirical Studies of International Institutions' (1998) 52 *International Organization* 729–57.

Martineau, Anne-Charlotte, 'La technique du balancement par l'Organe d'appel de l'OMC (études de la justification dans les discours juridiques)' (2007) 123 *Revue du Droit Public* 991–1030.

Mathiason, John, *Invisible Governance. International Secretariats in World Politics* (Bloomfield, CT: Kumarian 2007).

Mavroidis, Petros C, 'Trade and Environment after the Shrimps-Turtles Litigation' (2000) 34 *Journal of World Trade* 73–88.

——, Amicus Curiae Briefs Before the WTO. Much Ado About Nothing, in: Armin von Bogdandy, Yves Mény, and Petros C Mavroidis (eds), *European Integration and International Co-ordination. Studies In Transnational Economic Law in Honour of Claus-Dieter Ehlermann* (The Hague: Kluwer 2002), pp 317–29.

Mayer, Franz C, Multilevel Constitutional Jurisdiction, in: Armin von Bogdandy and Jürgen Bast (eds), *Principles of European Constitutional Law* (Oxford, Munich: Hart, Beck 2010), pp 299–339.

Mayntz, Renate and Fritz W Scharpf, Der Ansatz des akteurzentrierten Institutionalismus, in: Renate Mayntz and Fritz W Scharpf (eds), *Steuerung und Selbstorganisation in staatsnahen Sektoren* (Frankfurt am Main: Campus 1995), pp 39–72.

McAdam, Jane, Interpretation of the 1951 Convention, in: Andreas Zimmermann (ed), *The 1951 Convention Relating to the Status of Refugees and its 1967 Protocol: A Commentary* (Oxford: Oxford University Press 2011), pp 75–115.

McDougal, Myres S, 'International Law, Power, and Policy: A Contemporary Conception' (1954) 82 *Recueil des Cours* 137–259.

——, *Studies in World Public Order* (New Haven, CT: Yale University Press 1960).

——, 'The International Law Commission's Draft Articles upon Interpretation: Textuality Redivivus' (1967) 61 *American Journal of International Law* 992–1000.

—— and Michael Reisman, 'The Prescribing Function in World Constitutive Process: How International Law is Made' (1980) 6 *Yale Studies in World Public Order* 249–84.

McDougal, Myres Smith, Harold D Lasswell, and Lung-Chu Chen, *Human Rights and World Public Order* (New Haven, CT: Yale University Press 1980).

McDougal, Myres Smith, Harold D Lasswell, and James C Miller, *The Interpretation of Agreements and World Public Order* (New Haven, CT: Yale University Press 1967).

McGrady, Benn, 'Necessity Exceptions in WTO Law: Retreaded Tyres, Regulatory Purpose and Cumulative Regulatory Measures' (2009) 12 *Journal of International Economic Law* 153–73.

McRae, Donald, Treaty Interpretation by the WTO Appellate Body: The Conundrum of Article 17(6) of the WTO Antidumping Agreement, in: Enzo Cannizzaro (ed), *The Law of Treaties Beyond the Vienna Convention* (Oxford: Oxford University Press 2011), pp 164–85.

Mearsheimer, John J, 'The False Promise of International Institutions' (1994) 19 *International Security* 5–49.

Melander, Göran, International Refugee Organization (IRO), in: Rüdiger Wolfrum (ed), *MPEPIL* (Oxford: Oxford University Press 2007).

Mendelson, Maurice, 'The Formation of Customary International Law' (1998) 272 *Recueil des Cours* 155–410.

Meng, Werner, *Extraterritoriale Jurisdiktion im öffentlichen Wirtschaftsrecht* (Heidelberg: Springer 1994).

Merkl, Adolf, 'Das Doppelte Rechtantlitz' (1918) 47 *Juristische Blätter* 425.

Merleau-Ponty, Maurice, Everywhere and Nowhere, in: *Signs* (Evanston: Northwesteren University Press 1964), pp 126–58.

——, *Die Abenteuer der Dialektik* (Frankfurt am Main: Suhrkamp 1968).

Milner, Helen V, *Interests, Institutions, and Information* (Princeton: Princeton University Press 1997).

Mitchell, Andrew D, 'Proportionality and Remedies in WTO Disputes' (2006) 17 *European Journal of International Law* 985–1008.

Mitrany, David, *A Working Peace System. An argument for the functional development of international organization* (London: Royal Inst. of Internat. Affairs 1943).

——, *The Functional Theory of Politics* (London: London School of Economics & Political Science 1975).

Möllers, Christoph, *Gewaltengliederung: Legitimation und Dogmatik im nationalen und internationalen Rechtsvergleich* (Tübingen: Mohr Siebeck 2005).

——, 'Transnationale Behördenkooperation. Verfassungs- und völkerrechtliche Probleme transnationaler administrativer Standardsetzung' (2005) 65 *Zeitschrift für ausländisches öffentliches Recht und Völkerrecht* 351–89.

——, Verfassungsgebende Gewalt—Verfassung—Konstitutionalisierung, in: Armin von Bogdandy and Jürgen Bast (eds), *Europäisches Verfassungsrecht* (Heidelberg: Springer 2009), pp 227–78.

Monk, Ray, *Ludwig Wittgenstein. The Duty of Genius* (London: Vintage 1991).

Moravcsik, Andrew, 'Taking Preferences Seriously: A liberal theory of international politics' (1997) 51 *International Organization* 513–53.

Morgenthau, Hans J, 'Positivism, Functionalism and International Law' (1940) 34 *American Journal of International Law* 261–84.

——, *Politics Among Nations the Struggle for Power and Peace* (New York: Knopf 1949).

——, *In Defense of the National Interest: A Critical Examination of American Foreign Policy* (New York: Knopf 1951).

Mouffe, Chantal, *On the Political* (London: Routledge 2005).

Moussalli, Michel, The Evolving Functions of the Office of the High Commissioner for Refugees, in: Vera Gowlland and Klaus Samson (eds), *Problems and Prospects of Refugee Law* (Geneva: The Graduate Institute of International Studies 1992), pp 81–103.

Muggah, Robert (ed), *No Refuge: The crisis of refugee militarization in Africa* (London: Zed 2006).

Müller, Friedrich, Richterrecht—rechtstheoretisch formuliert, in: Richterliche Rechtsfortbildung, *Festschrift der Juristischen Fakultät der Universität Heidelberg* (Heidelberg: 1986), pp 65–84.

——, *Strukturierende Rechtslehre*, vol 1 (Berlin: Duncker und Humblot 1994).

Müller, Harald, 'Arguing, Bargaining and All That: Communicative Action, Rationalist Theory and the Logic of Appropriateness in International Relations' (2004) 10 *European Journal of International Relations* 395–435.

——, Internationale Verhandlungen, Argumente und Verständigungshandeln. Verteidigung, Befunde, Warnung, in: Peter Niesen and B Herborth (eds), *Anarchie der kommunikativen Freiheit. Jürgen Habermas und die Theorie der internationalen Politik* (Frankfurt am Main: Suhrkamp 2007), pp 199–223.

Müllerson, Rein, 'On the Nature and Scope of Customary International Law' (1997) 2 *Austrian Review of International and European Law* 341–60.

Musalo, Karen, 'Claims for Protection based on Religion or Belief' (2004) 16 *International Journal of Refugee Law* 165–226.

Nadelmann, Ethan A, 'Global Prohibition Regimes: The Evolution of Norms in International Society' (1990) 44 *International Organization* 479–526.

Nagel, Thomas, *The Last Word* (Oxford: Oxford University Press 1997).

Nanda, Ved P, The Role of International Organizations in Non-contractual Lawmaking, in: Rüdiger Wolfrum and Volker Röben (eds), *Developments of International Law in Treaty Making* (Heidelberg: Springer 2005), pp 157–70.

Nanz, Patrizia and Jens Steffek, Zivilgesellschaftliche Partizipation und die Demokratisierung internationalen Regierens, in: Peter Niesen and Benjamin Herborth (eds), *Anarchie der kommunikativen Freiheit. Jürgen Habermas und die Theorie der internationalen Politik* (Frankfurt am Main: Suhrkamp 2007), pp 87–110.

Nascimento e Silva, Geraldo Eulalio do, 'Le Facteur Temps et les Traités' (1977) 154 *Recueil des Cours* 215–97.
Navari, Cornelia, 'The Concept of Practice in the English School' (2011) 17 *European Journal of International Relations* 611–30.
Ness, Gayl D and Steven R Brechin, 'Bridging the Gap: International Organizations as Organizations' (1988) 42 *International Organization* 245–73.
Nettesheim, Martin, 'Von der Verhandlungsdiplomatie zur internationalen Wirtschaftsordnung: Zur Entwicklung des internationalen Wirtschaftsrechts' (2000) 19 *Jahrbuch für Neue Politische Ökonomie* 48–76.
Neumann, Jan and Elisabeth Türk, 'Necessity Revisited: Proportionality in World Trade Organization law after Korea-Beef, EC-Asbestos and EC-Sardines' (2003) 37 *Journal of World Trade* 199–233.
Neumann, Ulfried, Theorie der juristischen Argumentation, in: Winfried Brugger, Ulfried Neumann, and Stephan Kirste (eds), *Rechtsphilosophie im 21. Jahrhundert* (Frankfurt am Main: Suhrkamp 2008), pp 233–60.
Neven, Damien J and Joseph H H Weiler, Japan—Measures Affecting the Importation of Apples: One Bad Apple?, in: Henrik Horn and Petros C Mavroidis (eds), *The American Law Institute Reporters' Studies on WTO Case Law* (Cambridge: Cambridge University Press 2007), pp 850–79.
Neves, Marcelo, 'Grenzen der Autonomie des Rechts in einer asymmetrischen Weltgesellschaft' (2007) 93 *Archiv für Rechts- und Sozialphilosophie* 363–95.
Nietzsche, Friedrich, *The Use and Abuse of History for Life* (New York: Cosimo 2006 [1873]).
Nollkaemper, André, *National Courts and the International Rule of Law* (Oxford: Oxford University Press 2011).
——, Inside or Out: Two Types of International Legal Pluralism, in: Jan Klabbers and Touko Piiparinen (eds), *Normative Pluralism and International Law* (forthcoming 2012),
Nolte, Georg, Between Contemporaneous and Evolutive Interpretation: The Use of 'Subsequent Practice' in the Judgment of the International Court of Justice Concerning the Case of Costa Rica v. Nicaragua (2009), in: Holger P Hestermeyer, Doris König, Nele Matz-Lück, Volker Röben, Anja Seibert-Fohr, Peter-Tobias Stoll, and Silja Vöneky (eds), *Coexistence, Cooperation and Solidarity*, vol II (Leiden: Nijhoff 2011), pp 1675–84.
——, Subsequent Practice as a Means of Interpretation in the Jurisprudence of the Appellate Body, in: Enzo Cannizzaro (ed), *The Law of Treaties Beyond the Vienna Convention* (Oxford: Oxford University Press 2011), pp 138–44.
Noortmann, Math, The International Law Association and Non-State Actors: Professional network, public interest group of epistemic community?, in: Jean d'Aspremont (ed), *Participants in the International Legal System: Multiple Perspectives on Non-State Actors in International Law* (London: Routledge 2010), pp 233–47.
North, Douglass C, *Institutions, Institutional Change and Economic Performance* (Cambridge: Cambridge University Press 1990).
O'Connell, Mary Ellen, 'New International Legal Process' (2004) 36 *Studies in Transnational Legal Policy* 79–107.

Oellers-Frahm, Karin, 'Multiplication of International Courts and Tribunals and Conflicting Jurisdiction: Problems and possible solutions' (2001) 5 *Max Planck Yearbook of United Nations Law* 67–104.

——, The Evolving Role of Treaties in International Law in: Russell Miller and Rebecca Bratspies (eds), *Progress in International Law* (Leiden: Nijhoff 2008), pp 173–95.

Oeter, Stefan, Souveränität—ein überholtes Konzept?, in: Hans-Joachim Cremer, Thomas Griegerich, Dagmar Richter, and Andreas Zimmermann (eds), *Tradition und Weltoffenheit des Rechts, Festschrift für Helmut Steinberger* (Berlin: Springer 2002), pp 259–90.

——, Theorising the Global Legal Order—An Institutionalist Perspective, in: Andrew Halpin and Volker Roeben (eds), *Theorising the Global Legal Order* (Oxford: Hart 2009), pp 61–83.

Ogden, Charles K and Ivor A Richards, *The Meaning of Meaning. A Study of the Influence of Language upon Thought and of the Science of Symbolism* (London: Routledge & Kegan 1972).

Ogorek, Regina, *Richterkönig oder Subsumtionsautomat?* (Frankfurt am Main: Klostermann 1986).

Olsen, Johan P, 'Maybe it is Time to Rediscover Bureaucracies' (2006) 16 *Journal of Public Administration Research and Theory* 1–24.

Onuf, Nicholas Greenwood, 'Do Rules Say What They Do? From Ordinary Language to International Law' (1985) 26 *Harvard International Law Journal* 385–410.

——, *World of Our Making: Rules and Rule in Social Theory and International Relations* (Columbia, SC: University of South Carolina Press 1989).

Orakhelashvili, Alexander, *Peremptory Norms in International Law* (Oxford: Oxford University Press 2006).

——, *The Interpretation of Acts and Rules in Public International Law* (Oxford: Oxford University Press 2008).

Orford, Anne, A Jurisprudence of the Limit, in: Anne Orford (ed), *International Law and its Others* (Cambridge: Cambridge University Press 2006), pp 1–33.

Ortino, Federico, *Basic Legal Instruments for the Liberalisation of Trade* (Oxford: Hart 2004).

——, 'Treaty Interpretation and the WTO Appellate Body Report in US—Gambling: A critique' (2006) 9 *Journal of International Economic Law* 117–48.

Palonen, Kari, *Die Entzauberung der Begriffe. Das Umschreiben der politischen Begriffe bei Quentin Skinner und Reinhart Koselleck* (Berlin: LIT Verlag 2003).

——, *Quentin Skinner: History, Politics, Rhetoric* (Cambridge: Polity 2003).

Paris, Roland, 'International peacebuilding and the "mission civilisatrice"' (2002) 28 *Review of International Studies* 637.

Paschke, Karl Th, UNO von innen—die Besonderheiten einer multinationalen Bürokratie, in: Sabine von Schorlemer (ed), *Praxishandbuch UNO. Die Vereinten Nationen im Lichte globaler Herausforderungen* (Berlin, Heidelberg: Springer 2003), pp 553–67.

Patterson, Dennis M, 'Dworkin on the Semantics of Legal and Political Concepts' (2006) 26 *Oxford Journal of Legal Studies* 545–57.

Paulson, Stanley L, Introduction, in: Stanley L Paulson and B Litschewski Paulson (eds), *Normativity and Norms. Critical Perspectives on Kelsenian Themes* (Oxford: Oxford University Press 1998), pp xxiii–liii.

Paulus, Andreas L, *Die internationale Gemeinschaft im Völkerrecht. Eine Untersuchung zur Entwicklung des Völkerrechts im Zeitalter der Globalisierung* (München: Beck 2001).

——, The International Legal System as a Constitution, in: Jeffrey L Dunoff and Joel P Trachtman (eds), *Ruling the World? Constitutionalism, International Law, and Global Governance* (Cambridge: Cambridge University Press 2009), pp 69–111.

Payandeh, Mehrdad, *Internationales Gemeinschaftsrecht* (Heidelberg: Springer 2010).

Payne, Rodger A, 'Persuasion, Frames and Norm Construction' (2001) 7 *European Journal of International Relations* 37–61.

Pelláthy, Gabriel S, The Evolving Definitions of IDPs and Links to Ethnic Cleansing in Europe, in: Steven Béla Várdy and T Hunt Tooley (eds), *Ethnic Cleansing in 20th-century Europe* (Boulder: Columbia University Press 2003), pp 757–72.

Pellet, Alain, Article 38, in: Andreas Zimmermann, Christian Tomuschat, and Karin Oellers-Frahm (eds), *Statute of the International Court of Justice: A Commentary* (Oxford: Oxford University Press 2006), pp 677–792.

Pereira, Ravi Afonso, 'Why Would International Administrative Activity Be Any Less Legitimate?—A Study of the Codex Alimentarius Commission' (2008) 9 *German Law Journal* 1693–718.

Perelman, Chaïm, *Logique Juridique. Nouvelle Rhétorique* (Paris: Dalloz 2001).

Peters, Anne, 'Humanity as the A and Ω of Sovereignty' (2009) 20 *European Journal of International Law* 513–44.

Petersen, Niels, 'Customary lLaw without Custom? Rules, principles, and the role of state practice in international norm creation' (2008) 23 *American University International Law Review* 275–310.

——, *Demokratie als teleologisches Prinzip* (Heidelberg: Springer 2009).

Petersmann, Ernst-Ulrich, 'The Transformation of the World Trading System through the 1994 Agreement Establishing the World Trade Organization' (1995) 6 *European Journal of International Law* 161–221.

——, *The GATT/WTO Dispute Settlement System: International Law, International Organizations and Dispute Settlement* (London: Kluwer 1997).

——, 'Time for a United Nations 'Global Compact' for Integrating Human Rights into the Law of Worldwide Organizations: Lessons from European Integration' (2002) 13 *European Journal of International Law* 621–50.

——, From 'Member-driven Governance' to Constitutionally Limited 'Multi-level Governance' in the WTO, in: Giorgio Sacerdoti, Alan Yanovich, and Jan Bohanes (eds), *The WTO at Ten: The Contribution of the Dispute Settlement System* (Cambridge: Cambridge University Press 2006), pp 86–110.

Pettit, Philip, *A Theory of Freedom. From the Psychology to the Politics of Agency* (Cambridge: Polity 2001).

Pierson, Paul, *Politics in Time. History, Institutions, and Social Analysis* (Princeton: Princeton University Press 2004).

Piiparinen, Touko, 'The Rise and Fall of Bureaucratic Rationalization: Exploring the Possibilities and Limitations of the UN Secretariat in Conflict Prevention' (2008) 14 *European Journal of International Relations* 697–724.

Pilloud, Claude and Yves Sandoz, *Commentary on the Additional Protocols of 8 June 1977 to the Geneva Conventions of 12 August 1949* (Geneva: Nijhoff 1987).

Plantey, Alain and François Loriot, *Fonction publique internationale. Organisations mondiales et européennes* (Paris: CNRS Éd. 2005).

Politis, Nicolas, *La justice internationale* (Paris: Hachette 1924).

Pollack, Mark A, 'Delegation, Agency, and Agenda Setting in the European Community' (1997) 51 *International Organization* 99–134.

Posner, Eric A, *The Perils of Global Legalism* (Chicago: University of Chicago Press 2009).

—— and John C Yoo, 'Judicial Independence in International Tribunals' (2005) 93 *California Law Review* 1–74.

Pouliot, Vincent, 'The Logic of Practicality: A Theory of Practice of Security Communities' (2008) 62 *International Organization* 257–88.

Prott, Lyndel V, 'Argumentation in International Law' (1991) 5 *Argumentation* 299–310.

Pufendorf, Samuel, *De Jure Naturae et Gentium (On the Law of Nature and of Nations)*, vol 1 (Oxford: Clarendon Press 1934 [1672]).

Putnam, Robert D, 'Diplomacy and Domestic Politics: The Logic of Two-Level Games' (1988) 42 *International Organization* 427–60.

Ralston, Jackson H, *International Arbitration from Athens to Locarno* (Stanford, CA: Standord University Press 1929).

Ranshofen-Wertheimer, Egon F, *The International Secretariat. A Great Experiment in International Administration* (Washington, DC: Carnegie Endowment for International Peace 1945).

Rasch, William, 'A Just War? Or Just a War?: Schmitt, Habermas, and the Cosmopolitan Orthodoxy' (2000) 21 *Cardozo Law Review* 1665–84.

Raustiala, Kal, 'Form and Substance in International Agreements' (2005) 99 *American Journal of International Law* 581–614.

Rawls, John, *The Law of Peoples* (Cambridge, MA: Harvard University Press 1999).

Raz, Joseph, Kelsen's Theory of the Basic Norm, in: *The Authority of Law* (Oxford: Oxford University Press 2009), pp 122–45.

Redgwell, Catherine, International Soft Law and Globalization, in: Barry Barton, Lila K Barrera-Hernández, Alstair R Lucas, and Anita Rønne (eds), *Regulating Energy and Natural Resources* (Oxford: Oxford University Press 2006), pp 89–107.

Regan, Donald, 'The Meaning of "Necessary" in GATT Article XX and GATS Article XIV: The myth of cost-benefit balancing' (2007) 6 *World Trade Review* 347–69.

Reiner, Marga and Elisabeth Camp, Metaphor, in: Ernest Lepore and Barry C Smith (eds), *The Oxford Handbook of Philosophy of Language* (Oxford: Oxford University Press 2006), pp 845–63.

Reinisch, August, The International Relations of National Courts: A Discourse on International Law Norms on Jurisdictional and Enforcement Immunity, in: August Reinisch and U Kriebaum (eds), *The Law of International Relations—Liber Amicorum Hanspeter Neuhold* (Utrecht: Eleven 2007), pp 289–309.

Reisman, Michael, 'International Lawmaking: A Process of Communication' (1981) 75 *American Society of International Law Proceedings* 101–20.

——, 'A Jurisprudence from the Perspective of the 'Political Superior' (1996) 23 *Northern Kentucky Law Review* 605–28.

——, 'Unilateral Action and the Transformations of the World Constitutive Process: The special problem of humanitarian intervention' (2000) 11 *European Journal of International Law* 3–18.

Reisman, William Michael (ed), *Toward World Order and Human Dignity. Essays in Honor of Myres S. McDougal* (New York: Free Press 1976).

Reus-Smit, Christian, 'The Strange Death of Liberal International Theory' (2001) 12 *European Journal of International Law* 573–93.

Risse, Thomas, '"Let's Argue!": Communicative Action in World Politics' (2000) 54 *International Organization* 1–39.

——, Transnational Governance and Legitimacy, in: Arthur Benz and Yannis Papadopoulos (eds), *Governance and Democracy: Comparing National, European and International Experiences* (London: Routledge 2006), pp 179–99.

—— and Kathryn Sikkink, The Socialization of International Human Rights Norms into Domestic Practices: Introduction, in: Thomas Risse, Stephen C Ropp, and Kathryn Sikkink (eds), *The Power of Human Rights. International Norms and Domestic Change* (Cambridge: Cambridge University Press 1999), pp 1–38.

Rittberger, Volker (ed), *Regime Theory and International Relations* (Oxford: Oxford University Press 1993).

Roberts, Anthea, 'Traditional and Modern Approaches to Customary International Law' (2001) 95 *American Journal of International Law* 757–91.

Romano, Cesare P R, 'The Proliferation of International Judicial Bodies: The Pieces of the Puzzle' (1999) 31 *NYU Journal of International Law & Politics* 709–51.

——, 'A Taxonomy of International Rule of Law Institutions' (2011) 2 *Journal of International Dispute Settlement* 241–77.

Rorty, Richard, *Philosophy and the Mirror of Nature* (Princeton: Princeton University Press 1979).

——, Wittgenstein, Heidegger, and the Reification of Language, in: Richard Rorty (ed), *Essays on Heidegger and Others*, vol 2 (Cambridge: Cambridge Universtiy Press 1991), pp 50–65.

Ross, Alf, *Theorie der Rechtsquellen* (Leipzig: Deuticke 1929).

Ruggie, John Gerald, 'International Responses to Technology: Concepts and Trends' (1975) 29 *International Organization* 557–83.

——, 'International Regimes, Transactions, and Change: Embedded Liberalism in the Postwar Economic Order' (1982) 36 *International Organization* 379–415.

Ruiz Fabri, Hélène, Drawing a Line of Equilibrium in a Complex World, in: Giorgio Sacerdoti, Alan Yanovich, and Jan Bohanes (eds), *The WTO at Ten: The Contribution of the Dispute Settlement System* (Cambridge: Cambridge University Press 2006), pp 125–42.

——, 'Le juge de l'OMC: Ombres et lumières d'une figure judiciaire singulière' (2006) 110 *Revue Générale de Droit International Public* 39–83.

—— and Constance Grewe, La constitutionalisation à l'épreuve du droit international et du droit européen, in: *Les dynamiques du droit européen en début de siècle. Études en l'honneur de Jean Claude Gautron* (Paris: Pedone 2004), pp 189–206.

Ruozzi, Elisa, L'application du principe de proportionnalité en droit de l'Organisation Mondiale du Commerce, in: Hélène Ruiz Fabri and Lorenzo Gradoni (eds), *La Circulation des Concepts Juridiques* (Paris: Société de législation comparée 2009), pp 475–92.

Salehyan, Idean and Kristian Skrede Gleditsch, 'Refugees and the Spread of Civil War' (2006) 60 *International Organization* 335–66.

Salerno, Francesco (ed), *Il ruolo del giudice internazionale nell'evoluzione del diritto internazionale e comunitario* (Padova: Cedam 1995).

Sandholtz, Wayne, *Prohibiting Plunder: How Norms Change* (Oxford: Oxford University Press 2007).

——, and Kendall Stiles, *International Norms and Cycles of Change* (Oxford: Oxford University Press 2009).

Sandholtz, Wayne and Alec Stone Sweet, Law, Politics, and International Governance, in: Christian Reus-Smit (ed), *The Politics of International Law* (Cambridge: Cambridge University Press 2004), pp 238–71.

Sarasin, Philipp, Diskurstheorie und Geschichtswissenschaft, in: Reiner Keller, Andreas Hirseland, Werner Schneider, and Willy Viehöver (eds), *Handbuch Sozialwissenschaftliche Diskursanalyse*, vol 1 (Wiesbaden: Verlag für Sozialwissenschaften 2006), pp 55–83.

Scelle, George, *Théorie juridique de la révision des traités* (Paris: Recueil Sirey 1936).

——, Le Phénomène Juridique du Dédoublement Fonctionnel, in: Walter Schätzel and H J Schlochauer (eds), *Rechtsfragen Internationaler Organisation. Festschrift für Hans Wehberg* (Frankfurt am Main: Klostermann 1956), pp 324–42.

Schachter, Oscar, 'The Invisible College of International Lawyers' (1977) 72 *Northwestern University Law Review* 217–26.

——, 'The Twilight Existence of Nonbinding International Agreements' (1977) 71 *American Journal of International Law* 296–304.

——, New Custom: Power, Opinio Juris and Contrary Practice, in: Jerzy Makarczyk (ed), *Theory of International Law at the Threshold of the 21st Century. Essays in Honour of Krzysztof Skubiszewski* (The Hague: Kluwer Law International 1996), pp 531–40.

Scharpf, Fritz Wilhelm, *Games Real Actors Play. Actor-centered institutionalism in policy research* (Boulder: Westview Press 1997).

Schatzki, Theodore R, Introduction: Practice Theory, in: Theodore R Schatzki, Karin Knorr Cetina, and Eike von Savigny (eds), *The Practice Turn in Contemporary Theory* (London: Routledge 2001), pp 1–14.

Scheuerman, William E, 'Carl Schmitt and the Road to Abu Ghraib' (2006) 13 *Constellations* 108–24.

Schill, Stephan W, 'International Investment Law and the Host State's Power to Handle Economic Crises. Comment on the ICSID dcision in LG& E v. Argentina' (2007) 24 *Journal of International Arbitration* 265–86.

——, *The Multilateralization of International Investment Law* (Cambridge: Cambridge University Press 2009).

—— and Benedict Kingsbury, Public Law Concepts to Balance Investors' Rights with State Regulatory Actions in the Public Interest—The Concept of Proportionality, in: Stephan W Schill (ed), *International Investment Law and Comparative Public Law* (Oxford: Oxford University Press 2010), pp 75–105.

——, 'System-Building in Investment Treaty Arbitration and Lawmaking' (2011) 12 *German Law Journal* 1083–110.

Schlieben-Lange, Brigitte, 'Die Französische Revolution und die Sprache' (1981) 41 *Zeitschrift für Literaturwissenschaft und Linguistik* 90–123.

Schlink, Bernhard, *Abwägung im Verfassungsrecht* (Berlin: Duncker & Humblot 1976).

——, Der Grundsatz der Verhältnismäßigkeit, in: Peter Badura and Horst Dreier (eds), *Festschrift 50 Jahre Bundesverfassungsgericht* (Tübingen: Mohr Siebeck 2001), pp 445–65.

Schmitt, Carl, *Die Wendung zum diskriminierenden Kriegsbegriff* (Berlin: Duncker und Humblot 1938).
——, *Der Begriff des Politischen. Text von 1932 mit einem Vorwort und 3 Corollarien* (Berlin: Duncker & Humblot 1963).
——, *The Concept of the Political* (Chicago: Chicago University Press 1996).
Schnyder, Félix, 'Les aspects juridiques actuels du problème des réfugiés' (1965) 114 *Recueil des Cours* 341–450.
Schrijver, Nico, *The Evolution of Sustainable Development in International Law: Inception, Meaning and Status* (Leiden: Nijhoff 2008).
Schücking, Walther (ed), Die Organisation der Welt, in: Wilhelm van Calker (ed), *Staatsrechtliche Abhandlungen. Festgabe für Paul Laband zum 50. Jahrestage der Doktor-Promotion* (Tübingen: Mohr 1908), pp 533–617.
——, *Das Werk vom Haag* (München: Duncker & Humblot 1912).
Schwingel, Markus, *Pierre Bourdieu* (Hamburg: Junius 1995).
Scobbie, Iain, 'Res Judicata, Precedent, and the International Court: A Preliminary Sketch' (1999) 20 *Australian Yearbook of International Law* 299–318.
Scott, James Brown, *The Hague Peace Conferences of 1899 and 1907* (Baltimore: Johns Hopkins 1909).
——, 'A Permanent Court of International Justice (Editorial Comment)' (1921) 15 *American Journal of International Law* 53–5.
Scott, John, *Power* (Cambridge: Polity Press 2001).
Searle, John R, A Taxonomy of Illocutionary Acts, in: *Expression and Meaning: Studies in the Theory of Speech Acts* (Cambridge: Cambridge University Press 1979), pp 1–19.
Sebastian, Thomas, 'World Trade Organization Remedies and the Assessment of Proportionality: Equivalence and Appropriateness' (2007) 48 *Harvard International Law Journal* 337–82.
Sen, Amartya, *The Idea of Justice* (Cambridge, MA: Harvard University Press 2009).
Shahabuddeen, Mohamed, *Precedent in the World Court* (Cambridge: Cambridge University Press 1996).
Shany, Yuval, *Regulating Jurisdictional Relations Between National and International Courts* (New York: Oxford University Press 2007).
——, 'No Longer a Weak Department of Power? Reflections on the Emergence of a New International Judiciary' (2009) 20 *European Journal of International Law* 73–91.
Shelton, Dinah (ed), *Commitment and Compliance. The Role of Non-Binding Norms in the International Legal System* (Oxford: Oxford University Press 2000).
——, Introduction: Law, Non-Law and the Problem of 'Soft Law', in: Dinah Shelton (ed), *Commitment and Compliance. The Role of Non-Binding Norms in the International Legal System* (Oxford: Oxford University Press 2000), pp 1–19.
Shklar, Judith N, *Legalism* (Cambridge, MA: Harvard University Press 1964).
Simma, Bruno, 'From Bilateralism to Community Interest in International Law' (1994) 250 *Recueil des Cours* 221–384.
—— and Philip Alston, 'The Sources of Human Rights Law: Custom, Jus Cogens, and General Principles' (1988) 12 *Australian Yearbook of International Law* 82–108.
Simma, Bruno, Stefan Brunner, and Hans-Peter Kaul, Article 27, in: Bruno Simma (ed), *The Charter of the United Nations: A Commentary* (Oxford: Oxford University Press 2002), pp 476–523.

Simmons, Beth A and Lisa L Martin, International Organizations and Institutions, in: Walter Carlsnaes, Thomas Risse, and Beth A Simmons (eds), *Handbook of International Relations* (London: Sage Publications 2002), pp 192–211.

Simon, Denys, *L'Interprétation judiciaire des traités d'organisations internationales* (Paris: Pedone 1981).

Simpson, Gerry, 'Imagined Consent: Democratic Liberalism in International Legal Theory' (1994) 15 *Australian Yearbook of International Law* 103–28.

——, *Great Powers and Outlaw States. Unequal Sovereigns in the International Legal Order* (Cambridge: Cambridge University Press 2004).

Sinclair, Ian MacTaggart, *The Vienna Convention on the Law of Treaties* (Manchester: Manchester University Press 1984).

Skinner, Quentin, 'Rhetoric and Conceptual Change' (1999) 3 *Finnish Yearbook of Political Thought* 60–72.

Skouteris, Thomas, *The Notion of Progress in International Law Discourse* (The Hague: Asser 2010).

——, The Force of a Doctrine: Art. 38 of the PCIJ Statute and the Sources of International Law, in: Fleur Johns, Richard Joyce, and Sundhya Pahuja (eds), *Events: The Force of International Law* (Abingdon: Routledge 2011), pp 69–80.

Skran, Claudena M, Historical Development of International Refugee Law, in: Andreas Zimmermann (ed), *The 1951 Convention Relating to the Status of Refugees and its 1967 Protocol: A Commentary* (Oxford: Oxford University Press 2011), pp 3–36.

Slaughter, Amy and Jeff Crisp, 'A Surrogate State? The role of UNHCR in protracted refugee situations' (2009) *New Issues in Refugee Research, Research Paper No. 168, UNHCR.*

Slaughter, Anne-Marie, 'A Typology of Transjudicial Communication' (1994) 29 *University of Richmond Law Review* 99–137.

——, 'International Law and International Relations' (2000) 285 *Recueil des Cours* 13–249.

——, 'A Liberal Theory of International Law' (2000) 94 *Proceedings of the American Society of International Law* 240–49.

——, *A New World Order* (Princeton: Princeton University Press 2004).

—— and Laurence R Helfer, 'Why States Create International Tribunals: A Response to Professors Posner and Yoo' (2005) 93 *California Law Review* 899–956.

Smrkolj, Maja, 'International Bureaucracies and Individualized Decision-Making: An Example of UNHCR's Refuge Status Determination' (2008) 9 *German Law Journal* 1779–803.

Snidal, Duncan, 'Political Economy and International Institutions' (1996) 16 *International Review of Law and Economics* 121–37.

Somek, Alexander, 'Legal Formality and Freedom of Choice. A Moral Perspective on Jhering's Constructivism' (2002) 15 *Ratio Juris* 52–62.

——, Ermächtigung und Verpflichtung: Ein Versuch über Normativität bei Hans Kelsen, in: Stanley L Paulson and Michael Stolleis (eds), *Hans Kelsen: Staatsrechtslehrer und Rechtstheoretiker des 20. Jahrhunderts* (Tübingen: Mohr Siebeck 2005), pp 58–79.

——, 'The Concept of 'Law' in Global Administrative Law: A Reply to Benedict Kingsbury' (2009) 20 *European Journal of International Law* 985–95.

Sorel, Jean-Marc and Valérie Boré-Eveno, Article 31, in: Olivier Corten and Pierre Klein (eds), *The Vienna Conventions on the Law of Treaties: A Commentary* (Oxford: Oxford University Press 2011), pp 804–37.

Sørensen, Max, *Les sources du droit international. Étude sur la jurisprudence de la Cour Permanente de Justice Internationale* (Copenhague: Munksgaard 1946).

Spiermann, Ole, *International Legal Argument in the Permanent Court of International Justice. The rise of the international judiciary* (Cambridge: Cambridge University Press 2005).

Staden, Andreas von, 'Democratic Legitimacy of Review Beyond the State: The Need for an Appropriate Standard of Review' (2011) *Jean Monnet Working Paper* 10/11.

Steffek, Jens, 'The Legitimation of International Governance: A Discourse Approach' (2003) 9 *European Journal of International Relations* 249–76.

Stein, Ted L, 'The Approach of the Different Drummer: The Principle of the Persistent Objector in International Law' (1985) 26 *Harvard International Law Journal* 467–82.

Sterling-Folker, Jennifer, Realist Global Governance: Revisiting *cave! hic dragones* and beyond, in: Alice D Ba and Matthew J Hoffmann (eds), *Contending Perspectives on Global Governance. Coherence, Contestation and World Order* (London: Routledge 2005), pp 17–38.

Stewart, Richard B and Michelle Ratton Sanchez Badin, 'The World Trade Organization and Global Administrative Law' (2011) 9 *International Journal of Constitutional Law* 556–86.

Stoessinger, John G, *The Refugee and the World Community* (Minneapolis: University of Minnesota Press 1956).

Stone Sweet, Alec and Judd Mathews, 'Proportionality Balancing and Global Constitutionalism' (2008) 47 *Columbia Journal of Transnational Law* 73–165.

Strange, Susan, Cave! Hic Dragones: A Critique of Regime Analysis, in: Stephen D Krasner (ed), *International Regimes* (Ithaca, NY: Cornell University Press 1983), pp 337–54.

Sunstein, Cass R and Adrian Vermeule, "Interpretation and institutions" (2003) 101 *Michigan Law Review* 885–951.

Swart, Mia, 'Judicial Lawmaking at the Ad Hoc Tribunals: the Creative Use of the Sources of International Law and "Adventurous Interpretation"' (2010) 70 *Zeitschrift für ausländisches öffentliches Recht und Völkerrecht* 459–86.

Sweetser, Arthur, 'The World's Civil Service' (1945) 30 *Iowa Law Review* 478–89.

Sztucki, Jerzy, 'The Conclusions on the International Protection of Refugees Adopted by the Executive Committee of the UNHCR Programme' (1989) 1 *International Journal of Refugee Law* 285–318.

——, Who is a Refugee? The Convention definition: universal or obsolete?, in: Frances Nicholson and Patrick Twomey (eds), *Refugee Rights and Realities: Evolving international concepts and regimes* (Cambridge: Cambridge University Press 1999), pp 55–80.

Tarullo, Daniel K, 'Logic, Myth, and the International Economic Order' (1985) 26 *Harvard International Law Journal* 533–52.

Taylor, Charles, To Follow a Rule . . . in: Craig Calhoun, Edward LiPuma, and Moishe Postone (eds), *Bourdieu: Critical Perspectives* (Chicago: University of Chicago Press 1993), pp 45–60.

Teitel, Ruti G, 'Humanity's Law: Rule of Law for the New Global Politics' (2002) 35 *Cornell International Law Journal* 355–87.

——, *Humanity's Law* (New York: Oxford University Press 2011).

—— and Robert Howse, 'Cross-Judging: Tribunalization in a fragmented but interconnected global order' (2009) 41 *NYU Journal of International Law & Politics* 959–90.

Tesón, Fernando R, *Humanitarian Intervention. An Inquiry into Law and Morality* (Ardsley, NY: Transnational Publishers 2005).

Teubner, Gunther, *Recht als autopoietisches System* (Frankfurt am Main: Suhrkamp 1989).

——, 'Global Bukowina' : Legal Pluralism in the World Society, in: *Global Law Without a State* (Aldershot: Dartmouth 1997), pp 3–28.

——, 'Globale Zivilverfassungen: Alternativen zur staatszentrierten Verfassungstheorie' (2003) 63 *Zeitschrift für ausländisches öffentliches Recht und Völkerrecht* 1–28.

Thirlway, Hugh W A, *International Customary Law and Codification. An Examination of the Continuing Role of Custom in the Present Period of Codification of International Law* (Leiden: Sijthoff 1972).

Tomuschat, Christian, 'International Law: Ensuring the Survival of Mankind on the Eve of a New Century' (2001) 281 *Recueil des Cours* 13–438.

Trachtman, Joel P, 'The Domain of WTO Dispute Resolution' (1999) 40 *Harvard International Law Journal* 333–78.

——, 'The World Trading System, the International Legal System and Multilevel Choice' (2006) 12 *European Law Journal* 469–85.

Trebilcock, Michael J and Robert Howse, *The Regulation of International Trade* (London: Routledge 2005).

Treves, Tullio, Judicial Lawmaking in an Era of 'Proliferation' of International Courts and Tribunals: Development or Fragmentation of International Law?, in: Rüdiger Wolfrum and Volker Röben (eds), *Developments of International Law in Treaty Making* (Berlin: Springer 2005), pp 587–620.

Trevisanut, Seline, 'The Principle of Non-Refoulement at Sea and the Effectiveness of Asylum Protection' (2008) 12 *Max Planck Yearbook of United Nations Law* 205–46.

——, La convention des Nations Unies sur le droit de la mer et le droit de l'environnement: développement intrasystémique et renvoi intersystémique, in: Hélène Ruiz Fabri and Lorenzo Gradoni (eds), *La Circulation des Concepts Juridiques* (Paris: Société de législation comparée 2009), pp 397–426.

Triepel, Heinrich, *Völkerrecht und Landesrecht* (Leipzig: Hirschfeldt 1899).

Türk, Volker, *Das Flüchtlingshochkommissariat der Vereinten Nationen (UNHCR)* (Berlin: Duncker und Humblot 1992).

——, The Role of UNHCR in the Development of International Refugee Law, in: Frances Nicholson and Patrick Twomey (eds), *Refugee Rights and Realities: Evolving international concepts and regimes* (Cambridge: Cambridge University Press 1999), pp 153–74.

——, 'UNHCR's supervisory responsibility' (2001) 14 *Revue Québécoise de Droit International* 135–58.

—— and Elizabeth Eyster, 'Strengthening Accountability in UNHCR' (2010) 22 *International Journal of Refugee Law* 159–72.

Ulbert, Cornelia and Thomas Risse, 'Deliberately Changing the Discourse: What Does Make Arguing Effective?' (2005) 40 *Acta Politica* 351–67.

van Damme, Isabelle, *Treaty Interpretation by the WTO Appellate Body* (Oxford: Oxford University Press 2009).

Venzke, Ingo, 'International Bureaucracies in a Political Science Perspective—Agency, Authority and International Institutional Law' (2008) 9 *German Law Journal* 1401–28.

——, 'Legal Contestation about "Enemy Combatants": On the Exercise of Power in Legal Interpretation' (2009) 5 *Journal of International Law & International Relations* 155–84.

Venzke, Ingo, 'Making General Exceptions: The Spell of Precedents in Developing Art. XX into Standards for Domestic Regulatory Policy' (2011) 12 *German Law Journal* 1111–40.

——, Antinomies and Change in International Dispute Settlement: An Exercise in Comparative Procedural Law, in: Rüdiger Wolfrum and Ina Gätzschmann (eds), *International Dispute Settlement: Room for Innovations* (Heidelberg: Springer 2012, forthcoming).

——, 'The Role of International Courts as Interpreters and Developers of the Law: Working out the Jurisgenerative Practice of Interpretation' (2012) 34 *Loyola of Los Angeles International and Comparative Law Review* 119–51.

Verbeek, Bertjan, International Organizations. The ugly duckling of international relations theory?, in: Bob Reinalda and Bertjan Verbeek (eds), *Autonomous Policy Making by International Organizations* (London: Routledge 1998), pp 11–26.

Verdirame, Guglielmo, 'The Genocide Definition in the Jurisprudence of the AdHoc Tribunals' (2000) 49 *International and Comparative Law Quarterly* 578–98.

Verdross, Alfred, *Die Verfassung der Völkerrechtsgemeinschaft* (Wien: Springer 1926).

——, Die allgemeinen Rechtsgrundsätze des Völkerrechts, in: Alfred Verdross (ed), *Gesellschaft, Staat und Recht. Untersuchungen zur Reinen Rechtslehre, Festschrift für Hans Kelsen* (Wien: Springer 1931), pp 354–60.

——, *Völkerrecht* (Wien: Springer 1950).

—— and Bruno Simma, *Universelles Völkerrecht. Theorie und Praxis* (Berlin: Duncker & Humblot 1984).

Vernant, Jacques, *The Refugee in the Post-war World* (London: Allen & Unwin 1953).

Vesting, Thomas, 'Kein Anfang und kein Ende. Die Systemtheorie des Rechts als Herausforderung für Rechtswissenschaft und Rechtsdogmatik' (2001) *JURA* 299–305.

——, *Rechtstheorie* (München: Beck 2007).

Villegas, Mauricio García, 'On Pierre Bourdieu's Legal Thought' (2004) 56–57 *Droit et Société* 57–71.

Vollrath, Ernst, *Was ist das Politische? Eine Theorie des Politischen und seiner Wahrnehmung* (Würzburg: Könighausen & Neumann 2003).

Voßkuhle, Andreas, 'Gibt es und wozu nutzt eine Lehre vom Verfassungswandel?' (2004) 43 *Der Staat* 450–9.

Vukas, Budislav, Generally Accepted International Rules and Standards, in: Alfred H Soons (ed), *Implementation of the Law of the Sea Convention through International Institutions* (Honolulu: The Law of the Sea Institute 1990), pp 405–21.

Wagner, Kristen, 'UNHCR's Involvement in the Great Lakes Refugee Crisis' (2009) 21 *Pace International Law Review* 365–86.

Waibel, Michael, 'Demystifying the Art of Interpretation (Review Essay)' (2011) 22 *European Journal of International Law* 571–88.

Waldron, Jeremy, The Rule of Law as a Theatre of Debate, in: Justine Burley (ed), *Dworkin and his Critics* (Malden, MA: Blackwell Publishers 2004), pp 319–36.

Walker, Neil, 'Beyond Boundary Disputes and Basic Grids: Mapping the Global Disorder of Normative Orders' (2008) 6 *International Journal of Constitutional Law* 373–96.

Waltz, Kenneth N, *Man, the State, and War. A Theoretical Analysis* (New York: Columbia University Press 1959).

Watson, Alan, *The Evolution of Law* (Oxford: Blackwell 1985).

Weber, Max, Politik als Beruf (1919), in: *Gesammelte Politische Schriften* (Tübingen: Mohr 1971).

——, Wissenschaft als Beruf (1917/19), in: Horst Baier (ed), *Max Weber Gesamtausgabe*, vol 17 (Tübingen: Mohr Siebeck 1992).

——, *Wirtschaft und Gesellschaft* (Paderborn: Voltmedia 2006 [1922]).

Wehberg, Hans, 'Friedrich von Martens und die Haager Friedenskonferenzen' (1910) 20 *Zeitschrift für internationales Recht* 343–57.

——, *Die internationale Friedensbewegung*, Staatsbürgerbibliothek Heft 22 (Mönchengladbach: Volksvereins-Verlag 1911).

——, *Das Problem eines internationalen Staatengerichtshofes* (München: Duncker & Humblot 1912).

——, 'Die Organisation der Staatengemeinschaft nach dem Kriege—Das Problem einer wahren Repräsentation der Völker' (1944) 44 *Die Friedens-Warte* 49–74.

Weil, Prosper, 'Le droit international en quête de son identité' (1992) 237 *Recueil des Cours* 9–370.

Weiler, Joseph H H, 'The Transformation of Europe' (1991) 100 *Yale Law Journal* 2403–83.

——, 'A Quiet Revolution: The European Court of Justice and its Interlocutors' (1994) 26 *Comparative Political Studies* 510–34.

——, Epilogue: Towards a Common Law of International Trade, in: Joseph H H Weiler (ed), *The EU, the WTO and the NAFTA. Towards a common law of international trade?* (Oxford: Oxford University Press 2000), pp 201–32.

——, 'The Rule of Lawyers and the Ethos of Diplomats. Reflections on the Internal and External Legitimacy of WTO Dispute Settlement' (2001) 35 *Journal of World Trade* 191–207.

——, 'The Geology of International Law—Governance, Democracy and Legitimacy' (2004) 64 *Zeitschrift für ausländisches öffentliches Recht und Völkerrecht* 547–62.

——, Law, Culture, and Values in the WTO—Gazing into the Crystal Ball, in: Daniel L Bethlehem, Donald RcRae, Rodney Neufeld, and Isabelle Van Damme (eds), *The Oxford Handbook of International Trade Law* (Oxford: Oxford University Press 2009), pp 749–72.

Weinrib, Ernest J, 'Legal Formalism: On the Immanent Rationality of Law' (1988) 97 *Yale Law Journal* 949–1016.

Weis, Paul, 'Le concept de réfugié en droit international' (1960) 87 *Journal du Droit International* 929–1001.

——, 'The 1967 Protocol relating to the Status of Refugees and Some Questions of the Law of Treaties' (1967) 42 *British Yearbook of International Law* 39–70.

Weiss, Thomas G, *International Bureaucracy. An analysis of the operation of functional and global international secretariats* (Lexington, MS: Lexington Books 1975).

—— and Amir Pasić, 'Reinventing UNHCR: Enterprising Humanitarians in the Former Yugoslavia' (1997) 3 *Global Governance* 41.

Wendt, Alexander, 'The Agent-Structure Problem in International Relations Theory' (1987) 41 *International Organization* 335–70.

——, 'Anarchy is What States Make of It: The Social Construction of Power Politics' (1992) 46 *International Organization* 391–425.

——, *Social Theory of International Politics* (Cambridge: Cambridge University Press 2000).

Wendt, Alexander, 'Driving with the Rearview Mirror: On the Rational Science of Institutional Design' (2001) 55 *International Organization* 1019–49.

White, Hayden, 'The Question of Narrative in Contemporary Historical Theory' (1984) 23 *History and Theory* 1–33.

Wiener, Antje, Die Wende zum Dialog: Konstruktivistische Brückenstationen und ihre Zukunft, in: Gunther Hellmann, Klaus Dieter Wolf, and Michael Zürn (eds), *Die neuen Internationalen Beziehungen. Forschungsstand und Perspektiven in Deutschland* (Baden-Baden: Nomos 2003), pp 133–59.

——, 'Contested Compliance: Interventions on the Normative Structure of World Politics' (2004) 10 *European Journal of International Relations* 189–234.

—— and Uwe Puetter, 'The Quality of Norms is What Actors Make of It. Critical Constructivist Research on Norms' (2009) 5 *Journal of International Law & International Relations* 1–15.

Wilde, Ralph, *International Territorial Administration: How the Truseeship and the Civilizing Mission Never Went Away* (Oxford: Oxford University Press 2008).

Williamson, Oliver E, *The Mechanisms of Governance* (New York: Oxford University Press 1996).

Winkler, Markus, 'Die normativität des Praktischen' (2009) *Juristenzeitung* 821–29.

Wittgenstein, Ludwig, *Philosophical Investigations* (Oxford: Blackwell 1958).

——, *On Certainty* (Oxford: Blackwell 1969).

——, *Philosophische Untersuchungen* (Frankfurt am Main: Suhrkamp 1984).

Wolfrum, Rüdiger, Die Kontrolle der auswärtigen Gewalt, in: *Veröffentlichungen der Vereinigung der Deutschen Staatsrechtler*, vol 56 (Berlin: de Gruyter 1997), pp 38–66.

——, Article XX GATT 1994, General Exceptions [Chapeau], in: Rüdiger Wolfrum, Peter-Tobias Stoll, and Karen Kaiser (eds), *Max Planck Commentaries on World Trade Law*, vol 2 (Leiden: Nijhoff 2006), pp 66–79.

—— and Volker Röben (eds), *Developments of International Law in Treaty Making* (Berlin: Springer 2005).

Wouters, Jan and Bart De Meester, *The World Trade Organization. A Legal and Institutional Analysis* (Antwerp: Intersentia 2007).

Xu, Yi-Chong and Patrick Moray Weller, *The Governance of World Trade. International Civil Servants and GATT/WTO* (Cheltenham: Elgar 2004).

Yasseen, Mustafa K, 'L'interprétation des traités d'après la Convention de Vienne sur le droit des traités' (1976) 151 *Recueil des Cours* 1–114.

Young, Stephen B, 'Between Sovereigns: A Reexamination of the Refugee's Status' (1982) 3 *Michigan Yearbook of International Legal Studies* 339–72.

Zamboni, Mauro, *Law and Politics. A Dilemma for Contemporary Legal Theory* (Heidelberg: Springer 2007).

Zangl, Bernhard, Das Entstehen internationaler Rechtstaatlichkeit?, in: Stephan Leibfried and Michael Zürn (eds), *Transformationen des Staates?* (Frankfurt am Main: Suhrkamp 2006), pp 123–50.

Zemanek, Karl, The Metamorphosis of *Jus Cogens*: From an Institution of Treaty Law to the Bedrock of the International Legal Order, in: Enzo Cannizzaro (ed), *The Law of Treaties Beyond the Vienna Convention* (Oxford: Oxford University Press 2011), pp 381–409.

Zieck, Marjoleine, *UNHCR and Voluntary Repatriation of Refugees: A Legal Analysis* (Dordrecht: Kluwer 1997).

——, *UNHCR's Worldwide Presence in the Field* (Nijmegen: Wolf Legal Publishers 2006).

——, *UNHCR's Parallel Universe: Marking the Contours of a Problem* (Amsterdam: Amsterdam University Press 2010).

——, Article 35 of the 1951 Convention/Article II of the 1967 Protocol, in: Andreas Zimmermann (ed), *The 1951 Convention Relating to the Status of Refugees and its 1967 Protocol: A Commentary* (Oxford: Oxford University Press 2011), pp 1459–510.

Zimmermann, Andreas and Rainer Hofmann (eds), *Unity and Diversity in International Law* (Berlin: Duncker & Humblot 2006).

Zink, Karl Friedrich, Zur Bestimmung des Begriffs 'Verfolgung' im Sinne des Abkommens vom 28. Juli 1951 über die Rechtsstellung der Flüchtlinge, in: Martin Kornrumpf (ed), *Zweites Internationales Asyl-Colloquium* (Köln: Heymanns 1965), pp 115–22.

Zolo, Danilo, 'Hans Kelsen: International Peace through International Law' (1998) 9 *European Journal of International Law* 306–24.

Zorn, Philipp, *Die beiden Haager Friedenskonferenzen von 1899 und 1907* (Stuttgart: Kohlhammer 1914).

Zürn, Michael, *Regieren jenseits des Nationalstaates: Globalisierung und Denationalisierung als Chance* (Frankfurt am Main: Suhrkamp 1998).

——, 'Global Governance and Legitimacy Problems' (2004) 39 *Government and Opposition* 260–87.

Zwaan, Karin, *UNHCR and the European Asylum Law* (Nijmegen: Wolf 2005).

Index

abuse of rights 181
acceptance (of interpretative claims) 5, 17, 37, 40, 48, 55, 58, 60–3, 86, 122, 198, 218–22
accountability 223, 240–1, 250 *see also* legitimacy
actors, scope of 17, 64–71, 237 *see also* legal discourse, participants
Ador, Gustav 90
Aegean Sea Continental Shelf 39 n117, 232
Aga Khan, Sadruddin 103–4
agency slack 81
Ago, Roberto 2, 66
agorae 254–5
agreement *see also* sources (of international law), treaty
  enforcement of 78–9
  genuine 61–2, 218
  subsequent 233–9
  tacit 24
Agreement Establishing the World Trade Organization 150, 168, 177, 234–5
Agreement on Sanitary and Phytosanitary Measures 74, 168
Agreement on Technical Barriers to Trade 74, 168
Alvarez, José 144, 180
amicus curiae 67, 119–21, 126, 195, 244, 256
Anti-Dumping Agreement 171
Appellate Body 8, 39, 50, 63, 149–50, 153–5, 160, 167–95, 233–4
Arbitration Regarding the Iron Rhine 231, 233
Arendt, Hannah 255
arguing, logic and practice of 217–24 *see also* communicative action
argument, definition of 219
argumentative self-entrapment 218
Austin, John L 54–5
authority *see also* semantic authority; ultimate authority
  and power 57, 61–2
  of international institutions 8, 10, 70–1, 76–87, 119–22, 169–71, 247
  delegation 63, 77–82
  international public 243–5
  justification 13, 62–4, 224, 229–30, 240–5, 247
  spheres 257–8, 265
autonomy
  individual 248
  of domestic courts 69
  of international bureaucracies 76–8, 82–7
  of international courts 69, 169
  of international institutions 238
  public 251
  regulatory 189–93, 258
autopoiesis 35, 38

Barnett, Michael 82, 105
Begriffsjurisprudenz 3
Bentham, Jeremy 20
Benvenisti, Eyal 68, 131
Berman, Paul Schiff 34–5
Bernhardt, Rudolf 4
Bodin, Jean 21 n14
Boré-Eveno, Valérie 51
Bourdieu, Pierre 42
Boyle, Alan 226, 229
Brandom, Robert 49, 56, 64, 221 n122 *see also* semantic pragmatism
Broches, Aron 138
Brown Scott, James 142
Bull, Hedley 206, 213
Bundesverfassungsgericht *see* German Constitutional Court
Bureaucracies *see* international bureaucracies
Busse, Dietrich 58

Cançado Trindade, Antônio Augusto 201
Carr, Edward Hallett 212–13
Charter of the United Nations *see* United Nations Charter
Chimni, Bhupinder 11–12
China—Publications and Audiovisual Products 8, 39, 179
Chinkin, Christine 227
civil servants 82–5, 97
classical liberalism 16, 18, 20, 52, 56, 248
Clausewitz, Carl von 205–6
Codex Alimentarius Commission 74
Cold War 92, 95, 106
colonialism 207–8
Committee on Trade and Environment 168
communicative action 217–23
Conclusions on International Protection 115–17
consent 1–2, 4, 6, 8–9, 16, 19–29, 47–51, 57, 64, 82, 131, 170, 196, 201, 225–32, 237–9, 247, 248, 255
constative speech acts *see* speech acts, constative
constitution
  interpretation of 53
  constitutional doctrine 189, 258
  domestic constitutions 36, 249, 258, 259 n285
  of the international legal order 204 *see also* constitutionalism in international law
  United Nations Charter 52

constitution (*cont.*)
World Trade Organization 189
constitutional change 6 n23
constitutional judiciary 30, 249, 258 *see also* German Constitutional Court
constitutionalism in international law 52, 204–5, 216
constraint (in interpretation) 5, 37, 43–4, 48–9, 54–7
constructivism 43–5, 85
content (of legal commitments) 54, 57, 63–4, 197, 237, 248
contestability 46–9
context (meaning) 2–3, 50, 54, 62, 85, 114, 133, 176, 179, 262
Convention against Torture 124
Convention on the Elimination of All Forms of Racial Discrimination 127
Convention on the Rights and Duties of States 20
Coşeriu, Eugeniu 40
cosmopolitanism 10, 67, 214, 250–2
Court of Justice of the European Union 161, 251–2
courts *see* domestic courts; international courts
Cover, Robert 33 n83, 34, 60 n229
Crawford, James 66
culture of formalism 49, 223 *see also* formalism
customary international law *see* sources (of international law), custom

Davidson, Donald 56, 220 n121
de Vitoria, Francisco 204
de Wet, Erika 87
deformalization 229 *see also* culture of formalism; formalism; soft law
delegation of authority *see* authority, delegation of
democratic legitimacy *see* legitimacy
Derrida, Jacques 29 n60
dictionary 184
Diderot, Denis 28
direct effect (doctrine of) 260
displaced persons 90, 92, 98, 102–4, 108, 126, 133
Dispute Regarding Navigational and Related Rights 231–3
Dispute Settlement Understanding 79, 168–9, 178, 191
Article 3(2) 26, 170, 176
Article 19(2) 170
Article 11 172, 178
Article 17 (6) 178
Article 21(5) 177–8, 193
Article 22(4) 183
distinction between law-creation and law-application 19, 31, 54–6, 117, 237
distinction between *lex lata* and *lege ferenda* 32, 54–5, 237
distinction between law and non-law 35, 37, 48, 198, 226 *see also* legal discourse; soft law; validity
distinction between permissible and impermissible interpretations 51, 54–5 *see also* constraint (in interpretation); contents (of legal commitments)
domestic courts 68–9, 118, 122, 131–2, 227, 238, 258–60
due process 195
Dworkin, Ronald 54 n199

Encyclopédie (French Revolution) 28–9, 246
English School (of International Relations) 213
entrapment, *see* **argumentative self-entrapment**
European Convention of Human Rights and Fundamental Freedoms 121, 137, 183, 258–9
European Court of Human Rights 39, 121, 135, 137, 183, 258–9
European Court of Justice *see* Court of Justice of the European Union
evolution 37–41, 43, 107, 189, 231–4 *see also* interpretation, evolutive
Executive Committee 80, 89, 104–5, 114–19, 123–4
expectations
cognitive 5 n18
normative 5, 146, 192
expertise 78, 82, 85–8, 118–19, 224

Falk, Richard 68
Faust 1–3, 46, 264
Finnemore, Martha 82, 105
Fischer-Lescano, Andreas 66
Fish, Stanley 17
Food and Agricultural Organization 74
force
behind the law 1, 3–4, 6, 17, 51–2
binding force 26, 49, 149
normative force 6, 16–17, 56, 64 *see also* normativity
of ideas 213
of justice 14, 207
formalism 6, 12, 33, 37, 49, 131, 223, 229, 241
foundation *see* legitimacy, foundation
fragmentation 9, 67–8, 132, 194
French Revolution 19–20, 27–9, 58–9, 246
functionalism (in international relations) 33, 82–4, 163, 175, 226

Gallie, Walter Bryce 47
General Agreement on Tariffs and Trade 148–9
Article III 152–5, 167, 173–4, 186
Article XX 138, 150–94, 207, 257
Article XXIII 136–7
GATT secretariat 79, 148–9, 154, 164–5

general principles of law *see* sources (of international law), general principles
generic terms 8, 39, 102, 104, 179, 232–3
Geneva Convention Relating to the Status of Refugees 8, 75, 93, 100, 109–34, 203, 227
  Article 35 78, 112, 117, 119–20
German Constitutional Court 182, 251, 258–60
Giddens, Anthony 44
global administrative law 240–3
global goals 76, 82–3, 202–7, 211, 215, 222, 229
global governance 10, 22, 226, 229, 241–3
good offices 98–103
Goodwin-Gill, Guy 103, 110, 124
Görgülü 258
Grahl-Madsen, Atle 125
grammar 11, 47–8, 59 *see also* structure
Guidelines on International Protection 63, 69, 116–20, 129–30, 258

Habermas, Jürgen 13 n47, 52, 216–223
Handbook on Procedures and Criteria for Determining Refugee 116–19, 124, 127
Hart, Herbert Lionel Adolphus 22, 46, 55
Hegel, Georg Wilhelm Friedrich 21 n15, 56
hegemony 61–2, 209, 216, 222
hermeneutics 3, 50–1
Heuven Goedhart, Gerrit J van 97
historical school of law 41
Hobbes, Thomas 20, 21 n14
Hocké, Jean-Pierre 105
House of Lords 118, 128–30
Howse, Robert 156, 251
Hudec, Robert 148
Hudson, Manley O 6–7, 142–3,
human dignity 32, 123, 203
humanitarian assistance 75, 87–90, 99, 102–8
humanitarian intervention 202–3
humanitarianism 33, 101–3, 199–203, 207–10
humanity 25, 201, 203–4, 207–11
human rights discourse 52, 67, 73, 108, 122–4, 127, 129–31, 201, 205
Hurrell, Andrew 214–6

imperialism 207–8
implied powers 70
indeterminacy 37, 46–9, 60, 196, 197
Institut de Droit International 69, 140, 231
institutional design 9, 13, 242, 252–6
institutionalism 8, 44
instrumentalism 208, 229
intent 2–3, 26 n45, 55, 56, 81, 128, 136, 153–5, 230–4, 239 *see also* consent
Inter-American Court of Human Rights 121
interface norms 256 *see also* relationship between international and domestic law
internally displaced persons 104, 126
internal point of view 225
international adjudication *see* international courts
international bureaucracies 69–70, 75–87, 119, 132–3, 224, 238–41, 245, 254
International Centre for the Settlement of Investment Disputes 138, 258
International Committee of the Red Cross 90, 98
International Convention for the Abolition of Import and Export Prohibitions and Restrictions 151
International Court of Justice 39, 50, 66, 70, 73, 145, 174, 179, 203, 231, 238
  Statute
  Article 38 12, 16, 22–6, 32, 65, 146, 226
  Article 59 26
international courts 7, 70–1, 135–47, 234, 239, 244 *see also* judicial lawmaking; precedents; semantic authority
  history 140–44
International Criminal Tribunal for Rwanda 135, 137
International Criminal Tribunal for the Former Yugoslavia 135–7
international institutions *see* international courts; international bureaucracies
International Labour Organization 87, 132
International Law Association 66, 140
International Law Commission 2–3, 65–6, 236–9 *see also* Treaties over Time
international lawmaking *see* lawmaking
international legal order 7, 19, 20–1, 52, 68, 135, 197, 214, 227, 245
International Maritime Organization 74
international protection 75, 87–90, 95–103, 107–9 *see also* Conclusions on International Protection
International Refugee Organization 89, 92–3, 97
International Tribunal for the Law of the Sea 135
Interpretation *see also* indeterminacy; content (of legal commitments); rhetoric; semantic struggle; subsequent practice
  evolutive; evolutionary 38–9, 137, 179, 232–9
  form 49–54
  nature 14, 17, 19, 49–54
  outward show 10, 17, 46, 49–54, 71, 116, 131, 196–8, 262
  rules 2–4, 17, 49–54, 176, 198, 225, 231, 236–40 *see also* Vienna Convention on the Law of Treaties
  substance 48, 54–8

interpretative community 40, 55, 211
interpretative declarations 113, 236
intertemporal law 230–2
Island of Palmas 230 n159

Jackson, John 136–7
Jellinek, Georg 21 n15, 144
Jennings, Robert 22
Jhering, Rudolf von 3 n10, 41, 262–4
judicial decisions 17, 23, 26–7, 144–7, 155, 161, 171, 192, 233 *see also* precedents; stare decisis
judicial lawmaking 136–50, 170, 172, 194
jurisgenesis, concept of 33–4
jus cogens 66, 203–5
justice 14, 47, 97, 196–224, 245 *see also* rhetoric of justice
justification of authority *see* legitimacy

Kadi 260
Kälin, Walter 78, 108, 126
Kant, Immanuel 19–20, 29–31, 56, 143, 145, 264
Karl, Wolfram 237
Keller, Rudi 39–41
Kelsen, Hans 5–6, 21 n14, 30, 31, 38, 60, 143–5, 204, 208–11
Kennedy, David 47, 133, 209–10
Kingsbury, Benedict 53
Klabbers, Jan 4, 72, 229
knowledge 1, 33, 75, 78, 85–8, 263
  absolute 263
Koh, Harold 33
Kolb, Robert 51
Korea—Beef 181, 184–8
Koskenniemi, Martti 21 n14, 47–9, 60–1, 196, 209–11, 223
Krasner, Steven 42
Krever, Tor 210
Krisch, Nico 259
Kundera, Milan 200
Kyoto Protocol 66

language *see also* indeterminacy; linguistic turn
  and law 38–42, 54–7
  design 19, 28, 58, 59, 244
  evolution 38–42
  normativity in 54–7, 217–23
  reification 30 n62, 264
  theory of 5 n18, 30 n62, 54–7, 217–23
Lauterpacht, Hersch 3–4, 17, 51 n185, 66, 68, 142, 204,
Law of Treaties *see* Vienna Convention on the Law of Treaties
Lawmaking *see also* consent; content (of legal commitments); evolution; judicial lawmaking; positivism; semantic authority; semantic change; sources
  by way of interpretation 8–9, 18, 30–1, 47–57, 112–4, 117, 132, 136–50, 196–8, 214, 217–22, 227, 234, 245, 248, 263 *see also* interpretation
  charge of 54–5, 170
  communicative practice 12, 18–37, 63–5, 87, 117, 197, 246
  exercise of authority 6, 58–60, 63–4, 81, 224
  incremental 18, 22, 30, 197
  political-legislative 7–9, 37, 111–12, 143, 165–8, 170, 191, 194, 254
League of Nations 22, 89–92, 142–3, 151, 208, 212
legal discourse 9, 27, 45, 48–50, 59, 63–4, 71, 82–3, 132–3, 144, 171–2, 191–2, 195, 198, 201–3, 208–10, 238 *see also* theory of legal discourse
  participants and actors 28, 32, 48, 76–87, 144–147, 238, 258, 263
legal normativity *see* normativity; language, normativity
legal pluralism 35–6, 251 n247 *see also* normative pluriverse
legal positivism *see* positivism
legalism 71
legitimacy *see also* sovereignty
  and interpretation 188–95, 217–22
  and legality 223–45
  democratic 10, 247–60, 264
  foundation 13, 18, 20, 27–9, 216, 240, 246, 248, 255
  functional 238 *see also* functionalism
  narrative of 6, 9, 13, 142, 224, 230, 232
  social 64, 71, 83, 94, 256
  sources of 12–13, 27–9, 217, 222–3, 257
legitimate expectations 71 n282, 137, 130, 192, 194, 242, 258
liberalism 202–5, 213 *see also* classical liberalism
  embedded 156
  hegemonic 216
like product 152–6, 186
Lindt, Auguste 99–101
linguistic turn 27, 30–1, 35, 55, 145, 216, 218–22
Lotus 21–2
Luhmann, Niklas 29 n60, 35–40

Mephistopheles 46, 264 *see also* Faust
Martens, Friedrich von 141
Marxism 21 n13, 41
material assistance 98–101, 108, 131
McAdam, Jane 124, 128
McDougal, Myres 3–4, 32
meaning *see also* content (of legal commitments); semantic pragmatism
  change *see* semantic change

contestation 2–4, 7, 11, 28, 46–9, 58–64, 147, 161 *see also* contestability; semantic struggles
deduction 51
generation (creation) 1–6, 10–12, 16, 27–31, 34, 38, 40, 46–9, 55–7, 62–3, 145, 170, 197, 218–19
influencing (shaping) 27–29, 58–62, 82 *see also* semantic authority
ordinary 2–3, 31, 50–2, 176, 179 n218, 232, 237
plain 48
true 6, 17
Merleau-Ponty, Maurice 41
metaphors 18, 38, 144
mission creep 70, 147
Mitrany, David 82–3
Montevideo Convention *see* Convention on the Rights and Duties of States
Morgenthau, Hans 211–2
Mouffe, Chantal 61, 209

Nansen, Fridtjof 90–1
narrative of legitimacy *see* legitimacy, narrative of
natural law 22, 25, 214
necessity (in Article XX GATT) 151, 159–67, 181–8, 190–1, 193–4
neo-pragmatism *see* semantic pragmatism
New Haven School 31–3, 37, 203
Nietzsche, Friedrich 199
Nolte, Georg 239
normativity 1–6, 12–13, 49, 56–7, 62–4, 136–8, 146, 216, 224 *see also* language, normativity in; constraints (in interpretation); content (of legal commitments)
normative pluriverse 13, 240, 245–61, 262, 265

O'Connell, Mary Ellen 33–4
Orakhelashvili, Alexander 51
ordinary meaning *see* meaning, ordinary
original intentionalism 136, 230–3 *see also* intent

performative speech acts *see* speech acts, performative
Permanent International Court of Justice 21–2, 141–3, 147
persuasion 59, 62–3, 87
pluralism *see* legal pluralism; normative pluriverse
politics 40, 57–62, 83, 126, 211–15
as ethics 60 n233
as technique 60 n233
of interpretation 58–62, 126, 218
sites of 254–5
Politis, Nicolas 142
positivism 6, 9, 12–13, 18–19, 21–2, 32–3, 56, 196, 202–3, 216, 229
power *see also* authority; hegemony
and authority 57–64
asymmetry of 8–9
balance of 211
definition of 58, 63–4, 211
of words 28–9, 59–60, 219
of ideas 85
public 248
relations (structures) of 9, 14, 61–2, 74, 76, 206, 209, 211, 214–15, 222, 223, 264
symbolic 11, 59–60
practice, concept of 41–2, 45, 62–3, 213
pragmatism (in international relations) 42–5 *see also* semantic pragmatism
precedents 17, 27, 63, 71, 119–20, 137–9, 144–7, 158, 160–1, 167, 171–4, 178, 191–4, 202, 232
progress 72, 197–201, 206–7, 214–8, 238
progressive development (of international law) 65, 110 n198, 215, 227
Project on International Courts and Tribunals 135
proportionality 180–93, 242, 258
Protection Guidelines 63, 116–20, 129–30, 258
Protocol relating to the Status of Refugees 95, 108, 112, 113–5, 120
Proudhon, Pierre-Joseph 209
publicness
of international law 23, 243
of procedures 244, 256

Quintilianus 59

rational choice 43–4, 77–8, 189
Rawls, John 203
realism
in international relations 43, 75–6, 211–14
legal 29–31, 145
moral 62
Redgwell, Catherine 228
refugee, definition of 91–5, 97–103, 115, 122–34
regime debate 42–4, 77
Reisman, Michael 32–3, 203
relationship between international and domestic law 6–10, 257–61
res judicata 145
reservations (to treaties) 227, 236
responsibility (of interpreter) 13, 262
rhetoric 58–9
rhetoric of justice 97, 198–223
Root, Elihu 141
Ruggie, John 156
rule of law 28–9
rule-following 38, 56–7

Sandholtz, Wayne 34, 202, 206
Savigny, Friedrich Carl von 41
Scelle, George 68
scepticism (in international law) 207–11
Schmitt, Carl 21 n14, 59, 208–11
Schnyder, Felix 100–2
semantic authority 45, 62–4, 117, 119–22, 147, 169–71, 221, 224, 246, 254–6
semantic change 4, 6–8, 14, 27–9, 40, 46–9, 55–7, 74–5, 87–8, 109, 122, 150, 167, 200–1, 205, 214–20, 232–3, 257
semantic pragmatism 5, 27, 30, 38, 47, 56, 62, 64, 145, 216, 236
semantic struggle 2, 11, 28–9, 37, 46, 57–9, 62, 64, 67, 86, 89, 103, 109, 122, 126, 131, 134, 152, 192, 194–5, 198, 206, 211, 224, 240, 245, 262 *see also* meaning, contestation
semantic theory 4 n16, 55–7 *see also* language, theory of; meaning
sense (meaning) 1–4, 17, 51, 53
Shany, Yuval 136
Shklar, Judith 71
Slaughter, Anne-Marie 69, 202, 205
social fact 21 n14, 33, 202–3, 222
socialization 9, 38, 44, 84, 213, 257
soft law 22 n22, 27, 198, 225–30, 238, 240
Solange 259 n290, 260
Sorel, Jean-Marc 51
sources (of international law) *see also* International Court of Justice, Statute, Article 38
- custom 14, 23–4, 34, 68
- doctrine of 1–2, 6, 10, 16–30, 32–5, 37, 38, 41, 53, 63, 196–8, 205, 225–30, 243–4, 245, 248, 257
- general principles 23–6
- metaphor of 18, 38
- treaty 8, 23–4, 114–15, 227–8

sovereignty 20–1, 27–8, 32, 59, 102, 201–2, 240, 246–52
- popular sovereignty 27, 59, 246–52

spaces of reason 13
speech acts 54, 219, 222 n126
- constative 54
- performative 10, 54, 206

SPS Agreement *see* Agreement on Sanitary and Phytosanitary Measures
Standing Committee 80
stare decisis 146
states *see also* sovereignty
- as subjects of international law 1–2, 13, 16, 19–20
- as normative foundation 8, 13, 19, 52–3, 196 *see also* legitimacy, foundation
- disaggregated 67–9
- role in interpretation 73–4, 89, 239–40

state consent 2, 6, 19–25, 47, 131, 196, 201, 232, 239, 248, 255 *see also* consent
Statute of the International Court of Justice *see* International Court of Justice
Statute of the United Nations High Commissioner for Refugees
- Para 1 88, 106
- Para 8 88, 95, 106, 110–11
- Para 9 96
- Para 13 94
- Para 15 85

structural coupling 36
structure
- in space of interpretation (of discourse) 4, 28, 63, 75, 89, 185 *see also* grammar
- of international legal argument 47, 196, 201 *see also* indeterminacy
- of society 11, 42–6 *see also* grammar
- power structures 76, 212

Suarez, Francisco 204
subsequent practice 198, 225, 230–40 *see also* Vienna Convention on the Law of Treaties, Article 31(3)(b)
subsumption, idea of 31, 198 *see also* meaning, deduction
supervisory function 78, 87, 110–14, 120, 131
systems theory 35–7, 40
Sztucki, Jerzy 110

tacit agreement *see* agreement, tacit
TBT Agreement *see* Agreement on Technical Barriers to Trade
Teitel, Ruti 201
Teubner, Gunther 36
texts 1–9, 12, 17, 51, 53–6, 128, 159, 234, 254 n261, 262 *see also* sources (of international law), treaty
textual fetish 50, 131
theory of legal discourse 217–20
Tomuschat, Christian 67
trade and environment 164, 167–8, 177
transnational legal processes, theory of 33–5
travaux préparatoires 3–4, 128
Treaties over Time (ILC project) 239
treaty law *see* sources (of international law), treaty
Triepel, Heinrich 21 n15, 30
Türk, Volker 107–8

ultimate authority 21, 26, 28, 246, 248–52, 259
United Nations Charter
- Article 13(1) 65 n251, 110 n198
- Article 27(3) 73
- Article 39 72
- Article 100 84
- as a constitution 52–3, 204 *see also* constitutionalism
- Chapter VII 72

United Nations Convention on the Law of the Sea 74, 135
United Nations High Commissioner for Refugees 8, 27, 63–8, 70, 72–134, 207, 210, 227–8, 239, 244, 250, *see also* Statute of the United Nations High Commissioner for Refugees
Uruguay Round 79, 167, 177

validity, test of 27, 31, 35, 37
validity claims (of speech acts) 218–22
Verdross, Alfred 204
Vernant, Jacques 123
Vienna Convention on the Law of Treaties 2–3 *see also* interpretation, rules
  Article 2(1)(a) 23
  Article 9 16
  Article 31 2–3, 51
  Article 31(1) 50
  Article 31(3)(a) 235
  Article 31(3)(b) 198, 225, 230–40 *see also* subsequent practice
  use by Appellate Body 50, 149, 169, 173

Waldheim, Kurt 104
Waldock, Sir Humphrey 2
Weber, Max 40, 82, 85–6, 144
Wehberg, Hans 51 n185, 139, 141–2
Weiler, Joseph H H 153
Weiss, Paul 123
Wittgenstein, Ludwig 1, 11, 30, 38, 199
world citizenship *see* cosmopolitanism
World Customs Organization 74
World Health Organization 74, 238
World Trade Organization 8, 16–17, 63, 74, 79, 135–95, 201, 210, 233–5, 239, 247, 250, 256, 257–9
WTO Agreement *see* Agreement Establishing the World Trade Organization

zeroing 8, 171–2
Zink, Karl Friedrich 123

The manufacturer's authorised representative in the EU for product safety is Oxford University Press España S.A. of el Parque Empresarial San Fernando de Henares, Avenida de Castilla, 2 – 28830 Madrid (www.oup.es/en or product.safety@oup.com). OUP España S.A. also acts as importer into Spain of products made by the manufacturer.

www.ingramcontent.com/pod-product-compliance
Ingram Content Group UK Ltd.
Pitfield, Milton Keynes, MK11 3LW, UK
UKHW022024150926
475595UK00013B/282
* 9 7 8 0 1 9 8 7 1 2 9 7 8 *